D0609498

Studies in Economic Theory

Editors

Charalambos D. Aliprantis
Department of Mathematical Sciences
IUPUI
402 N. Blackford Street
Indianapolis, IN 46202-3216
USA

Nicholas C. Yannelis
Department of Economics
University of Illinois
Champaign, IL 61820
USA

Donald G. Saari

Geometry
of
Voting

With 120 Figures

Springer-Verlag
Berlin Heidelberg New York London Paris Tokyo
Hong Kong Barcelona Budapest

Prof. Dr. Donald G. Saari
Northwestern University
Department of Mathematics
2033 Sheridan Road
Evanston, IL 60208-2730
USA

ISBN 3-540-57199-X Springer-Verlag Berlin Heidelberg New York Tokyo
ISBN 0-387-57199-X Springer-Verlag New York Berlin Heidelberg Tokyo

© Springer-Verlag Berlin · Heidelberg 1994
Printing in Germany

42/7130-5 4 3 2 1 0 - Printed on acid-free paper

For

Lillian

Whatever the issue, whatever the procedure
She's got my vote!

My object in living is to unite
My avocation and my vocation
As my two eyes make one in sight

Robert Frost; Two Tramps at Mudtime

PREFACE

I confess; I am one of those political junkies who remains glued to the TV watching election returns late into the night even when in a country where I don't know the candidates, the issues, or even the language. Since a child, supposedly sleeping but really captivated by my parents' political discussions continuing well into early morning hours, I've been intrigued by politics. But, rather than combining my avocation and vocation, I stumbled into the fascinating area of voting theory by trying to understand Arrow's Theorem and the mathematics of "information theory." It turns out that there are unexpected relationships among these research topics.

Years ago, skeptical about my colleague Len Evens' comment that voting systems don't do what we think they do, I bought Arrow's book [Ar]; for years it collected dust at the far end of a bookshelf surrounded by numerous other good intentions. Then, to master the material when I finally did read it, I tried to unravel the combinatorics by proving the theorem geometrically. The result was the geometric explanation and extension for Arrow's Theorem reported in [S1, 14] and in Sect.4.4. In this way "voting" became an avocation where even a couple of papers [S3, 4] were written.

The real stimulus for the research described in this book, however, comes from that portion of information theory modeling certain economic, computer, and engineering concerns. Based on the insightful work of (my eventual coauthors) Leo Hurwicz and Stan Reiter, there seemed to be interesting mathematics connected with the design of organizations and the communication of information. In simplified terms, an organization accomplishes its specified goals with a division of labor, but how is this determined? More abstractly, given a body of data, a pool of talent, certain resources, etc., the design issue is to characterize all ways the information can be structured and aggregated to attain a specified objective. Namely, we want to understand all possible "divisions of labor."

Each division of labor answers the fundamental questions "Who does what?" and "Who says what to whom?" On an assembly line, each worker has specific tasks ("Who does what?") and the partially completed product is passed on to the next in line ("Who says what to whom?"). A computer program assigns processors particular tasks and the partial computations are passed on to specified other processors. The chain of command in the military, a university, and a corporation provide different answers to these fundamental questions. Embellishments come from topics such as "incentives;" e.g., to investigate the integrity of organizational structures, appended to the first question is, "How can I ensure he does what he is supposed to do?" Dogging the heels of the second is, "Is she telling the truth? Would she be personally better off by distorting the information?"

Voting enjoys a particularly simple organizational structure. Each voter ranks the alternatives ("Who does what?") while the tallying procedure ("Who says what to whom?") aggregates the beliefs and registers the outcome. Because of its simplicity, I adopted this topic as a natural way to develop insight into the mathematical structures of information. After all, "What could be easier than interpreting an election?" What an awakening! While voting theory does provide the desired insight, it is a complicated, counterintuitive, difficult and fascinating subject! This is manifested by its incredibly large literature (e.g., see [K3]) where one quickly learns about the many talented people who have carefully examined its varied facets – yet each result seems only to deepen the mystery! The mathematical approaches range from the axiomatic to the concrete, from statistical, analytic, and computational to topological (e.g., [C]).

As my mathematical foundations are in dynamics and the Newtonian N-body problem, my "tool bag" includes those techniques popularly called "Chaos." So, to analyze voting, I developed an approach motivated by "chaotic" principles with an emphasis on geometry. The ultimate goal, of course, is to find "everything that could ever occur" with sincere voting. (How this objective connects with chaos is described in [S7].) To my surprise, this wishful hope actually was attained; a method (starting in [S9, 12, 16, 18]) now exists to characterize for any number of candidates all possible election paradoxes and outcomes that can occur with any choice of positional voting methods.

The purpose of this book is to describe, in an expository manner and with minimal mathematical entry requirements, a portion of this research program. Rather than discussing the connections with "chaos," my emphasis is on what can be learned about choice and information theory by identifying "voting" with geometry. As it turns out, much is gained; for instance, the geometry provides an immediate way to overcome the complicated combinatorics that normally frustrate progress in this research area. Consequently, instead of restricting attention just to specified systems, it now is possible to simultaneously evaluate *all* positional methods. Of greater interest, once the voting paradoxes are intimately connected to geometric constructs, intuition replaces the mystery. The importance for related topics is that the geometry converts the near cliche concerning "higher dimensions of information" into a working tool.

In writing this book, a choice had to be made between describing the most complete and recent results involving any number of candidates, or providing geometric intuition; eventually I opted for the latter. This decision required emphasizing two and three-candidate elections. The mathematical reason for this restriction is similar to what happens in algebra; the complexity escalates with the degree of the problem. For algebra, even elementary school students can solve linear equations, secondary students master quadratic equations, certain high school students discover the clever complex variable technique to solve cubic equations, but the structure of higher order equations is left to the mysterious delights of Galois Theory and other advanced techniques often first taught in a mathematics graduate program. Nevertheless, knowledge about the quadratic case provides insight into the more complicated setting. Similarly, in voting, analyzing two-candidate elections is stuff for elementary school. But, already with three candidates, the complexity of the problem can invite a solid migraine. With more than three candidates, the analysis (at least in its current form) depends upon the symmetry structures (the algebraic orbits) of the wreath product of permutation groups. (See the concluding notes.) As such, this material is not ready for polite company; until civilized, let it remain in research journals! Nevertheless, knowledge about the three-candidate case provides accurate intuition for the general setting.

So, this book analyzes three-candidate elections. A surprise is how the intricacies of voting can be identified with the comfortable, familiar geometry of our three-dimensional world. Consequently, even though this book is written in an expository fashion, previously unpublished results can be and are included. After the introductory material, each section contains new results and/or new explanations for old assertions. Almost all conclusions extend to an arbitrarily number of candidates – just remember, with more candidates much more can happen.

In addition to introducing this new geometric approach, this book is written with the hope of attracting people to this fascinating, important area. Therefore, to help test understanding, or to facilitate using this material in a course, exercises follow each section starting in Chap. 2. As an introduction to what can go wrong, Chap. 1 catalogues the woes of the Chair of a hypothetical academic department. (For the convenience of the reader, the examples introduced in this first section are used throughout the book.) The second section builds on this fable to raise issues; this is followed by a selective history. The last section reminds the reader of useful mathematical properties.

The actual geometry of voting starts in Chap. 2. After introducing standard terms but with a geometric formulation, new results start in the fourth section. Here, a geometric theory is developed to describe why different methods can lead to radically different election outcomes with the same voters' preferences. Thanks to the geometry, everything that could possibly happen for three candidates is described; after the structures are developed, deriving new conclusions becomes as simple as drawing lines on a triangle. In the fifth section – which gives a critical analysis of pairwise voting – I introduce "coordinate representations for profiles" which make it possible to "see" all possible profiles that support a particular election outcome. Once we can "see" all profiles, new flaws with pairwise voting become readily apparent. In this manner, it becomes easy to cast serious doubt about using the widely accepted Condorcet winner, to find extensions of Black's single-peakedness, to uncover flaws with agendas, etc., and to develop an informational explanation for the "paradox of voting." The last section starts the analysis of comparing the election outcomes for a pair of candidates when ranked "head-to-head" or as part of a larger group of candidates. Again, thanks to another coordinate representation for profiles, new results become geometrically immediate.

Chapter 3 delves deeper into a comparison of positional and pairwise voting. The first section uses a geometric interpretation of "neutrality" to create a form of "super-neutrality." (Most procedures fail super-neutrality, and the cost is that they admit new kinds of troubling paradoxes.) The second section introduces a geometric analysis of the Borda Count to extract its various strengths. Also, a technique borrowed from "chaos" (the dictionaries) is described. The natural next issue, comparing the Borda Count with other positional methods, is the theme of the third section. Outlined in the fourth and fifth sections is how to extend the geometric analysis beyond positional and pairwise voting in order to address a wider variety of techniques and issues.

While Chaps. 2 and 3 emphasize single profile issues, Chap. 4 describes what happens in those fascinating scenarios involving several profiles. The first two sections, for example, create the geometry to analyze what can happen when subcommittees join, voters abstain or change their opinions, or the procedure is being manipulated. As a sampler, associated with a new, geometric proof of the Gibbard-Satterthwaite Theorem is a technique to analyze how susceptible a procedure is to being manipulated. In the third section, which emphasizes proportional voting, new geometric techniques are developed to explain the serious problems of apportionment methods – it turns out that most procedures admit reasonable outcomes only through a fortuitous balance of compensating errors! Consequently, we must anticipate problems. Indeed, legal issues raised about the current apportionment of Congressional seats for the USA are mentioned. The last two sections highlight axiomatic conclusions. First, a geometric proof of Arrow's Theorem is given to expose the informational reasons for the conclusion. This not only provides a benign (compared to the more popular draconian) interpretation of Arrow's conclusion, but also leads to the sharpest possible extension. Then, ways to avoid the negative conclusion are developed. The concluding section provides a geometric, axiomatic representation for basic voting systems.

The "Notes" following Chap. 4 are intended to provide references and places for the interested reader to learn more about this topic. Also, an outline is offered that indicates how the conclusions in this book can be extended in several ways.

Remember, this is a research monograph that, hopefully, is written in an accessible manner. As such, the organization is based on the natural progression dictated by the mathematical development of certain techniques. However, readers new to this field seeking an overview may wish to read the material in different orders. To assist such readers, with the exception of Sect. 2.5, the basic notions of each section are introduced in the first half; therefore, the reader can read the second half at a later date to discover added applications and more sophisticated developments. Secondly, certain sections, such as those on symmetry and related systems (Sects. 3.1, 3.4, 3.5, 4.5), are critical for a deeper understanding of the problems in voting, but they can be skipped on a first reading.

A road map of possible ways to use this book follows:

1. The fundamental sections include Sect. 1.1, which introduces the problems and identifies certain basic examples, Sect. 1.4, which reviews the needed geometry, and Sects. 2.1 - 3 which introduce the geometric notation.

2. The next section could be Sect. 2.5 (2.5.1 - 2.5.7, 2.5.10) to learn about the reasons for cycles, extensions of Black's single-peakedness, problems with the Condorcet winner, and the new coordinate representations.

3. This could be followed by an introduction to Arrow's Theorem in Sects. 4.4- 4.4.5 (with a proof in Sects. 4.4.6, 4.4.7). (Actually, the material on Arrow's Theorem only requires Sect. 2.1, the introduction for Sect. 2.2, and Sects. 2.5.1-2.5.2.)

4. For an introduction to the comparisons of systems, start with the procedure line (Sects. 2.4.1 - 2.4.4) to see why different methods can cause different election conclusions, and then to Sects. 2.6.1 - 2.6.4 to discover why the pairwise ranking of a pair can differ from its relative ranking within a positional setting.

5. Sects. 3.2 - 3.2.3 (and Sect. 3.2.4 for the more adventurous) show how the discussed problems are resolved with the Borda Count. Insight into the advantages of the Borda Count over other methods can be obtained with the introduction to Sect. 3.3.

All together, the above constitutes about 100 pages of material. At this point, depending on individual interest, the reader could approach either Sect. 4.2 to learn about monotonicity and the geometric reasons for the important Gibbard-Satterthwaite Theorem, Sects. 4.3.1-4.3.3, 4.3.5-4.3.6, 4.3.8-4.3.12, to obtain insight into proportional representation and apportionment problems, Sects. 3.4.1-3.4.4, 3.5.1-3.5.5 to see how to apply this analysis to other systems, or Sect. 4.1 to see the geometric reasons for other kinds of election paradoxes.

Recall that the initial motivation for examining these topics was to use voting theory to help understand other aggregation and information problems. While the techniques differ, the notion of "dimension of information" with its associated emphasis on the geometric structure of procedures provides useful insight to expose and analyze problems experienced in other research areas. Much of this work is still in preliminary stages, but as a sample from statistics, see the work of Haunsperger [Ha] where she uncovered many new kinds of difficulties with the Kruskal-Wallis test while showing that this procedure is the optimal nonparametric method. For functional analysis problems emphasizing economics and demonstrating a large class of new obstacles confronting Adam Smith's "supply and demand story," the reader could consult [S17].

When writing an expository - research book, one quickly learns the critical importance of colleagues and friends! This is particularly so when a program doesn't work or a computer goes astray threatening to shred days of work, and I'm rescued by my far more knowledgeable colleagues Len Evens, John Franks, and, in particular, Clark Robinson. If you like the computer generated pictures,

thanks go to Jack Lin and Hollie Howard, Northwestern University undergrad-
uates who programmed them with PiCTeX, and to Katri Saari who suggested
some of them; all three (and Margarete Hendrickson) critiqued various portions of
the manuscript. Thanks for encouragement, suggestions, comments, references,
information, critiques, etc., etc., go to Roko Aliprantis, Jean-Pierre Aubin, Steve
Brams, Len Evens, Eric Friedlander, Ken Janda, Ehud Kalai, Jerry Kelly, Mark
Mahowald, Ken Mount, Diana Richards, Clark Robinson, Maurice Salles, Mark
Satterthwaite, Carl Simon, Steve Williams, and several others. Particular thanks
go to my NSF project director Larry Rosenberg and the financial support from
NSF that made this research possible!

Donald G. Saari
Northwestern University
Evanston, Illinois
September, 1993

Typeset with $\mathcal{A}\mathcal{M}\mathcal{S}$-TeX

CONTENTS

CHAPTER I

FROM AN ELECTION FABLE
TO ELECTION PROCEDURES

What could be easier than interpreting an election? Even nursery school children use voting to select their juice of choice before nap time. After all, it just involves counting where the candidate with the most votes wins. What is so difficult about something as elementary as that?

There is no mystery about two-candidate elections, but the story changes radically once there are three or more alternatives. Here, as anyone who has followed elections might suspect, if something can go wrong it probably will. Multicandidate elections can admit all sorts of complexities characterized by a wide selection of counter-intuitive outcomes. These complexities must be taken seriously because they can generate doubt about the meaning – even the integrity – of an election. A selection of these paradoxes – counter-intuitive conclusions – is outlined in the introductory electoral fable.

As shown in subsequent chapters, this fable describes only a small portion of what can go wrong. Outcomes can be manipulated, a candidate can be penalized by receiving extra support, procedures don't do what we expect them to do. Nevertheless, even this sampler suggests why voting paradoxes have made this research area a fascinating, essential, and complicated topic. The source of the fascination is clear; it derives from the troublesome, unexpected consequences that can plague even simple, standard processes.

What defines the essential nature of this topic is that these troubling outcomes can and do occur in actual elections; one example is the 1970 New York senatorial election which conservative Buckley won even though over 60% of the voters would have preferred one of the two more liberal candidates. Indeed, it is not difficult to find "real world" paradoxes where it is arguable that the election ranking contradicts the voters' true desires. With the accompanying change of power, such an outcome can lead to unpopular and unintended changes in policy, differences in the allocations of resources, and even the direction of a society. Even more bothersome are those situations where the longer term effects of a "real life voting paradox" results in violence, death, and even the loss of democracy.[1] There is no debate; the goal of understanding and deriving the properties

---

[1] In 1970, the Marxist Salvador Allende won the election for President of Chile even though the polls indicated that the voters would have preferred either of the other two more moderate candidates. (See [Fr].) There is no excuse for the resulting action precipitated by the American CIA leading to the overthrow and death of Allende, nor for the dark period of dictatorial abuse that followed. Yet, one must wonder whether these events would have happened if the election

of voting procedures is an important topic with significant consequences.

"Voting" is not new; it has been around at least for a couple of millennia and probably much longer. So, while deferring to the more worthy claimant for the title of "the world's oldest profession," voting theory clearly qualifies for any "top ten list." Yet, in spite of its lengthy history, much mystery remains. This is due to the serious, hidden technical difficulties inherent in the analysis of these paradoxes. In later chapters, I explain these complexities by identifying them with the geometric properties of higher dimensional spaces.

1.1 An Electoral Fable

Anyone who has ever tried to coordinate the decision making processes for a group knows that it can be an hair-losing proposition. For the uninitiated, let me indicate why this is so by describing the woes of a conscientious, hardworking chairman from a mythical academic department.

Start with the annual departmental fall banquet where, to save money, only one beverage was to be served. In this hypothetical 15-member department:

A. Six specified to the chair that they preferred milk to wine to beer (denoted by milk $\succ$ wine $\succ$ beer).

B. Five specified beer $\succ$ wine $\succ$ milk.

C. Four specified wine $\succ$ beer $\succ$ milk.

The department's choice was obvious; using a *plurality vote* – where each person votes for her or his favorite beverage – the group's plurality ranking was

$$\text{milk} \succ \text{beer} \succ \text{wine}$$

with a tally of 6:5:4.

Scrupulously following the wishes of the department, the chair announced that milk, their beverage of choice, would be served at the banquet. For unexplained reasons, milk was not available that particular evening, so the chair did the obvious; he ordered beer, the department's second choice.

During the banquet, the naturally inquisitive wine lovers discovered that beer *wasn't* the department's second choice. Instead, after questioning their colleagues, they learned that two-thirds of the faculty (ten to five) actually preferred wine to beer!

Voters	Wine $\succ$	Beer
A	6	–
B	–	5
C	4	–
Total	10	5

---

outcome had better reflected the voters' intentions.

With suspicions aroused, the meddling wine lovers continued to compile information about their colleagues' preferences. Before the end of the evening, they found that contrary to the announced decision, milk was *not* the departmental top choice – instead, it was crystal clear that wine was the beverage of choice! In fact three-fifths of the faculty (nine to six) preferred wine to milk and three-fifths preferred beer to milk.

Voters	Wine	≻	Milk		Voters	Beer	≻	Milk
A	–		6		A	–		6
B	5		–		B	5		–
C	4		–		C	4		–
Total	9		6		**Total**	9		6

Something was seriously wrong! These results distinctly indicate that the department's "true ranking" was

$$\text{wine} \succ \text{beer} \succ \text{milk}.$$

Why, then, was the "false" ranking of milk ≻ beer ≻ wine announced? The morning after the banquet, rumors floated that the chair reversed the department's true preference ranking so that the outcome would favor his overly aggravated ulcer. Once impugned, trust is lost and suspicions grow. In practical terms, this meant that all of our chair's previous announcements became suspect. After all, only the chair counted the ballots; only he knew how the department really voted. Questions were raised.

> *Was Bob truly our departmental choice to fill the one vacant tenure track position, or did the chair reverse the election outcome so that Bob, his brother-in-law, would finally have a job?*
>
> *Who really got elected to the departmental Budget Committee?*

The unrest in our hypothetical department resulted in a clamor for a departmental meeting — but, to ensure the honesty of the outcomes, the faculty insisted that all votes must be by a public show of hands. The purpose of the meeting was to decide among the three competing proposals:

1. *"The chair is to be commended for his efforts."*
2. *"So that future elections are accurately tallied, the chair is to teach remedial math."*
3. *"The dean must take immediate steps to replace the chair!"*

After far too many corridor debates, the opinions within the department split evenly among the three rankings:

a. Five for 1 ≻ 2 ≻ 3.
b. Five for 2 ≻ 3 ≻ 1.

c.   Five for $3 \succ 1 \succ 2$.

Our chair was worried; to protect what remained of his tarnished reputation, he decided that the meeting agenda should ensure that his case would receive a complete, fair hearing. Now, an *agenda* lists the alternatives in the order in which they are to be compared. For instance, with the agenda $[1, 2, 3]$, the first two alternatives, 1 and 2, are compared, and the winner of a majority vote is then advanced to be compared with the third listed alternative, 3. To provide the optimal hearing for his case, the Chair decided to emphasize the positive by focusing the initial debate between his preferred choices; the first vote would be between proposals (1) and (2). Then, the winning alternative would be matched against the dreaded (3). Thus the Chair put forth the agenda $[1, 2, 3]$.

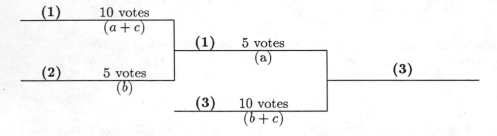

Fig. 1.1.1. The agenda [1, 2, 3].

His strategy failed miserably. As the above tree diagram shows, where letters indicate how each set of voters voted, the feared (3) was overwhelmingly adopted. The faculty left the meeting satisfied that the true departmental opinion had emerged; after all, both votes were decided by the decisive tallies of ten to five.

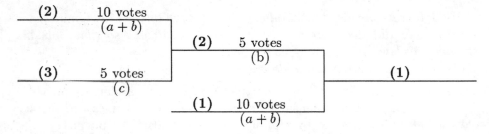

Fig. 1.1.2. The agenda [2, 3, 1].

What a missed opportunity! Had our chair been more Machiavellian, he could have left the meeting with substantial "proof" that his colleagues sincerely appreciated his continuing efforts on their behalf. With even minimal knowledge about voting procedures, not only would his preferred choice of (1) have been selected, but the votes would have been sufficiently decisive to prove that any departmental dissent must be due to a small, dissident minority. The outcome of the $[2, 3, 1]$ agenda pairing the winner of (2) versus (3) against (1) is in Fig. 1.1.2.

1.1.1 Time for the Dean

Even before she was approached, the Dean of the College had had serious doubts about our chair's integrity. Her suspicions were aroused by an earlier incident when he chaired a committee to choose a student representative for the Dean's Council.

When assigned to this post, our chair inherited an unwieldy large committee of 26. In the name of efficiency, he created two smaller subcommittees of 13 each. Then, to ensure a fair hearing for each of the three finalists — Ann, Barb, and Carol — our chair asked each subcommittee to conduct an unofficial preliminary vote – a *straw ballot* – with a *runoff procedure*. A runoff involves two votes; the two top-ranked candidates from the first election are advanced to the second one. The majority winner of the second ballot — the runoff election — is the selected candidate.

Using the runoff, both subcommittees selected Ann. As one should expect, even though the committee members were instructed to keep all results strictly confidential, Ann's good fortune was widely publicized on the front page of the student newspaper. A victory party was thrown for her that evening.

After the two subcommittees completed their straw votes, our chair convened the full committee to reach the formal conclusion with the runoff procedure. Everyone knew about Ann's victorious straw ballots, so it was commonly accepted that the full committee's final vote was a mere formality – Ann would be the student representative. But, after our chair tabulated the secret ballot, he had the temerity to announce that Barb, who just happened to be his department's candidate, won the election by a substantial margin!

(The rankings of the 13 voters of the first subcommittee were split in the following manner:

a. Four had the ranking Ann $\succ$ Barb $\succ$ Carol.
b. Three had the rankings Barb $\succ$ Ann $\succ$ Carol.
c. Three had the ranking Carol $\succ$ Ann $\succ$ Barb.
d. Three had the ranking Carol $\succ$ Barb $\succ$ Ann.

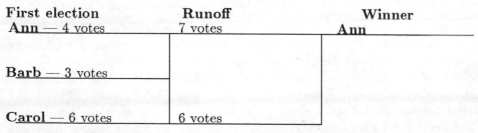

First election	Runoff	Winner
Ann — 4 votes	7 votes	**Ann**
Barb — 3 votes		
Carol — 6 votes	6 votes	

Fig. 1.1.3. The first subcommittee runoff

For this subcommittee, the outcome of the first election was Carol $\succ$ Ann $\succ$ Barb by a vote of 6 : 4 : 3. In the runoff, Ann beat Carol by a vote of seven to six.

The rankings of the 13 members in the second subcommittee were split so that

a. Four had the ranking Ann ≻ Barb ≻ Carol.
b. Three had the ranking Barb ≻ Ann ≻ Carol.
c. Three had the ranking Carol ≻ Ann ≻ Barb.
d. Three had the ranking Barb ≻ Carol ≻ Ann.

Here the outcome among the three candidates was Barb ≻ Ann ≻ Carol by a vote of 6 : 4 : 3. In the runoff between Ann and Barb, Ann beat Barb by a vote of seven to six.

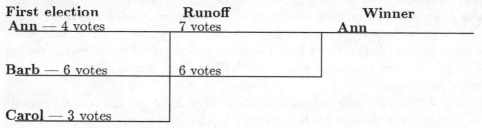

Fig. 1.1.4. The second subcommittee runoff

Even though Ann won with both subcommittees, she was *bottom-ranked* at the end of the first vote for the joint committee of all 26 voters. In this vote, the outcome was Barb ∼ Carol ≻ Ann by a vote of 9 : 9 : 8. In the runoff, Barb was the decisive winner over Carol by a vote of 17 to 9.)

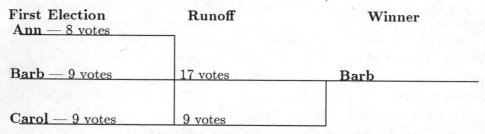

Fig. 1.1.5. The full committee runoff

1.1.2 The Departmental Election

During this autumn of his discontent, our chair's reputation suffered serious blows – the scandal associated with the Dean's Council election, the beverage brouhaha, and the devastating "no confidence" vote from the department. Across campus it quickly became accepted that his reckless, unethical behavior no longer could be tolerated! Drastic action had to be taken. After consulting with the Political Science Department about procedures, the dean announced a departmental election to select a new chair. This election would be tallied according to a method proposed in 1770 by the French mathematician J. C. Borda.

The *Borda Count* (BC) is where, with n candidates, $n - i$ points are assigned to a voter's ith-ranked candidate, $i = 1, \ldots, n$. The number of points assigned to each candidate are counted, and the election ranking is determined by these sums where "more is better." So, with $n = 5$ candidates, four points are given to a voter's top-ranked candidate, three for a second-ranked candidate, two for a third-ranked candidate, one for a fourth-ranked candidate, and zero for the bottom-ranked candidate. In the particular setting of $n = 3$ candidates, 2, 1, 0 points are assigned, respectively, to a voter's top-ranked, second-ranked, and bottom-ranked candidates.

After intense campaigning in the department, a coffee-room survey showed that

- 7 of the faculty members preferred Abbott $\succ$ Boyce $\succ$ Chair,
- 7 preferred Boyce $\succ$ Abbott $\succ$ Chair, and
- only our beleaguered chair preferred Chair $\succ$ Abbott $\succ$ Boyce.

In this de facto two-person race, the tally would be

	Abbott	Boyce	Chair
	$(7 \times 2) = 14$	$(7 \times 1) = 7$	0
	$(7 \times 1) = 7$	$(7 \times 2) = 14$	0
	1	0	2
Total	22	21	2

Thus, Boyce would lose the election as the outcome would be Abbott $\succ$ Boyce $\succ$ Chair with the tally of 22 : 21 : 2. (The first row are the Abbott supporters where the $14 = 7 \times 2$ points reflects the seven first-place votes, the $7 = 7 \times 1$ reflects the seven second-place votes, and $0 = 7 \times 0$ are the last-place votes. Similarly, the second row are the tallies from the seven Boyce supporters, while the last row reflects the Chair's ballot.)

To prevent Boyce's defeat, Boyce's supporters decided to act "strategically" by voting as though each of them preferred Boyce $\succ$ Chair $\succ$ Abbott. In this manner, each voter could provide Boyce with a two point, instead of a single-point, differential over Abbott. This would lead to an election ranking of Boyce $\succ$ Abbott $\succ$ Chair with a tally of 21 : 15 : 9.

	Abbott	Boyce	Chair
	14	7	0
	0	14	7
	1	0	2
Total	15	21	9

Abbott's supporters, of course, suspected this might happen, so each of them adopted the strategy of marking their ballots Abbott $\succ$ Chair $\succ$ Boyce in order to give an edge to Abbott. *The chair was re-elected.*

	Abbott	Boyce	Chair
	14	0	7
	0	14	7
	1	0	2
	———	———	———
Total	15	14	16

1.2 The Moral of the Tale

Although the dean of this far-fetched story was misinformed, she was correct in taking decisive action once she suspected that the chair was unethically misrepresenting sincere election outcomes. Elections play a central role in the everyday decision processes of modern society. We use them to choose our leaders, to determine the outcome of primary elections, to select from among the many legislative proposals, to accept members for professional organizations, to choose the winners of prizes, fellowships or scholarships, to fill scarce tenure track positions in academic departments, to invite potential members to join fraternities, sororities, and other social organizations, to resolve a family debate over what to name a pet mongrel, to coordinate our more pedestrian daily choices ranging from the selection of a dinner beverage to whose car will be used to go to the theater, and even to crown the MVP and the mythical national champion for certain sports.

Elections form such an integral part of our daily life that there is a critical obligation to preserve faith in the process. This concern is manifested on election day with the armies of poll watchers fighting to thwart that age-old charge of *"Vote early, vote often!"* to guarantee that the ballots counted are the ballots cast, and to ensure that a potential voter is not, in fact, an eternal resident of a local cemetery. We see this concern reflected through the outrage generated by press stories about "ballot stuffing," even with a popularity contest to choose an "All Star" sports team. At all levels and in all contexts, it is natural to insist on preventive actions to ensure honest elections. This is rightfully so. Elections are treated seriously; they form an important class of group decision instruments to replace might in battle with the right of the ballot.

Elections serve as useful decision tools only as long as we trust them. An election outcome not to our liking may be somewhat more palatable if we believe it reflects the sincere wishes of the people. For these reasons, the dean in our fable was correct in taking prompt, direct action to ensure her colleagues of the integrity of the process.

While our mythical dean is justified in her swift action, we have an advantage over her. We know that, in fact, the chair of our fable was an honest agent who did nothing whatsoever to vitiate the electoral process. The true culprits were hidden mathematical subtleties which exercised their pernicious effects upon the election procedures. This raises an important challenge; does our concern for the sanctity of the election process extend beyond guarding against human malfeasance? If we honestly wish and expect our elections to reflect the "true beliefs of the people," shouldn't we worry about those mathematical peculiarities that can do more to frustrate this lofty goal than even the craftiest actions of a cigar chomping precinct captain?

In order to protect against humans stealing elections, we first need to learn how they can do it. Similarly, to prevent election procedures from selecting the alternative popularly viewed as being decidedly inferior, we need to know what can go wrong and why. We need to understand the mathematical sources for the various paradoxes and undesired election outcomes. We need to understand the structural reasons why certain procedures are more easily manipulated than others. The development of a mathematical theory to provide the structural foundation for these procedures is the basic theme of this book.

1.2.1 The Basic Goal

The ultimate goal is to choose a procedure that always honors the beliefs of the voters. This sounds simple, but what are these "true wishes?" After all, each voting procedure is intended to provide an accurate measurement. Even with the same profile, different procedures lead to different conclusions, so which "correct one" should be embraced?

The complexity of this issue is illustrated with the beverage example. For instance, instead of using either a plurality vote or a decision based on the majority votes, suppose the chair selects the beverage with a runoff election. Here, Beer and Milk are advanced to the runoff where Beer wins by a vote of 9 : 6. Thus, for the beverage example:

Election Method	Winning alternative
Plurality election	Milk
Pairwise comparison	Wine
Runoff	Beer

According to this table, each alternative can be touted as the "sincere" choice for the same group of people. The disturbing conclusion is that *the chosen beverage depends more on choice of the decision procedure than on the voters' wishes.* So, which beverage should be selected?

To further demonstrate this difficulty, consider the departmental election. Had our chair wished to teach remedial mathematics, he could have ensured this outcome by using the remaining agenda of [3, 1, 2]. This agenda pitches (1) versus (3) in the first vote, and the winner is matched against (2) in the second vote. As true with the other agendas, by use of [3, 1, 2], alternative (2) would be selected by such landslide proportions that the legitimacy of the outcome probably would not have been questioned by any reasonable observer.

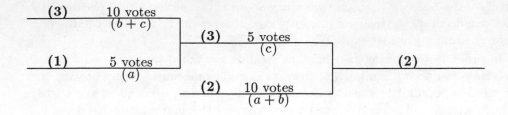

Fig. 1.2.1. The agenda [3, 1, 2]

In other words, with the three possible agendas, this particular division of the departmental preferences has the curious characteristic that whichever alternative is voted on last always emerges victorious. Moreover, each outcome is supported by decisive votes. Again, we reach the disturbing conclusion that the election outcome depends more upon the choice of a procedure (the agenda) than the voters' views.

Agenda	Winning Alternative
[2, 3, 1]	1
[1, 3, 2]	2
[1, 2, 3]	3

To have any hope of reconciling this problem, we need to understand how the outcomes of procedures relate to voters' preferences.[2] This is the thrust of the mathematical approach developed here. With such a mathematical foundation, new concepts and issues can be analyzed, so the reader can determine which method is appropriate for a particular purpose.

1.2.2 Other Political Issues

The mathematical investigation of voting and other political science issues is an old, yet relatively new topic. The rich supply of important topics that almost beg to be analyzed with mathematical techniques ensures that this is an area ready to explode with activity! It is easy to make this prediction; when almost daily seismic readings of the literature prove the existence of activity coming from various locations, "The Big One" has to be expected. It is not clear when it will happen, but it will.

A glance at the daily newspaper furnishes a ready list of issues. For instance, immediately after the 1992 Presidential elections in the USA, pundits, politicians, spin artists and academics tried to interpret the election outcome. Did Clinton receive a mandate? If so, to do what? What did the election outcome really mean? The initial reaction of Republican Senator Dole was to combine the

---

[2]Other areas are concerned about this same issue. For instance, in computer design, voting methods often are used to decide priority for projects. Clearly, one hopes that the outcome reflects the intention of the "voters."

Bush and Perot vote to argue the extreme position that 57% of the voters were against Clinton. A familiar Democratic response was that the combined Perot and Clinton vote of 62% created a clear mandate for "Change." Polling services offered their instant analysis by claiming that about 34% of the Perot voters had Clinton as second choice, and 34% preferred Bush.

The 1992 election is typical; elections are followed by a careful analysis of the vote. At times, the goal is propaganda to put a "spin" on a negative outcome. More often, because the voting process is a crude communication procedure, the goal is to determine the voters' aggregated message. Whether an election is for a chair of a department, a congressman, or a President, the vote often is and should be interpreted as reflecting the will of the people. So, if re-election is intended, it is worth deciphering the message hidden behind the vote.

Further support for this comment comes from the Peruvian election in mid-November, 1992. The outcome was carefully watched by the international community as a barometer about how the Peruvian people were accepting President Fujimori's extreme actions. At balance was restoration of much needed foreign aid and investments that were suspended in April, 1992, after President Fujimori seized near dictatorial powers. (He justified his drastic action as necessary to effectively combat the Shining Path terrorist group.) Presumably because Fujimori's allies won a majority of seats in congress, the election was interpreted as indicating a wide-spread support for the President. Indeed, the Japanese agreed to give Peru $100 million of new loans and the USA stated that Peru was back on the path toward democracy. But, did Fujimori's allies really receive a majority support of the people? That his allies won a majority of the seats in congress could reflect properties of the voting procedure because, in fact, they received only about 38% of the vote.

As suggested, this inverse problem of using the election tally to decipher the intent of the voters is sufficiently critical to qualify as an important theoretical question. A desirable tool of analysis, then, is one that can extract from a given procedure all possible divisions of voters' preferences leading to a specific conclusion. Does the answer vary with the choice of a procedure? These kinds of issues can be answered; as part of our mathematical development of voting procedures, "coordinate representations" for profiles are introduced that allow us to "see" all possible profiles that support a given election outcome.

1.2.3 Strategic Behavior

"Strategic behavior" is an academic growth area that grew from the wedding of game theory with decision analysis. Be careful, this charming area is seductive; it is difficult not to become hooked on this approach even after only a brief exposure to its powers. This is because insight into a vast number of critical issues can be obtained by using basic mathematical techniques.

Strategic voting is not new; often it is encouraged with the admonition, "Don't waste your vote; vote for –." In the 1988 Democratic Party Presidential primaries, candidate Jesse Jackson tried to counter this advice by encouraging his Black and liberal supporters to vote their convictions. Actually, such counter comments are common in multicandidate elections. We heard this from the third party Presidential candidate Anderson when he urged his supporters to send a message to Washington, and from Perot's claim that votes for Bush or Clinton would be "wasted."

Actually, "strategic voting" to avoid wasting your vote could be treated as a version of informed, sincere voting; after all, the voter only votes for candidates he or she believes can be elected. The negative side of strategic action is where advantage is taken of structural peculiarities of a procedure to force an unwanted outcome upon the electorate. While it is not clear whether this is a serious practical problem, it is such an attractive issue that has spawned numereous research papers. New questions can be generated just by changing the identity of who is trying to manipulate the system and who is not, who has certain information and who does not. For instance, in the departmental meeting from the fable, what would happen if some of the faculty voted strategically? How should they vote to succeed? In the departmental election, what is the best response of Boyce's supporters once they discovered that Abbott's fans would vote strategically? What if they did not have this information?

My analysis of strategic behavior differs from standard treatments in that I believe the main issue is to understand the structures of voting procedures. From this perspective, strategic action becomes an embellishment; it is an action taken by some agents to exploit this structure to obtain a personally better conclusion. So, by first unraveling the structure of procedures, it becomes possible (Chap. 4.) to determine all possible ways paradoxes occur and procedures can be manipulated.

A word of caution. While manipulative behavior is an important concern, it must never become the single deciding factor in the choice of a system. As an analogy, "carjacking" can be prevented by driving a beat up, uncomfortable, unattractive automobile belching smoke, but few people do this. Precautions are necessary, but extremes are stupid. Similarly, corporations with decentralized decision activities provide opportunities for manipulation, but very few embrace a Stalinist, or even more severe approaches to solve this difficulty.[3] Precautions are necessary, but extremes can be counterproductive. All election methods can be manipulated, some more than others, but it is unrealistic to select a procedure just on its manipulative features. Precautions are necessary, but adopting extreme methods that already can seriously distort the voters' true intentions with sincere voting is total nonsense! Part of the conflict is that, in a mathematical sense that will be made more precise, the closer a procedure is to being "strategy proof," the closer it is to using only a single dimensional aspect of the available information. This does not suggest a very robust system capable of capturing what the voters really want.

---

[3] However, an important paper on incentives by Eric Maskin [Ma] imposes death sentences upon violators.

1.2.4 Some Procedures Are Better than Others

Actually, some procedures are better for certain purposes than for others. But, based on the mathematical development that follows, the commonly used plurality vote turns out to be one of the worse methods that could ever be adopted. Yet, mindful of the importance of being positive, some nice things can be said even about this maligned procedure. In fact, for any method, arguments can be advanced, situations created, criteria imposed to "prove" that that procedure is "optimal." (See Sect. 4.3.) Then, by emphasizing a different, carefully edited set of arguments and criteria, it is possible to discredit any "competing" method.

There is a corollary to this observation; caution and extreme skepticism must be exercised whenever you encounter a "salesman" from academics or a political party selling election reforms – particularly around election time. Accepting an election reform should be treated like the selection of a major purchase, such as an used car from an unknown dealer – be sure to learn what really is being sold. We recognize the danger of buying a flashy car complete with the latest electronics and sex appeal only to find that it won't run. Similarly, it is not hard to be enticed by flashy, positive attributes of a voting procedures that disguise the simple fact that it does not work – its election outcomes can abuse the intent of the voters. For instance, while being reasonably immune to manipulative strategies, a procedure may produce outlandish outcomes. While being promoted in terms of properties that promise to promote democratic principles, the election outcomes of a reform procedure may vitiate the true intent of the voters. In light of this realistic concern, hopefully the theory developed here will assist in a more informed consumer selection of voting processes.

After these warnings, it is reasonable to wonder what method I think is best. Based on what will be described, the Borda Count appears to be optimal. It has flaws; I indicated one of them in the fable with the manipulation of the election for a new chair. However, as we know from the Gibbard-Satterthwaite result (described in Sect. 4.3 in the context of positional voting procedures), all nondictatorial methods involving three or more alternatives can be manipulated. Therefore, not only the BC, but all other procedures reside in this hall of shame.

So, why the BC? As the properties will indicate, the BC appears to be the unique voting method to represent the true wishes of the voters. As a preview of its properties, consider what happens when the BC is used with the beverage example. Here, each voter with the preference Milk $\succ$ Wine $\succ$ Beer contributes two points for Milk, one point for Wine and zero points for Beer. Continuing this process for each voter, the final tally is

	Wine	Beer	Milk
	6	0	12
	5	10	0
	8	4	0
Total	19	14	12

The BC election ranking of the beverages *reverses* the plurality ranking to become consistent with how these voters majority rank the three pairs! (As explained later, consistency of the BC outcomes with the pairwise votes is no accident.) Consequently, had our chair used the BC, he could have avoided all of his difficulties within the department.

The consistency extends; had the BC been used with the runoff procedure, then wine would win the runoff election between wine and beer. The following table indicates what occurs with the beverage example when the BC is used with the different procedures.

Borda Count outcome	
Election method	**Winning alternative**
Borda election	Wine
Pairwise comparison	Wine
Runoff	Wine

Among other positive features of the BC, I will show that it is the unique method to minimize the number and kinds of paradoxes, to minimize the likelihood of a paradox, to minimize the likelihood that a small group can successfully manipulate the outcome, to minimize the possibility of voters' errors adversely changing the outcome, and so forth. All of this is described elsewhere in this book with an emphasis on the structural reasons.

Even though there are several strong arguments proving that the BC is "optimal," it need not be the "best" choice for everyone. As a personal example, with my focus on the mathematical analysis of these procedures, I have not spent any energy advocating the adoption of the BC – even in my own academic department. However, within days after I gave a colloquium lecture on the mathematics of voting procedures to my colleagues, they adopted the BC for our important elections.[4] As a result, our results more accurately reflect the general views of the department. In retrospect, this might serve as a second reason for my reluctance to promote the BC; the biased outcomes of the previous procedure were personally more favorable. In other words, the choice of a procedure can and must be treated as an important strategic variable.

1.3 From Aristotle to "Fast Eddie"

This book is about the theoretical aspects of voting, not the history or literature of the subject. Yet, the history has many fascinating stories that can be used to motivate certain topics. Therefore, a selective description of the early years of voting theory is outlined. Hopefully this sampler will encourage the reader to refer to the references for a complete account.

It is reasonable to expect voting to predate written history. For the same reason that boys in a school yard squabble over how many players are on each

---

[4] To minimize the temptation to manipulate when k out of n candidates are selected, we occasionally use the weights $(k, k-1, \ldots, 1, 0, \ldots, 0)$.

team, one can imagine competing prehistoric tribes quickly assessing the strength of the opposition to determine whether action or diplomacy would serve best – this count is a crude form of voting. The same tense connection using a vote count to assess the opposition's strength continues throughout history. But problems can arise when a majority vote does not mean that the "winning side" enjoys a superiority in exercising power. When this happens, the balance between might and right may tilt – even in holy places such as the Catholic Church.

1.3.1 Selecting a Pope

During the period of time often identified with the controversy between King Henry II of England and Thomas Becket, precise procedures for the election of a pope had yet to be established. Not only was there a lack of agreement about what constituted a winner and who was a voter, but a form of "weighted voting" was used where the votes of the wiser, spiritually more meritorious cardinals received added importance. It is not clear, however, how wisdom and holiness were measured. With all of the ambiguity, it is no wonder that two popes – a Pope and an Anti-Pope – were elected in 1130 creating a schism within the Church. The election of 1159 was no better. Even though Roland received a majority vote of the Cardinals, he was hesitant to accept the papacy without the unanimous vote that seems to have been tacitly expected. Finally he was persuaded to accept the decision.

Controversy is expected to accompany debated elections, but not necessarily of the wild type witnessed in 1159. At reluctant Roland's investiture, jealous competitor Octavian "snatched the mantle like a robber, tore it with his own hands from Alexander's shoulders, and attempted among cries and confusion to carry it off. But one of the Senators ... was moved to anger, and throwing himself bodily on the ranting man, seized the mantle from his hand." Perhaps anticipating such an event, Octavian then enrobed himself with a second mantle supplied by a confederate. Alas, in the excitement he put it on backwards and upside down – definitive proof to Cardinal Boso that "just as [Octavian's] mind was twisted and his intentions devious, he wore his mantle awry in testimony of his own condemnation." Then, for political reasons rather than to shield his embarrassing attire, Octavian quickly was surrounded by his armed supporters; in the resulting violence many of Roland's allies fled for their lives. Following this period of confusion between might and right, Roland became Pope Alexander III with Octavian serving as the competing Pope Victor IV.[5] So, who was the real pope?

What more proof is required about the need for carefully established election procedures? Procedures are needed to spell out who can vote and what it takes

---

[5] Most of this material comes from Cardinal Boso's delightfully biased account of his friend Pope Alexander III. See, for example, *Boso's Life of Alexander III*,[E]; the quotes are from page 44 of this reference. Also see the important reference [U]. In addition, I had the advantage of conversations with Prof. R. Kieckhefer from the Northwestern University Department of Religion.

to be a winner. The Catholic Church recognized and resolved this problem by creating the method during the Third Lateran Council in 1179 that is still in use. The qualitative ("who is holier than whom?") weighted voting approach was abandoned; the new rules specify that only cardinals can vote and each cardinal has a single vote. Anyone can be a candidate for the papacy, but to win you need one more than two-thirds of the vote. Compliance of the faithful with the election result is ensured by invoking the threat of swift excommunication.

Why the two-thirds vote? Why not, say, 63%? As my colleague R. Kieckhefer speculates, "My own hunch is that the clever folk who devised these procedures were less concerned about the fairness of the outcome than about its stability. They were sick and tired of malcontents changing their minds after an election and claiming that for one reason or another the election hadn't been proper, then setting up a rival candidate as antipope and producing a schism. So the question was: how can we devise a procedure that will minimize the risk of there being an effective rival claimant after the election has taken place."

The stability ensured by the two-thirds plus one rule follows from simple arithmetic. In order to successfully create a schism, a competitor needs to convert to his side a majority of the pope's original supporters. In other words, "For really serious problems to arise now, a newly elected pope will have to be so clumsy as to alienate more than half of the cardinals who originally elected him. That, of course, did happen – whence the Great Schism of 1378. Which is only to say that mere mathematics can never ensure against disaster when it's pitted against human nature. But at least now there's a greater safeguard against foreseeable damage."

1.3.2 Procedure Versus Process

This connection between power and vote is a natural one. Through time the disenfranchised have gained the vote primarily through might rather than by appealing to justice or reason. History is full of examples where the king, emperor, dictator, or the group in power, after a realistic assessment of the costs, opted for diplomacy over defeat by offering the right to vote to another select group. This natural phenomenon ranges from the formal voting methods offered to the aristocrats in Sparta around 750 BC, to the suffrage movement of the twentieth century and on to numerous examples in contemporary society with changes in developing countries and former dictatorships. But once the vote is granted, how is it conducted? The earlier processes typically involved voting either *yes* or *no*.

One fifth century BC approach, an obvious precursor for the mindless early morning TV game shows, is where each candidate appeared in front of an assembly to be judged by the crowd's level of approval as demonstrated by shouting. In lieu of the electronic sound meters, that required another couple of millennia to be invented, a small group of men would sit in a nearby building charged with ranking the relative loudness of the shouts. Thus, this approach constituted an early form of our computerized tallying of ballots to offer quick conclusions. A difficulty with this counting method, however, is the obvious incentive it provides for a candidate to court big-lunged supporters. Aristotle joins many of us in viewing this procedure as childish; presumably his opinion would extend to the morning game shows.

Among the many other processes was the traditional show of hands and the Athenian move toward an added degree of anonymity by dropping pebbles into different containers. ([St] is one of several excellent references about the early history of voting.) What we find throughout the early history of this subject, starting from the Greek and Roman Forums through the seventeenth century, is an emphasis on process – who can vote, how they cast their vote, who can be a candidate, who is a winner, and how to avoid fraud and manipulation. While we find comments already in Aristotle's *Politics* about legislative procedures, not much is expressed about voting methods. In fact, what differences arise in the elections involve for the most part the setting of various quotas, different kinds of runoffs, and establishing the thresholds levels required for victory.

1.3.3 Jean-Charles Borda

The mathematician Jean-Charles Borda appears to be the first to recognize that while the mathematics of voting seems to be trivial, it is not. He was the first to formally investigate the subtle effects of using various voting methods. It is worth noting that his attempts to find a method to capture the true views of the voters were first advanced on June 16, 1770, and then again in 1784. These are the years building toward the French revolutionary period, and this theme supporting the voter was pioneered by a person born to nobility. The Borda Count plays a central role in voting theory, so it is worth spending a couple of paragraphs to say something about the man.[6]

J.-C. Borda was the tenth of 16 children born on May 4, 1733, to parents of nobility – Jean-Antoine de Borda and Jeanne-Marie-Théré de Lacroix. That he was an accomplished, influential scientist during those eventful days of the late 1700s is attested to by his election to the Paris Académie des Sciences in 1756 at the age of 23. Readers of this book probably associate Borda with voting, but this work constituted such a minor portion of his contributions that his biographer Mascart devotes less than seven of 636 pages to it. Instead, most of Borda's research involved the mathematical and experimental investigation of fluid dynamics. To provide a feeling for his work, a small sample of his varied contributions follows.

On the theoretical level Borda critiqued Newton's theory of fluid resistance by showing that, contrary to Newton's belief, the resistance is proportional to

---

[6] Other than letters in the collected works of Laplace and correspondence from the Académie of Sciences, I could find very little about Borda except where his name is attached to various ideas in fluid mechanics. In fact, I have yet to find a picture of him. This scarcity of reliable information reflects the unfortunate lack of readily available biographical material about Borda. The best Borda reference I found – the source for most of my comments – is Jean Mascart, *La vie et les travaux du Chevalier Jean-Charles de Borda* [M]. (The quote given below from this book (page 128) and the material I used was translated for me by Katri Saari.) In addition to Mascart's reference, see Duncan Black's classic *The Theory of Committees and Elections* [Bl], and [D]. Also, I have benefited from correspondence with A. Urken about his ongoing research on the history of Borda and Condorcet.

the square of the fluid velocity and the sine of the angle of incidence. He made many contributions to the modern theory of physics. He introduced the Borda mouthpiece, or "Borda harp," and then he computed the "jet" properties for the associated fluid contraction. He wrote on the calculus of variations, developed trigonometric tables to accompany his development of a surveying instrument – the *cercle de réflection.* The role of this instrument in astronomy adds to his role as one of the founders of the Bureau des Longitudes in 1795. The list goes on, but the point is made; Borda was an accomplished scientist, physicist, and mathematician.

Let's admit it. With his important contributions to weights, the pendulum, navigation, geodesy, scientific instruments, fluid flow – both theoretically and as applied to ships, serving on the commission to establish the metric system, his work earning his reputation as one of the founders of modern French mathematical physics, and on and on, we are almost forced to conjure an image of an introverted, absent-minded, sedentary academic balancing his time between a quiet study surrounded by books and a lab where he shuffled around attired in a stained lab coat. Contrast that image with Borda's active role in the French navy where he attained the rank of *capitaine de vaisseau* on March 13, 1779. Remember, the period of the 1770s and 1780s was not the time where the occasional summer vacation warrior could enlist in a national guard; these were years of active naval conflict between England and France. In addition to his normal military duties, Borda took part in scientific voyages and he even participated in the American War for Independence! Indeed, for his actions in the American war, he was in the short lived "Order of Cincinnatus."[7] Then, in 1782, Borda was captured by the English while in charge of a flotilla of six ships in the Antilles. Although the subsequent English imprisonment broke his health, he remained intellectually active until his death on February 19, 1799, as evidenced by his presentation on voting theory in 1784. So, in addition to his valued contributions to mathematics and physics as well as to voting theory, Borda is treated as an important figure in the history of the French navy. With his many contributions, he can give anyone an inferiority complex.

Back to voting theory. Borda's biographer Jean Mascart starts his brief description of this work by describing Borda's 1784 paper which was based on his much earlier 1770 presentation and that, to escalate the confusion, is published in an Academie volume dated 1781 (but, of course, published years later). Mascart says:

> "It is truly remarkable to see a noble, whose family was dispersed by the Revolution, preoccupy himself since 1770 with the correct means to assure the loyalty and sincerity of a vote. 'It is a generally held opinion,'[Borda] says in starting and against which I don't know if anyone has ever made an objection, 'that in an election, the plurality of votes always indicates the desires of the electors; in other words, that the candidate who has

---

[7]In personal correspondence, A. Urken states his suspicion that Borda was an honorary, rather than a full member.

obtained the plurality is necessarily the one that the electors prefer to his opponents. But, I will show that this opinion, which is true if the election is held between only two subjects, can infer an error in all other cases.'"

To support his insightful claim, Borda [Bo, D] develops an example similar to the beverage example from the fable. The thrust of his argument is to use the example to show that the candidate who beats all other candidates in pairwise contests can be plurality bottom-ranked, while the candidate who loses all pairwise contests can be plurality top-ranked. Clearly, such a procedure is flawed. Then Borda demonstrates the superiority of his 3, 2, 1 point system by showing that, at least for this example, the "correct" candidate is elected. His argument must have been persuasive because the Borda Count was adopted by the French Academy until in the 1800s a new member, Napoleon Bonaparte, exerted influence to have it overturned.

When an opportunity for a debate exists, it usually generates one – particularly in academic circles. Borda's method begs for controversy to answer the questions: *"Why these particular choices of weights?" "Why not use, say, 4, 1, 0, or 5, 4, 1?"* Justifications for the BC weights were offered by Borda and by Laplace, but their philosophical responses are not satisfying; the questions remain. Another fault of Borda's method, as shown in the fable, is that the BC can be manipulated. The reported reaction from Borda asserting that his method is intended only for honest people is lame (Chap. 2 of [Bl]); anyway, such a restriction disqualifies its use in modern society. Thus, the debate continues. These questions, which have remained open for the last couple of centuries, are answered here.

1.3.4 Beyond Borda

The next person to get involved was an impressive intellectual of that time and a fellow Academie member, M. Condorcet. (With Condorcet's better press, there is no need to describe his fascinating contributions. See, for instance, [B].) Condorcet argues that a candidate who wins all of the pairwise elections should be selected; an argument that remains central to this field. Observe that Condorcet's concept is an immediate extension of the election phenomenon developed, used, and illustrated in Borda's earlier lecture and publication. Presumably following the occasionally accepted scientific protocol whereby credit and the naming of a process is awarded to a popularizer rather than the actual discoverer, this solution concept is called a "Condorcet winner." (See Sect. 2.5.) A new concept introduces a new issue: *which is the more natural, representative solution concept – the Condorcet or the Borda winner?* The debate continues; so how can I resist entering?

An important insightful Condorcet contribution, which he used to prove that a Condorcet winner need not always exist, is the disturbing example from the departmental meeting. This division of the voters, which proves that sincere pairwise elections can create cycles, has been rediscovered many times since by important contributors to this area. (See [Bl].) In fact, this election paradox plays an important role motivating Arrow's theorem (Sect. 4.4) where Arrow proves the impossibility of ever constructing a method for three or more alternatives that satisfies certain desirable, yet seemingly innocuous properties. The geometric implications of this paradox are described in several sections; an informational explanation is given in Sect. 4.4.

Once history moves beyond those creative days of Borda and Condorcet, there exist several excellent descriptions about the development of this subject chronicling who did what and why. From these accounts, we learn about Lewis Carroll's contributions, presumably developed between reporting on Alice's exciting and delightful adventures, the debates of proportional voting (see Sect. 4.3), etc. Moreover, surveys of modern work (e.g. [F1, NiR, Nu, Mo1, Pl, Se2]) are easily found. Indeed, this intellectually attractive subject which now is a couple hundred years old has attracted the imagination of large numbers of researchers, so it has spawned an incredibly large literature! This underscores the value of J. Kelly's compilation [K3] of publications.

So far, perhaps reflecting a natural academic arrogance, I have emphasized theoretical developments. What about the practicing politicians? Do the clever, successful politicians know about the various voting paradoxes? Of course they do, and probably long before us academics! In fact, a case can be made demonstrating how this knowledge has served them well. (However, Riker [R1-2] is among the few scholars who has studied how "paradoxes" have been converted to political advantage.) Indeed, I suspect that some of the deep, insightful voting paradoxes discovered by academics are restatements of properties already being used to the advantage of clever politicians.

Where can illustrating examples be found? Anywhere where smart politicians are in conflict with one another. My favorite political dig, and the source of several of my examples, is the city of Chicago where politics has been elevated to a popular spectator sport. Indeed, it is probably the only major metropolitan area where opposing alderman are sufficiently well known to become the featured stars of a popular commercial depicting a "Council Wars" debate over the merits of an advertised food product. And, many of the politicians form colorful character studies. For example, while disagreeing with much of his politics, one of my favorites is Edward Vydolyak, whose alleged attempts to manipulate the system through clever "reform movements," political action, coalition development, and even changing and creating political parties earned him the title of "Fast Eddie." Academics have much to learn about voting procedures from the "Fast Eddies" of the world.

1.4 What Kind of Geometry?

The beverage example exhibits a particular division of voters' preferences where milk, the winning alternative, loses in a pairwise comparison with each of the other two choices. If this were the only division of voters' preferences causing such a troublesome outcome, the example could be dismissed as a curious anomaly. The discomforting fact is that such election behavior is not exceptional.

If the beverage paradox is not unusual, it should be easy to construct many different illustrating examples. Try it; you won't like it. Try, for instance, to create a different example of voters' preferences where the plurality election ranking is $c_1 \succ c_2 \succ c_3$ even though the pairwise election results are $c_2 \succ c_1$, $c_3 \succ c_1$, $c_3 \succ c_1$. Or, try to create an example involving n_1 voters with the ranking $c_1 \succ c_2 \succ c_3$, n_2 voters with the ranking $c_3 \succ c_1 \succ c_2$, n_3 voters with the ranking $c_3 \succ c_2 \succ c_1$, and n_4 voters with the ranking $c_2 \succ c_1 \succ c_3$. Finally, try to construct such an example using just the three rankings $c_1 \succ c_2 \succ c_3$, $c_2 \succ c_3 \succ c_1$, $c_3 \succ c_1 \succ c_2$.

The challenge problems make it clear that analyzing voting procedures by creating concrete examples can be difficult. The complexity is due to the combinatorics of the many available options. To further illustrate, often near election day the radio and television airways are clogged with advice to *"Have your say! Vote!"* The reason is clear; by not voting, a voter risks being responsible for an election outcome that he doesn't want. But, is this always true? Can situations arise where by not voting a voter ensures an election outcome that he prefers to what would have occurred had he voted? Is it possible to argue to a particular voter, *"Don't vote! Only by staying home can you win!"* Procedures admitting such situations exist. (See Chapter 4.) But, to verify that such perverse, counter-intuitive behavior exists is not easy. If you don't believe me, try to find one. Moreover, because these paradoxes are counter-intuitive, how does one know what to look for? This underscores the major problem – where does one start?

The same is true for manipulative strategies. We know from the startling Gibbard-Satterthwaite Theorem that, with three or more alternatives, all non-dictatorial procedures allow situations where a voter can force the outcome into a personally better one by voting strategically. Why is this true? How does one identify these manipulative situations? We saw from the fable how to do this with the BC, but how is this done with the plurality vote? Does the agenda procedure for the departmental meeting allow for such opportunities? If so, for whom? How does one start the analysis?

What we want is a way to systematically explore, discover, and prove the existence of new voting properties. We want a method of analysis where the basic ideas become sufficiently transparent so that us mere mortals can hope to offer theoretical advances. In order to create such techniques, we need to find a way to avoid the difficult, frustrating combinatorics that traditionally accompany the development of voting theory. This is done here where much of this heavy computational work is palmed off onto the related geometry.

Somewhat surprisingly, at least for three-candidate problems, the mathematical entry requirements to achieve these goals are realistic. (While the mathematics involves reasonably standard mathematics known to most readers, it is used in different and new contexts.) To assist the development of intuition, much of the discussion is accompanied by familiar two and three-dimensional geometric figures. What follows is a brief outline of some of the needed mathematical tools. The reader familiar with the connection between convexity and linear mappings should move on to Chap. 2.

1.4.1 Convexity And Linear Mappings

An important geometric concept used repeatedly throughout this book is *convexity*.

Convexity. A set is convex if for any two points in the set, the straight line connecting these points also is in the set.

As examples, the first two sets in Fig. 1.4.1 are convex. Intuitively, convexity is ensured because all "bulges" are outwards. Consequently, for any two points chosen in a set, the connecting straight path also is in the set.

The third set in Fig. 1.4.1 fails convexity because the line connecting the two points is partially outside of the shaded region. So, refining the above intuition, a convex set can't have an inward dent. With a dent, as in the third figure, it is easy to find two points near the indentation where part of the connecting line falls outside of the set.

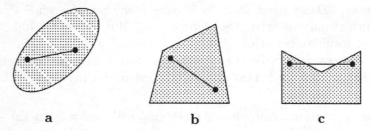

a   b   c

Fig. 1.4.1. Convex and non-convex sets. **a** Convex. **b** Convex.
 c Not convex because of the inward bulge

A common technical problem for what follows is to divide a convex set into convex subsets. By experimenting with the regions of Fig. 1.4.1, it becomes clear that the boundary between two subsets must be a straight line. If it isn't, then the bulge of one subset is an indentation for the other.

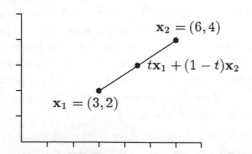

Fig. 1.4.2. The representation of the connecting line

Linear Mappings. Because it is frequently used in this book, I'll recall how to algebraically represent the line segment connecting two given points. Suppose they are $\mathbf{x}_1 = (3,2)$ and $\mathbf{x}_2 = (6,4)$. Let t, $0 \leq t \leq 1$, represent the position on the connecting line segment that is the proportion t of the distance from $\mathbf{x}_2$ to $\mathbf{x}_1$, or $1 - t$ of the distance from $\mathbf{x}_1$ to $\mathbf{x}_2$. Combining these facts, the representation for the line is

$$t\mathbf{x}_1 + (1 - t)\mathbf{x}_2 = t(3,2) + (1 - t)(6,4) = (6 - 3t, 4 - 2t), \quad t \in [0,1] \quad (1.4.1)$$

So, with the interpretation of t, when $t = 0$ we should be at $\mathbf{x}_2$, which is what Eq. 1.4.1 yields. Similarly, when $t = 1$, we are at $\mathbf{x}_1$. Other t values extend the line beyond these defining points.

More general than a straight line is a linear mapping – it generalizes the single variable equation $y = ax$ where a is a given constant and where x is the input, or independent variable, and y is the output, or dependent variable. In voting, the inputs often correspond to the number of voters with each of the possible rankings of the candidates, and the outputs represent the election tallies. The algebra we need, then, is the set of linear equations defined by specified constants $a_{i,j}$

$$
\begin{aligned}
y_1 &= a_{1,1}x_1 + a_{1,2}x_2 + \ldots a_{1,n}x_n \\
y_2 &= a_{2,1}x_1 + a_{2,2}x_2 + \ldots a_{2,n}x_n \\
&\quad \ldots \\
&\quad \ldots \\
y_m &= a_{m,1}x_1 + a_{m,2}x_2 + \ldots a_{m,n}x_n
\end{aligned}
\quad (1.4.2)
$$

and the associated problems of determining when the system admits unique solutions, when it admits solutions, etc. In other words, we need the kind of mathematics associated with the familiar phrase "m equations in n unknowns."

As an illustration, with specified values for the y_j's, the problem is to solve the system of m equations in n unknowns. If $m > n$, then, in general, there are no solutions. The system of three equations and two unknowns

$$
\begin{aligned}
2 &= 2x_1 + 3x_2 \\
6 &= 2x_1 + 3x_2 \\
4 &= 3x_1 - x_2
\end{aligned}
$$

demonstrates the difficulty; it is impossible to satisfy the first and second equations simultaneously. A solution is possible only should the y values lie in the n-dimensional image set defined by the equations.

With $m = n$ equations and unknowns, we should expect an unique solution except for the rare choice of $a_{i,j}$ coefficients where no solution exists. To illustrate a setting where the unique solution assertion does not hold, no solution exists for

$$4 = x_1 + x_2, \quad 5 = x_1 + x_2,$$

while the system

$$4 = x_1 + x_2, \quad 8 = 2x_1 + 2x_2$$

admits the infinite number of solutions $x_1 = 4 - x_2$.

Finally, if $m < n$, then we must expect the solution set to be a $n - m$ dimensional set. For instance, the system

$$3 = 2x_1 + 3x_2 + 4x_3, \quad 2 = 3x_1 - x_2 + x_3$$

has a line of solutions determined by various choices of x_3.

The matrix representation for Eq. 1.4.2 is given by

$$
\begin{pmatrix} y_1 \\ y_2 \\ \cdots \\ y_m \end{pmatrix}
=
\begin{pmatrix}
a_{1,1} & a_{1,2} & \cdots & a_{1,n} \\
a_{2,1} & a_{2,2} & \cdots & a_{2,n} \\
& \cdots & \cdots & \\
a_{m,1} & a_{m,2} & \cdots & a_{m,n}
\end{pmatrix}
\begin{pmatrix} x_1 \\ x_2 \\ \cdots \\ x_n \end{pmatrix}
\tag{1.4.3}
$$

where the solution properties are expressed in terms of the properties of the matrix $((a_{i,j}))$.

Properties of Linear Mappings. An important (and the defining) property of a linear function f is

$$f(a\mathbf{x}_1 + b\mathbf{x}_2) = af(\mathbf{x}_1) + bf(\mathbf{x}_2) \tag{1.4.4}$$

where a and b are scalars. This powerful property asserts that a linear combination of inputs is transferred into the same linear combination of outputs. As a consequence, a linear function maps a straight line to a straight line because

$$f(t\mathbf{x}_1 + (1-t)\mathbf{x}_2) = tf(\mathbf{x}_1) + (1-t)f(\mathbf{x}_2) \tag{1.4.5}$$

There is an immediate, useful consequence of this delightful separation property of Eq. 1.4.5 that is enjoyed by linear mappings.

Convexity Property. *If $\mathcal{A}$ is a convex set in the domain and if f is a linear function, then the image of $\mathcal{A}$ is a convex set in the image space. Conversely, if f is a linear mapping with a convex domain and if $\mathcal{D}$ is a convex set in the image set, then $f^{-1}(\mathcal{D})$ is a convex set.*

Outline of the proof. The assertion holds because the convexity of $\mathcal{A}$ ensures that the line segment connecting any two points in $\mathcal{A}$ must also be in $\mathcal{A}$. According to Eq. 1.4.5, the connecting straight line must accompany the image of the two points in $f(\mathcal{A})$. But, every point in the image set $f(\mathcal{A})$ has a preimage, so the conclusion follows.

In the other direction, if $\mathbf{q}_1, \mathbf{q}_2 \in \mathcal{D}$, then by the convexity of this set, the line segment defined by these points also is in $\mathcal{D}$. Now, suppose $\mathbf{p}_i$ are such that $f(\mathbf{p}_i) = \mathbf{q}_i$, $i = 1, 2$. As the domain is convex, the line segment defined by these two points is in the domain. By linearity, this line segment is mapping to the line segment defined by $\mathbf{q}_1$, $\mathbf{q}_2$. Consequently, the line segment defined by $\mathbf{p}_1, \mathbf{p}_2$ is in $f^{-1}(\mathcal{D})$. $\square$

For reasons that will become apparent in subsequent chapters, convex sets play an important role in the analysis of election procedures. The natural relationship – connecting the number of voters that have each ranking of the candidates with the election tallies – is a linear function. (Here, the $a_{i,j}$ coefficients reflect the choice of the voting system and the preferences of the voters; the x values represent the number of voters.) As linear functions map convex sets to convex sets, for many procedures the convexity of sets of preferences ensures the convexity of sets of election outcomes.

1.4.2 Convex Hulls

Many convex sets are defined by specified vertices $\{\mathbf{v}_i\}_{i=1}^n$.

Convex Hull. *The convex hull of a specified set of vertices $\{\mathbf{v}_i\}_{i=1}^n$ is the smallest convex set containing all vertices. A way to represent the convex hull is*

$$\mathcal{CH}(\{\mathbf{v}_i\}) = \{\sum_{i=1}^{n} \lambda_i \mathbf{v}_i \mid \lambda_i \geq 0, \sum_{i=1}^{n} \lambda_i = 1\} \tag{1.4.6}$$

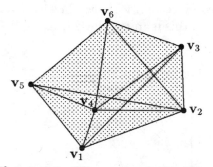

Fig. 1.4.3. The convex hull of the vertices $\{\mathbf{v}_i\}_{i=1}^6$

Equation 1.4.6 generalizes the straight line representation of Eq. 1.4.1. The t values from Eq. 1.4.1 provide all possible linear combinations between the two defining points. With more vertices, there are more possible locations, and they are given by the wider choice of λ values. Because the definition in Eq. 1.4.7 includes all possible choices of λ values, it includes choices where only two of the λ_i values are not zero, say λ_1 and λ_2. Here, $\lambda_1 = 1 - \lambda_2$, so Eq. 1.4.7 becomes $\lambda_2 \mathbf{v}_2 + (1 - \lambda_2)\mathbf{v}_1$; this is the equation of a straight line connecting the two vertices $\mathbf{v}_1$, $\mathbf{v}_2$. This description leads to the geometric construction of the convex hull. Just connect all of the vertices with straight lines, and then shade in the resulting figure. A two-dimensional example is given in Fig. 1.4.3.

The Mapping of Convex Hulls. By combining the separation property for linear mappings along with the above geometric construction of a convex hull defined by the vertices $\{\mathbf{v}_i\}_{i=1}^n$ we have a simple way to construct the image of a convex hull. First find the images $\{f(\mathbf{v}_i)\}_{i=1}^n$ and then find the convex hull defined by these points. For example, the convex hull for the four points

$(0,0), (1,0), (0,1), (1,1)$ is the square on the left-hand side of Fig. 1.4.4. Suppose the linear mapping is given in matrix form by

$$\begin{pmatrix} y_1 \\ y_2 \end{pmatrix} = f(\begin{pmatrix} x_1 \\ x_2 \end{pmatrix}) = \begin{pmatrix} 2 & 1 \\ 1 & 3 \end{pmatrix} \begin{pmatrix} x_1 \\ x_2 \end{pmatrix},$$

which has the linear equation form

$$y_1 = 2x_1 + x_2, \quad y_2 = x_1 + 3x_2.$$

To find the image set, just find the image of each vertex, or

$$(0,0) \rightarrow f(0,0) = (0,0), \quad (1,0) \rightarrow f(1,0) = (2,1)$$
$$(0,1) \rightarrow f(0,1) = (1,3), \quad (1,1) \rightarrow f(1,1) = (3,4).$$

The image set is the convex hull of these image points, as illustrated in Fig. 1.4.4.

This illustrates a common geometric theme used in this book. When dealing with a convex set of profiles defined by certain vertices, the election outcomes of the vertex profiles are determined. In this manner, the convex hull of all possible election outcomes can be constructed.

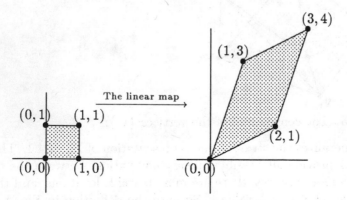

Fig. 1.4.4. Transferring a convex hull

While more sophisticated mathematical results are used, the above provides entry for the reader.

CHAPTER II
GEOMETRY FOR POSITIONAL AND PAIRWISE VOTING

A plurality election is simple; just count how many voters have each candidate top-ranked. It is surprising that using this elementary description to analyze the procedure quickly introduces mathematical complications that severely limit what can be learned.

How can this be? In part, the difficulty is due to the enormous number of ways voters' preferences can be arranged. For instance, with the beverage example a voter has six ways to rank the three choices. So, two voters create $6^2 = 36$ possible arrangements. With 15 voters, as in the example, the number of possible assignments grows to the hundreds of billions – $6^{15} = 470, 184, 984, 576$. To appreciate this number, one might try to count to 6^{15}, but it would take awhile because 6^{15} seconds of time is about 14,899 years. As another measure, the printed listings for these 15 voters would require a library to hold the more than $340,000$ books of 500 pages each.[1] And, even for the reader who maintains interest in this series to the last page of the last book, much more is required. This is because to develop a theory, we need to consider all possible arrangements of voters' choices for any number of voters.

So, even for three candidates, the overwhelming numbers of possible voter arrangements deny the possibility for anyone to develop an accurate intuition of what can happen based just on experience or constructing examples. In other words, with three or more candidates the associated combinatorics introduce a complexity that defies a simple analysis of voting; different mathematical approaches must be developed.

Contributing to the combinatoric complexity are the "gaps" between the integers. Without the gaps, calculus type techniques apply; with the spaces the more difficult techniques of combinatorics and discrete mathematics are required. To avoid these pitfalls, we might use a model that fills these holes; but which one?

---

[1] This value of 6^{15} is correct but misleading; it arises if one computes the rankings by preserving the identity of the voters. This is not necessary. For instance, if only Anneli and Claudia interchange preferences then there is no change in the election outcome. Thus, a different way to compute the number of different rankings is to impose an anonymity condition – the identities of the voters are not relevant, it only matters how many voters have each ranking. Using this anonymity assumption, "only" $14,484$ different profiles result from the 15 voters. But, where did this value come from? This computation, in itself, underscores the complexities associated with a discrete analysis. Moreover, when one considers what happens with $1, 2, \ldots, 15, \ldots$ voters, millions upon millions of different voter arrangements emerge.

The problem with constructing models to span the spaces is that there are too many choices. As an analogy, just as anyone rushing to clean a room before a dinner party learns, the empty spaces in a hall closet can be filled in highly imaginative, unexpected ways. However, many of these clever space-filling techniques are counter-productive – as when a collapsing top shelf dumps dirty underwear, several partially completed manuscripts, and an unstrung tennis racket upon a stunned dinner guest. This same difficulty extends to the mathematics; the spaces between the integers can be filled in highly imaginative ways with various mathematical structures. Some are useful, but others share striking similarities with the closet shelf; they could dump irrelevant, unwanted structures upon the intended objectives. Thus the first task is to introduce a representation for the integer counting process that filters out those mathematical structures that are, at best, redundant.

The representation developed here is a natural, geometric one where the number of candidates is identified with the geometric dimension of a space. In this manner the mysteries of election paradoxes and the properties of election procedures can be explained with simple geometric constructions and elementary mathematical arguments. In fact, it quickly becomes clear that the differences between two and three candidate elections can be understood in terms of the geometric difference exhibited by different dimensional spaces.

To identify elections with geometry, the first three sections of this chapter are devoted toward introducing the appropriate notation and geometry for positional voting procedures. Related results about other possible procedures are in the exercises. Then, for the rest of the chapter, the power of this geometric approach is used to compare election outcomes over different subsets of candidates with different voting procedures.

2.1 Ranking Regions

With two candidates, a voter votes only for his or her top-ranked candidate. It seems reasonable to use this procedure with any number of candidates. Or, is it?

Definition 2.1.1. A *plurality election* is where each voter casts a single point for his top-ranked candidate. The ranking of each candidate is determined by the total number of points assigned to her. If candidate c_i receives more votes than candidate c_j, then c_i is ranked higher than c_j. This is denoted as $c_i \succ c_j$. If both candidates, c_i, c_j, receive the same number of votes, then they are tied. This is denoted as $c_i \sim c_j$. $\square$

With three candidates $\{c_1, c_2, c_3\}$, the vote total defines the array (n_1, n_2, n_3) where n_j is the number of points assigned to candidate c_j, $j = 1, 2, 3$. By exploiting our familiarity with the three dimensional world, treat (n_1, n_2, n_3) as a point in the three dimensional space $R^3 = \{(x_1, x_2, x_3) \mid -\infty < x_j < \infty, j = 1, 2, 3\}$. This requires identifying values along the x_j axis of R^3 with the election tally for candidate c_j; $j = 1, 2, 3$. Each component of (n_1, n_2, n_3) is non-negative, so the point is in the *non-negative orthant* of R^3,

$$R^3_+ = \{(x_1, x_2, x_3) \in R^3 \mid x_j \geq 0\}$$

In the obvious manner, the entries (n_1, n_2, n_3) determine the rankings of the candidates. For instance, $(45, 75, 80)$ indicates that c_1 receives 45 votes, c_2 receives 75 votes, and c_3 receives 80 votes leading to the election ranking $c_3 \succ c_2 \succ c_1$. Because an ordinal ranking of the candidates depends only on the relative sizes of the coordinates of a vector, any positive multiple of the tally preserves the election ranking. So, while a multiple of 1000 separates $(3, 5, 2)$ from $(3000, 5000, 2000)$, both vote totals define the same election ranking $c_2 \succ c_1 \succ c_3$.

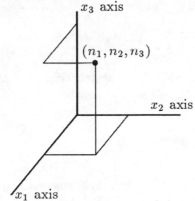

Fig. 2.1.1. The election tally

2.1.1 Normalized Election Tally

A useful mathematical technique is, "When in doubt, exploit a mathematical invariance." To apply this advice to the scalar invariance, observe that the ranking associated with (n_1, n_2, n_3) remains the same after each term is divided by the total number of votes cast, $\sum_{j=1}^{3} n_j$. Therefore the election ranking for (n_1, n_2, n_3) is determined by the *normalized election vector*

$$\mathbf{q} = \left(\frac{n_1}{\sum_{j=1}^{3} n_j}, \frac{n_2}{\sum_{j=1}^{3} n_j}, \frac{n_3}{\sum_{j=1}^{3} n_j} \right) \tag{2.1.1}$$

An interpretation of the normalized election vector is that the jth component, q_j, specifies the portion of the total tally received by the jth candidate, $j = 1, 2, 3$. Indeed, the components of the normalized election vector,

---

HATFIELD WINS $\frac{2}{3}$ OF THE VOTE!!
McCoy refuses to concede;
clan will fight on!

rather than the actual tallies, dominate the morning headlines after election night.

Example 2.1.1. The election ranking assigned to the normalized election vector $(\frac{1}{6}, \frac{1}{2}, \frac{1}{3})$ is $c_2 \succ c_3 \succ c_1$. A common denominator for these three fractions is any multiple of 6, so the normalized vector could be from an election involving six voters, or 12,000,000 voters. In the former case, the integer tally is $(1, 3, 2)$, and in the latter case it is $(2,000,000, 6,000,000, 4,000,000)$. □

It follows from the definition of the normalized election vector $\mathbf{q} = (q_1, q_2, q_3)$, where

$$q_k = \frac{n_k}{\sum_{j=1}^{3} n_j} \tag{2.1.2}$$

that

$$q_k \geq 0 \text{ and } \sum_{k=1}^{3} q_k = 1$$

These conditions make sense. As q_k identifies the fraction of the total vote received by c_k, q_k must be non-negative. All votes must be accounted for, so

$$\sum_{k=1}^{3} q_k = 1$$

These properties, $\sum_{k=1}^{3} q_k = 1$ and $q_k \geq 0, k = 1, 2, 3$, suggest identifying the election ranking with a point in the *unit simplex* in R_+^3 defined by

$$Si(3) = \{\mathbf{x} = (x_1, x_2, x_3) \in R_+^3 \mid x_j \geq 0, \sum_{j=1}^{3} x_j = 1\} \tag{2.1.3}$$

and illustrated in Fig. 2.1.2. This simplex, called the *representation triangle*, is the equilateral triangle passing through the three unanimity outcomes $\mathbf{e}_1 = (1, 0, 0)$, $\mathbf{e}_2 = (0, 1, 0)$, $\mathbf{e}_3 = (0, 0, 1)$. Each point in the representation triangle, $Si(3)$, uniquely defines a particular ranking of the candidates.

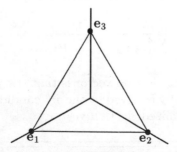

Fig. 2.1.2. The simplex of normalized election outcomes

As only the representation triangle is need, the coordinate axes are suppressed in what follows; this leads to a figure like that in Fig. 2.1.3.

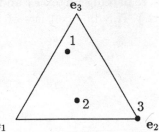

Fig. 2.1.3. Normalized election outcomes

Example 2.1.2. In Fig. 2.1.3, each of the three identified points represents a normalized election vector.

Point	Coordinate	Ranking
1	$(\frac{7}{20}, \frac{4}{20}, \frac{9}{20}) \in Si(3)$	$c_3 \succ c_1 \succ c_2$
2	$(\frac{2}{5}, \frac{2}{5}, \frac{1}{5}) \in Si(3)$	$c_1 \sim c_2 \succ c_3$
3	$(0, 1, 0) \in Si(3)$	$c_2 \succ c_1 \sim c_3$

Point 3 at $\mathbf{e}_2 = (0, 1, 0)$ requires c_2 to receive an unanimous vote. □

As in love, "closer is better," so the ranking assigned to $\mathbf{q} \in Si(3)$ (the representation triangle) is determined by how close $\mathbf{q}$ is to each vertex. Namely, the closer $\mathbf{q}$ is to vertex $\mathbf{e}_k$, the better candidate c_k fares in the election. This "closer is better" relationship is easy to understand. If c_k receives a large vote relative to the other candidates, then q_k has a large value, so $\mathbf{q} = (q_1, q_2, q_3)$ is closer to the vertex $\mathbf{e}_k$. (Remember, $\mathbf{e}_k$ represents an unanimous vote for c_k.) Conversely, the closer $\mathbf{q} = (q_1, q_2, q_3)$ is to $\mathbf{e}_k$, the larger the vote proportion, q_k, received by c_k.

2.1.2 Ranking Regions

The "closer is better" relationship divides $Si(3)$ into "ranking regions" where each geometric region is identified with a unique election ranking. The idea is straightforward. For instance, the election ranking $c_3 \sim c_1 \succ c_2$ occurs iff the election tally is $q_3 = q_1 > q_2$. As such, the ranking region for $c_3 \sim c_1 \succ c_2$ is

$$\mathcal{R}(c_3 \sim c_1 \succ c_2) = \{\mathbf{q} \in Si(3) | q_3 = q_1 > q_2\}$$

Using all possible inequalities involving q_1, q_2, q_3, the representation triangle $Si(3)$ is partitioned into 13 different ranking regions. Six of these regions correspond to election rankings without ties between candidates, six represent election rankings with a tie vote between a pair of candidates, and the last region represents the election ranking with a tie among all three candidates.

A geometric construction of the ranking regions relates the "closer is better" relationship with pairs of candidates. Start with a $c_j \sim c_k$ region. For instance, the line $q_1 = q_2$, indicating a tie vote between c_1 and c_2, connects the mid-point between the vertices e_1 and e_2 with the remaining vertex e_3 and it is called the "c_1, c_2 *indifference line.*" (See Fig. 2.1.4.) This line consists of all points equal distance from the two vertices.

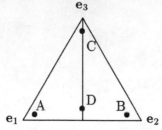

Fig. 2.1.4. The $c_1 - c_2$ indifference line

The $c_j \sim c_k$ line separates the $c_j \succ c_k$ region from the $c_k \succ c_j$ region. In particular, a point to the left of the $c_1 \sim c_2$ line, such as point A in Fig. 2.1.4, is closer to e_1 than to e_2, so it is in the binary ranking region $c_1 \succ c_2$. Correspondingly, a point to the right of this line, such as B in the figure, represents $c_2 \succ c_1$. However, further refinements of the rankings is not delineated by the $c_1 \sim c_2$ line. For instance, while C clearly is close enough to the vertex e_3 to define the relationship

$$q_3 > q_1 = q_2$$

it is not obvious from Fig. 2.1.4 what other points are in the same ranking region $c_3 \succ c_1 \sim c_2$. Similarly, D is sufficiently near the mid-point of e_1 and e_2 to ensure that $q_1 = q_2 > q_3$, but what are all other points in the ranking region $c_1 \sim c_2 \succ c_3$?

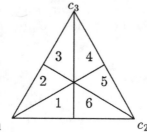

Fig. 2.1.5. The representation triangle

To further refine the ranking regions, all three $c_i \sim c_j$ indifferent lines are drawn to obtain Fig. 2.1.5. (Note that the vertex e_j is replaced with the name of the candidate, $c_j, j = 1, 2, 3$.) So, the intersections of the large "binary relations" triangles create the six smaller triangular ranking regions defining strict rankings. This process of intersecting the larger binary triangles (of the type in Fig. 2.1.4) to obtain the smaller triangle ranking regions of Fig. 2.1.5 is a geometric representation of how the binary rankings of pairs define a transitive[2] ranking of the candidates.

---

[2] This means that if $c_i \succ c_j$ and $c_j \succ c_k$, then $c_i \succ c_k$. So, with "transitivity" the binary rankings of certain pairs of candidates imposes a particular ranking on other pairs of candidates. These ideas are described in Sect. 2.3.

The six small triangles in Fig. 2.1.5 represent the strict rankings with no tie vote or indifference among candidates. As the remaining election rankings involve a tie vote, the associated ranking regions must be on the indifference lines. For instance, one ranking region is where all three indifference lines intersect at $(\frac{1}{3}, \frac{1}{3}, \frac{1}{3})$. This barycentric point serves two purposes. The first is to define the ranking region of *complete indifference*, $\mathcal{I} = c_1 \sim c_2 \sim c_3$. The second is to divide each indifference line into two segments; one segment ends in a vertex and the other ends at the midpoint of a leg of the equilateral triangle. The first segment is the ranking region where the tied pair is bottom-ranked (and the vertex identifies the top-ranked candidate), while the second segment has the tied pair top-ranked. In this manner, the six line segments and $\mathcal{I}$ account for the seven rankings with a tie vote among two or more candidates.

Example 2.1.3. In Fig. 2.1.5, the line segment separating the regions labeled 3 and 4 corresponds to the ranking $c_3 \succ c_1 \sim c_2$. The line segment separating the regions 2 and 3 is the ranking region for $c_1 \sim c_3 \succ c_2$. $\square$

The above provides a geometric representation for the "transitive rankings." Geometric representations for other kinds of binary rankings are developed in the exercises.

2.1.3 Exercises

2.1.1. Geometrically, show that the intersection of the binary ranking regions $c_1 \succ c_2$ and $c_3 \succ c_2$ contains three ranking regions. Next show that the intersection of the binary regions $c_1 \succ c_2$ and $c_2 \succ c_3$ defines a unique ranking region. The flexibility admitted by one situation, but not by the other, plays an important role in proving Arrow's Theorem in Sect. 4.4.

2.1.2. Geometric relationships among binary rankings can be created by dividing objects other than the simplex $Si(3)$. To see this, start with the candidates c_1, c_2 and the interval $[-1, 1]$. Suppose positive values from this interval imply that $c_1 \succ c_2$ while negative values represent $c_2 \succ c_1$. With three candidates, there are three pairs of candidates, so we need three intervals to represent the different binary rankings. To do this, consider the three coordinate axes of R^3 where points along the x, y, and z axis correspond, respectively, to binary ranking for $\{c_1, c_2\}$, $\{c_2, c_3\}$, $\{c_3, c_1\}$ and where a positive value for a component means the first listed candidate in the corresponding pair is preferred. To see the implied interaction among these binary rankings, place a $[-1, 1]$ interval on each axis; this defines a cube.

a. Determine the intersections of all the binary relationships to show that there are 27 ranking regions in this cube. Which ones are *not* transitive?

b. A set of binary rankings is acyclic if $c_i \succ c_j$ and $c_j \succ c_k$ hold, then $c_k \not\succ c_i$. Find the regions from the divided cube that need to be excluded to ensure that the remaining binary relationships are acyclic.

c. Find a two dimensional plane that passes through the origin of the cube so that all of the ranking regions on this plane are transitive.

2.1.3. Show that if each q_j of $\mathbf{q} = (q_1, q_2, q_3) \in Si(3)$ is a fraction, then $\mathbf{q}$ corresponds to a normalized plurality election tally. What are the numbers of voters for any supporting example?

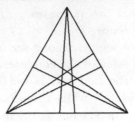

Fig. 2.1.6. The quasitransitive regions

2.1.4. The ranking regions of Fig. 2.1.5 are determined by the requirement that $c_1 \sim c_j$ iff $q_i = q_j$. Other definitions of binary indifference create different types of ranking regions. For instance, one could say that c_i is indifferent to c_j when the point totals are "*almost the same.*" More specifically, let $\epsilon > 0$ be a specified constant. Say that $c_i \sim c_j$ iff

$$\frac{1-\epsilon}{1+\epsilon} \leq \frac{x_i}{x_j} \leq \frac{1+\epsilon}{1-\epsilon};$$

and $c_i \succ c_j$ iff $\frac{x_i}{x_j} > \frac{1+\epsilon}{1-\epsilon}$.

a.   Prove that the relationship " $\sim$ " is symmetric. Namely, if $c_i \sim c_j$, then $c_j \sim c_i$.

b.   Prove that $\succ$ is transitive. That is, if $c_i \succ c_j$ and $c_j \succ c_k$, then $c_i \succ c_k$. Also show that $\succ$ is asymmetric; i.e., if $c_i \succ c_j$ then $c_j \not\succ c_i$..

c.   On the simplex $Si(3)$, graph the c_1, c_2 binary indifference region. (You should get a triangle with vertex at $\mathbf{e}_3$ that straddles the c_1, c_2 indifference line from Fig. 2.1.5.) Next, by computing all of the c_i, c_j indifference regions, show that Fig. 2.1.6 provides a geometric representation of how the binary relationships interact. In this figure, identify all nineteen regions. In particular, identify the rankings for the six ranking regions that are not admitted by Fig. 2.1.5.

d.   Prove that with this binary relationship, it is possible to have the rankings $c_1 \sim c_2, c_2 \sim c_3, c_1 \succ c_3$. Thus, "$\sim$" is not transitive.

e.   Identify the regions of Fig. 2.1.6 with corresponding regions of the cube from Example 2.1.3. Which cube regions are *not* in the quasitransitive triangle?

This *quasitransitive* relationship can be used with the normalized tally of a plurality election to determine the election rankings. As above, the election ranking is given by the ranking region that contains the normalized election tally.

2.1.5. Suppose the normalized election ranking (q_1, q_2, q_3) satisfies the inequalities $q_1 > q_2 > q_3$. A normal interpretation of the election ranking $c_1 \succ c_2 \succ c_3$ is that even should c_1 beat c_2 by a single vote, c_1 is designated the top-ranked candidate. As an alternative, suppose in order to be elected, the normalized tally for a top-ranked candidate must beat the second-ranked candidate by a specified fractional amount. This motivates the following threshold method.

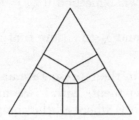

Fig. 2.1.7. The distinct winner threshold method

The *"Distinct winner"* threshold procedure is determined by specified values $\gamma_2 \geq \frac{1}{2}$, $\gamma_3 \geq \frac{2}{3}$. For c_i to win:

1. She must have the most votes.
2. If c_j has the second highest vote, then $\frac{q_i}{q_i+q_j} \geq \gamma_2$.

For candidates c_i, c_j to be tied for top-ranked:

1. There must be no single winner.
2. Each of c_i, c_j must have more votes than the remaining candidate.
3. The normalized vote tallies must satisfy $\frac{q_i+q_j}{\sum_{k=1}^{3} q_k} = q_i + q_j \geq \gamma_3$. Otherwise, the three candidates are in a three way tie.

a. Show that the associated ranking regions are transitive and that they admit a representation of the form given in Fig. 2.1.7. By use of elementary trigonometry of the 30°–60°–90° triangle (see Sect. 1.4), describe what happens if $\gamma_3 = \frac{1-\gamma_2}{\sqrt{3}}$ and if $\gamma_3 \geq \frac{1-\gamma_2}{\sqrt{3}}$.

b. What happens to the representation for $\frac{1-\gamma_2}{\sqrt{3}} > \gamma_3 \geq \frac{1}{3}$? In particular, describe the regions where no election outcome is defined. Change the definition distinguishing between whether two or three candidates are top-ranked to handle this situation.

2.1.6. The *"Universal"* threshold method requires the winning candidate to receive a certain fraction of the total vote. The threshold values are specified numbers $\delta_2 \geq \frac{1}{3}$, $\delta_3 \geq \frac{2}{3}$. For candidate c_j to win, she must have the largest normalized vote tally and $q_j \geq \delta_2$. If no winner exists, then the two candidates with the largest number of votes, c_i, c_j, are tied for top-rank iff $q_i + q_j \geq \delta_3$. Otherwise, all three candidates are tied.

a. Show that for one particular choice of δ's, the ranking regions are as illustrated in Fig. 2.1.8.

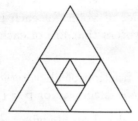

Fig. 2.1.8. The universal threshold method

b.   This threshold method becomes what method if $\delta_2 = \frac{1}{3}$? What happens if $\delta_2 \geq \frac{1}{2}$?

c.   Find the relationship between δ_2 and δ_3 to ensure that an election outcome always is defined.

2.1.7. Recall that the rational points in the representational triangle are *dense*. This means that if $\mathbf{q}' \in Si(3)$ has components with irrational values, then arbitrarily close to $\mathbf{q}'$ are choices of $\mathbf{q} \in Si(3)$ where all the components are rational numbers. Equivalently, there exists a sequence of points in $Si(3)$ with rational components, $\{\mathbf{q}_n\}_{n=1}^{\infty}$, such that $\mathbf{q}_n \to \mathbf{q}'$ as $n \to \infty$.

a. The components of

$$\mathbf{q}' = (\frac{\sqrt{2}}{4}, \frac{\sqrt{2}}{4}, 1 - \frac{\sqrt{2}}{2}) \approx (0.3535538\ldots, 0.3535538\ldots, 0.2928932\ldots) \in Si(3)$$

have irrational values. Find a sequence of rational points in $Si(3)$ that approach $\mathbf{q}'$.

b.   Argue that all points in $Si(3)$, whether the components have rational or irrational values, can be viewed as being the limit of a sequence of normalized election tallies.

2.2 Profiles and Election Mappings

Next we create a geometric representation for voters similar to that developed for election tallies. Each voter is assumed to have a *strict linear ordering* of the candidates; namely, the voter compares each pair of candidates in a transitive manner without registering indifference between any two candidates.

A voter's *type* is defined by his ranking of the candidates; the six ways three candidates can be strictly ranked define the six voter types. Denoting each type by the identifying numbers from Fig. 2.1.5, they are listed below.

Type	Ranking	Type	Ranking
1	$c_1 \succ c_2 \succ c_3$	4	$c_3 \succ c_2 \succ c_1$
2	$c_1 \succ c_3 \succ c_2$	5	$c_2 \succ c_3 \succ c_1$
3	$c_3 \succ c_1 \succ c_2$	6	$c_2 \succ c_1 \succ c_3$

An "*integer profile*" lists the number of voters of each type. A related approach, specifying the fraction of all voters that are of each type, is used here.

Definition 2.2.1. Let p_j denote the fraction of all voters that are of the jth type, $j = 1, \ldots, 6$. A (normalized) *profile* is the vector $\mathbf{p} = (p_1, \ldots, p_6)$. $\square$

The vector $(\frac{1}{6}, 0, \frac{1}{3}, 0, \frac{1}{2}, 0)$ is a normalized profile where $\frac{1}{6}$ of all voters are of type-1, $\frac{1}{3}$ are of type-3, $\frac{1}{2}$ are of type-5, and there are no voters of the remaining three types. As the smallest common denominator is six, the total number of voters for an associated integer profile must be a multiple of six.

As the definition requires $p_j \geq 0$ and $\sum_{j=1}^{6} p_j = 1$, a profile is a (rational) point in the unit simplex

$$Si(3!) = \{\mathbf{y} = (y_1, \ldots, y_6) \in R^{3!} \,|\, y_j \geq 0, \sum_{j=1}^{6} y_j = 1\} \qquad (2.2.1)$$

Thus, a profile can be identified with a point in the unit simplex of R_+^6. The host space R_+^6 is six-dimensional, and the restricting equation $\sum_{j=1}^{6} x_j = 1$ reduces $Si(6)$, *the space of normalized profiles*, to a five-dimensional geometric object.

We have a problem. It is easy to draw a one-dimensional object, a bit harder to draw a two-dimensional figure, and, with practice, artistically talented people can create a recognizable two-dimensional drawing of a three-dimensional figure. But should a drawing of a four or higher dimensional object be required, well, we experience the frustrations of the citizens from Abbott's *"Flatland"* ([Ab]) in attempting to visualize objects from an unknown higher dimensional world. More honestly stated, there is not a simple sketch for the five-dimensional simplex of profiles $Si(6)$. Nevertheless, its geometric properties play such an important role in the analysis of voting that they need to be exploited and understood.

Some properties of $Si(6)$ are easy to establish because they respect our intuition from the more familiar three-dimensional world. For instance, a point $\mathbf{q} \in Si(3)$ is on an edge of the representational triangle iff ("if and only if") one of the three components of $\mathbf{q} = (q_1, q_2, q_3)$ is zero iff some candidate receives no votes. Similarly, a profile $\mathbf{p} = (p_1, \ldots, p_6) \in Si(6)$ is on an edge of $Si(6)$ iff some p_j components are zero iff there are no voters of certain voter types. Restricting a profile $\mathbf{p}$ to the boundary, then, suggests that it has special properties.

The *unanimity profile* $\mathbf{E}_i$, where all voters are of the ith type, $i = 1, \ldots, 6$, plays an important role. (For example, $\mathbf{E}_3 = (0, 0, 1, 0, 0, 0)$ is where all voters have the type-three ranking $c_3 \succ c_1 \succ c_2$.) Just as the normalized outcome $\mathbf{e}_j$ serves as a vertex for $Si(3)$, the six unanimity profiles, $\{\mathbf{E}_i\}_{i=1}^{6}$, are the vertices for $Si(6)$. That is, $Si(6)$ is the convex hull defined by these vertices (see Sect. 1.4); a fact that is underscored by the obvious relationship

$$\mathbf{p} = (p_1, p_2, \ldots, p_6) = \sum_{j=1}^{6} p_j \mathbf{E}_j, \text{ where } \sum_{j=1}^{6} p_j = 1. \qquad (2.2.2)$$

Consequently, *the p_j values are the convex weights defining the profile* $\mathbf{p}$.

In general, two points define an one-dimensional line, three points define a two-dimensional plane, and k points define a $k-1$ dimensional surface. Thus, using the convex representation Eq. 2.2.2, if k of the six components of $\mathbf{p}$ are non-zero, then $\mathbf{p}$ belongs to a $k-1$ dimensional boundary of $Si(6)$. For example, the profile $(\frac{1}{6}, \frac{1}{3}, 0, \frac{1}{6}, \frac{1}{6}, \frac{1}{6})$ belongs to a four-dimensional surface of $Si(6)$ defined by the five vertices $\mathbf{E}_1, \mathbf{E}_2, \mathbf{E}_4, \mathbf{E}_5, \mathbf{E}_6$, while $(\frac{1}{2}, 0, 0, \frac{1}{3}, 0, \frac{1}{6})$ is relegated to a more restrictive two-dimensional edge of $Si(6)$ defined by the unanimity profiles $\mathbf{E}_1, \mathbf{E}_4$ and $\mathbf{E}_6$.

Later in the chapter, geometric coordinate systems for profiles are introduced to allow us to "see" the sets of profiles that define different election outcomes. A primitive yet useful representation of a profile is obtained by listing the component values from a profile in the appropriate ranking region of the representation triangle.

Example 2.2.1. In this example, profiles from the introductory fable are expressed as normalized profiles in $Si(6)$.

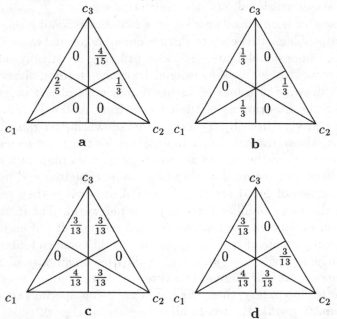

Fig. 2.2.1. Representations of four profiles

- In the beverage part of the fable, let c_1 be milk, c_2 be beer, and c_3 be wine. The resulting beverage profile $\mathbf{p}_b = (0, \frac{6}{15}, 0, \frac{4}{15}, \frac{5}{15}, 0)$ is given in the representation triangle of Fig. 2.2.1a.

- For the contentious departmental meeting, if c_j represents the jth alternative, the profile is $\mathbf{p}_m = (\frac{1}{3}, 0, \frac{1}{3}, 0, \frac{1}{3}, 0)$. This profile is represented in Fig. 2.2.1b. The consequences of its geometrically symmetrical arrangement are discussed in Chap. 3.

- For the selection of a member to the Dean's Council, let c_1, c_2, c_3 represent, respectively, the candidates Ann, Barb, and Carol. In this manner the profiles $\mathbf{p}_{DC(1)} = (\frac{4}{13}, 0, \frac{3}{13}, \frac{3}{13}, 0, \frac{3}{13})$ (Fig. 2.2.1c) and $\mathbf{p}_{DC(2)} = (\frac{4}{13}, 0, \frac{3}{13}, 0, \frac{3}{13}, \frac{3}{13})$ (Fig. 2.2.1d) represent, respectively, the profiles of the first two subcommittees. Observe the geometric similarity between these two profiles. The (normalized) profile for the committee of the whole is $\mathbf{p}_{DC} = (\frac{8}{26}, 0, \frac{6}{26}, \frac{3}{13}, \frac{3}{13}, \frac{6}{26})$.
  □

2.2.1 The Election Mapping

We have the voters, we have the candidates, so let's start the election. As the purpose of an election is to convert a profile into an election tally, it defines a mapping from $Si(3!)$, the five-dimensional space of voters' preferences, to $Si(3)$, the two-dimensional space of election outcomes. The definition of the mapping is immediate. For instance, with the profile $(\frac{1}{6}, 0, \frac{1}{3}, 0, \frac{1}{2}, 0)$, c_1 is top-choice for $\frac{1}{6}$ of the voters, c_3 is top-choice for $\frac{1}{3}$ of the voters, and c_2 is top-choice for $\frac{1}{2}$ of the voters, so the normalized election vector is $(\frac{1}{6}, \frac{1}{2}, \frac{1}{3})$. As $(\frac{1}{6}, \frac{1}{2}, \frac{1}{3})$ is in the ranking region $c_2 \succ c_3 \succ c_1$, this is the election ranking.

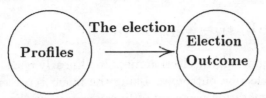

The formal definition of the election mapping is a geometric version of counting. In a plurality election, a type-1 voter votes only for his top-ranked candidate c_1. This ballot is equivalent to registering the voter's vote with the *vector ballot* $\mathbf{e}_1 = (1, 0, 0)$ to indicate that one point is tabulated for the candidate c_1 and none for the other candidates. Similarly a type-4 voter has c_3 top-ranked, so the associated vector ballot is $\mathbf{e}_3 = (0, 0, 1)$. While a voter's vector ballot depends on his type, the only three vector ballots are $\{\mathbf{e}_j\}_{j=1}^3$. Re-expressing the plurality outcome for the above profile of $(\frac{1}{6}, 0, \frac{1}{3}, 0, \frac{1}{2}, 0)$ in this notation, the outcome of the election mapping is

$$\frac{1}{6}\mathbf{e}_1 + \frac{1}{2}\mathbf{e}_2 + \frac{1}{3}\mathbf{e}_3 = (\frac{1}{6}, \frac{1}{2}, \frac{1}{3})$$

We need to be picky about the notation in order to avoid problems when analyzing voting processes. The failing of a vector ballot is that it doesn't identify the voter type; e.g., both type-5 and 6 voters have c_2 top-ranked, so their vector ballot is the same $\mathbf{e}_2$. A better notation would indicate the voter type of the vector ballot. To realize this goal, observe that each vector ballot $\mathbf{e}_j$ is a permutation of $\mathbf{e}_1$; e.g., $\mathbf{e}_2 = (0, 1, 0)$ is obtained by interchanging the first and second coordinate of $\mathbf{e}_1 = (1, 0, 0)$ while $\mathbf{e}_3 = (0, 0, 1)$ is found by interchanging the first and the third coordinate of $\mathbf{e}_1$.

Definition 2.2.2. Let $[\mathbf{e}_1]_j$ denote the permutation of $\mathbf{e}_1$ that represents the vector ballot for the jth voter type. $\square$

Example 2.2.2. The top choice of a type-four voter is c_3; thus the vector ballot is $\mathbf{e}_3$. As such, $[\mathbf{e}_1]_4 = \mathbf{e}_3$. Similarly, to reflect that a type-5 voter votes for c_2, the notation is $[\mathbf{e}_1]_5 = \mathbf{e}_2$. $\square$

With this notation, an election outcome is determined by computing what fraction of voters from the profile $\mathbf{p} \in Si(3!)$ cast each vector ballot. The resulting sum, the election tally, is a normalized election vector in $Si(3)$. Thus the election mapping

$$f : Si(6) \rightarrow Si(3) \tag{2.2.3}$$

is defined by

$$f(\mathbf{p}, \mathbf{e}_1) = \sum_{j=1}^{6} p_j [\mathbf{e}_1]_j \tag{2.2.4}$$

What aids in the analysis of elections are the "linear" properties of the election mapping f and the special case of unanimity profiles where

$$f(\mathbf{E}_j, \mathbf{e}_1) = [\mathbf{e}_1]_j, \quad j = 1, \ldots, 6 \tag{2.2.5}$$

As Eq. 2.2.4 is a linear equation, the election mapping linearly transforms a sum of profiles into a sum of election outcomes. Using the linear representation of a profile (Eq. 2.2.2), the separation property of linear equations (Eq. 1.4.4), and Eq. 2.2.5, we recapture Eq. 2.2.4.

$$f(\mathbf{p}, \mathbf{e}_1) = f(\sum_{j=1}^{6} p_j \mathbf{E}_j, \mathbf{e}_1) = \sum_{j=1}^{6} p_j f(\mathbf{E}_j, \mathbf{e}_1) = \sum_{j=1}^{6} p_j [\mathbf{e}_1]_j \tag{2.2.6}$$

Example 2.2.3. The plurality election outcomes for each of the above profiles are given next.

- For the beverage example from the fable,

$$f(\mathbf{p}_b, \mathbf{e}_1) = \frac{6}{15}[\mathbf{e}_1]_2 + \frac{4}{15}[\mathbf{e}_1]_4 + \frac{5}{15}[\mathbf{e}_1]_5$$

$$= \frac{6}{15}\mathbf{e}_1 + \frac{4}{15}\mathbf{e}_3 + \frac{5}{15}\mathbf{e}_2 = (\frac{6}{15}, \frac{5}{15}, \frac{4}{15})$$

  This normalized election vector is in the ranking region for $c_1 \succ c_2 \succ c_3$.
- For the profile $\mathbf{p}_m$ from the departmental meeting, the outcome is

$$f(\mathbf{p}_m, \mathbf{e}_1) = \frac{1}{3}[\mathbf{e}_1]_1 + \frac{1}{3}[\mathbf{e}_1]_3 + \frac{1}{3}[\mathbf{e}_1]_5 = (\frac{1}{3}, \frac{1}{3}, \frac{1}{3})$$

  which is in the ranking region $\mathcal{I}$ representing $c_1 \sim c_2 \sim c_3$.
- The ranking for the first Dean's Council subcommittee is $f(\mathbf{p}_{DC(1)}, \mathbf{e}_1) = (\frac{4}{13}, \frac{6}{13}, \frac{3}{13})$ or $c_2 \succ c_1 \succ c_3$.
- The outcome for the second subcommittee is $f(\mathbf{p}_{DC(2)}, \mathbf{e}_1) = (\frac{4}{13}, \frac{3}{13}, \frac{6}{13})$ or $c_3 \succ c_1 \succ c_2$.
- For the full committee, the outcome is $f(\mathbf{p}_{DC}, \mathbf{e}_1) = (\frac{8}{26}, \frac{9}{26}, \frac{9}{26})$ or $c_2 \sim c_3 \succ c_1$. Notice that although c_1 (Ann) is one of the two top-ranked candidates for each subcommittee, she is bottom-ranked in the committee of the whole. □

2.2.2 The Geometry of Election Outcomes

As developed, a normalized profile is a rational point from $Si(6)$. However, the components of many (indeed, most) points in $Si(6)$ have irrational values. While these points cannot be identified with integer profiles, they can, as indicated in the exercises, be identified with limits of integer profiles and/or with profiles from a weighted voting system. For instance, recall from the pope selection discussion (Sect. 1.3) that a *weighted* voting system is where some voters are "more equal than others."

In weighted voting, the ith voter is assigned a weight, δ_i, and the voter's ballot is counted as though δ_i voters voted in the same manner. In a law firm, for instance, a partner's ownership share can determine her voting weight. As there is no restriction on the value of δ_i, it could be an integer, say $\delta_i = 2$, a fraction, such as $\delta_i = \frac{3}{8}$, or even be an irrational value such as $\sqrt{2}$ or the *golden mean* $\delta_i = \frac{1+\sqrt{5}}{2}$. The modification of Eq. 2.2.6 to include weighted voting is immediate.

Among the many situations where weighted voting is appropriate, consider a group consisting of members with diverse talents. When faced with a particular decision, it is reasonable for the better informed to have a greater say in the final outcome. To do so, each person can distribute some of his or her voting power to other decision makers. This defines an iteration where, at the end of each round, each voter decides how to redistribute his or her changed level of influence. (See, for example, [De].) In the limit, the voting power of certain agents can be an irrational number.

So, by defining an election as a mapping from *all points* in $Si(6)$, not just the rational ones, we can model and analyze a much richer class of problems. *This assumption holds unless specifically stated otherwise!*

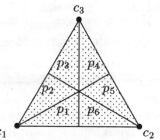

Fig. 2.2.2. The plurality election outcomes

It remains to understand what kinds of normalized election outcomes can occur. By identifying elections with a linear mapping, this geometric representation uses the discussion of Sect. 1.4. The domain, or space of normalized profiles $Si(6)$, is the convex hull defined by the vertices $\{\mathbf{E}_j\}$. Therefore, as argued in Sect. 1.4, the set of normalized election outcomes is the convex hull defined by $\{f(\mathbf{E}_j, \mathbf{e}_1)\}_{j=1}^6$. Consequently, any election outcome can be represented by $\sum_{j=1}^6 \lambda_j f(\mathbf{E}_j, \mathbf{e}_1)$ for some choice of $\lambda_1, \ldots, \lambda_6$ where $\lambda_j \geq 0$ and $\sum_{j=1}^6 \lambda_j = 1$. There is no mystery here; by comparing this expression with Eq. 2.2.4, it follows immediately that $\lambda_j = p_j$ for $j = 1, \ldots, 6$.

As the election outcomes of the unanimity profiles are the vertices of the representation triangle (Eq. 2.2.5), the space of normalized election outcomes is the full simplex $Si(3)$ as indicated in Fig. 2.2.2. Namely, any point in the *convex hull* defined by $\{f(\mathbf{E}_j, \mathbf{e}_1) = [\mathbf{e}_1]_j\}_{j=1}^3$, is the election outcome for some choice of $\mathbf{p} \in Si(6)$.

2.2.3 Exercises

2.2.1. Show that $f(\mathbf{p}, \mathbf{e}_1) = (p_1 + p_2, p_5 + p_6, p_3 + p_4)$.

2.2.2. In the definition of the election mapping, it is asserted that the election outcome is a *normalized* election tally. Justify this comment. In other words, prove that because $\mathbf{p} \in Si(6)$, the election outcome $f(\mathbf{p}, \mathbf{e}_1)$ satisfies the two required conditions for a point to be in $Si(3)$.

2.2.3. Suppose three voters are assigned the weights $\delta_1 = \frac{\pi}{2} = \frac{3.14159\ldots}{2}$, $\delta_2 = 1$, $\delta_3 = 0.500$.

a.   If the voters are of the respective types one, three, five, find the weighted election outcome.

b.   Express the profile of part a as a normalized profile in $Si(6)$.

c.   Show for these weights that whatever voter-one wants, voter-one gets. Namely, *show that voter-one is a dictator*. Show that if voter-one does not vote, then voter-two becomes a dictator.

d.   A voting vector can be extended from strict preferences to all preferences by averaging the number of votes cast over all ways indifference can be broken. In this manner, a voter with the ranking $c_1 \sim c_3 \succ c_2$ would cast the ballot $(\frac{1}{2}, 0, \frac{1}{2}) = \frac{1}{2}([\mathbf{e}_1]_2 + [\mathbf{e}_1]_3)$. Show that the above weights define a *sequential dictatorship*. Namely, voter-one always gets his way unless he is indifferent between two candidates. In this situation, voter-two's preferences dominate. Finally, voter-three's views are manifested only when the first two voters are indifferent.

2.2.4. A theme from voting theory is to analyze what occurs as the number of voters becomes large. In this spirit find a sequence of normalized profiles (where the coordinates have rational values) so that the election ranking always is $c_1 \succ c_2 \succ c_3$ but the normalized tallies approach the point from Ex 2.1.6. (So, the limit ranking is $c_1 \sim c_2 \succ c_3$.) Find one such sequence so that the normalized profiles approach a specific normalized profile, and then find another sequence which does not approach a single normalized profile.

2.2.5. For the three threshold methods from the Exercises of Sect. 2.1, let $\delta_2 = \frac{1}{2}$, $\gamma_2 = \frac{3}{5}$, $\epsilon = 0.21$.

a.   Find a profile $\mathbf{p}_1$ so that c_1 is top-ranked with the Universal but not with the Distinct or Quasi transitive threshold methods.

b.   Find a profile $\mathbf{p}_2$ so that c_2 is top-ranked with the Distinct, but not with the Universal or Quasi-transitive threshold methods.

c. Can a profile be found where c_3 is top-ranked with the Quasi-transitive threshold method but not with the other two?

2.3 Positional Voting Methods

Mankind need not live by the plurality vote alone; there are other ways to tally ballots. To see why we should even bother to raise this issue, consider an one-voter profile election with, say, a type-one voter $\mathbf{p} = \mathbf{E}_1$. The vector ballot is $\mathbf{e}_1$, so c_1 wins with an unanimous vote. In no manner does this outcome reflect the second-ranked status of c_2; in fact, based only on the outcome, it is equally reasonable to believe that this voter is of type-2 with the ranking $c_1 \succ c_3 \succ c_2$. This may, or may not matter for anyone other than c_2's father, but the missing information becomes important when analyzing paradoxes such as the beverage example. Here, the troublesome outcome happened because the procedure failed to utilize the critical information that each voter treated "Wine" as either a first or a second-ranked option. So, are there other procedures that better capture the true intent of the voters? If so, they must transmit information about a voter's middle- and bottom-ranked candidates.

Definition 2.3.1. Vector $\mathbf{W} = (w_1, w_2, w_3) \in R^3$ is a *voting vector* if its components satisfy the inequalities

$$w_i \geq w_{i+1}, \quad i = 1, 2, \text{ and } w_1 > w_3 \tag{2.3.1}$$

A *positional voting method* is defined by a voting vector $\mathbf{W} = (w_1, w_2, w_3)$. In tallying a voter's ballot, w_j points are assigned to the voter's jth-ranked candidate, $j = 1, 2, 3$. The ranking of the candidates is determined by the number of points assigned to each of them. $\square$

The first inequality of Eq. 2.3.1 ensures that a lower ranked candidate does not receive more points than a higher ranked one. The second inequality guarantees that the tally is able to distinguish a voter's rankings among the candidates. For instance, there is no suspense on election night if $(1, 1, 1)$ is used – the only possible election outcome is the complete tie $\mathcal{I} = c_1 \sim c_2 \sim c_3$.

Example 2.3.1. a. A *plurality vote* is the positional voting method defined by the voting vector

$$\mathbf{W}_P = \mathbf{e}_1 = (1, 0, 0) \tag{2.3.2}$$

b. The *antiplurality* positional voting method is defined by the voting vector

$$\mathbf{W}_{AP} = (1, 1, 0) \tag{2.3.3}$$

With the antiplurality vote, a voter is instructed to vote for his two top-ranked candidates. Actually, this is just a kinder and gentler way to camouflage the true intent of having each voter vote *against* his bottom-ranked candidate. (With three candidates, voting for the two top-ranked candidates is the same as voting against the bottom-ranked candidate.) Thus this system is equivalent to using the voting vector $(0, 0, -1)$. When expressed in this fashion, the procedure clearly is a negative version of the plurality vote. The source of the name *antiplurality vote* now is obvious.

c. One of the earliest positional voting methods, the procedure used to select a new chair in the fable, is the BC. The BC is defined by the voting vector

$$\mathbf{W}_{BC} = (2, 1, 0) \tag{2.3.4}$$

It is interesting to note that

$$\mathbf{W}_{BC} = (2, 1, 0) = (1, 0, 0) + (1, 1, 0)$$
$$= \mathbf{W}_P + \mathbf{W}_{AP} \tag{2.3.5}$$

So, according to Eq. 2.3.5, the BC appears to split the difference between the plurality and antiplurality votes. □

2.3.1 The Difference a Procedure Makes

There is a practical WGAD ("Who gives a damn?") question associated with the infinite number of positional voting methods. What difference does it make if an election is tallied with a plurality vote, an antiplurality vote, the BC, or something else? Won't the outcomes be essentially the same?

The answer is No. As shown in the fable, when different voting methods are used to tally the same ballots, the outcomes can appear to have nothing to do with each other! For instance, had the chair used the BC rather than the plurality vote to rank the beverages, he might have enjoyed a stress-free life. To recall, the BC tally for the beverage example with the profile $\mathbf{p}_b = (0, \frac{6}{15}, 0, \frac{4}{15}, \frac{5}{15}, 0)$ is

Voter type	p_j	Borda tally		
		Water	Beer	Wine
2	$\frac{6}{15}$	$2(\frac{6}{15})$	0	$\frac{6}{15}$
4	$\frac{4}{15}$	0	$\frac{4}{15}$	$2(\frac{4}{15})$
5	$\frac{5}{15}$	0	$2(\frac{5}{15})$	$\frac{5}{15}$
Total	1	$\frac{12}{15}$	$\frac{14}{15}$	$\frac{19}{15}$

Thus, the BC ranking for the beverage example is Wine $\succ$ Beer $\succ$ Water; a ranking that agrees with the binary majority vote comparisons while completely reversing the plurality ranking of Water $\succ$ Beer $\succ$ Wine. The message is clear; the choice of the voting system matters.

The message might be clear, but there remains considerable fog surrounding the choice of a voting system. To improve the visibility, we need a theory for positional voting. This requires a functional representation for the election.

The tally for a positional voting system can be modeled in a manner similar to that in Eq. 2.2.2. With a specified voting vector $\mathbf{W} = (w_1, w_2, w_3)$, the vector ballot representing a voter of type $c_2 \succ c_1 \succ c_3$ is (w_2, w_1, w_3) to indicate that c_1 is second-ranked so she receives w_2 points, c_2 is top-ranked so she gets w_1 points, and the bottom-ranked position of c_3 means she is assigned only w_3 points. As in Sect. 2.2, the vector ballot for each voter type is an appropriate permutation of $\mathbf{W}$. Let $[\mathbf{W}]_j$ be the vector ballot (the appropriate permutation of $\mathbf{W}$) for a type j voter. For instance, $[\mathbf{W}]_4 = (w_3, w_2, w_1)$ reflects the voter's preference of $c_3 \succ c_2 \succ c_1$. The outcome for a unanimity profile captures the notation

$$f(\mathbf{E}_j, \mathbf{W}) = [\mathbf{W}]_j \quad , j = 1, 2, \ldots, 6$$

As the election tally just counts the proportion of all voters casting a particular vector ballot, the election mapping for profile $\mathbf{p}$ is the linear mapping

$$f(\mathbf{p}, \mathbf{W}) = \sum_{j=1}^{6} p_j f(\mathbf{E}_j, \mathbf{W}) = \sum_{j=1}^{6} p_j [\mathbf{W}]_j \qquad (2.3.6)$$

Example 2.3.2. a. For the BC and $\mathbf{p}_b$, we have

$$\begin{aligned}
f(\mathbf{p}_b, \mathbf{W}_{BC}) &= p_2 [\mathbf{W}_{BC}]_2 + p_4 [\mathbf{W}_{BC}]_4 + p_5 [\mathbf{W}_{BC}]_5 \\
&= \frac{6}{15} [\mathbf{W}_{BC}]_2 + \frac{4}{15} [\mathbf{W}_{BC}]_4 + \frac{5}{15} [\mathbf{W}_{BC}]_5 \\
&= \frac{6}{15} (2, 0, 1) + \frac{4}{15} (0, 1, 2) + \frac{5}{15} (0, 2, 1) \\
&= (\frac{12}{15}, \frac{14}{15}, \frac{19}{15})
\end{aligned}$$

b. For the antiplurality method and $\mathbf{p}_b$ we have

$$\begin{aligned}
f(\mathbf{p}_b, \mathbf{W}_{AP}) &= \frac{6}{15} [\mathbf{W}_{AP}]_2 + \frac{4}{15} [\mathbf{W}_{AP}]_4 + \frac{5}{15} [\mathbf{W}_{AP}]_5 \\
&= \frac{6}{15} (1, 0, 1) + \frac{4}{15} (0, 1, 1) + \frac{5}{15} (0, 1, 1) \\
&= (\frac{6}{15}, \frac{9}{15}, \frac{15}{15})
\end{aligned}$$

With both positional methods, the beverage ranking is Wine $\succ$ Beer $\succ$ Water. Thus, the antiplurality method joins the BC in offering a beverage ranking that is consistent with the binary rankings. $\square$

2.3.2 An Equivalence Relationship for Voting Vectors

By definition, there are an infinite number of different voting vectors. The numbers are significantly reduced by appealing to a natural equivalence relationship.

Theorem 2.3.1. *Let* $\mathbf{W}_1$ *and* $\mathbf{W}_2$ *be voting vectors that satisfy the relationship*

$$\mathbf{W}_1 = a\mathbf{W}_2 + b(1,1,1) \tag{2.3.7}$$

for scalars b *and* $a > 0$. *For any profile* $\mathbf{p}$, *the election ranking for* $f(\mathbf{p}, \mathbf{W}_1)$ *is the same as that for* $f(\mathbf{p}, \mathbf{W}_2)$.

The conclusion of this theorem is intuitively clear. After all, as the $b(1,1,1)$ term just adds the same constant value of b to each candidate's final tally, it does not, in any manner, affect the final ranking. Similarly, the multiple a only changes the vote tally by this a multiple – the final ranking remains unchanged.

Proof. When a profile is held fixed, the election mapping becomes a linear mapping of the voting vector. So, by exploiting the linear separation property of a linear mapping, it follows that

$$\begin{aligned}
f(\mathbf{p}, \mathbf{W}_1) &= f(\mathbf{p}, a\mathbf{W}_2 + b(1,1,1)) = af(\mathbf{p}, \mathbf{W}_2) + bf(\mathbf{p}, (1,1,1)) \\
&= af(\mathbf{p}, \mathbf{W}_2) + (b, b, b)
\end{aligned} \tag{2.3.8}$$

The fact that $f(\mathbf{p}, (1,1,1)) = (1,1,1)$ is a direct computation. $\square$

Example 2.3.3. For $\mathbf{p} = (\frac{1}{3}, 0, \frac{1}{6}, \frac{1}{2}, 0, 0)$, the BC outcome is

$$\begin{aligned}
f(\mathbf{p}, \mathbf{W}_{BC}) &= \frac{1}{3}[(2,1,0)]_1 + \frac{1}{6}[(2,1,0)]_3 + \frac{1}{2}[(2,1,0)]_4 \\
&= \frac{1}{3}(2,1,0) + \frac{1}{6}(1,0,2) + \frac{1}{2}(0,1,2) \\
&= (\frac{5}{6}, \frac{5}{6}, \frac{8}{6})
\end{aligned}$$

If $a = 1$, $b = 2$ then

$$\begin{aligned}
f(\mathbf{p}, \mathbf{W}_{BC} + 2(1,1,1)) &= f(\mathbf{p}, (4,3,2)) \\
&= \frac{1}{3}(4,3,2) + \frac{1}{6}(3,2,4) + \frac{1}{2}(2,3,4) \\
&= (2\frac{5}{6}, 2\frac{5}{6}, 2\frac{8}{6}) = (2,2,2) + f(\mathbf{p}, \mathbf{W}_{BC})
\end{aligned}$$

Finally, if $a = 3$, $b = 0$, then

$$f(\mathbf{p}, 3(2,1,0)) = \frac{1}{3}(6,3,0) + \frac{1}{6}(3,0,6) + \frac{1}{2}(0,3,6) = 3f(\mathbf{p}, \mathbf{W}_{BC}). \square$$

It is left for the exercises to prove that Eq. 2.3.7 defines an equivalence relationship among the voting vectors.

Definition 2.3.2. Two voting vectors $\mathbf{W}_1, \mathbf{W}_2$ are equivalent, $\mathbf{W}_1 \approx \mathbf{W}_2$, if there exist scalars b and $a > 0$ so that Eq. 2.3.7 is satisfied. $\square$

Example 2.3.4. a. To see that the antiplurality voting vector $\mathbf{W}_1 = (1,1,0)$ is equivalent to the voting vector $\mathbf{W}_2 = (0,0,-1)$, let $a = 1$, $b = -1$ in Eq. 2.3.7.

b. *A voting vector $\mathbf{W} = (w_1, w_2, w_3)$ is equivalent to the BC iff it has the property*

$$w_1 - w_2 = w_2 - w_3;$$

that is, if the difference between successive weights is the same. One direction of this assertion follows immediately by choosing $a = w_1 - w_2$ and $b = w_3$. Arithmetic shows that

$$a(2,1,0) = (2(w_1 - w_2), w_1 - w_2, 0) = (w_1 - w_2 + (w_2 - w_3), w_2 - w_3, 0)$$
$$= (w_1 - w_3, w_2 - w_3, 0)$$

so $a\mathbf{W}_{BC} + b(1,1,1) = \mathbf{W}$. Conversely, if $\mathbf{W} = a\mathbf{W}_{BC} + b(1,1,1)$, then $\mathbf{W} = (2a + b, a + b, b)$. This means that $w_1 - w_2 = w_2 - w_3 = a$. $\square$

The Exploitation of the Equivalence Relationship. Definition 2.3.2 defines an equivalence relationship, and, as asserted in Sect. 2.1, equivalence relationships are meant to be exploited. This particular relationship allows a single voting vector to represent each class of equivalent voting methods. Consequently, assume that all voting vectors are in the *normalized form*

$$\mathbf{w}_s = (1 - s, s, 0) \text{ for } 0 \le s \le \frac{1}{2} \tag{2.3.9}$$

To transform $\mathbf{W} = (w_1, w_2, w_3)$ into its normalized form, start with $b = -w_3$ to define the equivalent voting vector

$$(w_1 - w_3, w_2 - w_3, 0)$$

Next, sum the components of the new vector, and divide each component by this sum. This is the same as choosing the scalar multiple

$$a = 1/([w_1 - w_3] + [w_2 - w_3]) = 1/(w_1 + w_2 - 2w_3)$$

The new, equivalent voting vector is of the form $\mathbf{w}_s = (1 - s, s, 0)$ where

$$s = (w_2 - w_3)/(w_1 + w_2 - 2w_3) \tag{2.3.10}$$

Observe that Eq. 2.3.10 is particularly simple for voting vectors where $w_3 = 0$. In this situation, $s = \frac{w_2}{w_1 + w_2}$, so the value of s indicates the portion of the weights assigned to a second-ranked candidate. The condition $s \le \frac{1}{2}$ captures the requirement that a top-ranked candidate receives at least as many points as a second-ranked candidate; i.e., $1 - s \geq s$. This restriction on s follows from the above derivation and the inequality

$$w_1 - w_3 \geq w_2 - w_3$$

By exploiting the equivalence relationship for voting vectors, we end up with *the line segment of voting vectors* $\{(1 - s, s, 0) \in R_+^3 \mid s \in [0, \frac{1}{2}]\}$ in three space depicted in Fig. 2.3.1. However, I often represent this segment simply by the interval of s values $[0, \frac{1}{2}]$.

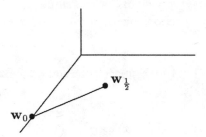

Fig. 2.3.1. The line segment of voting vectors

Example 2.3.5. The plurality voting vector $(1, 0, 0)$ already is in a normalized form where $s = 0$; thus $\mathbf{w}_0$ represents the plurality vote.

For the BC, $w_1 = 2, w_2 = 1$, and $w_3 = 0$, so, according to Eq. 2.3.10

$$s = 1/(2 + 1) = \frac{1}{3}$$

Thus, the normalized form for the BC is $\mathbf{w}_{\frac{1}{3}} = (\frac{2}{3}, \frac{1}{3}, 0)$. As required by Example 2.3.4b, the difference between successive components is a fixed value.

For the antiplurality vote, $w_1 = w_2 = 1, w_3 = 0$, so

$$s = 1/(1 + 1) = \frac{1}{2}$$

Therefore $\mathbf{w}_{\frac{1}{2}}$ is the normalized version of the antiplurality vote. $\square$

The normalized $\mathbf{w}_s$ representation allows us to have some fun. With a little imagination, one could develop an argument justifying why any choice of a voting system is the "natural extension" of the majority vote. After all, in the pairwise vote, zero points are given to a voter's bottom-ranked candidate, and one point is left to be divided among the remaining candidates. With two candidates, only one candidate remains, so, by default, she receives the full point. However, in a three person election, two candidates are not bottom-ranked, so $\mathbf{w}_s$ specifies how to split this point between them. To support selecting a particular $\mathbf{w}_s$, one just needs to concoct a convincing argument why that choice of s is the "correct one." With a little imagination sufficiently supplemented by bovine by- products, any value of s can be justified.

2.3.3 The Geometry of $\mathbf{w}_s$ Outcomes

To develop the basic message that the choice of a positional system matters, a geometric representation is created for the $\mathbf{w}_s$ outcomes by using Sect. 1.4. Namely, the space of profiles is the convex hull of the vertices $\{\mathbf{E}_j\}_{j=1}^6$ (the unanimity profiles) and the election mapping is linear. According to Sect. 1.4, the linear mapping transforms the convex hull $Si(6)$ into the convex hull $\mathcal{CH}(\mathbf{w}_s)$ in $Si(3)$. This convex hull of normalized $\mathbf{w}_s$ election outcomes is defined by the vertices $\{f(\mathbf{E}_j, \mathbf{w}_s) = [\mathbf{w}_s]_j\}_{j=1}^6$.

Equivalently, take a voting vector $\mathbf{w}_s$ and plot the six point $\{[\mathbf{w}_s]_j\}_{j=1}^6$. The normalized weight for a bottom-ranked candidate is zero, so each vector is on the boundary of $Si(3)$. Next, connect the dots with straight lines and shade in the region defined by the lines as illustrated in Fig. 2.3.2. In this manner, the geometry associated with the plurality vote (Fig. 2.2.2) generalizes to all other positional procedures.

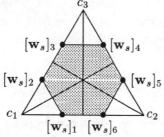

Figure 2.3.2. The convex hull $\mathcal{CH}(\mathbf{w}_s)$

Conversely, any point in $\mathcal{CH}(\mathbf{w}_s)$ can be expressed as a combination

$$\sum_{j=1}^6 p_j [\mathbf{w}_s]_j$$

for some choice of $(p_1, \ldots, p_6)$, $p_j \geq 0$, $\sum_{j=1}^6 p_j = 1$. Hence, the convex weights define a profile where p_j of the voters are of type-j. Consequently, *any point in the convex set $\mathcal{CH}(\mathbf{w}_s)$ is an election outcome for some profile*, and the weights for the convex representation of this point define the associated profile.

Theorem 2.3.2. a. *Let voting vector $\mathbf{w}_s$ be given, and let $\mathcal{CH}(\mathbf{w}_s)$ be the convex hull of $\{[\mathbf{w}_s]_j\}_{j=1}^6$. For any normalized profile $\mathbf{p}$, the normalized election outcome is in $\mathcal{CH}(\mathbf{w}_s)$. Moreover, any point in $\mathcal{CH}(\mathbf{w}_s)$ is the normalized election vector for some profile $\mathbf{p} \in Si(3!)$.*

b. *If $0 \leq s_2 < s_1 \leq \frac{1}{2}$, then*

$$\mathcal{CH}(\mathbf{w}_{s_1}) \subset \mathcal{CH}(\mathbf{w}_{s_2}) \qquad (2.3.11)$$

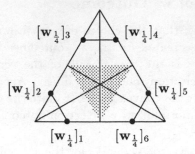

Fig. 2.3.3. A comparison of the hulls $\{CH(\mathbf{w}_s)\}_{s=0,\frac{1}{4},\frac{1}{2}}$

The proof of part a follows from the discussion preceding the theorem. The proof of part b is immediate once the points are plotted on $Si(3)$. The basic fact is that if $s_2 < s_1$, then each $[\mathbf{w}_{s_2}]_j$ is closer to the appropriate vertex $[\mathbf{e}_1]_j$ of the representation triangle than is $[\mathbf{w}_{s_1}]_j$. This is illustrated in Fig. 2.3.3 where the full simplex $Si(3)$ is $CH(\mathbf{w}_0)$, the shaded region is $CH(\mathbf{w}_{\frac{1}{2}})$ and the hull defined by the connected lines is $CH(\mathbf{w}_{\frac{1}{4}})$. In subsequent chapters, the geometric differences in the geometry of these hulls force differences in the properties of the voting procedures. $\square$

An Optimal Solution. On election day, a candidate wants to win with the largest possible election outcome. To do so, she needs to convert the voters to her way of thinking. Thus she searches for an ideal profile $\mathbf{p}$ to give her the strongest possible outcome. What is this profile?

The answer is simple for the plurality vote; the "best" outcome (a unanimous vote) for c_1 occurs if all voters are of type-1, so the optimal profile is $\mathbf{E}_1$. This is no surprise; in fact it is reasonable to expect the unanimity profile $\mathbf{E}_1$ to be optimal for c_1 for all choices of $\mathbf{w}_s$. This is false. For instance, with the antiplurality vote, the unanimity profile $\mathbf{E}_1$ forces c_1 into a tie with c_2! Surely with $\mathbf{w}_{\frac{1}{2}}$ other profiles allow c_1 to do better! More generally, for a given $\mathbf{w}_s$, find the normalized profile that maximizes the normalized election outcome for c_1.

Geometrically, the best election outcome for c_1 is where the normalized election outcome $\mathbf{q}$ is the closest to the vertex $\mathbf{e}_1$ subject to the constraint $\mathbf{q} \in CH(\mathbf{w}_s)$. To minimize the distance from $\mathbf{e}_1$ to a point $\mathbf{q} \in CH(\mathbf{w}_s)$, $\mathbf{q}$ must be on the line segment connecting $[\mathbf{w}_s]_1$ and $[\mathbf{w}_s]_2$. (See Fig. 2.3.3.)

If $s \neq 0$, then the vertex $\mathbf{e}_1$, and the points $[\mathbf{w}_s]_1, [\mathbf{w}_s]_2$ define an equilateral triangle. (This is because the angle at $\mathbf{e}_1$ is 60° and $[\mathbf{w}_s]_1$ and $[\mathbf{w}_s]_2$ are the same distance from $\mathbf{e}_1$.) In this triangle, the $c_2 \sim c_3$ line is the perpendicular bisector of the leg connecting $[\mathbf{w}_s]_1$ and $[\mathbf{w}_s]_2$. From the geometry, the bisector point $(1 - s, s/2, s/2)$ is the unique point in $CH(\mathbf{w}_s)$ closest to $\mathbf{e}_1$. As this point is on the boundary of $CH(\mathbf{w}_s)$, only voters of the indicated types (types-one and -two) are involved, and they are evenly divided. Thus the only profile supporting this outcome is $\frac{1}{2}(\mathbf{E}_1 + \mathbf{E}_2) = (\frac{1}{2}, \frac{1}{2}, 0, 0, 0, 0)$. Consequently, unless $s = 0$, *the optimal situation for c_1 requires the voters to be evenly split between type-1 and type-2, and the normalized tally is $(1 - s, s/2, s/2)$ with the election ranking*

$c_1 \succ c_2 \sim c_3$. If $s = 0$, the outcome can be any split among type-1 and 2 voters.

2.3.4 Exercises

2.3.1. Show that the relationship defined by Eq. 2.3.7 is an equivalence relationship. Namely, show that:
1. (Reflexive) A voting vector $\mathbf{W}$ is equivalent to itself.
2. (Symmetry) If $\mathbf{W}_1 \approx \mathbf{W}_2$, then $\mathbf{W}_2 \approx \mathbf{W}_1$.
3. (Transitivity) If $\mathbf{W}_1 \approx \mathbf{W}_2$ and $\mathbf{W}_2 \approx \mathbf{W}_3$, then $\mathbf{W}_1 \approx \mathbf{W}_3$.

2.3.2. a. The antiplurality method $(1, 1, 0)$ is equivalent to $(0, 0, -1)$. Show that this system is equivalent to where the negative of plurality vote is applied to *reversed ranking order* of the candidates. This same argument can be applied to the general setting. Let $\mathbf{W} = (w_1, w_2, 0)$ be given. Define

$$\mathbf{W}^r = (0, -w_2, -w_1) \qquad (2.3.12)$$

to be the reversed or anti-$\mathbf{W}$ voting vector. Prove that $\mathbf{W}^r$ is a voting vector, and find an equivalent form for this vector where zero points are assigned to a bottom-ranked candidate. Rewrite $\mathbf{W}$ and $\mathbf{W}^r$ om their normalized forms to discover the relationship between their s-values.

b. Show that the BC is the unique voting system where $\mathbf{w}_s = \mathbf{w}_s^r$. This requires proving that

$$\mathbf{w}_s \approx \mathbf{w}_s^r \text{ iff } s = \frac{1}{3} \qquad (2.3.13)$$

c. Show that any point on the $Si(3)$ edge between $\mathbf{e}_1$ and $(\frac{1}{2}, \frac{1}{2}, 0)$ corresponds to a voting vector $\mathbf{w}_s$ for some choice of s. Likewise, show that on an edge of $Si(3)$, any point between a vertex of $Si(3)$ and the $c_i \sim c_j$ point on this edge also defines a voting vector $\mathbf{w}_s$ where this point is $[\mathbf{w}_s]_k$ for the appropriate ranking region $\mathcal{R}(k)$. What is this ranking region?

d. For a given voting vector $\mathbf{w}_s$, the line passing through $[\mathbf{w}_s]_1$ and $\mathcal{I}$ intersects the boundary of $Si(3)$ in $\mathcal{R}(4)$. This intersection point is $[\mathbf{w}_t]_4$ for some choice of t. Show that $\mathbf{w}_t \approx \mathbf{w}_s^r$. (Draw the picture)

2.3.3. a. Following Theorem 2.3.1, it is asserted that adding the value $b(1, 1, 1)$ does not affect the election ranking. Show that the adding this term *does change the normalized election tally*. In particular, if $\mathbf{q}, \mathbf{q}_b$ represent, respectively, the normalized election outcome for $f(\mathbf{p}, \mathbf{W})$ and $f(\mathbf{p}, \mathbf{W} + b(1, 1, 1))$, show that $\mathbf{q}_b$ is on the line starting from the complete indifference point $\mathcal{I}$ and passing through $\mathbf{q}$. This line is divided into two parts by $\mathbf{q}$; which part contains $\mathbf{q}_b$ if $b > 0$?

b. In the Distinct winner threshold method for $\gamma_2 = \frac{3}{5}$, candidate c_1 wins with the normalized plurality tally of $\mathbf{q} = (\frac{8}{14}, \frac{5}{14}, \frac{1}{14})$. Find values of b so that for the same profile, the outcome of would have been a tie between c_1, c_2 if the tally had been based on the "equivalent" voting vector $(1, 0, 0) + b(1, 1, 1)$. Find values of b so that the outcome would have been a three way tie. (Thus, the assertion of equivalence does not hold for the threshold methods.)

c. Re-do part c where the outcome is determined by the Universal threshold method with $\delta_2 = \frac{8}{15}$.

2.3.4. In the introduction of the plurality and the antiplurality method, it was suggested that the BC "splits the difference" between these methods. Using the normalized voting vectors, argue that $\mathbf{w}_{\frac{1}{4}} \approx (3,1,0)$ is the method that "splits the difference" between the plurality and the antiplurality methods. Then, by using different equivalent representations for the plurality and antiplurality vectors, show that any voting vector (w_1, w_2, w_3), $w_2 \neq w_1, w_3$, can be "viewed as splitting the difference" between the plurality and antiplurality methods.

2.3.5. a. Show that $\mathcal{CH}(\mathbf{w}_s)$ is a triangle (actually, an equilateral triangle) iff $s = 0, \frac{1}{2}$. That is, the convex hull is a triangle only for the plurality and the antiplurality methods. In particular, show that $\mathcal{CH}(\mathbf{w}_s) = Si(3)$ iff $\mathbf{w}_s$ represents the plurality vote. Then show that $\mathcal{CH}(\mathbf{w}_s)$ is the triangle connecting the midpoints of each leg of $Si(3)$ iff the method is the antiplurality procedure.
b. Show that the line segment connecting $[\mathbf{w}_s]_1$ and $[\mathbf{w}_s]_3$ is perpendicular to the base connecting the vertices $\mathbf{e}_1$ and $\mathbf{e}_2$ iff $s = \frac{1}{3}$. Equivalently, this shows that this line segment is parallel to the c_1, c_2 indifference line if and only if the procedure is the BC.

2.3.6. a. Suppose the election for each of the three threshold procedures is tallied with $\mathbf{w}_s$. Show that for a given $\mathbf{w}_s$, $s \neq 0$, that there are sufficiently large values for $\epsilon_2, \gamma_2, \delta_2$ so that it is impossible for a single winner to emerge. Find the largest values for $\epsilon_2, \gamma_2, \delta_2$ in terms of the value of s so that a single candidate can emerge as the "winner." What about the threshold values distinguishing between a pair being designated for top-ranked and a three way tie?
b. Consider the profile $(\frac{1}{2}, \frac{1}{2}, 0, 0, 0, 0)$ and let $\gamma_2 = \frac{2}{3}$ for the Distinct winner procedure. Find the values of s so that this method will select the single candidate c_1.

2.3.7. Suppose $\mathbf{q}_1, \mathbf{q}_2$ are two normalized election outcomes for the voting vector $\mathbf{w}_s$. The maximum distance that could occur between two such vectors indicates the maximum difference in an election outcome. Find this maximum distance in terms of the value of s. Find profiles associated with each outcome.

2.3.8. In weighted voting, suppose we have the profile $(\pi, 1, 0, 2, \pi, 1)$.
a. Find the normalized version of this profile.
b. For what choices of s do we have the ranking $c_1 \sim c_2 \succ c_3$?
c. Show that the BC ranking is $c_2 \succ c_1 \succ c_3$. Show that this ranking is "robust", that is, for any small change in the profile, the ranking remains the same. Show that the plurality ranking for this profile is *not* robust; an arbitrarily small change in the profile can change the ranking.

2.3.9. There are procedures where the smallest number of points are assigned to a higher ranked candidate. For instance, we could assign the first-place candidate one point, the second-place two points, and the third-place three points. Show that these methods can be included in this discussion by allowing negative values for a in Eq. 2.3.7. Show that the above procedure is another form of the BC.

2.4 What a Difference a Procedure Makes; Several Different Outcomes

Different voting methods can create conflicting election outcomes with the same voters' preferences. But why? What is the source of this irritating fact? The explanation involves the differences between the plurality and the antiplurality methods. These procedures manifest extremes in philosophy where the former totally ignores a voter's second-ranked candidate while the latter accords her the preferential treatment of a top-ranked candidate. These differences are reflected geometrically by the fact that $\mathbf{w}_0$ and $\mathbf{w}_{\frac{1}{2}}$ are the endpoints of the line segment of voting vectors $\mathbf{w}_s$, $s \in [0, \frac{1}{2}]$. Another geometric measure is the nested arrangement ensured by Theorem 2.3.2 where for $s \in (0, \frac{1}{2})$,

$$\mathcal{CH}(\mathbf{w}_{\frac{1}{2}}) \subset \mathcal{CH}(\mathbf{w}_s) \subset \mathcal{CH}(\mathbf{w}_0) = Si(3).$$

The two limiting convex hulls are the shaded areas depicted in Fig. 2.4.1. The joint plurality, antiplurality outcome for a profile $\mathbf{p}$ is

$$(f(\mathbf{p}, \mathbf{w}_0), f(\mathbf{p}, \mathbf{w}_{\frac{1}{2}})) \in Si(3) \times Si(3)$$

where the notation indicates that the plurality election outcome is in the left-hand simplex of Fig. 2.4.1 while the antiplurality outcome is in the right-hand one.

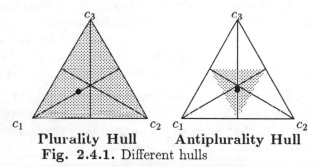

Plurality Hull   Antiplurality Hull
Fig. 2.4.1. Different hulls

A direct computation shows for profile $\mathbf{p}_m = (\frac{1}{3}, 0, \frac{1}{3}, 0, \frac{1}{3}, 0)$ that

$$(f(\mathbf{p}_m, \mathbf{w}_0), f(\mathbf{p}_m, \mathbf{w}_{\frac{1}{2}})) = ((\frac{1}{3}, \frac{1}{3}, \frac{1}{3}), (\frac{1}{3}, \frac{1}{3}, \frac{1}{3})),$$

so the normalized tally in each simplex is the barycentric point $\mathcal{I}$. Now suppose a type-1 voter joins $\mathbf{p}_m$ to create the new profile $\mathbf{p}'$. The arrival of this voter breaks the tie in different ways.

For the plurality election, the new outcome moves from $\mathcal{I}$ toward $[\mathbf{w}_0]_1 = (1, 0, 0)$ to reflect the vector ballot cast by the new type-one voter. Geometrically, the tally moves from $\mathcal{I}$ toward the c_1 vertex along the indifference line $q_2 = q_3$ to end up in the ranking region $c_1 \succ c_2 \sim c_3$. On the other hand, the impact this voter has on the antiplurality vote is to move the election vector from $\mathcal{I}$

toward $[\mathbf{w}_{\frac{1}{2}}]_1 = (\frac{1}{2}, \frac{1}{2}, 0)$. As the outcome moves along a different indifference line $q_1 = q_2$, the new election ranking is $c_1 \sim c_2 \succ c_3$. The exact amount of movement depends upon the number of original voters. For instance, if 15 voters defined the original profile $\mathbf{p}_m$, then the 16 voters define the normalized profile $\mathbf{p}' = \frac{15}{16}\mathbf{p}_m + \frac{1}{16}\mathbf{E}_1$. The linearity of election mappings leads to

$$
\begin{aligned}
f(\mathbf{p}', \mathbf{w}_s) =& f(\frac{15}{16}\mathbf{p}_m + \frac{1}{16}\mathbf{E}_1, \mathbf{w}_s) = \frac{15}{16}f(\mathbf{p}_m, \mathbf{w}_s) + \frac{1}{16}f(\mathbf{E}_1, \mathbf{w}_s) \\
=& \frac{15}{16}(\frac{1}{3}, \frac{1}{3}, \frac{1}{3}) + \frac{1}{16}[\mathbf{w}_s]_1.
\end{aligned}
$$

This equation is a special case of the general situation where if $\mathbf{p}, \mathbf{p}_1$ are, respectively, the profiles of the old and new voters, and if t is the proportion of new to all voters, then

$$
f((1-t)\mathbf{p} + t\mathbf{p}_1, \mathbf{w}_s) = (1-t)f(\mathbf{p}, \mathbf{w}_s) + tf(\mathbf{p}_1, \mathbf{w}_s). \tag{2.4.1}
$$

In Fig. 2.4.1, the two election outcomes $f(\mathbf{p}', \mathbf{w}_0)$, $f(\mathbf{p}', \mathbf{w}_{\frac{1}{2}})$ are indicated by dots in the appropriate simplex. As dictated by Eq. 2.4.1, any other voting method $\mathbf{w}_s, s \in (0, \frac{1}{2})$, moves the outcome from $\mathcal{I}$ toward $[\mathbf{w}_s]_1 = (1-s, s, 0)$ to create the election ranking $c_1 \succ c_2 \succ c_3$. What happens, then, is that the same profile $\mathbf{p}'$ defines three different election outcomes where the outcome depends on the geometric properties of the voting vector $\mathbf{w}_s$. The choice of a procedure matters!

With some imagination, modifications of the above construction lead to a diverse selection of other results. For instance, by adding different mixtures of voter types to $\mathbf{p}_m$, a wide selection of outcomes can emerge. Again, we must expect different procedures to define different outcomes for the same profile. But, how different can they be? The next theorem asserts that there are no limits.

Theorem 2.4.1. *Let voting vectors $\mathbf{w}_{s_1} \neq \mathbf{w}_{s_2}$ be given. Let β_1, β_2 be any two rankings of the three candidates – these rankings may be the same, or they may differ. There exists a profile so that when $\mathbf{w}_{s_j}$ is used to tally the ballots of the voters, the outcome is β_j; $j = 1, 2$.*

This is a shocking conclusion! It is intuitively clear that situations exist where differences in procedures can alter the election outcome. But, this much stronger conclusion asserts that there are no restrictions on how disparate the outcomes can be! Indeed, it even admits the possibility that a minuscule change in the weights assigned to the candidates can results in arbitrarily large differences in the election rankings!

How can this be true? An explanation must involve the only way voting vectors disagree – by the amount of weight assigned to a second-ranked candidate. This difference in weights is captured in the proof (at the end of the section) by the independent directions defined by the voting vectors.

Example 2.4.1. a. As the beverage example demonstrates, there is a profile where the plurality ranking is $c_1 \succ c_2 \succ c_3$, but the BC ranking is the reversed $c_3 \succ c_2 \succ c_1$.

b. Consider the two voting vectors $(5, 4, 0) \approx \mathbf{w}_{\frac{4}{9}}$ and $(5, 3, 0) \approx \mathbf{w}_{\frac{3}{8}}$. According to the theorem, there is a profile so that the $\mathbf{w}_{\frac{4}{9}}$ outcome is $\mathcal{I}$ while the $\mathbf{w}_{\frac{3}{8}}$ outcome is $\beta_2 = c_2 \succ c_1 \succ c_3$. Also, there is a profile so that the $\mathbf{w}_{\frac{4}{9}}$ outcome is $c_2 \succ c_3 \succ c_1$ while the $\mathbf{w}_{\frac{3}{8}}$ outcome is $c_1 \sim c_2 \succ c_3$.

c. Suppose $s_1 \geq 0$, and $\frac{1}{2} \geq s_2 = s_1 + 0.0000001$. The voting vectors $\mathbf{w}_{s_1}$ and $\mathbf{w}_{s_2}$ are essentially the same because they agree up to the seventh decimal place. Nevertheless, according to the theorem, there exists a profile where the $\mathbf{w}_{s_1}$ ranking is $c_3 \succ c_2 \succ c_1$ while the $\mathbf{w}_{s_2}$ ranking is the reversed $c_1 \succ c_2 \succ c_3$. So, even if two procedures are almost identical, their election outcomes can be radically different! □

2.4.1 How Bad It Can Get

Just imagine the mischief a young, modern Machiavelli could have once armed with this theorem. Suppose our modern Machiavelli discovers that the present attitudes of the electorate define the profile $\mathbf{p}$ which, when tallied with the required procedure $\mathbf{w}_s$, leads to the election outcome $f(\mathbf{p}, \mathbf{w}_s) = \beta_1$. This is fine if β_1 suits Machiavelli's purposes. If not, then he has at least two options. The first is to campaign so that the election day profile of $\mathbf{p}'$ leads to the desired outcome of $f(\mathbf{p}', \mathbf{w}_s) = \beta_2$. Alternatively, young Machiavelli could search for a different voting vector $\mathbf{w}_{s'}$ which, with the original profile $\mathbf{p}$, delivers the desired election outcome $f(\mathbf{p}, \mathbf{w}_{s'}) = \beta_2$. Then acting in the name of "responsible government," Mr. I. M. Machiavelli could promote the "virtues" of $\mathbf{w}_{s'}$ by starting a reform movement to replace $\mathbf{w}_s$ with $\mathbf{w}_{s'}$. [3]

This assertion that "anything can happen" is disturbing. After all, Theorem 2.4.1 appears to cast serious doubts about cherished democratic procedures that have painfully evolved over centuries. A standard way to handle this problem is to try to ignore it by speculating that *"Sure, maybe these assertions are true, but so what! They're probably useless because they never would occur in the 'real world'!"* In other words, motivated by the outlandish Example 2.4.1.c, it's natural to conjecture that if the rankings β_1, β_2 are sufficiently dissimilar, then the profiles supporting the conclusion of Theorem 2.4.1 must be, in some practical sense, highly restricted and nonrobust.

If such a conjecture could be validated for all choices of $\mathbf{w}_{s_1}, \mathbf{w}_{s_2}$, it would emasculate the theorem. Without "robustness" a described behavior would be so special – like a tie vote – that even small changes in a profile could destroy the conclusion. A natural issue, then, is to determine which conclusions are likely. However as shown at the end of this section, unless tie votes are involved,

---

[3] It is not difficult to find situations where it is arguable that "reform proposals" were motivated more by how a new procedure would change election outcomes than by a thoughtful study of the merits and fairness of one method over another. For example, the debate in certain states as well as in Chicago during parts of the 1970s and 1980s over "runoff" elections appeared to be dictated more by who would win than by which procedure is better. In 1992, the same argument surfaced in my home town of Evanston, Illinois.

robustness happens. Weird as it may seem, this robustness is compatible with the sensitivity exhibited by Example 2.4.1c. (Can the reader anticipate how?)

A more immediate issue motivated by Theorem 2.4.1 is to determine what else can occur. After all, if two procedures can admit two arbitrarily different election outcomes, then how bad can it be when three, or four, ..., or seven, or ... different procedures are applied to the same profile? To address this issue, let

$$Sup(\mathbf{p}) = \{ \text{ all election rankings of the 3 candidates that can arise}$$
$$\text{from profile } \mathbf{p} \text{ with changes in the positional voting method}\}$$

be the set of election rankings supported by profile $\mathbf{p}$; it is important to understand the properties of $Sup(\mathbf{p})$. As an illustration, the profile $\mathbf{p}'$ from the introductory example of this section defines $Sup(\mathbf{p}') = \{c_1 \succ c_2 \sim c_3, c_1 \succ c_2 \succ c_3, c_1 \sim c_2 \succ c_3\}$. In general, how many and what kind of entries can be in $Sup(\mathbf{p})$? How does $Sup(\mathbf{p})$ vary with changes in the profile $\mathbf{p}$? For a given $\mathbf{p}$, which voting vectors yield which rankings in $Sup(\mathbf{p})$? These questions are answered next.

2.4.2 Properties of $Sup(\mathbf{p})$

The next theorem, basic for our analysis of $Sup(\mathbf{p})$, uses geometric notation that should be explained in advance. Common sense suggests that if $f(\mathbf{p}, \mathbf{w}_{s_1})$ and $f(\mathbf{p}, w_{s_2})$ have radically different rankings, then the election tallies must be near $\mathcal{I}$. So, consider a ball of radius $\rho > 0$ with center $\mathcal{I}$. As such a ball intersects all ranking regions, if the only restriction on the outcomes is that they are in some ball $\mathcal{B}(\mathcal{I}, \rho)$, then any ranking can occur. This is what happens. Incidentally, a measure of the seriousness of the problem is the admissible value for ρ; can ρ have large values or is the conclusion insignificant because ρ must have a very small value?

Theorem 2.4.2. a. *Let voting vectors* $\mathbf{w}_{s_1} \neq \mathbf{w}_{s_2}$ *be given. There exists* $\rho > 0$ *so that the following is true. In the simplex* $Si(3)$, *construct the ball of radius* ρ *and center* $\mathcal{I}$, $B(\mathcal{I}, \rho)$. *(See Fig. 2.4.2.) In this ball, select any two election points* $\mathbf{q}_j$; $j = 1, 2$. *There is a one-dimensional line of profiles,* $\mathcal{L}_{\mathbf{w}_{s_1}, \mathbf{w}_{s_2}}(\mathbf{q}_1, \mathbf{q}_2) \subset Si(6)$, *so that if* $\mathbf{p} \in \mathcal{L}_{\mathbf{w}_{s_1}, \mathbf{w}_{s_2}}(\mathbf{q}_1, \mathbf{q}_2)$, *then*

$$f(\mathbf{p}, \mathbf{w}_{s_1}) = \mathbf{q}_1, \quad f(\mathbf{p}, \mathbf{w}_{s_2}) = \mathbf{q}_2. \tag{2.4.2}$$

b. *For profile* $\mathbf{p} \in Si(6)$ *and* $\mathbf{w}_s$, *the election vector* $f(\mathbf{p}, \mathbf{w}_s) \in Si(3)$ *is on the line segment connecting* $f(\mathbf{p}, \mathbf{w}_0)$ *and* $f(\mathbf{p}, \mathbf{w}_{\frac{1}{2}})$. *More precisely,*

$$f(\mathbf{p}, \mathbf{w}_s) = (1 - 2s)f(\mathbf{p}, \mathbf{w}_0) + 2s f(\mathbf{p}, \mathbf{w}_{\frac{1}{2}}), \quad s \in [0, \frac{1}{2}]. \tag{2.4.3}$$

The line segment defined by Eq. 2.4.3, the procedure line for profile $\mathbf{p}$, *is denoted by* $PL(\mathbf{p})$.

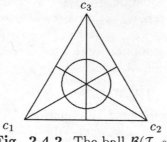

Fig. 2.4.2. The ball $\mathcal{B}(\mathcal{I}, \rho)$

The first assertion significantly improves upon Theorem 2.4.1. It ensures that not only can the election rankings for the two procedures be selected in an arbitrary fashion, but, with only the restriction about the value of ρ, even the normalized election tally for each procedure can be randomly chosen! Moreover, the theorem goes on to assert that the conclusion is not due to some isolated, single profile; instead, a whole line of profiles, $\mathbf{p} \in \mathcal{L}_{\mathbf{w}_{s_1}, \mathbf{w}_{s_2}}(\mathbf{q}_1, \mathbf{q}_2)$, defines the same two randomly chosen election tallies!

The more important assertion, b, maintains that *the procedure line* $PL(\mathbf{p})$ completely specifies the normalized election tally for each $\mathbf{w}_s$. In words, once we know $f(\mathbf{p}, \mathbf{w}_0)$ and $f(\mathbf{p}, \mathbf{w}_{\frac{1}{2}})$, we know all remaining outcomes $f(\mathbf{p}, \mathbf{w}_s)$! Indeed, the election outcome for $\mathbf{w}_s$, $f(\mathbf{p}, \mathbf{w}_s)$, is the point on the procedure line $PL(\mathbf{p})$ that is $2s$ of the distance from $f(\mathbf{p}, \mathbf{w}_0)$ to $f(\mathbf{p}, \mathbf{w}_{\frac{1}{2}})$. So, the outcome for each $f(\mathbf{p}, \mathbf{w}_s)$ is uniquely determined by how $PL(\mathbf{p})$ is positioned within the representation triangle. This positioning, in turn, is completely determined by the location of its endpoints – the plurality and antiplurality election outcomes. This leads to the important conclusion that *with just the two computations needed to find the end points of* $PL(\mathbf{p})$, *all possible* $\mathbf{w}_s$ *election outcomes for the given profile are determined!*

Proof of Part b. Because $\mathbf{w}_s = (1 - s, s, 0) = (1 - 2s, 0, 0) + (s, s, 0)$ can be expressed as $\mathbf{w}_s = (1 - 2s)(1, 0, 0) + 2s(\frac{1}{2}, \frac{1}{2}, 0)$, or

$$\mathbf{w}_s = (1 - 2s)\mathbf{w}_0 + 2s\mathbf{w}_{\frac{1}{2}}, \tag{2.4.4}$$

we have that $f(\mathbf{p}, \mathbf{w}_s) = f(\mathbf{p}, (1 - 2s)\mathbf{w}_0 + 2s\mathbf{w}_{\frac{1}{2}})$. The election mapping f is linear in both variables, so the linear separation property Eq. 1.4.4 ensures that

$$f(\mathbf{p}, \mathbf{w}_s) = (1 - 2s)f(\mathbf{p}, \mathbf{w}_0) + 2sf(\mathbf{p}, \mathbf{w}_{\frac{1}{2}}). \quad \square$$

Outline of the Proof of Part a. To see why part a is true, notice for given $\mathbf{q}$ and $\mathbf{w}_s$ that the vector equation

$$f(\mathbf{p}, \mathbf{w}_s) = \mathbf{q}$$

represents three linear equations (one for each component of $\mathbf{q}$) in the six unknowns $p_1, \ldots, p_6$. There is a reduction; once two components of $\mathbf{q}$ are known, the third can be determined from the equation $q_1 + q_2 + q_3 = 1$. (This is the equation defining $\mathbf{q} \in Si(3)$.) Therefore $f(\mathbf{p}, \mathbf{w}_s) = \mathbf{q}$ represents two independent equations in six unknowns.

We are not interested in one vector equation, but two of them. Using the above argument, these two vector equations

$$f(\mathbf{p}, \mathbf{w}_{s_1}) = \mathbf{q}_1, \quad f(\mathbf{p}, \mathbf{w}_{s_2}) = \mathbf{q}_2$$

reduce to four equations in six unknowns. A fifth equation, $\sum_{j=1}^{6} p_j = 1$, is mandated by the constraint $\mathbf{p} \in Si(6)$. Consequently, the voting problem can be equated with an algebraic problem involving five linear equations in six unknowns. From high school algebra, the general situation is that there is a line of solutions expressed in terms of one of the p_j variables. (See Sect. 1.4.) The technical rank condition ensuring this conclusion is given at the end of the section.

2.4.3 The Procedure Line

When Theorem 2.4.2 is viewed from the standpoint of elections, the conclusion totally violates intuition. After all, it asserts there need not be any relationship between the election outcomes for two different procedures with the same profile. Yet, once expressed as an algebraic system – five equations in six unknowns – the assertion is converted into a familiar form where the conclusion must be expected.

In a similar fashion, a natural explanation can be offered for the procedure line $PL(\mathbf{p})$. By holding a profile $\mathbf{p}$ fixed but varying the choice of $\mathbf{w}_s$, f becomes a linear mapping of the *voting vectors*. Moreover, as indicated by Eq. 2.4.3, the set of positional voting vectors is the convex hull defined by the two vertex voting vectors $\mathbf{w}_0, \mathbf{w}_{\frac{1}{2}}$. Therefore, according to Sect. 1.4, the linear election mapping picks up the line of voting vectors with vertices $\mathbf{w}_0, \mathbf{w}_{\frac{1}{2}}$, and transforms it into the procedure line of election outcomes with vertices $f(\mathbf{p}, \mathbf{w}_0)$ and $f(\mathbf{p}, \mathbf{w}_{\frac{1}{2}})$. (See Fig. 2.4.3.) This transformation, then, underscores how the different $\mathbf{w}_s$ election outcomes along the procedure line reflect the different emphasis each $\mathbf{w}_s$ places on who is the voter's second-ranked candidate.

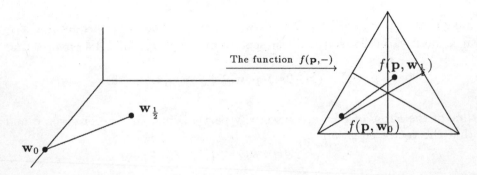

Fig. 2.4.3. The image of the line segment of voting vectors for fixed $\mathbf{p}$

Much more is possible. The relative lack of constraints on the choices for $f(\mathbf{p}, \mathbf{w}_0)$ and $f(\mathbf{p}, \mathbf{w}_{\frac{1}{2}})$ (Theorem 2.4.2a) combined with the fact that these two outcomes uniquely determine the procedure line $PL(\mathbf{p})$ lead to the conclusion that there are minimal restrictions on how $PL(\mathbf{p})$ is positioned. The only constraint is that the endpoints are in the ball $\mathcal{B}(\mathcal{I}, \rho)$ associated with $\mathbf{w}_0, \mathbf{w}_{\frac{1}{2}}$, so *any line segment in this ball is a procedure line $PL(\mathbf{p})$ for some set (a line) of profiles!* This introduces considerable freedom in the choices of the $\mathbf{w}_s$ election outcomes. Later in this section I resolve the annoyance that nothing has been stated about the value of ρ.

This constitutes a powerful tool for voting theory because the properties of $Sup(\mathbf{p})$ are completely determined by the properties of the $PL(\mathbf{p})$. Consequently, deep results about $Sup(\mathbf{p})$ can be obtained simply by drawing line segments in the representation triangle $Si(3)$; the theorem ensures that such a segment is a $PL(\mathbf{p})$ for some $\mathbf{p}$. To illustrate, draw a line segment where one endpoint is at $\mathcal{I}$. Obviously, this segment can enter only one ranking region. (To see this, draw the picture.) This trivial geometric fact translates into the deep assertion that *if either the plurality or the antiplurality ranking is a complete tie, then, with this profile, there is a single ranking that is the outcome for all other choices of a positional voting method. Consequently, should just one other $\mathbf{w}_s$ have $\mathcal{I}$ as the outcome for this profile, then the outcome for all procedures is a complete tie.*[4]

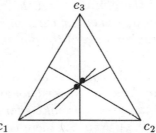

c_3

c_1 c_2

Fig. 2.4.4. Nearby points on $PL(\mathbf{p})$ with reversed rankings

To further illustrate the power of the procedure line, I'll use it and Fig. 2.4.4 to explain the conflict between common sense and the conclusion of Example 2.4.1c. If s_1 and s_2 are close in value, Eq. 2.4.3 requires $f(\mathbf{p}, \mathbf{w}_{s_1})$ and $f(\mathbf{p}, \mathbf{w}_{s_2})$ to be near-by points on the procedure line $PL(\mathbf{p})$. Thus, supporting common sense, the normalized election tallies are essentially the same. On the other hand, "essentially the same" normalized election outcomes need not translate into "exactly the same" ordinal rankings; the difference provides a window of opportunity to create outcomes exhibiting conflicting outcomes.

The key geometric fact is that near $\mathcal{I} \in Si(3)$, all 13 ranking regions are arbitrarily close to one another. (This makes sense; the complete tie can be broken in any one of 12 different ways.) So, no matter how close the two tallies

---

[4]Suppose $f(\mathbf{p}, \mathbf{w}_0)$ and $f(\mathbf{p}, \mathbf{w}_s)$, $s \neq 0$ are at $\mathcal{I}$. Solving Eq. 2.4.3 for $f(\mathbf{p}, \mathbf{w}_{\frac{1}{2}})$ leads to the conclusion that the antiplurality outcome is $\mathcal{I}$. Substituting the plurality and the antiplurality outcomes into Eq. 2.4.3 leads to the stated conclusion.

are to one another, the procedure line can be placed in $Si(3)$ so that $f(\mathbf{p}, \mathbf{w}_{s_1})$ and $f(\mathbf{p}, \mathbf{w}_{s_2})$ are in specified ranking regions. (See Fig. 2.4.4.) This is a geometric explanation of the conflict, where close election tallies define radically different election rankings.

Discovering new statements about $Sup(\mathbf{p})$ and their proofs now almost becomes a game. Just draw lines in the representation triangle and examine how they cross the various ranking regions. Thus, while the conclusions of the following theorem are deep, the approach to find them mimics the actions of a child placing sticks on a diagram to discover how many regions can be crossed.

Theorem 2.4.3. a. *The jth election ranking is in $Sup(\mathbf{p})$ if and only if $PL(\mathbf{p}) \cap \mathcal{R}(j) \neq \emptyset$.*

b. *Let k be an integer satisfying $1 \leq k \leq 7$. There exists a profile $\mathbf{p}$ so that $Sup(\mathbf{p})$ has precisely k rankings. Conversely, if $Sup(\mathbf{p})$ has k rankings, then $1 \leq k \leq 7$. If either the plurality or the antiplurality ranking involves a tie, then $Sup(\mathbf{p})$ has, at most, six rankings.*

c. *Let k be an integer satisfying $0 \leq k \leq 4$. There exists a profile $\mathbf{p}$ so that $Sup(\mathbf{p})$ has precisely k strict rankings. Conversely, if $Sup(\mathbf{p})$ has k strict rankings, then $0 \leq k \leq 4$. The number of rankings in $Sup(\mathbf{p})$ with a tie satisfies the inequality $0 \leq k \leq 3$.*

d. *If the election ranking of the plurality and the antiplurality vote are the reversal of each other, then $Sup(\mathbf{p})$ has either three or seven entries. In the first case, the entries of $Sup(\mathbf{p})$ are the rankings of the plurality vote, the antiplurality vote, and $\mathcal{I}$.*

e. *The election ranking for $\mathbf{p}$ is the same for all choices of $\mathbf{w}_s$ iff the plurality and the antiplurality ranking are the same. Indeed, for any ranking β, there exists a profile $\mathbf{p}$ so that not only is β the common ranking for all $\mathbf{w}_s$ elections, but also $f(\mathbf{p}, \mathbf{w}_0) = f(\mathbf{p}, \mathbf{w}_s)$ for all $s \in [0, \frac{1}{2}]$. Namely, there is a line of profiles whereby the normalized election tally is the same specified value for all procedures.*

The original question about the size of $Sup(\mathbf{p})$ is answered; according to part b, $Sup(\mathbf{p})$ can have anywhere from one to seven entries.[5] Part e offers good news; it specifies necessary and sufficient conditions so that all voting procedures record the same election ranking. Contrary to intuition, a unanimity profile does *not* satisfy this condition!

Proof. Part a is immediate as $PL(\mathbf{p}) \cap \mathcal{R}(j) \neq \emptyset$ iff there is a $\mathbf{w}_s$ so that $f(\mathbf{p}, \mathbf{w}_s) \in \mathcal{R}(j)$ iff the jth ranking is in $Sup(\mathbf{p})$.

---

[5] Much more can happen with additional candidates. For instance, using the same kind of geometric arguments in a higher dimensional space, it turns out for ten candidates that there is a profile where $84,830,767$ different rankings can emerge just by varying the choice of the positional voting method ([S15]). Moreover, each candidate can be top-ranked with some procedure and bottom-ranked with another. So, which one of these more than 84 million conflicting rankings best reflects the "true views" of the voters?

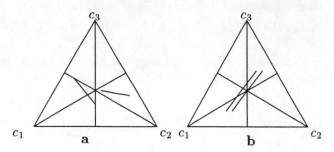

Fig. 2.4.5. Various positions of the position line.
a. Choices of $PL(\mathbf{p})$. **b.** Parallel position lines

To prove parts b and c, just experiment with the positioning of line segments in $Si(3)$ to see how many and few ranking regions the segment intersects. For instance, the choice of $PL(\mathbf{p_1})$ in the left-hand side of Fig. 2.4.5a borders on two indifference lines and intersects five regions so $Sup(\mathbf{p_1})$ consists of the five rankings $\{c_1 \sim c_2 \succ c_3, c_1 \succ c_2 \succ c_3, c_1 \succ c_2 \sim c_3, c_1 \succ c_3 \succ c_2, c_1 \sim c_3 \succ c_2\}$. The other line segment, $PL(\mathbf{p_2})$, is in $\mathcal{R}(5)$, so $Sup(\mathbf{p_2}) = \{c_2 \succ c_3 \succ c_1\}$. The proof of the theorem follows immediately because any line segment (in the $\mathbf{w_0}$, $\mathbf{w_{\frac{1}{2}}}$ disk) is a procedure line for some profile.

To see how to prove part d, let the plurality ranking be in $\mathcal{R}(1)$ and the antiplurality ranking in $\mathcal{R}(4)$. The associated procedure line either passes through $\mathcal{I}$, which forces $PL(\mathbf{p})$ to meet $\{\mathcal{R}(1), \mathcal{R}(4), \mathcal{I}\}$, or $PL(\mathbf{p})$ passes on one side of $\mathcal{I}$, so it meets seven regions. These two situations are depicted in Fig. 2.4.5b.

For part e, all of the election rankings agree iff $PL(\mathbf{p})$ is contained in a single ranking region iff the plurality and the antiplurality rankings agree.

Similarly, the normalized election tallies all agree iff the limit $PL(\mathbf{p})$ becomes a point $\mathbf{q}$. This situation holds iff $f(\mathbf{p}, \mathbf{w_0}) = f(\mathbf{p}, \mathbf{w_{\frac{1}{2}}}) = \mathbf{q}$. According to Theorem 2.4.2, for any $\mathbf{q}$ in the described disk, there is a line of profiles defining this outcome. Because the disk is centered at $\mathcal{I}$, $\mathbf{q}$ can be chosen in any of the 13 ranking regions. $\square$

2.4.4 Using the Procedure Line

To review: the mystery why different election outcomes can arise with the same profile is answered by using the arguments of Sect. 1.4. For a given profile $\mathbf{p}$, the mapping $f(\mathbf{p}, -)$ picks up the line of election vectors and repositions it as the procedure line defined by $\mathbf{p}$. Using the parametric representation $PL(\mathbf{p}) = \{(1 - 2s)f(\mathbf{p}, \mathbf{w_0}) + 2sf(\mathbf{p}, \mathbf{w_{\frac{1}{2}}}) \mid s \in [0, \frac{1}{2}]\}$, the different points on $PL(\mathbf{p})$ manifest the changing emphasis a procedure places on a second-ranked candidate. The only issue is the positioning of $PL(\mathbf{p})$; here, algebra allows considerable freedom in the choice of the endpoints $f(\mathbf{p}, \mathbf{w_0}), f(\mathbf{p}, \mathbf{w_{\frac{1}{2}}}) \in \mathcal{B}(\mathcal{I}, \rho)$. Once $PL(\mathbf{p})$ is specified, all related properties, such as what rankings are in $Sup(\mathbf{p})$, which voting methods give rise to which rankings, etc., follow immediately. Moreover, because the rankings in $Sup(\mathbf{p})$ are determined by the straight line segment $PL(\mathbf{p})$, the entries of $Sup(\mathbf{p})$ are related. All of this is illustrated in the next example.

Example 2.4.2. For the profile $\mathbf{p}'$ from the introductory example of this section, the plurality and antiplurality outcomes are indicated by dots in Fig. 2.4.1. When both dots are placed in the same simplex, the procedure line $PL(\mathbf{p}')$ is the connecting line segment. Thus $Sup(\mathbf{p}') = \{c_1 \succ c_2 \sim c_3, c_1 \succ c_2 \succ c_3, c_1 \sim c_2 \succ c_3\}$.

The introductory example starts with $\mathbf{p}_m$; the profile from the departmental meeting for which $f(\mathbf{p}_m, \mathbf{w}_0) = f(\mathbf{p}_m, \mathbf{w}_{\frac{1}{2}}) = \mathcal{I}$. As the two election vectors agree, we have that $PL(\mathbf{p}_m) = \{(\frac{1}{3}, \frac{1}{3}, \frac{1}{3})\}$, so the outcome must be $\mathcal{I}$ for all voting vectors. Thus $Sup(\mathbf{p}_m) = \{c_1 \sim c_2 \sim c_3\}$.

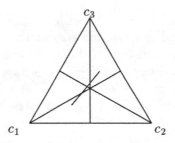

Fig. 2.4.6. An example of the procedure line

Next, $Sup(\mathbf{p})$, $PL(\mathbf{p})$, are found for $\mathbf{p} = (0, \frac{7}{18}, 0, \frac{5}{18}, \frac{6}{18}, 0)$. With this profile, all voters rank c_3 in either first or second position. As $f(\mathbf{p}, \mathbf{w}_0) = (\frac{7}{18}, \frac{6}{18}, \frac{5}{18})$ and $f(\mathbf{p}, \mathbf{w}_{\frac{1}{2}}) = (\frac{7}{36}, \frac{11}{36}, \frac{18}{36})$, we have that

$$PL(\mathbf{p}) = \{(1 - 2s)(\frac{7}{18}, \frac{6}{18}, \frac{5}{18}) + 2s(\frac{7}{36}, \frac{11}{36}, \frac{18}{36})$$
$$= (\frac{14(1 - s)}{36}, \frac{12 - 2s}{36}, \frac{10 + 16s}{36}) \mid s \in [0, \frac{1}{2}]\}.$$

(2.4.5)

From the geometric positioning of this line, given in Fig. 2.4.4, it follows immediately that

$$Sup(\mathbf{p}) = \{c_1 \succ c_2 \succ c_3, \ c_1 \succ c_2 \sim c_3, \ c_1 \succ c_3 \succ c_2, \ c_1 \sim c_3 \succ c_2,$$
$$c_3 \succ c_1 \succ c_2, \ c_3 \succ c_1 \sim c_2, \ c_3 \succ c_2 \succ c_1\}.$$

Observe the strict relationship among the rankings in $Sup(\mathbf{p})$ as the value of s varies; the ordering is imposed by the straight line geometry of $PL(\mathbf{p})$. For instance, the relative rankings of two adjacently ranked candidates are reversed by first going through a tie vote.

Using elementary algebra and Eqs. 2.4.3, 2.4.5, we can determine which choices of $\mathbf{w}_s$ define which rankings from $Sup(\mathbf{p})$. For instance, in order for $\mathbf{w}_s$ to define the election ranking $c_1 \succ c_2 \succ c_3$, the components of $\mathbf{q}$ must satisfy

$q_1 > q_2 > q_3$. So, according to Eq. 2.4.5, s must satisfy $\frac{14(1-s)}{36} > \frac{12-2s}{36} > \frac{10+16s}{36}$, or $s \in [0, \frac{1}{9})$. In this manner, the complete listing is

s for $\mathbf{w}_s$	Ranking	s for $\mathbf{w}_s$	Ranking
$s \in [0, \frac{1}{9})$	$c_1 \succ c_2 \succ c_3$	$s \in (\frac{2}{15}, \frac{1}{6})$	$c_3 \succ c_1 \succ c_2$
$s = \frac{1}{9}$	$c_1 \succ c_2 \sim c_3$	$s = \frac{1}{6}$	$c_3 \succ c_1 \sim c_2$
$s \in (\frac{1}{9}, \frac{2}{15})$	$c_1 \succ c_3 \succ c_2$	$s \in (\frac{1}{6}, \frac{1}{2})$	$c_3 \succ c_2 \succ c_1$
$s = \frac{2}{15}$	$c_1 \sim c_3 \succ c_2$		

This listing identifies which $\mathbf{w}_s$ lead to which of the seven rankings admitted by this profile $\mathbf{p}$. Among the properties that become apparent (for this particular $\mathbf{p}$) is that the more emphasis $\mathbf{w}_s$ places on the identity of a voter's second-ranked candidate, the better c_3 (everyone's top or second-ranked candidate) fares. In particular, changing procedures to provide increased recognition of a voter's second-ranked candidate forces the rankings to approach $c_3 \succ c_2 \succ c_1$. So, while the $\mathbf{w}_0$ (plurality) ranking of $c_1 \succ c_2 \succ c_3$ relegates c_3 to last place, the $(7, 1, 0) \approx \mathbf{w}_{\frac{1}{8}}$ ranking of $c_1 \succ c_3 \succ c_2$ allows c_3 to advance to a middle ranking, and the BC $(2, 1, 0) \approx \mathbf{w}_{\frac{1}{3}}$ ranking of $c_3 \succ c_2 \succ c_1$ finally elevates c_3 to the top-ranked position. $\square$

It is clear from this example that the normalized plurality and antiplurality election outcomes uniquely determine the properties and entries of $Sup(\mathbf{p})$. The following assertion, stating how $Sup(\mathbf{p})$ can change, is based on this fact.

Corollary 2.4.4. a. *Because $f(-, \mathbf{w}_0)$ and $f(-, \mathbf{w}_{\frac{1}{2}})$ are continuous functions of the profile, the procedure line varies continuously with changes in $\mathbf{p}$.*
b. *With changes in $\mathbf{p}$, there are two ways the entries of $Sup(\mathbf{p})$ can change.*
i. *The plurality ranking is the reverse of the antiplurality ranking and the procedure line passes through the point of complete indifference $\mathcal{I}$.*
ii. *The plurality and/or the antiplurality ranking changes. This requires passing through a ranking involving tie votes.*

Proof. Part a is obvious, so only part b needs to be proved. If the plurality and/or the antiplurality ranking changes, then the end-points of the procedure line must move into different regions. This creates new entries for $Sup(\mathbf{p})$.

The proof of the rest of this assertion involves the geometry of the ranking regions; they are either triangles, connected line segments, or the point $\mathcal{I}$. By experimenting with the positioning of line segments in $Si(3)$, it is clear that if the end-points are in ranking regions that are not the reverse of one another, then the procedure line always intersects the same ranking regions. Another way the procedure line can change ranking regions is if the end-points of the line segment are in ranking regions that are the reverse of one another. Here, the union of the ranking regions that meet $PL(\mathbf{p})$ is *not* a convex set. With the loss of convexity, the line can pass through the point $\mathcal{I}$. This completes the proof. $\square$

Example 2.4.3. Suppose all we know about a profile $\mathbf{p}$ involving a large number of voters is that $\mathcal{I} \in Sup(\mathbf{p})$; thus, for some $\mathbf{w}_s$, the outcome is a complete tie.

We want to determine what can happen if another voter arrives. This voter, then, makes a small change in $\mathbf{p}$ to create the profile $\mathbf{p}'$. (See Eq. 2.4.1.)

Using Theorem 2.4.3d, this information requires $Sup(\mathbf{p})$ to have one, two, or three entries depending on whether the procedure line is the point $\mathcal{I}$, has an endpoint on $\mathcal{I}$, or has $\mathcal{I}$ as an interior point. In the first case, the new voter breaks the tie, and, as in the introductory example, the new $Sup(\mathbf{p}')$ admits precisely three entries. In the second case ($|Sup(\mathbf{p})| = 2$)), either the plurality or the antiplurality outcome must be a complete tie while the other is not. If the new voter is of type j, then this endpoint will move either in the direction $[\mathbf{w}_0]_j$ or $[\mathbf{w}_{\frac{1}{2}}]_j$. By experimenting with possible choices for $PL(\mathbf{p})$, it can be seen that $Sup(\mathbf{p}')$ can have anywhere from one to five entries. Finally, in the last case, $|Sup(\mathbf{p}')| = 3, 7$. The reader should verify these assertions. $\square$

2.4.5 From Procedure Lines to Scoring Shells

Why should we be constrained to positional voting vectors? Why not explore a colorful, more imaginative world where the number of points assigned to a candidate need not satisfy the staid, orderly requirement of $w_i \geq w_{i+1}$ imposed upon the positional vectors? Why not assign, say, 2 points to a top-ranked candidate, -3 points for a second-ranked candidate and 11 points for a bottom-ranked candidate to define the *scoring vector* $(2, -3, 11)$. (The only requirement imposed upon a scoring vector is that not all the terms are the same.)

Why scoring vectors? Why not! Adopt the adventurous spirit that if the vector can be defined, there probably is an use for it. This is the case; as indicated below (and in Sect. 4.5) scoring rules help define an important class of choice procedures. However, to answer the WGAD question, we first need a theory. As an important bonus, the theory answers the remaining, nagging question about positioning the procedure line, $PL(\mathbf{p})$ within the representation triangle.

The same arguments defining the equivalence relationship $\mathbf{W}_1 \approx \mathbf{W}_2$ among voting vectors leads to a similar equivalence relationship for scoring vectors; the scoring ranking remains the same if $\mathbf{W}_1 = a\mathbf{W}_2 + b(1,1,1)$. By adhering to our practice of exploiting equivalence relationships, the *normalized form for scoring vectors* is defined in the same manner as for normalized voting vectors.

Definition 2.4.1. A normalized scoring vector $\mathbf{sc} = (sc_1, sc_2, sc_3)$, is where

$$\sum_{j=1}^{3} sc_j = 1, \quad sc_j \geq 0, \, j = 1, 2, 3,$$

and at least one sc_j term is zero. In tallying a ballot with $\mathbf{sc}$, sc_j points are assigned to the voter's jth ranked candidate, $j = 1, 2, 3$. $\square$

So, to convert the above scoring vector $(2, -3, 11)$ to a normalized form, first add the value 3 to each component to obtain $(5, 0, 14)$ and then divide by the sum of the terms to obtain a vector $(\frac{5}{19}, 0, \frac{14}{19})$ in the simplex.

According to Definition 2.4.1, a normalized scoring vectors is the weighted sum of the vertices $\mathbf{e}_1 = (1,0,0)$, $\mathbf{e}_2 = (0,1,0)$, and $\mathbf{e}_3 = (0,0,1)$ given by

$$\mathbf{sc} = sc_1(1,0,0) + sc_2(0,1,0) + sc_3(0,0,1) = \sum_{j=1}^{3} sc_j \mathbf{e}_j.$$

The *scoring election outcomes* are computed just as for a standard election. For instance, with $\mathbf{sc} = (\frac{1}{3}, 0, \frac{2}{3})$ and the profile $\mathbf{p} = \frac{1}{2}\mathbf{E}_5 + \frac{1}{2}\mathbf{E}_6$ (so, all voters have c_2 top-ranked, but they are evenly split between how the other two candidates are ranked), the outcome is $f(\mathbf{p}, \mathbf{sc}) = (\frac{1}{2}, 0, \frac{1}{2})$ with the ranking $c_1 \succ c_3 \succ c_2$.

Of interest for our purposes is the representation of a scoring election; a representation that follows from the linearity of the procedures

$$f(\mathbf{p}, \mathbf{sc}) = \sum_{j=1}^{6} p_j f(\mathbf{E}_j, \mathbf{sc}) = \sum_{j=1}^{6} p_j [\sum_{i=1}^{3} sc_i f(\mathbf{E}_j, \mathbf{e}_i)].$$

Next, interchange the order of summation in the final double summation to obtain

$$f(\mathbf{p}, \mathbf{sc}) = \sum_{i=1}^{3} sc_j f(\mathbf{p}, \mathbf{e}_i). \tag{2.4.6}$$

This equation shows that $f(\mathbf{p}, \mathbf{sc})$ is a convex sum of the outcomes $\{f(\mathbf{p}, \mathbf{e}_i)\}_{i=1}^{3}$.

To understand Eq. 2.4.6, we first need to interpret the scoring elections $\{f(\mathbf{p}, \mathbf{e}_j)\}$. The first term, $f(\mathbf{p}, \mathbf{e}_1)$ is the plurality election; an election based only on the identities of the voters' top-ranked candidates. As such, the outcome measures who the voters like the most. Similarly, $f(\mathbf{p}, \mathbf{e}_2)$ is a form of a plurality election determined by who the voters rank in second place. This outcome, therefore, can be thought of as measuring mediocrity. Finally, $f(\mathbf{p}, \mathbf{e}_3)$ reflects who the voters like the least. The computation of these three terms is as easy as computing the plurality outcome; just count. According to Eq. 2.4.6, $f(\mathbf{p}, \mathbf{sc})$, then, is a weighted combination of these specialized outcomes. If the weights satisfy the comfortable ordering $sc_1 \geq sc_2 \geq sc_3$, then the weighted ordering defines a positional voting method. Therefore, *a positional voting vector is a scoring vector, but most scoring vectors are not positional voting vectors.*

With the above interpretations, it is time to offer the reader a challenge. Is it possible for the most liked candidate (the $f(\mathbf{p}, \mathbf{e}_1)$ top-ranked candidate) to also be the most disliked (the $f(\mathbf{p}, \mathbf{e}_3)$ top-ranked candidate)? Is it possible for the same candidate to receive all three titles (most liked, most mediocre, most disliked)?

From this description, it is possible to envision uses for scoring rules. We could, for instance, design an election procedure where the candidate who receives at least half of the total number of $\mathbf{w}_s$ votes wins. Without a winning candidate, a runoff should be held between two of the candidates. But, which two? Perhaps it could be the $\mathbf{w}_s$ top-ranked candidate and the $f(\mathbf{p}, \mathbf{e}_2)$ top-ranked candidate.

Or, perhaps we could drop the least favored candidate, the $f(\mathbf{p}, (0, 0, 1))$ winner, and have the runoff between the remaining two.

Example 2.4.4. Consider the procedure where a plurality winner is selected if she receives over half the vote. If a runoff is needed, the candidate most voters have bottom-ranked (the $f(\mathbf{p}, \mathbf{e}_3)$ "winner") is dropped from further consideration. Is this procedure the same as a standard runoff where the plurality bottom-ranked candidate is dropped and the runoff is between the two top-ranked candidates?

These runoffs appear to be essentially the same, but the profile from the beverage example $(0, \frac{6}{15}, 0, \frac{4}{15}, \frac{5}{15}, 0)$ proves that the outcomes can differ. The plurality ranking is

$$\text{milk} \succ \text{beer} \succ \text{wine} ,$$

where, because milk fails to receive a majority vote, a runoff is needed. In the standard procedure, wine is dropped and beer beats milk in the runoff. However, for the proposed scheme, the eliminated candidate is determined by the $f(\mathbf{p}, (0, 0, 1))$ ranking. Surprisingly, this ranking for "what beverage is least liked" is the same as the plurality ranking! (The tally is $(\frac{9}{15}, \frac{6}{15}, 0)$.) Namely, more people have milk bottom-ranked than beer than wine. So, milk is dropped, and the runoff is between beer and wine.

It is easy to invent all sorts of "angry voters" scenarios based on this peculiarity where, in the "new, improved" procedure, the top-ranked candidate from the first stage is barred from the runoff! It is interesting to determine what other choices of $\mathbf{w}_s$ admit these same kind of election problems. $\square$.

Other applications of scoring rules are designed in much the same manner. In order to understand the consequences of such processes, the obvious goal, then, is to find the relationship between positional voting and scoring vector outcomes. The development of a theory follows the standard theme of *m equations and n unknowns* where, according to a straightforward computation, the relevant equations are

$$
\begin{aligned}
f(\mathbf{p}, \mathbf{e}_1) &= (p_1 + p_2, p_5 + p_6, p_3 + p_4) \\
f(\mathbf{p}, \mathbf{e}_2) &= (p_3 + p_6, p_1 + p_4, p_2 + p_5) \\
f(\mathbf{p}, \mathbf{e}_3) &= (p_4 + p_5, p_2 + p_3, p_1 + p_6)
\end{aligned}
\tag{2.4.7}
$$

These equations are *not* independent because the x, the y, and the z components of these three equations sum to unity. Thus, once two of the vectors $f(\mathbf{p}, \mathbf{e}_i)$ and $f(\mathbf{p}, \mathbf{e}_j)$ are computed, the third vector is determined immediately from the relationship

$$f(\mathbf{p}, \mathbf{e}_k) = (1, 1, 1) - [f(\mathbf{p}, \mathbf{e}_i) + f(\mathbf{p}, \mathbf{e}_j)]. \tag{2.4.8}$$

To illustrate, if $f(\mathbf{p}, \mathbf{e}_1) = (\frac{1}{3}, \frac{1}{6}, \frac{1}{2})$ and $f(\mathbf{p}, \mathbf{e}_2) = (\frac{1}{3}, \frac{1}{3}, \frac{1}{3})$, then it must be that

$$f(\mathbf{p}, \mathbf{e}_3) = (1, 1, 1) - [f(\mathbf{p}, \mathbf{e}_1) + f(\mathbf{p}, \mathbf{e}_2)] = (\frac{1}{3}, \frac{1}{2}, \frac{1}{6}).$$

Equation 2.4.8 answers the question whether a candidate can, simultaneously, be most liked, most mediocre, and most disliked. She cannot; she may win any two of these titles, but not the third. To see why, notice that by being $f(\mathbf{p}, \mathbf{e}_j)$ top-ranked, she receives more than $\frac{1}{3}$ of the vote. So, by winning two titles, her component in the bracket on the right hand side of Eq. 2.4.8 exceeds two-thirds; therefore, she receives less than one-third of the vote for the last election.

What adds to the adventure of using scoring methods is that any two values $f(\mathbf{p}, \mathbf{e}_i)$ are free to be chosen subject only to the usual requirement that they are inside of a disk centered at $\mathcal{I}$. Consequently all of the unexpected results associated with the procedure line extend to the scoring hull. This means, for instance, that we can develop the appropriate geometry to anticipate all sorts of surprises with runoffs and other procedures. This time, however, the location of the vertices for the hull is not shrouded in mystery. The following theorem describes the precise constraints.

Theorem 2.4.5. *Let $\mathbf{q}_1, \mathbf{q}_2 \in Si(3)$ be such that each component in the sum $\mathbf{q}_1 + \mathbf{q}_2$ is bounded above by unity. To each vector, assign one of the scoring vectors $\mathbf{e}_1, \mathbf{e}_2, \mathbf{e}_3$, say $\mathbf{q}_1 \rightarrow \mathbf{e}_i$ and $\mathbf{q}_2 \rightarrow \mathbf{e}_j$. There exists a line of profiles so that if $\mathbf{p}$ is chosen from this line, then*

$$f(\mathbf{p}, \mathbf{e}_i) = \mathbf{q}_1, \quad f(\mathbf{p}, \mathbf{e}_j) = \mathbf{q}_2.$$

Example 2.4.5. Let $\mathbf{q}_1 = (\frac{1}{2}, 0, \frac{1}{2})$ and $\mathbf{q}_2 = (\frac{1}{3}, \frac{1}{3}, \frac{1}{3})$. Because all three components of $(\frac{1}{2}, 0, \frac{1}{2}) + (\frac{1}{3}, \frac{1}{3}, \frac{1}{3}) = (\frac{5}{6}, \frac{1}{3}, \frac{5}{6})$ are bounded by unity, the theorem ensures there is a line of profiles whereby $f(\mathbf{p}, \mathbf{e}_1) = \mathbf{q}_2$, $f(\mathbf{p}, \mathbf{e}_3) = \mathbf{q}_1$. From Eq. 2.4.8, the last term is $f(\mathbf{p}, \mathbf{e}_2) = (\frac{1}{6}, \frac{2}{3}, \frac{1}{6})$. On the other hand, there are no profiles leading to the choices of $\mathbf{q}_1 = (\frac{1}{2}, 0, \frac{1}{2})$, $\mathbf{q}_3 = (0, \frac{1}{3}, \frac{2}{3})$ because the sum of the third component exceeds unity. $\square$

2.4.6 Scoring Shell Geometry

To find the geometric representation of scoring election outcomes, we turn to the familiar tools of Sect. 1.4. To use these tools, we would want the space of scoring rules to be the convex hull of the vertices $\{\mathbf{e}_j\}_{j=1}^3$, but it is not. Instead, the normalization requirement that at least one scoring vector component is zero forces the set of scoring vectors to inhabit only the boundary of this convex hull. These three edges define the *scoring shell*. In the left hand side of Fig. 2.4.7, the scoring shell are the three edges of the equilateral triangle (the shaded area) connecting pairs of vertices. However, no point in the shaded area is a (normalized) scoring vector. To use Sect. 1.4, somehow this region needs to become a convex hull. So, if we need a convex hull, invent one. Let the *scoring hull* be the convex hull defined by the scoring vector vertices $\{\mathbf{e}_j\}_{j=1}^3$. In the right hand side of Fig. 2.4.7, the scoring hull *is* the full shaded equilateral triangle.

For a fixed profile, it is easy to extend the election mapping from a linear mapping of the scoring vectors to a linear mapping of the scoring hull. Now that we have a convex hull for a domain and a linear mapping, the convexity property of Sect. 1.4 applies. The image set is a convex set in $Si(3)$; it is called the *scoring hull outcomes* where its edges, the *scoring shell outcomes*, is the set of normalized scoring election outcomes. To obtain the scoring shell outcomes, just connect pairs of points from $\{f(\mathbf{p}, \mathbf{e}_j)\}_{j=1}^{3}$ with straight lines. (See the right hand side of Fig. 2.4.7.) In Fig. 2.4.7, the heavy line on the boundary of each shaded simplex is the interval of positional voting vectors. (Compare this figure with Fig. 2.4.3.)

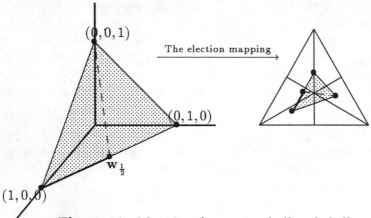

Fig. 2.4.7. Mapping the scoring hull and shell

From the Geometry of the Scoring Shell to $\mathcal{B}(\mathcal{I}, \rho)$. Observe that the positional voting vectors form an interval in one of the edges of the scoring shell. There should be a way to exploit this geometry, and there is. The key is that $f(\mathbf{p}, (\frac{1}{3}, \frac{1}{3}, \frac{1}{3})) = \mathcal{I}$ for all choices of $\mathbf{p}$. Because $(\frac{1}{3}, \frac{1}{3}, \frac{1}{3})$ is an interior point of the scoring hull, $\mathcal{I}$ must be an interior point of the scoring hull outcomes for all $\mathbf{p}$. As just one consequence, it is impossible for the scoring shell to be on one side of an indifference line. Thus, *with the three rankings from* $\{f(\mathbf{p}, \mathbf{e}_j)\}_{j=1}^{3}$, *it is impossible for the relative ranking of a pair of candidates to be the same strict ranking.* This is a geometric proof of the earlier assertion that a candidate cannot be simultaneously the most liked, the most mediocre, and the most disliked. In fact, the geometry leads to the stronger pairwise assertion that it is impossible for $c_i \succ c_j$ for each of the three elections. (If there were a pair $\{c_i, c_j\}$ where $c_i \succ c_j$ for all three elections, then, contrary to the assertion, the scoring hull would be on the $c_i \succ c_j$ side of the indifference line $c_i \sim c_j$.)

Additional geometry to exploit comes from the equilateral triangle shape of the scoring hull. For example, $\mathbf{w}_{\frac{1}{2}}$ is the midpoint of the bottom edge, so the line connecting $\mathbf{w}_{\frac{1}{2}}$ and $\mathbf{e}_3$ must pass through $(\frac{1}{3}, \frac{1}{3}, \frac{1}{3})$. (This is the dashed line in Fig. 2.4.7.) But, linear mappings map lines to lines, so $f(\mathbf{p}, \mathbf{e}_3)$ must be on the straight line starting from $f(\mathbf{p}, \mathbf{w}_{\frac{1}{2}})$ and passing through $\mathcal{I}$. (This is the dashed line in the scoring hull outcomes in the figure.) In fact, using the separation property of linear mappings (Eq. 1.4.4), the precise position of $f(\mathbf{p}, \mathbf{e}_3)$ can be determined. To do so, notice that the solution to $(1-t)\mathbf{w}_{\frac{1}{2}} + t\mathbf{e}_3 = (\frac{1}{3}, \frac{1}{3}, \frac{1}{3})$ is $t = \frac{1}{3}$, so *the distance from* $(\frac{1}{3}, \frac{1}{3}, \frac{1}{3})$ *to* $\mathbf{e}_3$ *is twice the distance from* $\mathbf{w}_{\frac{1}{2}}$ *to*

$(\frac{1}{3}, \frac{1}{3}, \frac{1}{3})$. Linear mappings preserve this ratio (Eq. 1.4.4), so the distance from $\mathcal{I}$ to $f(\mathbf{p}, \mathbf{e}_3)$ is twice the distance from $f(\mathbf{p}, \mathbf{w}_{\frac{1}{2}})$ to $\mathcal{I}$. Therefore, by knowing either $f(\mathbf{p}, \mathbf{w}_{\frac{1}{2}})$ or $f(\mathbf{p}, \mathbf{e}_3)$, the other value can be found.

Using the same kind of arguments, but applied to the bottom edge of the scoring hull, we have that $f(\mathbf{p}, \mathbf{e}_2)$ must be on the line starting at the plurality outcome and passing through the antiplurality outcome. This is the procedure line. So, to find $f(\mathbf{p}, \mathbf{e}_2)$, extend the procedure line by doubling its length. The endpoint is $f(\mathbf{p}, \mathbf{e}_2)$. Actually, $f(\mathbf{p}, \mathbf{e}_2)$ is easier to compute, so to determine the proceure line, compute $f(\mathbf{p}, \mathbf{e}_1), f(\mathbf{p}, \mathbf{e}_2)$; the midpoint between these points is the antiplurality endpoint $f(\mathbf{p}, \mathbf{w}_{\frac{1}{2}})$.

Example 2.4.6. It follows from the above discussion that once the procedure line is known, then so is the scoring shell. For instance, suppose $f(\mathbf{p}, \mathbf{w}_0) = \mathbf{q}_0 = (0.9, 0.1, 0)$ and $f(\mathbf{p}, \mathbf{w}_{\frac{1}{2}}) = \mathbf{q}_{\frac{1}{2}} = (0.5, 0.1, 0.4)$. According to the above, $f(\mathbf{p}, \mathbf{e}_2)$ is found by extending the procedure line so it has double the length. Do this by first finding the direction of the procedure line – the direction from the plurality election to the antiplurality outcome, $\mathbf{q}_{\frac{1}{2}} - \mathbf{q}_0 = (-0.4, 0, 0.4)$. The doubling requirement leads to increment $2(\mathbf{q}_{\frac{1}{2}} - \mathbf{q}_0) = (-0.8, 0, 0.8)$. Add this increment to the base point $f(\mathbf{p}, \mathbf{e}_1)$ to obtain

$$f(\mathbf{p}, \mathbf{e}_2) = 2(f(\mathbf{p}, \mathbf{w}_{\frac{1}{2}}) - f(\mathbf{p}, \mathbf{w}_0)) + f(\mathbf{p}, \mathbf{w}_0) = 2f(\mathbf{p}, \mathbf{w}_{\frac{1}{2}}) - f(\mathbf{p}, \mathbf{w}_0). \quad (2.4.9)$$

So, the above define $f(\mathbf{p}, \mathbf{e}_2) = 2(0.5, 0.1, 0.4) - (0.9, 0.1, 0) = (0.1, 0.1, 0.8)$. Using a similar algebraic approach, we have that

$$f(\mathbf{p}, \mathbf{e}_3) = (1, 1, 1) - 2f(\mathbf{p}, \mathbf{w}_{\frac{1}{2}}), \quad (2.4.10)$$

or, with the example, $f(\mathbf{p}, \mathbf{e}_3) = (0, 0.8, 0.2)$. $\square$

Next, I offer an important consequence of these equations and the geometry. Part a of the next theorem specifies those $\mathbf{q}_0, \mathbf{q}_{\frac{1}{2}} \in Si(3)$ that are admissible election outcomes $f(\mathbf{p}, \mathbf{w}_s) = \mathbf{q}_s$, $s = 0, \frac{1}{2}$, for some profile. Consequently, this assertion finally answers the nagging questions about the location of the procedure line and the size of the region asserted in Theorem 2.4.1. As already suggested, this region is quite large!

Theorem 2.4.6. a. Let $\mathbf{q}_0, \mathbf{q}_{\frac{1}{2}} \in Si(3)$. In order for there to exist a profile $\mathbf{p}$ so that $f(\mathbf{p}, \mathbf{w}_s) = \mathbf{q}_s$, $s = 0, \frac{1}{2}$, it is necessary and sufficient that the following two conditions are satisfied.

   i. Each component of $\mathbf{q}_{\frac{1}{2}}$ is bounded above by $\frac{1}{2}$.
   ii. Each component of $\mathbf{q}_{\frac{1}{2}}$ is at least as large as half the corresponding component of $\mathbf{q}_0$.

   b. The procedure line $PL(\mathbf{P})$ uniquely determines the scoring shell and hull outcomes. Conversely, for a profile, the scoring shell outcome uniquely determines the procedure line.

c. The ranking of $f(\mathbf{p}, \mathbf{e}_3)$ is the reverse of the ranking of $f(\mathbf{p}, \mathbf{w}_{\frac{1}{2}})$.

d. If for some j we have $f(\mathbf{p}, \mathbf{e}_j) = \mathcal{I}$, then the scoring hull and scoring shell outcomes are on a straight line passing through $\mathcal{I}$. If $f(\mathbf{p}, \mathbf{e}_j) = \mathcal{I}$ holds for two values of j, then it holds for all three; the scoring hull, the scoring shell, and the procedure line become the point $\mathcal{I}$.

Thus, for example, from part d it follows that if the above runoff procedure is applied to a profile where $f(\mathbf{p}, \mathbf{w}_0) = f(\mathbf{p}, \mathbf{w}_{\frac{1}{2}}) = \mathcal{I}$, then $f(\mathbf{p}, \mathbf{e}_3) = \mathcal{I}$; the procedure cannot identify a candidate to drop. Actually, in this situation $f(\mathbf{p}, \mathbf{sc}) = \mathcal{I}$ for all choices of scoring rules, so no scoring rule would be of any help.

From part c we have that the embarrassing situation described in Example 2.4.4, where the plurality top-ranked candidate is barred from competing in the runoff, never happens if the first election is antiplurality ranked. It is an exercise using Theorem 2.4.5 for the possible positioning of the scoring hull to show that this is true only for $\mathbf{w}_{\frac{1}{2}}$. For any other $\mathbf{w}_s$, the $f(\mathbf{p}, \mathbf{w}_s)$ election ranking could agree with the $f(\mathbf{p}, \mathbf{e}_3)$ ranking.

From part a of the theorem it follows that there does not exist a profile with the outcomes $\mathbf{q}_0 = (.2, .4, .4)$, $\mathbf{q}_{\frac{1}{2}} = (.45, .15, .4)$. This is because the c_2 component of $\mathbf{q}_{\frac{1}{2}}$ is smaller than half of the corresponding $\mathbf{q}_0$ component. However, there are profiles supporting the nearby pair of outcomes $\mathbf{q}_0 = (.2, .4, .4)$, $\mathbf{q}_{\frac{1}{2}} = (.4, .2, .4)$. The important contribution of part a is that it removes the final obstacle for the design of procedure lines.

As another illustration, suppose $\mathbf{q}_0 = (0.4, 0.1, 0.5)$. The problem is to find all admissible values of $\mathbf{q}_{\frac{1}{2}} = (x, y, z)$. According to part a, the constraints are

$$0.5 \geq x \geq 0.2 \quad 0.5 \geq y \geq 0.05$$
$$0.5 \geq z \geq 0.25 \quad x + y + z = 1.$$

This example illustrates the enormous flexibility to choose a procedure line even when one endpoint is fixed.

Proof of Part a. The first condition on $\mathbf{q}_{\frac{1}{2}}$ merely requires $\mathbf{q}_{\frac{1}{2}} \in \mathcal{CH}(\mathbf{w}_{\frac{1}{2}})$. The second requirement ensures that some component of $f(\mathbf{p}, \mathbf{e}_2)$, as expressed in Eq. 2.4.9, is not negative. What remains is to prove the existence of a profile $\mathbf{p}$. But, according to Theorem 2.4.5, such a profile exists as long as each component of $f(\mathbf{p}, \mathbf{e}_1) + f(\mathbf{p}, \mathbf{e}_2)$ is bounded by unity. Using Eq. 2.4.9, the existence is ensured as long as this condition is satisfied by $\mathbf{q}_0 + [2\mathbf{q}_{\frac{1}{2}} - \mathbf{q}_0] = 2\mathbf{q}_{\frac{1}{2}}$. But this condition, which requires each component of $\mathbf{q}_{\frac{1}{2}}$ to be bounded by $\frac{1}{2}$, just describes $\mathcal{CH}(\mathbf{w}_{\frac{1}{2}})$.

Proof of Part b. This is a restatement of the discussion preceding the theorem.

Proof of Part c. A line segment passing through $\mathcal{I}$ has its endpoints in ranking regions that are the reverse of one another. This completes the proof.

Proof of Part d. The point $\mathcal{I}$ must be in the interior of the scoring hull outcomes. If a vertex agrees with $\mathcal{I}$, then this requirement can be satisfied only if the hull is a line segment. To show the second part, if the two points are $f(\mathbf{p}, \mathbf{e}_1)$ and $f(\mathbf{p}, \mathbf{e}_2)$, then the mid-point between them, $f(\mathbf{p}, \mathbf{w}_{\frac{1}{2}})$ also is stuck at $\mathcal{I}$. Using Eq. 2.4.8 to determine $f(\mathbf{p}, \mathbf{e}_3)$, we find that it, too, is at the indifference point.

If some other pair of vertices of the scoring hull outcomes is stuck at $\mathcal{I}$, then carry out the same approach using the midpoint of the appropriate edges of the scoring shell. $\square$

2.4.7 Robustness of the Paradoxical Assertions

Returning to the procedure line, we must wonder whether these assertions about how the election rankings can change with the voting procedure are of practical concern, or just a "Gee Whiz" fact to be invoked as a last attempt to salvage a boring cocktail conversation. The answer is suggested by Theorems 2.4.2, 2.4.6. With the immense freedom of choice allowed for the normalized election tallies of the plurality and antiplurality outcomes, we must expect the conclusions to be robust and likely. In fact, extrapolating from Example 2.4.2, it appears that only profiles endowed with a remarkable uniformity of views among the voters are immune from the conclusions.

A practical test as to whether these assertions are likely to occur is if actual election examples can be found to illustrate Theorems 2.4.1, 2.4.2. This is easy; in fact, practical examples should be expected to emerge from most closely contested election among three (or more) candidates.

Example 2.4.7. As indicated above, a plurality method favors a candidate who is top-ranked among a sizable, unified portion of the electorate, while other methods favor more subtle distinctions of the electorate. So, depending upon the demographics and political unity, different political groups will find different choices of $\mathbf{w}_s$ to be to their political advantage. But, election procedures are mathematical tools without an ideological bias. Thus, an advantage enjoyed by a group with a specific procedure can change with the demographics and the degree of political unity.

To illustrate, the 1983 primary election for the Mayor of Chicago was closely contested among Jane Byrne, Richard Daley and Harold Washington. The polls indicated that Washington would lose a "head-to-head" election with either other candidate. Yet, because of unified Afro-American support and because the plurality method does not recognize a voter's second-ranked candidate, Washington became the first Afro-American Mayor of Chicago. Choices of $\mathbf{w}_s$ which give increased recognition to a voter's second-ranked candidate, such as the BC, may have forced Washington to lose.

In the 1987 campaign, Mayor Washington appeared to be sufficiently popular to beat any competitor with almost any method; he easily won reelection. Unfortunately, he died soon after. The resulting political scramble for a successor divided the Afro-American community into two factions. Consequently in the election to fill the remainder of Washington's term, the plurality vote with its inability to reflect "second-choices" now worked against this same community;

Richard Daley won. It is arguable that had a different positional method been used, such as the BC, an Afro-American would have been elected. So, in the short time span of five years, the voting method that initially showered success upon the united Afro-American community, now worked against the divided group. Indeed, the need for a single candidate to emerge with the plurality vote appears to be keeping this community divided.

A 1991 example comes from the "crook or klan" Louisiana gubernatorial race. Former Governor Edwards was labeled a "crook" and a womanizer, while David Duke had been a leader of the Ku Klux Klan and a member of the neo-Nazi party.[6] It is reasonable to suspect that the incumbent Governor Roemer would have beaten either of the other two in a head-to-head race – even though he had changed political parties and made controversial decisions during his term. But, the plurality method does not recognize a voter's second-ranked candidate, so Roemer came in last. In the highly publicized "crook or klan" run-off, Edwards beat Duke. □

The Mathematics of Robustness. The mathematics needed to prove which assertions are robust and which are unlikely is immediate. The goal is to determine whether a small change in the profile can alter the election outcome, so the analysis must involve the geometry of the five-dimensional space of profiles $Si(6)$. The relevant properties are consequences of Theorem 2.4.2 and "m equations with n unknowns" with its $n - m$ dimensional space of solutions. In our case, a particular procedure line defines a line of profiles. By taking the union of lines, we create sets of profiles supporting particular kinds of outcomes. In this manner, straightforward approaches from our three-dimensional world are used to extract properties of the unfamiliar five-dimensional space of profiles.[7]

The idea is to start with procedures $\mathbf{w}_{s_1} \neq \mathbf{w}_{s_2}$, specified election outcomes $\mathbf{q}_1, \mathbf{q}_2$, and then exploit the fact that, with five equations in six unknowns, the set of profiles yielding $\mathbf{q}_1, \mathbf{q}_2$ is a line in profile space $Si(6)$. This solution line $L_{\mathbf{w}_{s_1}, \mathbf{w}_{s_2}}(\mathbf{q}_1, \mathbf{q}_2)$ cannot extend forever because if it did, it would admit negative values for the the non-negative p_j's. Thus, the ends of $L_{\mathbf{w}_{s_1}, \mathbf{w}_{s_2}}(\mathbf{q}_1, \mathbf{q}_2)$ are on the boundary of $Si(6)$. Because $\mathbf{p} \in Si(6)$ is a boundary point iff some voter types have no voters, each end-point is characterized by having a different zero component.

A line is uniquely determined by two points, so once two profiles are found that define the same $\mathbf{q}_1, \mathbf{q}_2$ outcomes, we know all of them. For instance, a direct computation proves that $f(\mathbf{w}_s, \mathbf{p}_m) = (\frac{1}{3}, \frac{1}{3}, \frac{1}{3})$ for $s = 0, \frac{1}{2}$ where $\mathbf{p}_m = (\frac{1}{3}, 0, \frac{1}{3}, 0, \frac{1}{3}, 0)$ is a boundary point of $Si(6)$. The same conclusion holds for a different boundary point $\mathbf{p}_m^r = (0, \frac{1}{3}, 0, \frac{1}{3}, 0, \frac{1}{3})$. By knowing two profiles where $f(\mathbf{p}, \mathbf{w}_0), f(\mathbf{p}, \mathbf{w}_{\frac{1}{2}})$ both equal to $\mathcal{I}$, we now know all profiles defining this

---

[6]The comments about Edwards are based on alleged scandals during his earlier term as governor.

[7]A different profile representation is developed in the following sections.

outcome; they are the points on the line

$$L_{\mathcal{I}} = (1-t)\mathbf{p}_m + t\mathbf{p}_m^r = (\frac{1-t}{3}, \frac{t}{3}, \frac{1-t}{3}, \frac{t}{3}, \frac{1-t}{3}, \frac{t}{3}) \qquad (2.4.11)$$

for $t \in [0,1]$. The importance of $L_{\mathcal{I}}$ is specified in the following assertion.

Corollary 2.4.7. *If* $\mathbf{p} \in L_{\mathcal{I}}$, *then all* $\mathbf{w}_s$ *have the outcome* $f(\mathbf{w}_s, \mathbf{p}) = \mathcal{I}$. *Conversely, if* $\mathbf{p} \notin L_{\mathcal{I}}$, *then there exists a* $\mathbf{w}_s$ *so that* $f(\mathbf{w}_s, \mathbf{p}) \neq \mathcal{I}$.

Proof. The procedure line for both profiles is the point $\mathcal{I}$. These two boundary profiles define the line $L_{\mathcal{I}}$. Therefore, the procedure line for any $\mathbf{p} \in L_{\mathcal{I}}$ is the point $\mathcal{I}$. The conclusion follows. $\square$

A word of caution; for a specified $\mathbf{w}_s$, this corollary does not mean that only the profiles from $L_{\mathcal{I}}$ define the outcome $\mathcal{I}$. After all, for each $\mathbf{w}_s$, the equation $f(\mathbf{p}, \mathbf{w}_s) = \mathcal{I}$ corresponds to three linear equations in six variables (What are they?), so $f(\mathbf{p}, \mathbf{w}_s) = \mathcal{I}$ defines a *three-dimensional* profile subset of $Si(6)$. Different choices of $\mathbf{w}_s$ define different three-dimensional sets of profiles, and $L_{\mathcal{I}}$ is the intersection of all of them.

A conclusion similar to that described in the corollary holds for any $\mathbf{w}_{s_1} \neq \mathbf{w}_{s_2}$ and election outcomes $\mathbf{q}_1, \mathbf{q}_2$. The associated line of profiles, $L_{\mathbf{w}_1, \mathbf{w}_2}(\mathbf{q}_1, \mathbf{q}_2)$, is uniquely determined by its end points on $Si(6)$. To find this line, just find two different profiles that support the specified outcomes; the line passing through these profiles is $L_{\mathbf{w}_1, \mathbf{w}_2}(\mathbf{q}_1, \mathbf{q}_2)$.

The profile set leading to specified election rankings β_1, β_2 is found by using all election vectors $\mathbf{q}_1 \in \mathcal{R}(\beta_1), \mathbf{q}_2 \in \mathcal{R}(\beta_2)$. Each pair $\mathbf{q}_1, \mathbf{q}_2$ defines a line of profiles, so the union of the lines $L_{\mathbf{w}_{s_1}, \mathbf{w}_{s_2}}(\mathbf{q}_1, \mathbf{q}_2)$ defines the set of profiles leading to a specific pair of rankings.

Theorem 2.4.8. *Let* $\mathbf{w}_{s_1} \neq \mathbf{w}_{s_2}$ *and rankings* β_1, β_2 *be given. The set of profiles supporting the* $\mathbf{w}_{s_1}$ *ranking of* β_1 *and the* $\mathbf{w}_{s_2}$ *ranking of* β_2 *is the union of parallel straight line segments*

$$P_{s_1, s_2}(\beta_1, \beta_2) = \cup_{\substack{\mathbf{q}_1 \in \mathcal{R}(\beta_1) \\ \mathbf{q}_2 \in \mathcal{R}(\beta_2)}} L_{\mathbf{w}_{s_1}, \mathbf{w}_{s_2}}(\mathbf{q}_1, \mathbf{q}_2) \subset Si(6). \qquad (2.4.12)$$

This convex region is uniquely defined by its vertices on the boundary of $Si(6)$.

The proof of this theorem is given at the end of this section. A more immediate concern is to interpret what this theorem means about the robustness of election outcomes. The guiding idea is depicted in Fig. 2.4.8 where the shaded region is the union of parallel lines created by varying an end point. The line is one-dimensional and the end point varies over a one-dimensional line, so the resulting shaded area is two-dimensional. If the endpoint could range over a two dimensional domain, then a three-dimensional region would emerge. This suggests that the geometric dimension of $P_{s_1, s_2}(\beta_1, \beta_2)$ is found by adding unity (the dimension of the line segment) to the number of degrees of freedom allowed for an endpoint of the lines. As already argued, the degrees of freedom for the endpoint is the degrees of freedom available to move $\mathbf{q}_1, \mathbf{q}_2$; this value is the dimension of the ranking regions $\mathcal{R}(\beta_j)$.

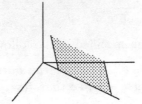

Fig. 2.4.8. A union of parallel straight lines

Corollary 2.4.9. *The set* $P_{s_1, s_2}(\beta_1, \beta_2)$ *has dimension*

$$1 + dim(\mathcal{R}(\beta_1)) + dim(\mathcal{R}(\beta_2)).$$

In particular, if β_1 *and* β_2 *are strict rankings, then the set of profiles forms an open five-dimensional subset of* $Si(6)$.

"Robustness" traditionally means that if a profile is changed by a sufficiently small amount in *any* direction, then the outcome is not significantly altered. Consequently, a sufficiently small change in the profile keeps the election ranking unchanged. So, if a profile set has the same dimension as $Si(6)$ (five), then the corresponding outcome must be robust. On the other hand, if a set of profiles has dimension less than five, then there are directions where only a trivial change in the profile defines a new election ranking.

Corollary 2.4.10. *Let* $\mathbf{w}_{s_1} \neq \mathbf{w}_{s_2}$ *and* β_1, β_2 *be given. If* β_1, β_2 *are strict election rankings, then there is an open set of profiles in* $Si(6)$ *where the* $f(\mathbf{p}, \mathbf{w}_{s_j})$ *election ranking is* β_j, $j = 1, 2$.

Therefore, the assertion of Theorem 2.4.1 is robust for rankings β_1, β_2 that do not involve ties. But, robustness is lost if either ranking does have a tie. This makes sense because the tie vote can be broken with arbitrarily small changes in the profile. In fact, there is a correspondence between the number of candidates tied in the two election rankings and the number of directions within the space of profiles available to break the tie vote.

This robustness assertion about election rankings doesn't correspond with intuition that if $\mathbf{w}_{s_1}$ is essentially the same as $\mathbf{w}_{s_2}$, then the corresponding election rankings also must be essentially the same. The only possible reconciliation is for the five-dimensional set of profiles to be, in some refined sense, "small." For instance, if these profiles constitute a five-dimensional set with "small" (five-dimensional) volume, then many natural choices of probability distributions would assign this event a small likelihood of occurring. This is what happens. A discussion of the profile sets is deferred until the coordinate representations are introduced.

2.4.8 Proofs

To conclude, the proofs of the major conclusions are given.

Proof of Theorem 2.4.2 a As described above, the proof of this part of the theorem reduces to the examination of the five equations in six unknowns. A standard method of solving these equations is to express them in a matrix form

$$A(\mathbf{p}^t) = (q_1^1, q_2^1, q_1^2, q_2^2, 1)^t$$

where $\mathbf{p}^t$ indicates the transpose of the row vector (so it is a column vector) and q_i^j is the ith component of $\mathbf{q}_j$. Matrix A is

$$A = \begin{pmatrix} s_1 & 0 & 0 & s_1 & 1-s_1 & 1-s_1 \\ 1-s_1 & 1-s_1 & s_1 & 0 & 0 & s_1 \\ s_2 & 0 & 0 & s_2 & 1-s_2 & 1-s_2 \\ 1-s_2 & 1-s_2 & s_2 & 0 & 0 & s_2 \\ 1 & 1 & 1 & 1 & 1 & 1 \end{pmatrix}. \tag{2.4.13}$$

As $s_1 \neq s_2$, one s_j value is not zero and the other is not $\frac{1}{2}$. So, assume that $s_1 \neq 0$, $s_2 \neq \frac{1}{2}$. By moving the fifth row to become the second row and the fourth row to become the third row, the matrix equation is

$$\begin{pmatrix} s_1 & 0 & 0 & s_1 & 1-s_1 & 1-s_1 \\ 1 & 1 & 1 & 1 & 1 & 1 \\ 1-s_2 & 1-s_2 & s_2 & 0 & 0 & s_2 \\ 1-s_1 & 1-s_1 & s_1 & 0 & 0 & s_1 \\ s_2 & 0 & 0 & s_2 & 1-s_2 & 1-s_2 \end{pmatrix} (\mathbf{p}^t) = \begin{pmatrix} q_1^1 \\ 1 \\ q_2^2 \\ q_1^2 \\ q_2^1 \end{pmatrix}.$$

By using elementary row operations on this matrix (which corresponds to standard algebraic manipulations of the five original algebraic equations), the matrix is reduced to the form

$$\begin{pmatrix} 1 & 0 & 0 & 1 & \frac{1-s_1}{s_1} & \frac{1-s_1}{s_1} \\ 0 & 1 & 1 & 0 & \frac{-1}{s_1} & \frac{-1}{s_1} \\ 0 & 0 & 2s_2-1 & s_2-1 & 1-s_2 & 1 \\ 0 & 0 & 0 & \frac{s_1-s_2}{2s_2-1} & \frac{s_2-s_1}{2s_2-1} & \frac{2(s_2-s_1)}{2s_2-1} \\ 0 & 0 & 0 & 0 & \frac{s_1-s_2}{s_1} & \frac{s_1-s_2}{s_1} \end{pmatrix}. \tag{2.4.14}$$

It follows from the reduced matrix of Eq. 2.4.14 that a solution exists for any $\mathbf{q}_1$, $\mathbf{q}_2$. For instance, from the last row, we have that

$$p_5 = -p_6 + c_5$$

where c_5 is a scalar depending on the row reduction and the values of $\mathbf{q}_j$, and where the value of p_6 is free to be varied. Similarly, from the fourth row, we have that

$$p_4 = -p_5 + 2p_6 + c_4 = 3p_6 + c_4 + c_5.$$

The equations for the remaining variables can be read off in a similar manner. The resulting solution defines a line in R^6 where the defining variable is p_6. The slope of this line is uniquely determined by the values of s_1, s_2, while the positioning of the line is determined by $s_1, s_2, \mathbf{q}_1, \mathbf{q}_2$. Also notice that for values of s_1 close to s_2, some of the coefficients of the equations are either very small or very large.

There is a problem. From the expression for p_5, it is obvious some solutions require a negative number of type-five voters. Independent of one's personal opinions about these voters, such an outcome is not permitted for a profile. Therefore, we need to verify that if appropriate restrictions[8] are imposed on the values of $\mathbf{q}_1, \mathbf{q}_2$, there are solutions with non- negative coefficients.

The resolution of this problem is simple. As already shown, the algebraic system

$$F(\mathbf{p}) = (f(-, \mathbf{w}_{s_1}), f(-, \mathbf{w}_{s_2})) : Si(6) \to Si(3) \times Si(3) \tag{2.4.15}$$

has maximum rank, so solutions exist for any $(\mathbf{q}_1, \mathbf{q}_2)$. Now, $\mathbf{p}' = (\frac{1}{6}, \frac{1}{6}, \ldots, \frac{1}{6})$ is the barycentric point of $Si(6)$ and it is a solution for the equation $F = (\mathcal{I}, \mathcal{I})$. By continuity of solutions, if $(\mathbf{q}_1, \mathbf{q}_2)$ is near $(\mathcal{I}, \mathcal{I})$, then there is a solution near the interior point $\mathbf{p}'$. This completes the proof.

Re-expressing the last argument in a geometric fashion, note that we have a linear mapping F and a convex hull $Si(6)$ defined by the vertices $\{\mathbf{E}_j\}_{j=1}^6$; this suggests using the material from Sect. 1.4. Because $\mathbf{p}' = (\frac{1}{6}, \frac{1}{6}, \ldots, \frac{1}{6})$ is an interior point of the $Si(6)$ hull, its image $F(\mathbf{p}') = (\mathcal{I}, \mathcal{I})$ must be in the interior of the F image set. Now, either the image is a lower dimensional linear space passing through this point, or it is a higher dimensional space with $\mathcal{F}(\mathbf{p}') = (\mathcal{I}, \mathcal{I})$ as an interior point. If the later holds, then there is a ball of profiles about $\mathbf{p}'$ that is mapped to the image space. The latter case does hold because of the analysis of Eq. 2.4.14. $\square$

Proof of Theorem 2.4.1. Theorem 2.4.2 a asserts that values of $\{\mathbf{q}_i\}_{i=1}^2$ can be chosen in an arbitrary fashion from $B(\mathcal{I}, \rho)$. But, $B(\mathcal{I}, \rho)$ intersects all 13 ranking regions, so for any choice of β_1, β_2 a value of $\mathbf{q}_1, \mathbf{q}_2$ can be selected from that ranking region. $\square$

Proof of Corollary 2.4.7. This proof involves the mapping $\mathcal{F}$ defined in the proof of Theorem 2.4.2 and the inverse mapping theorem. The theorem asserts that if $\mathcal{F}$ has the rank of the image space (which it does), and if Σ is a smooth surface (manifold) in the image of $\mathcal{F}$ with dimension $4 - k$, then $\mathcal{F}^{-1}(\Sigma)$ is (locally) a smooth surface of dimension $5 - k$. In this statement, notice that the value 4 is dictated by the dimension of the image space, and the value 5 is the dimension of the domain. In the statement of the corollary, the values of $\mathbf{q}_1, \mathbf{q}_2$ can vary over a four-dimensional surface, so the value of k is zero. This means that the image contains a five-dimensional open set. The rest of the assertion follows from the

---

[8]These restrictions explain why the profile sets are small for s_1 close to s_2 in value.

linear form for $\mathcal{F}$; the inverse image of a point is a linear space of the appropriate dimension.

Proof of Theorem 2.4.5. The simplest proof is to use the linear mapping

$$F = (f(-, \mathbf{e}_1), f(-, \mathbf{e}_2)) : Si(6) \to Si(3) \times Si(3)$$

and the ideas from Sect. 1.4. The conclusion follows by computing $\{F(\mathbf{E}_j)\}_{j=1}^{6}$ and then considering the convex combinations.

Proof of Theorem 2.4.8. In $Si(3) \times Si(3)$, the ranking regions are defined by the intersection of hyperplanes. The mapping converting profiles into election outcomes is linear. Thus, the inverse image of a hyperplane and/or a hyperplane and the outcomes on one side of this hyperplane, is a convex set in $Si(6)$ defined by hyperplanes. The conclusion follows by taking the intersection of these regions.

2.4.9 Exercises

2.4.1. Show that while $f(\mathbf{p}, \mathbf{w}_0) = (1, 0, 0)$ and $f(\mathbf{p}, \mathbf{w}_{\frac{1}{2}}) = (0, \frac{1}{2}, \frac{1}{2})$ have common solutions, but there does not exist a solution where all of the coefficients are non-negative. In other words, prove there exist admissible plurality and admissible antiplurality outcomes that cannot be obtained simultaneously. Does this example satisfy Theorem 2.4.6?

2.4.2. Let profile $\mathbf{p}$ be so that for a positional voting method $\mathbf{w}_s$, $s \neq 0, \frac{1}{2}$, the election outcome is $f(\mathbf{p}, \mathbf{w}_s) = \mathcal{I}$. Prove for $\mathbf{p}$ that only two other rankings emerge for any other choice of a positional voting method. What happens to the scoring outcomes? (Show they, too, are on a line.) What happens if the hypothesis is changed so that the above $\mathbf{w}_s$ has either $s = 0$ or $s = \frac{1}{2}$? What is the dimension of the set of profiles leading to these two conclusions?

2.4.3. a. Suppose $f(\mathbf{p}, \mathbf{w}_0) = (\frac{5}{10}, \frac{4}{10}, \frac{1}{10})$ and $f(\mathbf{p}, \mathbf{w}_{\frac{1}{2}}) = (\frac{4}{10}, \frac{5}{10}, \frac{1}{10})$. Find $f(\mathbf{p}, \mathbf{w}_{\frac{1}{3}})$.

b. Suppose $f(\mathbf{p}, \mathbf{w}_0) = (\frac{3}{8}, \frac{3}{8}, \frac{2}{8})$ and $f(\mathbf{p}, \mathbf{w}_{\frac{1}{3}}) = (\frac{6}{16}, \frac{5}{16}, \frac{5}{16})$. Find $f(\mathbf{p}, \mathbf{w}_{\frac{1}{2}})$ and $f(\mathbf{p}, \mathbf{w}_{\frac{1}{4}})$.

c. Suppose $f(\mathbf{p}, \mathbf{w}_{\frac{1}{4}}) \in \mathcal{R}(c_1 \succ c_3 \succ c_2)$ and that $f(\mathbf{p}, \mathbf{w}_{\frac{1}{3}}) \in \mathcal{R}(c_3 \succ c_1 \sim c_2)$. Find all admissible rankings for $f(\mathbf{p}, \mathbf{w}_{\frac{1}{2}})$ and $f(\mathbf{p}, \mathbf{w}_0)$.

2.4.4. a. Suppose $f(\mathbf{p}, \mathbf{w}_0) \in \mathcal{R}(c_3 \succ c_2 \succ c_1)$ and $f(\mathbf{p}, \mathbf{w}_{\frac{1}{2}}) \in \mathcal{R}(c_1 \succ c_2 \succ c_3)$. By varying the choice of the $\mathbf{w}_s$ there are three different listing of rankings that can occur with $\mathbf{p}$. List them. Suppose that $f(\mathbf{p}, \mathbf{w}_{\frac{1}{2}}) = (\frac{4}{15}, \frac{5}{15}, \frac{6}{15})$ and $f(\mathbf{p}, \mathbf{w}_0) = (\frac{13}{30}, \frac{9}{30}, \frac{8}{30})$. List all possible rankings that ever could occur with any choice of $\mathbf{w}_s$. Find choices of $\mathbf{w}_s$ that lead to each of these possible rankings.

b. According to Theorem 2.4.3, associated with a profile $\mathbf{p}$ anywhere from one to seven different election rankings can result where the different rankings depend upon the choice of the positional voting method. Find the relationship that exists among these rankings. (This relationship is determined by the plurality ranking and the antiplurality ranking for $\mathbf{p}$.)

c. Show that if $|Sup(\mathbf{p})| > 1$, there is at least one ranking with a tie vote.

2.4.5. Carry out the details of the row reduction part of the proof of Theorem 2.4.2, but do so carrying along the values of q_i^j. In this way, find the equations for the line of profiles in terms of the values of p_6 and $\{q_i^j\}_{i,j=1}^2$.

2.4.6. a. Using the proof of Corollary 2.4.7, consider the set of profiles leading to a ranking where β_1 has a tie outcome between one pair of candidates, but β_2 admits no ties. Show that this set is of dimension 4. Consider all possibilities of the different β_1, β_2 with various ties votes and determine the dimension of the supporting set of profiles.

b. Find the set of all profiles where for *all choices of* $\mathbf{w}_s$ the election ranking is $c_1 \succ c_2 \succ c_3$. (Hint: In the discussion, we found the set of profiles where the outcome always is $\mathcal{I}$. Using similar ideas, find the profiles where the outcome is $c_1 \sim c_2 \succ c_3$ for $\mathbf{w}_0$, but for $\mathbf{w}_{\frac{1}{2}}$ the ranking is $c_1 \succ c_2 \succ c_3$. Now, do the same, but reverse the roles of $\mathbf{w}_0$ and $\mathbf{w}_{\frac{1}{2}}$. Then, do the same where the different rankings are $c_1 \succ c_2 \succ c_3$ and $c_1 \succ c_2 \sim c_3$. These sets form the boundary in $Si(6)$ for the indicated region.)

2.4.7. Show that the optimal choice of ρ in the statement of Theorem 2.4.2 depends upon the choice of the values of s_1, s_2. Show that the maximum value for ρ is associated with the extreme values of $s = 0, \frac{1}{2}$.

2.4.8. Show that there exist profiles so that the $\mathbf{w}_s$, $s \neq \frac{1}{2}$, agrees with the $\mathbf{e}_3$ ranking. (Hint: Use geometry! First draw the line connecting $f(-, \mathbf{e}_3)$ and $f(-, \mathbf{w}_{\frac{1}{2}})$. There is freedom in the choice of $f(\mathbf{p}, \mathbf{w}_0)$, so chose it so that $f(-, \mathbf{w}_0)$ is in the same ranking region as $f(-, \mathbf{e}_3)$. Now, by varying the location of $f(\mathbf{p}, \mathbf{w}_{\frac{1}{2}})$, show that $f(\mathbf{p}, \mathbf{w}_s)$ can be moved into the same ranking region.)

2.4.9. For the beverage example, we know that the BC and the antiplurality rankings are consistent with the pairwise rankings. For this profile, find all choices of $\mathbf{w}_s$ that have this property. Find all $\mathbf{w}_s$ where the ranking agrees with the plurality ranking.

2.4.10. Suppose the $\mathbf{p}$ ranking for $\mathbf{w}_{s-1} \neq \mathbf{w}_{s-2}$ have a tie vote between c_1 and c_2. Show that for this profile, *all* scoring and positional rankings have a tie vote between these two candidates. Does the same conclusion hold if the two $\mathbf{w}_{s_j}$ are replaced with any two scoring vectors?

2.4.11. Show that there exists a profile so that each candidate is top-ranked with some choice of $\mathbf{w}_s$. Show that there is a profile where each candidate is bottom-ranked depending on which $\mathbf{w}_s$ is used. Show that there is a profile where c_3 always is bottom-ranked, but some positional methods have c_1 top-ranked, while others have c_2 top-ranked. Show that these conclusions are robust.

2.4.12. For $\mathbf{w}_s, s \in [0, \frac{1}{2}]$, find a $\mathbf{sc}$ so that the $f(\mathbf{p}, \mathbf{sc})$ ranking *always* reverses the $f(\mathbf{p}, \mathbf{w}_s)$ ranking. Next, show that if $\mathbf{sc}$ is not used, then there always exists a $\mathbf{p}$ so that the two rankings agree. Prove that $f(\mathbf{p}, \mathbf{w}_{\frac{1}{2}} = \mathcal{I}$ iff $f(\mathbf{p}, \mathbf{e}_3) = \mathcal{I}$.

2.4.13. a. If $f(\mathbf{p}, \mathbf{w}_0) = (0.2, 0.5, 0.3)$, find all admissible values for $f(\mathbf{p}, \mathbf{w}_{\frac{1}{2}})$.

b. The plurality vote for U.S. President in 1992 was $(0.43, 0.38, 0.19)$. Find all the procedure lines that could accompany this outcome.

c. For a given $f(\mathbf{p}, \mathbf{w}_{\frac{1}{2}}) = \mathbf{q}_{\frac{1}{2}}$, find a relationship specifying all admissible $\mathbf{q}_0$.

2.4.14. a. Show that the scoring hull outcomes for $\mathbf{p}$ is the full representation triangle iff $\mathbf{p} = \mathbf{E}_j$ for some choice of j.

b. Show that for a profile $\mathbf{p}$ there exist scoring rules $(1 - s_1, 0, s_1)$, and $(0, 1 - s_2, s_2)$, $s_1, s_2 \in (0, 1)$ with the same normalized election outcome iff the procedure line is a point.

2.4.15. Show by using the scoring hull that if c_1 has more first-place and more second-place votes than any other candidate, then she is top-ranked with all positional ranking methods. What can you say about a candidate who receives more second and more third-place votes? How about first and third-place votes?

2.5 Why Can't an Organization Be More Like a Person?

The beverage brouhaha, which initiated the season of dissent within the hypothetical department of the fable, started with the winer's discovery that the department's plurality ranking conflicts with how these same voters rank the three pairs of beverages. The radical disagreement among these rankings raises interesting theoretical questions. How does a majority vote ranking of a pair relate to its relative ranking within a positional election outcome? How and when are the majority vote rankings of the pairs related to one another?

In this section, geometric techniques are developed to answer questions of this kind about pairwise vote rankings and to explain the emergence of election paradoxes. In doing so, coordinate representations for profiles are introduced to allow us to "see" which profiles lead to which election outcomes.

2.5.1 Pairs and the Irrational Behavior of Organizations

When comparing candidates, it is natural to use pairwise competitions. In this manner, distracting side issues are avoided because the merits of a candidate are directly compared with those of her competitor. This kind of reasoning is used to support the adoption of agendas and other pairwise procedures. (Recall that an agenda lists the candidates, say $[c_1, c_3, c_2]$. The majority vote winner of the first pair, $\{c_1, c_3\}$, is advanced to be compared via a majority vote election with the next listed candidate, c_2. The winner of the last election wins.) Once the value of using pairwise comparisons is embraced, the first goal is to identify those profiles that escape the difficulties described in Sect. 1.1-2. Namely, we want to characterize those profiles where the same candidate wins with any reasonable pairwise comparison procedure. Such a candidate must be able to beat everyone else.

Definition 2.5.1. Candidate c_k is a *Condorcet winner* if she wins all pairwise majority vote elections against all other candidates. Candidate c_j is a *Condorcet loser* if she loses all pairwise elections against the other candidates. □

In the beverage example, wine is the Condorcet winner and milk is the Condorcet loser. Of course, there can be at most one Condorcet winner and one Condorcet loser.

Part of the attraction of a Condorcet winner is the comfort of using the familiar pairwise, majority vote elections. This concept captures a sense of rugged individualism because c_k is the Condorcet winner iff she beats all comers. With all of this electoral strength, it is obvious that she will be victorious whenever a reasonable procedure based on pairwise comparisons is used. (Namely, exclude those perverse methods that ignore certain candidates or reward the loser of a contest, rather than the winner.) For instance, a Condorcet winner wins with any agenda. For these kinds of reasons, it is widely accepted that whenever a Condorcet winner exists, she should be selected.

As described later in this section and in the next chapter, this concept suffers several negatives; impediments that are sufficiently serious to cause pause for reflection. As a first flaw, a Condorcet winner and/or Condorcet loser need not exist. Condorcet demonstrated this limitation by creating "the Condorcet profile" $\mathbf{p}_m$ illustrated with the departmental meeting of the fable. With $\mathbf{p}_m$, each alternative loses to one candidate while beating another. The existence problem, then, is not because of an absence of pairwise winners; instead, there are too many of them. (This example also proves that an agenda winner need not be a Condorcet winner.) Consequently a "Condorcet winner" is a "sometimes" concept – sometimes it can be used; sometimes it can't. This in itself suggests that the arguments supporting a Condorcet winner should be critically re-examined, and this is done here.

The Money Pump. The Condorcet cycle $c_1 \succ c_2$, $c_2 \succ c_3$, $c_3 \succ c_1$ created by $\mathbf{p}_m = (\frac{1}{3}, 0, \frac{1}{3}, 0, \frac{1}{3}, 0, \frac{1}{3})$ is particularly bothersome because it violates our intuition and expectations about rational behavior. Some of us, after all, claim to be "rational individuals" who proudly affiliate only with rational behaving groups. Using a Turing test, this means it would be impossible to decide whether a given set of outcomes are the decisions of a rational individual, or those of a group of rational people.

To discuss rational behavior, we need a working description. Standard definitions require the preference rankings to be as orderly as points on a line. If three points satisfy the inequalities $p_1 \le p_2$ and $p_2 \le p_3$, then we must have $p_1 \le p_3$. Similar predictable behavior, *transitivity*, is expected of personal and group preferences; we expect a person with preferences $c_1 \succ c_2$ and $c_2 \succ c_3$ to have the ranking $c_1 \succ c_3$.[9]

So, if Susie prefers strawberries to apple pie, and apple pie to raspberries, we might dismiss her as acting irrational should she prefer raspberries to strawberries. Maybe; but maybe not. Reasonable scenarios (see the exercises) can justify

---

[9] Not all binary relationships are transitive. For instance, let S be the people in a room and define the binary relationship $s_1 \mathcal{L} s_2$ to mean that s_1 loves s_2. Now, it may be that "Klaus $\mathcal{L}$ Katri", and "Katri $\mathcal{L}$ John," but it need not be true that "Klaus $\mathcal{L}$ John."

such nontransitive actions as being sophisticated; well, maybe pseudosophisti-
cated.

Transitivity of preferences may, or may not adequately model rational behavior, but it is a reasonable starting assumption. After all, if voters are not
rational, then it is trivial to show that all sorts of chaotic outcomes could and
should happen! Consequently, to have any hope for orderly outcomes, a critical
assumption in choice theory is to require transitive preferences for the voters.

The standard justification for this assumption is the "Dutch Book" or "money
pump" which argues that an individual with intransitive rankings quickly will
learn to exchange them for transitive preferences. To see why, suppose cyclic
Susie *does* prefer raspberries to strawberries. If offered a choice between strawberries and raspberries, she will, of course, choose raspberries. Now, along comes
Mike. For a small fee, Mike will arrange for Susie to choose between raspberries
and apple pie. This option involves a preferred choice, so, presumably, she would
pay. Then, clever Mike would offer another deal for "soon to be poor" Susie!
Again for a small fee, she could choose between apple pie and strawberries.

raspberries $\succ$ strawberries   apple pie $\succ$ raspberries

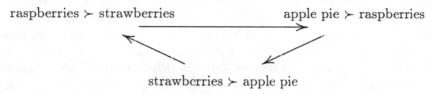

strawberries $\succ$ apple pie

The money pump now is in full operation. Should Susie pay and select strawberries, Mike would dangle another opportunity that can't be refused; she can, for
a small fee, choose between strawberries and raspberries! Susie's choices would
be right back to where they started, but her wallet would be lighter. Around
the cycle Mike would go, trying to pump out all of Susie's money. However,
if you know Susie like I know Susie, you know that this strategy will fail; she
would instantly detect and foil Mike's devious intentions by adopting transitive
preferences.

If Mike could try to pump money from Susie, why would he not attempt to con
an organization? After all, the (sincere voting) cycle defined by $\mathbf{p}_m$ offers plenty
of opportunities.[10] Would a group learn? The immediate issue, however, is to
understand why such an option could even arise with an organization of rational
voters. To poorly paraphrase the scholarly Professor Higgens of *"My Fair Lady"*
fame, "why can't an organization be more like a person?" Any explanation must
delve into the mysteries of how the simple aggregation of heterogeneous transitive
opinions can destroy transitivity. [11]

---

[10] Suppose each of the three members $\{A, B, C\}$ of a condo organization has $100. For a fee,
the manager, M, offers to assess some member $5; one dollar (say, in services) goes to each of
the two unassessed members while the remaining $3 is the manager's fee. With the advantage
to the majority, one can see how a money pump cycle would be set up. At the end of the first
vote where B, C voted against A, we have $A - \$95$, $B - \$101$, $C - \$101$, $M - \$3$; at the end of
the second vote A, C vote down B to obtain $A - \$96$, $B - \$96$, $C - \$102$, $M - \$6$; and so forth.

[11] This conflict between individual/group behavior is central to the social sciences. The

2.5.2 Confused, Irrational Voters

Would you trust a surgeon, a dentist, or a lawyer who consistently makes decisions while ignoring critical available information? Of course not. Similar deficiencies plague the pairwise vote procedure; as I will show in several different ways, this voting method systematically ignores vital, available information. So, can we trust pairwise voting?

To understand the lost information, envision the pairwise vote procedure as an accommodating servant trained to ignore all peculiarities of the guests. Consequently, this servant - the pairwise vote - serves the confused, irrational, cyclic voter with the same service and respect as the more staid, transitive individual who has painfully learned the lessons of the money pump. But, there are informational costs in the servant's inability to distinguish; by not knowing whether a guest is transitive or intransitive, it is impossible for the servant to coordinate requests or anticipate future ones.

I will illustrate this with an example. When three voters consider a proposal A, where two are in favor and one is against, then the fair outcome is a $2 : 1$ vote in favor of A. So, suppose out of three confused, cyclic voters, two have the preferences $A = \{c_1 \succ c_2, c_2 \succ c_3, c_3 \succ c_1\}$, while the third cyclic voter has the exact opposite persuasion of $A^c = \{c_2 \succ c_1, c_1 \succ c_3, c_3 \succ c_2\}$. Although confused (with respect to our definition of rational behavior), each voter has a distinct ranking of each pair, so the three pairwise election outcomes are well defined. Moreover, this confused voter profile has two in favor of Proposition A and one against. Posed in terms of this single issue, the outcome is obvious; the only fair outcome is a $2 : 1$ majority vote in favor of A. This is the pairwise election outcome.

The Condorcet profile of transitive voters, $c_1 \succ c_2 \succ c_3, c_2 \succ c_3 \succ c_1, c_3 \succ c_1 \succ c_2$, supports the same pairwise election outcomes. Actually, there is no mystery here; it is exactly as it should be. This is because, with anonymity and an emphasis on pairwise rankings, *it is impossible for the procedure to distinguish between the Condorcet profile of transitive voters and the group of confused voters.* Therefore, the "fair" outcome must be the cycle specified above. The identification between the two profiles is illustrated in the following table where the kth row lists the pairwise ranking of the kth transitive voter, while a subscript j on the pairs indicates how to reassign these pairs to construct the jth cyclic voter, $j, k = 1, 2, 3$.

$$
\begin{array}{lll}
(c_1 \succ c_2)_1 & (c_2 \succ c_3)_2 & (c_1 \succ c_3)_3 \\
(c_2 \succ c_1)_3 & (c_2 \succ c_3)_1 & (c_3 \succ c_1)_2 \\
(c_1 \succ c_2)_2 & (c_3 \succ c_2)_3 & (c_3 \succ c_1)_1
\end{array}
$$

The table underscores the central informational flaw of the pairwise vote; this electoral servant cannot distinguish whether it is dealing with transitive or

---

essence of the argument developed here and in other sections extends to other aggregation processes.

intransitive voters![12] As such, *the procedure ignores the critical assumption that the voters have transitive preferences!* No wonder we encounter cycles and other problems of pairwise voting; they just manifest this enormous loss of information about the basic transitivity assumption. Indeed, it turns out that for almost all profiles defining cycles and problems with pairwise voting, the pairwise rankings can be reassigned to create an alternative profile involving confused voters to illustrate that the outcome is "reasonable" when irrationality is admitted.

This informational gap is not suffered with positional voting methods. These procedures (other than the plurality and antiplurality vote) *require the voter to specify a transitive ranking* – they can't accommodate confused voters – so the transitivity assumption is built into the procedure. As such, (Chap. 3) we must anticipate that certain positional methods possess distinct advantages over pairwise voting.[13]

2.5.3 Information Lost from Pairwise Majority Voting

Asserting that information is lost is one matter; characterizing it is another. This is done is by describing the geometry of pairwise voting.

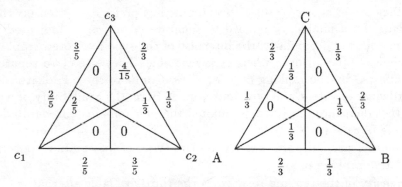

Fig. 2.5.1. Majority votes as projections

Start with the profile representation of $\mathbf{p}_b$ (the beverage example) where p_j is placed in the ranking region $\mathcal{R}(j)$, $j = 1, \ldots, 6$, of the representation triangle in Fig. 2.5.1. All voter types with the relative ranking $c_1 \succ c_2$ are to the left of the $c_1 \sim c_2$ indifference line, while those with the relative ranking $c_2 \succ c_1$ are to the right. Thus, the majority vote tallies for c_1 and c_2 are, respectively, the sum

---

[12]This is not obvious. In a discussion with Diana Richards, we noted that a tacit assumption in the literature is the transitivity of strategic actions. As the procedure can't detect rationality, there are many situations where transitivity can be ignored to admit all sorts of added strategies; e.g., for the manipulation of "single issue" problems, etc.

[13]This "lost information" theme explains paradoxes arising with $n \geq 4$ candidates where the positional vote rankings of $k(< n)$ candidate subsets are compared. By ranking k-candidate subsets, the procedure has no way to determine whether it is dealing with transitive voters, or with voters only capable of a transitive ranking for subsets of k candidates. With all of the lost information, we must anticipate discrepancies between the rankings of the $\binom{n}{k}$ subsets of k candidates and the ranking of all n candidates. This is the case; see [S9, S11, S16, S18].

of the numbers in the simplex listed to the left and to the right of the $c_1 \sim c_2$ line. The tally $(\frac{2}{5}, \frac{3}{5})$ defining the ranking $c_2 \succ c_1$, is listed below the c_1, c_2 edge of the simplex.

Geometrically, the pairwise vote should be thought of as a projection. After all, the $\{c_j, c_k\}$ majority vote is obtained by first projecting the simplex entries to the c_j, c_k edge and then summing the projected values. In this manner, the $\{c_2, c_3\}$ and $\{c_1, c_3\}$ majority vote outcomes can be computed; they are listed next to the appropriate edge in the figure.

A reason why the pairwise and plurality votes for the beverage example are at such extreme odds with one another is that the plurality vote ignores a voter's second choice. Clearly, we cannot trust a procedure that systematically ignores vital facts! This warning also applies to the pairwise vote. To better understand the lost information, we need to see what aspects of the geometry identify where the pairwise vote ignores the transitivity of rankings.

A pairwise election only uses the relative rankings of the two alternatives. For instance, in the beverage example comparison of $\{c_1, c_2\}$, only one voter type (type-two) has the ranking $c_1 \succ c_2$. However, we know more about these voters; not only do they prefer $c_1 \succ c_2$ (milk $\succ$ beer), but they prefer it so intensely that should c_3 (wine) be available, c_3 is used to separate c_1 and c_2 as indicated by the ranking $c_1 \succ c_3 \succ c_2$. Similarly, the intensity of the type-five voters' ranking $c_2 \succ c_1$, becomes apparent only when c_3 is available; They use c_3 to separate c_1, c_2 as manifested by the ranking $c_1 \succ c_3 \succ c_2$. Compare these two situation with the third class of voters, the type four-voters. Here, the availability of wine does not further delineate the $\{c_1, c_2\}$ ranking; the pair remains unseparated in the full ranking of $c_3 \succ (c_2 \succ c_1)$.

So, *with another available alternative*, the two types of information concern

1. The relative ranking $c_i \succ c_j$
2. The intensity of the ranking *relative to the third available alternative*

Strong intensity is where the ranking of the pair is separated by the third alternative. *Weak intensity* is where the pair remains intact; the undivided pair is compared with the third alternative.[14] These definitions of weak and strong intensity are based on objective, pragmatic criteria. Instead of juggling voters' subjective comments about the extremes in a comparison, where one voter's "like, awesome!" might equate with another voter's "well, somewhat," the measure of intensity is conditioned on information revealed by how a voter ranks a third alternative relative to the pair. Of even greater importance, *the intensity of pairwise comparisons is a minimal way to signal that the voters have transitive rankings*. After all, the intensity information is not available without transitivity; a cyclic voter has only binary rankings with weak intensities.

---

[14] With $n > 3$ candidates, the three intensity levels for $c_1 \succ c_2$ depend on whether the transitive ranking has zero, one, or two candidates separating c_1 and c_2. In the natural manner, this extends to conditions for subsets of $2 < k < n$ candidates. Incidentally, "intensity" is closely related to "conditional probability" where the likelihood of events A and B can change when the comparison is subject to event C occurring.

In pairwise voting, the projection stage drops all information about the intensity – and, hence, the knowledge that the voters have transitive preferences. Is this ignored information vital or superfluous? If the latter, then the above comments can be dismissed as an annoying digression. But, if it is the former, then we must worry about the validity of the outcomes for any procedure based on pairwise elections – this includes the Condorcet winner as well as agendas. Clearly, we need guidelines to indicate when the lost information is superfluous and can be ignored, and when it is critical for the integrity of the conclusion.

Observe the emphasis on whether or not another alternative is available. In the beverage example, if only milk (c_1) and beer (c_2) are available, then there is no debate; the voters really do prefer $c_2 \succ c_1$. (With only two available alternatives, the pairwise rankings are transitive.) However, if wine (c_3) is a choice, then, as indicated above, the intensity of the pairwise comparisons is an important informational variable - if only to indicate that voters have transitive rankings. With three alternatives where the pairwise rankings are intended to select the "best choice," the ranking of $\{c_1, c_2\}$ must, in some way, reflect the availability of c_3. But, for intensity to be a pragmatic measure, the third alternative must be an honest option. The intensity of my ranking *Crime and Punishment* $\succ$ *War and Peace* is not reflected by comparing them to the non-existent *The Algebraic Closing Lemma* by H. Poinchoff (1976).

Fourth Graders. To argue that the intensity of comparisons is a natural concept, I'll relate an audience's reaction when I introduced the profile $\mathbf{p}_m$ during a lecture. As part of the Pittsburgh Public School System's celebration of the annual national *Mathematics Awareness Week*, the Director of Mathematics, Dr. D. Briars, invited me to discuss "recent developments in mathematics" to several high school classes. This was enjoyable, but a sense of trepidation set in when I discovered I was also scheduled to talk to Ms. Chamberlin's fourth grade class at the East Hill School. *What does one say to fourth graders!*

Searching for a way to survive my allotted forty minutes, I decided to show the class some "counting surprises;" they were voting paradoxes involving the rankings of three popular (at least for the trendy nine year old set) TV shows that I denote here as A, B, C. The proposed problem was to determine which show a hypothetical group of children should watch. The Condorcet cycle, $\mathbf{p}_m$, was introduced as:

- Five children like A better than B better than C.
- Five children like B better than C better than A.
- Five children like C better than A better than B.

Upon seeing the data, the students immediately argued that *no* show was preferred to any other! They pointed out that each show is in first-place, second-place, and last-place the same number of times, so the only fair ranking is $A \sim B \sim C$. When I tried to create controversy by computing the pairwise ranking $A \succ B$ by the vote of 10 : 5, these fourth graders beat me to my punch line by instantly arguing that, sure, and then $B \succ C$ and $C \succ A$ by the same vote. Not only did they see the symmetry of the profile (see Sect. 3.1 and Fig. 2.5.1b), but these 9 year olds seized upon, and then emphasized the subtle difference between a pairwise vote when only two alternatives are available and when there exists a viable third alternative.

With only two alternatives, say A, B, there is no debate – both the fourth graders and the rest of us agree that the hypothetical group overwhelmingly prefers $A \succ B$ with a 10 : 5 vote. However, once C becomes a viable third alternative, information about the intensity level of the pairwise comparisons is available and must be used to indicate that these voters are transitive rather than confused. In some sense, with all of the data, we should end up with the pairwise ranking $A \sim B$ *conditioned on the availability of* C. The pairwise vote cycle, then, is just an artifact of the fact that data, vital to the decision process, is lost. This is further supported by the fact that all positional methods, where the transitivity of the rankings is built into the procedure, yield the completely tied ranking of $\mathcal{I}$.

(To illustrate the intensity levels, observe that the binary ranking $B \succ A$ is strong as manifested by the voters use of C to separate the pair into the ranking $B \succ C \succ A$. On the other hand, the two voter types with the pairwise ranking $A \succ B$ exhibit a a weak intensity because the pair is compared as a unit with the third alternative C; C is either placed after the pair (for the type-one ranking of $(A \succ B) \succ C$), or before it (for the type-three ranking of $C \succ (A \succ B)$).)

The need to distinguish between the ranking of a pair in isolation and when accompanied by another alternative was explained to me by an incredibly short boy from that fourth grade classroom. Because I remained "puzzled" by my Condorcet cycle example, he took pity on me by carefully offering, "Let me explain. Nobody is better; they are all the same. It is like the rock and the scissors and the paper. The rock can dull the scissors and the scissors can cut the paper and the paper can cover the rock, so nothing is better than the others." He is correct, of course.

2.5.4 Geometry of Pairwise Voting

To demonstrate that the intensity information is vital, we need to devise a pairwise procedure that can avoid cycles by using this information; this is described in Sects. 3.1-3.2. But before offering remedies, we need to understand what is being corrected; we need to determine what can go right and wrong with the loss of intensity (and transitivity) data. Moreover, because pairwise voting is so commonly used, it is important to know what kinds of difficulties to anticipate. My emphasis is to use geometric constructions along with from algebra about "m equations in n unknowns".

Using the above "projection and summation" description, a pairwise vote converts a profile from $Si(6)$ into a value in $[-1, 1]$. Thus the $\{c_1, c_2\}$ majority vote mapping $f_{\{c_1, c_2\}} : Si(6) \to [-1, 1]$ is

$$f_{\{c_1, c_2\}}(\mathbf{p}) = \sum_{j=1}^{3} p_j - \sum_{j=4}^{6} p_j. \tag{2.5.1}$$

If $f_{\{c_1,c_2\}}(\mathbf{p}) > 0$, the first summation has the larger value. This means more voters are to the left of the $c_1 \sim c_2$ line than to the right, so c_1 beats c_2. Similarly, if $f_{\{c_1,c_2\}}(\mathbf{p}) < 0$, then c_2 beats c_1. The last possibility, $f_{\{c_1,c_2\}}(\mathbf{p}) = 0$, corresponds to the tie ranking of $c_1 \sim c_2$.

Similar equations hold for the other two pairs. By using the profile to determine who would vote for whom, we have

$$f_{\{c_2,c_3\}}(\mathbf{p}) = p_1 + p_5 + p_6 - \sum_{j=2}^{4} p_j,$$

$$f_{\{c_3,c_1\}}(\mathbf{p}) = \sum_{j=3}^{5} p_j - (p_1 + p_2 + p_6), \qquad (2.5.2)$$

where a positive value for $f_{\{c_i,c_j\}}(\mathbf{p})$ corresponds to the majority ranking $c_i \succ c_j$.

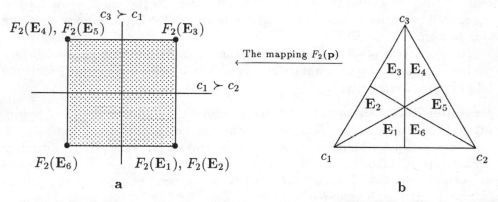

Fig. 2.5.2. The unanimity profile representation of majority vote outcomes. **a.** Majority outcomes. **b.** The profile space

To develop the techniques and intuition needed to analyze issues about all three pairs, start with the simpler problem of comparing the values of $x = f_{\{c_1,c_2\}}(\mathbf{p})$ and $z = f_{\{c_3,c_1\}}(\mathbf{p})$. The potential values are $-1 \le x \le 1$, $-1 \le z \le 1$; so (x, z) is a point in the square $[-1,1] \times [-1,1]$ depicted in Fig. 2.5.2a. The goal is to find the image subset - those (x, z) points that are election outcomes.

It is worth reviewing why $[-1,1] \times [-1,1]$ is a square. For each x value in the interval $[-1, 1]$, there is no a priori reason to restrict the accompanying z value; it could be anything from $[-1, 1]$. Thus, for each x, the potential (x, z) combinations are represented by passing the vertical line interval $[-1, 1]$ of potential z values through the x point. The union of all such line intervals, obtained by varying the value of $x \in [-1, 1]$, is the square.

The equations for the two pairs define the mapping

$$F_2 = (f_{\{c_1,c_2\}}, f_{\{c_3,c_1\}}) : Si(6) \to [-1,1] \times [-1,1]. \qquad (2.5.3)$$

A majority vote outcome is based on three equations (the two in Eq. 2.5.3 and the profile constraint $\sum_{j=1}^{6} p_j = 1$ from $\mathbf{p} \in Si(6)$) in six variables, so the algebraic techniques of Sects. 1.4, 2.4 apply.

The set of all possible election outcomes is the image set of F_2, so we need to characterize it. This seems to be a difficult task, but it is not. The mapping F_2 is linear, the domain $Si(6)$ is the convex hull defined by the vertices $\{\mathbf{E}_j\}_{j=1}^{6}$ of unanimity profiles, so, according to the convexity property of Sect. 1.4, the set of election outcomes is the convex hull defined by the outcomes $\{F_2(\mathbf{E}_j)\}_{j=1}^{6}$.

To compute an unanimity outcome, observe that one candidate from each pair receives all of the vote. Thus, the unanimity election points are of the form $(\pm 1, \pm 1)$; they are vertices of the square in Fig. 2.5.2. The vertex of $F_2(\mathbf{E}_j)$ is defined by the pairwise rankings of the unanimity profile $\mathbf{E}_j$. For example, $\mathbf{E}_3$ requires all voters to have the ranking $c_3 \succ c_1 \succ c_2$, so c_1 wins all of the votes in the $\{c_1, c_2\}$ election while c_3 receives all of them in the $\{c_3, c_1\}$ election. Thus, $F_2(\mathbf{E}_3) = (1, 1)$. Similarly, the outcomes of the other unanimity profiles are as indicated in the figure. The shaded area – the full square – is the convex hull defining the F_2 image set of election outcomes. As the image set is the full square, all potential values from $[-1, 1]^2$ are actual election outcomes; anything can happen.

The important point is that elections can be easily understood just by computing the unanimity outcomes. This approach is further illustrated with the following profile restrictions.

Example 2.5.1. An important theme in choice theory is the design of appropriate profile restrictions. The hope is that by not admitting all voter types, election relationships might emerge. A convenient way to view profile restriction is that certain unknowns in the original system of m equations in n unknowns are being restricted. Figure 2.5.2 helps us understand how profile restrictions can be designed and analyzed.

a. If only voters of types three and six are allowed, the original system of Eq. 2.5.3 becomes a "three equation, two unknown (p_3, p_6) system." Such a system is overdetermined, so, from algebra, not all outcomes are admitted. In words, certain choices of $q_{1,2}$ and $q_{3,1}$ have no solutions, so these election outcomes cannot occur. Indeed, this profile restriction forces the $\{c_1, c_2\}$ tally to always agree with the $\{c_3, c_1\}$ tally; i.e., $q_{1,2} = q_{3,1}$. This assertion follows because the election outcomes must be on the line $y = x$ connecting the $F_2(\mathbf{E}_6)$ vertex $(-1, -1)$ with the $F_2(\mathbf{E}_3)$ vertex $(1, 1)$. (This line is the convex hull of the two vertices.) Election relationships occur, then, because the image set is a proper subset of the full square; not everything can happen. However, this election relationship bears the cost that only those profiles, $(0, 0, p_3, 0, 0, 1 - p_3)$, constrained to live in a highly restrictive, one-dimensional edge of $Si(6)$ are admitted. So, this restriction means we can say much about very little.

b. It is possible to incur the cost of a profile restriction without receiving any benefits of election relationships. For instance, exclude all type-one and five voters. (The admissible profiles are on a three-dimensional surface of $Si(6)$ defined by the unanimity vertices $\{\mathbf{E}_2, \mathbf{E}_3, \mathbf{E}_4, \mathbf{E}_6\}$. From an algebraic viewpoint, the restriction converts Eq. 2.5.3 into a system of three equations in four unknowns.) This profile restriction fails to admit election relationships because the images of the four remaining unanimity profiles ($\{\mathbf{E}_2, \mathbf{E}_3, \mathbf{E}_4, \mathbf{E}_6\}$) are the four vertices of the square. As the image set is the full square, anything can happen.

c.   Instead of the restriction in part b, impose a minimal restriction where just type-three voters are excluded. This converts Eq. 2.5.3 into a system of three equations in *five* unknowns; geometrically, the admitted profiles are in a four-dimensional boundary surface of $Si(6)$. Accompanying the expulsion of the type-three voters is the $(1,1)$ vertex of the square.   As the convex hull of the remaining three vertices, a triangle, is a *proper* subset of the square, there are election relationships; not everything can happen! Thus, by comparing parts b and c, it becomes clear that it is not the size of your profile restriction that matters, but how you use it. $\square$

All Three Pairs of Candidates. As the real issue is to compare the outcomes of all three pairs of candidates, let's turn to it. Because $f_{\{c_i, c_j\}}(\mathbf{p}) \in [-1, 1]$, the three pair outcome is a point in

$$[-1, 1] \times [-1, 1] \times [-1, 1] = [-1, 1]^3.$$

To understand the geometry of the image set, recall that $[-1, 1] \times [-1, 1]$ is a square. Each point in $[-1, 1] \times [-1, 1]$ identifies an outcome for two pairwise rankings. There is no a priori reason to restrict the third outcome, so we must admit the possibility that it can be any value from $[-1, 1]$. Thus, through each point in the square, pass the third interval $[-1, 1]$ in an orthogonal direction. By varying the point in the square, a cube emerges. In this manner, $[-1, 1]^3$ is identified with a three-dimensional cube. The mapping for the three pairwise elections,

$$F_3 = (f_{\{c_1, c_2\}}, f_{\{c_2, c_3\}}, f_{\{c_3, c_1\}}) : Si(6) \to [-1, 1]^3,$$

converts profiles into cube points. To understand the pairwise elections, we need to characterize the F_3 image set.

Before computing the image set, it is instructive to describe the various ranking regions of the cube. A point in the positive orthant (i.e., a point (x, y, z) where all components have positive values) corresponds to the cycle $c_1 \succ c_2, c_2 \succ c_3, c_3 \succ c_1$. This is called a *positive cycle* to indicate that this cyclic point resides in the positive orthant. Similarly, a point in the negative orthant defines the reversed, or *negative cycle* $c_2 \succ c_1, c_1 \succ c_3, c_3 \succ c_2$. With the exception of $(0, 0, 0)$, any boundary point of these two orthants (on a coordinate axis or plane) represents a quasi-transitive ranking. (See Example 2.1.2.) The remaining cube points define transitive rankings.[15]

---

[15] With $n \geq 3$ candidates, the pairwise comparisons defines a cube in a $\binom{n}{2}$ dimensional space. The analysis of the corresponding mapping, $F_n : Si(n!) \to [-1, 1]^{\binom{n}{2}}$, is much the same as developed below for $n = 3$. Differences are caused by the higher dimensional geometry which

By exploiting convexity, the F_3 image space of election outcomes is found by first plotting the unanimity outcomes $\{F_3(\mathbf{E}_j)\}_{j=1}^6$, and then constructing the associated convex hull. Using the earlier F_2 argument about unanimous votes, it follows that $F_3(\mathbf{E}_j)$ is of the form $(\pm1, \pm1, \pm1)$; it is a vertex of the cube $[-1,1]^3$. As before, the assignment of $F_3(\mathbf{E}_j)$ to a particular vertex is determined by the three pairwise rankings defined by $\mathbf{E}_j$.

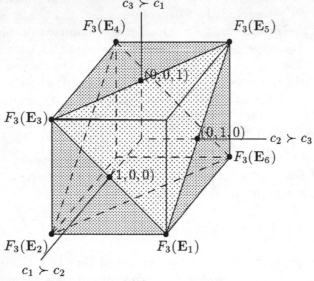

Fig. 2.5.3. The representation cube for the three pairs of candidates

The cube $[-1,1]^3$ has more vertices (eight) than $Si(6)$ has unanimity profiles (six), so two cube vertices miss out in the assignment process. They are, of course, the cyclic vertices $(1,1,1)$ and $(-1,-1,-1)$. The convex hull of the remaining six vertices, depicted in Fig. 2.5.3, is the image set of F_3; this set consisting of all possible pairwise election outcomes is called the *representation cube*.

So, start with the cube and then discard the two $[-1,1]^3$ vertices that are not assigned anything. This means that the representation cube is a mutilated version of $[-1,1]^3$. The first step of the surgery on $[-1,1]^3$ is to slice through the vertices with odd indices, $\{F_3(\mathbf{E}_j)\}_{j=1,3,5}$, and discard the resulting corner piece. (The scar from this operation is the lightly shaded region in the figure.) Next, slice through the even vertices, $\{F_3(\mathbf{E}_j)\}_{j=2,4,6}$ (indicated by the dashed, hidden lines), and throw away that corner. (According to standard equations for volumes of tetrahedrons, the slicing process eliminates $\frac{1}{3}$ of the original volume of the cube.) All remaining points are election outcomes for some $\mathbf{p} \in Si(6)$; this is the representation cube.

The operation of discarding large regions of $[-1,1]^3$ is not sufficiently discriminatory to make F_3 transitive. For instance, because the lightly shaded

admits many other possibilities; e.g., there are ranking regions corresponding to all imaginable pathologies associated with binary relationships. Moreover, all relationships are admissible election outcomes!

area passes through the points $(1,0,0), (0,1,0)$, and $(0,0,1)$, the representation cube includes a portion of the cycle generating positive orthant. Similarly, the triangular hidden line region passes through the negative orthant. The convex geometry forces the representation cube to meet all 27 ranking regions, so, with respect to admissible pairwise election rankings, "anything can happen!"[16]

2.5.5 The Geometry of Cycles

Elections are best understood when we can see the relationship between profiles and election outcomes. To attain this goal by exploiting the geometry of the representation cube, I start by analyzing certain election points.

The point $(1,0,0)$, corresponding to the rankings $c_1 \succ c_2, c_1 \sim c_3, c_2 \sim c_3$, is on the edge of the representation cube midway between $F_3(\mathbf{E}_3)$ and $F_3(\mathbf{E}_1)$. By linearity,

$$(1,0,0) = \frac{1}{2}(F_3(\mathbf{E}_1) + F_3(\mathbf{E}_3)) = F_3(\frac{\mathbf{E}_1 + \mathbf{E}_3}{2}),$$

so this election outcome occurs iff the profile evenly splits the voters between types-one and three. Similarly, the outcomes $(0,1,0)$ and $(0,0,1)$ occur, respectively, with the profiles $\frac{\mathbf{E}_1 + \mathbf{E}_5}{2}$ and $\frac{\mathbf{E}_3 + \mathbf{E}_5}{2}$.

More ambitiously, a point is in the triangular lightly shaded region T_1 – the equilateral triangle on the plane $x + y + z = 1$ defined by the odd vertices $F_2(\mathbf{E}_1), F_2(\mathbf{E}_3), F_2(\mathbf{E}_5)$ – iff all voters are of types-one, three, and five. By linearity, $(x, y, z) \in T_1$ is expressed as

$$x(1,0,0) + y(0,1,0) + z(0,0,1)$$
$$= xF_3(\frac{\mathbf{E}_1 + \mathbf{E}_3}{2}) + yF_3(\frac{\mathbf{E}_1 + \mathbf{E}_5}{2}) + zF_3(\frac{\mathbf{E}_3 + \mathbf{E}_5}{2})$$
$$= F_3(\frac{x+y}{2}\mathbf{E}_1 + \frac{x+z}{2}\mathbf{E}_3 + \frac{y+z}{2}\mathbf{E}_5), \tag{2.5.4}$$

so the unique supporting profile, $(\frac{x+y}{2}, 0, \frac{x+z}{2}, 0, \frac{y+z}{2}, 0)$, involves only odd voter types. Similarly, a point (x, y, z) on the hidden, opposing triangular surface T_2 (the part of the plane $x + y + z = -1$ denoted by the dashed lines in Fig. 2.5.4), is uniquely supported by profiles with even voter types $(0, -\frac{x+y}{2}, 0, -\frac{y+x}{2}, 0, -\frac{x+z}{2})$. So, at least in the special settings of T_1, T_2, each election outcome is uniquely identified with a profile.

What makes these special cases interesting is that they define the vertices of the region of troublesome pairwise outcomes. For instance, the positive orthant

---

[16]There are three rankings for each pair – one is a tie vote and the other two has one candidate winning – so there are $3^3 = 27$ potential rankings. With n candidates, there are $3^{\binom{n}{2}}$ ranking regions for the majority vote comparisons, and all can occur! The geometric reason is the same; the convex hull connecting all unanimity outcomes meets all ranking regions. For $n = 3$, each cycle generating regions is a tetrahedron with volume $\frac{1}{6}$. Thus the cyclic regions constitute only $\frac{1}{16}$ of the total volume of the image set. Later in this section, I show that $\frac{1}{16}$ of all profiles support cycles.

corresponds to the positive cycles. One boundary of this cyclic region is the portion of T_1 where all components of $(x, y, z) \in T_1$ are positive. Therefore, this triangular portion consists of the extreme *positive cycles*. From the geometry, the profile for such a cycle can involve only odd voter types. Because $(\frac{1}{3}, \frac{1}{3}, \frac{1}{3}) \in T_1$ is the point farthest from any transitive ranking, it is the "most" positive cyclic election outcome. In particular, $(\frac{1}{3}, \frac{1}{3}, \frac{1}{3})$ arises iff the profile is the Condorcet profile $\mathbf{p}_m = (\frac{1}{3}, 0, \frac{1}{3}, 0, \frac{1}{3}, 0)$ from the departmental meeting. Similar comments apply to the portion of T_2 that meets the negative orthant and the election outcome $(-\frac{1}{3}, -\frac{1}{3}, -\frac{1}{3})$ with its unique, even-voter profile $\mathbf{p}_m^r = (0, \frac{1}{3}, 0, \frac{1}{3}, 0, \frac{1}{3})$.

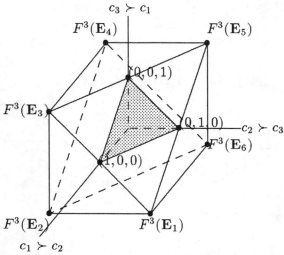

Fig. 2.5.4. Can cycles (the shaded region) be avoided?

This geometry provides answers for questions about pairwise elections. For instance, if c_1 demonstrates electoral strength by overwhelmingly beating c_2, does this preclude the possibility of a cycle? (No.) How extreme can the victory margins of the pairwise majority votes be while still admitting a cycle? How large are the sets of profiles supporting certain outcomes? A sample of answers based on the geometry of the representation cube follows. In this statement, the assertions that different choices of $\mathbf{q}$ are supported by profile sets with different dimensions come from a "m equations in n unknowns define a $n-m$ dimensional space of solutions" argument. In reading this theorem, it is worth identifying the position of each $\mathbf{q}$ in Figs. 2.5.4, 2.5.5.

Theorem 2.5.1. a. *Any choice of rankings for the each of the three pairs of candidates has supporting profiles.*

b. *Choose $\mathbf{q}$ in the representation cube. If $\mathbf{q}$ is an interior point, then there is a two-dimensional linear subspace of normalized profiles in $Si(6)$ that support $\mathbf{q}$. If $\mathbf{q}$ is on one of the surface boundaries of the representation cube, then the outcome is supported by a unique profile.*

c. *For any value of $\epsilon > 0$, there are profiles where a cycle occurs even though c_1 beats c_2 with more than $1 - \epsilon$ of the total vote. On the other hand, it is* *impossible to have a cycle where each candidate beats another candidate by receiving more than two-thirds of the vote.*

Compare the last part of statement c with the Pope selection (Sect. 1.3); requiring the winner to receive one more than two-thirds of the vote eliminates the danger of a cycle. For $n \geq 2$ candidates, the value $\frac{2}{3}$ is replaced by $\frac{n-1}{n}$.

Idea of the Proof. To prove the first part of c, choose $(1 - \frac{\epsilon}{2}, \frac{\epsilon}{4}, \frac{\epsilon}{4})$ from the cyclic region of T_1. This point is in the representation cube, so the conclusion follows. (A supporting profile can be found by using Eq. 2.5.4.) The second part of c follows by using the "most cyclic" point $(\frac{1}{3}, \frac{1}{3}, \frac{1}{3})$. For example, $x = \frac{1}{3}$ means that c_1 beats c_2 with two-thirds of the vote.

The proof for the assertion about a $\mathbf{q} \in T_1$ is given above. For the remaining assertions, suppose a profile is in the two-dimensional boundary of the representation cube where $x = 1$. From the geometry, such a result requires *all* voters to prefer $c_1 \succ c_2$; consequently, there can be no voters of types four, five or six. Thus a supporting profile must be in the two-dimensional boundary surface of $Si(6)$ defined by $\{\mathbf{E}_1, \mathbf{E}_2, \mathbf{E}_3\}$. The remaining conclusions follow with similar arguments. $\square$

2.5.6 From Group Coordinates to Profile Restrictions

A standard trick from geometry is to invent convenient coordinate systems that reflect and simplify the particular properties being studied. For instance, cartesian coordinates[17] are used to analyze rectangular objects while spherical coordinates are introduced to study spheres. Applying this theme to voting theory, I'll develop a coordinate system for profiles so that we can "see" which profiles define which pairwise election outcomes. The idea is to divide the voter types into natural groupings, and then determine the election outcomes if only the voters of each particular group vote. The value of $\mathbf{q}$, then, is based on the election outcomes for the two subgroups and the proportion of all voters in each subgroup.

First, divide the voter types into the "odds" and "evens" as identified by the subscripts. Thus the odd group consists of all voters of types $\{1, 3, 5\}$ while the evens are the voter types $\{2, 4, 6\}$. As shown above, if a profile consists only of odd voters, the outcome is in T_1. Similarly, if only even voters are in a profile, the outcome is T_2. The two election outcomes are

$$F_3((p_1, 0, p_3, 0, p_5, 0)) = (p_1 + p_3 - p_5, p_1 + p_5 - p_3, p_3 + p_5 - p_1)$$
$$F_3((0, p_2, 0, p_4, 0, p_6)) = -(p_4 + p_6 - p_2, p_2 + p_4 - p_6, p_2 + p_6 - p_4).$$
$$(2.5.5)$$

---

[17] These coordinates are attributed to R. Des Cartes (1595-1650). As true with most discoveries, other philosophers, such as I. M. Des Horst, experimented with related systems. While I have not found reliable publication dates for Des Horst's work, it is doubtful that Des Horst came before Des Cartes.

While Eq. 2.5.5 specifies the precise values of the election outcomes, the geometry usually is more useful. For example, if $\alpha \in T_1$ is close to $F_3(\mathbf{E}_1)$, then, clearly, the type-one voters dominate the odd group.

To describe $F_3(\mathbf{p})$ for $\mathbf{p} = (p_1, \ldots, p_6)$, first consider the outcome when only the odd voters vote. Here we have a slight problem because $(p_1, 0, p_3, 0, p_5, 0)$ is not a profile when $p_1 + p_3 + p_5 = d < 1$. However, if the "evens" fail to vote, then the profile defined by the odd voters becomes $\frac{1}{d}(p_1, 0, p_3, 0, p_5, 0)$. This motivates the definition of the *cyclic group coordinate representation of a profile*, (α, β, d).

$$d = p_1 + p_3 + p_5$$

$$a_i = \frac{p_i}{d}, \; i = 1, 3, 5, \quad \alpha = (a_1 + a_3 - a_5, a_1 + a_5 - a_3, a_3 + a_5 - a_1) \in T_1$$

$$b_j = \frac{p_j}{1-d}, \; j = 2, 4, 6, \quad \beta = -(b_4 + b_6 - b_2, b_2 + b_4 - b_6, b_2 + b_6 - b_4) \in T_2.$$
$$(2.5.6)$$

By definition, $\mathbf{p} = d(a_1, 0, a_3, 0, a_5, 0) + (1-d)(0, b_2, 0, b_4, 0, b_6)$, so by the linearity of F_3 it follows that

$$F_3(\mathbf{p}) = d\alpha + (1-d)\beta. \qquad (2.5.7)$$

Stated in words, α is the odd's outcome, β is the even's outcome, d measures the relative strength of one subgroup over the other, and the election is a weighted sum of α, β as determined by d. Geometrically, plot $\alpha \in T_1$, and $\beta \in T_2$, and then find the point on the line segment joining α and β that is d of the distance from β to α. Thus, *the line segment and the designated point represent the profile.*

Actually, the designated point does double duty because it also designates the election outcome $F_3(\mathbf{p}) = \mathbf{q}$. (See the bottom portion of Fig. 2.5.5.) A virtue of the cyclic coordinates, then, is that both a profile and its election point are jointly represented. Justification for calling (α, β, d) a *coordinate representation* of $\mathbf{p}$ follows.

Proposition 2.5.2. *There is a smooth, one to one mapping between profiles* $\mathbf{p} \in Si(6)$ *with the set of points* (α, β, d) *where* $\alpha \in T_1, \beta \in T_2, d \in [0, 1]$.

The analytic relationships between the two profile representations are given by Eq. 2.5.5 and the equations following Eq. 2.5.4. Even though the α and β values translate immediately into a_i, b_j values, the geometric positioning of α, β (the line segment) and the designated point (the value of d) are more suggestive of the properties $\mathbf{p}$. For instance, an α near the vertex $F(\mathbf{E}_3)$ requires most of the odd voters to be of type-3 and a large d value (where the designated point is close to the T_1 surface) means there are more odd voters than even voters. Similarly, if β is on an edge of T_2, then there are no voters of a particular even type. From this reasoning, it follows that the boundaries of $Si(6)$ are identified with the edges of T_1, T_2 and/or where the d values are 0 and 1. For instance, the edge of the representation cube connecting $F_3(\mathbf{E}_1)$ with $F_3(\mathbf{E}_2)$ corresponds to the one-dimensional edge of $Si(6)$ of normalized profiles of the form $(p, 1 - p, 0, 0, 0, 0)$, $p \in [0, 1]$.

The power of cyclic coordinates. To illustrate the power of cyclic group coordinates, I'll use them to extend Theorem 2.5.1, and to describe the set of all profiles defining cycles. As a starting point, observe that the theorem offers only crude descriptions about supporting sets of profiles. For instance, it asserts that **q** in the interior of the representation cube is supported by a two-dimensional set of profiles in $Si(6)$. But, *which* two-dimensional set; *what kinds* of profiles are involved? These more interesting issues are answered immediately with the (α, β, d) profile representation.

The approach is simple; because *any line segment* passing through **q** defines a profile where $F_3(\mathbf{p}) = \mathbf{q}$, the cone of all such line segments defines the set of supporting profiles. For a particular line segment, its T_1 endpoint is the α values, its T_2 endpoint is the β values, and the relative distance of **q** from β defines d. The geometric positioning of α and β determines which voter types dominate in the profile, while the proximity of the designated point to T_1 or T_2 explains the proportion of odd and even voters.

The geometry lets us "see" the trade-offs needed between voters of different types in order to realize a specified **q**. Recall, all profile lines with **q** as an outcome must pass through **q**. So, if one endpoint, say α, is moved, then **q** serves as a pivot point forcing the other endpoint, β, to move in an opposite direction. This is similar to grabbing a pencil at a specified point; when the eraser is moved in one direction, the pencil point moves in the other. These different directions correspond to different mixtures of odd and even voters.

A large or small value of d means that the pencil is held either near the eraser or the pencil point. Here, a slight change in the short end of the pencil (from the pivot point) forces a large change in the other end. For voting, this means that if, say, d has a value near unity, then a small change in the distribution of the even voters must be compensated by a large change in the distribution of odd voters in order for the resulting profile to support the specified **q**.

The cone of all possible line segments passing through **q** with endpoints in T_1, T_2 is the *(group coordinate) set of all profiles supporting* **q**. Because **q** is fixed, once α is selected, the values of β, d are uniquely determined. Consequently, the two degrees of freedom in choosing α depict the two-dimensional surface of profiles ensured by Theorem 2.5.1. So, not only does each line segment illustrate which voter types are required, but also *the size of the α and β cones indicate the relative size of the set of supporting profiles.*

The size of a set of supporting profiles is indicated by either the α or the β cone; the one that should be used depends upon the value of d. To see why, suppose out of $10,000$ voters, only three are of the even type. With this $d = \frac{9,997}{10,000}$ value, it does not matter much how the even voters are distributed; it is the distribution of the odd voters that really counts. In fact, for a specified **q**, it is clear that there is a very restricted set of ways the voters can be distributed. Stated in geometric terms, because of the **q** pivoting action, if $d \geq \frac{1}{2}$, a small change in α creates a large change in β. Therefore, the smaller α cone is a better indicator of the size of the set of profiles. Similarly, if $d \leq \frac{1}{2}$, the β cone is the better indicator.

Example 2.5.2. a. The integer profile $(5, 3, 7, 2, 1, 1)$ defines the normalized profile $(\frac{1}{4}, \frac{3}{20}, \frac{7}{20}, \frac{1}{10}, \frac{1}{20}, \frac{1}{10}) \in Si(6)$. According to Eq. 2.5.6, this profile has the cyclic group coordinates representation $(\alpha = (\frac{11}{13}, \frac{-1}{13}, \frac{3}{13}), \beta = -(\frac{1}{7}, \frac{3}{7}, \frac{3}{7}), d = \frac{13}{20})$.

Conversely, suppose we need a profile that "nearly" defines a cycle, but the actual outcome is the transitive $c_1 \succ c_2, c_2 \succ c_3, c_1 \succ c_3$ (or, $x > 0, y > 0, z < 0$). To design this profile geometrically, choose α in the cyclic region near the $F_3(\mathbf{E}_1) - F_3(\mathbf{E}_3)$ edge, β in the negative cyclic region near the $F_3(\mathbf{E}_2) - F_3(\mathbf{E}_6)$ edge, and d near $\frac{1}{2}$. One such profile is $(\alpha = (\frac{5}{10}, \frac{4}{10}, \frac{1}{10}), \beta = -(\frac{5}{10}, \frac{1}{10}, \frac{4}{10}), d = \frac{6}{10})$. By use of Eqs. 2.5.4 - 6, this corresponds to $a = (0.45, 0, 0.3, 0, 0.25, 0), b = (0, 0.25, 0, 0.3, 0, 0.45)$ which defines $(0.27, 0.1, 0.18, 0.12, 0.15, 0.18) \in Si(6)$.

As an alternative construction for this example, choose $\mathbf{q}$ to satisfy the specified condition and then find the coordinate representation of any line segment passing through $\mathbf{q}$. There are, of course, a cone of examples. The main point is that *with the cyclic coordinate system, constructing profiles to illustrate specified outcomes becomes a simple exercise.*

b. Cyclic group coordinates can be used to compare the relative sizes of the profile sets supporting different election outcomes. To see this, consider $\mathbf{q}_1 = (0.9, 0, 0)$ and $\mathbf{q}_2 = (0.1, 0.1, 0.1)$. Theorem 2.5.1 asserts that both $\mathbf{q}_j$ outcomes are supported by a two-dimensional set of profiles; we want to know whether one set larger than the other. The answer comes from comparing the size of the α cones defined by each $\mathbf{q}_j$.

The endpoints of a profile line through $\mathbf{q}_j$ must be on the T_i regions, so the proximity of the pivot point $\mathbf{q}_1$ to a surface of the representation cube severely restricts the size of its cone. It is equivalent to using a small child's teeter-totter – where, because of the low pivot point, you become well acquainted with your knees. Similarly with $\mathbf{q}_1$, even when β is on the boundary of T_2, the restrictive pivot action of $\mathbf{q}_1$ keeps α close to the same T_1 edge. Again, on a teeter-totter, the maximum height of one end is determined by the pivot point and when the other end is on the "boundary," the ground. Similarly, the line going through the T_2 corner $(1, -1, -1)$ and $\mathbf{q}_1$ is $(1-t)(1, -1, -1) + t(0.9, 0, 0) = (1 - 0.1t, -1 + t, -1 + t)$, so it reaches T_1 (the $x + y + z = 1$ plane) where $t = \frac{2}{1.9}$. Thus $\alpha = (0.895, 0.053, 0.053)$. By considering the other possible extreme locations for $\beta \in T_2$, the full cone of α values is the triangle defined by the vertices $(0.895, 0.053, 0.053), (1, -0.053, 0.053), (1, 0.053, -0.053)$. This cone of profiles is so small that its size needs to be exaggerated in Fig. 2.5.5.

Compare the fate of $\mathbf{q}_1$ with that of $\mathbf{q}_2$. Here, as the election outcome (and pivot point) $\mathbf{q}_2$ is sufficiently far from the edges of T_1 or T_2, $\mathbf{q}_2$ admits considerable latitude in the choice of profile lines. In other words, the more central location of $\mathbf{q}_2$ introduces wider swings in the admissible profile line segments. Consequently, we must (accurately) expect $\mathbf{q}_2$ to be supported by a larger two-dimensional set of profiles than $\mathbf{q}_1$. By drawing the three lines from the T_2 vertices through $\mathbf{q}_2$, the α cone is the triangle with three vertices obtained by permuting the three values $-0.4, 0.7, 0.7$. (Thus, for example, if there is an odd voter-type with less than $\frac{1-0.4}{2} = 0.3$ of all of the odd voters, then α is not in this triangle and q_2 is not an admissible outcome.) This much larger triangle, reflecting the larger numbers of profiles, is the lightly shaded region of Fig. 2.5.5.

To underscore why care is needed when comparing the relative sizes of α cones, observe that the profile cone for the election point $q_3 = -(0.1, 0.1, 0.1)$ is obtained by reversing the roles of the odd and even voter types for q_2, so both outcomes must have the same size sets of supporting profiles. However, the α cone for q_3 is all of T_1, while the β cone in T_2 is similar to the q_2 α cone of T_1. This is because $-(0.1, 0.1, 0.1)$ is closer to T_2 than to T_1 ($d < \frac{1}{2}$), so the pivot action of q is more sensitive to small changes of the T_2 endpoint. Thus, the smaller cone in the closer region, T_2, is the better indicator of the size of the profile set.

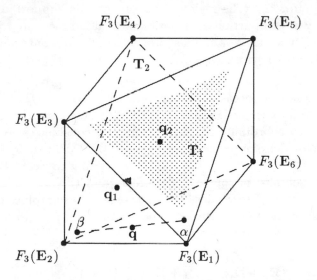

Fig. 2.5.5. The $\alpha - \beta$ line at the bottom of the figure represents a profile. For Example 2.5.2, the light shaded area is the α cone for $q_2 = (.1, .1.1)$; the small dark region is the profile cone for $q_1 = (.9, 0, 0)$.

c. The coordinate representation makes it easy to see relationships between the group profile representation and election outcomes. For instance, choose any two points $\alpha \in T_1, \beta \in T_2$. Unless these points satisfy $\beta = -\alpha$ (which is a necessary and sufficient condition for the connecting line segment to pass through the origin), at least a portion of the connecting line misses both the positive and the negative orthants. Consequently, *for any $\beta \neq -\alpha$, there is an open interval of d values where the election outcomes of the (α, β, d) profiles are transitive.* This statement illustrates the importance of the variable d.

d. I have placed the blame for "cycles" on the inability of the pairwise voting procedures to recognize the intensity of pairwise comparisons. To illustrate this comment, observe for $\alpha \in T_1$ that each pair of candidates has two of the three voter types with a weak ranking, while the third voter type has a strong ranking.

Moreover, if α is near the center, then there is a reasonable balance among the number of voters of each type. (This balance is what permits a reassignment of the binary rankings of the transitive voters to create an example of intransitive voters.) So, we must expect the intensity of pairwise comparisons to provide valuable information; if it is ignored, we must expect the negative consequences where α is in the positive cyclic region. Similar comments hold for β and negative cycles.

Now, compare the profiles defining $\mathbf{q}_1$ (which is not a cycle) and $\mathbf{q}_2$ (which is a cycle). All profiles supporting $\mathbf{q}_1$ have α near the $F_3(\mathbf{E}_1) - F_3(\mathbf{E}_3)$ edge and β near the $F_3(\mathbf{E}_2)$ vertex. This restriction on the supporting profiles keep the endpoints away from the cyclic region, so it is clear these profiles must come from transitive rankings. In contrast, a large portion of the profiles for $\mathbf{q}_2$ must have the α and β endpoints in cyclic regions; this outcome is supported by profiles where the intensity of comparison information is vital. In fact, *all profiles in the* $\mathbf{q}_2$ *cone are of the type where one must worry about the consequences of not using the intensity of pairwise comparison information.*

e. The geometry of the cones suffices to analyze most problems about profiles. There are, however, occasions where we need more precise comparisons of profile sets defining specified outcomes. To illustrate how this information can be obtained with coordinate representations; I'll consider cycles. The positive cycles are defined by outcomes in the convex hull defined by the vertices $(1,0,0)$, $(0,1,0)$, $(0,0,1)$, $(0,0,0)$. This means, according to Sect. 1.4, that the supporting profile set also is convex. To understand this profile set, we just need to find the vertices. The vertices of this profile set are profiles defining the vertices of the hull in the representation cube, so they are easy to find with the cyclic coordinate representation. They are

$$\frac{1}{2}(\mathbf{E}_1 + \mathbf{E}_3), \; \frac{1}{2}(\mathbf{E}_3 + \mathbf{E}_5), \; \frac{1}{2}(\mathbf{E}_5 + \mathbf{E}_1),$$
$$\frac{1}{2}(\mathbf{E}_1 + \mathbf{E}_4), \; \frac{1}{2}(\mathbf{E}_3 + \mathbf{E}_6), \; \frac{1}{2}(\mathbf{E}_5 + \mathbf{E}_2).$$

Now that the profile vertices are known, determinants or other techniques (I prefer the "wedge product," an extension of the "vector cross product" of R^3) can be used to compute the volume. In this way, we have that *the profile set supporting the positive cycles constitutes* $\frac{1}{2^5} = \frac{1}{32}$ *of all profiles in* $Si(6)$. *The profile set supporting a cycle, then, is* $\frac{1}{16}$ *of all profiles.*

So, if each profile is equally likely (that is, if there is a uniform distribution over the profiles in $Si(6)$), then the probability of a cycle is $\frac{1}{16}$. Actually, now that the profile set defining cycles is identified, it is a standard calculus computation to determine this probability for any other specified distributions of profiles!

I must caution, this assertion does not mean that for any number of voters, $\frac{1}{16}$ of the profiles are in the cyclic region. To illustrate the problem, I'll use the simpler example where the unit interval is evenly divided into the three regions, $A = [0, \frac{1}{3}), B = [\frac{1}{3}, \frac{2}{3}), C = [\frac{2}{3}, 1)$. Now consider the set of all fractions with the same denominator n. Even though they are evenly divided within the unit interval, each of the three regions does not have the same proportion of fractions. For instance, for $n = 2$, the sole point $\frac{1}{2} \in B$. For $n = 3$, B and C each have a point, but A is empty. For $n = 4$, each region has a single point. For $n = 5$, A and C each have one point while B has two. In other words, the number theoretic problems (remainder problems) relating n (the number of voters) with the number of regions (3) create asymmetric distributions for small values of n. However, for sufficiently large values of n, such problems disappear. For all practical purposes, the points for large values of n are equally divided.

The same number theoretic problem occurs in the distribution of fractional profiles within the six regions of $Si(6)$. Consequently, the probabilities shift with changing numbers of voters. Moreover, tie votes, which are unlikely with large number of voters, are more probable with certain small numbers of voters. But, this is only a number theoretic peculiarity that has little to do with the structure of voting procedures. Now that we understand the source of the difficulty, we can safely ignore it. □

2.5.7 Black's Conditions for Avoiding Cycles

As determined by the example, *all possible profiles that avoid cycles can be found by varying the α, β line segments and choosing d values as required by the geometry.* These restrictions, as indicated by Fig. 2.5.6, are obtained by characterizing all (α, β, d) profiles where the election point stays out of the positive and negative orthants of the figure. To show how to do this, I'll start with the simple but useful situations where the line segment *completely misses* both the positive and negative orthants. Obviously, for this to be true, the endpoints α, β must also remain outside of these orthants.

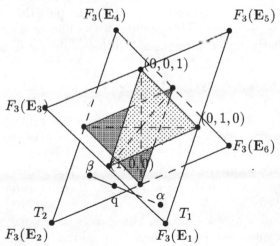

Fig. 2.5.6. The shaded areas represent the two cyclic regions.

Definition 2.5.1. The *cyclic triangle* of T_j, $j = 1, 2$, is the set of points of T_j where all components have the same sign.

If a profile involves no more than three voter types, p_i, p_j, p_k, voter type-j is *dominant* if $p_j \geq p_i + p_k$. $\square$

As discussed in Example 2.5.2d, a profile with an endpoint in a cyclic triangle involves a reasonably equal mixture of voter types where, for each pair of candidates, one voter type has a strong comparison, and the other two have weak intensity comparisons. These are the type of profiles where a redistribution of the pairwise rankings define irrational voters. The next theorem shows that cycles are identified with such situations. The d values should be treated as indicating the balance of odd and even voters that avoids cycles.

Theorem 2.5.3. a.   *The coordinate α is in the cyclic triangle iff there is not a dominant voter type for the profile $(a_1, 0, a_3, 0, a_5, 0)$. Similarly, β is in the cyclic triangle of T_2 iff there is not a dominant voter type for the profile $(0, b_2, 0, b_4, 0, b_6)$.*
   b. If either α or β is in the cyclic triangle, then there exists an open interval of choices of d so that the resulting profile defines a cyclic outcome.
   c.   If $\beta \neq -\alpha$, then there is an open interval of choice of d so that the (α, β, d) outcome is transitive. The outcome of $(\alpha, \beta = -\alpha, d = \frac{1}{2})$ is complete indifference. If $\alpha = -\beta$ is in the cyclic triangle, then all $d \neq \frac{1}{2}$ define cyclic rankings.

From the geometry, it is clear that the first assertion of part c requires d to have a value near $\frac{1}{2}$. In other words, cycles can be avoided for those profiles where the amount of information ignored is balanced between certain even and odd voter types. On the other hand, this result underscores the observation that cycles are manifestations of the ignored intensity information.

Proof. The proof of part a follows from Eq. 2.5.5. Part b follows immediately from the geometry because the line connecting α and β must pass through either the positive or the negative orthants. The portion of the line passing through such an orthant defines the asserted interval of d values. Part c follows from Example 2.5.1. $\square$

A simple way to avoid positive cycles (the cycles in the positive orthant, so $c_1 \succ c_2$) is to restrict α to a T_1 edge. According to the geometry of the representation cube (see Fig. 2.5.6), for example, if α is on the $F_3(\mathbf{E}_1)$ - $F_3(\mathbf{E}_3)$ edge, then for any β, the connecting profile line misses the positive orthant. Indeed, the worse case scenario requires $\alpha = (1, 0, 0)$ and $\beta = -\alpha = (-1, 0, 0)$ to force the profile line on the quasi- transitive x-axis. The geometry of the representation cube proves that if α is on a T_1 edge, then a profile (α, β, d) cannot define a positive cycle.

This restriction on α avoids positive cycles, but choices of β (such as in the cyclic triangle) force the connecting line segment to pass through the negative cyclic region. Using the philosophy that what is good for the odds is good for the evens, all possible cycles are avoided by further restricting β to a T_2 edge.

The edges of T_1, T_2 are identified with boundaries of $Si(6)$ with no voters of certain voter types. The following assertion now is immediate.

Theorem 2.5.4. *If profile* **p** *is such that there are no voters of at least one odd and one even voter types, then the pairwise majority votes do not define a cycle. Such a profile is in a three-dimensional boundary surface of* $Si(6)$.

The profile restrictions of the theorem that confine the profiles to the improbable, nonrobust three-dimensional boundary surfaces of $Si(6)$ suggest that this theorem is irrelevant. After all, even a tie vote between the two top-ranked candidates in a plurality election is supported by a larger *four*-dimensional subset of profiles! Anyway, it is obvious from the geometry of Fig. 2.5.4-5 that other, more general, robust conditions to avoid cycles are easy to derive.

These comments are correct, and some of the more general profile restrictions are derived below. However, it is interesting to note that special cases of Theorem 2.5.4 – situations which specify which even and odd voter types are excluded – continue to serve as standard assumptions for voting theory. These restrictions are the important Black *single-peakedness* conditions.

Black's condition requires the excluded rankings to have the same candidate bottom-ranked. In the terminology of the representation triangle, Black's condition requires the excluded even and odd voter types to be in adjacent ranking regions sharing an edge of the representation triangle. For example, the adjacent regions $\mathcal{R}(1), \mathcal{R}(6)$ share the bottom edge of the representation triangle, so one way to satisfy Black's condition is to exclude voter types $\{1, 6\}$. These two *excluded* rankings are the only ones with c_3 bottom-ranked, so the *admitted* voter types never bottom rank c_3. The other two choices of excluded types with Black's condition are $\{2, 3\}$ and $\{4, 5\}$.

The name *single peakedness* derives from a delightfully simple property exhibited by the graphs of each voter's cardinal rankings of the candidates. There is an ordering of the candidates along the line (more precisely, the candidate who never is bottom-ranked is placed in the middle) so that the graphs of the voter's cardinal rankings have a single peak. This is illustrated in Fig. 2.5.7 where the solid lines are graphs of admitted voter types and the dashed line with two peaks (on each end) is the graph of an excluded voter type.

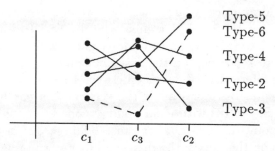

Fig. 2.5.7. Single peakedness where c_3 never is bottom ranked

Corollary 2.5.5. *If the profiles satisfy Black's single peakedness condition, then the majority vote election outcomes cannot define a cycle.*

2.5.8 Spatial Voting

When an election campaign centers about a single issue, say, foreign aid for the state of Superior, single peakedness becomes a natural condition. To see why, let each candidate's position (specifying the amount of aid) be denoted by a point on the line as indicated the labeled bullet in Fig. 2.5.8. The voter's *ideal point*, that is, the point characterizing the voter's stand on this issue, is denoted by a labeled dagger.

Fig. 2.5.8. A single issue and single-peakedness

Presumably, the closer a candidate is to a voter's ideal point, the better the voter likes her. This *Euclidean distance preference ranking* defines each voter's ranking of the three candidates where "closer is better." It now follows that the set of rankings must be single-peaked; no voter ranks the middle positioned candidate, c_2, at the bottom. Thus, the combination of a single issue and Euclidean preferences ensures single-peakedness.

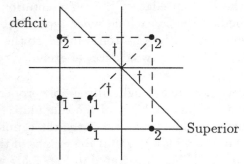

Fig. 2.5.9. Two issues and two candidates allow for cycles

The situation changes dramatically once there are two or more issues; say, aid to the state of Superior and the need to combat the deficit. To illustrate the wealth of new possibilities, start with two candidates and a single issue, say, aid to Superior. The candidates' position on this issue is defined by a point on the x-axis. With Euclidean preference, indifference between these two candidates is defined by the perpendicular bisector; this is the vertical line passing through the x axis in Fig. 2.5.9. So, voters with ideal points to the left of this line vote for c_1; voters with ideal points to the right vote for c_2. The second issue (deficit) is modeled by the points on the y-axis; the dividing line determining who votes for whom is, again, the perpendicular bisector which now is a horizontal line. When both issues are considered together, the divisions between voters is given in the figure by the slanted line; it is the perpendicular bisector of the dashed line connecting the positions taken by the two candidates.

The three lines intersect in a point, and they define six regions. These regions depict the differing ways a voter can rank the candidates depending on the mix of issues. Observe how this geometry resembles the division of the ranking regions in the representation triangle – even to the extent that the irrational voters with non-transitive rankings are excluded from the representation triangle while the inconsistent voters who rank the candidates as $c_j \succ c_k$ over both issues, but $c_k \succ c_j$ over the pair of issues are excluded from issue space. Hence, one must expect the similar arguments with related results to hold for spatial voting. This is the case; the following is a sample.

Theorem 2.5.6. *With $k \geq 2$ issues, there are $2^k - 1$ subsets of issues. Suppose the candidates never agree on any issue. For each of the $2^k - 1$ subsets of issues, choose a ranking for the candidates. There exist examples of ideal points for the voters so that the sincere outcome for the j set of issues is the selected ranking.*

Outline of proof. Equations similar to those for F_{c_j,c_k} designate the number of voters needed in each region. The assumption on the voters' preferences ensures the independence of the equations. The conclusion now follows from an "m equation and n unknown" argument. See [S17] for more details. □

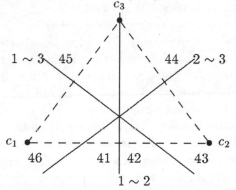

Fig. 2.5.10. Two issues and three candidates allow all rankings to occur

An advantage of spatial voting models is the visual representation of the profile. It allows us to see, for instance, how radically a voter's ranking can change with different sets of issues. But candidates know this, that's why each tries to introduce new sets of issues during a campaign. A disadvantage of spatial voting is the problem of seeing what election outcome corresponds to the profile. This information is available with the coordinate representation for profiles, so certain aspects can be transferred to spatial voting. For instance, observe that the spatial voting analogue of a Condorcet triplet is where there is a voter's ideal point in every other sector. This is represented by the daggers in Fig. 2.5.9. As true for the Condorcet cycle, the spatial voting winner always is one the same side of the bisecting line when they are examined in a clockwise manner. In the figure, these lines ensure that c_1 wins in each single issue election, but she looses when both issues are being considered. (So, the comparison between the number of spatial voting issues and the need for using the "intensity" information also holds.) Also observe that with just a rewording, Theorem 2.5.4 and Black's single-peakedness condition applies to the $k = 2$ issue setting to indicate when the rankings over issues must be compatible. (But, we also need an assumption on the candidates' relative ranking on each single issue.)

With more candidates, the voters rankings are found by using the perpendicular bisectors between the various pairs of candidates positions. This is, of course, another version of the discussion from Sect. 2.1 showing how general transitive preference are derived from binary preferences. Because the Euclidean preferences for each voter are transitive, the lines must intersect in specified ways. For instance, with three alternatives, they intersect in a point as indicated in Fig. 2.5.10. Of course, if the candidates' positions are on a line – as they must be with a single issue – the bisecting lines are parallel, so the intersection point is off at ∞. Again, the division of issue space resembles the representation triangle division – as it must. Consequently, all of the results described earlier transfer immediately to spatial voting.

To illustrate, in a clockwise manner, label the six regions with six consecutive integers in an increasing manner in the manner shown in the figure. Theorem 2.5.4 asserts that if there are no ideal points in at least one even sector and one odd sector, then pairwise voting will not create a cycle.

Before returning to pairwise voting, it is worth using these profile restrictions over three candidates to demonstrate the differences between positional voting methods. Over a single issue, the middle positioned candidate can never be more than middle ranked. Thus, she receives a point from each voter when the BC vector of $(2, 1, 0)$ is used. This means she receives at least one-third of all votes cast; so, unless the ranking is a complete tie, she has more than an average number of votes. Consequently, she cannot be bottom-ranked. With the antiplurality vote, this candidate receives a vote from everyone, so she must be, at worse, tied for top place. Using this kind of arguments, the procedure line and some computations, the following can be proved. (See [S17] for details.)

Theorem 2.5.7. *With three candidates and a single issue, the middle positioned candidate can never be* $\mathbf{w}_s$ *bottom-ranked for* $s \in (\frac{1}{3}, \frac{1}{2}]$. *For the BC, either the outcome is* $\mathcal{I}$ *or she is not bottom ranked. For* $s \in [0, \frac{1}{3})$, *all rankings are possible.*

With $k \geq 2$ *issues, there are* $2^k - 1$ *subsets of issues. Suppose the candidates positions are such that they never agree on any single issue. For each of the* $2^k - 1$ *subsets of issues, choose a ranking for the three candidates. There exist examples of ideal points for the voters so that the sincere plurality outcome for the* j *th set of issues is the selected ranking.*

2.5.9 Extensions of Black's Condition

While single peakedness is natural with a single issue, it looses status once there are two or more issues. So, we would like to extend Black's requirements. Even though Theorem 2.5.4 is more generous than Black's single peakedness conditions[18], it is overly restrictive. After all, the cycle generating region constitute

---

[18]The restriction of the theorem require all voters never to rank a particular voter candidate

two regular tetrahedrons with only 6.25% of the total volume of the representation cube, and the profiles supporting cycles is a convex set with only $\frac{1}{16}$ of $Si(6)$. So, why should we restrict attention to lower dimensional boundary profiles? All we need to do is to impose conditions so that the line connecting α and β misses the positive and negative orthant. Once the location of α is known, this trivially determines the β forbidden regions.

Example 2.5.3. The cyclic triangle divides the T_j spaces into four smaller equilateral triangles as labeled in Fig. 2.5.11. Clearly, in order to avoid cycles for all $d \in [0,1]$, neither α nor β can be in a cyclic triangle. (These are the shaded triangles in Fig. 2.5.5.) Can we do more; if α is in one of three labeled triangles, is it possible to choose β in certain T_2 labeled triangles to avoid cycles? It is. For instance, suppose $\alpha \in 1b$. Using the geometry of the representation cube, we must determine whether β is in $2b$ or not $2b$; that is the geometric question deciding whether a cycle is avoided. To see why, observe that if $\beta \notin 2b$ (so $\beta \in 2a \cup 2c$), then it is impossible for the profile line to pass through either cycle generating orthant. (For spatial voting, this determines the portion of even and odd voters that can be in various sectors of Fig. 2.5.7 while still avoiding cycles.)

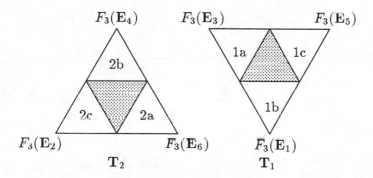

Fig. 2.5.11. Regions for avoiding cycles

Even sharper results are possible! With $\alpha \in 1b$, certain choices of $\beta \in 2b$ can avoid cycles. For instance, if $\beta = -\alpha$, the profile line passes through the origin, while missing the positive and negative orthants. (For a specified $\{c_i, c_j\}$, the condition $\beta = -\alpha$ imposes a balance among the voters with a strong $\{c_i, c_j\}$ comparison and those with a weak comparison.) To find other acceptable $\beta \in 2b$, observe that if a α-β profile line hits the positive cyclic region, it must pass through the $(x > 0,\ y > 0,\ z = 0)$ coordinate plane boundary. (To see this analytically, note that $\alpha \in 1b$ has the same sign pattern as $F_3(\mathbf{E}_1)$, so its coordinates satisfy $x > 0$, $y > 0$, $z < 0$, or $(+, +, -)$. Similarly, the β endpoint is in $2b$ with the $F_3(\mathbf{E}_4)$ sign pattern of $(-, -, +)$. By comparing the sign patterns, if follows

in a particular position. For example, if no voter has c_2 top-ranked, then this is equivalent to excluding voters of types five and six. For $n \geq 3$, the same geometric analysis admits still other kinds of conditions.

that for the line segment to enter the positive orthant, the z value must be zero while the x and y values must remain positive. Thus the profile line has the entries $(+, +, 0)$; this is the portion of the $z = 0$ coordinate surface spanned by the positive x and y axes.)

Now that we know where the profile line must hit to create a positive cycle, the goal is to find the $\beta \in 2b$ values where the α-β line misses the portion of the $z = 0$ plane where $x > 0$, $y > 0$. To discover these $\beta \in 2b$ values, first examine where the profile line just misses the $(+, +, 0)$ region because it hits a boundary edge. For instance, the $\beta \in 2b$ values where the profile line passes through the line $x > 0$, $y = 0$, $z = 0$, define a boundary between cyclic and non-cyclic choices of β; choosing β on one side of the boundary values forces the profile line through the positive orthant, while β values on the other side miss all positive cycles.

To construct such a boundary point, choose $\mathbf{q}$ on the positive x axis. As one endpoint of the profile line is at the specified value of $\alpha \in 1b$, the choice of $\mathbf{q}$ determines the corresponding β value. By varying the choice of $\mathbf{q}$ along this axis, the resulting β values trace a boundary between where the α-β line hits the positive cyclic region and where it misses it.

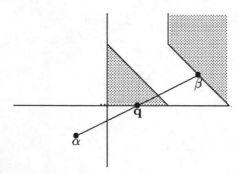

Fig. 2.5.12. Tracing out a β boundary

The boundary for β values that miss the positive orthant, then, is traced out by the T_2 endpoints of all line segments anchored at α which have $\mathbf{q}$ on the positive x axis or the positive y axis. (See Fig. 2.5.12.) The two boundary line segments in T_2 meet at $\beta = -\alpha$ and they have the parametric equations $-\alpha + u(\alpha - \mathbf{a})$ where $u \in [0, 1]$ and $\mathbf{a}$ is either $(1, 0, 0)$ or $(0, 1, 0)$. Also observe that if β is on the boundary, then the α-β profile line has no cycles. But, if β is in the region between the traced out lines, then the $\alpha - \beta$ line segment must pass through the positive cyclic region.

Similarly, a α-β connecting line passes through the negative cyclic region iff it passes through the boundary region defined by the negative x and y axes. Using the same tracing process, the boundary in $2b$ allowing points on α-β to meet the negative orthant are given by parametric equations $-\alpha + u(\alpha - \mathbf{a})$ where $u \in [-1, 0]$ and $\mathbf{a}$ is either $(1, 0, 0)$ or $(0, 1, 0)$.

Thus, region $2b$ is divided into four subregions by the two lines passing through

$-\alpha$ with the representation

$$-\alpha + u(\alpha - \mathbf{a}), \quad u \in [-1,1], \mathbf{a} = (1,0,0), (0,1,0).$$

For β in two of the subregions of $2b$, any point on the α-β line represents a transitive ranking. If β is in either of the other two regions, then there are segments of the α-β line that correspond to cycles.

So, which of the four regions define cycles, and which do not? This involves algebraic computations to prove that the region where $\beta_3 > \frac{\alpha_3}{\alpha_i}\beta_i$, $i = 1,2$ can admit positive cycles. The region where both inequalities are reversed is where negative cycles can occur. A similar analysis holds for the remaining regions. Clearly, this analysis characterizes all profile lines where, for all $d \in [0,1]$, no cycles arise.

Geometry helps to avoid the tedious algebra. Because a line is defined by two points, it follows from the boundary equation $-\alpha + u(\alpha - \mathbf{a})$, that each boundary line in $2b$ is defined by the two defining points $-\alpha$, $-\mathbf{a}$ (where $u = 0, 1$). So, as indicated in Fig. 2.5.13, for a specified $\alpha \in T_1$, plot the point $-\alpha \in T_2$. Now, there are only two vertices of the cyclic triangle near $-\alpha$; these are the two $-\mathbf{a}$ values. From each vertex, draw a dashed line through $-\alpha$; these two lines divide the small triangle into four regions. By the construction of the lines (using the value $u = 1$), the region adjacent to the cyclic region is where the profile line must pass through the positive orthant; this is a β forbidden region. The second region is on the opposite side. These "α cyclic regions" are the darker shaded regions in the figures. The β values on the dashed line avoid cycles, but there is a unique d value where a quasi-transitive outcome occurs. (This is where the line hits one of the axes.) $\square$

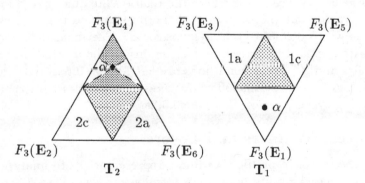

Fig 2.5.13. Refined regions for avoiding cycles

What follows is an analytic description of the above geometric argument. The purpose of the following definition is to generalize the description relating the above geometric division of the $2b$ region when $\alpha \in 1b$.

Definition 2.5.2. For voter type j, the *j reversed voter type* is given either by $j + 3$ or $j - 3$; whichever value is between 1 and 6.

Denote the two positive components of $\alpha \in T_1$ by i and j, and let $\mathbf{a}_k$ denote the unit vector along the positive k axis, $k = i, j$. (So, $\mathbf{a}_k$ is one of the vertices of the T_1 cyclic triangle.) The two lines in T_2 defined by $-\alpha + u_k(\alpha - \mathbf{a}_k)$, $k = i, j$, cross at $-\alpha$ and they define four regions where each region is determined by the signs of u_i, u_j. We say the $\beta \in T_2$ is α -cyclic if β is in a region where both u_i, u_j have the same sign. $\square$

On the representation triangle, the reversed voter type for j is given by the ranking region directly opposite $\mathcal{R}(j)$. A special case of α-cyclic regions is given in the example; they are the darker shaded regions of Fig. 2.5.10. Geometrically, the α cyclic regions can be constructed as indicated in the example.

Theorem 2.5.8. *Suppose profile* **p** *is such that there are dominant odd and even voter types where the voter types are not the reversal of one another. The profile* **p** *does not admit cycles for the majority vote elections.*

If **p** *is such that there are dominant odd and even voter types which are the reversal of one another, and if* β *is not* α-*cyclic, then* **p** *does not admit cycles.*

It is a fairly elementary exercise to prove that Theorem 2.5.4 is a special case of Theorem 2.5.8. This is because if there are no voters of one odd and one even voter type, then at least one of the remaining voter types from each group must be dominant. The only problem is if the voter types are reversals of one another. In this situation, we need to use the α cyclic condition. But, if α is on a T_1 edge, then $\beta = -\alpha$ must be on a T_2 edge. One of the dashed lines connecting $-\alpha$ with a vertex of the cyclic triangle includes the full T_2 edge. Thus, the conclusions follows.

Now that the basic geometric ideas are outlined, it is clear that sharper conditions involving restrictions of the d values can be derived. The derivation uses the same kind of geometric reasoning where the relationship among α, β and d is determined by tracing out the boundary of the positive and negative cyclic regions as used above to define α-cyclic regions for β. The main difference is that the boundaries are used to determine restrictions on the d values in terms of the position of α and β. These conditions are left for the interested reader. Of course, even stronger descriptions follow by using the exact description of the profile set generating cycles given in Example 2.5.2e.

2.5.10 Condorcet Winners and Losers

It is time to use the power of profile coordinate representations to analyze the Condorcet winner; related results hold for a Condorcet loser. The difference between this analysis and the generalization of Black's condition is that now we seek conditions to ensure that the election outcome is *in* a specified geometric region rather than missing it. As for potential problems, recall that while the Condorcet winner wins with any reasonable pairwise election procedure, the outcome uses a procedure that cannot distinguish between transitive or confused voters – it ignores all intensity information. Consequently, it is reasonable to worry whether a Condorcet winner is an appropriate solution concept. Is a Condorcet winner always the overwhelming favorite of the voters, or can she be a compromise candidate? When do the profiles support a Condorcet winner, and when do they suggest that the Condorcet winner is not appropriate? Are there situations where, because of the ignored intensity information, we should question the Condorcet winner?

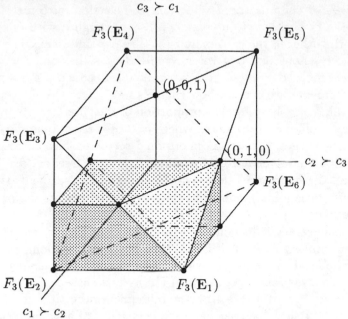

Fig. 2.5.14. The outcome space where c_1 is a Condorcet winner

To simplify the discussion, let c_1 be the Condorcet winner. This suggests dividing the voters into the "Yes" group consisting of those voter types with c_1 top-ranked, and the "No" group where c_1 is not top-ranked. The division defines a new group coordinate representation where the "Yes" group's outcome is a point α along the $F_3(\mathbf{E}_1)$–$F_3(\mathbf{E}_2)$ edge, $\mathcal{E}_1$, of the representation cube while the "No" group's outcome is a point in the tetrahedron (or polytrope), P_2, with vertices defined by the unanimity election outcomes $\{F_3(\mathbf{E}_j)\}_{j=3}^{6}$. As the *group strength* variable, d, is the distance from β to α, it is the fraction of all voters with c_1 top-ranked while $1-d$ is the fraction that just says No. The geometry is depicted in Fig. 2.5.14 where the shaded region are those election outcomes that crown c_1 as the Condorcet winner. This shaded region of the representation cube is the set of outcomes where $x > 0$ ($c_1 \succ c_2$) and $z < 0$ ($c_1 \succ c_3$).

Analytically, the c_1-*Condorcet group representation* is defined as

$$p_1 + p_2 = d; \quad a_i = \frac{p_i}{d}, i = 1, 2, \quad \alpha = (1, -1, a_1 - a_2) \in E_1$$

$$b_j = \frac{p_j}{1-d}, j = 3, 4, 5, 6, \quad \beta = \left(b_3 - \sum_{j=4}^{6} b_j, b_5 + b_6 - b_3 - b_4, \sum_{j=3}^{5} b_j - b_6\right) \in P_2$$

$$F_3(\mathbf{p}) = d\alpha + (1-d)\beta.$$

The exact values are important for computations, but I will emphasize the geometry of the c_1-Condorcet representation for a profile.

Use of c_1-Condorcet Coordinates. As true for the cyclic group coordinates, the c_1-Condorcet group coordinates have a smooth, invertible identification with profiles from $Si(6)$. So, a profile is a line segment where the designated point plays the dual role of defining the d value and the election outcome. Thus, a profile defining the c_1-Condorcet outcome $\mathbf{q}$ passes through $\mathbf{q}$ with one end on the edge $\mathcal{E}_1$ and the other in the convex hull P_2. The α point defines the relative split between the type-one and two voters, while β does the same for the four voter types not enamoured by c_1. As the designated outcome $\mathbf{q}$ plays a pivoting role for all line segments, we can see how changes in α affect the corresponding value of β. The value of d describes the proportion of the "Yes" group among all voters. Boundary profiles correspond to where α, β or d reach boundary values for their respective ranges. The two-dimensional set of profiles corresponding to a given $\mathbf{q}$ can be characterized by the single degree of freedom available to choose $\alpha \in \mathcal{E}_1$ and the freedom to choose d. The cone of line segments (which is on a plane because $\mathcal{E}_1$ is a line) defined in this manner represents the profile set supporting the outcome $\mathbf{q}$.

Armed with this geometric insight, we can analyze the profile set defining c_1 as the Condorcet winner. To start, if $d = 1$, then $F_3(\mathbf{p}) = \alpha$ is along $\mathcal{E}_1$, so c_1 is the Condorcet winner. Indeed, as long as $d > \frac{1}{2}$, the geometry ensures that the election point is in the c_1-Condorcet region. (The extreme case is if β is along the $F_3(\mathbf{E}_4)$–$F_3(\mathbf{E}_5)$ edge; here if $d < \frac{1}{2}$, then c_1 relinquishes the title of Condorcet winner.) Such results reflect the reasonable expectation that a Condorcet winner should be top-ranked by most voters. Indeed, the other extreme value is $d = 0$ where nobody has c_1 top- ranked; here c_1 is not a Condorcet winner because $F_3(\mathbf{p}) = \beta \in P_2$, and P_2, the convex hull of the unanimity outcomes $\{F_3(\mathbf{E}_j)\}_{j=3}^6$, misses the c_1 Condorcet region. Consequently, *if c_1 is the Condorcet winner, she must be top-ranked by at least one voter.*

How about the converse; can c_1 be the Condorcet winner even should only one voter have her top-ranked? This seems to be impossible because it implies that the Condorcet winner could be viewed by almost all voters as being mediocre or worse. But, it can happen. The geometric reason is that the midpoint of the P_2 line connecting $F_3(\mathbf{E}_3)$ with $F_3(\mathbf{E}_6)$ is on the boundary of the c_1-Condorcet region. Consequently, choosing β at this boundary point means that for any small positive value of d, the $\alpha \in \mathcal{E}_1$ value forces the election outcome into the c_1-Condorcet region. (See Fig. 2.5.14.)

We can learn more; the geometry dictates which profiles permit a mediocre c_1 to be crowned the Condorcet winner. If d has a small value, then for $\mathbf{q}$ to be in the c_1-Condorcet region, β must be near the origin of the representation cube. But, with β near the origin, most "No" voters must be evenly divided between type-3 (where $c_3 \succ c_1 \succ c_2$) and type-6 (where $c_2 \succ c_1 \succ c_3$). With this nearly even split over the excellence of c_2 and c_3, surely one of these two candidates would be selected over mediocre c_1. But, c_1 wins by Condorcet's standards. Therefore, not only is the Condorcet winner a "sometimes" concept, but the winner could be viewed by almost all voters as representing mediocrity.

The source of the problem is that the pairwise vote, in its attempt to be impartial in serving confused or rational voters, is ignorant of the intensity information. With this inadequacy, it cannot distinguish between the above profile $\frac{1}{2}(\mathbf{E}_3 + \mathbf{E}_6)$ and the profile $\frac{1}{2}(\mathbf{E}_1 + \mathbf{E}_4)$ where c_1 is top-ranked by half voters and bottom-ranked by the other half. For the second profile, by being top-ranked by half the voters, it is arguable that c_1 *does* manifest excellence. (The tie vote is decided in favor of c_1 with one voter having c_1 top-ranked.) To see the confusion that can occur when intensity information is ignored, the subscripts show how to reassign the binary rankings from $\frac{1}{2}(\mathbf{E}_3 + \mathbf{E}_6)$ to create $\frac{1}{2}(\mathbf{E}_1 + \mathbf{E}_4)$.

3	$(c_1 \succ c_2)_1$	$(c_3 \succ c_1)_4$	$(c_3 \succ c_2)_4$
6	$(c_2 \succ c_1)_4$	$(c_1 \succ c_3)_1$	$(c_2 \succ c_3)_1$

Can it be worse? Can an inferior candidate be a Condorcet winner? Fortunately, no. The larger the fraction of voters with c_1 bottom-ranked, the closer β is to the $F_3(\mathbf{E}_4)$–$F_3(\mathbf{E}_5)$ edge. Now, by considering the surface passing through the four vertices $\{F_3(\mathbf{E}_j)\}_{j=1,3,4,5}$, it follows that c_1 is the Condorcet winner iff more voters have her top-ranked than bottom-ranked. (The y axis is half way between $\mathcal{E}_1$ and the $F_3(\mathbf{E}_4) - F_3(\mathbf{E}_5)$ edge.) On the other hand, this difference between the c_1 lovers and haters can be as large or as small (but positive) as desired while still admitting c_1 as the Condorcet winner.

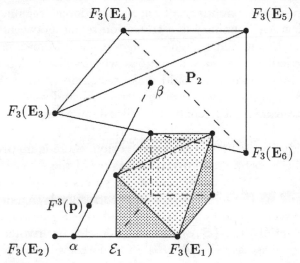

Fig. 2.5.15. The space where c_1 is a Condorcet winner
and c_3 is a Condorcet loser

If c_1 can be the Condorcet winner when almost everyone ranks her as mediocre, what happens to the other candidates? Could a candidate who is top-ranked by almost half of the voters be stigmatized with the name "Condorcet loser?" Yes. The shaded region depicted in Fig. 2.5.15 designates where c_1 is the Condorcet winner and c_3 is the Condorcet loser (so $x > 0, z < 0, y > 0$). For a small value of $\epsilon > 0$, the election point $\mathbf{q} = (\epsilon, \epsilon, -\epsilon)$ is close to the origin while being in the Condorcet c_1-winner – c_3-loser region. Now take a profile line where the P_2 endpoint is on the closest boundary of the P_2 hull. Such a point is near the midpoint of the $F_3(\mathbf{E}_3) - F_3(\mathbf{E}_6)$ connecting line. By choosing small values for ϵ, the fraction of voters with c_3 top-ranked can be made as close to $\frac{1}{2}$ as desired. On the other hand, because d has a small value, very few voters accept c_1 as top-ranked. Therefore, it can be that almost all voters view the Condorcet winner as mediocre (middle-ranked), but nearly half of the voters believe that the Condorcet loser represents excellence (top-ranked). Again, this Condorcet fault emerges because of the information lost about the intensity of the comparisons.

A reasonable counter response to these negative assertions about election outcomes near the origin is that c_1 is a compromise candidate for an electorate severely split between two candidates – in such a setting, compromise may make sense. By experimenting with the cone of line segments passing through a $\mathbf{q}$ near the origin, it becomes clear that all of the supporting profiles[19] reflect mixtures combining an electorate that is diametrically split between c_2 and c_3 (so c_1 may be a reasonable compromise) and an electorate where c_1 is either top or bottom-ranked (so the election approximates a "yes - no" vote on c_1). In these situations, arguments are easy to fashion to justify the selection of c_1.

The Boundary of the c_1-Condorcet Region. What we learn from the above is that if profiles exist which raise doubts about the validity of choosing c_1, they correspond to $\mathbf{q}$ values near the boundary of the c_1-Condorcet region. The informational reason is clear. A boundary is a transition region between where one or another candidate is chosen. Thus, slight changes in the information could alter an outcome. In particular, these are situations where information about the intensity of the pairwise comparisons could make a significant difference in who is selected. Therefore, one way to analyze the strengths and weaknesses of the Condorcet winner is to examine the cone of profiles supporting outcomes $\mathbf{q}$ that are near the boundary.

In examining the boundaries of the c_1-Condorcet region, there is no problem with $\mathbf{q} \in \mathcal{E}_1$; here all profiles show a unanimous acceptance of the superiority of c_1. The boundary point $(0, 1, -1)$ can only occur if the voters are split between types one $(c_1 \succ c_2 \succ c_3)$ and six $(c_2 \succ c_1 \succ c_3)$, so this corresponds to a de facto two candidate election between c_1 and c_2 where the Condorcet region selects the "majority" winner. (Incidentally, the $\{c_1, c_2\}$ comparisons for both voter types involve a weak intensity, so it is easy to justify the Condorcet winner for these profiles.)

A remaining boundary point is $(0, 1, 0)$ on the y axis. A $\mathbf{q}$ near this point must be supported by a profile where the voters are nearly evenly split between type-one $(c_1 \succ c_2 \succ c_3)$ and type-five $(c_2 \succ c_3 \succ c_1)$. For this profile, it is very difficult to accept c_1 rather than c_2 as the winner. In particular, the above argument justifying c_1 as a compromise candidate for $\mathbf{q}$ near the origin now works against

---

[19] This set is restricted by the combination of the pivot action of $\mathbf{q}$ (which is near the origin) and the restriction of α to an edge of the representation cube. What is traced out is a portion of a plane.

c_1 should $\mathbf{q}$ be near $(0, 1, 0)$. This is because $\mathbf{q}$ near $(0, 1, 0)$ must be supported by a profile where the electorate is severely split on its views of c_1; nearly half of the voters weakly prefer c_1 to c_2 while nearly half strongly prefer c_2 to c_1. (c_2 is top-ranked by nearly half of the voters, and she is not bottom-ranked by anybody.) Consequently c_2 is not a "compromise candidate;" clearly she is the voters' top-choice. This situation, more than any of the above, demonstrates how the informational limitations of the pairwise vote can compromise the integrity of the Condorcet solution concept.

The difficulty, of course, is that the pairwise vote attempts to serve both confused and rational voters on an equal standing; by trying to serve both types, it cannot assume there exists linkage among the pairwise rankings. So, when serving the two confused voters, $(c_3 \succ c_1, c_1 \succ c_2, c_2 \succ c_3)$ and $(c_2 \succ c_1, c_1 \succ c_3, c_2 \succ c_3)$, where the second confused voter accidentally has rankings that could be viewed as being transitive, the outcome is the only reasonable one. It is *not* when these outcomes are reassembled to create the original transitive voters. Transitivity must have consequences! Pairwise voting vitiates them.

Thus, if follows that a region surrounding the positive y axis should designate c_2, rather than c_1, as the winner. Similarly, a region around the negative y axis should be awarded to c_3. positive y axis should designate c_2, rather than c_1, as the winner. Continuing, the same argument suggests that the regions lost to c_1 should be compensated by awarding c_1 additional regions around the positive x and negative z axis. This covers all boundary regions.

Theorem 2.5.9. *If c_j is a Condorcet winner, then at least one voter has her top-ranked. Indeed, more voters must have c_j top-ranked than bottom-ranked.*

Conversely, for any value of $\epsilon > 0$, there exist profiles c_j is the Condorcet winner even though no more than ϵ of all voters have c_j top-ranked. More generally, there are profiles where c_j is the Condorcet winner even though the positive difference between those voters that have her top-ranked from those that have her bottom-ranked is bounded by ϵ.

For any value of $\epsilon > 0$, there are profiles where the Condorcet loser is top-ranked by more than $\frac{1}{2} - \epsilon$ of the voters.

There are profiles where even though no voter has c_2 bottom-ranked, almost half of the voters have c_2 top-ranked, and almost half of the voters have c_1 bottom-ranked, c_1 is the Condorcet winner.

2.5.11 A Condorcet Improvement

Although the concept of a Condorcet winner is appealing, it has serious faults caused by the pairwise vote procedure being ignorant of the fact it is dealing with transitive voters. The first is that a Condorcet winner is not always defined – this difficulty occurs if the election point is in a cyclic region. The second problem are those situations where it is difficult, if not impossible, to justify the Condorcet winner as representing the voters' top- choice – the selection of the Condorcet winner is indefensible. The obvious goal, therefore, is to modify the idea of a Condorcet winner by eliminating its failings while retaining its strengths. This is easy to do. To handle the nonexistence issue, just divide the cyclic outcomes among the three candidates; to handle the injustice issue, just reassign certain outcomes along the coordinate axes to the more deserving candidate.

The general principle in assigning candidates for points in the cyclic regions is clear – the better a candidate does in the majority vote tallies, the stronger the argument for choosing her. Conversely, the tie outcome $(\frac{1}{3}, \frac{1}{3}, \frac{1}{3})$ should be on the boundary of each candidate's region. Also, for reasons discussed in Chap 4.2, the set of election outcomes associated with a particular candidate must be convex.   These are minimal conditions required of any improvement over the Condorcet concept. The regions $C(c_j)$ in the representation cube are the outcomes where c_j is selected.

Definition 2.5.3. Three sets of election outcomes, $\{C(c_j)\}_{j=1}^3$, are called *Condorcet Improvements* if they are pairwise disjoint and satisfy the following conditions.

1. The election outcomes where all voters have c_j top-ranked is in $C(c_j)$.
2. Each set $C(c_j)$ is convex with $(\frac{1}{3}, \frac{1}{3}, \frac{1}{3})$ and $(0,0,0)$ as boundary points.
3. The election outcome where no voter has c_i or c_j bottom-ranked and half of the voters have each candidate top-ranked is a boundary point of $C(c_j)$ and $C(c_i)$.
4. The election points not in $\cup_{j=1}^3 C(c_j)$ has zero three-dimensional volume. $\square$

The first condition asserts that when all voters have c_1 top-ranked, she should be selected; this outcome must be in $C(c_j)$. The importance of the second condition, convexity, is described in Chapter 4. As for the two specified boundary points, clearly they cannot be assigned to any one candidate, so they should be boundary points of each $C(c_j)$. The third condition essentially asserts that when the profile reduces an election to a two-candidate situation, then majority vote principles should apply. The fourth condition requires decisiveness; it relegates those situations where an outcome is not defined to a lower dimensional set of profiles. These four conditions clearly are minimal – they do not even speak to the issue of the reassignment of Condorcet regions around each axis for a more deserving candidate. Nevertheless, they suffice to make the indicated corrections.

Theorem 2.5.10. *If the sets* $\{C(c_j)\}_{j=1}^3$ *are Condorcet Improvements, then these sets are uniquely defined by the three planes*

$$2x = y + z, \quad 2y = x + z, \quad 2z = x + y \qquad (2.5.8)$$

that can be identified, respectively, with the pairs $\{c_1, c_2\}, \{c_2, c_3\}, \{c_3, c_1\}$. *For each* $\{c_i, c_j\}$, *the associated plane divides the space of election outcomes into two parts; the side containing the coordinate axis identified with* $c_i \succ c_j$ *is the set of election outcomes assigned this binary ranking. The intersection of these planes define six symmetric, open regions of election outcomes; each open region corresponds to a transitive ranking. The region* $C(c_j)$ *is the union of the two regions (and their common boundary) where* c_j *is top-ranked.*

So, with the exception of ties (the outcomes on the three planes), there is a unique Condorcet Improvement. With simple algebra, the portions of the

c_1-Condorcet region that are reassigned to other candidates are easy to compute. For instance, the wedge bordering the y axis defined by the four vertices $(0,0,0), (0,1,0), (0,1,-1), (\frac{1}{3},1,-\frac{1}{3})$ is reassigned to c_2 as it should be. Likewise, a wedge from the c_1- Condorcet region about the negative y axis defined by the vertices $(0,0,0), (0,-1,0), (0,-1,-1), (-\frac{1}{3},-1,-\frac{1}{3})$ is appropriately reassigned to c_3. Similar regions are added to $C(c_1)$ around the positive x and negative z axes. Figure 2.5.16 indicates the region where c_1 is top-ranked. This figure should be compared with the one showing where c_1 is the Condorcet winner (the dashed lines in the figure).

Now consider how the Condorcet Improvement handles those indefensible situations where the Condorcet winner is not the voters' top choice. For example, suppose the voters are divided between type-one with the ranking $c_1 \succ c_2 \succ c_3$ and type-five with $c_2 \succ c_3 \succ c_1$. As already argued, even if there are slightly more type-one than type-five voters, c_2 should be treated as the voters' top choice. On the other hand, if almost all voters are of type-one, then c_1 should be elected. The problem is to determine an appropriate threshold dividing the selection of c_1 over c_2. According to the Condorcet Improvement procedure, the value is $\frac{2}{3}$; if c_1 receives one more than $\frac{2}{3}$ of the vote, the type-one voters' rankings need to be honored. (Compare this value with the Pope selection procedure.) However, once a more diversified selection of voters are admitted, the criteria for selecting a particular candidate are relaxed.

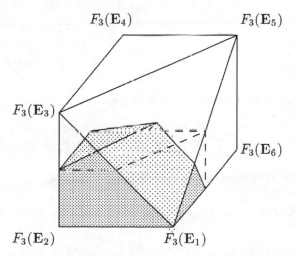

Fig. 2.5.16. The region where c_1 is a Condorcet Improved winner

Proof. The boundary region between $C(c_i)$ and $C(c_j)$ must be a plane. If not, then two points on the boundary region can be found where the connecting line would be in one of the other regions. If this line is in $C(c_i)$, then it cannot be in $C(c_j)$. Thus, $C(c_j)$ would not be convex violating the assumption.

A plane is defined by three points, so the boundary conditions completely specify the plane dividing $C(c_i)$ and $C(c_j)$. With a specific example of $C(c_1)$

and $C(c_2)$, the plane is $ax + by + cz = e$. Because the origin is on the plane (it is a boundary point for each region), $e = 0$. Because $(\frac{1}{3}, \frac{1}{3}, \frac{1}{3})$ is on the plane, $a + b + c = 0$. Finally, the point $(0, 1, -1)$ is the election point where the voters are evenly split between $c_1 \succ c_2 \succ c_3$ and $c_2 \succ c_1 \succ c_3$, so it is a point on the plane. Thus, $b = c$. This means that coefficients must satisfy $a = -2b = -2c$. By choosing $b = 1$, the conclusion follows.

The first condition for a Condorcet Improvement uniquely defines which plane and which side of this plane is assigned to a ranking $c_i \succ c_j$. The last condition precludes the possibility of choosing subsets of these regions. $\square$

Summary. Coordinate representations for profiles enable us to "see" which profiles define which outcomes. As such, the coordinate representations become easy to use, powerful tools to analyze various concepts and election outcomes. For instance, in this way we see the consequences of the pairwise vote systematically ignores information about transitivity and the intensity of pairwise comparisons. In this manner we now have an answer to the question, "Why can't an organization be more like a person?" It can once it stops relying upon procedures that toss away vital information.

2.5.12 Exercises

2.5.1. Show that if c_1 is not a Condorcet winner, then there is an pairwise election procedure where c_1 does not win. Characterize all pairwise procedures that always select a Condorcet winner when one exists.

2.5.2. Find all profiles where $F_2(\mathbf{p}) = (\frac{1}{2}, \frac{1}{3})$. Find all profiles where $F_3(\mathbf{p}) = (\frac{1}{2}, 0, \frac{1}{3})$. Convert the profile $(\alpha = (.2, .3, .5), \beta = -(.6, .3, .1), d = \frac{2}{3})$ into the corresponding $\mathbf{p} \in Si(6)$.

2.5.3. What are the maximum victory margins for $c_1 \succ c_2, c_2 \succ c_3$ that still allow the outcome $c_3 \succ c_1$?

2.5.4. Using the same kind of geometric argument showing that $([-1, 1] \times [-1, 1]) \times [-1, 1]$ is a cube, describe geometrically $Si(3) \times [-1, 1]$–the product of the representation triangle with a line segment.

2.5.5. The profile where four voters are of type-two, three of type-four, three of type-six defines a cycle. Find a corresponding set of confused voters leading to the same outcome.

2.5.6. Find the cone of profiles for $\mathbf{q} = (.8, .1, 0)$. Compare it with the cone for $(0, 0, 0)$. Describe the one-dimensional set of profiles supporting $(\frac{1}{2}, -\frac{2}{3}, 1)$.

2.5.7. By use of the argument following Theorem 2.5.8, show that some of the profiles admitted by Theorem 2.5.4 define quasi-transitive rankings.

2.5.8. For spatial voting and a single issue, suppose we know each voter's ideal point and suppose there are an odd number of voters. Furthermore, suppose candidate c_1 is the first to announce her position on these issues. Determine what should be her position so she will win any pairwise contest independent of what the other candidates declare. (This is the "median voter" theorem.) With two issues, suppose the odd number of voters' ideal points are known (and not on a line), candidates c_2 and c_3 have declared their positions. Find a stand for c_1 to ensure she wins.

2.5.9. For two issues, let the three voters' ideal points be $(0,0)$, $(4,0)$, $(2,3)$. Suppose the declared positions of c_1, c_3 are, respectively, $(0,1)$, $(4,1)$. Find all positions for c_2 so that the voters' preferences are single peaked and she is never bottom-ranked. (Hint: This happens if c_2's position is on the line connecting $(0,1)$ with $(4,1)$. Now, move c_2 so that the figure similar to Fig. 2.5.9 keeps the voters' ideal points in the same ranking regions.) Use this to generalize the statement about single peakedness over a single issue to certain two-dimensional configurations. Now, find positions for c_2 so that a cycle occurs.

2.5.10. Suppose Susie evaluates raspberries, strawberries and apple pie on the three criteria of calories, color and taste. Show it is possible to find transitive rankings for each so that when Susie aggregates, a cycle emerges. That is, show that a person who pairwise aggregates over several criteria can appear to be cyclic.

2.5.11. With two candidates and two issues, a, b, find positioning of three ideal points so that on issue a, c_1 wins, on issue b, c_2 wins, and on both issues, c_1 wins. With two candidates and three issues, a, b, c, find a positioning of the three voters' ideal points so that c_1 wins whenever a single issue or any two issues are considered, but c_2 wins when all three issues are considered. Create another example where c_1 wins whenever one or three issues are considered, but c_2 wins whenever two issues are considered.

2.5.12. If $\alpha = (0.8, 0.1, 0.1)$, find all β for which the profile line misses the cycle generating regions.

Suppose all we know is that α is defined by where 80% of the odd voters are type-three and no more than 10% are of type-one. Find the restrictions on β so that all α-β lines miss the cycle generating regions.

2.5.13. The outcome $\mathbf{q} = (0.1, 0.9, -0.1)$ crowns c_1 as the Condorcet winner. Using c_1-Condorcet coordinates, find the cone of supporting profiles. This profile set is two-dimensional, so indicate where both dimensions are captured in this cone. Are there profiles where it seems inappropriate to choose c_1 as the winner? Now compare the above with the cone of profiles supporting $(.1, 0, -.1)$. Which set appears to be larger? Why?

2.5.14. We know that with the agenda $< c_1, c_2, c_3 >$, c_3 wins if she is a Condorcet winner or if there is a cycle. On the other hand, wither of the other two candidates wins only by being a Condorcet winner. Use Example 2.5.2e to determine the portion of all $Si(6)$ profiles that crown c_1 the agenda winner. Compare this with the portion of all profiles where c_3 wins.

By use of the techniques of Example 2.5.2a, find the vertices of the convex set of profiles where c_1 is the Condorcet winner, c_3 is the Condorcet loser, but c_1 is not top-ranked with the Condorcet Improvement. (If the reader knows how to compute the volume of this set, do so.)

2.6 Positional Versus Pairwise Voting

So far I have explained why election outcomes can vary with the choice of the positional voting method and why the paradoxical cycles can occur with pairs of candidates. In this section, these ideas are combined to compare positional with pairwise vote outcomes. This material, then, is a step toward understanding the kinds of difficulties introduced in the fable.

To start, I will compare positional voting outcomes with the pairwise ranking of a particular pair of candidates. One result is that all positional methods allow "anything to happen" – the $\{c_i, c_j\}$ pairwise and positional rankings need not have anything to do with one another. As this negative assertion holds for all $\mathbf{w}_s$, we need more delicate ways to compare procedures. By doing so, it is shown that the plurality method is more apt to cause such chaotic behavior, and the BC is the unique method to impose a tone of temperance. Then, by combining the cyclic coordinates with the procedure line, we discover how to compare the rankings of positional methods with those for all three pairs of candidates. Watch out; more kinds of troublesome election outcomes exist than one might expect. As true throughout this book, while the goal is to understand the informational reasons for electoral problems, the analysis depends on developing an appropriate geometric representation.

2.6.1 Comparing Votes with a Fat Triangle

Comparing a positional and a majority ranking outcome of the pair $\{c_1, c_2\}$ involves comparing a point in the representation triangle $Si(3)$ – the positional election outcome – and a point in $[-1, 1]$ – the $\{c_1, c_2\}$ majority vote outcome. The analysis, then, is modeled as the mapping

$$F_4(-, \mathbf{w}_s) : Si(6) \to Si(3) \times [-1, 1] \qquad (2.6.1)$$

defined by

$$F_4(\mathbf{p}, \mathbf{w}_s) = (f(\mathbf{p}, \mathbf{w}_s), f_{\{c_1, c_2\}}(\mathbf{p})).$$

To visualize $Si(3) \times [-1, 1]$, start with the standard assumption that for a given $\mathbf{q}$ in the representation triangle, there is no a priori reason to restrict the potential $\{c_1, c_2\}$ vote outcome in $[-1, 1]$. Following the lead of the last section, pass the interval of pairwise vote outcomes, $[-1, 1]$, through $\mathbf{q} \in Si(3)$ in an orthogonal direction. By varying the choice of $\mathbf{q} \in Si(3)$, a "fat" equilateral triangle is traced out.

As we need to understand the image set of F_4, the convexity property ensures it is the convex hull defined by the six unanimity F_4 election outcomes. The identification process is easy because $F_4(\mathbf{E}_j, \mathbf{w}_s) = ([\mathbf{w}_s]_j, \pm 1)$, $j = 1, \ldots, 6$, where the choice of 1 or -1 depends, respectively, on whether the jth voter type has $c_1 \succ c_2$ or $c_2 \succ c_1$. The image hulls for the plurality and antiplurality methods are depicted in Fig. 2.6.1.

The plurality and antiplurality methods account for all six unanimity outcomes with only four points from $Si(3) \times [-1, 1]$. This is due to a "doubling up" effect where, for instance, the type-one and two unanimity outcomes agree, $F_4(\mathbf{E}_1, \mathbf{w}_0) = F_4(\mathbf{E}_2, \mathbf{w}_0) = ((1,0,0),1)$; i.e., $[\mathbf{w}_0]_1 = [\mathbf{w}_0]_2 = (1,0,0)$ and both voter types have the same $c_1 \succ c_2$ ranking of the pair. (This F_4 point is the dot at the bottom, back, and left of Fig. 2.6.1a. I reversed the usual geometric representation of the line interval $[-1, 1]$ to make the picture easier to analyze – at least for me.) All other positional election procedures $\mathbf{w}_s$, $s \in (0, \frac{1}{2})$, define six distinct F_4 unanimity election points. (See Fig. 2.6.2a.)

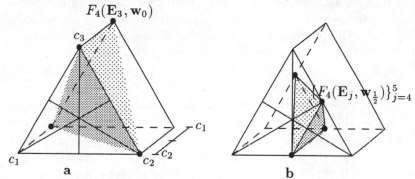

Fig. 2.6.1. Extreme hulls. **a.** The F_4 plurality hull.
b. The F_4 antiplurality hull

Figure 2.6.1 shows that the region of complete indifference, $((\frac{1}{3}, \frac{1}{3}, \frac{1}{3}), 0)$, is an interior point for the plurality and the antiplurality image sets. As shown later and as suggested by Fig. 2.6.2a, the same geometry holds for all positional methods. Some consequences are captured by the next statement.

Theorem 2.6.1. *For* $\mathbf{w}_s$, $s \in [0, \frac{1}{2}]$, *the indifference point* $((\frac{1}{3}, \frac{1}{3}, \frac{1}{3}), 0)$ *is an interior point of the image set of* $F_4(-, \mathbf{w}_s)$; *the image set meets all ranking regions in* $Si(3) \times [-1, 1]$. *Thus, for any ranking of* $\{c_1, c_2\}$ *combined with any (of the 13 possible) positional election ranking of the three candidates, there exists a profile* $\mathbf{p}$ *so that the majority vote of* $\{c_1, c_2\}$ *and the* $\mathbf{w}_s$ *election outcome are the chosen ones. Indeed, an election point* $\mathbf{q}$ *in the interior of the* $F_4(-, \mathbf{w}_s)$ *image set is supported by a two-dimensional set of profiles.*

Well, there it goes again! Flaunting our expectations, Theorem 2.6.1 asserts that anything can happen when the positional election outcome is compared with the majority vote outcome of a particular pair. The statement does not even provide a scapegoat to blame a particular positional method; instead, for *any* $\mathbf{w}_s$, there exist profiles where the positional ranking of $c_1 \succ c_3 \succ c_2$ is distinctly at odds with the same voters' pairwise ranking of $c_2 \succ c_1$. This means that the ranking of a scholarship competition could be Arvid $\succ$ Andrew $\succ$ Adam, even though most voters really prefer Adam to Arvid. As these examples involve strict rankings, the arguments of Sect. 2.4 show that the outcomes are likely, robust events; they are supported by an open five-dimensional subset of profiles.

The proof of the theorem depends upon the geometry of the F_4 image set; but this is a complicated figure! For example, the wedged surface to the left and back of Fig. 2.6.2a (partially outlined by hidden, dashed lines), W_s^1, is the convex hull defined by the three points $\{([\mathbf{w}_s]_j, 1)\}_{j=1}^3$ while the wedge to the right and front, W_s^2, is the convex hull of $\{([\mathbf{w}_s]_j, -1)\}_{j=4}^6$. The six remaining surface wedges connect the front and back faces of the fat triangle.

2.6.2 Positional Group Coordinates

To understand and prove Theorem 2.6.1, it helps to know which profiles define which F_4 outcomes; i.e., we need another group coordinate representation for the profiles. To define one, it is natural to group the voter types according to how a voter ranks the pair $\{c_1, c_2\}$. Thus, the *liberals*, or voter types $\{1, 2, 3\}$ that are to the left of $c_1 \sim c_2$ line, have the relative ranking $c_1 \succ c_2$ while the *conservatives*, or voter types $\{4, 5, 6\}$, are to the right of the $c_1 \sim c_2$ indifference line.

If only liberals vote, the outcome is in the convex hull W_s^1 defined by the vertices $\{F(\mathbf{E}_j, \mathbf{w}_s)\}_{j=1}^3$; similarly, the election outcome when only conservatives vote is in W_s^2. So, let $(\alpha_s \in W_s^1, \beta_s \in W_s^2, d \in [0, 1])$ represent, respectively, the $\mathbf{w}_s$ election outcome if only the liberals vote, if only the conservatives vote, and the proportion of all voters that are liberals. The analytic definition of these terms is

$$d = \sum_{j=1}^3 p_j, \quad a_i = \frac{p_i}{d}, \, i = 1, 2, 3; \quad \alpha_s = (\sum_{j=1}^3 a_j [\mathbf{w}_s]_j, \, 1) \in W_s^1$$

$$b_j = \frac{p_j}{1-d}, \, j = 4, 5, 6; \quad \beta_s = (\sum_{j=4}^6 b_j [\mathbf{w}_s]_j, \, -1) \in W_s^2$$

$$F_4(\mathbf{p}, \mathbf{w}_s) = d\alpha_s + (1 - d)\beta_s. \tag{2.6.2}$$

As in Sect. 2.5, a profile is represented as a line segment connecting α_s, β_s, and a designated point on the segment that is d of the distance from β_s to α_s. If $s \neq 0, \frac{1}{2}$, there is a smooth invertible relationship between $\mathbf{p} \in Si(6)$ and the *positional group coordinate representation*, (α_s, β_s, d), of the profile. Unfortunately, the invertibility does not extend to the plurality and antiplurality methods; instead, these extreme procedures assign a *subset* of profiles to a *single* (α_s, β_s, d) value. While this annoying fact makes it improper to call (α_s, β_s, d) a "coordinate representation" when $s = 0, \frac{1}{2}$, I do so anyway. (A similar singularity situation occurs with spherical coordinates when the radius of the sphere is zero.)

Even with these coordinates, the geometry of the image set remains too complicated to use. The easiest part of the geometry is the majority vote outcome; if $d > \frac{1}{2}$, then $c_1 \succ c_2$; if $d < \frac{1}{2}$, then $c_2 \succ c_1$. Geometrically, then, $d > \frac{1}{2}$ forces $\mathbf{q}_s$ to be closer to α_s than to β_s. (The converse relationship holds for $d < \frac{1}{2}$.) Thus, all information about who wins the $\{c_1, c_2\}$ pairwise vote and by how much is captured by how close $\mathbf{q}_s$ is to α_s or β_s. This information is retained if we view the fat triangle through the front triangular surface.

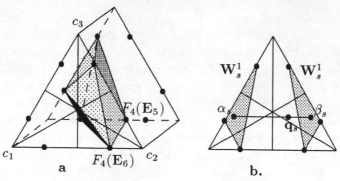

Fig. 2.6.2. Reducing the dimension. **a.** The image set of $F_4(-, \mathbf{w}_s)$.
b The collapsed region

Stated in practical terms, as the geometry allows us to ignore the pairwise vote direction, we can collapse the fat triangle to the front surface. Figure 2-6-2b is the result where the shaded areas are the wedges W_s^1, W_s^2. A potential problem is the effect on the d value. I suggested above that the relative distances among $\mathbf{q}$, α_s, and β_s remain the same whether they are compared in the fat triangle, or projected to the front surface. This assertion is true; d remains the same. (The reader can check this by using standard properties of similar triangles. See the exercises.)

This liberal-conservative coordinate representation is particularly easy to use and interpret with the collapsed fat triangle.

1. The point α_s can be any point in W_s^1. The closer α_s is to the ith vertex of W_s^1, the stronger the dominance of the ith voter type among the liberals. Similar statements apply to the conservatives for $\beta_s \in W_s^2$.

2. A profile $\mathbf{p}$ is represented by the line segment α_s - β_s and a designated point that is d of the distance from β_s toward α_s. As the designated point also identifies $\mathbf{q}_s$, the $\mathbf{w}_s$ election ranking is given by the ranking region containing $\mathbf{q}_s$.

3. The c_1, c_2 majority vote ranking is determined by the value of d; e.g., if the designated point $\mathbf{q}_s$ is closer to α_s than to β_s, the majority ranking is $c_1 \succ c_2$.

Triangle Abuse. The power of the coordinate representation is that we can "see" what profiles lead to what kinds of election outcomes. As true for the cyclic coordinate representation, the designated outcome $\mathbf{q}_s$ serves as a pivot creating a balance between the types of liberals and conservatives needed to support $\mathbf{q}_s$. In particular, it is interesting to see how this pivoting action and the triangular geometry of $Si(3)$ shape the possible election outcomes. Indeed, several paradoxes are consequences of the pointy head – fat bottom geometry of the representation triangle.

I start with the plurality vote; it is particularly easy to use because the wedges W_0^1, W_0^2 are, respectively, the left and right side edges of $Si(3)$. Thus any line segment connecting the side edges of the representation triangle represents a α_0 - β_0 profile line. Recall, a plurality vote ignores who is a voter's second-ranked candidate while the pairwise vote ignores the intensity of pairwise comparisons.

Surrounded by this wealth of ignorance, we must expect all sorts of paradoxical situations to arise. This happens, and the geometry displays them.

Start with $d = \frac{1}{2}$; this d value requires the pairwise ranking to be $c_1 \sim c_2$. Geometrically, $d = \frac{1}{2}$ requires $\mathbf{q}_0$ to be the midpoint of the α_0 - β_0 profile line. If α_0, β_0 are the same height above the base of the representation triangle, then the connecting line segment is parallel to the base. Using the properties of similar triangles, this positions $\mathbf{q}_0$ on the $c_1 \sim c_2$ indifference line (see Fig. 2.6.3) so the relative ranking of $\{c_1, c_2\}$ for the pairwise and plurality votes agree. Of course, the status of c_3 in the plurality ranking varies through three possible choices of $c_3 \succ c_1 \sim c_2$, $c_3 \sim c_1 \sim c_2$, $c_1 \sim c_2 \succ c_3$ by changing the common height of α_0 and β_0.

An informational interpretation makes it clear that the consistent outcomes is due to "canceling errors." As α_0 shares the same height with β_0, the geometry requires the α_0 and β_0 components of the profile to have a reasonably similar mix of strong and weak $\{c_1, c_2\}$ intensity comparisons and the frequency c_3 is top-ranked by the liberals and conservatives. It is this careful balance of the kind of information ignored by a pairwise vote (the intensity factor) and dropped by the plurality procedure (a voter's second-ranked candidate) between liberals and conservatives that cancels out any artificial advantage shown to one candidate over the other. So, the geometry allows the plurality and pairwise $\{c_1, c_2\}$ rankings to agree.

A geometrically more interesting case is if α_0 or β_0 is higher than the other point. From an informational viewpoint, such a profile presents a different mix for the intensity of the $\{c_1, c_2\}$ comparisons (for the pairwise vote) and a different distribution of how often c_3 is the second-ranked candidate (for the plurality vote). Without balancing the "lost" information, we must expect paradoxes.

To see the consequences, observe that when one endpoint is higher than the other, the resulting slant of the α_0 - β_0 profile line forces its midpoint off of the $c_1 \sim c_2$ indifference line; thus the pair's relative plurality ranking disagrees with the $c_1 \sim c_2$ pairwise ranking. For instance, the higher a liberal point is on W_0^1, the closer α_0 is both to the pointy head and the $c_1 \sim c_2$ indifference line. Similarly, the closer the conservative point approaches the fat bottom of the representation triangle, the farther β_0 strays from the indifference line. Thus, elementary geometry (or observation) ensures that the midpoint of the connecting line is in the $c_2 \succ c_1$ region. Consequently, if β_0 is lower than α_0 while $d = \frac{1}{2}$, then $\mathbf{q}_0$ is pulled to the right forcing the pair's relative plurality ranking to be $c_2 \succ c_1$. Similarly, if α_0 is lower than β_0, then $\mathbf{q}_0$ is pulled to the left creating the plurality ranking $c_1 \succ c_2$. By varying the relative heights of α_0, β_0 the midpoint can be forced into any of the thirteen regions of the representation triangle. Thus *any of the thirteen plurality rankings can accompany a pairwise outcome of $c_1 \sim c_2$*. Figure 2.6.3a depicts three different situations.

There is no reason to restrict attention to a pairwise tie vote $c_1 \sim c_2$ where $\mathbf{q}_0$ is the midpoint of the α_0 - β_0 line segment. Similar statements hold for almost any other d value. If, for example, c_1 beats c_2 by receiving 60% of the vote, then $d = 0.6$. This d value requires $\mathbf{q}_0$ to be closer to α_0 than β_0. Consequently, to

obtain the contradictory plurality relative ranking of $c_2 \succ c_1$, α_0 must be close
to the pointy head while β_0 is near the fat bottom; an extreme slant is needed
to force the designated point into the $c_2 \succ c_1$ region. On the other hand, should
the profile line be horizontal, or slant in the other direction, the liberal beats the
conservative in both the plurality and pairwise ($d > \frac{1}{2}$) elections. Using similar
arguments and varying the height of α_0 and β_0, it is clear that Theorem 2.6.1
holds for the plurality method.

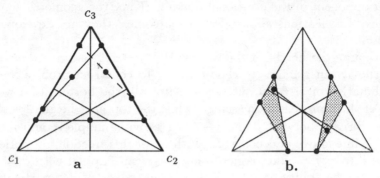

Fig. 2.6.3. Liberals and conservative coordinates.
a. Plurality ($s = 0$) voting. **b.** For $0 < s < \frac{1}{2}$

One way to appreciate the geometry is to use it to describe actual election
behavior. As soon as Ross Perot entered the race for the 1992 US Presidency,
there was considerable speculation in the press about which of the other two
candidates, George Bush or Bill Clinton, would be hurt the most. For example,
if a voter has (c_3) Perot top-ranked and (c_2) Bush second-ranked, then Bush
loses the vote. Geometrically, the more voters there are of this type, the closer
β_0 moves to the c_3 vertex. From the geometry, the resulting slant of the profile
line could force a (c_1) Clinton victory even if more people preferred Bush to
Clinton (as indicated by the polls in Spring, 1992). As a response, in June of
1992, the Bush forces tried to instill doubt about Perot's reliability. The goal,
of course, was to convert voters indecisive between Bush and Perot to vote for
Bush to push β_0 closer to the base of the representation triangle. Expressed
geometrically, they hoped to put an appropriate slant on the profile line to allow
a Bush victory even should more voters prefer Clinton. In July, 1992, Perot
withdrew (for a couple of months) leaving a two-person race.

The geometry changes if $0 < s < \frac{1}{2}$ as the wedges W_s^i become two-dimensional
triangles instead of simple lines (because $F_4(\mathbf{E}_1, \mathbf{w}_s) \neq F_4(\mathbf{E}_2, \mathbf{w}_s)$). The extra
direction in the wedges, which manifest the recognition accorded to a second-
ranked candidate, allows α_s, β_s to be moved horizontally as well as vertically.
(See Fig. 2-6-3b.) Consequently, even when $d = \frac{1}{2}$ and α_s and β_s have the
same height, the designated point need not be on the $c_1 \sim c_2$ indifference line.
By using the horizontal freedom to move α_s more to the left, the $\mathbf{w}_s$ election
outcome $\mathbf{q}_s$ is forced into the liberal region with its relative ranking of $c_1 \succ c_2$.
By varying the vertical and horizontal positions of α_s, β_s, the position of $\mathbf{q}_s$ can
be radically changed. It is this flexibility that almost encourages the pairwise

and $\mathbf{w}_s$ rankings of c_1, c_2 to disagree.

There is a trade-off; accompanying the new found freedom where α_s, β_s can be moved horizontally, a limit is imposed on the vertical movement – only for $s = 0$ is the pointy head of the representation triangle accessible. In particular, the upper limit for W_s^1 is determined by the c_3 value of $f(\mathbf{E}_3, \mathbf{w}_s) = [\mathbf{w}_s]_3 = (s, 0, 1 - s)$. This upper limit, of course, restricts the slant of a profile line. As we have seen, the greater the slant, the more likely it is for a pairwise winner to be ranked *below* her opponent in the positional ranking. Thus, the geometric upper bound should have implications about election outcomes; they are developed later in this section.

Even though the height of the wedges W_s^j, $j = 1, 2$, is limited, enough flexibility of movement remains to choose α_s, β_s to construct profiles that support any combination of election outcomes. After all, the bottom of a wedge is on the base of the representation triangle while the top is at height $1 - s > \frac{1}{2} > \frac{1}{3}$. The vertical range between 0 and $1 - s > \frac{1}{3}$ provides ample room to manipulate the α_s - β_s line above and below $\mathcal{I}$. With all of this freedom of motion, $\mathbf{q}_s$ can be moved into any ranking region – anything can happen with $d = \frac{1}{2}$. Again, thanks to the flexibility, it is clear that other values of d – particularly those values sufficiently close to $\frac{1}{2}$ – can be accompanied with any of the 13 positional rankings. This is a geometric proof of Theorem 2.6.1 for $\mathbf{w}_s$, $s \in [0, \frac{1}{2})$.

For the remaining procedure, $\mathbf{w}_{\frac{1}{2}}$, the wedge $W_{\frac{1}{2}}^1$ degenerates to the line connecting the midpoints of the left and bottom edges of $Si(3)$; similarly, $W_{\frac{1}{2}}^2$ is the line connecting the midpoints of the right and bottom edges. As true for the plurality method, the wedges form a pointy head and fat bottom, but in the reversed direction. The geometric arguments justifying the theorem are similar to those used for the plurality vote.

2.6.3 Profile Sets

To complete Theorem 2.6.1, we need a geometric way to demonstrate that a $F_4(-, \mathbf{w}_s)$ interior election point (i.e., a specified $\mathbf{q}_s$ and a specified majority $\{c_1, c_2\}$ outcome) is supported by a two-dimensional set of profiles. The construction uses the fact that a given $\{c_1, c_2\}$ majority vote uniquely defines $d = \sum_{j=1}^{3} p_j \in [0, 1]$.

Each profile line in the cone of profiles supporting a designated $\mathbf{q}_s$ (and, hence, passing through $\mathbf{q}_s$) can be described in the following manner. The points $\mathbf{q}_s$ and β_s (the W_s^2 endpoint) determine the slope of the line while the specified d value uniquely determines α_s, the W_s^1 endpoint. Consequently, with a specified d, the two-dimensional profile set is represented by the cone of all line segments passing through $\mathbf{q}_s$; the two-dimensional parameterization of the lines is given by the ways $\beta_s \in W_s^2$ can vary. Alternatively, this parameterization can use $\alpha_s \in W_s^1$.

As true with the other coordinate representations, the cone of β_s values is a convex set defined by its vertices. These vertices are on the three profile lines defined when α_s is one of the three vertices of W_s^1. (See Fig. 2.6.4.) If $d > \frac{1}{2}$, then the pivoting role of $\mathbf{q}_s$ makes the smaller set, the cone in W_s^1, a more descriptive set of supporting profiles.

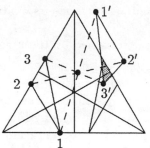

Fig. 2.6.4. The β_s profile values for a specified outcome

Example 2.6.1. In Fig. 2.6.4, $s = \frac{2}{5}$, $\mathbf{q}_s = (0.2, 0.3, 0.5)$ and $d = 0.4$ defines the $\mathbf{w}_{\frac{2}{5}}$ outcome of $c_3 \succ c_2 \succ c_1$ and the pairwise outcome is $c_2 \succ c_1$. Because $\mathbf{q}_s$ is closer to $W_{\frac{2}{5}}^2$ than to $W_{\frac{2}{5}}^1$ (as $d < \frac{1}{2}$), the pivoting action of $\mathbf{q}_s$ on the profile lines makes $W_{\frac{2}{5}}^2$ the better indicator of the size of the cone of profiles.

To find the vertices of the $\beta_{\frac{2}{5}}$ cone, start with $\alpha_{\frac{2}{5}} = [\mathbf{w}_{\frac{2}{5}}]_1 = (\frac{3}{5}, \frac{2}{5}, 0)$; this vertex of the wedge $W_{\frac{2}{5}}^1$ is labeled 1 in Fig. 2.6.4. According to Eq. 2.6.2, the corresponding $\beta_{\frac{2}{5}}$ value satisfies the equation

$$0.4(\frac{3}{5}, \frac{2}{5}, 0) + 0.6\beta_{\frac{2}{5}} = \mathbf{q}_{\frac{2}{5}} = (0.2, 0.3, 0.5),$$

or

$$\beta_{\frac{2}{5}} = (\frac{-2}{30}, \frac{7}{30}, \frac{25}{30}).$$

The negative component, $\frac{-2}{30}$, is meaningless in a profile representation; therefore no profile supports $\mathbf{q}_{\frac{2}{5}}$ where $\alpha_{\frac{2}{5}} = (\frac{3}{5}, \frac{2}{5}, 0)$. Nevertheless, this value is plotted as the point $1'$ in the figure.

To find $1'$ geometrically, draw the dashed line from 1 (the vertex $[\mathbf{w}_{\frac{2}{5}}]_1$) through $\mathbf{q}_{\frac{2}{5}}$; point $1'$ is on this line. (See the figure.) By the definition of d,

$$d = \frac{\|1' - \mathbf{q}_{\frac{2}{5}}\|}{\|1' - \mathbf{q}_{\frac{2}{5}}\| + \|\mathbf{q}_{\frac{2}{5}} - [\mathbf{w}_{\frac{2}{5}}]_1\|}$$

where $\|1' - \mathbf{q}_{\frac{2}{5}}\|$ is the distance from the sought after $1'$ to the designated outcome $\mathbf{q}_{\frac{2}{5}}$. So, $1'$ is on the dashed line a distance $\frac{1}{1-d}\|[\mathbf{w}_{\frac{2}{5}}]_1 - \mathbf{q}_{\frac{2}{5}}\|$ from $[\mathbf{w}_{\frac{2}{5}}]_1$.

Similarly, the vertices $2', 3'$, correspond, respectively, to $\alpha_{\frac{2}{5}} = [\mathbf{w}_{\frac{2}{5}}]_2$, $[\mathbf{w}_{\frac{2}{5}}]_3$. The intersection of the triangle formed by $1', 2', 3'$ with the wedge $W_{\frac{2}{5}}^2$ is the cone of admissible $\beta_{\frac{2}{5}}$ values. By using the four defining vertices of the $\beta_{\frac{2}{5}}$ cone, the corresponding cone of $\alpha_{\frac{2}{5}}$ values can be determined. $\square$

The profile line also can be used to "see" the three-dimensional set of profiles defining a specified $\mathbf{q}_s$. (See Corollary 2.4.9.) Because the outcome of the pairwise vote is not specified, the d value can vary. Therefore, the set of profiles is given by *all* profile lines passing through $\mathbf{q}_s$ with one endpoint in W_s^1 and the other in W_s^2.

For the above $\mathbf{q}_{\frac{2}{5}}$, this set is determined by the three boundary lines passing through $\mathbf{q}_{\frac{2}{5}}$ and a vertex $\{[\mathbf{w}_{\frac{2}{5}}]_j\}_{j=1}^3$; i.e., just extend the dashed lines in the figure to the boundary of the representation triangle. Here, only the 3 - 3' dashed line need to be extended, so the admissible β_s values are all points in W_s^2 above this extended line. The profiles are given by any line segment passing through $\mathbf{q}_{\frac{2}{5}}$ with β_s in this region and $\alpha_s \in W_{\frac{1}{2}}^1$. The significant advantage this geometric approach has over Corollary 2.4.9 is that now we can "see" what profiles lead to specified election outcomes, and we can compare the sets of supporting profiles for different results. (See the exercises.) Also, from the profile representation, we can "see" for each profile which candidate wins the pairwise election – just check whether α_s or β_s is closer to $\mathbf{q}_s$.

How Bad It Can Get. Can c_1 trounce c_2 in a majority vote election and still be plurality ranked below c_2? How decisive of a victory does c_1 need over c_2 to ensure she is not $\mathbf{w}_s$-ranked below c_2? Do the answers change with the choice of $\mathbf{w}_s$? What profile restrictions ensure compatibility between the majority vote and how the pair is $\mathbf{w}_s$-ranked? Answers for these kinds of questions follow from the coordinate representation.

I start by finding the pairwise vote needed by c_1 to ensure that she is plurality ranked above c_2. For instance, if c_1 beats c_2 by receiving 80% of the pairwise vote, will she be ranked above c_2 in the plurality contest? The analysis uses the fact that the pairwise vote is uniquely determined by the value of d. So, the goal is to find a $d = d_0^*$ value which ensures for all α_0, β_0 that the election outcome $\mathbf{q}_0$ is to the left of the $c_1 \sim c_2$ line. So, if it turns out that $d_0^* < .8$, then with the above 80% vote, c_1 is assured of being ranked over c_2. However, if $d_0^* > .8$, then there are profiles where c_1 is plurality ranked below c_2.

We know from the geometry that for a given $d \geq \frac{1}{2}$, c_1 can be $\mathbf{w}_0$-ranked below c_2 only if the profile line has a sufficiently steep slant. The more extreme the slant, the easier it is for the pairwise ranking to be reversed by the plurality vote. Therefore, to compute d_0^*, first find the profile line segment with the steepest slant. This is where $\alpha_0 \in W_0^1$ is as close as possible to the $c_1 \sim c_2$ indifference line while $\beta_0 \in W_0^2$ is as far from this line as possible. If $\mathbf{q}_0$ is the point where this profile line intersects the $c_1 \sim c_2$ line, then $\mathbf{q}_0$ defines the limiting $d = d_0^*$ value. This is the sought after value because d_0^* comes from the extreme situation where the $\mathbf{w}_0$ ranking of the pair is a tie vote. As no other profile line admits such an extreme slant, on any other profile line the point corresponding to d_0^* falls on the $c_1 \succ c_2$ side of the $c_1 \sim c_2$ line.

From the geometry, the extreme slant is when $\alpha_0 = F_4(\mathbf{E}_3, \mathbf{w}_0)$ and $\beta_0 \neq F_4(\mathbf{E}_4, \mathbf{w}_0)$. This choice places α_0 at the c_3 vertex, so the α_0 - β_0 profile line is in W_0^2 (the right hand edge of the representation triangle); thus, $d_0^* = 1$. In words, *no matter how decisive the victory c_1 has over c_2 – even if she wins by as close to an unanimous vote as desired – c_2 could be plurality ranked above c_1!* The geometry of the coordinate representation dictates the kind of profiles allowing such a biased outcome – almost all liberals are type-three.

To illustrate, suppose 9,999 of 10,000 voters have the ranking $c_3 \succ c_1 \succ c_2$ and only the last voter, who happens to be c_2, has the ranking $c_2 \succ c_1 \succ c_3$. There is no debate; the correct group ranking for this profile is $c_3 \succ c_1 \succ c_2$ and everyone, other than c_2, prefers c_1 to c_2. Yet, this obvious conclusion is flaunted by the plurality ranking of $c_3 \succ c_2 \succ c_1$. This, of course, manifests the fact that the plurality method totally ignores information about who is a voter's second-ranked candidate. Thus, c_1 joins a distinguished group of victims of the plurality method's elitist disregard for lower ranked candidates.

As other positional procedures do recognize lower ranked candidates, we must expect a sufficiently strong majority victory for c_1 to ensure that she is $\mathbf{w}_s$-ranked above c_2. The geometric analysis is similar; use extreme choices of $\alpha_s \in W_s^1$ and $\beta_s \in W_s^2$ to find the threshold value d_s^*. As already observed, a manifestation of the $\mathbf{w}_s$, $s \neq 0$, recognition of a voter's second-ranked candidate is the upper limit on W_s^j. This upper limit restricts the slant of the profile line, so we should expect more realistic values for d_s^*. This happens – sometimes. The following assertion simplifies the analysis.

Proposition 2.6.2. *Let $\rho(\mathbf{q})$ be the distance of point $\mathbf{q} \in Si(3)$ to the $c_1 \sim c_2$ indifference line. Then, for*

$$d = \frac{\rho(\beta_s)}{\rho(\alpha_s) + \rho(\beta_s)}, \tag{2.6.3}$$

the election outcome for the profile (α_s, β_s, d) is on the $c_1 \sim c_2$ indifference line.

Proof. The proof is based on the triangle created by passing a vertical line through α_s and an horizontal line through β_s. This large triangle is similar to the smaller, darker one in the figure created by the $c_1 \sim c_2$ indifference line, the α_s - β_s profile line, and the horizontal line passing through β_s. (See Fig. 2.6.5.) If h is the length of the hypotenuse of the first triangle (so h is the length of the α_s - β_s segment), then dh is the length of the hypotenuse of the smaller triangle; it is the distance from β_s to the point on the $c_1 \sim c_2$ line. Eq. 2.6.3 follows by comparing the ratio of the base and hypotenuse of the two similar triangles; a comparison that yields

$$\frac{h}{\rho(\alpha_s) + \rho(\beta_s)} = \frac{dh}{\rho(\beta_s)}. \quad \square$$

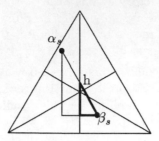

Fig. 2.6.5. Maximizing d values

With Proposition 2.6.2 and the geometry of the wedges, it is easy to find d_s^*. Let α_s be the point in W_s^1 closest to the $c_1 \sim c_2$ indifference line, and β_s the point farthest from this line. While $\beta_s = F_4(\mathbf{E}_5, \mathbf{w}_s)$, the location of α_s varies because the geometry of W_s^1 changes with the value of s. For $s \leq \frac{1}{3}$, the top vertex of W_s^1 is the closest to the indifference line; for $s \geq \frac{1}{3}$, the base vertex of the W_s^1 wedge now is the closest. Separating the two situations is the BC ($s = \frac{1}{3}$). So, for $s \in [0, \frac{1}{3}]$, choose $\alpha_s = F_4(\mathbf{E}_3, \mathbf{w}_s)$, for $s \in [\frac{1}{3}, \frac{1}{2}]$, choose $\alpha_s = F_4(\mathbf{E}_1, \mathbf{w}_s)$.

The choice of α_s, β_s defines an extreme mixture of voter types with a strong $c_2 \succ c_1$ ranking and a weak $c_1 \succ c_2$. Consequently, d_s^* *measures how* $\mathbf{w}_s$ *handles the intensity of comparison information. In particular, the smaller the value of* $1 - d_s^*$, *the less importance the procedure places upon the intensity information.* Adding force is the observation that if d_s has a value near d_s^* and if the $\{c_1, c_2\}$ pairwise ranking is reversed by the $\mathbf{w}_s$-ranking, then the profile is dominated by voters of the two identified types. Thus the reversal is caused because profile information is not being used by the pairwise and/or the positional method.

Theorem 2.6.3. *The value of* d_s^* *is*

$$d_s^* = 1 - s \text{ for } 0 \leq s \leq \frac{1}{3}$$

$$d_s^* = \frac{1-s}{2-3s} \text{ for } \frac{1}{3} \leq s \leq \frac{1}{2}. \qquad (2.6.4)$$

So, suppose in a $\{c_i, c_j\}$ *pairwise election,* c_i *receives the portion* $k \in [0, 1]$ *of the total vote. If* $k < d_s^*$, *then there are profiles where the* $\mathbf{w}_s$ *election ranking has* c_j *ranked above* c_i. *If* $k = d_s^*$, *then either* c_i *is* $\mathbf{w}_s$-*ranked above or tied with* c_j. *If* $k > d_s^*$, *then* c_i *must be* $\mathbf{w}_s$-*ranked above* c_j.

Let's see what all of this means. The normalized version of the voting vector $(4, 1, 0)$ is $\mathbf{w}_{\frac{1}{5}} = (\frac{4}{5}, \frac{1}{5}, 0)$, so $s = \frac{1}{5}$. Thus, according to the theorem, it is possible that even though Gina beats Dave by receiving 79% of the pairwise vote (the relevant fact is that $0.79 < d_{\frac{1}{5}}^* = 1 - s = .8$), it is possible for the $\mathbf{w}_{\frac{1}{5}}$ ranking to have Dave ranked above Gina. If this happens, however, it is because most of Gina's support comes from type-three voters (exhibiting a weak intensity in their Gina-Dave ranking), while Dave's support comes primarily from type-five votes with strong views in their Dave-Gina preferences. Should Gina receive one more than 0.8 of the pairwise vote, she is ensured of being $\mathbf{w}_{\frac{1}{5}}$-ranked above Dave. Similarly, because the voting vector $(1,1,0)$ defines $s = \frac{1}{2}$, it can be that even though Brigid receives 99% of the votes in a contest with Adrian, Adrian is antiplurality ranked above Brigid. (This is because $0.99 < d^*_{\frac{1}{2}} = \frac{1-\frac{1}{2}}{2-3\times\frac{1}{2}} = 1$.) But if Katri beats Spencer with $\frac{2}{3}$ of the vote, then, at the worse, she is at least BC tied with him. (For the BC, $s = \frac{1}{3}$, so $d^*_{\frac{1}{3}} = \frac{2}{3} = 1 - \frac{1}{3}$, or $d^*_{\frac{1}{3}} = \frac{1-\frac{1}{3}}{2-3\times\frac{1}{3}} = \frac{2}{3}$.)

Proof. To use the described choice of α_s, β_s (representing the extreme d values) with Eq. 2.6.3, we need the values of $\rho(\alpha_s)$, $\rho(\beta_s)$. The value of $\rho(\beta_s)$ is the distance between $\beta_s = (0, 1-s, s)$ and $(\frac{1-s}{2}, \frac{1-s}{2}, s)$, the closest point on $c_1 \sim c_2$.[20] For example, if $s \in [\frac{1}{3}, \frac{1}{2}]$, then

$$\rho(\alpha_s) = \rho((1-s, s, 0)) = \sqrt{((1-s) - \frac{1}{2})^2 + (s - \frac{1}{2})^2} = \sqrt{2}\frac{1-2s}{2}$$

while

$$\rho(\beta_s) = \rho((0, 1-s, s)) = \sqrt{(\frac{1-s}{2})^2 + (\frac{1-s}{2})^2 + (s-s)^2} = \sqrt{2}\frac{1-s}{2}.$$

The conclusion follows from Eq. 2.6.3. $\square$

2.6.4 Some Comparisons

Theorem 2.6.3 is disturbing! It means that even though c_1 beats c_2 with, say, 64% of the vote, c_2 could be $\mathbf{w}_s$-ranked above c_1. (But, as shown in the exercises, different profiles might be needed with different positional methods.) On the other hand, the BC has the minimum d^*_s value; a smaller pairwise victory will ensure the same ranking holds with the BC. Consequently, *if we desire maximum compatibility between how a pair is ranked in a pairwise contest and how it is ranked in a positional election, we must use the BC.* This assertion about the BC is consistent with the crude measure, $1 - d^*$, of attention paid by $\mathbf{w}_s$ to the intensity of pairwise comparisons.

Corollary 2.6.4. *If c_i beats c_j by receiving $\frac{2}{3}$ of the vote, then, at the worse, she is ensured of being BC tied with c_j. With any other choice of $\mathbf{w}_s$, there are profiles where c_j is $\mathbf{w}_s$ ranked above c_i. Indeed, there are profiles where c_i can beat c_j with as close to an unanimous vote as desired, yet c_j is plurality, or antiplurality ranked above c_i.*

The positional group representation makes it easy to find profiles where the plurality and antiplurality outcomes are indefensible – the election outcome denies what is obviously the group's true ranking. An example for the plurality

---

[20] For a point to be on the indifference line, the c_1, c_2 values must agree. To define the shortest distance, the selected point and β_s must define a line orthogonal to the indifference line. This condition requires both points to have the same c_3 value of s.

ranking is given above; similar examples hold for the antiplurality method. For instance, it follows from the geometry that antiplurality extreme situations involve type-two and six voters. So, suppose 9,999,999 of the 10,000,000 voters have the conservative ranking $c_2 \succ c_1 \succ c_3$, and the last voter has the ranking $c_1 \succ c_3 \succ c_2$. While the group's ranking should be $c_2 \succ c_1 \succ c_3$, the antiplurality ranking is $c_1 \succ c_2 \succ c_3$.

Upon reflection, these assertions about the plurality and antiplurality outcomes should not be surprising. While the plurality vote totally ignores the distinction between a voter's second and third-ranked candidates, the antiplurality method discards all information differentiating a voter's top and second-ranked candidate. Therefore, whenever the discarded information dominates or is critical for the profile, the outcome is suspect. (For each method, $1 - d^* = 0$.)

The symmetry of the s values defining d_s^* indicates that the BC ($s = \frac{1}{3}$) serves as a pivot point for positional voting methods. Methods for s near zero place little stock on the distinctions between a voter's second and third-ranked candidates; methods for s near $\frac{1}{2}$ place little value on distinctions between a voter's first and second-ranked candidates. Moreover, each admissible d^* value is be attained by a $s \in [0, \frac{1}{3}]$, and a $s' \in [\frac{1}{3}, \frac{1}{2}]$; in fact, $\mathbf{w}_s^r = \mathbf{w}_{s'}$. (See the exercises.)

2.6.5 How Likely Is It?

Common sense dictates that procedures with larger d_s^* values admit larger sets of profiles that cause these election anomalies; i.e., there is a stronger probability that the $\{c_1, c_2\}$ pairwise and $\mathbf{w}_s$-rankings disagree. Conversely, the BC (with its minimum d_s^* value) should minimize the likelihood that such contradictory outcomes occur. This intuition is accurate and the proof follows from the coordinate representation. (A reader who accepts this assertion and wishes to avoid the following technical discussion should skip to the subsection "Further Comparisons" following Fig. 2.6.6.)

With our ability to "see" profile sets, one way to determine which method is most likely to create paradoxes is to compare the cones of profiles leading to specified problems; the issue considered here is where the $\mathbf{w}_s$ ranking of $c_1 \succ c_2$ disagrees with the pairwise ranking $c_2 \succ c_1$. Following the approach of Example 2.5.2e with the fat triangle, the relevant set of election outcomes is the portion of the shaded region of Fig. 2.6.2 on the front half of the $[-1, 1]$ edge ($d \le \frac{1}{2}$) and on the left side of the representation triangle (where the $\mathbf{w}_s$ ranking is $c_1 \succ c_2$). As this set is convex, so is the supporting set of profiles. Thus, we just need to find the profile vertices. For reasons related to why Theorem 2.6.3 is specified in terms of two sets of s values, the probability analysis needs to be broken into the cases $s \le \frac{1}{3}$ and $s \ge \frac{1}{3}$. I will do the first case; the second is left to the reader. (The outcome for $\mathbf{w}_s$ and $\mathbf{w}_s^r$ are symmetrically equivalent.)

The fat triangle geometry is used only to identify the boundary outcomes for this set; the coordinate representation is used to find the corresponding profiles. For example, one edge in the outcome space is where both the pairwise and positional outcome is $c_1 \sim c_2$; this requires $d = \frac{1}{2}$. What we want, then, is to find all profiles where $d = \frac{1}{2}$ and $\mathbf{q}_s$ is on the $c_1 \sim c_2$ line. The vertex profiles have either α_s or β_s at an unanimity outcome and the remaining point at an extreme allowable position. Using these conditions and the coordinate representations, the vertex profiles can be found. The three that define a horizontal profile line are

$$\frac{1}{2}(\mathbf{E}_1 + \mathbf{E}_6), \quad \frac{1}{2}(\mathbf{E}_2 + \mathbf{E}_5), \quad \frac{1}{2}(\mathbf{E}_3 + \mathbf{E}_4),$$

and the two that allow a slanty profile line are

$$\frac{1}{2}(\mathbf{E}_1 + \frac{s}{1-s}\mathbf{E}_4 + \frac{1-3s}{1-2s}\mathbf{E}_5), \quad \frac{1}{2}(\mathbf{E}_6 + \frac{s}{1-s}\mathbf{E}_3 + \frac{1-3s}{1-2s}\mathbf{E}_2).$$

The first of the last two vertices is found in the following manner. Placing $\alpha_s = [\mathbf{w}_s]_1$, one extreme choice for β_s satisfying the specified constraints is $\beta_s = [\mathbf{w}_s]_6$. Now, draw a line from $[\mathbf{w}_s]_6$ perpendicular to the base of the representation triangle; a "similar triangle" argument of the kind used with Fig. 2.6.5 proves that any β_s value on this line satisfies the conditions. (Remember, $s \leq \frac{1}{3}$; these comments don't hold for $s > \frac{1}{3}$. For $s \geq \frac{1}{3}$, $\beta_s = [\mathbf{w}_s]_6$ is replaced with $\beta_s = [\mathbf{w}_s]_4$.) The intersection point of this line and the edge of the representation triangle defines the second extreme β_s value; this defines the first of the two extra profile vertices. The other one is determined in a similar fashion.

The next edge for the set of the election outcomes is where the shaded region of the fat triangle intersects the plane defined by the tied pairwise outcome $c_1 \sim c_2$. With profile coordinates, the profile vertices are where $d = \frac{1}{2}$ and there is an extreme $\mathbf{w}_s$ outcome with $c_1 \succ c_2$. So, for instance, if $\alpha_s = [\mathbf{w}_s]_1$, and β_s is placed on the edge defined by $[\mathbf{w}_s]_4$, $[\mathbf{w}_s]_5$, then we need to find the extreme choices of β_s with $d = \frac{1}{2}$ so that $\mathbf{q}_s$ is to the left of the $c_1 \sim c_2$ line. Using algebra, this leads to the two profile vertices

$$\frac{1}{2}(\mathbf{E}_1 + \mathbf{E}_4), \quad \frac{1}{2}(\mathbf{E}_1 + \frac{1-3s}{1-2s}\mathbf{E}_5 + \frac{s}{1-2s}\mathbf{E}_4).$$

One of these profiles vertices is an earlier one; the new vertices are

$$\frac{1}{2}[\mathbf{E}_2 + \mathbf{E}_6], \quad \frac{1}{2}[\mathbf{E}_2 + \mathbf{E}_4].$$

The final edge of the set of outcomes is the front part of the figure where the $\mathbf{w}_s$ $c_1 \sim c_2$ outcomes pass through the shaded region for $d < 1$. The extreme profiles are where the $\mathbf{w}_s$ relative ranking is $c_1 \sim c_2$ and $d < \frac{1}{2}$ has its smallest value. Using Eq. 2.6.4, they are

$$\frac{s}{1-s}\mathbf{E}_1 + \frac{1-2s}{1-s}\mathbf{E}_4, \quad \frac{1-2s}{2-3s}\mathbf{E}_2 + \frac{1-s}{2-3s}\mathbf{E}_6, \quad s\mathbf{E}_2 + (1-s)\mathbf{E}_4.$$

Thus, a profile has this election effect iff it can be expressed as a convex combination of the above profiles. Observe how the profile set changes with the choice of $\mathbf{w}_s$.

Those vertices not independent of s are on a line segment connecting vertices for the BC and plurality vote. Thus, one of these two procedures defines the profile region with maximum volume and the other has the minimum (at least for $s \in [0, \frac{1}{3}]$); everything else is between. To show that the plurality method maximizes and the BC minimizes the probability of this election paradox, just compute and compare both five-dimensional volumes. (This can be done with, say, integral calculus.) Instead, I will give a geometric illustration emphasizing the intuition.

From the above, the relevant profile vertices for $\mathbf{w}_0$ are

$$\frac{1}{2}(\mathbf{E}_1 + \mathbf{E}_6), \frac{1}{2}(\mathbf{E}_2 + \mathbf{E}_5), \frac{1}{2}(\mathbf{E}_3 + \mathbf{E}_4), \frac{1}{2}(\mathbf{E}_2 + \mathbf{E}_6)$$

$$\frac{1}{2}(\mathbf{E}_1 + \mathbf{E}_4), \frac{1}{2}(\mathbf{E}_1 + \mathbf{E}_5), \mathbf{E}_4$$

The first six vertices also serve for the BC. In addition, the BC has the vertices

$$\frac{1}{2}(\mathbf{E}_3 + \mathbf{E}_6), \frac{1}{3}\mathbf{E}_2 + \frac{2}{3}\mathbf{E}_6, \frac{1}{3}\mathbf{E}_2 + \frac{2}{3}\mathbf{E}_4.$$

The first five vertices on midpoints on five of the 15 possible $Si(6)$ edges, so both figures are geometrically similar. The edge of the hull for $\mathbf{w}_0$ connecting $\mathbf{E}_4$ with $\frac{1}{2}(\mathbf{E}_2 + \mathbf{E}_4)$ has one of the extra BC vertices, $\frac{1}{3}\mathbf{E}_2 + \frac{2}{3}\mathbf{E}_4 = \frac{2}{3}(\frac{1}{2}(\mathbf{E}_2 + \mathbf{E}_4)) + \frac{1}{3}\mathbf{E}_4$ near the common base region. In fact, it is so close to the common region that the added volume created by this BC vertex is less than a third of that created by the plurality vertex $\mathbf{E}_4$. As the second region created by the last BC vertex is geometrically similar, the sum of these two volumes is less than that added by the plurality. Consequently, the volume of the profile set for the BC outcome is smaller than that for the plurality.

(For intuition why this is so, see Fig. 2.6.6. The dark region represents a common region defined by midpoints. The light region of the first and third triangles are where a simplex vertex is added; this represents the plurality and antiplurality methods. The middle one, where the vertices are along an edge but not even to the midpoint of the regions, corresponds to the BC. As this point is not even at the midpoint, the area is less than half.)

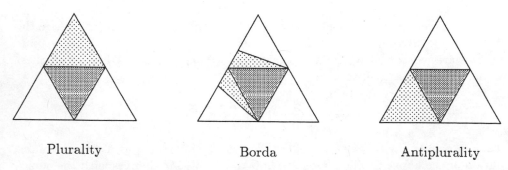

Plurality   Borda   Antiplurality

Fig. 2.6.6. Comparison of appended regions

Further Comparisons. As emphasized, we are faced with two informational problems: pairwise elections ignore the intensity of pairwise comparisons and positional place varying emphasis on the voter's second-ranked candidate. For positional methods, it isn't obvious whether a procedure over or undercompensates the information about a voter's second-choice. On the other hand, Theorem 2.6.3 and the above comments about the likelihood of a conflict in a pair's positional and pairwise ranking provide evidence that $\mathbf{w}_{\frac{1}{3}}$, the BC, is the optimal way for a positional method to capture this "second-choice" data. The informational reason for this positive assertion is that the BC is the only positional method that provides equal distinction between a voter's first and second-ranked candidates and second and third-ranked candidates.

As shown by the geometry, the profiles, such as a division between type-one and five voters, define the extreme setting for positional voting method; these situations combine extreme differences between the intensity of a particular pairwise comparison and who is top-ranked. Hence, another way to compare positional voting methods is to compare the threshold required with such extreme profiles before c_1 is ranked above c_2.

Procedure	Vote
Pope Selection	One more than $\frac{2}{3}$
Condorcet Improvement	One more than $\frac{2}{3}$
Borda Count	One more than $\frac{2}{3}$
$\mathbf{w}_s$, $s \in [0, \frac{1}{3})$	One more than $1 - s > \frac{2}{3}$
$\mathbf{w}_s$, $s \in (\frac{1}{3}, \frac{1}{2}]$	One more than $\frac{1-s}{2-3s} > \frac{2}{3}$

Thus the Catholic Church, Borda, and the Condorcet Improvement agree; *the other procedures impose stricter requirements upon the type-one voters before c_1 can prevail in the resulting ranking.* Again, this should be expected because these other methods place less value upon the intensity information.

As noted, for other profiles, the BC makes it easier for the pairwise winner to be BC ranked in the same way. Therefore, the arguments used to criticize the plurality and antiplurality methods do not apply to the BC. In fact, by use of the linearity of voting processes (such as used in the above probability argument), it follows that each positional voting method is a weighted compromise between the desirable manner the BC handles profiles and the deplorable way the plurality (or antiplurality) method can disregard voters' beliefs.

The Two-Thirds Rule. Sure, c_1 can win 99% of the majority vote over c_2 and still be plurality ranked below c_2, but when this happens, the plurality ranking *must be $c_3 \succ c_2 \succ c_1$.* After all, the only way $\mathbf{q}_0$ can be kept to the right of the $c_1 \sim c_2$ indifference line with $d = 0.99$ is if both α_0 and $\mathbf{q}_0$ are near the c_3 vertex. So, even if c_1 beats c_2 by a large margin, she may be $\mathbf{w}_s$-ranked below c_2. On the other hand, her pairwise victory margin may be sufficiently large to preclude certain $\mathbf{w}_s$ rankings from occurring. The natural issue, then, is to determine which pairwise majority votes prevent all 13 $\mathbf{w}_s$-rankings from occurring.

Again, the geometric way to resolve this problem is to find an extreme profile with the steepest slant that just barely satisfies the conditions. This means the profile line must pass through $\mathcal{I}$. So, on such a line with an extreme slope, find the $d = d^{\#}$ value where $\mathbf{q}_s = \mathcal{I} = (\frac{1}{3}, \frac{1}{3}, \frac{1}{3})$. By finding the extreme $d^{\#}$ value, $d > d^{\#}$ can never realize $\mathcal{I}$, or any ranking that requires the profile line to move toward one side or the other of the indifference point. Similarly, if $d = d^{\#}$, then any positioning of the profile line does not allow the distinguished point $\mathbf{q}_s$ to fall below $\mathcal{I}$ – not all rankings can be obtained.

This critical $d^{\#}$ value is found the same way as above; set β_s at $F_4(\mathbf{E}_5, \mathbf{w}_s)$, pass the profile line through $\mathbf{q}_s = (\frac{1}{3}, \frac{1}{3}, \frac{1}{3})$, and let α_s be the first boundary point of ∂W_s^1 that meets the profile line. The values of α_s, $\mathbf{q}_s$ determine the threshold $d^{\#}$ value. Surprisingly, the value is independent of the choice of s.

Theorem 2.6.5. *If c_i beats c_j in a majority vote by receiving at least $\frac{2}{3}$ of the vote, then there are restrictions on the choice of the associated $\mathbf{w}_s$ ranking. If c_i receives at least one vote more than $\frac{2}{3}$ of the total majority vote, then it is impossible for the $\mathbf{w}_s$ ranking to be $\mathcal{I}$. On the other hand, for any choice of $\mathbf{w}_s$, $\epsilon > 0$, and a ranking of the three candidates, there is a profile where c_i beats c_j by receiving at least $\frac{2}{3} - \epsilon$ of the vote (but less than $\frac{2}{3}$ of the vote) and the $\mathbf{w}_s$ ranking is the chosen ranking.*

Again, from the geometry, it is easy to determine the admissible rankings if a candidate does well in a majority vote election.

So far the analysis has emphasized the variable d; similar approaches can be used with the α_s, β_s variables. For example, suppose whenever c_1 beats c_2 by winning at least 55% of the vote, we want her to be $\mathbf{w}_s$-ranked above c_2. Here the $d = .55$ value is specified, the goal is to find profile restrictions on α_s, β_s that realize the stated objective. Such restrictions are obtained in a straightforward manner.

2.6.6 How Varied Does It Get?

We know from Sect. 2.4 that two different positional methods can define radically different election outcomes for the same profile. From this section, we now know that the ranking of a positional voting procedure and the majority ranking of a particular pair can be chosen at random. These results can be combined into a single statement.

Theorem 2.6.6. *Let $\mathbf{w}_{s_1} \neq \mathbf{w}_{s_2}$ be given. Choose any two rankings of the three candidates and any ranking of the pair $\{c_1, c_2\}$. There is a profile where the $\mathbf{w}_{s_j}$ ranking is the jth selected one, $j = 1, 2$, and the pairwise majority outcome is the selected ranking of a pair. Indeed, there exists a positive value ρ so that if $\mathbf{q}_i \in \mathcal{B}(\rho, \mathcal{I})$, $i = 1, 2$ and $q \in (-\rho, \rho)$ are chosen, then there exists a (unique) profile $\mathbf{p}$ so that*

$$f(\mathbf{p}, \mathbf{w}_{s_1}) = \mathbf{q}_1, \quad f(\mathbf{p}, \mathbf{w}_{s_2}) = \mathbf{q}_2, \quad f_{\{c_1, c_2\}}(\mathbf{p}) = q.$$

Outline of the Proof. One way to see the truth of this assertion is to first prove the theorem for $\mathbf{w}_0$, $\mathbf{w}_{\frac{1}{2}}$ and then use the procedure line. This is an algebraic exercise which requires showing the independence of the six equations (two for the plurality method, two for the antiplurality method, one for the pairwise vote, and one for the constraint equation) in six variables. The details are left to the reader. A more general, geometric argument is developed below. $\square$

Election outcomes can be more random than previously suggested! Theorem 2.6.6 asserts that there need not be any relationship between the positional and $\{c_1, c_2\}$ pairwise rankings. This means, for instance, that profiles can be found so that the ranking for *all* choices of $\mathbf{w}_s$ is $c_2 \succ c_3 \succ c_1$ while the pairwise ranking is the reversed $c_1 \succ c_2$. Indeed, by choosing $\mathbf{q}_1 = \mathbf{q}_2$ in Theorem 2.6.6 (as the procedure line becomes the point $\mathbf{q}_1$), the $\mathbf{w}_s$ outcomes share the same normalized tally!

Because these are surprising conclusions, the next goal is to find a geometric way to characterize the supporting set of profiles. By doing so, we obtain much more; we end up with a *geometric connection between the procedure line and the three pairwise election outcomes!* Consequently, it becomes possible to go beyond the restriction of Theorem 2.6.6 and its single pair of candidates to discuss what happens with all three pairs. (The algebraic proof of Theorem 2.6.6 uses a full system of six equations in six unknowns, so the following extension to all pairs of candidates is, by no means, obvious.)

2.6.7 Procedure Lines and Cyclic Coordinates

The relationship between the procedure line and the rankings of all three pairs of candidates is based on the fact that a plurality outcome $\mathbf{q}_0 = (q_1, q_2, q_3)$ is supported both by an odd and an even voter profile: $\mathbf{p}_o = (q_1, 0, q_3, 0, q_2)$ and $\mathbf{p}_e = (0, q_1, 0, q_3, 0, q_2)$. As a somewhat similar statement holds for all $\mathbf{w}_s$, this suggests characterizing a profile in terms of the positional outcomes of the odd and even voters. Namely, for a given profile $\mathbf{p}$, first find the $\mathbf{w}_s$ outcome if only the odd voters vote (denoted by α_s^c), if only the even voters vote (β_s^c), and then determine the portion of all voters that are even voters (d^c). The superscript reflects the dependency of this system upon the cyclic coordinates.

Analytically, the *cyclic-positional* coordinate representation for $\mathbf{p} \in Si(6)$ is

$$d^c = p_1 + p_3 + p_5,$$

$$a_j = \frac{p_j}{d^c} \text{ for } j = 1, 3, 5, \quad b_j = \frac{p_j}{1 - d^c} \text{ for } j = 2, 4, 6;$$

$$\alpha_s^c = \sum_{j=1,3,5} a_j [\mathbf{w}_s]_j, \quad \beta_s^c = \sum_{j=2,4,6} b_j [\mathbf{w}_s]_j \tag{2.6.5}$$

The combined distinguished point and outcome is

$$\mathbf{q}_s = f(\mathbf{p}, \mathbf{w}_s) = d^c \alpha_s^c + (1 - d^c) \beta_s^c. \tag{2.6.6}$$

The procedure line, of course, is uniquely defined by the values for $s = 0, \frac{1}{2}$. Actually, thanks to a simple geometric relationship between $(\alpha_{\frac{1}{2}}^c, \beta_{\frac{1}{2}}^c)$ and (α_0^c, β_0^c), once α_0^c, β_0^c are specified, the procedure line can be determined!

This makes sense; after all, the unique odd voter profile supporting α_0^c also defines $\alpha_{\frac{1}{2}}^c$. What is interesting is the simple geometric way $\alpha_{\frac{1}{2}}^c$ is constructed from α_0^c. To understand this relationship, start with the unanimity profile $\mathbf{p} = \mathbf{E}_1$ which defines $\alpha_0^c = (1, 0, 0)$ and $\alpha_{\frac{1}{2}}^c = (\frac{1}{2}, \frac{1}{2}, 0)$. The key is that the three points, $\alpha_0^c, \alpha_{\frac{1}{2}}^c, \mathcal{I}$, form a 30°- 60° - 90° right triangle. This same triangular description holds for the other two unanimity profiles $\mathbf{E}_j$, $j = 3, 5$. So, because α_0^c is a convex sum of (odd) unanimity outcomes, *the three points $\alpha_0^c, \alpha_{\frac{1}{2}}^c, \mathcal{I}$ always form a 30°- 60° - 90° right triangle* called the α^c triangle.

The construction of $\alpha_{\frac{1}{2}}^c$ is immediate. Once α_0^c is known, the $\alpha_{\frac{1}{2}}^c$ point is the remaining vertex of the α^c triangle. The orientation of the triangle is described next.

> To obtain the α^c triangle, draw a line segment from $\mathcal{I}$ that forms a $+60^\circ$ angle with the line defined by α_0^c-$\mathcal{I}$. The vertex $\alpha_{\frac{1}{2}}^c$ is the point on this new line that is distance $\frac{1}{2} \|\alpha_0^c - \mathcal{I}\|$ from $\mathcal{I}$.

To define the β^c triangle, so that $\beta_{\frac{1}{2}}^c$ can be found from β_0^c, a rotation of -60° is used instead of 60°. The proof of this assertion follows by examining what happens with the unanimity profiles for even voter types. For instance, $\mathbf{E}_2$ defines $\beta_0^c = (1, 0, 0)$ and $\beta_{\frac{1}{2}}^c = (\frac{1}{2}, 0, \frac{1}{2})$, the defined angle relative to the vertex $\mathcal{I}$ is -60°. These results are summarized in the next statement.

Proposition 2.6.7. *For the plurality point $(\alpha_0^c, \beta_0^c, d^c)$, the antiplurality representation $(\alpha_{\frac{1}{2}}^c, \beta_{\frac{1}{2}}^c, d^c)$ can be constructed in the following manner. The point $\alpha_{\frac{1}{2}}^c$ is the third vertex of the 30°-60°-90° α^c triangle; the other two vertices are $\mathcal{I}$ and α_0^c. The angle at vertex α_0^c is 30°; the directed angle from the α_0^c-$\mathcal{I}$ edge to the $\mathcal{I}$-$\alpha_{\frac{1}{2}}^c$ edge is 60°. Similarly, $\beta_{\frac{1}{2}}^c$ is the third vertex of a 30°-60°-90° β^c triangle where the other two vertices are $\mathcal{I}$ and β_0^c. The angle at vertex β_0^c is 30°; the directed angle from the edge α_0^c-$\mathcal{I}$ to the edge $\mathcal{I}$-$\alpha_{\frac{1}{2}}^c$ is -60°.*

The conclusion of Theorem 2.6.7 is represented in Fig. 2.6.7. In this figure, if $d^c = \frac{1}{2}$, then $\mathbf{q}_0$ is the midpoint of the line connecting α_0^c and β_0^c, so the plurality outcome is in $\mathcal{R}(1)$. Similarly, because $\mathbf{q}_{\frac{1}{2}}$ is the midpoint of the line connecting $\beta_{\frac{1}{2}}^c$ with $\alpha_{\frac{1}{2}}^c$, this outcome is in $\mathcal{R}(4)$. The procedure line is, of course, the segment connecting $\mathbf{q}_0$ and $\mathbf{q}_{\frac{1}{2}}$. By changing the size and orientation of each triangle (by changing the α_0, β_0 values), it is possible to construct a set of profiles where the procedure line passes through all seven ranking regions. Indeed, by using these four degrees of freedom (the orientation and size of each triangle), all sorts of conclusions about procedure lines are forthcoming. (A degenerate situation arises when $\alpha_0^c = \mathcal{I}$ (or, $\beta_0^c = \mathcal{I}$), as the triangle α^c is the point $\mathcal{I}$ – but the profile is $\frac{1}{3}(\mathbf{E}_1 + \mathbf{E}_3 + \mathbf{E}_5)$, so this outcome is expected.)

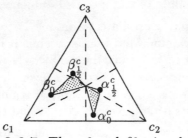

Fig. 2.6.7. The α^c and β^c triangles

Call the edge of the α^c triangle opposite $\mathcal{I}$ (the line connecting α_0^c with $\alpha_{\frac{1}{2}}^c$) the α^c *procedure line*; similarly, the β^c *procedure line* is the edge of the β^c triangle opposite the $\mathcal{I}$ vertex. To justify these terms, mimic the derivation of Eq. 2.4.3 to obtain

$$\alpha_s^c = (1 - 2s)\alpha_0^c + 2s\alpha_{\frac{1}{2}}^c,$$
$$\beta_s^c = (1 - 2s)\beta_0^c + 2s\beta_{\frac{1}{2}}^c. \tag{2.6.8}$$

Because $\mathbf{q}_s = d^c\alpha_s^c + (1 - d^c)\beta_s^c$, Eq. 2.6.8 provides a geometric way to construct the profile line to obtain desired outcomes.

Clearly, this coordinate representation offers a new way to analyze election outcomes. Because α_0^c, β_0^c, d^c uniquely determine $\mathbf{q}_0$ and $\mathbf{q}_{\frac{1}{2}}$, these coordinates also uniquely determine the procedure line. As α_0^c, β_0^c, d^c are determined by the size and positions of the triangles, the analysis reduces to manipulating these triangles. An example of how this is done follows.

Example 2.6.2. The best way to develop skill in using these coordinate systems is to experiment by varying the α^c and β^c triangles to obtain various conclusions about profile lines. To start with a simple problem, suppose we want to find all profiles where $\mathbf{q}_0 = \mathbf{q}_{\frac{1}{2}} = \mathcal{I}$; that is, we want to characterize the profile set where the procedure line is the point $\mathcal{I}$. As noted above, if only one point, say α_0^c, is $\mathcal{I}$, then the corresponding triangle α^c is the point $\mathcal{I}$. As $\beta_0^c \neq \mathcal{I}$, the profile line segments α_0^c-β_0^c and $\alpha_{\frac{1}{2}}^c$-$\beta_{\frac{1}{2}}^c$ both start at $\mathcal{I}$ and emanate into the representation triangle. So, the only way the desired outcome can occur is if $d^c = 1$; there are no even voters.

Next, assume that neither α_0^c nor β_0^c are at $\mathcal{I}$. To ensure that $\mathbf{q}_0 = \mathcal{I}$, the profile line connecting α_0^c and β_0^c must pass through $\mathcal{I}$; that is, $\mathcal{I}$ separates these points. In turn, the different orientations of the α^c and β^c triangles force $\alpha_{\frac{1}{2}}^c$ and $\beta_{\frac{1}{2}}^c$ to be on the same side of the α_0^c - β_0^c profile line. Therefore, the $\alpha_{\frac{1}{2}}^c$ - $\beta_{\frac{1}{2}}^c$ profile line cannot pass through $\mathcal{I}$; an assertion that violates the requirement $\mathbf{q}_{\frac{1}{2}} = \mathcal{I}$.

Thus, the only possibility is $\alpha_0^c = \beta_0^c = \mathcal{I}$ and $d^c \in [0, 1]$. This line,

$$d(\frac{1}{3}, 0, \frac{1}{3}, 0, \frac{1}{3}, 0) + (1 - d)(0, \frac{1}{3}, 0, \frac{1}{3}, 0, \frac{1}{3}) \in Si(6),$$

is the set of all profiles leading to the specified outcome.

A useful cyclic-positional coordinate technique is to start with a "regular" configuration, and then examine what happens when it is perturbed. I will illustrate this by showing how to construct the profile sets where the procedure line is a point and where the procedure line crosses seven different ranking regions.

One regular configuration is where the α^c and β^c triangles abut along specified legs. For instance, place the α^c and β^c triangles so that the $\alpha^c_{\frac{1}{2}}$ and $\beta^c_{\frac{1}{2}}$ legs (from $\mathcal{I}$) coincide; the geometry forces the α^c_0 and β^c_0 points to be on opposite sides of this line. (See Fig. 2.6.8.) Let $\mathbf{q}$ be the point of intersection between the lines connecting α^c_0 - β^c_0 and $\alpha^c_{\frac{1}{2}}$-$\beta^c_{\frac{1}{2}}$.

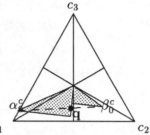

Fig. 2.6.8. A profile defining a singular procedure line

By construction, the triangles α^c_0 - $\alpha^c_{\frac{1}{2}}$ - $\mathbf{q}$ and β^c_0 - $\beta^c_{\frac{1}{2}}$ - $\mathbf{q}$ are similar. Because the ratio of congruent legs from each triangle must agree, we have that

$$\frac{\|\alpha^c_{\frac{1}{2}} - \mathbf{q}\|}{\|\beta^c_{\frac{1}{2}} - \mathbf{q}\|} = \frac{\|\alpha^c_0 - \mathbf{q}\|}{\|\beta^c_0 - \mathbf{q}\|}.$$

Adding unity to both sides and expressing the values in fractional form leads to

$$\frac{1}{d} = \frac{\|\alpha^c_{\frac{1}{2}} - \mathbf{q}\| + \|\mathbf{q} - \beta^c_{\frac{1}{2}}\|}{\|\beta^c_{\frac{1}{2}} - \mathbf{q}\|} = \frac{\|\alpha^c_0 - \mathbf{q}\| + \|\mathbf{q} - \beta^c_0\|}{\|\beta^c_0 - \mathbf{q}\|}. \qquad (2.6.9)$$

The numerator of each fraction is the distance from α^c_s to β^c_s, $s = 0, \frac{1}{2}$. Therefore, it follows by cross multiplying that if $d^c = d$, then $\mathbf{q} = \mathbf{q}_0 = \mathbf{q}_{\frac{1}{2}}$. In other words, *this configuration where the α^c and β^c triangles abut along the antiplurality legs and where the value of d is determined by the geometry of intersecting profile lines, always defines the singular setting where the procedure line is a point.*

Conversely, if the procedure line is the point $\mathbf{q}$, then $\mathbf{q} = \mathbf{q}_0 = \mathbf{q}_{\frac{1}{2}}$. This common point must be the intersection of the plurality profile line connecting α^c_0 - β^c_0, and the antiplurality profile line connecting $\alpha^c_{\frac{1}{2}}$-$\beta^c_{\frac{1}{2}}$. The d^c value is common to both profile representations and opposing angles formed by intersecting lines are equal, so similar triangles are formed. Using related geometric arguments, it now follows that the only way the intersection point is both $\mathbf{q}_0$ and $\mathbf{q}_{\frac{1}{2}}$ (where the same value of d^c applies) is if the two triangles abut in the above described manner.

The above discussion provides a simple way to find all profiles where the procedure line is a specified $\mathbf{q}$. First, draw the line from $\mathcal{I}$ through $\mathbf{q}$. Next, draw two lines passing through $\mathcal{I}$; the first forms an angle of $-60°$ (the locus of possible locations for α_0^c) and the second forms an angle of $60°$ (the locus of possible positions for β_o^c). Each point on the first line is a choice of α_0^c and the corresponding β_0^c is at the intersection of the $60°$ line with the line from α_0^c through $\mathbf{q}$ (the dashed line in Fig. 2.6.8). Observe the pivoting role played by $\mathbf{q}$; if either α_0^c or β_0^c is near the base of the representation triangle, the other point must be closer to $\mathcal{I}$.

In Sect. 2.4, I asserted that a procedure line is supported by a one-dimensional set of profiles; it now is possible to describe this profile set when the procedure line is a point $\mathbf{q}$. In terms of cyclic-positional coordinates, the vertices for this convex profile set correspond to where α_0^c and β_0^c are on an edge of the representation triangle. For example, if $\mathbf{q} = (0.4, 0.4, 0.2)$ then $\alpha_0^c \in \mathcal{R}(c_1 \succ c_2 \sim c_3)$, $\beta_0^c \in \mathcal{R}(c_2 \succ c_1 \sim c_3)$. The extreme value $\alpha_0^c = (1, 0, 0)$ sets up the equation $d^c(1, 0, 0) + (1 - d^c)(a, 1 - a, a) = (0.4, 0.4, 0.2)$ in the two unknowns d^c, a. The solution is $\beta_0^c = (a, 1 - a, a) = (0.25, 0.50, 0.25)$ and $d^c = 0.8$. Converting this profile representation to a more traditional form leads (via Eq. 2.6.5) to $\mathbf{p}_1 = (0.2, 0.2, 0, 0.2, 0, 0.4)$. Similarly, the other profile is $\mathbf{p}_2 = (0.4, 0, 0.2, 0, 0.2, 0.2)$. Consequently, the procedure line $PL(\mathbf{p}) = (0.4, 0.4, 0.2)$ iff $\mathbf{p} = t\mathbf{p}_1 + (1 - t)\mathbf{p}_2$ for $t \in [0, 1]$.

To demonstrate how to perturb a regular configuration, I will create profiles where the procedure line meets seven ranking regions where, say, $\mathbf{q}_{\frac{1}{2}} \in \mathcal{R}(4)$ while $\mathbf{q}_0 \in \mathcal{R}(1)$. Start with the regular configuration with the $\beta_{\frac{1}{2}}^c$ leg of the β^c triangle on the $c_3 \succ c_1 \sim c_2$ ranking region while the $\alpha_{\frac{1}{2}}^c$ leg is on the $c_2 \sim c_3 \succ c_1$ ranking region. These are the boundaries of $\mathcal{R}(4)$, so any $d^c \neq 0, 1$ defines a $\mathbf{q}_0 \in \mathcal{R}(4)$.

The geometry forces the plurality legs of the triangles to be on the $c_1 \sim c_3$ indifference line where $\beta_0^c \in \mathcal{R}(c_1 \sim c_3 \succ c_2)$ while $\alpha_0^c \in \mathcal{R}(c_2 \succ c_1 \sim c_3)$. (To see why this is so, construct the α^c, β^c triangles in a representation triangle.) Thus, for all d^c, $\mathbf{q}_0$ is on the $c_1 \sim c_3$ indifference line. Therefore, a small change in the orientation of either (or both) triangles breaks the tie vote. For instance, we could move α_0^c away from the c_2 vertex along the c_1-c_2 edge, or move β_0^c toward the c_1 vertex. In either case, the α_0^c - β_0^c profile line now crosses $\mathcal{R}(1)$. Thus, an appropriate choice of d^c defines the desired profile. (Indeed, the beverage example profile corresponds to a β_0^c perturbation.) I leave it to the reader to find the line of profiles that supports a specified $\mathbf{q}_0$ and $\mathbf{q}_{\frac{1}{2}}$.

With a d^c value to place $\mathbf{q}_0 = \mathcal{I}$, the original "regular" construction defines a boundary profile for the profile set where the procedure line crosses seven regions. Another boundary profile is where the plurality legs are along the edges of the $\mathcal{R}(1)$ region. Continuing in this way, it is not difficult to find all boundary profiles. This makes it possible to compare the size of the profile set where the procedure line crosses seven regions with the set of profiles where the procedure line is in a single ranking region. The results are surprising (and even more so once the number of candidates reaches, say, 10 or 11.) I leave this as an interesting exercise for the readers comfortable with the geometric constructions. □

Procedure Lines and Pairwise Rankings. The next goal is to relate the α_0^c, β_0^c outcomes to the pairwise rankings. This can be done because there is a one-to-one correspondence between points $\alpha \in T_1$ (from the cyclic coordinates) and the α_0^c values. For instance, if $\alpha_0^c = (a_1, a_5, a_3)$ (corresponding to $a_i = \frac{p_i}{d}$ from Eq. 2.5.6), then, according to Eq. 2.5.6, $\alpha = (a_1 + a_3 - a_5, a_1 + a_5 - a_3, a_3 + a_5 - a_1)$. A similar one-to-one correspondence is defined between $\beta \in T_2$ and the β_0^c values.

The analytic description is fine, but a geometric relationship can be more useful. To find the geometric connection, start with α_0^c and the pairwise outcome for $\{c_1, c_2\}$. If α_0^c is on the c_1-c_2 edge of the representation triangle, then only type-one and five voters are involved. Moreover, because c_3 receives no votes in the plurality election, the plurality and pairwise tallies agree. Consequently, the position of α_0^c on this edge is the same as that of $\alpha \in T_1$ along the $F_3(\mathbf{E}_1)$ - $F_3(\mathbf{E}_5)$ edge of the representation cube.

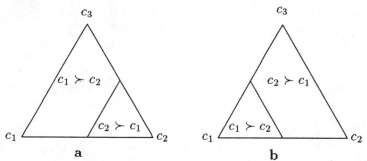

Fig. 2.6.9. Differences in rankings. **a.** $\{c_1, c_2\}$ ranking for α_0^c values. **b.** $\{c_1, c_2\}$ ranking for β_0^c

If α_0^c is not on the c_1 - c_2 edge of the representation triangle, then the profile includes type-three voters. These voters vote for c_1 over c_2 in a pairwise contest, so even if α_0^c is to the right of the $c_1 \sim c_2$ line, the pairwise outcome could be $c_1 \succ c_2$. Indeed, c_1 could beat c_2 in a pairwise election even without type-one voters. Here, α_0^c is above the midpoint on the c_2-c_3 edge of the representation triangle.

By use of the convexity property, the region where $c_1 \succ c_2$ in a pairwise vote when only odd voters vote is defined by the profiles $\frac{1}{2}(\mathbf{E}_1 + \mathbf{E}_5)$ and $\frac{1}{2}(\mathbf{E}_3 + \mathbf{E}_5)$. The indifference line for this region connects the midpoints of the c_1-c_2 and the c_2-c_3 edges of the representation triangle. This region, and the one for β_0^c outcomes, is illustrated in Fig. 2.6.9.

By carrying out this type of analysis for all pairs, the regions relating the α_0^c and β_0^c outcomes with the associated pairwise vote rankings are determined.

These regions are in Fig. 2.6.10. By comparing Fig. 2.6.10 with Fig. 2.5.5, the advantages of the cyclic-positional coordinates become clear. With a $120°$ rotation of one of the representation triangles in Fig. 2.6.10, Fig. 2.5.5 is recovered. Indeed, the position of α_0^c is precisely the positioning of $\alpha \in T_1$ after this rotation. Similarly, the geometric positioning of β_0^c identifies the geometric location of $\beta \in T_2$. As such, comparisons with procedure lines and pairwise rankings involve using two familiar geometric techniques.

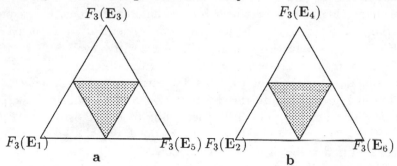

Fig. 2.6.10. Pairwise rankings. **a.** Pairwise rankings vs. α_0^c.
b. Pairwise rankings vs. β_0^c

The shaded regions in Fig. 2.6.10 identify the α_0^c and β_0^c outcomes where $\alpha \in T_1$, $\beta \in T_2$ are in the cyclic triangles. To see how to use these coordinates, suppose $\alpha_0^c = \beta_0^c = (\frac{1}{2}, 0, \frac{1}{2})$. Such a choice forces $\mathbf{q}_0 = (\frac{1}{2}, 0, \frac{1}{2})$ and the plurality ranking of $c_1 \sim c_3 \succ c_2$ for all choices of d^c. On the other hand, the line segment connecting the corresponding values of $\alpha = (1, 0, 0) \in T_1$, $\beta = (0, -1, 0) \in T_2$ has the representation

$$d^c(1, 0, 0) + (1 - d^c)(0, -1, 0) = (d^c, d^c - 1, 0),$$

so the pairwise rankings range from $\{c_1 \sim c_2, c_3 \succ c_2, c_1 \sim c_3\}$ to $\{c_1 \succ c_2, c_3 \sim c_2, c_1 \sim c_3\}$ to $\{c_1 \succ c_2, c_3 \sim c_2, c_1 \sim c_3\}$.

Another example is a geometric proof of Theorem 2.6.6. As shown in Example 2.6.2, the profile line $\alpha_0^c = \beta_0^c = \mathcal{I}$, $d \in [0, 1]$ defines the outcome $\mathbf{q}_0 = \mathbf{q}_{\frac{1}{2}} = \mathcal{I}$. The corresponding pairwise outcomes range from $d(\frac{1}{3}, \frac{1}{3}, \frac{1}{3}) + (1 - d)(-\frac{1}{3}, -\frac{1}{3}, -\frac{1}{3})$. To have the desired ranking of a specified pair, choose the d value so that we obtain either a positive or a negative cycle. Other values of $\mathbf{q}_0, \mathbf{q}_{\frac{1}{2}}$ near $\mathcal{I}$ are obtained by choosing α_0^c and β_0^c near $\mathcal{I}$. As this choice keeps α and β in the cyclic triangles, there are a large regions of values of d^c that will define either a positive or a negative cycle. $\square$

The following theorem indicates other kinds of conclusions that now can be obtained.

Theorem 2.6.8. *Choose one of the 13 possible rankings for a positional ranking method. Choose one of the 27 possible ways there are to rank the three pairs of candidates. There exists a profile where the pairwise rankings and the plurality outcome are the selected rankings.*

In words, "anything can happen with the plurality vote!" Of more immediate interest is the proof of this assertion; it emphasizes the geometric differences between the representation triangle and cube.

Outline of a Geometric Proof. Start with $\alpha_0^c = \beta_0^c = \mathcal{I}$. Because α_0^c and β_0^c coincide, this common point is the plurality outcome for any choice of d^c. However, this statement does not hold for the pairwise votes represented by points on a cube. Although $\alpha \in T_1$ and $\beta \in T_2$ are at the barycenter of their respective triangles, the connecting line passes through three different regions. Consequently, if $d^c < \frac{1}{2}$, the pairwise rankings define a negative cycle; if $d^c = \frac{1}{2}$, all pairs are tied, and if $d^c > \frac{1}{2}$, the pairwise rankings define a positive cycle.

The difference in the representation figures require different values of d^c are needed to keep $\mathbf{q}_0$ at $\mathcal{I}$ or $\mathbf{q}$ at $(0,0,0)$. To illustrate both the effect of the 120° rotation in Fig. 2.6.10 and the different effects of d^c, consider the profile leading to $\mathbf{q}_0 = \mathcal{I}$ where $\alpha_0^c = (1,0,0)$, (according to Fig. 2.6.10, $\alpha = F_3(\mathbf{E}_1)$) and $\beta_0^c = (0, \frac{1}{2}, \frac{1}{2})$ (so $\beta = \frac{1}{2}(F_3(\mathbf{E}_4) + F_3(\mathbf{E}_6))$. From the geometry of the triangle, the required value of d^c to ensure $\mathbf{q}_0 = \mathcal{I}$ is $d^c = \frac{1}{3}$, and the profile line passes through $\mathcal{I}$. However, for the cyclic coordinates, the rotation forces the line connecting $\alpha = (1,1,-1)$ and $\beta = (-1,0,0)$ to be nowhere near $(0,0,0)$. Thus, $\mathbf{q} = \frac{1}{3}(1,1,-1) + \frac{2}{3}(-1,0,0) = (-\frac{1}{3}, -\frac{2}{3}, 0)$, so the pairwise rankings are $c_2 \succ c_1, c_2 \succ c_3, c_3 \sim c_1$. To break the pairwise tie vote, it is clear from Fig. 2.5.3 that one just needs to perturb the choice of α_0^c.

The rest of the $13 \times 3 = 117$ combinations of rankings are obtained in a similar manner. The easiest geometric argument showing that everything can happen is to use values of α_0^c, β_0^c near $\mathcal{I}$ and d^c values near $\frac{1}{2}$. This keeps the $\mathbf{q}_0$ value near $\mathcal{I}$ (a boundary point for all $Si(3)$ ranking regions) and $\mathbf{q}$ near $(0,0,0)$ (a boundary point for all representation cube ranking regions). $\square$

The above result raises a new concern. Does this "anything can happen" conclusion extend to the comparisons of pairwise votes and the procedure line? Here, not everything can happen, there are some restrictions.

Theorem 2.6.9. *Suppose the procedure line is contained in a single ranking region, say, $\mathcal{R}(1)$ which corresponds to the ranking $c_1 \succ c_2 \succ c_3$. It is impossible for the pairwise rankings to have c_3 as the Condorcet winner, or c_1 as the Condorcet loser. Indeed, it is impossible to have any ranking that is on the boundary of these regions from the representation cube.*

So, while the plurality or antiplurality winner could be a Condorcet loser, such an ignoble outcome cannot hold *if a candidate is top-ranked by all positional procedures.*

Outline of the Proof. To see why this theorem is true, consider the special case where the procedure line is a point $\mathbf{q}^* = \mathbf{q}_0 = \mathbf{q}_{\frac{1}{2}}$. Recall from Example 2.6.2 that any supporting profile must have its α_0^c and β_0^c values restricted to particular lines; these lines of restriction are illustrated in Fig. 2.6.11. Because $\mathbf{q}_{\frac{1}{2}} \in \mathcal{CH}(\mathbf{w}_{\frac{1}{2}})$, $\mathbf{q}^*$ must be in the shaded region. For the representation cube, the pairwise outcomes are specified by the line connecting α and β in the figure.

Clearly, this line must miss several ranking regions of the representation cube; the missed regions are the ones indicated in the statement of the theorem.

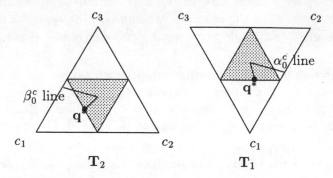

Fig. 2.6.11. Regions for α_0^c and β_0^c

More generally, requiring both $\mathbf{q}_0$ and $\mathbf{q}_{\frac{1}{2}}$ to be in the same ranking region imposes strong conditions upon the positioning of the α^c and β^c triangles. Suppose without loss of generality that the procedure line is in $\mathcal{R}(1)$. This means that the line connecting α_0^c and β_0^c as well as the line connecting $\alpha_{\frac{1}{2}}^c$ and $\beta_{\frac{1}{2}}^c$ must cross $\mathcal{R}(1)$. In turn, the geometry strongly constrains the positioning of the α^c and β^c triangles. For instance, one of the worse case scenario (as far as flexibility in choosing pairwise rankings) is if $\beta_{\frac{1}{2}}^c$ is near the $c_1 \sim c_2 \succ c_3$ region while $\alpha_{\frac{1}{2}}^c$ is near the $c_1 \succ c_2 \sim c_3$ region. This forces α_0^c, β_0^c to be near the $c_1 \sim c_3$ line. But, by examining Fig. 2.6.11, it is clear that the cyclic profile representation, satisfying these constraints, must miss several of the pairwise ranking regions; again, these are the regions indicated in the statement of the theorem.

A similar argument handles the remaining situation where α_0^c and β_0^c are near the boundaries of $\mathcal{R}(1)$ so that the line defining $\mathbf{q}_{\frac{1}{2}}$ also meets this region. Thus, there is a line passing through $\mathcal{I}$ in T_1, and a rotated line in T_2, so that both triangles are on the c_1 side of this line. The conclusion follows from the geometry. $\square$

2.6.8 Exercises

2.6.1. Show that Theorem 2.6.1 holds for any scoring vector.

2.6.2. For $\mathbf{q}_{\frac{1}{3}} = (0.3, 0.4, 0.5), d = 0.6$, find the cone of supporting profiles.

2.6.3. Find the combinations of $\alpha_s \in \partial W_s^1, \beta_s \in \partial W_s^2, d \in \{0,1\}$ that represent boundary regions of $Si(6)$. With this identification, extend Theorem 2.6.1 to discuss the kinds of boundary regions identified with the cone of profiles defined by a $\mathbf{q}_s$.

2.6.4. In collapsing the fat triangle to the representation surface, it is asserted that no change is made in the value of d. Justify this statement. (To do so, set up a triangle inside the fat triangle that is given by the vertices α_s, β_s, and the point defined when α_s is projected to the front representation triangle surface. Next, set up a similar triangle formed by $\mathbf{q}_s$ and its projection to the front surface.)

2.6.5. Equation 2.6.2 specifies (α_s, β_s, d) in terms of $\mathbf{p} \in Si(6)$. Find $\mathbf{p}$ as a function of α_s, β_s, d.

Suppose c_1 beats c_2 by winning 60% of the vote. Find the upper limit on α_0 to ensure that c_1 beats c_2 in the plurality ranking. Do the same for $\alpha_{\frac{1}{3}}$ and $\alpha_{\frac{1}{2}}$. Finally, find a general relationship between α_s and d to ensure that c_1 is $\mathbf{w}_s$ ranked above c_2.

2.6.6. Extend Theorem 2.6.1 to explain what happens with $\mathbf{q}_s$ on the boundary of the $F_4(-, \mathbf{w}_s)$ image set. For instance, suppose $d = \frac{1}{2}$ and $\mathbf{q}_s, s \in (0, \frac{1}{2})$, is on the c_1, c_2 edge of $Si(3)$. Show that the supporting set of profiles is either empty (so the outcome cannot occur), or $\mathbf{q}_s$ is the unique point $(\frac{1}{2}, \frac{1}{2}, 0)$ supported by a unique profile.

2.6.7. Caution is needed when using this analysis with the plurality and anti plurality procedures; procedures where (α_s, β_s, d) is not a true coordinate representation. For instance, show that if $\mathbf{q}_0$ is on the $Si(3)$ bottom edge and $d = \frac{1}{2}$, then the set of supporting profiles is empty if $\mathbf{q}_0 \neq (\frac{1}{2}, \frac{1}{2}, 0)$, but it is a *two-dimensional* set of profiles if $\mathbf{q}_0 = (\frac{1}{2}, \frac{1}{2}, 0)$. (Compare the outcome with Ex. 2.6.6.)

2.6.8. a. Suppose c_1 beats c_2 by winning 60% of the vote. Find the upper limit on α_0 to ensure that c_1 beats c_2 in the plurality ranking. Do the same for $\alpha_{\frac{1}{3}}$ and $\alpha_{\frac{1}{2}}$. Finally, find a general relationship between α_s and d to ensure that c_1 is $\mathbf{w}_s$ ranked above c_2.

b. Suppose c_1 beats c_2 by winning 60% of the vote. Find the set (geometrically) of all possible $\mathbf{w}_{\frac{1}{3}}$ normalized election *tallies* that can accompany this vote. Next, do the same for the plurality vote. Devise a technique so that if d is specified, then all associated $\mathbf{w}_s$ normalized tallies are found.

2.6.9. Find the set of all profiles supporting the positional election outcome $\mathbf{q}_{\frac{1}{5}} = (\frac{1}{3}, \frac{1}{3}, \frac{1}{3})$. Next, find the set for $\mathbf{q}_{\frac{1}{5}} = (\frac{1}{2}, \frac{1}{4}, \frac{1}{4})$. Compare these sets and explain why the location of $\mathbf{q}_{\frac{1}{5}}$ (which determines the amount of pivoting action) makes the second set smaller than the first. Use this argument to devise and prove a general statement about the sets of profiles supporting $\mathbf{q}_s$. Then, use the coordinate representation for profiles to describe what profiles dominate as $\mathbf{q}_s$ tends to the boundary of $\mathcal{CH}(\mathbf{w}_s)$. In doing so, explain what happens to the majority vote outcome of a particular pair.

2.6.10. In the discussion of d_s^*, it is stated that $1 - d_s^*$ serves as a crude measure of the ability of $\mathbf{w}_s$ to incorporate information about the intensity of pairwise comparisons. Give a justification for this statement. Next, critique it by showing, for example, that $\mathbf{w}_s$ does not give equal treatment for intensity of comparison information. Namely, if $s \neq \frac{1}{3}$, then some weak comparisons are treated more favorably than others.

2.6.11. Show that if $d^* \in (\frac{2}{3}, 1]$, then there are two s values, s_1 and s_2, that define d^*. Next, show that $\mathbf{w}_{s_1}^r = \mathbf{w}_{s_2}$.

2.6.12. Suppose c_1 beats c_2 by winning $d \in (\frac{1}{2}, 1]$ of the vote. Also suppose the plurality ranking has c_2 ranked above c_1. For this same profile, what can you say about the antiplurality ranking? Carry this one step further; observe that the value of d_s^* in Theorem 2.6.3 is determined by a particular profile which depends on whether $s \in [0, \frac{1}{3}]$, or $s \in [\frac{1}{3}, \frac{1}{2}]$. This suggests that a profile may allow the $\mathbf{w}_s$ ranking to reverse the pairwise ranking, but the $\mathbf{w}_s^r$ ranking will preserve it. In other words, associated with d_s^* describing what happens with $\mathbf{w}_s$, there is an associated value d_s^{*r} which indicates what happens with the same profile with $\mathbf{w}_s^r$. Find this value and explain what can occur. (Can you explain the difference in terms of the kind of information each procedure emphasizes?)

2.6.13. a. Theorem 2.6.5 specifies that if $d \geq d^{\#} = \frac{2}{3}$, then not all $\mathbf{w}_s$ rankings can occur. Nevertheless, there are several rankings that can occur. What are they? In other words, specify which $\mathbf{w}_s$ rankings can accompany a $c_1 \succ c_2$ pairwise victory where $d = d^{\#}$. What happens if $d > \frac{2}{3}$.?
b. Re-do Theorem 2.6.5, but now in the context of the three threshold methods described in the exercises of Sect. 2.1. Namely, for each threshold method, find the $d^{\#}$ value that avoids all possible rankings. (This value must be in terms of the specified threshold values.)

2.6.14. By use of the α^c, β^c triangles, find the set of profiles where the procedure line is the point $\mathbf{q} = (\frac{1}{4}, \frac{1}{4}, \frac{1}{2})$. Next, find the set of profiles where the procedure line is the point $\mathbf{q}' = (\frac{1}{6}, \frac{1}{6}, \frac{2}{3})$. Explain why there are difficulties for $\mathbf{q}'$. Find a general statement that includes what happened for $\mathbf{q}$ and for $\mathbf{q}'$.
    If the procedure line is a point, there must be a balance between the voter types. So, let $\mathbf{q}$ be on the $c_1 \sim c_2 \succ c_3$ line segment. First, find the set of profiles leading to this outcome, and then characterize the voter types that allow this conclusion.

2.6.15. Choose $\mathbf{q}_0 \in \mathcal{R}(2)$, $\mathbf{q}_{\frac{1}{2}} \in \mathcal{R}(5)$ so that the procedure line crosses only three ranking regions. Modify this profile so that the procedure line crosses seven ranking regions. Characterize the set of all profiles leading to this outcome.

2.6.16. a. Find (geometrically) a set of profiles where all $\mathbf{w}_s$ rankings are $c_1 \succ c_2 \succ c_3$ even though the pairwise rankings are $c_2 \succ c_1, c_1 \succ c_3, c_2 \succ c_3$. Do the same problem but where the pairwise rankings define a negative cycle.
b. Find a set of profiles where the $\mathbf{w}_0$ ranking is $c_1 \succ c_2 \succ c_3$, the $\mathbf{w}_{\frac{1}{2}}$ ranking is $c_3 \succ c_2 \succ c_1$, and the pairwise rankings define a positive cycle. Now, do so where the pairwise rankings are $c_1 \succ c_2$, $c_2 \succ c_3$, $c_1 \succ c_3$.

2.6.17. Choose an $\alpha_0^c \in \mathcal{R}(1)$, $\beta_0^c \in \mathcal{R}(3)$, and $d^c \in (0, 1)$ and compute the corresponding procedure line. Now interchange α_0^c with β_0^c and use $d = 1 - d^c$. How does this procedure line correspond to the original one.

2.6.18. State and prove a theorem similar to Theorem 2.6.8 but for the antiplurality method.

2.6.19. Find the $F_4(-, \mathbf{w}_0)$ image set if the pair of candidates is $\{c_2, c_3\}$.

CHAPTER III

FROM SYMMETRY TO THE BORDA
COUNT AND OTHER PROCEDURES

In this chapter I explore how geometric symmetry helps explain voting outcomes and procedures. For instance, the beverage example proves that the pairwise votes can reverse the plurality outcome, but why? The Condorcet profile shows that pairwise votes can create a cycle, but why? Certain profiles, such as a division between voters of types-one and five, create problems with voting procedures, but why? Some $\mathbf{w}_s$ procedures seem better than others, but is this true? In the first technical section, I show why some procedures lack certain symmetry properties; the cost is demonstrated with new paradoxes. The remaining sections return to the analysis of particular procedures.

3.1 Symmetry

In our search for a method to capture the voters' true beliefs, we need guidelines. Common sense dictates that if a procedure is sensitive to voters' preferences, then its election outcomes mirror methodical changes in voters' opinions. If each voter interchanges his ranking of Hollie and Rose, then the election ranking of Hollie and Rose is interchanged. If every voter completely reverses his ranking of the candidates, then the election outcome also should be completely reversed. A procedure failing to reflect these elementary symmetries clearly demonstrates a disturbing bias. As a result, the theory developed in this section leads to surprises: commonly used methods can violate these basic conditions. At the end of this section, I describe the unique symmetry admitted by the BC and I indicate why procedures without this symmetry exhibit a bias that produces disturbing election paradoxes. Consequently, the techniques developed in this (somewhat technical) section assist in understanding election procedures. Symmetry also is a powerful tool to analyze the higher dimensional aspects of profiles. So, as a first goal I use symmetries to answer some of the earlier questions about pairwise voting.

One Half or the Other. As described in Chap. 2, the image space for a two-candidate election is a line; if c_1 receives the portion $x \in [0,1]$ of the total vote, then c_2 receives the rest of it; $1 - x$. Similarly, the space of normalized profiles also is a line. With two candidates, a voter either prefers c_1 or c_2, so a profile $(y, 1 - y)$ indicates that $y \in [0,1]$ of the voters prefer c_1 while the rest, $1 - y$, prefer c_2. The election mapping, then, is the identity $f(x, 1 - x) = (x, 1 - x)$

that maps a line segment to a line segment. The winner is determined by which half of the line segment contains the normalized outcome.

Points on a line are boring; very little can be done with them. They can be moved to the right or left signifying that a candidate receives more or less of the vote. As for symmetries relative to the midpoint $(\frac{1}{2}, \frac{1}{2})$, a point $(x, 1-x)$ can stay where it is – this is the identity operation (a 0° rotation) – or its mirror image, $(1-x, x)$, can be computed – this is a 180° rotation about $(\frac{1}{2}, \frac{1}{2})$.

"Boredom," of course, can serve as a synonym for stability.[1] Indeed, it is the lack of adventure displayed by points on a line that generates the orderliness of a pairwise election. For instance, the properties of the line dictate that if $p_1 < p_2$, $p_3 < p_4$, then $p_1 + p_3 < p_2 + p_4$. As a consequence, suppose when Ann and Barb are evaluated by two subcommittees, each prefers Ann to Barb. When they convene as a full committee, Ann will be elected – there are no surprises of the kind encountered in the fable with the search for a Dean's Council representative.

Significant geometric differences emerge as soon as there are at least three candidates. To start, the space of normalized outcomes for a three-candidate election is transformed from the boring line to the two-dimensional representation triangle $Si(3)$. Similarly, the space of normalized profiles no longer is restricted to a line, or even to a two-dimensional set; it is the *five-dimensional* simplex $Si(3!)$. Higher dimensional spaces offer more places for an adventurous point to visit, so these larger spaces admit significantly more imaginative actions and symmetries than permitted by the staid line. Echoing the ancient curse, *"May you live in interesting times,"* these interesting new symmetries of higher dimensional spaces are the source of election paradoxes.

Try Thirds. Relative to its center point, a line can only be divided into halves. A higher dimensional space, on the other hand, can be divided into other sections; say thirds. So, the simplest symmetry not available to the line involves successive $\frac{360^o}{3} = 120^o$ counterclockwise rotations about $\mathcal{I}$ applied to a point $\mathbf{q}_0 \in Si(3)$. This rotation dynamic defines three symmetric points; the starting point $\mathbf{q}_0$, the point $\mathbf{q}_1$ which is 120° from $\mathbf{q}_0$, and the point $\mathbf{q}_2$ which is 120° from $\mathbf{q}_1$. (The 120° rotation of $\mathbf{q}_2$ returns to $\mathbf{q}_0$.) Call these three points $\{\mathbf{q}_0, \mathbf{q}_1, \mathbf{q}_2\}$ an *orbit* of the symmetry operation. (See Fig. 3.1.1.)

As the orbit $\{\mathbf{q}_0, \mathbf{q}_1, \mathbf{q}_2\}$ is the offspring of an action outlawed by the line, we must anticipate that it can be used to extract implications about voting. To do so, interpret the points as defining a profile where n voters are assigned to each of the three voter types; each voter type differs from the others by 120°. So, if $\mathbf{q}_0 \in \mathcal{R}(1)$, then

$$\mathbf{q}_0 \in \mathcal{R}(1), \; \mathbf{q}_1 \in \mathcal{R}(5), \; \mathbf{q}_2 \in \mathcal{R}(3).$$

(Observe that the orbit starting with $\mathbf{q}_0 \in \mathcal{R}(1)$ defines an "odd group" of voters.) This 120° symmetry assignment process for n = 5, displayed in Fig. 3.1.1,

---

[1] During 1992 election season, the Democratic Party of California wanted to present a united front to the electorate where part of the strategy was to avoid a divisive state party convention. "When the press wrote stories about how boring we were, we knew we'd succeeded," stated the party's political director Bob Mulholland to the *New York Times*. (Oct. 6, 1992)

defines $\mathbf{p}_m$ – the Condorcet triplet used for the agenda problems associated with contentious departmental meeting of the fable.[2] In this manner, the Condorcet triplet is identified with the simplest geometric configuration that cannot be represented on a line!

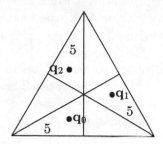

Fig. 3.1.1. The 120° orbit

Now that the higher dimensional symmetry of $\mathbf{p}_m$ is identified, what do we do with it? One answer is found by watching a child trying to push a square peg through a round hole; a way to mimic the child is to find a voting procedure where $\mathbf{p}_m$ doesn't fit. Because $\mathbf{p}_m$ is two-dimensional, this suggests using a single-dimensional procedure – the pairwise majority vote. As discussed in Sect. 2.5, this procedure squashes the two-dimensional aspects out of a profile by projecting the information to the appropriate edge of the representation triangle and then summing the terms. (Recall, the projection dismisses information about the intensity of the binary rankings.) But, no matter how hard we try to force $\mathbf{p}_m$ into becoming a single-dimensional object, a residue of its inherent two-dimensional symmetry is retained – the squashed two-dimensional symmetry becomes the majority vote cycle[3] characterized by the decisive $2:1$ victories:

$$c_1 \succ c_2, \ c_2 \succ c_3, \ \text{and} \ c_3 \succ c_1.$$

One way to see the important dimensional conflict between the profile and the procedure is to rotate Fig. 3.1.1. Ignore all labels; just consider the dots and indifference lines. The stripped figure has two dots to the left of the vertical indifference line, and one to the right. With respect to the two candidates identified by the bottom vertices, the two dots to the left have a weak pairwise

---

[2] In mathematical terms, the profile is based on the group action (orbit) of a particular subgroup of the permutation group S_3. The problems this profile encounters with pairwise votes arise because this subgroup of order 3 does not have its own subgroup of order 2.

[3] The same theme holds for all $n \geq 3$. Mimicking the construction of $Si(3)$ as the election space for three candidates, the election space for n candidates is the $(n-1)$ dimensional simplex $Si(n)$. If a profile $\mathbf{p}$ exhibits symmetries available only in $n-1$ dimensional spaces, we must expect $\mathbf{p}$ to create problems when subsets of $k < n$ candidates are ranked with elections. The idea is identical; because it is impossible to faithfully force the higher dimensional symmetries of $\mathbf{p}$ onto the lower dimensional subspaces of k candidate elections, cycles and other delightfully mysterious election behaviors must occur. Of equal importance, these symmetry profiles usually can be reconstructed to create a "confused voter" profile where voters can only rank k-candidate subsets in a transitive manner.

comparison while the one dot to the right has a strong intensity. Now, rotate the triangle 120° to obtain a new "bottom" edge of $Si(3)$. The rotated figure remains the same; there are two dots to the left of the (new) vertical line and one to the right. With respect to the candidates represented by the new bottom edge, the intensity of pairwise comparisons is the same. The identical geometry, with equivalent interpretations, continues with the final rotation of the figure.

The invariance of the picture with all of the rotations indicates the symmetry of $\mathbf{p}_m$. For the pairwise vote and for any rotation of the representation triangle, the candidate identified by the vertex to the left on the "bottom" edge beats the candidate to the right by $2:1$; this is the cycle. The dimensional argument, then, is that dividing the space into thirds according to the 120° rotation is incompatible with the pairwise division of the space into halves as required by a pairwise majority vote.

Of course, the same number of voters need not be assigned to each of the three voter types to get cycles; instead n_j voters could be assigned to the voter type identified by $\mathbf{q}_j$, $j = 0, 1, 2$. The perfect symmetry exhibited by $\mathbf{p}_m$ is destroyed, so a measure of how much the symmetry is broken would be useful. This measure is the positioning of α relative to $\mathcal{I}$ within the cyclic triangle of T_1. (See the cyclic coordinate representation introduced in Sect. 2.5.)

3.1.1 Partial Orbits and Intensity of Comparisons

As argued, the orbit $\{\mathbf{q}_0, \mathbf{q}_1, \mathbf{q}_2\}$ constitutes a two-dimensional geometric setting, complete with an balanced mixture of weak and string binary rankings. An informational interpretation is that the symmetry creates a profile that critically depends upon the kind of data the majority pairwise vote procedure ignores. But, all three points are not needed; it takes only two points to form the troublesome 120° angle prohibited by a line. Consequently, we must wonder whether a *pair* of points from the orbit can create other kinds of pairwise vote mischief.

The partial orbit $\mathbf{q}_0 \in \mathcal{R}(1)$, $\mathbf{q}_1 \in \mathcal{R}(5)$ defines the troubling profiles encountered in the critique of the Condorcet winner. If equal numbers of voters are placed at each of the two voter types, half of the voters have the ranking $c_1 \succ c_2 \succ c_3$ while the other half have $c_2 \succ c_3 \succ c_1$. As already argued, even if more than half of the voters are of type-one, it is easy to justify that c_2, rather than the Condorcet winner c_1, is the voters' top choice. Thus, this 120° difference identifies profiles that are critically dependent upon the information (intensity or transitivity) ignored by the pairwise vote.

The problems encountered by pairwise majority votes, therefore, are caused by the incompatibility of using a one-dimensional process with profiles that manifest higher dimensional properties. (These higher dimensional properties can be thought of as reflecting an heterogeneous mix of *transitive* voters' opinions.) In fact, all identified faults of the Condorcet winner, agendas, etc. can be attributed to the obviously impossible task of a myopic lower dimensional procedure accurately capturing the higher dimensional information about the heterogeneous nature of the voters. Simply stated, a pairwise majority vote, with its single-dimensional preoccupation, is blind to what is going on in other directions. If it were a child going out to play, its parents should be worried about traffic.

Can sophistication be added to a pairwise competition? Are there modifications that capture the higher dimensional realities of profiles? To see how this can be done, I will use the $\mathbf{q}_0$, $\mathbf{q}_1$ partial orbit.

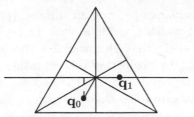

Fig. 3.1.2. The intensity procedure with a partial orbit

Interpret the $\mathbf{q}_i$ points as a cardinal, rather than an ordinal ranking of the candidates. This means that the relative values of the coordinates of a point $\mathbf{q}_i$ reflect an intensity of preference for the candidates. To avoid introducing bias, the points must be positioned in a "neutral position"; we do not want $\mathbf{q}_0$ closer to one indifference line than to another. The dividing angle between indifference lines is 60°, so $\mathbf{q}_0$ must be on the line through $\mathcal{I}$ that forms a 30° angle with each of the indifference lines $c_1 \sim c_2$ and $c_1 \sim c_3$. This choice, of course, forces $\mathbf{q}_1$, $\mathbf{q}_2$ to have the same unbiased 30° separation with respect to their neighboring indifference lines. If n_i voters are assigned to $\mathbf{q}_i$, $i = 0, 1$, then n_i is the magnitude – the number of voters representing a particular belief – and $\mathbf{q}_i$ is the vector direction characterizing this voter type. Thus the vectors $n_0\mathbf{q}_0$, $n_1\mathbf{q}_1$ incorporate information about the number and kinds of voters.

To develop an alternative election procedure for $\{c_1, c_2\}$, it is reasonable to retain the notion that a pairwise election is based on the sum of projected values. Projecting values to the bottom edge of $Si(3)$ is equivalent to projecting to a parallel line. Therefore, pass a line parallel to the c_1, c_2 edge of $Si(3)$ through $\mathcal{I}$; notice that $\mathbf{q}_1$ is on this line. (See Fig. 3.1.2.)

The problems with a standard pairwise vote is that only n_i, the magnitude of each $n_i\mathbf{q}_i$ vector, is projected; information embodied in the direction of $\mathbf{q}_i$ is totally ignored. To recapture this information about the heterogeneous mix of voters' opinions, project the full vector $n_i\mathbf{q}_i$, not just the value n_j, to the line. (This is the dashed line on the left side of Fig. 3.1.2.) Then, the *vector projected values* are summed to determine the pairwise election outcome.

All right; enough geometry. It is time to describe what this means in words and votes. The projected value of $n_1\mathbf{q}_1$ is n_1 (because $\mathbf{q}_1$ is on the line), while the projected value of $n_0\mathbf{q}_0$ is $\frac{1}{2}n_0$.[4] So, using this *vector projection procedure* with the integer profile $(n_0, 0, 0, 0, n_1, 0)$, c_1 gets $\frac{1}{2}n_0$ votes while c_2 receives n_1 votes. Thus, c_1 beats c_2 if and only if $\frac{1}{2}n_0 > n_1$. For this profile with a type-one, five

---

[4] The points $\mathcal{I}$ and $n_0\mathbf{q}_0$ define a 30° - 60° - 90° triangle. As the side opposite the 30° angle is half the value of the hypotenuse, the projected value is $\frac{1}{2}n_0$.

split, c_1 needs one more than two-thirds of the vote to be declared the winner. Thus, the geometry resolves the selection problem for this profile in the same way as the Condorcet Improvement and Pope selection procedures.

It remains to justify this situation where, in reality, the votes of type-one voters count only half that of type-five voters. Actually, not only are arguments easy to find, but we already explored some of them in Sect. 2.5. What the geometry does is to isolate which rankings provide an intense $\{c_1, c_2\}$ ranking (point q_1; the type-five voters) and which provide a weak $\{c_1, c_2\}$ ranking. It is this differences in intensity of beliefs that characterizes the heterogeneous mixture of opinions of a profile. Thus, by projecting *vectors* rather than just the length of the vector, information is reintroduced into the process. Of particular importance, *we reclaim the basic assumption that the voters have transitive preferences*. The geometry dictates how to measure the intensity information. In particular, it asserts (for $n = 3$) that two weaks do make a strong.

The geometric definition of a general procedure is immediate. For each voter type, put a unit vector in its ranking region of the representation triangle that straddles the bounding indifference lines. Then, multiply the vector by the number of voters of that type to define the *voter type vector*. With an election between c_i and c_j, draw a line through $\mathcal{I}$ parallel to the c_i - c_j edge of $Si(3)$; this is the c_i - c_j *projection line*. For the election, project each voter type vector to the c_i - c_j projection line, and then sum the projected values. The winner is the candidate who receives the most votes. An analytic definition with words instead of geometry follows.[5]

Definition 3.1.1. The *intensity of comparison* procedure for the pair $\{c_i, c_j\}$ is based on the summation of weights assigned to each candidate. The weights are determined in the following manner:

For each voter that strongly prefers c_i to c_j, assign c_i two points.

For each voter that weakly prefers $c_i \succ c_j$, assign c_i one point. □

Example 3.1.1. a. For the profile $\mathbf{p} = (\frac{1}{6}, 0, \frac{1}{2}, 0, \frac{1}{3}, 0)$ and the standard pairwise election, c_1 overwhelming beats c_2 by obtaining $\frac{1}{2} + \frac{1}{6} = \frac{2}{3}$ of the vote to c_2's $\frac{1}{3}$ of the vote. However, half of the voters have a weak $c_1 \succ c_2$ preference with their ranking $c_3 \succ (c_1 \succ c_2)$ and another $\frac{1}{6}$ have a weak c_1 preference with the ranking of $(c_1 \succ c_2) \succ c_3$. One has to wonder whether the overwhelming $\{c_1, c_2\}$ majority election outcome accurately reflects the views of the voters; after all, a third of them distinctly prefer c_2 over c_1 with their ranking $c_2 \succ c_3 \succ c_1$. Compare this outcome with the *intensity of comparison outcome* of a tie vote where c_1 receives $[\frac{1}{2} + \frac{1}{6}] = \frac{2}{3}$ points which agrees with c_2's point total of $2(\frac{1}{3})$. Similarly, the intensity of pairwise comparisons leads to the outcomes $c_3 \succ c_2$ and $c_3 \succ c_1$, so the intensity ranking is $c_3 \succ c_1 \sim c_2$.

b. It is clear that no candidate is preferred to any other with the Condorcet

---

[5] The analytic definition is based on the geometry of $Si(3)$. For $n > 3$ candidates, the geometric definition extends immediately, and the corresponding analytic definition reflects the new geometry of $Si(n)$.

profile $\mathbf{p}_m$. As the fourth-graders argued (Sect. 2.5), each candidate is ranked in top, middle, and bottom position by the same number of voters; the only realistic $\mathbf{p}_m$ outcome is a complete tie as given by the Condorcet Improvement. In fact, a reasonable measure of the ability of a procedure to escape a myopic, single-dimensional outlook is whether a complete tie is the $\mathbf{p}_m$ election outcome. This is the outcome of the intensity of comparison procedure. □

Comparison of Condorcet Improvement and Intensity. As shown, the intensity of comparison procedure agrees with the Condorcet Improvement procedure in treating certain troubling higher dimensional profiles. By construction, the Condorcet Improvement has a tempering effect; when the mix of voters' opinions approaches a true two-person contest, the Condorcet Improvement outcome tends to agree with Condorcet's solution concepts.

It is important to determine whether the intensity of comparison approach admits similar behavior. Actually, this is just one of many issues that should be investigated; does the intensity approach admit cycles? Can it elect a Condorcet loser? It turns out that none of these annoying problems arise. As asserted next, the reason the intensity approach and the Condorcet Improvement share important similarities is that they are equivalent.

Theorem 3.1.1. *The intensity of comparison pairwise procedure is an Condorcet Improvement.*

Corollary 3.1.2. *The pairwise rankings from the intensity of comparison procedure cannot create a cycle and the top-ranked candidate cannot be the Condorcet loser. (Similarly, the Condorcet winner cannot be bottom-ranked).*

The intensity of comparison approach reintroduces the assumption that the voters have transitive preferences with an immediate payoff that cycles do not occur. This suggests that whenever a procedure truly honors the assumption of transitive preferences, we can expect transitive outcomes.

Proof of the Theorem. All that we need to show is whether the intensity approach satisfies the defining axioms of the Condorcet Improvement. Most of these conditions involve computations (some are given above) to determine whether a tie vote emerges for certain profiles. The more difficult part is to establish that the ranking regions are convex. By definition, the vote total for c_i in an election with c_j is given by a linear equation of the profiles with fixed constant coefficients. Thus, the indifference profiles are on a lower dimensional linear surface dividing the profiles into the two convex sets where one or the other of the candidates is selected. The conclusion now follows from the convexity property.

A second part of the proof is to determine whether the three hyperplanes of profiles corresponding to indifference between some pair divides the space into six or eight regions. In the latter case, there would be a positive volume of outcomes with a cycle. But this last case occurs if and only if the three defining equations along with the equation $\sum_{j=1}^{6} p_j = 1$ are independent. A simple computation shows that they are not. □

3.1.2 Neutrality

An important symmetry condition is *neutrality*. Neutrality is the fairness property asserting that an election outcome does not depend upon the names of the candidates. For instance, with the candidates Anneli, Katri, and Lillian, suppose all voters thought Anneli was Katri and Katri was Anneli because they look so much alike. Once the correct identifications are made, there is no change in the voters' rankings or the election outcome, just in the names attached to the candidates. Thus, neutrality reduces the number of kinds of election outcomes; if two profiles are of the same kind except for the names of the candidates, then the outcomes are also the same with a name change.

To see the geometric symmetry involved with neutrality, observe that changing the names of c_1 and c_2 is the same as relabeling the vertices of the representation triangle. Alternatively, the name change is equivalent to flipping the representation triangle about the indifference line $c_1 \sim c_2$. (See Fig. 3.1.3a.) More complicated name changes such as $c_1 \to c_2$, $c_2 \to c_3$, $c_3 \to c_1$, can be viewed either as relabeling the vertices of $Si(3)$, or as rotating the representation triangle 120° about $\mathcal{I}$ so that each original vertex goes to the specified vertex. (Again, the 120° rotation appears.)

To simplify the notation, just use the subscripts. The name change $c_1 \to c_2$, $c_2 \to c_1$ could be represented by $(1,2,1)$. An even simpler notation emerges by recognizing that once c_1's name is assigned to someone else, she needs a new name. This suggests the shorter notation $(1,2)$ where we agree that the last name, 2, gets changed to the first one, 1. In this manner, the name changes $c_1 \to c_3$, $c_3 \to c_2$, $c_2 \to c_1$ is represented by $(1,3,2)$. The situation where no names are changed is represented by (1).

Permutations have interesting combinatoric properties. For instance, if $\sigma = (1,2,3)$ is applied twice, then candidate c_1's name is changed to c_2 on the first round and from c_2 to c_3 on the second round. Thus, after two rounds, we have that $c_1 \to c_3$. The name changes for all candidates from first to last is $c_1 \to c_3$, $c_2 \to c_1$, $c_3 \to c_1$. The natural way to compute these changes is $(1,2,3)(1,2,3) = (1,3,2)$ where the computation starts in the first block showing that $1 \to 2$ and then proceeds to the second unit where $2 \to 3$, so we have that $1 \to 3$. As c_1 is now called c_3, the old c_3 needs a new name. This is found by $3 \to 1$ in the first unit, and finally $1 \to 2$, so $3 \to 2$. A similar computation shows that $2 \to 1$.

Using the notation, suppose after using $\sigma = (1,2,3)$, we want to return to the original names. To reverse $1 \to 2$, $2 \to 3$, $3 \to 1$, we need $1 \to 3$, $3 \to 2$, $2 \to 1$. Therefore $\sigma^{-1} = (1,3,2)$. Observe that $\sigma\sigma^{-1} = (1)$ as the computation $(1,2,3)(1,3,2)$ shows.

Example 3.1.2. For the permutations $\sigma_1 = (1,3,2)$, $\sigma_2 = (2,3)$, we have that $\sigma_1^{-1} = (1,2,3)$, $\sigma_2^{-1} = (2,3)$. For computations we have $\sigma_1\sigma_2 = (1,3,2)(2,3) = (1,2)$ while $\sigma_2\sigma_1 = (2,3)(1,3,2) = (1,3)$. Therefore, $\sigma_1\sigma_2 \neq \sigma_2\sigma_1$. Until the reader is comfortable with this notation, it is worth describing all computations in words. For instance, σ_1 requires the names to be changed in a specific manner.

Once everyone has a name, they are changed again according to σ_2. Now, there is no reason to believe everyone ends up with the same name if σ_2 starts calling names first. This is the assertion $\sigma_1\sigma_2 \neq \sigma_2\sigma_1$.

Geometrically, $\sigma = (1, 2, 3)$ is a $120°$ rotation of $Si(3)$ about $\mathcal{I}$ in the counterclockwise direction. This rotation moves the ranking region $c_1 \succ c_2 \succ c_3$ to $c_2 \succ c_3 \succ c_1$. This new ranking can be obtained by a name change of the candidates. Indeed, a direct application shows that

$$\sigma(c_1 \succ c_2 \succ c_3) = c_{\sigma(1)} \succ c_{\sigma(2)} \succ c_{\sigma(3)} = c_2 \succ c_3 \succ c_1.$$

This makes sense; the new ranking must reflect the new names of each candidate. A similar name change holds for $\mathbf{q} = (q_1, q_2, q_3) \in Si(3)$ where the coordinates are reordered according to the new subscript $q_{\sigma(i)}$. As an illustration, if $\mathbf{q} = (\frac{1}{2}, \frac{1}{3}, \frac{1}{6})$, then, as the first coordinate becomes the second, the second becomes the third, and the third becomes the first, $\sigma(\mathbf{q}) = (\frac{1}{6}, \frac{1}{2}, \frac{1}{3})$.

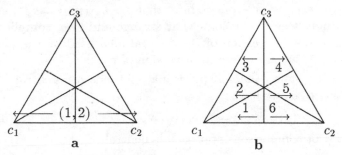

Fig. 3.1.3. Name changes. **a.** A $c_1 \to c_2$ name change.
b. $(1, 2)$ generates a permutation of the voter types

Changing the names of the candidates induces a corresponding change in the profile. How this is done is illustrated with Fig. 3.1.3 where the permutation $(1, 2)$ interchanges the names c_1 and c_2. As indicated in Fig. 3.1.3a, the representation triangle is flipped about the $c_1 \sim c_2$ indifference line. The effect, as shown in Fig. 3.1.3b, is to convert certain voter types into others. In particular, the name change of the candidates, $(1, 2)$, defines the name change in *voter types* $(1, 6)(2, 5)(3, 4)$. In general, a permutation of the candidate's names, σ, generates the permutation of voter types denoted by σ_T.

As a further illustration, the change in candidate's names, $\sigma = (1, 3, 2)$, defines the permutation of voter types $\sigma_T = (1, 3, 5)(2, 4, 6)$. This can be seen by using a $120°$ rotation of $Si(3)$ about $\mathcal{I}$ in a clockwise motion and noting which ranking regions are mapped on other ranking regions. $\square$

The notation allows an elegant description of neutrality. All neutrality requires is that a permutation of the names of the candidates in a profile leads to the same permutation of names in the outcome.

Definition 3.1.2. A voting procedure f satisfies *neutrality* if for any permutation of the names of the candidates σ and any profile $\mathbf{p}$ it follows that

$$f(\sigma_T(\mathbf{p})) = \sigma(f(\mathbf{p})). \quad \square \qquad\qquad (3.1.1)$$

Example 3.1.3. a. By use of neutrality, it follows from a computation that

$$\sigma(f_{\{c_i,c_j\}}(\mathbf{p})) = f_{\{c_{\sigma(i)},c_{\sigma(j)}\}}(\sigma_T(\mathbf{p})). \tag{3.1.2}$$

For example, if $\mathbf{p} = (\frac{1}{2}, 0, \frac{1}{3}, 0, \frac{1}{5}, 0)$ and $\sigma = (1,3)$, then $f_{\{c_1,c_2\}}(\mathbf{p}) = c_1 \succ c_2$. One interpretation of σ is that the voters confused the names of c_1 and c_3. Applying the name change of Eq. 3.1.2, the correct profile is $\sigma_T(\mathbf{p}) = (\frac{1}{3}, 0, \frac{1}{2}, 0, \frac{1}{6}, 0)$ and the election is $f_{\{c_3,c_1\}}(\sigma(\mathbf{p})) = c_3 \succ c_2$.

b. Consider $\mathbf{p}_m$ and the permutation $\sigma = (1,2,3)$. As $\sigma_T(\mathbf{p}_m) = \mathbf{p}_m$; the profile $\mathbf{p}_m$ is invariant with respect to the actions of σ. Geometrically, this invariance assertion is equivalent to the above description of rotating Fig. 3.1.1a and finding that the picture remains the same. The rest of the geometric picture, showing that the majority vote goes to the vertex to the right also is captured by neutrality; e.g., the first rotation is expressed as

$$\sigma(c_1 \succ c_2) = \sigma(f_{\{c_1,c_2\}}(\mathbf{p}_m)) = f_{\{c_{\sigma(1)},c_{\sigma(2)}\}}(\sigma_T(\mathbf{p}_m)) = f_{\{c_2,c_3\}}(\mathbf{p}_m).$$

As $\sigma(c_1 \succ c_2) = c_{\sigma(1)} \succ c_{\sigma(2)} = c_2 \succ c_3$, we have that $f_{\{c_2,c_3\}}(\mathbf{p}_m) = c_2 \succ c_3$.

This computation may seem to be somewhat strange and even complicated. However, it is just a formal expression of the natural idea used by the fourth-grade students (Sect. 2.5) when exposed to a version of $\mathbf{p}_m$.

c. A direct computation shows that all positional methods are neutral. This means that for any $\mathbf{w}_s$, $\mathbf{p}$, σ, we have

$$\sigma(f(\mathbf{p}, \mathbf{w}_s)) = f(\sigma_T(\mathbf{p}), \mathbf{w}_s). \tag{3.1.3}$$

Similarly, the intensity of comparisons approach is neutral. $\square$

I started this section asserting that an election procedure must not introduce bias. If all voters change their opinions in a consistent manner, then the election outcome must also change in the same fashion. "Neutrality" is our first measure of a consistent change and most procedures pass this test.

Theorem 3.1.3. *The Condorcet Improvement method, pairwise voting, the Condorcet winner concept, positional methods, the threshold methods of Chap. 2, scoring methods, and the intensity of comparison methods are neutral procedures.*

Another interpretation of neutrality is that certain permutations of voter types do not introduce new kinds of election outcomes; they just change the names of the candidates. It is reasonable to list them.

Neutrality profile symmetries		
Changes in names	σ	σ_T
none	(1)	(1)
$c_1 \to c_2$	$(1,2)$	$(1,6)(2,5)(3,4)$
$c_1 \to c_3$	$(1,3)$	$(1,4)(2,3)(5,6)$
$c_2 \to c_3$	$(2,3)$	$(1,2)(3,6)(4,5)$
$c_1 \to c_2 \to c_3$	$(1,2,3)$	$(1,5,3)(2,6,4)$
$c_1 \to c_3 \to c_2$	$(1,3,2)$	$(1,3,5)(2,4,6)$

3.1.3 Reversal of Fortune

Neutrality ensures that if each voter changes the names of the candidates, then the outcome reflects this name change. This fairness condition requires that the conditions for Judy to be elected are the same as those holding for Eric. As emphasized, this property also restricts the number of election outcomes that can occur, so it reduces the number of paradoxes.

A natural extension of neutrality[6] is where every voter's ranking is completely reversed; a voter with the ranking Martha $\succ$ Ruth $\succ$ Edna now has the ranking Edna $\succ$ Ruth $\succ$ Martha. Presumably, if every voter completely reverses his ranking, then this symmetry holds for the procedure – the election ranking also is completely reversed. If not, then the procedure exhibits an obvious bias.

Surely, as with neutrality, all standard procedures respect this reversal property! Well, maybe not. To understand when this reversal symmetry holds, we need to develop a theory in terms of the geometry and the permutations. First some definitions.

Definition 3.1.3. For a profile $\mathbf{p} = (p_1, p_2, p_3, p_4, p_5, p_6)$, let the *reversed profile* be

$$\mathbf{p}^r = (p_4, p_5, p_6, p_1, p_2, p_3).$$

The reversal of $\mathbf{q} \in Si(3)$ is the $180°$ rotation of $\mathbf{q}$ about $\mathcal{I}$. Alternatively, it is the unique point $\mathbf{q}^r \neq \mathbf{q}$ on the line defined by $\mathbf{q}$ and $\mathcal{I}$ that is the same distance form $\mathcal{I}$ (i.e., $\|\mathbf{q} - \mathcal{I}\| = \|\mathbf{q}^r - \mathcal{I}\|$). The reversal of a ranking region $\mathcal{R} \neq \mathcal{I}$, $\mathcal{R}^r$, is the ranking region diametrically opposite $\mathcal{R}$. (Also, $\mathcal{I}^r = \mathcal{I}$.) The reversal of a ranking α associated with ranking region $\mathcal{R}(\alpha)$ is the ranking identified with $\mathcal{R}^r$. $\square$

The permutation of voter types defined by $\mathbf{p} \to \mathbf{p}^r$ is a new object; it can *not* be obtained by combining permutations associated with the name changes of the candidates. If it could, its permutation representation, $(1, 4)(2, 5)(3, 6)$, would be in the above table.

The definitions of the reversal of a ranking region, $\mathbf{q} \in Si(3)$, and a profile are accomplished by geometrically finding what is "opposite." This is done by passing a line through $\mathcal{I}$ and finding the diametrically opposite object. For instance, $\mathbf{q} = (\frac{3}{10}, \frac{1}{2}, \frac{1}{5}) \in Si(3)$ is the $t = 1$ endpoint of the line $t\mathbf{q} + (1 - t)\mathcal{I}$,

---

[6]An interpretation of the permutation (i, j) is that every voter reverses his ranking of $\{c_i, c_j\}$ keeping everything else fixed. Neutrality requires the outcome of this subset to also be reversed. Now, because $(1, 2, 3) = (1, 2)(1, 3)$ and $(1, 3, 2) = (1, 3)(1, 2)$, it follows that all name changes can be viewed as successive applications of first choosing a pair of candidates, and then requiring every voter's ranking of this pair to be reversed. With neutrality, the outcome follows suit. Then, another pair is selected, and the process is repeated. The natural question is to determine what happens if, instead of a pair of candidates, we start with a larger subset of candidates. Again, each voter's rankings of this subset is reversed; everything else is kept fixed. We want to determine what happens to the election rankings. For $n = 3$ candidates, the only other subset is the full set, and this is studied next. However, for $n \geq 4$ candidates, this question extends to all k subsets of candidates where $2 \leq k \leq n$. There are surprising answers!

so the $t = -1$ point on the extended line is $\mathbf{q}^r = (\frac{11}{30}, \frac{1}{6}, \frac{14}{30})$. Other terms are defined in a similar manner; e.g., the reversal of $\mathbf{q} = (x, y, z)$ in the *representation cube* is $\mathbf{q}^r = (-x, -y, -z)$. From the geometry, properties such as $(\mathbf{p}^r)^r = \mathbf{p}$, $(\mathbf{q}^r)^r = \mathbf{q}$, and $(\mathcal{R}^r)^r = \mathcal{R}$ are immediate.

We now return to the central question; which election procedures F respect the reversal symmetries by satisfying

$$F(\mathbf{p}^r) = F^r(\mathbf{p})? \tag{3.1.4}$$

An immediate first answer follows.

Theorem 3.1.4. *Pairwise elections and the intensity of comparison approach preserve reversals. Namely,*

$$F_3(\mathbf{p}^r) = F_3^r(\mathbf{p}). \tag{3.1.5}$$

Proof. The proof of this theorem is immediate. For each $\{c_i, c_j\}$, all voters on the c_i side of the $c_i \sim c_j$ line for $\mathbf{p}$ are flipped to the c_j side for $\mathbf{p}^r$. This flipping preserves the intensity of comparisons. Thus, the vote received by c_i with $\mathbf{p}$ is the vote received by c_j with $\mathbf{p}^r$. $\square$

The natural reversal property, Eq. 3.1.4, is not enjoyed by all procedures. To demonstrate with the profile $\mathbf{p} = (\frac{1}{10}, \frac{2}{10}, \frac{1}{10}, \frac{1}{10}, \frac{4}{10}, \frac{1}{10})$, observe that the plurality outcome is $f(\mathbf{p}, \mathbf{w}_0) = (\frac{3}{10}, \frac{1}{2}, \frac{1}{5})$ with the ranking $c_2 \succ c_1 \succ c_3$. In this outcome, c_3 is bottom-ranked, so, presumably, she would be a beneficiary when *all* voters completely reverse their rankings. After all, should Eq. 3.1.4 be true, we would expect $f(\mathbf{p}^r, \mathbf{w}_0) = (\frac{3}{10}, \frac{1}{2}, \frac{1}{5})^r = (\frac{11}{30}, \frac{1}{6}, \frac{14}{30})$ with c_3 top-ranked. Instead, the actual outcome is $f(\mathbf{p}^r, \mathbf{w}_0) = (\frac{1}{2}, \frac{3}{10}, \frac{1}{5})$ with the ranking $c_1 \succ c_2 \succ c_3$. So, even though each voter completely reverses his ranking of the candidates, this reversal is not recognized by the plurality election.

The $\mathbf{w}_s$-Symmetries. To understand this weird behavior where the plurality method need not respect a reversal of opinions, we need to introduce the $\mathbf{w}_s$-symmetries. As the voting vectors $\mathbf{w}_s$ live on a line, we return to the limited geometry where the only admissible symmetry is a flip; a 180° rotation.[7] Nevertheless, unexpected relationships emerge.

The first task is to define a "flip" of $\mathbf{w}_s$; in particular, we need to identify which $\mathbf{w}_s$ serves as a pivot point. Whatever the definition of a flip, it is clear that the plurality procedure, $\mathbf{w}_0$, should be flipped to the antiplurality $\mathbf{w}_{\frac{1}{2}}$. The mechanics of converting $(1, 0, 0)$ to $(0, 0, -1)$ are obvious – just reverse $(1, 0, 0)$ to get $(0, 0, 1)$ and then multiply by -1. To convert the vector into its standard form, add $(1, 1, 1)$ and multiply by $\frac{1}{2}$. Using this approach with a general choice of $\mathbf{w}_s = (1 - s, s, 0)$, first we obtain $(0, s, 1 - s)$ and then $(0, -s, s - 1)$. To change this vector into an equivalent, normalized form, add $(1 - s)(1, 1, 1)$ and then multiply by the scalar $\frac{1}{2-3s}$ to obtain $\mathbf{w}_s^r$.

---

[7]On the other hand, if $n > 3$, then the set of positional voting methods are in the $(n - 2)$ dimensional simplex $Si(n - 1)$. Thus, more candidates admit more symmetries; in turn, the voting systems must inherit all the consequences associated with "interesting" spaces. Technically, this means that the BC admits symmetries in addition to the ones developed here.

Definition 3.1.4. The *reversal* of voting vector $\mathbf{w}_s$, $\mathbf{w}_s^r$, is

$$\mathbf{w}_s^r = (\frac{1-s}{2-3s}, \frac{1-2s}{2-3s}, 0). \quad \Box \tag{3.1.6}$$

The following statement provides several fundamental properties of this symmetry action. The first assertion provides geometric support for calling $\mathbf{w}_s^r$ the reversal of $\mathbf{w}_s$.

Theorem 3.1.5. a. *In $Si(3)$ consider the line passing through $[\mathbf{w}_s]_1$ and $\mathcal{I}$. This line intersects the boundary of $Si(3)$ at the point $[\mathbf{w}_s^r]_4$.*

b. *For $\mathbf{w}_s$, we have that $(\mathbf{w}_s^r)^r = \mathbf{w}_s$.*

c. *The relationship $\mathbf{w}_s = \mathbf{w}_s^r$ holds if and only if $s = \frac{1}{3}$. Namely, only the BC voting vector is its own reversal.*

Proof. Parts a and c are exercises in Sect. 2.3. Part b follows immediately from the geometry of part a. $\Box$

From the viewpoint of symmetry, part c of the theorem crowns *the Borda Count as the midpoint, the pivot point, of the positional voting methods.* This allows the voting vectors to be divided into those $\mathbf{w}_s$ that are to the left and to the right of the BC. The connection between the two sets of vectors is the reversal procedure – a form of a $180°$ flip where the BC is the pivot point. Observe that this type of assertion, where the BC is singled out for recognition when a new property is being discussed, or where the discussion centers on $s \in [0, \frac{1}{3}]$ and then on $s \in [\frac{1}{3}, \frac{1}{2}]$ is becoming common; some of the reasons are explained next. To be useful, the reversal of voting vectors should relate the $\mathbf{w}_s^r$ and $\mathbf{w}_s$ election outcomes.

Theorem 3.1.6. *For given $\mathbf{w}_s$, the normalized tallies satisfy*

$$f(\mathbf{p}^r, \mathbf{w}_s^r) = tf(\mathbf{p}, \mathbf{w}_s) + (1-t)\mathcal{I}, \quad t = -\frac{1}{2-3s}. \tag{3.1.7}$$

Expressed in terms of election rankings,

$$\mathcal{R}(f(\mathbf{p}^r, \mathbf{w}_s^r)) = \mathcal{R}((f(\mathbf{p}, \mathbf{w}_s))^r). \tag{3.1.8}$$

There are fascinating consequences of this theorem. For instance, it states that if we know everything that can happen with $\mathbf{w}_s$, then we also know everything that can happen with $\mathbf{w}_s^r$. As an application, we know from the beverage example of the fable that the profile $\mathbf{p} = (0, \frac{6}{15}, 0, \frac{4}{15}, \frac{5}{15}, 0)$ causes the plurality ranking, $c_1 \succ c_2 \succ c_3$, to conflict with the pairwise rankings $c_3 \succ c_1, c_3 \succ c_2, c_2 \succ c_1$. Because $\mathbf{w}_{\frac{1}{2}} = \mathbf{w}_0^r$, it follows from the theorem that there are profiles leading to the same conclusion for the antiplurality method. Indeed, according to Eq. 3.1.8, the ranking for $f(\mathbf{p}^r, \mathbf{w}_{\frac{1}{2}})$ is $(c_1 \succ c_2 \succ c_3)^r = c_3 \succ c_2 \succ c_1$. From Theorem 3.1.4, we know that the rankings of the pairs are reversed, so the pairwise rankings of $\mathbf{p}^r = (\frac{4}{15}, \frac{5}{15}, 0, 0, \frac{6}{15}, 0)$ are $c_1 \succ c_2, c_2 \succ c_3, c_1 \succ c_3$; the pairwise and antiplurality rankings are in direct contradiction.

Stated in words, the antiplurality and plurality methods share the same ranking problems. More generally, all the problems experienced by $\mathbf{w}_s$ for profile $\mathbf{p}$ are experienced by $\mathbf{w}_s^r$ with $\mathbf{p}^r$. Thus the sins of a positional procedure are visited upon its reversal, and they are equally likely for both procedures.

As indicated by the following proof, the value of t in Eq. 3.1.7 reflects the algebraic construction needed to go from $\mathbf{w}_s$ to $\mathbf{w}_s^r$.

Proof. Because $[\mathbf{w}_s^r]_4$ is on the line defined by $\mathbf{w}_s$ and $\mathcal{I}$, we have from algebra and Theorem 3.1.5 that

$$[\mathbf{w}_s^r]_4 = (1-t)\mathcal{I} + t\mathbf{w}_s, \quad t = -\frac{1}{2-3s}.$$

The more general expression is

$$[\mathbf{w}_s^r]_{j+3} = (1-t)\mathcal{I} + t[\mathbf{w}_s]_j, \, j = 1, \ldots 6, \quad t = -\frac{1}{2-3s}. \tag{3.1.9}$$

If $\mathbf{p}^r = (p_1^r, \ldots, p_6^r)$, then $p_{j+3}^r = p_j$. Using Eq. 3.1.9 and the definition of an election, we have that

$$f(\mathbf{p}^r, \mathbf{w}_s^r) = \sum_{j=1}^{6} p_{j+3}^r [\mathbf{w}_s^r]_{j+3} = \sum_{j=1}^{6} p_j [\mathbf{w}_s^r]_{j+3}$$

$$= \sum_{j=1}^{6} p_j \{(1-t)\mathcal{I} + t[\mathbf{w}_s]_j\}$$

$$= (1-t)\mathcal{I} + tf(\mathbf{p}, \mathbf{w}_s). \quad \square$$

Example 3.1.4. a. Let $\mathbf{p} = (\frac{1}{2}, 0, \frac{1}{3}, 0, \frac{1}{6}, 0)$. The plurality outcome is $c_1 \succ c_3 \succ c_2$ with the election point $\mathbf{q}_0 = (\frac{1}{2}, \frac{1}{3}, \frac{1}{6})$. The profile $\mathbf{p}^r = (0, \frac{1}{6}, 0, \frac{1}{3}, 0, \frac{1}{2})$ has the antiplurality outcome $c_2 \succ c_3 \succ c_1$. Using $s = 0$ with Eq. 3.1.7 leads to the value $t = -\frac{1}{2}$. Thus, we find the normalized outcome $\mathbf{q}_{\frac{1}{2}} = (\frac{1}{4}, \frac{5}{12}, \frac{1}{3}) = -\frac{1}{2}\mathbf{q}_0 + \frac{3}{2}\mathcal{I}$. As promised by the theorem, the reversal of the antiplurality ranking is the plurality ranking. A geometric argument is given below.

b. The dual relationship given by Eq. 3.1.5 means that if we understand the election results associated with $\mathbf{w}_s$, $s \in [0, \frac{1}{3}]$, then we understand the election results for all positional methods. For instance, in Sect. 2.6 I showed for $s \in [0, \frac{1}{3}]$ how to compute the probability that the $\mathbf{w}_s$ and the pairwise ranking of c_1, c_2 are in conflict. It follows from Theorem 3.1.6 that the answer for $\mathbf{w}_s^r$ agrees with that for $\mathbf{w}_s$; e.g., the antiplurality and plurality admit the same probability for this event. $\square$

The BC has a special role with Eq. 3.1.7; *the BC is the only positional voting method satisfying the reversal symmetry property Eq. 3.1.4.*

Corollary 3.1.7. *For the BC, the normalized outcomes satisfy*

$$f(\mathbf{p}^r, \mathbf{w}_{\frac{1}{3}}) = (f(\mathbf{p}, \mathbf{w}_{\frac{1}{3}}))^r. \tag{3.1.10}$$

For any other choice of $\mathbf{w}_s$, there exist choices of $\mathbf{p}$ where Eq. 3.1.10 does not hold.

Proof. That Eq. 3.1.10 holds for the BC is immediate from Eq. 3.1.7 with $s = \frac{1}{3}$. To see that this relationship does not hold for other choices of $\mathbf{w}_s$ consider $\mathbf{p} = (\frac{1}{2}, 0, 0, \frac{1}{2}, 0, 0)$ where the voters are evenly split between the rankings $c_1 \succ c_2 \succ c_3$ and the reversed ranking $c_3 \succ c_2 \succ c_1$. This profile involves a two-candidate conflict, so it is reasonable to expect the outcome to be the complete tie $c_1 \sim c_2 \sim c_3$. (This is the outcome of the pairwise majority votes, the intensity of comparison, and the Condorcet Improvement.) To see why this is the BC outcome, notice that $\mathbf{p}^r = \mathbf{p}$, so, according to Eq. 3.1.10, the BC election ranking must agree with its reversal – the only possible choice is $\mathcal{I}$. In fact, this argument shows that if a procedure respects the reversal symmetry, then $\mathcal{I}$ is the only possible outcome for $\mathbf{p}$.

It remains to check whether this reasonable outcome holds for other positional methods. It does not; in particular,

$$f(\mathbf{p}, \mathbf{w}_s) = \begin{cases} c_1 \sim c_3 \succ c_2 & s \in [0, \frac{1}{3}) \\ c_1 \sim c_2 \sim c_3 & s = \frac{1}{3} \\ c_2 \succ c_1 \sim c_3 & s \in (\frac{1}{3}, \frac{1}{2}] \end{cases},$$

the outcome is $f(\mathbf{p}, \mathbf{w}_s) = (\frac{1-s}{2}, s, \frac{1-s}{2})$. $\square$

It is worth describing how the above $\mathbf{p}$ was selected. If $\mathbf{w}_s$ ignores information about the reversal of profiles, then this fact should be apparent with a profile where the reversal property is critical. This suggests examining profiles satisfying $\mathbf{p} - \mathbf{p}^r$.

The symmetry relationship of Eq. 3.1.10 forces us to anticipate that *BC elections exhibit more regularity than any other positional method*. With the neutrality of positional methods, if two profiles differ by a permutation of names, then so does the election outcome. Only the BC can go further; if two profiles are the reversal of one another, the BC outcomes are the reversal of one another.

Even more is possible. By combining Corollary 3.1.7 and Theorem 3.1.3, it follows that *the BC has a stronger connection with the pairwise rankings than any other positional voting methods*. This is because both the BC and the pairwise rankings respect reversal symmetry; surprisingly, this is not true for any other positional voting method.

Corollary 3.1.8. *For any change of names σ, the BC and the pairwise votes satisfy the following symmetry relationships:*

$$\sigma(F_3(\mathbf{p}), f(\mathbf{p}, \mathbf{w}_{\frac{1}{3}})) = (F_3(\sigma_T(\mathbf{p})), f(\sigma_T(\mathbf{p}), \mathbf{w}_{\frac{1}{3}}))$$
$$(F_3(\mathbf{p}^r), f(\mathbf{p}^r, \mathbf{w}_{\frac{1}{3}})) = (F_3^r(\mathbf{p}), f^r(\mathbf{p}, \mathbf{w}_{\frac{1}{3}})). \tag{3.1.11}$$

Equation 3.1.11 does not hold for any other positional voting system.

3.1.4 Reversal Geometry

In an election, the procedure is fixed in advance; we can't change it after we know the profile. Therefore, although Eq. 3.1.7 is important and interesting, it is not what we want. Instead of relating $\mathbf{w}_s$ and $\mathbf{w}_s^r$ election outcomes, we want to relate election outcomes for a specified procedure. The more interesting issue is to find an equation, like Eq. 3.1.7, specifying the $f(\mathbf{p}^r, \mathbf{w}_s)$ outcome in terms of the $f(\mathbf{p}, \mathbf{w}_s)$ outcome. When all voters reverse their ranking, what is the new outcome?[8]

To explore this issue, I describe $\mathbf{p}$ and $\mathbf{p}^r$ in terms of cyclic-positional coordinate systems $(\alpha_s^c, \beta_s^c, d^c)$. So, we want to find the relationship between $\mathbf{p} = (\alpha_s^c, \beta_s^c, d^c)$ and $\mathbf{p}^r = (\alpha_s^c, \beta_s^c, d^c)^r = (\alpha_s^{cr}, \beta_s^{cr}, d^{cr})$. First consider the plurality method $s = 0$.

Theorem 3.1.9. *For a profile expressed in cyclic positional coordinates,* $\mathbf{p} = (\alpha_0^c, \beta_0^c, d^c)$, *the expression* $\mathbf{p}^r = (\alpha_0^{cr}, \beta_0^{cr}, d^{cr})$ *is obtained in the following manner:*

α_0^{cr} is a $120°$ rotation of β_0^c, β_0^{cr} is a $-120°$ rotation of α_0^c, and $d^{cr} = 1 - d^c$.

Proof. To see why β_0^{cr} is a $120°$ rotation of α_0^c, observe that $f(\mathbf{p}_o, \mathbf{w}_0) = \alpha_0^c = (a_1, a_2, a_3)$ uniquely defines the odd voter profile $\mathbf{p}_o = a_1\mathbf{E}_1 + a_2\mathbf{E}_5 + a_3\mathbf{E}_3$. Using the relationship $\mathbf{E}_j^r = \mathbf{E}_{j+3}$, it follows that $\mathbf{p}_o^r = a_1\mathbf{E}_4 + a_2\mathbf{E}_2 + a_3\mathbf{E}_6$ and the plurality election outcome is $\beta_0^{cr} = f(\mathbf{p}_o^r, \mathbf{w}_0) = (a_2, a_3, a_1)$. But, the vector (a_2, a_3, a_1) is obtained from (a_1, a_2, a_3) with the permutation $(1, 2, 3)$, or a $-120°$ rotation. The rest of the proof is derived in a similar manner. $\square$

Example 3.1.5. By using permutations and Theorem 3.1.9, $\mathbf{p}^r$ and its distinguished point are easy to compute. This is because the $-120°$ rotation is the same as a $\sigma_1 = (1, 2, 3)$ name change, and the $120°$ rotation agrees with a $\sigma_2 = (1, 3, 2)$ permutation. Thus, if $\mathbf{p} = ((0.4, 0.5, 0.1), (0.3, 0.25, 0.45), 0.6)$, then

$$\mathbf{p}^r = (\sigma_2((0.3, 0.25, 0.45)), \sigma_1((0.4, 0.5, 0.1)), 1 - 0.6)$$
$$= ((0.25, 0.45, 0.3), (0.1, 0.4, 0.5), 0.4).$$

It is this *double twist* effect, where portions of the profile are twisted in different directions, that permits all sorts of interesting conclusions. $\square$

The Reversal Set $R(\mathbf{q}_s)$. By satisfying the reversal symmetry, the BC should admit fewer kinds of election outcomes. To make sense of this statement, suppose $\mathbf{p}$ is a profile satisfying $f(\mathbf{p}, \mathbf{w}_{\frac{1}{3}}) = \mathbf{q}_{\frac{1}{3}}$. According to Eq. 3.1.10, we obtain the desired $f(\mathbf{p}^r, \mathbf{w}_{\frac{1}{3}}) = \mathbf{q}_{\frac{1}{3}}^r$. Namely, for the BC, the simple relationship specifying $f(\mathbf{p}^r, \mathbf{w}_{\frac{1}{3}})$ as the reversal of $f(\mathbf{p}, \mathbf{w}_{\frac{1}{3}})$ is exactly as it should be.

---

[8] Remember, reversal symmetry is studied to understand what an election outcome means - to determine any bias. There is no expectation that, in reality, all voters will reverse their rankings.

This satisfying BC relionship need not occur for any other $\mathbf{w}_s$. In fact, there is not even an equation relating $\mathbf{q}_s = f(\mathbf{p}, \mathbf{w}_s)$ with $f(\mathbf{p}^r, \mathbf{w}_s)$! Instead, the reversal of the profile set supporting $\mathbf{q}_s$ defines a *set of outcomes* rather than just a single outcome! So, the reversal of $\mathbf{q}_s$ could be one of many possibilities!

To understand this assertion, I show for the plurality method that some $\mathbf{q}_0$ even allow the *reversal set*

$$ R(\mathbf{q}_0) = \{ f(\mathbf{p}^r, \mathbf{w}_0) \,|\, \mathbf{p} \text{ so that } f(\mathbf{p}, \mathbf{w}_0) = \mathbf{q}_0 \} $$

to meet all 13 ranking regions! Instead of respecting common sense (i.e., Eq. 3.1.4), the rankings in the reversal set can be anything!

Imagine the conflicts that could be associated with this assertion. Suppose, for example, that a week before election day, the profile $\mathbf{p}$ (according to polls) would result in the plurality election ranking $c_1 \succ c_2 \succ c_3$. Now, c_3 not only is personally ambitious, but she fears the consequences should c_1 be elected. Therefore, rather than just trying to persuade more voters to vote for her, she plans to convince *all* voters to completely reverse their original ranking. Her strategy is obvious; in this way the new ranking would be $c_3 \succ c_2 \succ c_1$. However, complete success could frustrate her; even if each voter reverses his ranking, the plurality ranking could remain the same $c_1 \succ c_2 \succ c_3$!

The construction of the convex set $R(\mathbf{q}_0)$ follows our standard method; find the boundary vertices. To demonstrate this I construct $R(\mathbf{q}_0 = (0.4, 0.4, 0.2))$. First find the vertices of the profile set supporting $\mathbf{q}_0 = (0.4, 0.4, 0.2)$. The two vertices defined by $d^c = 0, 1$ are $\mathbf{p}_1 = (-, \beta^c = \mathbf{q}_0, d^c = 0)$ and $\mathbf{p}_2 = (\alpha_0^c = \mathbf{q}_0, -, d^c = 1)$ where the dash indicates that any value is admitted.

Half of the remaining vertex profiles are computed by placing α_0^c at a vertex and β_0^c on the opposite edge of the representation triangle. For instance, if $\alpha_0^c = (1, 0, 0)$, then the corresponding vertex profile is found by solving the three equations in three unknowns

$$ d^c(1, 0, 0) + (1 - d^c)(0, b_2, b_3) = (0.4, 0.4, 0.2); $$

the solution is $\mathbf{p}_3 = (\alpha_0^c = (1, 0, 0), \beta_0^c = (0, \frac{2}{3}, \frac{1}{3}), d^c = 0.4)$.

The other two profile vertices are found in a similar manner. To find the remaining profiles, the roles of β_0^c and α_0^c are reversed.

$$
\begin{array}{ll}
\mathbf{p}_1 = (-, \beta^c = \mathbf{q}_0, d^c = 0) & \mathbf{p}_2 = (\alpha_0^c = \mathbf{q}_0, -, d^c = 1) \\
\mathbf{p}_3 = ((1,0,0), (0, \frac{2}{3}, \frac{1}{3}), 0.4) & \mathbf{p}_4 = ((0, \frac{2}{3}, \frac{1}{3}), (1,0,0), 0.6) \\
\mathbf{p}_5 = ((0,1,0), (\frac{2}{3}, 0, \frac{1}{3}), 0.4) & \mathbf{p}_6 = ((\frac{2}{3}, 0, \frac{1}{3}), (0,1,0), 0.6) \\
\mathbf{p}_7 = ((0,0,1), (\frac{1}{2}, \frac{1}{2}, 0), 0.2) & \mathbf{p}_8 = ((\frac{1}{2}, \frac{1}{2}, 0), (0,0,1), 0.8)
\end{array}
$$

With the profiles, the next step is to compute $\mathbf{p}_j^r$ and, more importantly, the designated points. Using the symmetry properties described in Example 3.1.4, we find the following entries.

j	$\mathbf{p}_j^r$	$f(\mathbf{p}_j^r, \mathbf{w}_0)$
1	$((0.4, 0.2, 0.4), -, 1)$	$(0.4, 0.2, 0.4)$
2	$(-, (0.2, 0.4, 0.4), 0)$	$(0.2, 0.4, 0.4)$
3	$((\frac{1}{3}, 0, \frac{2}{3}), (0, 0, 1), 0.6)$	$(0.2, 0, 0.8)$
4	$((0, 1, 0), (\frac{2}{3}, \frac{1}{3}, 0), 0.4)$	$(0.4, 0.6, 0)$
5	$((\frac{1}{3}, \frac{2}{3}, 0), (1, 0, 0), 0.6)$	$(0.6, 0.4, 0)$
6	$((0, 0, 1), (0, \frac{1}{3}, \frac{2}{3}), 0.4)$	$(0, 0.2, 0.8)$
7	$((0, \frac{1}{2}, \frac{1}{2}), (0, 1, 0), 0.8)$	$(0, 0.6, 0.4)$
8	$((1, 0, 0), (\frac{1}{2}, 0, \frac{1}{2}), 0.2)$	$(0.6, 0, 0.4)$

By construction, $R(\mathbf{q}_0)$ is the convex hull of the designated points listed in the last column; it is plotted in Fig. 3.1.4. Observe; it meets all regions, so anything can happen!

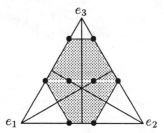

Fig. 3.1.4. The set $R(\mathbf{q}_0)$

The outcome indicated by Fig. 3.1.4, whereby $R(\mathbf{q}_0)$ meets all 13 ranking regions, is not an anomaly; it is the general situation. A startling assertion is the last sentence of the following theorem.

Theorem 3.1.10. *For $\mathbf{q}_0 \in Si(3)$, there are at least five different rankings of the candidates represented by points in $R(\mathbf{q}_0)$. If $\mathbf{q}_0$ is at the c_j vertex of the representation triangle (so, c_j enjoys an unanimous vote), then $R(\mathbf{q}_0)$ is the edge of $Si(3)$ opposite the c_j vertex. For $\mathbf{q}_0$ sufficiently close to $\mathcal{I}$, all 13 rankings of the candidates are represented by points in $R(\mathbf{q}_0)$.*

Proof. Both assertions follow from Theorem 3.1.9. A direct computation shows that

$$R(\mathbf{q}_0 = \mathcal{I}) = \mathcal{CH}(\mathbf{w}_{\frac{1}{3}}).$$

That is, $R(\mathbf{q}_0 = \mathcal{I})$ agrees with the BC convex hull. This discouraging comment about the plurality vote means that the normalized tallies of the reversal of a plurality complete tie agree with all possible BC outcomes! One profile vertex of $R(\mathcal{I})$ is based on the computation $d^c(1, 0, 0) + (1 - d^c)(0, \frac{1}{2}, \frac{1}{2}) = (\frac{1}{3}, \frac{1}{3}, \frac{1}{3})$; this defines the profile $\mathbf{p} = ((1, 0, 0), (0, \frac{1}{2}, \frac{1}{2}), \frac{1}{3})$. The reversal is $\mathbf{p}^r = ((\frac{1}{2}, 0, \frac{1}{2}), (0, 0, 1), \frac{2}{3})$ and its designated point is $(\frac{1}{3}, 0, \frac{2}{3})$. The other five points are found with a similar computation. Thus the vertices of $R(\mathcal{I})$ are defined by the six ways there are to permute $(\frac{2}{3}, \frac{1}{3}, 0)$, so $R(\mathcal{I})$ meets all 13 ranking regions.

If $\mathbf{q}_0 \neq \mathcal{I}$, the first claim follows by using the two vertex profiles defined by $d^c = 0, 1$; they are $\mathbf{p}_1 = (\alpha_0^c = \mathbf{q}_0, -, 1)$ and $\mathbf{p}_2 = (-, \beta_0^c = \mathbf{q}_0, 0)$. In each case, the profile and the designated point are determined by one entry. So, according to Theorem 3.1.9, there is a 120° angle between the designated points of $\mathbf{p}_1^r$ and $\mathbf{p}_2^r$. Thus the line connecting these designated points must meet five ranking regions. (For a specific example, consider the above discussion for $\mathbf{q}_0 = (0.4, 0.4, 0.2)$. The designated points for $\mathbf{p}_1^r$ and $\mathbf{p}_2^r$ are, respectively, on the ranking region $c_1 \sim c_3 \succ c_2$ and $c_2 \succ c_3 \sim c_1$.)

If $\mathbf{q}_0$ is at a vertex of the representation triangle, then the set of profiles supporting this outcome is a line segment with endpoints defined by $d^c = 0, 1$. The assertion in the theorem now follows from the geometry of the representation triangle and the above discussion.

A simple proof of the second assertion uses the relationship $R(\mathbf{q}_0 = \mathcal{I}) = \mathcal{CH}(\mathbf{w}_{\frac{1}{3}})$. All of the computations involve algebraic expressions, so, from continuity, if $\mathbf{q}_0$ is sufficiently close to $\mathcal{I}$, then $R(\mathbf{q}_0)$ remains close in appearance to $R(\mathcal{I})$. The conclusion follows. $\square$

There is some amusing geometry associated with the second conclusion. The distinguished point for a vertex profile $\mathbf{p}$, is, of course, at $\mathbf{q}_0$. What is interesting is that if a vertex $\mathbf{p}$ is not defined by $d^c = 0, 1$, then the distinguished point of $\mathbf{p}^r$ *must be on an edge of the representation triangle.* To see why this is so, observe that half of these profiles are determined by setting α_0^c at a vertex of the representation triangle, and β_0^c on the opposite edge. So, the "opposite twist" effect of reversing a profile forces both components of $\mathbf{p}_i^r$ to be on a common edge of the representation triangle. As the designated point is a convex combination of these two components, it must be on this edge of the representation triangle.

With a specific example, if $\alpha_0^c = (1, 0, 0)$, then β_0^c is on the c_2 - c_3 edge. The opposite twisting action forces both α_0^{cr} and β_0^{cr} of $\mathbf{p}^r$ to be on the c_1, c_3 edge of $Si(3)$; consequently, the designated point must also be on this edge. By appealing to neutrality, each edge of the representation triangle has one of these vertices of $R(\mathbf{q}_0)$. A similar argument holds for the other half of the vertices; these are the distinguished point obtained by setting β_0^c at the vertices of the representation triangle. Thus, except for degenerate choices of $\mathbf{q}_0$, there always are two vertices of $R(\mathbf{q}_0)$ on each edge of the representation triangle. No wonder the set is so large!

This description of $R(\mathbf{q}_0)$ indicates that the annoying "sufficiently close" comment from Theorem 3.1.10 can be replaced with a specific description. Let's see; to keep $R(\mathbf{q}_0)$ from meeting all 13 regions, we must prevent $\mathcal{I}$ from being in the interior of $R(\mathbf{q}_0)$. So, by following the "worse case" scenario approach of Sect. 2.5, it should be possible to find a condition on $\mathbf{q}_0$ to ensure that $R(\mathbf{q}_0)$ does not meet all 13 ranking regions.

Theorem 3.1.11. *A necessary and sufficient condition for $\mathcal{I} \notin R(\mathbf{q}_0)$ is that a* *candidate receives more than two-thirds of the vote. A necessary and sufficient condition for $R(\mathbf{q}_0)$ not to contain all 13 rankings is that one candidate receives at least two-thirds of the vote.*

The proof of this theorem uses the type of analysis introduced in Sect. 2.5, so the details and extensions (e.g., determining the conditions on $\mathbf{q}_0$ to ensure that only k rankings are represented in $R(\mathbf{q}_0)$) are left to the reader. As indicated by Fig. 3.1.5, the region of $\mathbf{q}_0$'s where the reversal can be anything is very large; again, it coincides with the space of normalized BC outcomes!

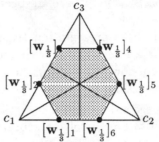

Fig. 3.1.5. The $\mathbf{q}_0$ values with 13 rankings in $R(\mathbf{q}_0)$

Here we go again; the condition posed in Theorem 3.1.11 follows the lead of the Catholic Church by requiring one more than two-thirds of the vote to avoid some sort of negative conclusion. By now the reader with an inquiring mind wants to know why the value $\frac{2}{3}$ keeps arising. Does the fact the BC is defined with this same fraction ($\mathbf{w}_{\frac{1}{3}} = (\frac{2}{3}, \frac{1}{3}, 0)$) have anything to do with its positive conclusions? (It does.) Does the same fraction serve as a dividing point when we consider $n \geq 4$ alternatives? (It does not.) Actually, I will leave this puzzle to the reader with the hint that, as indicated above, the point $\mathcal{I} = (\frac{1}{3}, \frac{1}{3}, \frac{1}{3})$ plays an important role in the geometric analysis.

3.1.5 Back to the Procedure Line

One way to extend the above theorems to all choices of $\mathbf{w}_s$ is to describe how the procedure line for $\mathbf{p}$ compares with the procedure line for $\mathbf{p}^r$. As shown in Sect. 2.6, the procedure line is uniquely determined by $\mathbf{p} = (\alpha_0^c, \beta_0^c, d^c)$ or by $(\alpha_{\frac{1}{2}}^c, \beta_{\frac{1}{2}}^c, d^c)$. The same assertion holds for $(\alpha_0^{cr}, \beta_0^{cr}, d^{cr})$. Notice the geometry; the long leg of the β^{cr} triangle is defined by the point β_0^{cr}, and $\beta_0^{cr} = (1, 3, 2)\alpha_0^c$ is obtained by rotating α_0^c through an angle of $-120°$. Once β_0^{cr} is known, the $\beta_{\frac{1}{2}}^{cr}$ leg is obtained by using another $-60°$ rotation and then taking $\frac{1}{2}$ of the length. (See Fig. 3.1.6.) From this construction, *it follows that α_0^c and $\beta_{\frac{1}{2}}^{cr}$ are on opposite sides of a line segment passing through $\mathcal{I}$.* By the properties of the $30°$- $60°$ - $90°$ triangle β^{cr}, it follows that

$$\|\beta_{\frac{1}{2}}^{cr} - \mathcal{I}\| = \frac{1}{2}\|\alpha_0^c - \mathcal{I}\|.$$

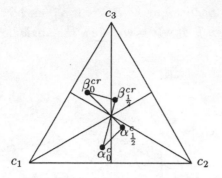

Fig. 3.1.6. Converting α_s^c to β_s^{cr}

A similar construction relates β_0^c to $\alpha_{\frac{1}{2}}^{cr}$. The main difference is that the twist is being made in the counter clockwise direction. That is, $\alpha_0^{cr} = (1, 2, 3)\beta_0^c$ is obtained by rotating β_0^c through a $120°$ angle. To go from the α_0^{cr} leg to the $\alpha_{\frac{1}{2}}^{cr}$ leg, another $60°$ rotation is required. Therefore, the rotation from α_0^c to $\beta_{\frac{1}{2}}^{cr}$ is a $180°$ angle.

Using this construction, we can find the rotations required to convert α_s^c into β_s^{cr}. An easy case is $s = \frac{1}{2}$. This is because there is a $-60°$ angle between $\alpha_{\frac{1}{2}}^c$ and α_0^c, a $-120°$ angle between α_0^c and β_0^{cr}, and another $-60°$ angle to $\beta_{\frac{1}{2}}^{cr}$. (See Fig. 3.1.6.) Thus, to convert $\alpha_{\frac{1}{2}}^c$ into $\beta_{\frac{1}{2}}^{cr}$, requires a $-240°$ rotation.

In much the same manner as used above, the geometry of how the α^c triangle is rotated into the β^{cr} triangle captures the conversion of α_s^c into β_s^{cr}. The only problem is to determine the angle between α_s^c and α_0^c.

Definition 3.1.5. Let Θ_s be the angle defined by $\mathbf{w}_0$ - $\mathcal{I}$ - $\mathbf{w}_s$. $\square$

Example 3.1.6. By definition, $\Theta_0 = 0°$, $\Theta_{\frac{1}{2}} = 60°$. To compute $\Theta_{\frac{1}{3}}$, observe that $\|\mathcal{I} - \mathbf{w}_{\frac{1}{3}}\| = \|(-\frac{1}{3}, \frac{1}{3}, 0)\| = \frac{\sqrt{2}}{3}$, while the distance $\|\mathbf{w}_{\frac{1}{3}} - \mathbf{w}_{\frac{1}{2}}\| = \|(\frac{1}{6}, -\frac{1}{6}, 0)\| = \frac{\sqrt{2}}{6}$. This means that the hypotenuse of the $\mathbf{w}_{\frac{1}{3}} - \mathbf{w}_{\frac{1}{2}}$ - $\mathcal{I}$ triangle is twice the length of the $\mathbf{w}_{\frac{1}{3}} - \mathbf{w}_{\frac{1}{2}}$ leg; consequently, it is a $30°$ - $60°$ - $90°$ triangle. As $\Theta_{\frac{1}{2}} = 60°$, it follows from the geometry that

$$\Theta_{\frac{1}{3}} = \Theta_{\frac{1}{2}} - 30^0 = 30^0.$$

As the $30°$ angle bisects the $\mathbf{w}_0$ - $\mathcal{I}$ - $\mathbf{w}_{\frac{1}{2}}$ angle, this provides still another measure showing that the BC is the "midpoint" of the positional voting methods. Also notice that since $\mathbf{w}_{\frac{1}{3}}$ is on the 30^0 line, it does not show a bias for one candidate over another. Therefore, the angle $\Theta - 30°$ *is a measure of the bias a positional method has for one candidate over another!* $\square$

Theorem 3.1.12. *In computing* $\mathbf{p}^r$ *from* $\mathbf{p}$, β_s^{cr} *is obtained by rotating* α_s^c *through an angle of* $-(120° + 2\Theta_s)$ *and* α_s^{cr} *is obtained by rotating* β_s^c *through* an angle of $120^0 + 2\Theta_s$. In particular, the BC pair $\alpha_{\frac{1}{3}}^c$ and $\beta_{\frac{1}{3}}^{cr}$ are on opposite sides of a line passing though $\mathcal{I}$. If $\mathbf{w}_{s'} = \mathbf{w}_s$, then the angle between α_s^c and $\beta_{s'}^{cr}$ is 180°.

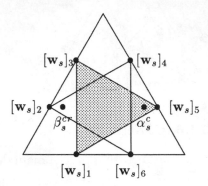

Fig. 3.1.7. Rotating α_s^c to obtain β_s^{cr}

While Theorem 3.1.12 appears to be complicated to use, it is not. As shown in Fig. 3.1.7, the point α_s^c is in the triangular convex hull $T_{1,s}$ defined by the vertices $\{[\mathbf{w}_s]_j\}_{j=1,3,5}$, and the point β_s^{cr} is in the triangle $T_{2,s}$ defined by $\{[\mathbf{w}_s]_j\}_{j=2,4,6}$. According to the reversal procedure and the permutation $(1,4)(2,5)(3,6)$, the equilateral triangle $T_{1,s}$ is rotated so that it becomes the equilateral triangle $T_{2,s}$ where the vertex $[\mathbf{w}_s]_j$ of $T_{1,s}$ is rotated to the vertex $[\mathbf{w}_s]_{j+3}$ of $T_{2,s}$. In this manner, the rotated position of α_s^c becomes the point β_s^{cr}. Likewise, when $T_{2,s}$ is rotated into $T_{1,s}$, the rotated location of $\beta_s^c \in T_{2,s}$ defines the point α_s^{cr}. The best way to "see" this, is to experiment with the triangles while carrying out the rotations for a specific computation. For an example problem, I suggest using Theorem 3.11 and the above geometric interpretation to devise a geometric proof of Theorem 3.1.6.

The Construction of $R(\mathbf{q}_s)$, $s \neq 0$. The construction of $R(\mathbf{q}_s)$ follows the lead of the construction of $R(\mathbf{q}_0)$ where Theorem 3.1.12 and the geometric description replace the $\pm 120^o$ rotations for the plurality (and antiplurality) method. So, for $\mathbf{q}_s \in \mathcal{CH}(\mathbf{w}_s)$, we need to determine the set $\{\mathbf{p} \mid f(\mathbf{p}, \mathbf{w}_s) = \mathbf{q}_s\}$. This convex set is determined by its vertices. As before, to find three of these vertices, α_s^c is placed at each of the vertices of $T_{1,s}$ and the corresponding d^c and $\beta_s^c \in T_{2,s}$ values are computed where β_s^c is on the boundary of $T_{2,s}$. Three more vertices are determined by setting β_s^c at vertices of $T_{2,s}$ and computing the corresponding d^c and α_s^c values. The last two vertices correspond to the d^c extreme values; when $d^c = 1$, $\alpha_s^c = \mathbf{q}_s$ and when $d^c = 0$, $\beta_s^c = \mathbf{q}_s$.

The $\mathbf{p}^r$ points are determined just by rotating the $T_{1,s}$ and $T_{2,s}$ triangles in the above indicated manner. The set $R(\mathbf{q}_s)$ is the convex hull defined by the distinguished points of these profiles.

Example 3.1.7. To illustrate this geometry, I will show that $R(\mathbf{q}_{\frac{1}{3}} = \mathcal{I}) = \{\mathcal{I}\}$. Following the above procedure, the line starting at $\alpha_{\frac{1}{3}}^c = [\mathbf{w}_{\frac{1}{3}}]_1$ and passing through $\mathbf{q}_{\frac{1}{3}} = \mathcal{I}$ meets the $T_{2,\frac{1}{3}}$ boundary at $\beta_{\frac{1}{3}}^c = [\mathbf{w}_{\frac{1}{3}}]_4$. This is because for the BC, the lines connecting the opposite points of $[\mathbf{w}_{\frac{1}{3}}]_j$ pass through $\mathcal{I}$. (This is due to the reversal symmetry.) Moreover, $d^c = \frac{1}{2}$. The reversal of $([\mathbf{w}_{\frac{1}{3}}]_1, [\mathbf{w}_{\frac{1}{3}}]_4, \frac{1}{2})$ is the same point $([\mathbf{w}_{\frac{1}{3}}]_1, [\mathbf{w}_{\frac{1}{3}}]_4, \frac{1}{2})$ with the same distinguished point $\mathcal{I}$. The identical analysis holds when the other seven vertices are computed. Thus, the assertion follows.

To see the bias introduced by other choices of $\mathbf{w}_s$, I will show next that when $s \neq \frac{1}{3}$, the set $R(\mathbf{q}_s = \mathcal{I})$ meets all 13 ranking regions of the representation triangle. (This is done above for $s = 0$.) Following the same approach, the line starting at $\alpha_s^c = [\mathbf{w}_s]_1$ and passing through $\mathcal{I}$ does *not* pass through $[\mathbf{w}_s]_4$. (Geometrically, this is because $\mathbf{w}_s$ does not satisfy reversal symmetry.) Instead, this line meets the boundary of $T_{2,s}$ at an interior point of the $[\mathbf{w}_s]_4$ - $[\mathbf{w}_s]_6$ edge if $s < \frac{1}{3}$, and at an interior point of the $[\mathbf{w}_s]_2$ - $[\mathbf{w}_s]_4$ edge if $s > \frac{1}{3}$. I will describe the case $s < \frac{1}{3}$, the other case follows with a similar argument. (I recommend the reader use Fig. 3.1.7 to follow the description.)

The rotation of this profile has $\beta_s^{cr} = [\mathbf{w}_s]_4$, but α_s^{cr} is an interior point of the $[\mathbf{w}_s]_1$ - $[\mathbf{w}_s]_3$ edge of $T_{1,s}$. Now, either by a simple computation or by the geometry, it is easy to show that $\mathcal{I}$ is *not* in the triangle determined by the three points $\{[\mathbf{w}_s]_j\}_{j=1,3,4}$. (Recall, the line connecting $[\mathbf{w}_s]_1$ and $[\mathbf{w}_s]_4$ misses $\mathcal{I}$.) This means that the distinguished point of this reversed profile is not at $\mathcal{I}$.

By neutrality, the distinguished points of the reversal of the profiles found by setting α_s^c at the other vertices of $T_{1,s}$ (that is, at $[\mathbf{w}_s]_3$, $[\mathbf{w}_s]_5$) must form angles of $\pm 120°$ with the first distinguished point. As such, $\mathcal{I}$ is at the center of the defined equilateral triangle. As this equilateral triangle meets all 13 ranking regions and as it is a subset of $R(\mathbf{q}_s = \mathcal{I})$, the assertion follows. $\square$

The results from the example are important, so they are highlighted in the following statement.

Theorem 3.1.13. a. *If $s \neq \frac{1}{3}$, then there exist $\mathbf{q}_s$ so that all 13 rankings are in $R(\mathbf{q}_s)$.*

b. *If $\mathbf{q}_{\frac{1}{3}} \in R(\mathbf{q}_{\frac{1}{3}})$, then $\mathbf{q}_{\frac{1}{3}} = \mathcal{I}$. On the other hand, for $s \neq \frac{1}{3}$, there is a ball of points about $\mathcal{I}$ so that any $\mathbf{q}_s$ in this ball satisfies*

$$\mathbf{q}_s \in R(\mathbf{q}_s). \qquad (3.1.12)$$

c. *If $s \neq 0, \frac{1}{2}$, and if $\mathbf{q}_s \in \partial\mathcal{CH}(\mathbf{w}_s)$, then $R(\mathbf{q}_s)$ is a point on the boundary of $\mathcal{CH}(\mathbf{w}_s)$ in a reversed ranking region.*

Part b asserts that unless you use the BC, there are profiles leading to a strict ranking with the peculiar property that when the profile is reversed, not only does the ranking remain the same, but so does the (normalized) election tally. Very disturbing!

By now the reader should realize the comments about the existence of "a ball of points about $\mathcal{I}$," such as in assertion b, are conservative statements. Instead, there could be a sizable set of such points. Consider the large set of outcomes where $\mathbf{q}_0 \in R(\mathbf{q}_0)$ is depicted in Fig. 3.1.8; a candidate needs to win more than half the votes in order to avoid this problem! In fact, by use of the geometry and the proof of Corollary 3.1.7, it can be shown that the convex set of points where $\mathbf{q}_s \in R(\mathbf{q}_s)$ has the three vertices $(\frac{1-s}{2}, s, \frac{1-s}{2})$, $(\frac{1-s}{2}, \frac{1-s}{2}, s)$, $(s, \frac{1-s}{2}, \frac{1-s}{2})$. The details of this statement, along with the obvious comparisons between what happens with various choices of $\mathbf{w}_s$ are left to the reader.

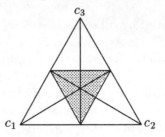

Fig. 3.1.8. The $\mathbf{q}_0$ values where $\mathbf{q}_0 \in R(\mathbf{q}_0)$

Proof. Part a is proved above for $\mathbf{q}_s = \mathcal{I}$. Because all of the computations are, in fact, based on linear expressions, a small change in $\mathbf{q}_s$ leads to a small change in $R(\mathbf{q}_s)$. Thus, the assertion holds for a ball of choices of $\mathbf{q}_s$ where the ball is centered at $\mathcal{I}$.

To prove part b, observe that $\mathcal{I} \in R(\mathbf{q}_s = \mathcal{I})$ is an interior point of this set should $s \neq \frac{1}{3}$. Again, a small perturbation of $\mathbf{q}_s$ results in a small change in $R(\mathbf{q}_s)$. Thus there is a small ball of choices of $\mathbf{q}_s$ so that the assertion holds.

Part c. If $\mathbf{q}_s \in \partial \mathcal{CH}(\mathbf{w}_s)$, $s \neq 0, \frac{1}{2}$, then $\mathbf{q}_s$ is uniquely expressed as a linear combination of a $[\mathbf{w}]_s$ with an odd subscript and an even subscript. This linear combination defines the unique $(\alpha_s^c, \beta_s^c, d^c)$ profile supporting $\mathbf{q}_s$. Thus, $R(\mathbf{q}_s)$ is the distinguished point for the reversal of this one profile. As both α_s^c and β_s^c correspond to vertices of $T_{1,s}$, $T_{2,s}$ respectively, α_s^{cr}, β_s^{cr} must also be vertices. Thus, the distinguished point is on the boundary of $\mathcal{CH}(\mathbf{w}_s)$. That the ranking of $R(\mathbf{q}_s)$ is the reversed of the ranking for $\mathbf{q}_s$ follows from the rotation geometry. $\square$

3.1.6 Reversal Bias Paradoxes

All right, what is so important about these theorems? We now know from the above that, with increasing intensity as the value of s moves away from $\frac{1}{3}$, the reversal of a profile need not reverse the election outcome. Is this a peculiarity, or does it tell us something new about elections? As I show next, the bias where a procedure does not satisfy the reversal symmetry has several damaging properties.

To see what are some of the consequences of violating reversal symmetry, start with the naive belief that the pairwise election rankings must agree with the ranking of all three candidates. This means that for any $\mathbf{p}$, if the $f(\mathbf{p}, \mathbf{w}_s)$ ranking is $c_i \succ c_j \succ c_k$, then the rankings of $F_3(\mathbf{p})$ must be the inherited $c_i \succ c_j, c_i \succ c_k, c_j \succ c_k$. But, with the possible exception of the BC, we cannot expect this to be true! If it were true, then, because $F_3(\mathbf{p}^r) = F_3^r(\mathbf{p})$, it would be necessary for the ranking of $f(\mathbf{p}^r, \mathbf{w}_s)$ to be the reversal of $f(\mathbf{p}, \mathbf{w}_s)$. This is not the case; we've shown that the rankings of $f(\mathbf{p}, \mathbf{w}_s)$ and $f(\mathbf{p}^r, \mathbf{w}_s)$ could remain the same! This suggests that, with the possible exception of the BC, the ranking defined by the pairs could be the exact opposite of the ranking defined by the positional voting method.

Similarly, suppose we would like to believe that the Condorcet winner never is bottom-ranked. Namely, we would like to believe when a Condorcet winner exists, there are restrictions on the choice of the $\mathbf{w}_s$ ranking. The reversal of such a profile either defines a new Condorcet winner, or a pair of top-ranked candidates. However, it is not clear what will be the $\mathbf{w}_s$ outcome for the reversed profile; by the refusal of $\mathbf{w}_s$, $s \neq \frac{1}{3}$, to honor reversal symmetry, the outcome could be anything! While this does not prove that many $\mathbf{w}_s$ choices can force the Condorcet winner to be bottom-ranked, it does offer a huge hint that this may be the case! (It is not a proof because the profiles where the rankings of $f(\mathbf{p}, \mathbf{w}_s)$ and $f(\mathbf{p}^r, \mathbf{w}_s)$ agree may define cycles.)

The problem, then, is that when $\mathbf{p}$ is reversed, so are the pairwise rankings. But, with the reversal of $\mathbf{p}$, anything can occur with the $\mathbf{w}_s$, $s \neq \frac{1}{3}$, ranking. As such, we must worry that *if a positional method other than the BC is used, a wide range of disturbing paradoxes occur.* As these other procedures ignore profile information about reversals (but the pairwise vote does not), this ignorance has to be accompanied by serious problems. However, a more refined approach needs to be developed to characterize this problems; this is discussed in Sect. 3.3.

There is a second kind of outcome suggested by these results. We must expect more paradoxes to occur and/or a greater likelihood of these paradoxes occurring with positional methods that are further away from the BC. The reason is simple; the set of outcomes $\mathbf{q}_s$ which do not satisfy reversal symmetry grows as s moves away from $\frac{1}{3}$. In turn, by use of the $(\alpha_s^c, \beta_s^c, d^c)$ coordinate systems, it can be seen that the size of the profile set leading to these disturbing outcomes also increases.

3.1.7 Borda Symmetry

The above development shows that the BC is more symmetric than any other positional voting procedure. With the added symmetry comes an added sense of predictability that the system better communicates the voters' beliefs.

To offer some insight as to why predictability occurs, remember that the purpose of a profile restriction, such as Black's single peakedness, is to restrict the kinds of election outcomes. The BC symmetry already restricts the potential outcomes. (See, for instance, Corollary 3.1.8.) The reason is similar to that of a profile restriction!

To see the connection, suppose we want to impose a profile restriction where $f(\mathbf{p}, \mathbf{w}_s) = f^r(\mathbf{p}^r, \mathbf{w}_s)$. For $s \neq \frac{1}{3}$, this is a severe profile restriction that cuts by two the dimension of the admissible profiles. However, for the BC, no restrictions are necessary because the desired outcome is ensured by symmetry.

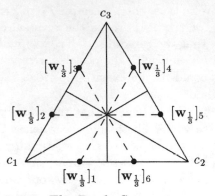

Fig. 3.1.9. The Borda Symmetry axes

As I will describe next, when these BC symmetries are expressed in terms of permutations, we obtain the following table.

Changes in voter types	Borda Profile Symmetries σ_T	Combinations
$c_1 \rightarrow c_2$	$(1,6)(2,5)(3,4)$	
$c_1 \rightarrow c_3$	$(1,4)(2,3)(5,6)$	
$c_2 \rightarrow c_3$	$(1,2)(3,6)(4,5)$	
180° rotation	$(1,5,3)(2,6,4)$	
-180° rotation	$(1,3,5)(2,4,6)$	
Reversal	$(1,4)(2,5)(3,6)$	
c_1 middle-ranked	$(1,5)(2,4)$	$c_2 \rightarrow c_3$ & Reversal
c_2 middle-ranked	$(2,6)(3,5)$	$c_1 \rightarrow c_3$ & Reversal
c_3 middle-ranked	$(1,3)(4,6)$	$c_1 \rightarrow c_2$ & Reversal
60° rotation	$(1,6,5,4,3,2)$	-180° & Reversal
-60° rotation	$(1,2,3,4,5,6)$	180° & Reversal

From this table and Fig. 3.1.9, it can be shown why the BC is more symmetric than any other positional voting method;[9] in fact, the BC satisfies a form of *super-neutrality*. To explain this statement, observe that an important consequence of neutrality is that it allows us to consider only situations where a particular candidate, say c_1, is top-ranked. Having a different candidate, say c_3, top-ranked, involves only a name change; it corresponds to flipping $Si(3)$ about an appropriate indifference line in Fig. 3.1.9. So, for strict rankings, we

---

[9]This is true for all $n \geq 3$. If every voter's ranking of a subset of k candidates, $2 \leq k \leq n$ is permuted in a specified manner, then we would expect the election ranking to be permuted in a similar manner. For each $k > 2$, the positional methods that satisfy this stronger neutrality condition admit various satisfying election relationships. However, *only the BC satisfies this condition for all $k \geq 2$*. Thus, the BC enjoys the properties of these other procedures and many others.

only have to consider $c_1 \succ c_2 \succ c_3$ and $c_1 \succ c_3 \succ c_2$ because the six specified symmetry changes in profiles and election outcomes lead to everything else. The BC does better than this; it also admits the election relationships guaranteed by Corollary 3.1.8. As such, it allows an analysis of $c_1 \succ c_2 \succ c_3$ to hold for its reversal–this is false for any other $\mathbf{w}_s$! Moreover, the BC imposes regularity and predictability on symmetries obtained by combining reversals and name changes! A listing of these symmetry relationships and what they correspond is in the table. As fewer profiles can force different BC outcomes, we must expect more election relationships to emerge for the BC than for any other $\mathbf{w}_s$[10]. In fact, according to these symmetries, a BC analysis need only involve a single ranking $c_1 \succ c_2 \succ c_3$.

Example 3.1.8. a. The last column of the table is obtained by combining permutations. For instance, if names are first changed according to $c_1 \to c_2$ and then followed by a reversal, we have the change in voter types given by

$$(1,6)(2,5)(3,4)(1,4)(2,5)(3,6) = (1,3)(1,6).$$

This last permutation corresponds to a new symmetry where voter types are changed

by keeping fixed a voter type that has c_3 middle-ranked, and

for each of the remaining four rankings, interchange the top and bottom-ranked candidates.

Geometrically, this is equivalent to flipping the representation triangle about the dashed line in Fig. 3.1.9 connecting $[\mathbf{w}_{\frac{1}{3}}]_2$ and $[\mathbf{w}_{\frac{1}{3}}]_5$ and then reading off which voter types are changed into others. Notice, types 2 and 5 remain fixed; types 1 and 3 and types 4 and 6 are interchanged. This is the permutation of voter types $(1,3)(4,6)$.

So, suppose the BC ranking of $\mathbf{p} = (p_1, p_2, p_3, p_4, p_5, p_6)$ is $c_2 \succ c_3 \sim c_1$. Now consider the profile $\sigma_T(\mathbf{p}) = (p_3, p_2, p_1, p_6, p_5, p_4)$ where $\sigma_T = (1,3)(4,6)$. According to the corollary, we have that the BC ranking associated with $\sigma_T(\mathbf{p})$ is obtained by first making the $c_1 \to c_2$ name change $c_1 \succ c_3 \sim c_2$ – and then taking the reversal to get $c_2 \sim c_3 \succ c_1$.

b. As another example, consider the two profiles $\mathbf{p}_1 = (\frac{2}{16}, \frac{5}{16}, \frac{1}{16}, \frac{1}{16}, \frac{3}{16}, \frac{4}{16})$, and $\mathbf{p}_2 = (\frac{5}{16}, \frac{1}{16}, \frac{1}{16}, \frac{3}{16}, \frac{4}{16}, \frac{2}{16})$. The BC ranking of $\mathbf{p}_1$ is $c_1 \succ c_2 \succ c_3$ and $\sigma_T(\mathbf{p}_1) = \mathbf{p}_2$ where σ_T is the -60° rotation obtained by rotating all of the ranking regions -60° about $\mathcal{I}$. (Remember, 60° rotations are *not* admitted by neutrality and name changes. From the table, this rotation is obtained by combining a 180° rotation with a reversal. Using these same operations on the ranking $c_1 \succ$

---

[10]Readers familiar with group theory will observe that the subgroup of profile symmetries guaranteed by neutrality is a S_6 subgroup of order six. The $6!/6 = 120$ cosets define 120 permutations of profiles that define different election outcomes. Including $\mathbf{w}_s$ as an admissible variable, the set of symmetries become $S_3 \times Z_2$; only the BC fully exploits this symmetry to define a S_6 subgroup of order 12 with 60 cosets. More information can be extracted from the symmetric group for $n > 3$ candidates, but this is beyond the scope of this book.

$c_2 \succ c_3$, we obtain the BC ranking for $\mathbf{p}_2$ which is $((1,2,3)(c_1 \succ c_2 \succ c_3))^r = (c_2 \succ c_3 \succ c_1)^r = c_1 \succ c_3 \succ c_2$. $\square$

We now have a simple geometric way to understand what is gained from the BC symmetries! A geometric way to understand neutrality is that the representation triangle can be repositioned in any way as long as $\mathcal{I}$ is placed over $\mathcal{I}$ and vertices are placed upon vertices. With the BC, the last restraint that vertices must end up on vertices is *relaxed!* It is replaced with the condition that indifference lines end up on indifference lines. This is what allows the previously unattainable rotations that are multiples of $\pm 60°$.

As another way to describe the added advantage of BC symmetry, observe the dashed lines in Fig. 3.1.9. With neutrality we can get any change obtained by flipping around the indifference lines and rotating vertices to vertices. The BC adds to all of this the ability to flip about the dashed lines on the figure.

Finally, to justify the superneutrality title for BC, consider $(f(\mathbf{p}, \mathbf{w}_s), F_3(\mathbf{p}))$. For any s, neutrality ensures that the outcomes are predictable for any profile change σ_T derived from a name change σ. Only the BC goes further to allow the outcome to be predictable with reversals of profiles and all combinations with name changes. By examining the geometry of Fig. 3.1.9, it is clear that the BC respects *all* permutations of voter types where two voter types that started out adjacent to each other remain adjacent. Only the BC allows this symmetry. Thus, the BC does satisfy a superneutrality.

3.1.8 Exercises

3.1.1. a. Compute the intensity outcome for all pairs for $\mathbf{p} = (\frac{1}{6}, 0, \frac{1}{3}, \frac{1}{4}, \frac{1}{6}, \frac{1}{12})$.
b. For the integer profile $(3,0,2,0,1,0)$, geometrically compute the c_1, c_3 intensity outcome.

3.1.2. Theorem 3.1.1 asserts that the intensity method is a Condorcet Improvement method. Find a Condorcet Improvement method that does not always agree with the intensity outcome.

3.1.3. a. Compute $(1,2,3)(1,3)$; $(1,3)(1,2,3)$. Geometrically move the representation triangle according to each computation to show why the answers differ according to the order they are performed.
b. To solve the algebra problem $\sigma_1 x = \sigma_2$, where x is an unknown permutation that is to be found, first multiply both sides of the equality on the *left* by σ_1^{-1} to obtain

$$\sigma_1^{-1}(\sigma_1 x) = \sigma_1^{-1}\sigma_2.$$

Multiplication of permutations is associative, which means that the left-hand side becomes $(\sigma_1^{-1}\sigma_1)x = (1)x = x$. Therefore, the solution is $x = \sigma_1^{-1}\sigma_2$. Use this approach to solve the following problems:

$$(1,2,3)x = (2,3); \quad (2,3)x = (1,2,3); \quad (1,2,3)x = (1,3,2); \quad (1,2)x = (2,3).$$

c. Modify the argument in b to show how to solve the problem $y\sigma_1 = \sigma_2$. (As part a shows, you cannot interchange the order of multiplication – the process is not commutative.) Use this approach to solve the following problems: $y(1,2,3) = (2,3)$; $y(2,3) = (1,2,3)$; $y(1,2,3) = (1,3,2)$; $y(1,2) = (2,3)$. (A set of points with an operation is called a *group* if all problems of the type $ax = b$, $ya = b$ can be solved in this general manner for any a, b.)

d. For permutations of voter types, solve

$$(1,3,5)(2,4,6)x = (1,2,3,4,5,6); \quad y(1,3,5)(2,4,6) = (1,2,3,4,5,6);$$
$$(1,2)(3,6)(4,5)x = (1,3)(4,6).$$

3.1.4. Is an agenda $< c_1, c_2, c_3 >$ neutral? There are two ways to analyze this problem. One is where the name change σ also changes the ordering in the agenda. The second, where the "fairness" issue becomes relevant, is where the name change does *not* change the $< c_1, c_2, c_3 >$ ordering. Compare both cases.

3.1.5. One reason $f(\mathbf{p}^r, \mathbf{w}_s) \neq \mathbf{q}_s^v$ is that for certain values of s, $\mathbf{q}_s^r$ need not even be in the representation triangle! Find the values of s for which this is true. For each s, find a $\mathbf{q}_s$ to illustrate this peculiar fact. Characterize those choices of $\mathbf{q}_s$ where $\mathbf{q}_s^r$ is in the representation triangle.

3.1.6. Suppose $\mathbf{w}_s$ has the alarming property that for any rankings of the three pairs and of the three candidates, there is a profile so that the rankings are attained by $(F_3(\mathbf{p}), F(\mathbf{p}, \mathbf{w}_s))$. Prove that the same property is satisfied by $\mathbf{w}_s^r$.

3.1.7. Find a $\mathbf{p}$ where the rankings of $f(\mathbf{p}, \mathbf{w}_0)$ and $f(\mathbf{p}^r, \mathbf{w}_0)$ both are $c_1 \succ c_2 \succ c_3$.

3.1.8. If $\mathbf{p}$ is such that the procedure line is a point $\mathbf{q}$, prove that the procedure line for $\mathbf{p}^r$ is the point $\mathbf{q}^r$.

3.1.9. If $\mathbf{p} = (\alpha_0 = (0.2, 0.3, 0.5), \beta_0 = (0.3, 0.4, 0.3), d = \frac{1}{4})$, find $\mathbf{p}^r$ and the procedure line for $\mathbf{p}^r$.

3.1.10. For $\mathbf{q}_0 = (0.4, 0.3, 0.3)$, find $R(\mathbf{q}_0)$.

3.1.11. Prove Theorem 3.1.11. Then, find conditions so that $R(\mathbf{q}_0)$ meets eight regions. Find a necessary and sufficient condition for $R(\mathbf{q}_{\frac{1}{2}})$ not to meet all 13 ranking regions. Do the same for $R(\mathbf{q}_{\frac{1}{4}})$.

3.2 From Aggregating Pairwise Votes to the Borda Count

Due to its familiarity and simplicity, pairwise majority voting retains its status as a favored procedure. Unfortunately, because of its single-dimensional myopia, we should seriously question the election outcomes. The good news is that these difficulties can be resolved. For instance, by using group coordinate representations, we identified those profiles that are associated with these troublesome election conclusions. Once the problems are identified, we can design reform procedures. This is, of course, the motivation and approach used to develop the Condorcet Improvement and the intensity of comparison approaches; both methods are designed to pay needed attention to the higher dimensional aspects of profiles and the fact that the voters' rankings are transitive. On the other hand, because these two procedures are motivated by different issues and philosophies, it is surprising that they are equivalent.

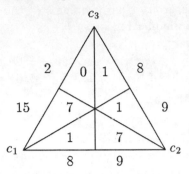

Fig. 3.2.1. Pairwise majority vote

Maybe there is still another approach. If cycles and other problems are created by retaining only the ordinal information about who won each pairwise election, maybe more acceptable conclusions can be achieved by recognizing how well each candidate does in each election. To illustrate, the profile indicated in Fig. 3.2.1 crowns c_2 as the Condorcet winner even though it is dubious that she is the voters' true top-choice. (The doubts are consequences of the dominating 120° symmetry where the voters have extreme views about c_2, but very few have c_1 bottom-ranked.) Indeed, an important indicator that a profile has these troublesome, higher dimensional properties is if the Condorcet winner, c_2, just barely wins each of her pairwise elections, while another candidate, c_1 in this case, barely loses to c_2 but wallops c_3.

If the pairwise tallies detect when the Condorcet winner may not be the voters' real choice, then perhaps these tallies, rather than just the ordinal ranking of who won, can help rank the candidates. So, a natural extension of the pairwise majority vote is to add up the tallies. After all, the pairwise tally indicates how *well* each candidate did in each contest. With the profile of Fig. 3.2.1, c_1 receives eight votes from the c_1 - c_2 election and 15 votes from the c_1 - c_3 contest for a total of 23 points. Similarly, c_2 receives 18 points, and c_3 receives a meager 10 points. Thus, the *aggregated* pairwise vote defines the more reasonable ranking of $c_1 \succ c_2 \succ c_3$ with the tally of 23 : 18 : 10.

Definition 3.2.1. For $\{c_i, c_j\}$, let $q_{i,j}$ be the fraction of voters that prefer c_i to c_j. The *aggregated pairwise vote* procedure is where $\sum_{j \neq i} q_{i,j}$ points are assigned to c_i and the candidates are ranked according to the point totals. $\square$

This aggregation method, which serves as another measure of the voters' intensity of support for one candidate over another, offers an immediate benefit; there are no cycles! To understand why, recall that cycles occur because the ordinal rankings fail to retain information about the intensity of each victory and the heterogeneous nature of the profile. On the other hand, with the aggregated pairwise vote procedure, information about the strength of each pairwise victory is introduced and cycles disappear. (Mathematically, the outcome is based on the values of three numbers on the line, so a transitive ranking must occur.) Observe how the motivating philosophy for the aggregated approach differs significantly from that used to develop "the intensity of comparison" approach, which favors the intensity level of the pairwise rankings, and the "Condorcet Improvement," which relies upon geometry to correct glaring faults of the Condorcet standards.

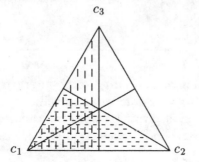

Fig. 3.2.2. c_1's aggregated vote

Keeping to the theme of this book, a geometric argument is developed for the aggregation procedure. The key to the geometry is depicted in Fig. 3.2.2. In the contest between c_1 and c_2, c_1 receives the sum of terms in the triangle with the vertically shaded components; in the $\{c_1, c_3\}$ contest, she receives the sum of points in the horizontally shaded regions. It is clear from the figure that c_1's vote total, the sum of numbers in both shaded regions, captures certain two-dimensional aspects of a profile. In fact, observe that c_1 receives a double count for the two ranking regions where she is top-ranked. Continuing, in those regions where c_1 is second-ranked, the vote is counted only once. Finally, no points are assigned to c_1 from those regions where c_1 is bottom-ranked.

This shady geometric reasoning shows how to compute the c_j outcome of the aggregated pairwise vote. Namely, double count the number of voters with c_j top-ranked, count the number of voters with c_j middle-ranked, and ignore those voters with c_j bottom-ranked. Equivalently, for each voter, assign two points to his top-ranked candidate, one to his middle-ranked candidate, and zero for his bottom-ranked candidate. Observe, *the aggregated pairwise majority vote is equivalent to the BC.*

Theorem 3.2.1. *The aggregated pairwise majority vote and the BC are equivalent.*

3.2.1 Borda and Aggregated Pairwise Votes

As another way to see the connection between the pairwise contests and the BC, suppose a voter has the ranking $c_1 \succ c_2 \succ c_3$. By using the BC, the weight he assigns to a candidate equals the sum of votes he would assign to her over the three pairwise (voting vector $(1, 0)$) elections. This is illustrated with the following assignments of points.

Method	Set of candidates	$\{c_1\}$	$\{c_2\}$	$\{c_3\}$
Majority	$\{c_1, c_2\}$	1	0	
Majority	$\{c_1, c_3\}$	1		0
Majority	$\{c_2, c_3\}$		1	0
		—	—	—
BC	$\{c_1, c_2, c_3\}$	2	1	0

Thus, *the BC voting vector is the aggregated version of the pairwise voting vector* (1,0). This "aggregated pairwise majority vote" interpretation, demonstrates why the BC (not the plurality vote or any other positional voting method) is the "natural" extension of the standard vote between two candidates. A precise relationship between the BC outcome and the aggregated pairwise vote tallies is

$$f(\mathbf{p}, \mathbf{w}_{\frac{1}{3}}) = \frac{1}{3}(\sum_{j \neq 1} q_{1,j}, \sum_{j \neq 2} q_{2,j}, \sum_{j \neq 3} q_{3,j}) \qquad (3.2.1)$$

where the multiple $\frac{1}{3}$, needed to normalize the total tally to unity, arises because there are three pairwise contests.

Example 3.2.1. Suppose the pairwise election outcomes for 30 voters are as given in the following table. Because the BC agrees with the aggregated pairwise vote outcome, the sum of each column is the (2, 1, 0) BC outcome for these voters.

	$\{c_1\}$	$\{c_2\}$	$\{c_3\}$
$\{c_1, c_2\}$	16	14	
$\{c_1, c_3\}$	16		14
$\{c_2, c_3\}$		20	10
BC tally	32	34	24

$\Box$

The connection of the BC with pairwise votes, as displayed by the symmetry properties of Sect. 3.1, Eq. 3.2.1 and Example 3.2.1, accurately supports a suspicion that the BC respects certain properties of pairwise elections. Some important results follow.

Theorem 3.2.2. *A Condorcet winner never is BC bottom-ranked, and a Condorcet loser never is BC top-ranked.*

A Condorcet winner always receives more than a third of the assigned BC points while a Condorcet loser always receives less than a third of the assigned BC points. Therefore, a Condorcet winner always is BC ranked above a Condorcet loser.

If all pairwise votes end in a tie, then the BC ranking is $\mathcal{I}$.

With reflection, these conclusions must be expected, and some of them must have been known by Borda.[11] After all, in order for c_j to be a Condorcet winner,

---

[11]See [D]. If $n \geq 4$, then the BC admits these and many other properties. See [S9, 11, 16-19].

she must win both pairwise elections, so her point total on the right hand side of Eq. 3.2.1 must exceed that of at least one other candidate. This happens, and the following elementary proof is fashioned from this description. Indeed, as shown by the following analysis, a *Condorcet winner must be favored by the BC.* Yet, while favored, the above example proves that she need not be top-ranked.

Proof. First, if all pairwise elections end in a tie vote, then it is obvious that the BC election outcome must be $\mathcal{I}$. Here, the aggregated pairwise vote sums the same values for each candidate.

If c_1 is the Condorcet winner, then

$$q_{1,j} = \frac{1}{2} + \epsilon_{1,j}, \quad q_{j,1} = \frac{1}{2} - \epsilon_{1,j}, \, j = 2, 3,$$

$$q_{2,3} = \frac{1}{2} + \alpha_{2,3}, \quad q_{3,2} = \frac{1}{2} - \alpha_{2,3}$$

where $\epsilon_{1,j} > 0$ is the amount over $\frac{1}{2}$ of c_1's victory over c_j. Similarly, the sign of fractional difference (from $\frac{1}{2}$), $\alpha_{2,3}$, determines whether c_2 or c_3 wins this pairwise contest.

Substituting these values into Eq. 3.2.1 leads to

$$f(\mathbf{p}, \mathbf{w}_{\frac{1}{3}}) = \frac{1}{3}(1 + \epsilon_{1,2} + \epsilon_{1,3}, 1 - \epsilon_{1,2} + \alpha_{2,3}, 1 - \epsilon_{1,3} - \alpha_{2,3}). \tag{3.2.2}$$

The first component of the BC tally requires c_1, the Condorcet winner to receive more than a third of the total tally. Now if c_2, instead of c_1, is BC top-ranked, then the inequality

$$\alpha_{2,3} > 2\epsilon_{1,2} + \epsilon_{1,3} > 0$$

determines the victory c_2 needs over c_3 to overcome the BC advantage given to the Condorcet winner c_1. But the sign of $\alpha_{2,3} > 0$ relegates c_3 to be BC bottom-ranked, and she receives less than $\frac{1}{3}$ of the total vote. Consequently, a Condorcet winner never can be BC bottom-ranked.

(As a simpler argument, because the Condorcet winner receives over one-third of the vote, she has more than the average number of points. Thus, some other candidate must receive less than one-third of the vote; that candidate is ranked below the Condorcet winner.)

A similar argument proves the other assertions such as the Condorcet winner must be BC ranked strictly above a Condorcet loser, and that a Condorcet loser cannot be top-ranked. □

One test of the BC is how it handles the partial $120°$ symmetry profiles where p of the voters have the ranking $c_1 \succ c_2 \succ c_3$ and the rest have the type five ranking $c_2 \succ c_3 \succ c_1$. The goal is to determine the value of p that gives the BC election victory to c_1. Recall that the Condorcet Improvement and the intensity of comparison approaches require $p > \frac{2}{3}$. The same threshold value holds for the BC because $f((p, 0, 0, 0, 1-p, 0), \mathbf{w}_{\frac{1}{3}}) = \frac{1}{3}(2p, 2-p, 1-p)$, so c_1 wins iff $2p > 2-p$ iff $p > \frac{2}{3}$. Again, c_1 needs one more than two-thirds of the vote.

As the next statement asserts, there is an excellent reason why the BC shares this threshold value with the Condorcet Improvement and intensity of comparison approaches. All three procedures are the same.

Theorem 3.2.3. *The BC, the aggregated pairwise majority vote and the intensity of comparison approaches are the same; all are Condorcet Improvement procedures.*

The simplest proof is to show that the BC agrees with the intensity of comparison approach. In a BC comparison of c_i with c_j where $c_i \succ c_k \succ c_j$, c_i is given two points while c_j is given zero. This ranking is where c_i is intensely preferred to c_j. Thus, the differential in point totals is twice that awarded to c_i for a ranking where $c_i \succ c_j$ and c_k is either top- or bottom-ranked. Similarly, c_k is given one point. But, this is the intensity of comparison method.

An alternative proof is offered that uses the relationship $q_{i,j} = 1 - q_{j,i}$. This identity permits the six $q_{i,j}$ variables to be expressed in terms of the three variables $q_{1,2}$, $q_{2,3}$, $q_{3,1}$.

Proof. It suffices to show that the profiles leading to each election outcome agree with that of the Condorcet Improvement. Using the notation of Sect. 2.5, recall that the $x \in [1, -1]$ component measures the c_1, c_2 pairwise vote where $x = 1, 0, -1$ corresponds, respectively, to c_1 getting all votes, a tie, and c_2 getting all votes. Indeed, $x = q_{1,2} - q_{2,1} = 2q_{1,2} - 1$. Similarly, $y = q_{2,3} - q_{3,2} = 2q_{2,3} - 1$, $z = q_{3,1} - q_{1,3} = 2q_{3,1} - 1$. With these equations, the Condorcet Improvement requirement for the relative ranking $c_1 \succ c_2$, given by $2x > y + z$, becomes $2q_{1,2} > q_{2,3} + q_{3,1}$.

According to Eq. 3.2.1, The BC admits the relative ranking $c_1 \succ c_2$ iff $q_{1,2} + q_{1,3} > q_{2,1} + q_{2,3}$. By expressing this relationship in terms of the three chosen variables, the BC condition also becomes $2q_{1,2} > q_{2,3} + q_{3,1}$. The proof is completed by observing that the equivalence of the procedures follows from neutrality and the fact that each gives the same relative (strict) ranking for c_1, c_2 for a profile. $\square$

A very fat triangle. When comparing the BC election outcomes with the three pairwise elections, the relevant mapping is

$$F_{\frac{1}{3}} = (F_3, f(-, \mathbf{w}_{\frac{1}{3}})) : Si(6) \to [-1, 1]^3 \times Si(3). \qquad (3.2.3)$$

In other words, for a given profile, first compute each of the three pairwise election tallies and then determine the BC tally. Just as the three pairwise elections can be viewed as defining a point in $[-1, 1]^3$, a cube (see Sect. 2.5), the four elections can be viewed as defining a point in the space $[-1, 1]^3 \times Si(3)$.

To obtain an inkling of what $[-1, 1]^3 \times Si(3)$ might look like, extend the ideas used to identify $[-1, 1]^3$ with a cube. Remember, the construction uses a freedom of choice approach where any point in $Si(3)$ could be associated with any specified point in the cube, $\mathbf{q} \in [-1, 1]^3$. So, in a direction orthogonal to the cube, pass a simplex $Si(3)$ through the specified $\mathbf{q} \in [-1, 1]^3$. Of course because a cube already uses up all of the available directions in our limited three-dimensional world and because the representation triangle is a two-dimensional object, the specifics of this construction require us to be in a five-dimensional space! This is no problem if our imagination is flexible enough to serve as the construction site. Now, by varying the choice of $\mathbf{q} \in [-1, 1]^3$, the moving simplex traces out the region in R^5.

While representations for $[-1, 1]^3 \times Si(3)$ are difficult in our limited three-dimensional world (some are given later in this section), we have an idea what the object looks like. In Sect. 2.6, we saw that the figure $[-1, 1] \times Si(3)$ is a fat triangle in three-space where the extra dimension is the line segment $[-1, 1]$. Similarly, $[-1, 1]^3 \times Si(3)$ is a very fat five-dimensional triangle where the fat direction is given by the cube $[-1, 1]^3$ instead of just the line segment. The goal is to determine where the image set of $F_{\frac{1}{3}}$ is situated within the very fat triangle.

What helps in our analysis is that the image set of $F_{\frac{1}{3}}$ cannot be the total fat triangle; we know from Theorem 3.2.3 and Eq. 3.2.1, that the pairwise election outcomes completely determine the BC tally! Thus the $F_{\frac{1}{3}}$ image set is in a three-dimensional subspace of the five-dimensional space.

Theorem 3.2.4. *The $F_{\frac{1}{3}}$ image set is the portion of a three-dimensional plane in a five-dimensional space R^5 given by the parametric representation*

$$(x, y, z; \frac{x-z}{6} + \frac{1}{3}, \frac{y-x}{6} + \frac{1}{3}, \frac{z-y}{6} + \frac{1}{3}) \qquad (3.2.4)$$

where

$$(x, y, z) \in [-1, 1]^3, \quad -1 \leq x + y + z \leq 1.$$

3.2.2 Geometric Representation

To understand the BC outcomes, we need to envision the image set. Here we have help. The fact that the $F_{\frac{1}{3}}$ image set is three-dimensional suggests that a geometric figure can be devised to represent the three pairwise election tallies along with the BC election outcome. That this can be done follows from the identification of the BC with the Condorcet Improvement. Therefore, the representation in Fig. 2.5.9 showing where c_1 is top-ranked for the Condorcet Improvement serves to show the region of pairwise tallies where c_1 is BC top-ranked. A refined representation, where the shaded region denotes the BC ranking $c_1 \succ c_2 \succ c_3$, is in Fig. 3.2.3.

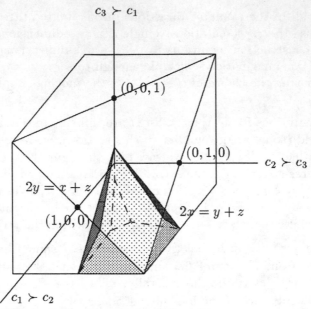

Fig. 3.2.3. The shaded region is the BC ranking $c_1 \succ c_2 \succ c_3$. Not all of the hidden lines are included.

To analyze the BC outcomes, the approach remains much the same. As the set of outcomes leading to a specified ranking is a convex set, we want to find the vertices. It follows from Eq. 3.2.4 that when the BC outcomes are characterized in the representation cube, the region has nine vertices. To illustrate, the region for the BC ranking of $c_1 \succ c_2 \succ c_3$ is the convex hull of the vertices

Vertices for the BC region $c_1 \succ c_2 \succ c_3$

$$(1, -1, -1), \ (0, 1, -1), (\frac{1}{3}, -\frac{1}{3}, -1), \ (1, 0, -1),$$

$$(-\frac{1}{3}, \frac{1}{3}, -1), \ (\frac{1}{3}, 1, -\frac{1}{3}), \ \pm(\frac{1}{3}, \frac{1}{3}, \frac{1}{3}), \ (1, \frac{1}{3}, -\frac{1}{3}). \qquad (3.2.5)$$

Finding these vertex values is an algebraic exercise using the equations for the boundaries of the F_3 image set (e.g., $x + y + z = \pm 1$) along with the equations defining indifference for pairs in the BC ranking. For instance, for the BC ranking $c_1 \sim c_2$, we have from Eq. 3.2.4 that the defining equations are $x - z = y - x$ or $2x = y + z$. Thus, by neutrality (using the permutation $\sigma = (1, 2, 3)$ and the fact that the positive y axis is identified with the pairwise ranking $c_2 \succ c_3$), we have that the other boundary set with the BC ranking $c_2 \sim c_3$ is $2y = x + z$. Consequently the BC region for $c_1 \succ c_2 \succ c_3$ is defined by the two inequalities

$$2x > y + z, \quad 2y > z + x. \qquad (3.2.6)$$

There are five remaining regions for BC strict rankings; each is geometrically similar to the region in Fig. 3.2.3. Each region can be determined with a similar computation, or by using the list of vertices in Eq. 3.2.5 along with neutrality. For instance, the BC region $c_2 \succ c_1 \succ c_3$ is obtained via the $\sigma = (1,2)$ permutation of $c_1 \succ c_2 \succ c_3$; the vertices of the original region are permuted to find the vertices of the new BC region. As $\sigma(c_1 \succ c_2) = c_2 \succ c_1$, $\sigma(c_2 \succ c_3) = c_1 \succ c_3$, $\sigma(c_3 \succ c_1) = c_3 \succ c_2$, it follows from the identification of the x, y, z coordinates that

$$\sigma((x, y, z)) = (-x, -z, -y). \tag{3.2.7}$$

Applying Eq. 3.2.7 (remember, Eq. 3.2.7 holds only for $\sigma = (1,2)$) to the vertices of Eq. 3.2.4, we obtain the vertices defining the BC region $c_2 \succ c_1 \succ c_3$. For instance, one of these vertices is $\sigma((1, \frac{1}{3}, -\frac{1}{3})) = (-1, \frac{1}{3}, -\frac{1}{3})$, $\sigma((1, 0, -1)) = (-1, 1, 0)$.

(As another way to derive Eq. 3.2.7, observe that $x > 0$ corresponds to the pairwise ranking $c_1 \succ c_2$. Now, $\sigma(c_1 \succ c_2) = c_{\sigma(1)} \succ c_{\sigma(2)} = c_2 \succ c_1$. The tally remains the same, so we have that $\sigma(x) = -x$. Similarly, we have for this permutation that $\sigma(y) = -z$, $\sigma(z) = -y$.)

The purpose of the vertices, of course, is to allow the comparison of pairwise results with BC rankings. For instance, it now is simple to find the vertices where the $c_1 \succ c_2, c_2 \succ c_3, c_1 \succ c_3$ outcomes do *not* correspond to the BC outcome $c_1 \succ c_2 \succ c_3$. Then, by use of cyclic coordinate representations, the vertices of the profile set can be determined. By standard methods of finding (five-dimensional) volume (calculus or determinant techniques) the portion of all profiles where the pairwise outcomes are suspect can be determined.

3.2.3 The Borda Dictionary

To understand the BC, we must determine which pairwise rankings can accompany a BC ranking.

Definition 3.2.2. For a profile $\mathbf{p}$, the election outcome $F_{\frac{1}{3}}(\mathbf{p})$ defines a unique election ranking for each of the sets $\{c_1, c_2\}$, $\{c_2, c_3\}$, $\{c_1, c_3\}$, $\{c_1, c_2, c_3\}$; the *word* defined by $\mathbf{p}$ is the listing of these four rankings.

The *Borda Dictionary*, $\mathcal{D}(\mathbf{w}_{\frac{1}{3}})$, is a collection of all words that occur for some profile.

The *Universal Set*, U^3, is the set of all $3^3 13 = 351$ ways to list a ranking for each of the four sets of candidates. $\square$

Example 3.2.2. The listing $(c_1 \succ c_2, c_2 \succ c_3, c_1 \succ c_3, c_1 \succ c_2 \succ c_3)$ is a word in the Borda Dictionary $\mathcal{D}(\mathbf{w}_{\frac{1}{3}})$ because these are the election rankings associated with, say, the profile $\mathbf{E}_1$. Somewhat less obvious is that the listing $(c_1 \succ c_2, c_2 \succ c_3, c_3 \succ c_1, c_1 \succ c_2 \succ c_3)$ also is a word in the BC Dictionary. To see why, observe that these pairwise rankings define the sign listing $(x, y, z) = (+, +, +)$ in the representation cube; this point is in the positive orthant. But, the shaded region of Fig. 3.2.3 (representing the BC ranking $c_1 \succ c_2 \succ c_3$) has a portion in the positive orthant of the representation cube. Thus, there are profiles leading to this list of outcomes. Alternatively, observe how easy it is to find positive x, y, z values where $x - z > y - z > z - y$. The conclusion now follows from Eq. 3.2.4.

The listing $(c_1 \succ c_2, c_3 \succ c_2, c_3 \succ c_1, c_1 \succ c_2 \succ c_3)$ is *not* a word in the Borda Dictionary because the pairwise rankings define the orthant with the sign pattern $(x, y, z) = (+, -, +)$; this particular orthant misses the shaded region of Fig. 3.2.3. Alternatively, the $(x, y, z) = (+, -, +)$ sign pattern and Eq. 3.2.4 requires the BC rankings to satisfy $x - z > 0, y - x < 0, z - y > 0$. (The negative value requires that candidate to receive less than $\frac{1}{3}$ of the total vote. Conversely, positive values indicate that a candidate receives over $\frac{1}{3}$ of the vote.) This requires c_2 to be BC bottom ranked, rather than the specifed middle-ranking.

As another example, $(c_2 \succ c_1, c_2 \succ c_3, c_3 \succ c_1, c_1 \succ c_2 \succ c_3) \notin \mathcal{D}(\mathbf{w}_{\frac{1}{3}})$. Thus, this is a listing of election rankings that never can occur with a BC election. There are several ways to prove this assertion; one is to note that it allows the Condorcet loser to be top-ranked (which violates Theorem 3.2.2). As another approach, use the geometry of Fig. 3.2.3. A third approach is to use Eq. 3.2.4.

Just the fact that one listing cannot be in the Borda Dictionary proves that

$$\mathcal{D}(\mathbf{w}_{\frac{1}{3}}) \subsetneq U^3. \quad \square \tag{3.2.8}$$

3.2.4 Borda Cross-Sections

While Fig. 3.2.3 provides a convenient way to determine what BC rankings can, and cannot accompany various pairwise rankings, it is not sufficiently refined to extract subtle features. The problem is that Fig. 3.2.3 is a two-dimensional representation of a three-dimensional object. So, to remove the complexity, find two-dimensional slices. This is done next.

To see what words can occur in the BC Dictionary, we can take sections of Fig. 3.2.3. For example, for $x = 0$ (a $c_1 \sim c_2$ pairwise outcome), the relevant regions from Fig. 3.2.3 is the intersection of the figure with the y-z plane. This intersection is given in Fig. 3.2.4a where the numbers indicate the BC ranking regions and the shaded area is where the BC ranking is $c_1 \succ c_2 \succ c_3$. (To find these regions, first substitute the $x = 0$ value into the boundary equations $x + y + z = \pm 1, 2x = y + z, 2y = x + z, 2z = x + y$, and then plot the resulting equations.)

To use this cross-section, notice that the positive orthant (determined by the dashed lines) is strictly included in the BC ranking of type-5. Thus, the only BC ranking that can accompany $c_1 \sim c_2$ $(x = 0)$, $c_2 \succ c_3$ $(y > 0)$, and $c_3 \succ c_1$ $(z > 0)$ is $c_3 \succ c_2 \succ c_1$. Other information from this cross-section is that the pairwise rankings represented by $x = 0, y < 0, z > 0$ can be accompanied by four different strict BC rankings; these are BC rankings of types 2, 3, 4, or 5. On the other hand, if the pairwise rankings define the sign pattern $(0, -, -)$ then the only possible choice for the BC outcome is the type-two ranking $c_1 \succ c_3 \succ c_2$.

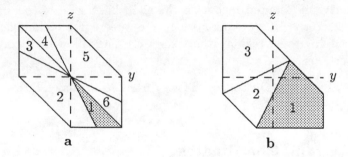

Fig. 3.2.4. BC-pairwise vote cross sections. **a.** $x = 0$. **b.** $x = \frac{1}{3}$

Another interesting cross-section is where $x = \frac{1}{3}$; this x value corresponds to c_1 winning two-thirds of the vote in her contest against c_2. As indicated in Fig. 3.2.4b, this x value is a bifurcation point; it is the smallest x value that does not admit BC rankings where $c_2 \succ c_1$. In fact, with this $x = \frac{1}{3}$ value, the BC ranking can be one of three strict rankings or one of four rankings with a tie vote, or $\mathcal{I}$. When $x > \frac{1}{3}$, several of these BC options immediately disappear. (These are all BC rankings where $c_1 \sim c_2$.)

Entries of the Borda Dictionary. What we want is a listing of all words in a Borda Dictionary. To start, as indicated by Example 3.2.2, we can use Eq. 3.2.4 or Fig. 3.2.3 to find all words where the BC ranking is $c_1 \succ c_2 \succ c_3$. Out of the 27 possible rankings of the pairs, only seventeen can occur. These pairwise rankings can be characterized by their (x, y, z) sign patterns

$$(+, \text{ any}, \text{ any}), (0, +, -),$$
$$(0, 0, -), (0, -, -)$$
$$(-, +, \ \ ), (-, 0, -), (-, -, \text{ any }). \qquad (3.2.9)$$

By applying the permutation tools of neutrality to this listing, we find all strict words in the Borda Dictionary.

If the BC ranking is $\mathcal{I}$, the admissible pairwise rankings are found either from the geometry or Eq. 3.2.4. For instance with the geometry the $\mathcal{I}$ region is the line in the representation cube connecting the points $\pm(\frac{1}{3}, \frac{1}{3}, \frac{1}{3})$. The only three words in the BC dictionary of this type, then, are

$$(c_1 \succ c_2, c_2 \succ c_3, c_3 \succ c_1, \mathcal{I}), (c_1 \sim c_2, c_2 \sim c_3, c_3 \sim c_1, \mathcal{I})$$
$$(c_2 \succ c_1, c_3 \succ c_2, c_1 \succ c_3, \mathcal{I}) \qquad (3.2.10)$$

Next consider the BC rankings with one tie; e.g., the BC ranking region $c_1 \succ c_2 \sim c_3$ is on the left hand side of Fig. 3.2.3 passing through the five vertices $(1, 0, -1), (1, \frac{1}{3}, -\frac{1}{3}), \pm(\frac{1}{3}, \frac{1}{3}, \frac{1}{3}), (\frac{1}{3}, -\frac{1}{3}, -1)$. From the geometry or Eq.

3.2.4, the five combination of pairs that accompany this BC ranking can be determined. Similarly, the slanted region on the right-hand side of the shaded region corresponding to the BC ranking $c_1 \sim c_2 \succ c_3$ meets five regions defined by the pairs. (Identifying these regions is an exercise.) The following theorem is based on these assertions.

Theorem 3.2.5. *The Borda Dictionary, $\mathcal{D}(\mathbf{w}_{\frac{1}{3}})$ has 135 words. Thus, it contains 38.5% of the 351 entries in U^3.*[12]

3.2.5 The BC Cyclic Coordinates

By use of Fig. 3.2.3 or one of the sections (as in Fig. 3.2.4), it is easy to construct profiles illustrating certain pairwise votes where the BC outcome is $c_1 \succ c_2 \succ c_3$. For example, to have an extreme vote for the pairs c_1, c_2 and c_2, c_3, place a point near a vertex in the shaded region. Then, either the cyclic or the c_1-Condorcet coordinates for a profile could be used to create an example. More generally, a fixed BC outcome is given by a point in the shaded region. Then, by use of a group coordinate representation for a profile, the cone of profiles defining the desired combination of pairwise and BC results can be computed. Thus, by use of the c_1-Condorcet coordinates, we see the supporting two-dimensional profile set.

A first limitation in using Fig. 3.2.3 is that the geometry of the shaded region is sufficiently complicated to frustrate the analysis without having to compute a section. For extreme situations, we may want to place the BC outcome near a boundary, but some boundary regions are difficult to envision. Secondly, in Fig. 3.2.3, the emphasis is on the pairwise votes; there is no information about the exact BC tally. Consequently, this figure is of little help should we wish the emphasis of an example to be on a specific BC election tally. To resolve both problems, we emphasize the representation triangle geometry rather than the representation cube by using the *Borda cyclic coordinates*.

Recall from Sect. 2.6 that in the BC cyclic coordinates, the voters are divided into the "odds" and "evens" with the analytic expression

$$d = p_1 + p_3 + p_5, \quad a_j = \frac{p_j}{d}, j = 1, 3, 5, \quad \alpha_{\frac{1}{3}} = \sum_{j=1,3,5} a_j[\mathbf{w}_{\frac{1}{3}}]_j$$

$$b_j = \frac{p_j}{1-d}, j = 2, 4, 6, \quad \beta_{\frac{1}{3}} = \sum_{j=2,4,6} b_j[\mathbf{w}_{\frac{1}{3}}]_j$$

$$f(\mathbf{p}, \mathbf{w}_{\frac{1}{3}}) = d\alpha_{\frac{1}{3}} + (1-d)\beta_{\frac{1}{3}}. \tag{3.2.11}$$

---

[12] With more candidates, the BC Dictionary uses very few of the entries from the universal set. For instance, with $n \geq 6$ candidates, the BC dictionary has fewer than $\frac{1}{10^{50}}$ of the admissible entries of U^n. As 10^{50} is much larger than 6^{15}, this number admits all sorts of "Gee Whiz!" statements of the type used in Sect. 2.1 to indicate the number of libraries required just to hold the listings of how one BC word can be varied to get all of the paradoxes admitted by other procedures.

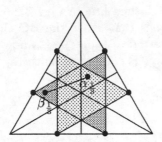

Fig. 3.2.5. The Borda cyclic coordinates

Geometrically, $\alpha_{\frac{1}{3}}$ is a point in the lightly shaded equilateral triangle of Fig. 3.2.5; it is the outcome if only the odd voters vote. Similarly, $\beta_{\frac{1}{3}}$, the outcome if only the even voters vote, is a point in the darker triangle. The actual outcome is the point on the connecting line that is d of the distance from $\beta_{\frac{1}{3}}$ to $\alpha_{\frac{1}{3}}$. So, in the fashion described with other group coordinate representations, insight into the kinds of profiles support different BC outcomes can be obtained.

It remains to understand how to extract information about pairwise election outcomes from the BC cyclic coordinates. (The following argument differs from that of Sect. 2.6.) First I will describe how this is done, and then I will justify the technique. So, with the BC cyclic coordinates $(\alpha_{\frac{1}{3}}^c, \beta_{\frac{1}{3}}^c, d^c)$, the goal is to determine the c_i - c_j pairwise vote. Without loss of generality, I will find the c_1 - c_2 vote. For the odd voters, there are two voter types (1 and 3) that share a weak c_1-c_2 ranking and only one voter type (5) with the strong relative ranking ($c_2 \succ c_1$). The key is the strong voter type (5 in this case), indicated in Fig. 3.2.5 by a dot at the vertex. Draw a line through $\alpha_{\frac{1}{3}}$ parallel to the edge of the triangle opposite the dot. (In Fig. 3.2.5, this is the solid line passing through $\alpha_{\frac{1}{3}}^c$. This line is parallel to the edge defined by vertices with a weak, intense ranking.) The point where this line crosses the c_1 - c_2 edge of the odd triangle, x_α, is the odd voters' c_1 - c_2 election outcome. The triangle is rotated so that this edge is in the standard position. The value assigned to x_α depends on its location. For instance, if x_α is at the midpoint of the edge, then $x_\alpha = 0$, but if it is at the left endpoint, $x_\alpha = 1$.

The same approach holds the even voters (where the sole even voter type with strong ranking is type-two) to determine the point x_β. The pairwise election outcome, then, is $x = d^c x_\alpha + (1 - d^c) x_\beta$. Similarly, $y = d^c y_\alpha + (1 - d^c) y_\beta$, $z = d^c z_\alpha + (1 - d^c) z_\beta$. For example, the choice of $\alpha_{\frac{1}{3}}^c$, $\beta_{\frac{1}{3}}^c$ illustrated in Fig. 3.2.6 must admit the pairwise ranking $c_1 \succ c_2$ independent of the choice of d^c.

This geometric approach follows from properties of triangles. If only the odd voters voted, then c_2 would received a_5 points while c_1 would receive $a_1 + a_3$ points. Now, draw a line from $[\mathbf{w}_{\frac{1}{3}}]_5$ through $\alpha_{\frac{1}{3}}^c$; this line passes through the far edge of the triangle. (This is the dashed line in Fig. 3.2.6.). This point of intersection is the BC election outcome if only voters of types-one and three voted. Indeed, the distance from this constructed point and $\alpha_{\frac{1}{3}}$ is a_5 of the length of the constructed line segment (the dashed line in Fig. 3.2.6.). It now follows from the properties of similar triangles that x_α is the BC election outcome if all a_3 type-three voters become converted to type-one (so now there are $a_1 + a_3$ type-one voters.) This election outcome is equivalent to the c_1 - c_2 pairwise vote for the odd voters.

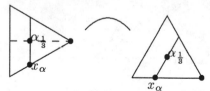

Rotation of the BC odd cycle to get c_1, c_2 pairwise ranking.

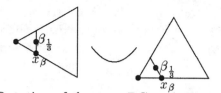

Rotation of the even BC cycle.

Fig. 3.2.6. The c_1, c_2 pairwise vote from the BC cyclic coordinates

3.2.6 The Borda Vector Space

The geometry of Fig. 3.2.2 helps, but often we need the analytic form of Eq. 3.2.4. While Eq. 3.2.4 satisfies our purposes, an alternative representation in terms of vectors is useful. After all, the $F_{\frac{1}{3}}$ image set is a portion of a three-dimensional plane in a higher dimensional space, so it is worth describing this plane by identifying its orientation.

Of two reasons to study this plane, the first is that it is used to discuss other positional voting methods in the next section. Of more importance, when $n > 3$ candidates are considered, the number of BC election relationships grows rapidly. Thus, an efficient way to describe the BC outcomes is to generalize this alternative representation based on "perpendicular directions."

Equation 3.2.4 can be expressed as

$$V + I = (x, y, z; \frac{x - z}{6}, \frac{y - x}{6}, \frac{z - y}{6}) + (0, 0, 0; \frac{1}{3}, \frac{1}{3}, \frac{1}{3}).$$

The first vector, V, expresses how the election tallies differ from complete indifference, while I is the vector of complete indifference. The more important first vector, V, is on a linear space passing through the origin of R^6. This is the BC linear space we need to describe. To do so, it suffices to describe the normal vectors (i.e., the orthogonal vectors) to this three-dimensional plane. The first normal vector,

$$(0, 0, 0; 1, 1, 1),$$

just expresses the fact that the sum of the last three components of V is zero; thus this normal vector is a consequence of the normalization of the tallies.

The three *BC normal vectors* describe the BC election relationships.

$$\mathbf{Z}_1 = (\frac{1}{6}, 0, -\frac{1}{6}; 1, 0, 0),$$

$$\mathbf{Z}_2 = (-\frac{1}{6}, \frac{1}{6}, 0; 0, 1, 0),$$

$$\mathbf{Z}_3 = (0, -\frac{1}{6}, \frac{1}{6}, 0; 0, 0, 1).$$

Because $\sum_{j=1}^{3} \mathbf{Z}_j = (0, 0, 0; 1, 1, 1)$, any two of these vectors along with the normalization of the tallies determines the third BC normal vector. So, the vector $(0, 0, 0; 1, 1, 1)$ recaptures the fact that $[-1, 1]^3 \times Si(3)$ is part of a five-dimensional subspace of R^6, and the three BC normal vectors define the three-dimensional plane containing the $F_{\frac{1}{3}}$ image space. The dependency condition on the BC normal vectors means that the plane is three, rather than two-dimensional, and it characterizes the BC election outcomes. Namely, if V is a vector from a BC election, then it must be that

$$< V, \mathbf{Z}_j >= 0, \quad j = 1, 2, 3, \tag{3.2.12}$$

where $< A, B >$ is the standard dot product defined as

$$< A, B >= \sum_{j=1}^{6} A_j B_j, \ A = (A_1, \dots, A_6), \ B = (B_1, \dots, B_6).$$

Example 3.2.3. Suppose c_1 is not the Condorcet winner because she is tied in each of her two pairwise contests. Can she be BC top or bottom-ranked? The tied pairwise elections requires $x = z = 0$. If she is BC bottom-ranked, then she receives less than one-third of the total vote, so the appropriate component of V (the fourth) must be negative. Similarly, if she is top-ranked, then this component is positive. So, to answer the question, we just need to see if a vector $V = (0, y, 0; a, b, c)$ satisfies Eq. 3.2.12 where $a \neq 0$. It does not because

$$< V, \mathbf{Z}_1 >= 0 \cdot \frac{1}{6} + y \cdot 0 + 0 \cdot (-\frac{1}{6}) + a \cdot 1 = a \neq 0.$$

Therefore, we have that *if a candidate ties in both the pairwise elections, then either she is BC middle-ranked, or the BC election ranking is* $\mathcal{I}$. She receives exactly one-third of the total vote.

This result can be obtained more simply from Eq. 3.2.4. The fact that $x = z = 0$ requires the c_1 BC tally to be $\frac{0-0}{6} = 0$. From Fig. 3.2.3, which describes the $x = 0$ section, and $x = z = 0$, the BC outcome is on the horizontal y axis. However, this axis meets only regions 2, 5, and $\mathcal{I}$. □

Summary of Borda properties. From Sects. 3.1, 3.2, we have the following.

If it is required that the positional voting method reverses its outcome when all the voters reverse their ranking, then the BC must be used.

If the idea of pairwise voting is attractive, but the obvious pitfalls are to be avoided, then the BC must be used.

Because the BC is a Condorcet Improvement, if the Condorcet winner is not BC top-ranked, it is because the pairwise voting procedure ignores critical information about the heterogeneous nature of the voters' preferences. In particular, it misses all information about the intensity of voters' beliefs in pairwise rankings; it is unaware of the critical fact that the voters are transitive.

The BC does not have the same bias shown by other positional procedures when voters permute their preferences.

3.2.7 Exercises

3.2.1. a. If the pairwise votes are $c_2 \succ c_2$ by $21 : 19$, $c_1 \succ c_3$ by $22 : 18$ and $c_3 \succ c_2$ by $35 : 5$, find the BC ranking.
b. Find a BC ranking where the Condorcet-loser is in second place. Analyze the geometry of the profile to determine whether the BC ranking, or the Condorcet designation, is more appropriate.

3.2.2. Complete the proof of Theorem 3.2.2.

3.2.3. Find an example of a Condorcet Improvement procedure that does not always agree with the BC outcome.

3.2.4. Equation 3.2.5 provides the vertices for the BC region $c_1 \succ c_2 \succ c_3$. Find the vertices for the BC region $c_2 \succ c_3 \succ c_1$.

3.2.5. Find the $x = \frac{1}{2}$ section of the BC-pairwise vote. The $x = \frac{1}{3}$ section of Fig. 3.2.4b allows the BC ranking of $c_1 \succ c_3 \succ c_2$ to be accompanied by four strict pairwise ranking regions. Is there an x section where this BC ranking meets fewer pairwise regions?

3.2.6. a. Use the techniques leading to Theorem 3.2.5 to find all pairwise rankings that can accompany $c_1 \sim c_2 \succ c_3$. Do the same for the ranking $c_1 \succ c_2 \sim c_3$. With the help of neutrality, find the number of BC words that can occur if there is one tie vote in the ranking of all three candidates.
b. Find all the pairwise rankings that can accompany the BC ranking $c_3 \succ c_1 \succ c_2$. For instance, one might use Eq. 3.2.9 and a name change.

3.2.7. a. By use of the BC cyclic coordinates, find a profile for $\mathbf{q}_{\frac{1}{3}} = (\frac{1}{2}, \frac{1}{6}, \frac{1}{3})$ where the odd voter outcome is as cyclic as possible.
b. Let $\mathbf{p} = (\alpha_{\frac{1}{3}} = (\frac{5}{18}, \frac{4}{9}, \frac{5}{18}), \beta_{\frac{1}{3}} = (\frac{1}{6}, \frac{1}{2}, \frac{1}{3}), d = \frac{3}{5})$. Find the pairwise vote for c_1, c_2.
c. Impose the Black's single peakedness condition on profile. Does this restrict the BC election rankings?

3.2.8. a. Is $(0.2, 0.3, 0.5, \frac{17}{60}, \frac{21}{60}, \frac{22}{60})$ is an admissible BC outcome? Use the BC vector space to prove your answer.

b. Suppose c_1 is the BC winner but not the Condorcet winner; c_2 is. Find a bound on the c_1 pairwise victory over c_3 in terms of the c_1, c_2 vote and the c_2, c_3 outcome.

3.2.9. a. Use the cross-section approach to find all BC rankings that can accompany the pairwise ranking $c_1 \sim c_2$, $c_3 \succ c_2$, and $c_3 \succ c_1$.
b. Suppose a pairwise vote is on the boundary of the negative cyclic region because one pairwise ranking is a tie. Identify the corresponding BC ranking by using a cross-section approach.
c. It is asserted that the $c = \frac{1}{3}$ section is a bifurcation. Prove this assertion by finding the cross-sections for x slightly less than and slightly greater than $\frac{1}{3}$. How many BC rankings can occur in each case?

3.2.10. The point $c = \frac{1}{2}, y = \frac{1}{3}, z = 0$ defines what BC outcome? By use of cyclic coordinates, find the cone of profiles leading to this outcome.

3.3 The Other Positional Voting Methods

In Sect. 3.2, the basic properties of the BC are developed, but how should they be interpreted? Are these conclusions coveted properties that become justifiable BC bragging rights, or are they embarrassing flaws that underscore serious BC inadequacies? After all, the universal set U^3 admits 351 different listings of rankings, and the BC realizes about 38% of them. Is this 38% figure large or small relative to other positional voting methods? The only way such questions can be answered is to understand what else is available. We need to determine the related properties of all other positional voting methods. This is done here.

To compare the BC with other positional methods, we need to determine the relationship among positional and pairwise election outcomes. That is, we need to analyze the image set of

$$F_s = (F_3, f(-, \mathbf{w}_s)) : Si(6) \to [-1,1]^3 \times Si(3), \quad s \in [0, \frac{1}{2}].$$

In the previous section I showed that the image of $F_{\frac{1}{3}}$ is three-dimensional. As proved below, if $s \neq \frac{1}{3}$, then the F_s image set is *five-dimensional and it meets all possible combinations of rankings regions*. This means that unless the BC is used to tally an election, "anything can happen!"

Theorem 3.3.1. *The image of F_s is five-dimensional iff $s \neq \frac{1}{3}$. In particular, the ranking region $(c_1 \sim c_2, c_2 \sim c_3, c_1 \sim c_3, \mathcal{I})$ is an interior point of the image set. Thus, for $\mathbf{w}_s \neq \mathbf{w}_{\frac{1}{3}}$,*

$$\mathcal{D}(\mathbf{w}_s) = U^3. \tag{3.3.1}$$

A first answer emerges; while the BC realizes about 38% of the entries in the universal set U^3, all other positional voting methods must include 100% of the 351 different listings! Therefore, *all non-BC methods admit all possible election paradoxes*. As an example, the troubling beverage paradox holds not only for the plurality and antiplurality methods, but for all non-BC procedures. This theorem means that

$$\mathcal{D}(\mathbf{w}_{\frac{1}{3}}) \subsetneqq \mathcal{D}(\mathbf{w}_s) = U^3, \quad \forall s \neq \frac{1}{3}. \qquad (3.3.2)$$

To describe Eq. 3.3.2 in a different manner, suppose a critic of the BC argues that a conflict between a particular BC ranking and the associated pairwise rankings demonstrates a potential flaw of the BC. (As we've discovered, a more careful analysis using profiles probably would show the flaw is in the pairwise rankings, not the BC outcome.) According to Eq. 3.3.2, the exact same argument using the same listing of rankings holds for all other choices of positional voting methods! Thus, if the BC has a flaw, it is universal; it must be suffered by all positional methods.

On the other hand, any other positional procedure has words that never can be used with the BC. They are, of course, the listings of election rankings that are proscribed for the BC in Sect. 3.2. As examples, listings that allow a Condorcet loser to be top-ranked are permitted by any other positional method; only the BC outlaws such an event. A listing indicating that the Condorcet winner is bottom-ranked, or that a Condorcet winner is ranked below a Condorcet loser are admissible election outcomes for all positional voting methods $\mathbf{w}_s$, $s = \frac{1}{3}$; only the BC prohibits such annoying election embarrassments. In other words, other procedures admit flaws that never occur with the BC. Actually, these conclusions should be expected from the discussion (at the end of Sect. 3.1) indicating the negative consequences accompanying a procedure that fails reversal symmetry.

Example 3.3.1. a. One could use the numbers from the weekly lotto game to select rankings for the three pairs of candidates and the three-candidate set. Next, assign a non-BC positional method $\mathbf{w}_s$ to the three-candidate subset. According to Theorem 3.3.1, there exists a profile where the randomly selected outcome is the sincere election outcome. It is difficult to accept that such randomly assigned rankings accurately reflect the voters' beliefs.

b. For $\mathbf{w}_s$, $s \neq \frac{1}{3}$, there exists a profile so that the election rankings are given by

$$\{c_1 \succ c_2, \; c_2 \succ c_3, \; c_1 \succ c_3, \; c_2 \succ c_3 \sim c_1\}.$$

There are two reasons such a listing could never arise with the BC. The first is that the Condorcet winner, c_1, is (tied for) bottom-ranked, and the second is that the Condorcet loser, c_3, is not strictly ranked below the Condorcet winner.

c. According to the results of the last section, it is impossible for the BC to admit a beverage paradox. More abstractly, it is impossible for the BC ranking to be $c_1 \succ c_2 \succ c_3$ when the pairwise rankings are $c_3 \succ c_2, c_3 \succ c_1, c_2 \succ c_1$. On the other hand, according to Theorem 3.3.1, for any non-BC positional voting method, there exists a profile supporting this outcome. In particular, this conclusion holds for $s = \frac{1}{3} + 0.00000000001$, a system that is essentially the BC.

This last comment is intended to generate skepticism about the conclusion of Theorem 3.3.1. After all, if two voting systems are essentially the same, then differences in outcomes should become apparent only with specially constructed profiles employing a cast of thousands. This is correct; the following shows how to analyze such issues. □

To understand the profiles that lead to different conclusions and whether these rankings are rare anomalies or serious concerns, we need a geometric description of the F_s image set. Following the established scheme of Sect. 1.4, the image set is the convex hull of the unanimity profile outcomes

$$\{F_s(\mathbf{E}_j, \mathbf{w}_s) = (F_3(\mathbf{E}_j), f(\mathbf{E}_j, \mathbf{w}_s))\}_{j=1}^6.$$

A straightforward algebraic argument establishes that any five of these vectors are independent if $s \neq \frac{1}{3}$; this proves the first part of Theorem 3.3.1. Applying the multiple $\frac{1}{6}$ to the sum of these vectors leads to the complete indifference ranking, which clearly is an interior point. This completes the proof of the theorem.

In describing the geometry, again we stumble upon the problem of representing a higher dimensional object in a lower dimensional picture. One way to understand what positional election tallies can accompany specified pairwise election tallies is to adopt the approach of the last section. Instead of examining the full five-dimensional space, concentrate on sections representing an issue of particular interest. This construction is a valuable tool, so it is carried out in detail while considering natural election issues. For example, we know from Sect. 3.2 that if the three pairwise elections end in tie votes, then the BC ranking must also be a tie vote. What happens for other positional voting methods? This question is examined first.

3.3.1 What Can Accompany a F_3 Tie Vote?

We are interested in analyzing the set of profiles $\mathbf{p} \in Si(6)$ that lead to $F_3(\mathbf{p}) = (0, 0, 0)$ where each pairwise election ends in a tie vote. The dimension counting argument of Chap. 2 indicates we must expect a two-dimensional set of profiles,

$$F_3^{-1}(\mathbf{0}) = \{\mathbf{p} \,|\, F_3(\mathbf{p}) = (0, 0, 0)\}.$$

The object is to obtain sufficient information about $F_3^{-1}(\mathbf{0})$ to determine the effect these profiles have upon the positional voting elections.

Assertion. $F_3^{-1}(\mathbf{0})$ *is a convex, two-dimensional subset of* $Si(6)$.

The proof of the assertion follows from the results in Sect. 1.4 and Chap. 2. Of the several ways to obtain sharper conclusions, two are offered here. The more technical approach is given first because it re-enforces a continuing theme about the subtle, yet important role played by symmetry. Then the more general approach, based on the coordinate representations of profiles, is described.

The basic symmetry for voting is inherited from neutrality, and, as we must expect, neutrality influences the symmetry structure of $F_3^{-1}(\mathbf{0})$. In particular, a name change of candidates does not, in any manner, influence the pairwise election outcomes because everyone is tied with everyone else. In technical terms, if permutation σ is a name change, if σ_T is the associated permutation for the profiles (see Sect. 3.1), and if $\mathbf{p} \in (F_3(\mathbf{0}))^{-1}$, then $\sigma_T(\mathbf{p}) \in (F_3(\mathbf{0}))^{-1}$.

The symmetries of neutrality are not sufficiently discriminating for our needs; we need symmetry operations that:

a.   Preserve the tie pairwise election outcomes.

b.   They need not preserve the positional election rankings.[13]

From Sect. 3.1, this symmetry is the *reversal permutation*. As asserted in Theorem 3.1.4, $F_3(\mathbf{p}) = (F_3(\mathbf{p}^r))^r = F_3(\mathbf{p}^r)$ where the last equality holds because the reversal of a tie is a tie. Thus, if $\mathbf{p} \in F_3^{-1}(\mathbf{0})$, then $\mathbf{p}^r \in F_3^{-1}(\mathbf{0})$. In particular,

$$\text{if } \mathbf{p} = \mathbf{p}^r, \text{ then } \mathbf{p} \in F_3^{-1}(\mathbf{0}). \tag{3.3.3}$$

The symmetry arguments determine the structure of $F_3^{-1}(\mathbf{0})$. For instance, the profile $\mathbf{E}_1$ can be used with Eq. 3.3.3 and $\mathbf{E}_1^r = \mathbf{E}_4$ to create a vertex of $F_3^{-1}(\mathbf{0})$. Namely, according to Eq. 3.3.3, the profile $\frac{1}{2}(\mathbf{E}_1 + \mathbf{E}_4) \in F_3^{-1}(\mathbf{0})$. Indeed, using the arguments of Chap. 2 and Sect. 3.1, this profile is a vertex of $F_3^{-1}(\mathbf{0})$. The other vertices are determined in a similar fashion.

Proposition 3.3.2. *The convex set* $F_3^{-1}(\mathbf{0}) \subset Si(6)$ *is the convex hull defined by*

$$\frac{1}{2}(\mathbf{E}_1 + \mathbf{E}_4), \quad \frac{1}{2}(\mathbf{E}_2 + \mathbf{E}_5), \quad \frac{1}{2}(\mathbf{E}_3 + \mathbf{E}_6).$$

For any $\mathbf{w}_s$ we now can determine all possible $\mathbf{w}_s$ positional election outcomes, $P_0(s)$, that accompany tie votes for all pairwise elections. Namely,

$$P_0(s) = \{f(\mathbf{p}, \mathbf{w}_s) \,|\, \mathbf{p} \in F_3^{-1}(\mathbf{0})\}.$$

By convexity, $P_0(s)$ is a convex hull defined by the $\mathbf{w}_s$ image of the three profile vertices specified in Proposition 3.3.2. For example,

$$f(\frac{1}{2}(\mathbf{E}_1 + \mathbf{E}_2), \mathbf{w}_s) = \frac{1}{2}(f(\mathbf{E}_1, \mathbf{w}_s) + f(\mathbf{E}_4, \mathbf{w}_s)) = (\frac{1-s}{2}, s, \frac{1-s}{2}),$$

so the election outcome is the midpoint on the line connecting $f(\mathbf{E}_1, \mathbf{w}_s)$ with $f(\mathbf{E}_4, \mathbf{w}_s)$. This connecting line is a dashed line in Fig. 3.3.1. Similarly, the three vertices of $P_0(s)$ are given by the three vectors that can be constructed from the entries $\frac{1-s}{2}, s, \frac{1-s}{2}$. As illustrated in Fig. 3.3.1, each vertex is determined by the intersection of an indifference line with the dashed line connecting $f(\mathbf{E}_i, \mathbf{w}_s)$ and $f(\mathbf{E}_i^r, \mathbf{w}_s)$. Notice that these vertices form an equilateral triangle. Illustrations are in Fig. 3.3.1.

---

[13] Theoretically, this requires finding the group of permutations that preserves $F_3^{-1}(\mathbf{0})$. This is the BC symmetry group described in Sect. 3.1.

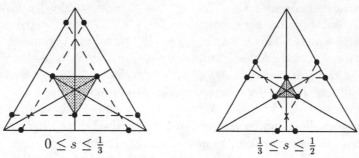

$$0 \le s \le \tfrac{1}{3} \qquad\qquad \tfrac{1}{3} \le s \le \tfrac{1}{2}$$

Fig. 3.3.1. The $\mathbf{w}_s$ outcomes with ties for the three pairs

The size of $P_0(s)$ decreases as s approaches $\tfrac{1}{3}$. The largest regions (corresponding to the largest deviation in election outcomes) occur for $s = 0, \tfrac{1}{2}$, the plurality and antiplurality vote. Observe the interesting reversal when s passes through the BC value of $\tfrac{1}{3}$; if $s < \tfrac{1}{3}$, then the vertices are along one set of indifference regions, but if $s > \tfrac{1}{3}$, the vertices are along the remaining set of indifference regions. This bifurcation point; a point where $P_0(s) = \mathcal{I}$, is the BC voting vector. This collapse of $P_0(s)$, of course, illustrates the symmetry of Eq. 3.1.7.

A simple explanation of this interesting inversion is that only for the BC does the line connecting $f(\mathbf{E}_1, \mathbf{w}_s)$ and $f(\mathbf{E}_4, \mathbf{w}_s)$ pass through $\mathcal{I}$; if $s < \tfrac{1}{3}$, then the line passes on one side of $\mathcal{I}$ and if $s > \tfrac{1}{3}$, it passes on the other side. But these connecting lines isolate the vertices of $P_0(s)$, so the inversion must be expected. Observe that this geometric argument is based on the fact that $\mathbf{w}_s^r = \mathbf{w}_s$ iff the positional voting method is the BC. Thus, the argument displays how the reversal symmetry of positional voting methods (Sect. 3.1) plays a critical role in election outcomes.

Example 3.3.2. a. The design of examples now is elementary. For example, suppose we want an profile to illustrate a tie with each pair and an extreme positional election tally supporting the ranking $c_1 \succ c_2 \sim c_3$. The choice of a profile depends upon whether $s < \tfrac{1}{3}$, or $s > \tfrac{1}{3}$. If $s < \tfrac{1}{3}$, it follows from Fig. 3.3.1a that the election outcome is where the $c_2 \sim c_3$ indifference line meets the left edge of the shaded triangle. This point is midway between the $\tfrac{1}{2}(\mathbf{E}_1 + \mathbf{E}_4)$ and the $\tfrac{1}{2}(\mathbf{E}_2 + \mathbf{E}_5)$ outcomes. Thus, the desired profile is $(\tfrac{1}{4}, \tfrac{1}{4}, 0, \tfrac{1}{4}, \tfrac{1}{4}, 0)$. A similar argument, but now using Fig. 3.3.1b., shows that the profile for $s > \tfrac{1}{3}$ is $\tfrac{1}{2}(\mathbf{E}_3 + \mathbf{E}_6)$.

More generally, using the profile vertices of $F_3^{-1}(\mathbf{0})$, it follows that a profile where the pairwise elections end in a tie is given by

$$\sum_{j=1}^{3} \lambda_j (\tfrac{1}{2}(\mathbf{E}_j + \mathbf{E}_{j+3})), \quad \lambda_j \ge 0, \ \sum_{j=1}^{3} \lambda_j = 1. \tag{3.3.4}$$

By varying the values of λ_j, different $\mathbf{w}_s$ outcomes are created.

b. *Proof of Theorem 3.3.1.* Figure 3.3.1 (and the supporting analysis) can be used to prove Theorem 3.3.1. First, if $s \neq \frac{1}{3}$, the set of $\mathbf{w}_s$-positional election outcomes that accompany a complete pairwise tie vote is given by the non-degenerate triangle. This triangle meets all 13 ranking regions of the representational triangle, so it follows immediately that any $\mathbf{w}_s$-positional ranking can accompany the pairwise rankings of $c_1 \sim c_2$, $c_2 \sim c_3$, $c_1 \sim c_3$. By the continuity and linearity of F_s, slight changes in the profile off of the set $F_3^{-1}(\mathbf{0})$ lead to slight changes in the outcomes. With an appropriate slight change in the profile, the pairwise ranking can be changed to any specified three rankings for the pairs. (Only ties are being broken, so not much of a change is required.) However, if the change is sufficiently small (in normalized profiles), then the $\mathbf{w}_s$ triangle is altered only slightly. With sufficiently small chages, the triangle still meets all 13 $Si(3)$ ranking regions. This proves that $\mathcal{D}(\mathbf{w}_s) = U^3$.

The size of the shaded positional election triangle determines the maximum size of a profile change. For instance, the plurality shaded region is so large that even with vast changes in a profile, the new profile could still be in the shaded region. However, for $s = \frac{1}{3} + 0.000001$, the shaded region is so small that only an incredibly small change in a profile will keep the outcome in the shaded zone. Now, if $\|\mathbf{p}_1 - \mathbf{p}_2\|$ is very small, the common denominator of all terms must be very large in value. This means that an accompanying integer profile must involve an enormous number of voters. Consequently, *in order for all possible outcomes to occur for values of s close to $\frac{1}{3}$, a very large number of voters may be required.*

The assertion that the F_s image set is five-dimensional for $s \neq \frac{1}{3}$ also follows from the geometry. At each point (at least around $(0,0,0)$) in the three-dimensional space $[-1,1]^3$, the associated set of possible $\mathbf{w}_s$-positional election outcomes is a two-dimensional equilateral triangle. The conclusion follows by a dimension count. $\square$

3.3.2 A Profile Coordinate Representation Approach

Why does $P_0(s)$ form an equilateral triangle? How are sections for other values of $F_3(\mathbf{p})$ determined? These questions are answered while introducing an alternative approach to construct sections of potential positional election outcomes.

The first step in computing $P_0(s)$ requires finding the appropriate set of profiles. Once the restriction on the profiles is determined, the election outcomes can be computed in the (now) standard way. In Sect. 2.4, it is shown how to find the cone of profiles leading to specified $F_3(\mathbf{p})$ outcomes in terms of the even and odd coordinate representation. For example, it follows from the geometry that the (α, β, d) representation of the vertices of this cone for the outcome $(0,0,0)$ are $((1,1,-1),(-1,-1,1),\frac{1}{2})$, $((1,-1,1),(-1,1,-1),\frac{1}{2})$, and $((-1,1,1),(1,-1,-1),\frac{1}{2})$. Translating these coordinates into the $Si(6)$ representation, we see that the vertices of the cone of supporting profiles are $\{\frac{1}{2}(\mathbf{E}_j + \mathbf{E}_{j+3})\}_{j=1}^3$. These are, of course, the same vertices found by use of symmetry. So, why is $P_0(s)$ an equilateral triangle? It is because the set of relevant profiles has the same geometry.

The profile coordinate representation serves as an alternative way to find, $P_{\mathbf{q}}(s)$, the set of $\mathbf{w}_s$ positional election that can accompany $F_3(\mathbf{p}) = \mathbf{q}$. To illustrate the ideas, I will do this for the special case where c_1 beats each of the other candidates by winning two-thirds of the vote and c_2 and c_3 end up in a tie; these pairwise outcomes define $\mathbf{q} = (\frac{1}{3}, 0, -\frac{1}{3})$. We need to determine the cone of profiles supporting this outcome.

By use of elementary algebra, the three vertices for the $(\frac{1}{3}, 0, -\frac{1}{3})$ cone are

$$((-\frac{1}{3}, 1, \frac{1}{3}), (1, -1, -1), \frac{1}{2}), ((1, 1, -1), (-\frac{1}{3}, -1, \frac{1}{3}), \frac{1}{2}),$$
$$(1, -\frac{1}{3}, \frac{1}{3}), (-\frac{1}{3}, \frac{1}{3}, -1), \frac{1}{2}).$$

When expressed in $Si(6)$ coordinate representation, the vertices are

$$(\frac{1}{6}, \frac{1}{2}, 0, 0, \frac{1}{3}, 0), (\frac{1}{2}, \frac{1}{6}, 0, \frac{1}{3}, 0, 0), (\frac{1}{6}, \frac{1}{6}, \frac{1}{3}, 0, 0, \frac{1}{3}). \qquad (3.3.5)$$

Once the vertices of the cone of profiles is known, the $P_{\mathbf{q}}(s)$ set can be computed by finding the $f(-, \mathbf{w}_s)$ outcome for each vertex. They are

$$(\frac{2}{3}(1 - s), \frac{1}{3} - \frac{s}{6}, \frac{5s}{6}), (\frac{2}{3}(1 - s), \frac{5s}{6}, \frac{1}{3} - \frac{s}{6}), (\frac{1}{3}(1 + s), \frac{1}{3} - \frac{s}{6}, \frac{1}{3} - \frac{s}{6}).$$

The set $P_{(\frac{1}{3}, 0, -\frac{1}{3})}(0)$ (plurality outcomes) is displayed in Fig. 3.3.2a while the antiplurality outcomes, $P_{(\frac{1}{3}, 0, -\frac{1}{3})}(\frac{1}{2})$, are given in Fig. 3.3.2b. The BC outcome corresponding to this pairwise outcome is a single, decisive point; the plurality and antiplurality outcomes offer indeterminacy of a set of possible values.

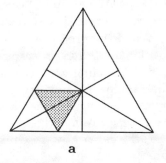 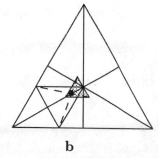

a   b

Fig. 3.3.2. Sections when $F_3 = (\frac{1}{3}, 0, -\frac{1}{3})$. **a.** $0 \le s \le \frac{1}{3}$. **b.** $\frac{1}{3} \le s \le \frac{1}{2}$

Figure 3.3.2b displays other properties of $P_{\mathbf{q}}(s)$. Each of the three dashed lines, where one dashed line coincides with the $c_2 \sim c_3$ line, is a procedure line for the appropriate vertex of the profile cone. These three lines intersect at the BC outcome. (Remember, the BC outcome is uniquely determined by the pairwise election tallies, so it must be a point.) Thus, again, the geometry forces an inversion of the $P_{\mathbf{q}}(s)$ regions corresponding to $s < \frac{1}{3}$ and $s > \frac{1}{3}$. Secondly, by using the rules of finding outcomes on the procedure line (see Sect. 2.4), the set $P_{\mathbf{q}}(s)$ can be determined. Notice, the pairwise outcome defines a cone of procedure lines where each procedure line must pass through the unique BC outcome.

More specifically, for a given $\mathbf{q}$ giving the pairwise outcomes, compute the unique BC outcome (see Sect. 3.2) $\mathbf{q}_{\frac{1}{3}}$ and the vertices $f(\mathbf{p}, \mathbf{w}_0)$, representing the plurality outcomes. Draw lines passing through the plurality vertices and the BC outcome. Each line contains a vertex for the set $P_{\mathbf{q}}(s)$; it is the point

$$f(\mathbf{p}, \mathbf{w}_s) = (1 - 3s)f(\mathbf{p}, \mathbf{w}_o) + 3s\mathbf{q}_{\frac{1}{3}}. \qquad (3.3.6)$$

From the three vertices, the set $P_{(\frac{1}{3}, 0, -\frac{1}{3})}(s)$ can be determined.

Some of the conclusions that follow from the geometry of the two figures and from the method of construction are listed next.

Theorem 3.3.3. a. *Suppose the pairwise election tallies are given by* $\mathbf{q}$.
  a. $P_{\mathbf{q}}(\frac{1}{3})$ *is a point in* $P_{\mathbf{q}}(s)$ *for all* s.
  b. *If* $s_1 < s_2 \leq \frac{1}{3}$ *or if* $\frac{1}{3} \leq s_2 < s_1 \leq \frac{1}{2}$, *then*

$$P_{\mathbf{q}}(s_2) \subsetneqq P_{\mathbf{q}}(s_1). \qquad (3.3.7)$$

  c. *If* $s \neq \frac{1}{3}$, *then the dimension of* $P_{\mathbf{q}}(s)$ *equals the dimension of* $F_3^{-1}(\mathbf{q})$.
  d. *For any* $\mathbf{q}$, *there exists a profile* $\mathbf{p}$ *so that*

$$F_3(\mathbf{p}) = \mathbf{q}, \; f(\mathbf{p}, \mathbf{w}_s) = f(\mathbf{p}, \mathbf{w}_{\frac{1}{3}}), \quad \forall s. \qquad (3.3.8)$$

Part d asserts that *for any BC election tally, there exists a profile so that this is the normalized tally for all possible positional election outcomes.* This conclusion is a consequence of part a and the positional line. Because the BC outcome is in $P_{\mathbf{q}}(s)$ for all choices of s, choose the plurality outcome to agree with the BC outcome. Then, by the properties of the procedure line, this must be the common outcome for all possible positional election processes.

What we have seen so far is that *only the BC ranking can be related, in any manner, to the rankings of the pairs.* The ranking for any other choice of a positional procedure need not reflect in any manner whatsoever the rankings of the pairs. Instead, there is a set of possible outcomes. When this set meets other ranking regions, we have paradoxes! However, the closer a $\mathbf{w}_s$ resembles the BC, the faster it sheds its troubles.

3.3.3 What Pairwise Outcomes Can Accompany a $\mathbf{w}_s$ Tally?

So far the emphasis has been to select the three pairwise election outcomes and then determine the accompanying set of positional outcomes $P_{\mathbf{q}}(s)$. Another kind of section is to select the $\mathbf{w}_s$ election outcome $\mathbf{q}_s$ and then compute the accompanying set of binary outcomes $B_{\mathbf{q}}(s)$. I will illustrate the ideas in the special setting where the $\mathbf{w}_s$ outcome is $\mathcal{I}$; extensions to the general value of $\mathbf{q}_s$ follows in the same manner, so they are left to the reader.

We already know that a complete tie in the pairwise elections need not mean that there is a complete tie in the $\mathbf{w}_s$ election. The converse question is to interpret the meaning of a $\mathbf{w}_s$ outcome of $\mathcal{I}$; what kinds of binary (pairwise) election outcomes can arise? The approach follows that developed above. Namely,

$$B_{(\frac{1}{3},\frac{1}{3},\frac{1}{3})}(s) = \{F_3(\mathbf{p}) \,|\, \mathbf{p} \in (f(-,\mathbf{w}_s))^{-1}(\mathcal{I})\}.$$

Thus, all we need are the profile vertices of $(f(-,\mathbf{w}_s))^{-1}(\mathcal{I})$.

The vertices of $f(-,\mathbf{w}_s))^{-1}(\mathcal{I})$ are those profiles in this set with as many voter types as possible without voters. Only the BC allows a profile with only two voter types to support $\mathcal{I}$, so a profile vertex for any other $\mathbf{w}_s$ must involve voters from three voter types. Two such profiles are immediate; they are

$$\mathbf{p}_m = (\frac{1}{3},0,\frac{1}{3},0,\frac{1}{3},0), \ \mathbf{p}_m^r = (0,\frac{1}{3},0,\frac{1}{3},0,\frac{1}{3}).$$

As a consequence of neutrality, the $\mathbf{w}_s$ outcome for each of these profiles is a cycle. In particular, independent of the value of s, two vertices of $B_{(\frac{1}{3},\frac{1}{3},\frac{1}{3})}(s)$ are

$$(\frac{1}{3},\frac{1}{3},\frac{1}{3}), \quad -(\frac{1}{3},\frac{1}{3},\frac{1}{3}). \tag{3.3.9}$$

The set $f(-,\mathbf{w}_s))^{-1}(\mathcal{I})$ has six more vertices; the choice of the required three voter types depends on the geometry admitted by $s < \frac{1}{3}$, or $s > \frac{1}{3}$. The idea is to modify a profile vertex defining a BC outcome of $\mathcal{I}$. Such a BC profile is based on profile reversals such as given by $\frac{1}{2}(\mathbf{E}_1 + \mathbf{E}_1^r) = \frac{1}{2}(\mathbf{E}_1 + \mathbf{E}_4)$.

If $s < \frac{1}{3}$, the line of profiles $t\mathbf{E}_1 + (1-t)\mathbf{E}_4$ defines a line of election results that misses $\mathcal{I}$; this is the dashed line starting from the left corner of Fig. 3.3.1a. To pull the election ranking to $\mathcal{I}$, we need a voter of type-five or six. A direct computation shows that if a profile $\mathbf{p} = (p_1,0,0,p_4,p_5,0)$ leads to the $\mathbf{w}_s$ outcome of $\mathcal{I}$ with tally $(\frac{1}{3},\frac{1}{3},\frac{1}{3})$, then

$$p_1 = \frac{1}{3(1-s)}, p_4 = \frac{1}{3} + \frac{s^2}{3(1-s)(1-2s)}, p_5 = \frac{1/3 - (p_1+p_4)s}{1-s},$$

$$0 \le s \le \frac{1}{3}. \tag{3.3.10}$$

These equations make sense. For instance, when $s = 0$, the profile reduces to $(\frac{1}{3},0,0,\frac{1}{3},\frac{1}{3},0)$ which clearly defines the plurality outcome of $\mathcal{I}$. At the other extreme, when $s = \frac{1}{3}$, we have that $p_5 = 0$ and the profile $(\frac{1}{2},0,0,\frac{1}{2},0,0)$ associated with the BC outcome of $\mathcal{I}$ is recovered. Thus, the expression for p_5 truly measures the degree to which a BC vertex needs to be modified to create a profile vertex for $(f(-,\mathbf{w}_s))^{-1}(\mathcal{I})$.

We now can obtain all of the remaining six vertices for $(f(-,\mathbf{w}_s))^{-1}(\mathcal{I})$ should $0 \le s \le \frac{1}{3}$. To see how to do this, notice that type-five voters help the type-four voters force the election outcome toward the right-hand edge of the representation triangle. (See a representation triangle.) If the profile had involved the three voter types one, four, and six, then the type-six voters would assist the type-one voters in moving the outcome toward the bottom edge of $Si(3)$. Thus, to get the $\mathcal{I}$ outcome, a permutation is involved. Namely, if $\sigma = (1,4)(5,6)$ and $\mathbf{p}$ is the above designed profile, then $\sigma_T(\mathbf{p})$ is the desired profile with type-one, four, and six voters. The following gives the list of all profile vertices where any voter type not mentioned has zero voters.

Types	Vertices $a = \frac{1}{3(1-s)}$	$0 \leq s \leq \frac{1}{3}$ $b = \frac{1}{3} + \frac{s^2}{3(1-s)(1-2s)}$	$1 - (a+b)$ $= \frac{2}{3} - \frac{1-2s+s^2}{3(1-s)(1-2s)}$
$1,4,5$	p_1	p_4	p_5
$1,4,6$	p_4	p_1	p_6
$2,4,5$	p_2	p_5	p_4
$2,3,5$	p_5	p_2	p_3
$1,3,6$	p_3	p_6	p_1
$2,3,6$	p_6	p_3	p_2

$$(3.3.11)$$

These eight profiles are the profile vertices for $(f(-,\mathbf{w}_s))^{-1}(\mathcal{I})$ should $0 \leq s \leq \frac{1}{3}$.

The vertices for $\frac{1}{3} \leq s \leq \frac{1}{2}$ can be obtained from the above table by using Theorem 3.1.6, the fact that $\mathcal{I}^r = \mathcal{I}$ and the reversal permutation $(1,4)(2,5)(3,6)$.

Types	Vertices $a = \frac{1}{3(1-s)}$	$\frac{1}{3} \leq s \leq \frac{1}{2}$ $b = \frac{1}{3} + \frac{s^2}{3(1-s)(1-2s)}$	$1 - (a+b)$ $= \frac{2}{3} - \frac{1-2s+s^2}{3(1-s)(1-2s)}$
$1,2,4$	p_4	p_1	p_2
$1,3,4$	p_1	p_4	p_3
$1,2,5$	p_5	p_2	p_1
$2,5,6$	p_2	p_5	p_6
$3,4,6$	p_6	p_3	p_4
$3,5,6$	p_3	p_6	p_5

$$(3.3.12)$$

With these vertices for $f(-,\mathbf{w}_s))^{-1}(\mathcal{I}), s \in [0, \frac{1}{2}]$, it is an exercise to determine the pairwise election outcomes that can accompany a $\mathbf{w}_s$ ranking of $\mathcal{I}$. Namely, determine the F_3 image of each vertex; $B_{\mathcal{I}}(s)$ is the convex hull of the eight F_3 image points. The set $B_{\mathcal{I}}(s)$ for $s = 0, \frac{1}{2}$ is illustrated in Fig. 3.3.3.

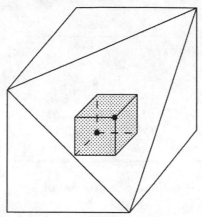

Fig. 3.3.3. The pairwise vote outcomes with the plurality ranking $\mathcal{I}$

The shaded region $B_{\mathcal{I}}(s)$ for $s = 0, \frac{1}{2}$ given in Fig. 3.3.3 is the cube with vertices $(\pm\frac{1}{3}, \pm\frac{1}{3}, \pm\frac{1}{3})$. This cube dramatically indicates how widely the pairwise tallies can deviate from the plurality ranking of $\mathcal{I}$. For example, because $(\frac{1}{3}, -\frac{1}{3}, -\frac{1}{3}) \in B_{\mathcal{I}}(0)$, it follows that there exist profiles where, even though c_1 beats both c_2 and c_3 in pairwise competitions by winning two-thirds of the vote in each case, and c_3 beats c_2 by getting two-thirds of the vote, the plurality election ends in a complete tie vote! (As this point is a vertex, it is trivial to show that $(0, \frac{1}{3}, \frac{1}{3}, 0, 0, \frac{1}{3})$ is the supporting profile.) It is difficult to justify the complete tie plurality outcome as reflecting the views of the voters! The general case is described next.

Theorem 3.3.4. a. For $0 \leq s \leq \frac{1}{3}$,

$$B_{\mathcal{I}}(\mathbf{w}_s) = B_{\mathcal{I}}(\mathbf{w}_s^r). \tag{3.3.13}$$

b. The points $\pm(\frac{1}{3}, \frac{1}{3}, \frac{1}{3})$ are vertices of each $B_{\mathcal{I}}(\mathbf{w}_s)$. The remaining six vertices of $B_{\mathcal{I}}(\mathbf{w}_s)$, $0 \leq s \leq \frac{1}{3}$, are

Voter types	F_3 image
$1, 4, 5$	$(2a - 1, 1 - 2b, 1 - 2a)$
$1, 4, 6$	$(2b - 1, 1 - 2a, 2a - 1)$
$2, 4, 5$	$(2a - 1, 2b - 1, 1 - 2a)$
$2, 3, 5$	$(1 - 2a, 2a - 1, 1 - 2b)$
$1, 3, 6$	$(1 - 2b, 1 - 2a, 2a - 1)$
$2, 3, 6$	$(1 - 2a, 2a - 1, 2b - 1)$

$$(3.3.14)$$

where the values of a and b are given in Eq. 3.3.11, 3.3.12. The remaining six *vertices of $B_{\mathcal{I}}(\mathbf{w}_s^r)$ are*

Voter types	F_3 image
$1, 2, 4$	$(1 - 2a, 2b - 1, 2a - 1)$
$1, 3, 4$	$(1 - 2b, 2a - 1, 1 - 2a)$
$1, 2, 5$	$(1 - 2a, 1 - 2b, 2a - 1)$
$2, 5, 6$	$(2a - 1, 1 - 2a, 2b - 1)$
$3, 4, 6$	$(2b - 1, 2a - 1, 1 - 2a)$
$3, 5, 6$	$(2a - 1, 1 - 2a, 1 - 2b)$

$$(3.3.15)$$

   c. *If $s \neq \frac{1}{3}$, then $B_{\mathcal{I}}(\mathbf{w}_s)$ is a three-dimensional object. The set $B_{\mathcal{I}}(\mathbf{w}_{\frac{1}{3}})$ is the line connecting the two points $\pm(\frac{1}{3}, \frac{1}{3}, \frac{1}{3})$.*

Proof. Equations 3.3.13, 3.3.14 follow from a direct computation. As to be expected from $F_3(\mathbf{p}^r) = (F_3)^r(\mathbf{p})$ (Theorem 3.1.4), the vertices in Eq. 3.3.15 are obtained by reversing the value for the corresponding entry of Eq. 3.3.14. Equation 3.3.13 is a direct consequence of this reversal operation. $\square$

   How do we interpret this theorem? It shows that that there are an abundance of different pairwise election tallies that can accompany a non-BC positional voting ranking of $\mathcal{I}$. As the value of s gets closer to $\frac{1}{3}$, the six variable vertices of $B_{\mathcal{I}}(\mathbf{w}_s)$ start approaching the point $(0, 0, 0)$, so the three-dimensional region approximates a straight line. In other words, the closer $\mathbf{w}_s$ is to being the BC, the stronger the restrictions on the choices of the pairwise tallies that can accompany the $\mathbf{w}_s$ ranking $\mathcal{I}$. (With the above argument, this means that to create a "paradox," a large number of voters may be needed.) These restrictions tend to the situation whereby either a positive or negative cycle occurs where the winning margin for each pair is the same. Here we can accept the positional ranking $\mathcal{I}$; all others are highly questionable.

3.3.4 Probability Computations

It is obvious that with any reasonable probability distribution and enough voters, the BC is the most likely to respect any condition requiring consistency with the pairwise rankings. After all, the cones illustrate the many profiles where the $\mathbf{w}_s$ rankings differ from the pairwise rankings once $s \neq \frac{1}{3}$. Indeed, from these cones, the profile vertices of the associated set of profiles is a straightforward computation. Then, with any probability distribution, calculus techniques provide the actual values for the probability.

   Because of the ease, I was tempted to report this analysis, but I did not for two reasons. This first is that we already know what the answer will be from the cones and geometric techniques developed here. Anyway, probability comparisons are crude measures; a more useful approach is to be able to "see" the actual set of profiles defining different outcomes. This more refined approach is described with the coordinate representations. So, why invest in hamburger when prime steak is available?

The second reason is that a probability comparison with pairwise rankings seems silly. It seems to be an attempt to announce that "two wrongs make a right!" We already know that the pairwise rankings are suspect, and the last couple of sections have demonstrated the serious bias and difficulties that can accompany a non-BC outcome. What does such a comparison mean? Is it measuring where both procedures are at fault but in different ways? So, a better approach is to use the profile cones.

Extensions. There are many other issues that require finding the pairwise votes that can accompany the outcome $f(\mathbf{p}, \mathbf{w}_s) = \mathbf{q}_s$. As an illustration, for the procedure $(3, 1, 0)$ $(s = \frac{1}{4})$, we might wish to determine the $\mathbf{q}$ normalized pairwise election tally for a ranking $c_1 \succ c_2 \succ c_3$ that will ensure that c_1 could win both pairwise elections. More generally, we might be interested in finding all pairwise tallies, $B_{\mathbf{q}_s}(\mathbf{w}_s)$, that accompany a $f(\mathbf{p}, \mathbf{w}_s) = \mathbf{q}_s$ outcome.

The approach is the same; as

$$B_{\mathbf{q}_s}(\mathbf{w}_s) = \{F_3(\mathbf{p}) \mid \mathbf{p} \in (f(-, \mathbf{w}_s))^{-1}(\mathbf{q}_s),$$

we must determine the vertices for the profile set $(f(-, \mathbf{w}_s))^{-1}(\mathbf{q}_s)$. These vertices are found by using the same three voter type profiles used above. (Replacing profiles $\mathbf{p}_m, \mathbf{p}_m^r$ is an appropriate convex combination of $\mathbf{E}_1, \mathbf{E}_3, \mathbf{E}_5$ and $\mathbf{E}_2, \mathbf{E}_4, \mathbf{E}_6$.) Now, however, certain profile vertices can drop out depending on the value of $\mathbf{q}_s$. For instance, it is impossible to find a profile $(p_1, 0, 0, p_4, p_5, 0)$ if $\mathbf{q}_s$ is not in the convex hull defined by $\{[\mathbf{w}_s]_j\}_{j=1,4,5}$. Thus, as $\mathbf{q}_s$ approaches extreme regions, a radical difference in the geometry of $B_{\mathbf{q}_s}(\mathbf{w}_s)$ emerges. These issues are left for the reader to explore.

Summary. From the above analysis, it is clear there need not be any relationships among a non-BC election ranking and the rankings of the three pairs of candidates. Only the BC can maintain any integrity among these rankings! When one examines the actual tallies, it becomes clear that the closer a positional voting method approximates the BC, the closer the tallies come into accord. Indeed, for a positional method close to the BC to admit certain paradoxes, a large number of voters might be required. These results provide strong support to an assertion that the BC is the unique positional voting method to preserve the voters' wishes.

3.3.5 Exercises

3.3.1. If a procedure line is a point $\mathbf{q}$, then this point has all of the properties of the BC outcome. (Why?) Use this argument to prove and extend Theorem 2.6.9.

3.3.2. Find the set of $\mathbf{w}_s$ outcomes for the pairwise vote $(\frac{1}{4}, 0, 0)$. Which choices of s allow all 13 outcomes to occur? Find the cone of all profiles supporting this outcome.

3.3.3. Find the values of $(x, 0, 0)$ which restrict the accompanying plurality outcomes to only three rankings. What values of $(x, y, 0)$ reduce the outcome to one ranking? In both cases, compare the plurality outcome with the BC outcome.

3.3.4. Compare the cones of profiles supporting $B_{\mathcal{I}}(\mathbf{w}_s)$ for $s = 0, \frac{1}{3}$.

3.3.5. Show that for any $\mathbf{q}$, $B_{\mathbf{q}}(\mathbf{w}_{\frac{1}{3}})$ is a line parallel to $B_{\mathcal{I}}(\mathbf{w}_{\frac{1}{3}})$. Show for any $\mathbf{q}$ and $s \neq \frac{1}{3}$ that $B_{\mathbf{q}}(\mathbf{w}_{\frac{1}{3}}) \subsetneq B_{\mathbf{q}}(\mathbf{w}_s)$ and that if $0 < s < \frac{1}{3}$, then $B_{\mathbf{q}}(\mathbf{w}_s) \subsetneq B_{\mathbf{q}}(\mathbf{w}_0)$. What does this say about the sets of supporting profiles?

3.3.6. (For those readers comfortable with calculus.) Show that $a(s), b(s)$ as defined in Eq. 3.3.11 are increasing functions on $[0, \frac{1}{3}]$. Then, use Eq. 3.3.14 to show that if $0 < s_1 < s_2 \leq \frac{1}{3}$, then

$$B_{\mathcal{I}}(\mathbf{w}_{s_2}) \subsetneq B_{\mathcal{I}}(\mathbf{w}_{s_1}). \tag{3.3.16}$$

What is the relationship for $\frac{1}{3} \leq s_2 < s_1 \leq \frac{1}{2}$? Show that Eq. 3.3.16 holds in general; that is, it holds when $\mathcal{I}$ is replaced by $\mathbf{q}$. What do these relationships mean about supporting sets of profiles?

3.4 Multiple Voting Schemes

So far, I have used the standard assumption that each voter has a *strict* transitive ranking of the candidates. But, anyone who has stood in an election booth confronted with pages of names of obscure candidates while silently wondering *"Who are these people?"* recognizes the conflict between reality and this convenient assumption. To compound the problem, even should everyone have a strict ranking, we all can cite examples of an obstinate voter who accompanies his refusal to rank the candidates with kind advice about where to spend eternity. Finally, there are situations when, for whatever reason, a voter doesn't want to rank all of the candidates.

What do we do? We could insist that the equivocating voters "get off the fence" and make a decision by choosing a strict ranking. This is easy to enforce; just invalidate any ballot not complying with the rules. The virtue of this "tough love" approach is to force the voters to think through the issues. But, let's be honest; it is important to understand what to do if voters do not use strict rankings. Anyway, this more general question introduces a nice theoretical issue.

The strict ranking assumption restricts attention to six voter types, so a new theory requires extending the earlier ideas to hold for all 13 transitive rankings. The goal is to determine which "extended positional voting procedures" best capture the voters' true wishes. There is a bonus attached to extending positional methods. Because the analysis utilizes the geometric techniques developed in the previous sections, I only need to outline the issues and questions; the technical details are left to the reader.

3.4.1 From Multiple Methods to Approval Voting

Labels for the seven new voter types are defined in Fig. 3.4.1 where the one missing region, $\mathcal{R}(13) = \mathcal{I}$, characterizes a voter who is either totally confused or an indifferent wimp. While many such voters exist, they do not create an obstacle to the analysis because (in a reasonable system) they do not affect the outcome. So, by ignoring such studied indifference, the following six new types emerge.

Voter type	Ranking	Unanimity profile
7	$c_1 \succ c_2 \sim c_3$	$\mathbf{E}_7$
8	$c_1 \sim c_3 \succ c_2$	$\mathbf{E}_8$
9	$c_3 \succ c_2 \sim c_1$	$\mathbf{E}_9$
10	$c_2 \sim c_3 \succ c_1$	$\mathbf{E}_{10}$
11	$c_2 \succ c_1 \sim c_3$	$\mathbf{E}_{11}$
12	$c_1 \sim c_2 \succ c_3$	$\mathbf{E}_{12}$

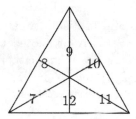

Fig. 3.4.1. The added voter types

The six new voter types can be subdivided into the "singleton-type" (types $\{7, 9, 11\}$) where one candidate is preferred while the other two are treated with indifference, and the "binary-type" (types $\{8, 10, 12\}$) where no difference is seen between the two top-ranked candidates. The assignment of voting vectors to each of the three types is

Voter type	Voting vector	
Strict ranking	$\mathbf{W}_0 = (w_1, w_2, w_3)$	
Singleton	$\mathbf{W}_1 = (w_1^1, w_2^1, w_3^1),\ w_2^1 = w_3^1$	(3.4.1)
Binary	$\mathbf{W}_2 = (w_1^2, w_2^2, w_3^2),\ w_1^2 = w_2^2$	

The listing illustrates that three kinds of voting vectors are needed to accommodate the three classes of voter types. Such a system is imaginatively called *a multiple positional voting system.*

Example 3.4.1. a. *Truncated voting.* Multiple voting systems emerge even when not intended. A typical situation involves an obstinate voter who casts a truncated ballot listing only his top choice. A convenient way to handle these ballots is to throw them out. But, to avoid ill will or a broken nose, it might be wiser to tally the ballot. If the voting vector is $\mathbf{W} = (3, 1, 0)$, then maybe the truncated ballots could be tallied by crediting the lone candidate with 3 points and zero points for the others. Such a benign attitude defines the vector $\mathbf{W}_1 = (3, 0, 0)$. Alternatively, one might divide the remaining point among the bottom two candidates to define $\mathbf{W}_1' = (3, \frac{1}{2}, \frac{1}{2})$.

To further complicate the departmental election, suppose some voters can't or won't choose between their top choices of say, Martha and Helvi. Such ballots can be handled by "splitting the difference" of the four available points to define $\mathbf{W}_2 = (2, 2, 0)$.

b. *Cumulative voting.* The State of Illinois, among other places, experimented with "cumulative voting." (See [SMR].) As an illustrating example of this procedure, let each voter have three points to split among the candidates in units of either integers or $\frac{3}{2}$. The assignment of points, of course, reveals the voter's preferences. For instance, a voter with strict preferences for the candidates uses $\mathbf{W}_0 = (2, 1, 0)$; a voter of the singleton type chooses $\mathbf{W}_1 = (3, 0, 0)$, and a binary type voter uses $\mathbf{W}_2 = (\frac{3}{2}, \frac{3}{2}, 0)$. (A voter using $(1, 0, 0)$ or $(1, 1, 0)$ is called a fool; such voters are ignored here.)

c. *Approval voting.* In the late 1970's, Approval Voting (AV) was independently invented by R. Weber, by S. Brams and P. Fishburn, and by others. Since then, AV has been carefully analyzed and widely promoted by Brams and Fishburn [BF1, BF2]. Because AV requires a voter to choose either "Yes" or "No" for each candidate, it follows that $\mathbf{W}_1 = (1, 0, 0)$ and $\mathbf{W}_2 = (1, 1, 0)$. On the other hand, it is not clear how a voter with strict preferences should vote; consequently, with AV, $\mathbf{W}_0$ is not well defined.

Just from the clever choice of the name, approval voting has to sound attractive: a voter can either approve or disapprove of each candidate. Yet, when this freedom is combined with the undefined $\mathbf{W}_0$, new kinds of election difficulties crop up.[14] After all, without a $\mathbf{W}_0$, AV forces a decisive voter to climb back on the fence and start equivocating. Namely, with a positional method, an undecided voter is forced to clarify his views; with AV, a voter with a clear ranking of the candidates is forced to develop indifference among them. These comments are supported by the emphasis in the AV literature describing strategies, such as "a voter's mean utility," to use to vote "sincerely."

To analyze AV, the set of the voters with a strict ranking of type j is split into two subgroups; those adopting the singleton type, j_1, and those who use a binary persuasion, j_2. For AV, then, there are $12 + 6 = 18$ voter types. (For the same reasons described earlier, the ranking region $\mathcal{I}$ is ignored.) $\square$

We now encounter a technical problem; the voting vectors must be normalized. (This reduces an infinite number of choices into a single equivalent one.) As true for positional voting methods, "equivalence" means that the election ranking is preserved for all profiles.

There is no problem normalizing the vector $\mathbf{W}_0$; convert $\mathbf{W}_0$ into a standard $\mathbf{w}_s$, $s \in [0, \frac{1}{2}]$ form. To demonstrate the difficulty in normalizing $\mathbf{W}_1$ and $\mathbf{W}_2$, suppose for the truncated voting example $\mathbf{W}_0 = (3, 1, 0)$ is identified with $\mathbf{w}_{\frac{1}{4}} = (\frac{3}{4}, \frac{1}{4}, 0)$. With a truncated ballot, the voter only identifies his top-ranked candidate. Presumably, this means that $\mathbf{W}_1 = (3, 0, 0)$. But if the normalized form of this $\mathbf{W}_1$ is $\mathbf{w}_0 = (1, 0, 0)$, the normalization *increases* the power of this

---

[14] For instance, the AV inherits the inability of the plurality and the antiplurality methods to relate to the higher dimensional aspects of a profile. Arguably, these profile characteristics can cause a procedure to choose the incorrect election rankings.

voter's ballot. To see this, the $\mathbf{W}_0$, $\mathbf{W}_1$ outcome for the profile $\frac{7}{13}\mathbf{E}_1 + \frac{6}{13}\mathbf{E}_9$ is $c_1 \succ c_3 \succ c_2$ with the tally $(\frac{21}{13}, \frac{7}{13}, \frac{18}{13})$, but the normalized $\mathbf{w}_{\frac{1}{4}}$, $(1,0,0)$ outcome is $c_3 \succ c_1 \succ c_2$ with the tally $(\frac{21}{52}, \frac{7}{52}, \frac{24}{52})$. As the ranking is not preserved, the normalization is incorrect.

As an example, with the AV, suppose $\mathbf{W}_1 = (1,0,0)$ is normalized to $\mathbf{w}_0 = (1,0,0)$ and $\mathbf{W}_2 = (1,1,0)$ to $\mathbf{w}_{\frac{1}{2}} = (\frac{1}{2}, \frac{1}{2}, 0)$ and consider the profile $\frac{1}{2}\mathbf{E}_7 + \frac{1}{2}\mathbf{E}_{11}$. The election outcome with $\mathbf{W}_1$, $\mathbf{W}_2$ is $\mathcal{I}$ with the tally $(\frac{1}{2}, \frac{1}{2}, \frac{1}{2})$, but if $\mathbf{w}_0$, $\mathbf{w}_{\frac{1}{2}}$ are used, the election ranking is $c_1 \succ c_2 \sim c_3$ with the tally $(\frac{1}{2}, \frac{1}{4}, \frac{1}{4})$. The normalization does not preserve the ranking, so it is wrong.

Normalization process. *Let $\mathbf{W}_0$, $\mathbf{W}_1$, $\mathbf{W}_2$ be the multiple voting vectors assigned to the three kinds of voter types. Let the scalars a and b define the normalized voting vector $\mathbf{w}_s = a\mathbf{W}_0 + b(1,1,1)$. The normalized form for the singleton and binary voter types are, respectively, $\mathbf{w}^1 = a\mathbf{W}_1 + b(1,1,1)$ and $\mathbf{w}^2 = a\mathbf{W}_2 + b(1,1,1)$.*

In other words, the scalars used to normalize one voting vector are used to normalize all of them. It is left to the reader to show that the normalization process preserves the election rankings.

Example 3.4.2. For the truncated voting example, the normalized voting vectors are $\mathbf{w} = (3,0,0) \approx \mathbf{w}_{\frac{1}{4}} = (\frac{3}{4}, \frac{1}{4}, 0)$, $\mathbf{W}_1 = (3,0,0) \approx \mathbf{w}^1 = (\frac{3}{4}, 0, 0)$, and $\mathbf{W}_1' = (3, \frac{1}{2}, \frac{1}{2}) \approx \mathbf{w}^1 = (\frac{3}{4}, \frac{1}{8}, \frac{1}{8})$, $\mathbf{w}^2 = (2,2,0) \approx \mathbf{w}^2 = (\frac{1}{2}, \frac{1}{2}, 0)$. For AV, the vectors specified above are in a normalized form. For the cumulative voting example, $\mathbf{W}_0 \approx \mathbf{w}_{\frac{1}{3}}$, $\mathbf{w}^1 = (1,0,0)$, and $\mathbf{w}^2 = (\frac{1}{2}, \frac{1}{2}, 0)$. $\square$

3.4.2 No Good Deed Goes Unpunished

"Fairness" often is used to promote multiple voting systems. After all, why discard a colleague's truncated ballot? Another attractive argument used to motivate cumulative voting and AV is that multiple systems appear to create a fairer, more responsive procedure by allowing a voter to more accurately represent his true preferences. Clearly, a better approximation is obtained by using cardinal rather than ordinal rankings. A closely related third theme, coming from Chap. 2, is that the pairwise vote has problems because it ignores vital information. Are other kinds of information being ignored by non-multiple procedures? Why not use methods that incorporate as much information as possible? There is no debate; these noble arguments and positive intentions are "good deeds." Consequently it is worth digressing to understand the promised punishment.

Often (but not always) multiple systems introduce new kinds of voting problems. What I find particularly disturbing is that these troubles are direct consequences of the good intentions motivating the adoption of a multiple system! After all, the added opportunities for voters to better express themselves suggest that, in some way, multiple systems promote basic democratic principles. Yet, it is the additional options that vitiate the noble objectives by forcing election outcomes that distinctly violate the voters' wishes! These added options permitting a voter to better express his or her views can distort the outcome so that it is counter to the voters' beliefs. What a paradox!

To understand this problem, we can use standard algebraic intuition. As even elementary school students learn, when the number of variables increases, so does the complexity of the system – extra variables introduce new problems and difficulties. With two equations in two unknowns, the image sets and solution sets are reasonably simple. But, nobody would anticipate a similar statement to apply for two equations in five unknowns. Instead, with five unknowns, we must expect new kinds of complexities to torment the analysis.

This algebraic intuition is relevant because, as developed here, voting theory is intimately connected with algebra and geometry. In fact, this intuition, while not expressed in terms of variable counting, already is firmly established in choice theory. Support comes from profile restrictions used to obtain election relationships. As shown in Chap. 2 with single peakedness conditions, etc., "nice" election relationships emerge. This is because effective profile restrictions are equivalent to decreasing the number of variables.

Armed with this common sense, observe that for multiple systems, the number of variables is *increased*, not decreased. Thus, instead of realizing sharper election relationships, we must expect the added variables to cause new problems. For example, a positional voting system is based on six variables; with a multiple system the number of variables is doubled to twelve. (So, a positional method is a profile restriction of a multiple system.)

Must There Be Problems? The Causes. It is not necessary for a multiple system to cause problems. To illustrate, there is not much difference between the image sets of $f_1(x,y) = x + 2y$, $f_2(x,y) = 2x - y$ and $g_1(x,u,v) = x + 2(u + v)$, $g_2(x,u,v) = 2x - (u + v)$, because the second system comes from the first by substituting $y = u + v$. Indeed, this kind of algebraic dependency creates the election relationships enjoyed by the BC. (Technically, these dependencies reduce the number of effective equations.) Therefore, it is worth wondering whether multiple systems enjoy a similar phenomenon with carefully coordinated choices of $\mathbf{w}_s, \mathbf{w}^1, \mathbf{w}^2$. They can, and when they do we must anticipate that the advantages of a multiple system can be bought at a minimal extra cost.

Some Voters Are More Equal than Others. It is not really the number of variables that creates problems; as demonstrated in Example 2.5.1, it is the geometry of the image set. In a sense already described in this chapter, the "smaller" the dimension and size of the image set, the more consistency we can expect among the election relationships. The problem with admitting more variables, then, is that they tend to force the image set to grow. This must be expected with multiple systems; after all, we are trying to force a higher dimensional space of profiles into the usual $[-1,1]^3 \times Si(3)$ range space.

The "size" problem emerges dramatically with multiple voting systems because the image can be larger than the representation triangle! To see why, start with the election mapping

$$f(\mathbf{p}_j, \mathbf{w}_s, \mathbf{w}^1, \mathbf{w}^2) = \sum_{j=1}^{6} p_j[\mathbf{w}_s]_j + \sum_{j=7,9,11} p_j[\mathbf{w}^1]_j + \sum_{j=8,10,12} p_j[\mathbf{w}^2]_j \quad (3.4.2)$$

where $[\mathbf{w}^k]_j$ has the obvious definition. The domain is

$$Si(12) = \{\mathbf{p} = (p_1, \ldots, p_{12}) \in R_+^{12} \,|\, p_j \geq 0, \sum_{j=1}^{12} p_j = 1\}. \quad (3.4.3)$$

Proposition 3.4.1. *If the sum of the components for each of* $\mathbf{W}, \mathbf{W}_1, \mathbf{W}_2$ *are the same, then the image set of Eq. 3.4.2 is a subset of the two-dimensional representation triangle. In the contrary case, the image set is a three-dimensional convex set.*

Proof. The proof is simple; the image set is the convex hull defined by the twelve points

$$\{[\mathbf{w}_s]_j\}_{j=1}^{6}, \{[\mathbf{w}^1]_j\}_{j=7,9,11}, \{[\mathbf{w}^2]_j\}_{j=8,10,12}.$$

If all vectors are in the representation triangle, then the convex hull must be two-dimensional. If the sum of the components of either $\mathbf{w}^1$ or $\mathbf{w}^2$ differ from unity, then the permutations of these particular vectors are either above (where the sum is greater than unity), or below (where the sum is less than unity) the representation triangle. This forces the convex hull to be three-dimensional. $\square$

Example 3.4.3. To illustrate, the truncated voting example has all of the $[\mathbf{w}_{\frac14}]_j$ and $[(\frac34, \frac18, \frac18)]_j$ terms on $Si(3)$ (because the sum of the components adds to unity), but the three vectors $[(\frac34, 0, 0)]_j$ are below the representation triangle because the sum of the components equals $\frac34$. Consequently, if truncated ballots are counted as $(\frac34, \frac18, \frac18)$, then the image is in the representation triangle, while if $(\frac34, 0, 0)$ is used, we have a three-dimensional image with six vertices on the plane $x + y + z = 1$ and three more on the plane $x + y + z = \frac34$.

A striking example comes from AV. Here, the vertices associated with $(1, 0, 0)$ are in the plane $x + y + z = 1$, while those vertices derived from $(1, 1, 0)$ are in the plane $x + y + z = 2$. The AV image set, given in Fig. 3.4.2, is a copy of the representation cube. $\square$

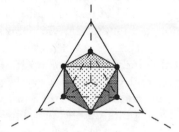

Fig. 3.4.2. The 3-dimensional image set for AV

For positional voting, the image space always is in the two-dimensional representational triangle; but for multiple voting, it need not be. An outline of some of the consequences of this thickness follows; the reader is encouraged to find other issues and to develop the geometry needed to establish the supporting arguments.

- With k voters, a voter of the jth type adds $\frac{1}{k}[\mathbf{w}]_j$ points toward the final outcome. The value $\frac{1}{k}$ doesn't change, but a multiple system allows the choice of $\mathbf{w}$ (in the vector ballot $[\mathbf{w}]_j$) to become an option for the voter. By simple geometry (or common sense), it is clear that a longer vector has a greater impact on the final election ranking. For example, being able to use $(2,0,0)$ rather than $(1,0,0)$ is a legal license to vote twice. There is no question; if the multiple procedure has a three-dimensional image space, *some voters are more equal than others.* This lack of equality may be by design; e.g., to penalize voters not using a strict ranking of the candidates, choose $\mathbf{w}^1$, $\mathbf{w}^2$ so that the sum of points is less than unity.

- One way to determine whether the election rankings reflect the views of the voters is to compare the rankings of the pairs of candidates with the three-candidate outcome. This is done with help from the dictionaries and cross sections of Sects. 3.2, 3.3. Recall, given the tallies of the pairwise rankings, we can compute the cross section for all positional outcomes. Correspondingly, for a specified positional election tally, the set of associated binary outcomes can be found. Now, when the image set of a multiple system is three-dimensional, it is clear that the corresponding sections are much larger. (The reader is encouraged to choose a system and compute some of these sections.) As "large" usually translates into "more paradoxes and problems," we must expect new types of problematic election outcomes.

3.4.3 Comparisons

Just as the plurality and antiplurality methods define the extreme limits for positional voting, AV is an extreme multiple method. Consequently, AV is an excellent choice to demonstrate the kinds of voter paradoxes caused by the added variables. (Of course, these problems are shared by other multiple methods; this is addressed in the exercises.) As a way to compare what can happen with the AV, assume that the plurality election outcome is $(\frac{1}{2}, \frac{1}{4}, \frac{1}{4})$; a situation that requires half of the voters have c_1 top-ranked, and the rest are split between the other two candidates. This point is the dot in Fig. 3.4.4a. So, who should be top-ranked?

The procedure line is used to address this kind of issue for positional voting methods, where, because c_1 is either a Condorcet winner, or very close to being one, the BC tally for c_1 is at least $\frac{1}{3}$ of the total number of points. (Thus, c_1 cannot be BC bottom-ranked.) With two points on the procedure line, we know all the associated positional outcomes. However, one must expect the added variables available for the AV to allow an even larger set of outcomes. It does; the shaded region is the set of AV outcomes that can accompany this c_1 plurality outcome.[15] So, even though it is arguable that c_1 should be at least second-ranked, any of the 13 rankings are admissible AV outcomes. This is due to the added variables.

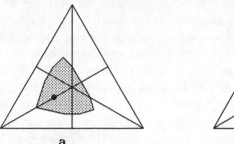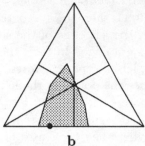

a   b

Fig. 3.4.3. Comparison of AV outcomes. **a.** AV outcomes for majority $\mathbf{w}_0$ vote. **b.** AV outcomes and Pope selection

(This region is created by finding the vertices of the convex hull of profiles leading to this plurality outcome. For example, one vertex is $\frac{1}{2}\mathbf{E}_1 + \frac{1}{4}\mathbf{E}_3 + \frac{1}{4}\mathbf{E}_5$. From the profile vertices, the corresponding AV outcomes are computed. The set of all AV outcomes, then, is the convex set defined by these AV vertices.)

As a more extreme example, the dot on the bottom edge of Fig. 3.4.3b corresponds to the Pope selection process where c_1 passes the two-thirds vote barrier, c_2 is in second place, and c_3 receives no votes. This decisive sentiment of the voters, which finally sends the correct colored smoke up the chimney, need not be reflected by an AV outcome. The decisive sentiment of the voters makes it difficult to justify selecting any candidate other than c_1. However, as illustrated by the shaded area of possible accompanying AV outcomes, any of the three candidates could be top-ranked if the AV is used. Again, the large region of election outcomes is due to the added options available to the voters.

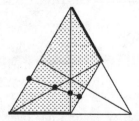

Fig. 3.4.4. Finding AV indetermancy

The above examples suggest that the AV is *indeterminate* in the sense that each profile defines not one outcome, but many of them.[16] To see why this

---

[15] In fact, the AV outcome is three-dimensional. To simplify the viewing, all election outcomes are normalized.

[16] For a discussion about the pros and cons of *indeterminacy*, see [SvN1, SvN2, BFM]. K. Saari offers a different argument supporting the AV indeterminacy where she uses game theory to select among the different outcomes. The flavor of her argument can be captured with

indeterminacy occurs for *all possible* profiles, $\mathbf{p} \in Si(6)$, consider Fig. 3.4.4. In this figure, the profile is $\lambda\mathbf{E}_1 + (1-\lambda)\mathbf{E}_4$ where $\lambda = 1$ is an unanimity profile; yet it supports the dark bottom line of AV outcomes that intersects three ranking regions. Thus, *even if the voters are unanimous in their beliefs, the AV outcome can be indeterminate.* A similar statement holds for $\mathbf{E}_4$ and $\lambda = 0$.

If $\lambda \in (0,1)$, then the AV outcome is in the shaded region where one vertex must be on the left edge of the shaded region (an edge of $Si(3)$), and one must be on the right edge. In fact, the four vertices are determined in the following way. First, let all type-one voters and type-four voters use $(1,0,0)$. The value of λ determines the point on the left edge of the representation triangle. Next, let all of the voters use $(1,1,0)$; the λ value determines the point on the right edge of the shaded region. The remaining two vertices are determined in a similar way, but where one type uses $(1,0,0)$ while the other type uses $(1,1,0)$. The convex region defined by these four dots is the AV hull.

Incidentally, if $\lambda > 0$, then the AV hull intersects $\mathcal{R}(c_2 \succ c_1)$. Thus, even should almost all of the voters have the ranking $c_1 \succ c_2 \succ c_3$, it is possible for c_2 to be AV top-ranked. This, of course, is due to the extra variables made available by multiple systems. Ironically, the added options available to the voters can vitiate the good intentions motivating the design of the procedure.

3.4.4 Averaged Multiple Voting Systems

How should $\mathbf{W}_1$ and $\mathbf{W}_2$ be chosen? To keep the image space two-dimensional, the sum of the components for each of these vectors must be the same as for $\mathbf{W}_0$. To avoid introducing undue bias for one candidate over another, the choices should use the obvious averages. For example, with a given $\mathbf{W}_0$, a type-seven voter, with his indecision between whether he is really of type-one or type-two, should be assigned the average, or $\mathbf{W}_1 = [\mathbf{W}_1]_7 = \frac{1}{2}[\mathbf{W}_0]_1 + \frac{1}{2}[\mathbf{W}_0]_2$. Similarly, a type-twelve voter should be assigned $\mathbf{W}_2 = [\mathbf{W}_2]_{12} = \frac{1}{2}[\mathbf{W}_0]_1 + \frac{1}{2}[\mathbf{W}_0]_6$. Because all three vectors are uniquely determined by the choice of $\mathbf{w}_s$, this is called the *averaged $\mathbf{w}_s$-multiple voting system*.

With the truncated ballot example of $\mathbf{W}_0 = (3,1,0)$, the averaged $\mathbf{W}_0$-multiple system is $\mathbf{W}_1 = (3, \frac{1}{2}, \frac{1}{2})$ and $\mathbf{W}_2 = (2,2,0)$. Similarly, the averaged plurality multiple voting system is where the voting vector, $\mathbf{w}_0$, is the assigned voting vector and the antiplurality vector, $\mathbf{w}^2 = \mathbf{w}_{\frac{1}{2}}$, is used with indecisive voters. The improvement the averaged plurality system has over the AV is that by keeping the image set on the representational triangle, it reduces the number and kinds of paradoxes: it prohibits any voter from becoming more equal than others. It is left to the reader to compare the geometry of averaged multiple voting systems with the original system.

---

her illustrating example of the 1992 primary election in New York among Abrams, D'Amato, Holtzman, and Ferraro. The last two are women, and both lost in part because of a split among the women voters. This need not have been the situation with AV. A similar conclusion holds for the BC.

It remains to determine which system "best" reflects the pairwise rankings. Here we just mimic the derivations used to relate the BC with the pairwise majority votes. The derivation of Sect. 3.2 establishes that $(2,1,0)$ agrees with the number of points a $c_1 \succ c_2 \succ c_3$ voter would assign each candidate over the three pairwise elections. To determine what happens for an indecisive voter, give a type-seven voter with the ranking $c_1 \succ c_2 \sim c_3$ a single point to split in each pairwise election. This leads to the following:

Set	$\{c_1\}$	$\{c_2\}$	$\{c_3\}$
$\{c_1, c_2\}$	1	0	
$\{c_1, c_3\}$	1		0
$\{c_2, c_3\}$		$\frac{1}{2}$	$\frac{1}{2}$
	—	—	—
Total	2	$\frac{1}{2}$	$\frac{1}{2}$

$$(3.4.4)$$

Thus, $\mathbf{w}^1 = (2, \frac{1}{2}, \frac{1}{2})$. Similarly, by examining how many points a voter with the ranking $c_1 \sim c_2 \succ c_3$ assigns to each candidate, we arrive at the vector $\mathbf{w}^2 = (\frac{3}{2}, \frac{3}{2}, 0)$. This is *the Averaged BC (ABC) multiple voting system.*

All of the earlier results about the central role played by the BC within positional voting systems extends to multiple voting systems. For example,

- If the pairwise majority vote ranking is a complete tie, then the ABC outcome must be $\mathcal{I}$. No other averaged $\mathbf{w}_s$ system has this property.
- A Condorcet winner always receives over $\frac{1}{3}$ of the total number of ABC points cast; a Condorcet loser receives less than $\frac{1}{3}$. Consequently, a Condorcet winner never can be ABC bottom-ranked; a Condorcet loser never can be ABC top-ranked, and a Condorcet loser never can be ABC-ranked equal to or above a Condorcet winner. This is the only averaged positional voting method for which these statements are true. For all other averaged $\mathbf{w}_s$ systems, the Condorcet winner can be bottom-ranked while the Condorcet loser can be top-ranked.
- The ABC dictionary is a proper subset of the dictionary for any other multiple voting system.
- Choose an admissible choice of outcomes for the three binary elections. Next, compute the sections of the associated averaged $\mathbf{w}_s$ outcomes. The section of ABC outcomes is a proper subset of the section for any other averaged $\mathbf{w}_s$ outcome. Indeed, the ABC outcomes are a subset of the section for any multiple system.
- The procedure line for averaged $\mathbf{w}_s$ systems is defined in the same manner as for positional methods. Namely, the averaged plurality and antiplurality outcomes are computed; the connecting line is the procedure line for average systems. The averaged $\mathbf{w}_s$-outcome is at the point $1 - 2s$ of the length of the line measured from the averaged plurality outcome. As true for the positional procedure line, the positioning of the ABC outcome is pivotal.

The strong arguments justifying the use of the BC extend to support the use of the ABC multiple voting system when indecisive voters must be accommodated.

Namely, the ABC system admits fewer paradoxes and disturbing situations where the outcome violates the voters wishes. In fact, the above containment assertions mean that any criticism or fault of the ABC is a fault for all multiple systems. The converse, of course, is not true. Many problems of the the average $\mathbf{w}_s$, $s \neq \frac{1}{3}$ system are not admissible with the ABC.

3.4.5 Procedure Strips

As some final suggestions how to analyze multiple systems, I will show how to compare the *AV procedure strip* with the averaged procedure strip. To do so for a given profile, compute the procedure line and then the convex hull of admitted AV outcomes. (A convex hull emerges for the AV because each strict voter type must be divided into two different groups.) This is illustrated in Fig. 3.4.5 for the beverage profile.

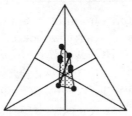

Fig. 3.4.5. The procedure line and AV procedure strip

This drawing shows that while seven rankings can occur with different choices of $\mathbf{w}_s$, all 13 rankings are admissible outcomes for the AV. This figure suggests several relationships.

- For $\mathbf{p} \in Si(6)$, the procedure line is a subset of the AV procedure strip. Any $\mathbf{w}_s$-ranking is an admissible AV outcome. Thus the AV inherits all paradoxes and faults admitted by any positional voting system.

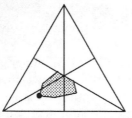

Fig. 3.4.6. The AV hull for a $\mathbf{p}$ specific tally

- For all profiles $\mathbf{p} \in Si(6)$, the AV hull intersects at least three ranking regions. For any profile, then, the AV never can promise a single outcome; AV always has an element of indeterminacy. This is illustrated in Fig. 3.4.4, where the unanimity profile $\mathbf{E}_1$ has three different AV outcomes. It is further illustrated in Fig. 3.4.6 with the integer profile $(4, 4, 2, 2, 0, 6)$ where the *procedure line* is the single point $(\frac{4}{9}, \frac{3}{9}, \frac{2}{9})$ and the pairwise rankings are $c_1 \succ c_2, c_1 \succ c_2, c_2 \succ c_3$. Thus, for all $\mathbf{w}_s$, the normalized election tally is the same fixed value with the ranking $c_1 \succ c_2 \succ c_3$; a ranking that coincides with the pairwise *rankings*. The shaded area, which indicates the eight admissible AV outcomes for this profile, introduces a wide variety of paradoxes and troubling election outcomes. For instance, even though c_3 is the Condorcet loser and bottom-ranked for all positional methods, she can be AV tied for top spot.

3.4.6 Exercises

3.4.1. Show that the indifferent type-13 can influence the outcome of a threshold election.

3.4.2. Create an example where the procedure line is a fixed point in $\mathcal{R}(1)$ but where the AV hull is in all 13 ranking regions.

3.4.3. Find the three-dimensional set of cumulative election outcomes.

3.4.4. Find the averaged plurality and the AV hulls for $\frac{1}{2}(\mathbf{E}_1 + \mathbf{E}_2)$. To show the difference, the full three-dimensional nature of the AV hull must be displayed.

3.4.5. Prove all of the bulleted comments.

3.4.6. Show that the normalization procedure preserves election ranking.

3.4.7. Compute the set of AV outcomes described in Fig. 3.4.3 a and b. Also, find all possible positions of the procedure line. Observe how the procedure line always is a subset of the shaded region.

3.4.8. The indicated set of AV outcomes for a fixed λ in Fig. 3.4.4 appears to be a one-dimensional line segment. Show that, in general, it is a two-dimensional object. Find λ values where it is a line. Also show that for the indicated profile, it is no accident that each of the dots is on a line defining the representation triangle. Use this geometry to find a quicker way to determine the set of AV outcomes.

3.4.9. Suppose the BC $(2,1,0)$ is used in an election where truncated voting is anticipated. There are three ways to handle such a ballot; one could use the ABC, one could assign one point to the only candidate on the ballot, or one could assign two points to this candidate. Choose a profile and compare the different outcomes. By using the methods of this section, critique the different choices.

3.4.10. Use Table 3.4.4 to show that the pairwise tallies of the pairwise elections determines the ABC outcome.

3.4.11. Compare the convex hull of election outcomes for a $\mathbf{w}_s$ procedure and an averaged $\mathbf{w}_s$ procedure.

3.4.12. A procedure occasionally used extends the cumulative voting method by allowing the voter to split a specified number of points in any desired manner. Thus, each voter has all $\mathbf{w}_s$ options. To analyze this method, compute the hull of outcomes for $\mathbf{p} = (0, \frac{2}{5}, 0, \frac{4}{15}, \frac{1}{3}, 0)$ Prove that this procedure has more than one ranking for each profile; and that the procedure line always is properly contained in the hull of outcomes.

3.5 Other Election Procedures

Positional methods are not the only ways to rank and choose candidates. Instead, we could use an agenda or a standard runoff election. We could create imaginative runoffs where the candidate dropped from further consideration is determined by how she fares in a separate positional or scoring election. We could invent procedures based on how the candidates perform with different scoring methods, and on and on. Indeed, armed with only a little imagination, it is possible to generate almost an infinite number of new methods. However, each procedure must be analyzed to determine what can go right and what can go wrong. In this section, an easier way to do this analysis is outlined.

3.5.1 Other Procedures

Recall the two steps in the traditional way to analyze a procedure. First we need to design a profile to create special election outcomes for the relevant subsets of candidates. These outcomes are chosen to demonstrate strengths or failings of the procedure. For instance, to show that a Condorcet winner can lose a runoff election, we need to create a profile where the Condorcet winner is bottom-ranked in the first election. Thus, the traditional steps of analysis can be represented with the following diagram.

$$\boxed{\textbf{Profiles}} \rightarrow \boxed{\begin{array}{c}\textbf{Election} \\ \textbf{outcomes}\end{array}} \rightarrow \boxed{\begin{array}{c}\textbf{Procedure} \\ \textbf{outcome}\end{array}}. \qquad (3.5.1)$$

The serious difficulty with the traditional approach is to find a profile where the election outcomes vary in desired ways over the different subsets of candidates. But, we already have this information; it is given by the dictionaries and the geometry of the F_s image sets. This suggests that we may be able to bypass the technically difficult first step.

Example 3.5.1. As described in Chap. 1, an agenda lists how the candidates are compared in the pairwise competitions. So, $< c_1, c_3, c_2 >$ advances the $\{c_1, c_3\}$ majority winner to a runoff with c_2. In practice, two separate elections are held. After all, the contestants for the second election are not known until the results of the first one are disclosed.

An advantage of being a theoretician is that we can ignore the above practical concern. Instead, we are faced with the design problem. For instance, suppose we want to show that with a cycle, the last listed candidate always wins; this means we need election outcomes $c_1 \succ c_2$, $c_2 \succ c_3, c_3 \succ c_1$. This easy part is the left-half of the diagram; the hard part is finding a supporting profile. The profile design is the first part of the diagram.

For a plurality runoff election, the two plurality top-ranked candidates are advanced to a runoff. In practice this also requires two separate elections. Now, suppose we want to show that the Condorcet winner can lose. We know the kind of election rankings that are needed; they are $(c_1 \succ c_2, c_1 \succ c_3, c_2 \succ c_3, c_2 \succ$

$c_3 \succ c_1$). So, this listing, which is the second part of the diagram, is easy. The difficult portion is the first part of the diagram – finding a supporting profile. $\square$

The purpose of Example 3.5.1 is to emphasize that election procedures can be described as the composition of two mappings. The first mapping, which usually causes the difficulty, converts profiles into election tallies and rankings. The much simplier second mapping combines the election outcomes in a specified manner to determine the outcome of the procedure. This two step process is significantly simplified by recognizing that the first mapping – the positional election outcomes – is extensively analyzed in the previous sections. Consequently, to study election methods, *results from the previous sections* – rather than profiles – become the inputs for the second mapping.

To carry out this program, we need to distinguish whether the election procedure is based on the rankings of the subsets of candidates, on the actual tallies, or on some combination. Each situation should be consider separately as it different spaces for the election outcomes. (An example of a combination is the common method that declares a candidate the winner if she receives more than 50% of the plurality vote. If not, then the two top-ranked candidates amove on to a runoff. To study this method, we need to compare a normalized election tally of one procedure (the plurality election) with the pairwise ordinal rankings.)

3.5.2 Ordinal Procedures

An *ordinal election procedure* is based on positional and scoring election rankings of the sets of candidates. Once the election procedures are specified, Eq. 3.5.1 becomes

$$Si(6) \xrightarrow{\text{F}} \mathcal{D}(\mathbf{w}_s) \xrightarrow{\text{G}} \boxed{\textbf{Procedure outcome}}.$$

The image space for G can be almost anything. For instance, if we want to select candidates rather than to rank them, the image can be $\mathcal{P}^3$, the set of all non-empty subsets of the three candidates. If rankings of candidates are desired, the natural choice of an image space is the set of all 13 rankings.

The best way to illustrate the ideas is with specific examples. So, define a $\mathbf{w}_s$-*simple runoff* to be where the candidates are $\mathbf{w}_s$ ranked, and the two top-ranked candidates are compared in a runoff election. Properties of this runoff are immediate. For instance, because $\mathcal{D}(\mathbf{w}_s) = \mathcal{U}^3$ if and only if $s \neq \frac{1}{3}$, it follows that *the only restriction on a non-BC simple runoff is that a Condorcet loser never wins*. This negative assertion follows because the two top-ranked candidates in the $\mathbf{w}_s$-election need not be related, in any manner, with the pairwise majority vote ranking. For example, the Condorcet winner could be bottom-ranked at the first stage to make her ineligible for the runoff, etc. On the other hand, if a Condorcet loser is advanced to the runoff, she loses in the pairwise election.

With a judicious choice of a $\mathbf{w}_s$, relationships do emerge. Here we exploit the election relationships admitted by the BC that force some regularity upon the BC simple runoffs. For instance, as already noted in 1884 by Nanson [N], because a Condorcet winner cannot be BC bottom-ranked, she must be advanced to the runoff. In the runoff she wins. *This assertion is true only for the BC.*

To be more inventive, notice that a runoff winner is determined by the election ranking of a particular pair of candidates; the rankings for the other two pairs do not matter. To exploit this observation, recall that an agenda outcome is determined by the rankings of two pairs of candidates; the ranking of the third pair is immaterial. From this statement, we should expect that we can choose the rankings of the pairs so that, for a fixed profile, the runoff and an agenda select different candidates!

Theorem 3.5.1. a. *A Condorcet loser never can be the winner of a simple runoff. If a Condorcet winner exists, she is guaranteed to be the winner of a $\mathbf{w}_s$-runoff election iff $\mathbf{w}_s$ is the BC.*

b. *If $\mathbf{w}_{s_1} \neq \mathbf{w}_{s_2}$, then there exists a profile where the winners of the two simple runoff elections do not agree.*

c. *Specify an agenda and a $\mathbf{w}_s$ simple runoff where $s \neq \frac{1}{3}$. Choose two candidates, say c_1 and c_2. There exists profiles so that c_1 is the winner of the agenda and c_2 is the winner of the simple runoff. For the BC simple runoff, this assertion is true only for the agenda $< c_2, c_3, c_1 >$.*

Proof. Part b follows by using the procedure line. Choose rankings so that different candidates are dropped at the first stage and one dropped candidates is the winner of the other runoff election.

For part c and the agenda $< c_2, c_3, c_1 >$, the specified outcomes occur for the word $(c_2 \succ c_1, c_1 \succ c_3, c_3 \succ c_2, c_2 \succ c_1 \succ c_3)$. This word is in all dictionaries. For c_1 to win with the agenda $< c_1, c_3, c_2 >$ or with $< c_1, c_2, c_3 >$, she needs to beat both candidates; thus c_1 must be the Condorcet winner. So, for c_2 to win the runoff, she must avoid being compared with c_1. To avoid comparing c_1 with c_2 in the runoff, c_1 must be bottom-ranked in the first election, and, for c_2 to win, we need $c_2 \succ c_3$ in a pairwise match. Such a situation is impossible for the BC (because it forces the Condorcet winner, c_1, to be bottom-ranked), but many words of this type, such as $(c_1 \succ c_2, c_1 \succ c_3, c_2 \succ c_3, c_3 \succ c_2 \succ c_1)$, are admitted by all other choices of $\mathbf{w}_s$. $\square$

3.5.3 Scoring Runoffs

The idea of a runoff is to drop the candidate least supported by the voters, and then to compare the remaining two candidates. Presumably, because she has the least amount of support, the $\mathbf{w}_s$ bottom-ranked candidate is dropped from further consideration in a $\mathbf{w}_s$-runoff. But, there are other measures of who should not be advanced.

One way to identify the candidate to be dropped is to find who is "least preferred" as indicated by a scoring election outcome. An important example is the *Coombs Runoff* which drops the "winner" of the $(0, 0, 1)$ contest because she is bottom-ranked by more voters than any other candidate. Another choice might be winner of the $(0, \frac{1}{2}, \frac{1}{2})$ scoring election; here one might argue that this candidate is viewed most often as being either mediocre or bottom-ranked. The scoring vector $(0, \frac{1}{6}, \frac{5}{6})$ imposes a compromise by placing a heavier emphasis on a voter's bottom-ranked candidate. As another choice, $(\frac{1}{3}, 0, \frac{2}{3})$ helps the middle ranking candidate; its use is justified by the belief that moderation in the pursuit of mediocrity is a sin. In general, *let a* $\mathbf{w}_s$–sc *runoff be where if a candidate receives over half of all the* $\mathbf{w}_s$ *votes cast, then she is the winner. Otherwise, the winner of the* sc *election is dropped from further consideration, and the other two candidates are matched in a runoff.*

There are natural questions, such as whether a $\mathbf{w}_s$-runoff outcome must coincide with a $\mathbf{w}_s$–sc outcome, or whether these procedures can elect a Condorcet loser or winner.

Theorem 3.5.2. a. *The winner of a* $\mathbf{w}_s$-runoff *always is the same as the* $\mathbf{w}_s$–sc *election iff* sc $\approx$ $-\mathbf{w}_s$. *Indeed, if* sc $\not\approx$ $-\mathbf{w}_s$, *then there are profiles where the candidate not advanced to the runoff is the* $\mathbf{w}_s$ *top-ranked candidate.*

b. *A Condorcet loser never wins in a* $\mathbf{w}_s$ – sc *runoff. If* sc $\neq (0, \frac{1}{3}, \frac{2}{3})$, *then the Condorcet winner can lose. On the other hand, if* sc $= (0, \frac{1}{3}, \frac{2}{3})$ *and a runoff is required, then the Condorcet winner (if one exists) wins.*

c. *The winner of a* $\mathbf{w}_s$–sc *election and an agenda need not agree.*

The proof of this theorem is an immediate application of results concerning scoring methods. To illustrate part b, select the plurality winner if she receives over half the vote. Otherwise, drop the "winner" of a $(0, 1, 2)$ election and have a runoff between the remaining two candidates. *If a Condorcet winner exists, she will be selected.*

3.5.4 Comparisons of Positional Voting Outcomes

Instead of eliminating candidates, maybe they should be compared with different positional elections. *A* $\mathbf{w}_{s_1}$, $\mathbf{w}_{s_2}$ *comparison procedure,* $s_1 < s_2$, *is where the candidates are ranked with each of the two procedures. If the same candidate is top-ranked in both outcomes, she is chosen. Otherwise, a runoff is held between the top-ranked candidate from each procedure.* As an illustration using the plurality, antiplurality comparison with the beverage profile, the runoff is between milk and wine where the Condorcet winner, wine, wins.

Theorem 3.5.3. a. *If* $\mathbf{w}_{s_1}$, $\mathbf{w}_{s_2}$ *are not the same as* $\mathbf{w}_{s_3}$, $\mathbf{w}_{s_4}$, *then there are profiles where the outcomes of the two comparison procedures do not agree.*

b. *For a given* $\mathbf{w}_{s_1}$ – $\mathbf{w}_{s_2}$ *comparison procedure, there are examples where the Condorcet winner is not selected. A Condorcet loser cannot be selected iff* $s_1 \leq \frac{1}{3} \leq s_2$.

Proof. The proof of the theorem is based on the positioning of the procedure line. For example, if in part a it turns out that $s_1 < s_3$, then choose a procedure line so that c_1 is top-ranked in the $\mathbf{w}_{s_1}$ and $\mathbf{w}_{s_2}$ rankings, but c_2 is top-ranked in the $\mathbf{w}_{s_3}$ and $\mathbf{w}_{s_4}$ elections. If the two comparison procedures do not have this separation property, because, say, $s_3 \leq s_2 < s_4$, then choose the procedure line so that c_1 is top-ranked in the $\{\mathbf{w}_{s_j}\}_{j=1}^3$ elections, and c_2 is $\mathbf{w}_{s_4}$ top-ranked in the last election. As we know from Sect. 2.6, the procedure line can be selected to satisfy this condition while supporting the pairwise outcome of $c_2 \succ c_1$. This leads to the stated conclusion.

To illustrate the first part of part b, choose the procedure line so that the Condorcet winner is not top-ranked for either procedure. (This always is possible.) Indeed, as long as $\mathbf{w}_s \neq \mathbf{w}_{\frac{1}{3}}$, the Condorcet loser could be $\mathbf{w}_s$ top-ranked. In fact, this is true for both procedures as long as the procedure line does not require the BC to have the Condorcet loser top-ranked. Such positioning of the procedure line always can be done as long as on this line both procedures are on the same side of the BC ($\mathbf{w}_{\frac{1}{3}}$). $\square$

So far we have considered what can happen by comparing the outcomes of two particular positional methods. The above theorem demonstrates that conflict, controversy, and other delightful forms of academic entertainment can accompany such methods. To retire to a more settled situation, we may wish to choose those candidates supported by the rankings of all positional methods.

Definition 3.5.1. An election ranking is **p**-specific if it is the common election ranking for all choices of $\mathbf{w}_s$. A candidate is **p**-favored if she is top-ranked for all $\mathbf{w}_s$. A candidate is **p**-inferior if she is bottom-ranked in all $\mathbf{w}_s$ rankings. $\square$

Who can argue against a **p**-favored candidate? After all, whether you are pro or anti-choice for positional methods that emphasize a voter's second-ranked candidate, the same candidate emerges victorious with all procedures. This candidate, therefore, has survived the gauntlet of the infinite number of ways there are to weight preferences. What more could be required of her? Similarly, by the universal rejection of a **p**-inferior candidate, it is difficult to justify her selection. The adoption of a **p**-specific procedure seems attractive. However, what are its properties?

Theorem 3.5.4. *a. A* **p**-*inferior and/or favored candidate need not exist. There exist profiles where the* **p**-*favored candidate exists but a Condorcet winner does not. Conversely, there exist profiles where a Condorcet winner exists but a* **p**-*favored candidate does not.*

b. A **p**-*favored candidate can never be a Condorcet loser; a* **p**-*inferior candidate can never be a Condorcet winner. There exist profiles where the* **p** *favored candidate is not the Condorcet winner; there exist examples where the* **p**-*inferior candidate is not the Condorcet loser.*

As true with the Condorcet concepts, the **p**-favored and inferior candidates are "sometime" concepts; sometime they exist, sometime they don't. And, in those situations where both solutions exist, they need not agree. However, a Condorcet winner is determined with only partial information; it does not use the assumption that voters are transitive or the intensity of pairwise rankings. On the other hand, the **p**-favored candidate survives all possible ways to use this intensity information. Therefore, those situations where a **p**-favored candidate is not the Condorcet winner should be viewed as exposing additional Condorcet faults.

The basic idea of the proof is to use results about the procedure line from Sects. 2.4, 2.6. For example, for c_1 to be the **p**-favored candidate, the procedure line just needs to be in $\mathcal{R}(1) \cup \mathcal{R}(7) \cup \mathcal{R}(2)$ – the union of the ranking regions where c_1 is top-ranked. So, place this line in such a manner that the pairwise ranking conditions are satisfied. From Sect. 2.6, we know that this can be done. Also observe that the positive features of a **p**-specific ranking are due to the fact that they are satisfied by the BC.

3.5.5 Plurality or a Runoff?

Every so often, a community caught in the spirit of electoral reform must decide whether to replace one procedure with another. To demonstrate how such an issue can be analyzed, consider replacing the standard plurality election with a runoff. (There are better systems.) The question is to determine which system is "better." By "better," we want the system that is more apt to represent the true view of the voters. In the debate over this issue, the "facts" can be debatable. For instance, in an editorial urging voters to reject a runoff, the *Evanston Review* argued that the plurality system "already affords each mayoral candidate a fair chance at being elected. A runoff won't make it any fairer."[17] Can it?

From the above theory it is easy to construct arguments showing why a runoff is an improvement. In fact, using the plurality dictionary and the plurality ranking of $c_1 \succ c_2 \succ c_3$, we know that the accompanying pairwise rankings can be anything. The analysis involves comparing the outcomes of the two procedures with the different possibilities. For instance, if either c_2 or c_3 is a Condorcet winner, or if c_1 is the Condorcet loser, there is strong reason to doubt the choice of the plurality election. On the other hand, with the runoff, c_1 is forced into a comparison with c_2. So, if c_2 is the Condorcet winner, or if c_1 is the Condorcet loser, then the second election resolves the plurality inequity. In fact, *whenever the pairwise rankings define a transitive ranking, the runoff winner is closer to meeting the voters' beliefs than the plurality winner.*

If the pairwise rankings define a positive cycle, then c_1 is the winner with either procedure. All that remains, therefore, is to analyze which election outcome better represents the voters' views if there is a negative cycle. This requires examining the supporting set of profiles. In particular, to find an advantage for the plurality vote, we need to examine the profile cone where c_2 barely beats c_1, but c_1 beats c_3 and c_3 beats c_2 by large margins.

---

[17]October 29, 1992, issue of the *Evanston Review*. An advertisement in this issue argued that the plurality system provided opportunities for minority and independent candidates to be elected; in a runoff they don't have a chance. Is this true? If so, is it at the cost of frustrating the true intent of the voters? Evanston voters adopted the runoff and when this so-called "minority-bashing" procedure was first used, L. Morton came in second in the first election (so she would have lost a plurality vote) but won the April 20, 1993, runoff to become Evanston's first Afro-American mayor.

From this analysis, the "even" voter types dominate and the supporting boundary profile has slightly less than half of the voters of type-two, while the rest of the voters are split between being of type-four and six with slightly more of type-six. Because this profile involves an extreme mixture between the binary rankings and the intensity of the rankings, it should isolate a weakness of the pairwise vote. (The BC ranking for such a profile, with its ability to account for the intensity variable in an unbiased fashion, is the reasonable $c_1 \succ c_3 \succ c_2$.) Here, the plurality outcome, rather than the runoff, better captures the voters beliefs.

So, there are situations where the plurality outcome appears is more reasonable than that of the runoff, but there are many more situations where the roles are reversed. An analysis of the trade-off requires a more accurate comparison of the two procedures. This means we need to examine the kinds of profiles that can define all of the different outcomes. Here, the the results clearly indicate that the runoff serves the voters better than the plurality procedure. For instance, the geometry shows that corresponding to the sets of profiles where c_1 should win are nearly symmetrical sets where c_2 should win. (The plurality ranking is $c_1 \succ c_2 \succ c_3$ while the negative cycle has c_2 beating c_1 and c_1 beating c_3 by substantial margins, while c_3 barely beats c_2.) And then, there are the large sets of profiles where the transitive ranking disagrees with the plurality ranking.

3.5.6 Cardinal Procedures

Using the election tallies, we can invent other kinds of procedures. For instance, let $q_{i,j}$ be the fraction of all points received by c_i in a pairwise contest with c_j where, of course, $q_{i,i} = 0$. In Sect. 3.2, this information was used by assigning to the ith candidate $\sum_{j=1}^{3} q_{i,j}$ points and then ranking the candidates according to the totals. This method has several solid properties, but, one might argue that it lacks imagination. For instance, we may wish to reward a strong performance in an election by awarding more than the $q_{i,j}$ points. How should this be done?

One choice is to award the ith candidate $(q_{i,j}/q_{j,i})^3 = [q_{i,j}/(1-q_{i,j})]^3$ points.[18] Thus, for example, the cubed total for c_1 is $(q_{1,2}/q_{2,1})^3 + (q_{1,3}/q_{3,1})^3$ points. That this method can lead to reasonable results can be seen with the profile $(\frac{1}{6}, 0, \frac{1}{2}, 0, \frac{1}{3})$ which leads to the pairwise rankings $c_1 \succ c_2, c_2 \sim c_3, c_3 \succ c_1$, the BC ranking $c_3 \succ c_1 \sim c_2$ (with the BC tally $(\frac{5}{18}, \frac{5}{18}, \frac{8}{18})$), and the cubed ranking $c_3 \succ c_1 \succ c_2$ with the tally $(2^3 + (\frac{1}{5})^3, 1 + (\frac{1}{2})^3, 5^3 + 1)$.

However, this procedure overly magnifies a strong performance. Indeed, it allows a candidate to win by just winning the unanimous voting in a single pairwise election. For instance, suppose, as illustrated in Fig. 3.5.1, there are 100 voters; 99 of whom prefer $c_1 \succ c_2 \succ c_3$ and the last voter has the ranking $c_2 \succ c_3 \succ c_1$. It is clear that c_1 is the favored candidate, but, because c_2 beats c_3

---

[18]While it is very different, this choice has the flavor of the "rule of an Anglo-Saxon parliamentary election" asserting that, in general, the ratio of seats received by two major parties approximately equals the cube of the ratio of votes they received. See [T1,2].

with a unanimous vote, c_2 receives an infinite number of points; this more than suffices for c_2 to win the election.

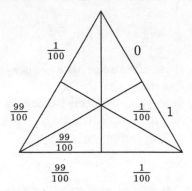

$\frac{1}{100}$ 0

$\frac{99}{100}$ $\frac{1}{100}$ 1

$\frac{99}{100}$

$\frac{99}{100}$ $\frac{1}{100}$

Fig. 3.5.1. Problems with generalized methods

To be more realistic, an upper bound needs to be assigned to the number of points.

Definition 3.5.2. Let $G : [0, 1] \to [0, 1]$ be a nondecreasing mapping satisfying the symmetry condition

$$G(q) = 1 - G(1 - q). \tag{3.5.2}$$

A G – *binary process* is determined by the tally

$$\frac{1}{3}(G(q_{1,2}) + G(q_{1,3}), G(q_{2,3}) + G(q_{2,1}), G(q_{3,1}) + G(q_{3,2})). \quad \square \tag{3.5.3}$$

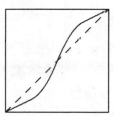

Fig. 3.5.2. Two choices of G functions

To reinforce a strong performance by offering more points, we could choose a G similar to that given in Fig. 3.5.2. The dashed line is the standard $G(x) = x$ while the solid line provides added emphasis for "winning" at the expense of the losing candidate. However, whatever the choice, Eq. 3.5.2 ensures a form of "neutrality" for tied elections because

$$G(\frac{1}{2}) = \frac{1}{2}. \tag{3.5.4}$$

What should be the choice of G? We already know that $G(q) = q$ defines a procedure equivalent to the BC. (See Sect. 3.2.) The next choice are other linear expansions. To satisfy Eq. 3.5.4, the equation must assume the form

$$G(q) = a(q - \frac{1}{2}) + \frac{1}{2}, \quad a > 0.$$

However, it is not difficult to see (so, it is an exercise) that this system always defines the BC; it is equivalent to the system where $a = 1$.

If linear choices of G offer nothing new, then we need to examine non-linear choices. They permit introducing magnifying and contracting effects. For example, the choice

$$G_3(q) = (q - \frac{1}{2})^3 + \frac{1}{2}$$

combines both by tempering how many points are assigned for values of q near $\frac{1}{2}$, and then magnifying the impact of larger victories. It is not difficult to justify this choice; values of q near $\frac{1}{2}$ are close to tie votes where the value may reflect small statistical fluctuations. To dampen this effect, it is wise to assign values near $\frac{1}{2}$. On the other hand, there is little doubt which candidate the voters prefer if the victory margin is large. Consequently, argument supporting the choice of G_3 are easy to find.

As we have learned, it is not difficult to advance convincing arguments to support disastrous procedures. So, to analyze G-binary procedures, we need to determine the properties and profiles that lead to different kinds of outcomes. This is done by following the lead of Chap. 2. For example, if the regions leading to different election outcomes are depicted in the representation cube, then it becomes easy to compare the G-binary outcomes with the outcomes associated with the Condorcet, Borda, and other procedures. Moreover, the cyclic coordinate system of the representation cube, makes it a standard exercise to relate profiles with G-binary outcomes.

Example 3.5.2. To analyze G_3, I will describe all outcomes leading to the ranking $c_1 \succ c_2 \succ c_3$. Using the coordinate system of the representation cube, the election tallies for the candidates with the G_3-binary system are

$$(x^3 - y^3, y^3 - z^3, z^3 - x^3). \tag{3.5.5}$$

Thus, the specified ranking is determined by the set of points of the representation cube satisfying the two inequalities

$$x^3 - y^3 \geq y^3 - z^3, \quad y^3 - z^3 \geq z^3 - x^3.$$

The nonlinear form of G_3 forces the boundary regions to be curved surfaces, rather than portions of planes. A more sensible scheme to represent the figure, therefore, is to use sections.

The following cross-sections are based on increasing values of y. (Recall, larger y values reflect an increased support for c_2 over c_3.) In doing so, the figures are drawn to represent what you would see from the vantage point of the positive y axis. This requires the positive x axis to be to the *left*, rather than in its natural position on the right. The slanted lines are, of course, the portions of the cube that are sliced off by the equations $x + y + z = \pm 1$.

Fig. 3.5.3. Some y sections

By use of algebra, it follows that no portion of this $c_1 \succ c_2 \succ c_3$ region exists for $y \leq -(\frac{1}{3})^{\frac{1}{3}}$. This makes sense; such extreme y values indicates that c_2 is soundly beat by c_3; in fact, the victory is so one-sided that it is impossible for c_2 to be G_3 ranked over c_3. Instead, the G_3 boundary for the $c_1 \succ c_2 \succ c_3$ region starts at a section $y = -(\frac{1}{3})^{\frac{1}{3}}$ at the point $((\frac{1}{3})^{\frac{1}{3}}, -(\frac{1}{3})^{\frac{1}{3}}, -1)$.

The first picture in Fig. 3.5.3 is the section for $y = -\frac{1}{2}$, a situation corresponding to where c_3 receives a full $\frac{3}{4}$ of the vote in her victory over c_2. Nevertheless, the sliver of a shaded region indicates the small set of pairwise outcomes (and, hence, the small profile set) supporting the $c_1 \succ c_2 \succ c_3$ conclusion. Candidate c_1's sizable victory is reflected by the $c_1 \sim c_2$ indifference curve which starts in the upper left hand corner. The terrible defeat of c_2 by c_3, along with the multiplier effect of G_3 is indicated by the extremes required of c_1's victory over c_3 in order for the indicated G_3 ranking to prevail. Notice, z needs to be nearly -1 for the ranking to hold; namely, c_2 needs a combination of a nearly total victory over c_3 along with the multiplier effect of G_3 in order to preserve $c_1 \succ c_2 \succ c_3$.

The second figure represents the section $y = 0$ where the c_2, c_3 election ends in a tie. Here, the G_3 indifference lines become straight lines, and the shaded region corresponds to $c_1 \succ c_2 \succ c_3$. Comparisons with the Borda outcomes and the Condorcet outcomes become particularly simple. For instance, a slight positive change in the y value will result in only minor changes in the shaded region. But, every point in the region $x > 0, y > 0, z < 0$ corresponds to the pairwise rankings $c_1 \succ c_2, c_2 \succ c_3, c_1 \succ c_3$. Thus, there are large sets of profiles where the strong pairwise rankings supporting the Condorcet winner c_1 are ignored by the G_3 outcomes. Similarly, for $y = 0$, the region where the Borda outcome is $c_1 \succ c_2 \succ c_3$ includes the $x > 0, z < 0$ quadrant. Thus, there exist wide regions of disagreement.

In Fig. 3.5.4, the sections for $y = \frac{1}{2}$, and $y = 1$ are computed. It is interesting to compare how the increased strength of c_2's victory over c_3 (as indicated by large y values) makes it much easier for her to ensure she is G_3 ranked over c_3. In particular, compare the evolution of the $c_2 \sim c_3$ indifference line through the different y values. The expense of c_2's solid victory over c_3 is the scrambling required by c_1 in her victory over c_3 to ensure she still remains G_3 ranked above c_2. This is indicated by the evolution of the $c_1 \sim c_2$ line in the different figures.

$$y = \tfrac{1}{2} \qquad\qquad\qquad y = 1$$

Fig. 3.5.4. Cross sections

Comparisons of these regions with those of the Condorcet and Borda rankings provides all sorts of conclusions; they are left for the reader. As a parting comment, it is interesting to compare how the G_3 system handles a profile with a $p\mathbf{E}_1 + (1-p)\mathbf{E}_5$ split. We know that the BC requires $p > \tfrac{2}{3}$ before c_1 is ranked above c_2. The G_3 method imposes an even stronger requirement upon c_1; she needs about 90% of the vote!

We might wonder whether the lessons learned from the G_3 system hold for all other G systems. For instance, can certain G_3 systems lead to cycles? A selection of immediate results follows.

Theorem 3.5.5. *A G binary procedure always has transitive outcomes. There does not exist a G-binary process where the Condorcet winner must be top-ranked and/or where the Condorcet loser must be bottom-ranked. If $g(q) \neq a(q - \tfrac{1}{2}) + \tfrac{1}{2}$ for some $a > 0$, then there are profiles where the G-binary outcome differs from the BC outcome.*

If all pairwise rankings end in a tie vote, then, for any G, the G-binary outcome is $\mathcal{I}$.

For any G-binary process defined by a G that is strictly increasing near $q = \tfrac{1}{2}$, the Condorcet winner always is strictly ranked above the Condorcet loser. On the other hand, if G is not increasing in a neighborhood of $q = \tfrac{1}{2}$, then it is possible for the Condorcet winner to be tied with the Condorcet loser. The Condorcet winner never is G ranked below the Condorcet loser.

Proof. According to Eq. 3.5.2, each candidate is assigned a fixed value on the line. The transitivity statement follows from the properties of the line.

All pairwise rankings are ties if and only if $\mathbf{q} = \mathbf{0}$ in the representation cube coordinates if and only if all $q_{i,j} = \tfrac{1}{2}$. The fact that the G-binary outcome is $\mathcal{I}$ follows from Eq. 3.5.3.

To compare the properties of the G-binary procedure with the Condorcet winner, it suffices to consider what happens on the boundaries of the c_1-Condorcet region in the representation cube. A point on the positive y axis represents the outcomes $q_{2,3} = \frac{1}{2}(1+y)$, $q_{3,2} = \frac{1}{2}(1-y)$ and $q_{i,j} = \frac{1}{2}$ for all other choices of i and j. Thus, the election outcome of Eq. 2.5.3 is

$$\left(\frac{1}{3}, \frac{1}{3}(G(\frac{1}{2}(1+y)) + \frac{1}{2}), \frac{1}{3}(G(\frac{1}{2}(1-y)) + \frac{1}{2})\right).$$

If G is strictly increasing at $q = \frac{1}{2}$, then the second term has the largest value while the third term has the smallest. Consequently, the ranking is $c_2 \succ c_1 \succ c_3$. This statement remains true even for values of x and y where y is sufficiently close to $\frac{1}{2}$ and $\frac{1}{2} < x < y$. In other words, there are points in the region where the pairwise rankings define $c_1 \succ c_2 \succ c_3$ but the G-binary rankings is $c_2 \succ c_1 \succ c_3$. From this we have that a Condorcet winner need not be top-ranked. If G is not increasing in a region about $\frac{1}{2}$, then the votes remain tied, so the Condorcet winner is not ranked above the Condorcet loser. In either case, we have that the Condorcet winner need not be top-ranked. A similar argument shows that a Condorcet loser need not be G-binary bottom-ranked. $\square$

Summary. The analysis and comparison of voting procedures becomes fairly easy with the $\mathbf{w}_s$ dictionaries and the F_s image sets. By knowing in advance all of the relationships admissible among the election outcomes of the different sets of candidates, it becomes particularly easy to determine strengths and weaknesses of different procedures, to compare them, and to modify then. Only certain kinds of procedures are discussed above, others are analyzed in a similar fashion.

3.5.7 Exercises

3.5.1. By using the dictionaries and procedure lines, show that it is possible for c_1 to be the $\mathbf{w}_0$-runoff winner, c_2 to be the $\mathbf{w}_{\frac{1}{2}}$-runoff winner, and c_3 to be the winner of an agenda. Find a set of profiles supporting these outcomes.

3.5.2. Prove Theorem 3.5.2. Find conditions on $\mathbf{sc}_1$, $\mathbf{sc}_2$ so that c_j could be the winner of a $\mathbf{w}_s$ - $\mathbf{sc}_j$ runoff, $j = 1, 2$, while c_3 could be the winner of an agenda.

3.5.3. Suppose $\mathbf{sc} \not\approx \mathbf{w}_s$. Show that there exists examples where c_2 is the $\mathbf{w}_s$ winner and c_3 is the $\mathbf{w}_s$-$\mathbf{sc}$ winner. What does this mean with respect to the winners of a plurality runoff and a Coombs runoff?

3.5.4. Find appropriate conditions on s_1 and s_2 so that it is possible for c_1 to be the Condorcet winner, c_2 to be the winner of a $\mathbf{w}_0$-runoff, and c_3, the Condorcet loser, to be the winner of a $\mathbf{w}_{s_1}$ - $\mathbf{w}_{s_2}$ comparison procedure.

3.5.5. Use the geometry of Fig. 3.5.5 to explain the location of the position line whereby c_1 is the Condorcet winner and c_2 is the $\mathbf{p}$-preferred candidate. Characterize the set of profiles leading to such a conclusion. Use this geometry to prove Theorem 3.5.4.

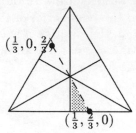

Fig. 3.5.5. c_2 can be **p**-specific

3.5.6. Explain the role of the BC in establishing the properties of Theorem 3.5.4.

3.5.7. Carry out the geometric analysis to compare the $\mathbf{w}_0$-runoff with the plurality election. Compare the Borda outcomes with the $\mathbf{w}_{\frac{1}{3}}$-runoff outcomes.

3.5.8. As a new procedure, first find the $\mathbf{w}_{s_1}$ tally of the candidates, and then the $\mathbf{w}_{s_2}$ tally. The ranking of the candidates is based on the average outcome from these two methods. What is this procedure? Now, consider the procedure where the candidates are ranked with the average between a $\mathbf{w}_s$ and a $\mathbf{sc}$ election. What is this procedure?

3.5.9. Show that $G(q) = a(q - \frac{1}{2}) + \frac{1}{2}$ for $a > 0$ is the same as the BC.

3.5.10. Find the $c_1 \succ c_2 \succ c_3$ region for $G_{\frac{1}{3}}(q) = (q - \frac{1}{2})^{\frac{1}{3}} + \frac{1}{2}$. To do so, find different y sections and then plot a couple of points on each indifference curve. Use these sections to compare the outcomes of a $G_{\frac{1}{3}}$ system, a G_3 system, the standard pairwise elections, and the BC. Arguments justifying $G_{\frac{1}{3}}$ must differ radically from those used for G_3. Here, small changes in outcomes near a tie vote are magnified. Therefore, we need to appeal to arguments such as "political stability." The idea is that votes which are close could lead to unstable governments. Thus it is advantageous to magnify differences from a tie situation. Do the sections justify this argument?

3.5.11. Suppose $G(q)$ is not the constant function. Show that there exist profiles where the Condorcet winner is not G-binary top-ranked and there are profiles where the Condorcet loser is not G-binary bottom-ranked. Notice that this assertion is a stronger statement than Theorem 3.5.5. (In that theorem, we needed that G is strictly increasing near $q = \frac{1}{2}$; here we just need that G is increasing *somewhere*.)

3.5.12. Show that c_1 is a **p**-favored candidate if and only if she is both plurality and antiplurality top-ranked. Extend this statement so it holds for other **p**-specific properties.

CHAPTER IV

MANY PROFILES;
MANY NEW PARADOXES

I now turn from the single profile consequences of election outcomes to describe the fascinating properties of voting theory involving several profiles. A natural example is the electoral fable controversy about the Dean's Council caused by combining the two profiles – one for each subcommittee. Beyond constructing amusing "paradoxes," the importance of multiprofile issues is, for instance, to understand what can happen if a voter votes strategically, or if he doesn't vote. (The voter's options are to vote sincerely, strategically, or abstain; each option defines a different profile.) Other multiprofile issues include a concern about the consequences should more voters vote. What happens if voters change preferences? Can forming a coalition cause problems? In fact, as I show, important theorems in social choice theory, such as the Arrow Impossibility Theorem, are based on the properties a procedure must exhibit with changes in profiles.

My emphasis is to develop geometric arguments that can be used to analyze a wide spectrum of multiprofile issues. The appropriate geometric traits emphasize "connection" properties of the profile space $Si(6)$. To simplify the analysis, the simpler two-dimensional geometry of the representation triangle is exploited whenever possible.

4.1 Weak Consistency: The Sum of the Parts

The Dean's Council paradox characterizes a class of particularly troubling paradoxes. After all, each subcommittee reached the same conclusion, but, when they gathered as a full committee, the sincere outcome changed. This example shows that voting can contradict the saying about "the whole being greater than the sum of the parts." Instead, even when the parts are in agreement, the common conclusion can differ radically. Why? What kinds of procedures admit such inconsistent, perverse behavior? As I show, rather than being abnormal, this phenomenon where *the outcome of the whole differs from the parts must be anticipated with procedures that rely on the election rankings of more than one subset of candidates.* Such inconsistencies, therefore, must be expected with agendas, runoffs, and so forth.

I will suggest the relevant geometry with a runoff. Let $\mathcal{RO}(c_j)$ be the profile set ensuring the selection of c_j, and let $\mathbf{p}_i \in \mathcal{RO}(c_j)$, $i = 1, 2$, be the normalized profile for the ith subcommittee. (In words, each group selects c_1 in a runoff election.) The normalized profile for the full committee is

$$\mathbf{p}_\lambda = \lambda\mathbf{p}_1 + (1 - \lambda)\mathbf{p}_2$$

where $\lambda \in [0,1]$ represents the portion of all voters that belong to the first subcommittee. Namely, the normalized profile for the full committee, $\mathbf{p}_\lambda$, is a point on the line segment connecting $\mathbf{p}_1$ and $\mathbf{p}_2$. Conversely, every point on the connecting line represents the normalized committee profile for some division of the voters (i.e., for some value of λ) into two subcommittees.

The geometric explanation for paradoxes of the Dean's Council type now is immediate. If $\mathbf{p}_1$, $\mathbf{p}_2 \in \mathcal{RO}(c_1)$ but $\mathbf{p}_\lambda$ is not, then, according to the definition of convexity (Sect. 1.4), $\mathcal{RO}(c_1)$ *is not a convex set.* Conversely, if $\mathcal{RO}(c_1)$ is a convex set, then such a disturbing event never can occur! Consequently, it is when convexity is violated that these multi-profile paradoxes arise.

Definition 4.1.1. Let the collection of nonempty subsets of three candidates be $\mathcal{P} = \{\{c_1\}, \{c_2\}, \{c_3\}, \{c_1, c_2\}, \{c_1, c_3\}, \{c_2, c_3\}, \{c_1, c_2, c_3\}\}$. A choice procedure, $f : Si(6) \to \mathcal{P}$, is *weakly consistent* if when $f(\mathbf{p}_1) = f(\mathbf{p}_2)$, then

$$f(\lambda\mathbf{p}_1 + (1 - \lambda)\mathbf{p}_2) = f(\mathbf{p}_1), \lambda \in [0, 1]. \quad \square \tag{4.1.1}$$

What a weakly consistent[1] procedure does is to ensure that paradoxes of the Dean's Council type cannot occur. The condition requires that if two groups reach the same conclusion, such as Ann from the fable, then that is their joint outcome. The goal is to understand what procedures are, and are not, weakly consistent.

Weakly Consistent Procedures. The following statement, which follows almost immediately from Definition 4.1.1, is a central tool for our analysis.

Proposition 4.1.1. *A choice procedure f is weakly consistent iff for each set of candidates $\alpha \in \mathcal{P}$, the profile set $f^{-1}(\alpha)$ is a convex subset in $Si(6)$.*

The power of this proposition is that it converts the election issue of weak consistency into a geometric property about profile sets. If each outcome is supported by a convex profile set, then there is no need to worry about weak consistency. On the other hand, if even one outcome is supported by a non-convex set of profiles, weak consistency is violated! Geometrically, a "non-convex" set carries with it the notion of residing in a "higher dimensional" space. Thus, the blame for a procedure failing to be weakly consistent can be attributed to the higher dimensional properties of profiles.

Example 4.1.1. The widely used choice procedure, where the $\mathbf{w}_s$ top-ranked candidate is selected, is weakly consistent. The technical argument relies on the fact that the intersection of convex sets is a convex set. To use this property,

---

[1] The term "strongly consistent" is reserved for the much more restrictive condition that is used in Sect. 4.4 to find an axiomatic representation for positional methods.

observe that the set of normalized election outcomes where c_1 is $\mathbf{w}_s$ top-ranked is characterized by c_1 beating each of the other two candidates. This set is

$$[\mathcal{C}_{c_1 \succ c_2} = \{\mathbf{q} \in Si(3) \text{ where } c_1 \succ c_2\}] \cap [\mathcal{C}_{c_1 \succ c_3} = \{\mathbf{q} \in Si(3) \text{ where } c_1 \succ c_3\}].$$

As $\mathcal{C}_{c_1 \succ c_j}$ are the points in the representation triangle on one side of the binary indifference line $c_1 \sim c_j$, $\mathcal{C}_{c_1 \succ c_j}$ is convex. Thus, $\mathcal{C}_{c_1 \succ c_2} \cap \mathcal{C}_{c_1 \succ c_3}$, which defines the normalized outcomes where c_1 is top-ranked, is convex. To use only outcomes that are realized by $\mathbf{w}_s$, restrict attention to the convex hull $\mathcal{CH}(\mathbf{w}_s)$. Therefore,

$$\mathcal{C}_{c_1 \succ c_2} \cap \mathcal{C}_{c_1 \succ c_3} \cap \mathcal{CH}(\mathbf{w}_s)$$

is the set of normalized $\mathbf{w}_s$ election outcomes where c_1 is top-ranked. As this set is the intersection of three convex sets, it is convex.

The next step is to use the linear form of the election mapping and the comments of Sect. 1.4. Recall, for a linear mapping the inverse image of a convex set is a convex set. The election mapping $f(-, \mathbf{w}_s)$ is linear; and the set of desired election outcomes $\mathcal{C}_{c_1 \succ c_2} \cap \mathcal{C}_{c_1 \succ c_3} \cap \mathcal{CH}(\mathbf{w}_s)$ is convex, so the profile set supporting the selection of c_1 is convex. A similar argument shows that this convexity assertion holds for all $\alpha \in \mathcal{P}$.

The conditions of the proposition are satisfied, so we have established that this standard choice function is weakly consistent. Geometrically, these comments are illustrated by the convex shaded portion of Fig. 4.1.1a which defines the set of election outcomes where c_1 is plurality top-ranked.

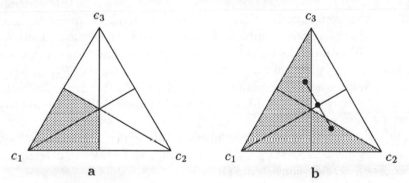

Fig. 4.1.1. Checking for convexity. **a.** c_1 is plurality top-ranked.
b. Is there convexity in a runoff?

For a different procedure, suppose two members are to be selected for, say, the U.S.A. Olympic Frisbee Team. Presumably, they are the two top-ranked candidates of a $\mathbf{w}_s$ election. Is this weakly consistent? To answer the question, observe that this procedure selects a *pair* of candidates, $\alpha \in \mathcal{P}$, rather than a singleton.

Without loss of generality, assume that the two top-ranked candidates are c_1 and c_2. Using the same kind of argument as above, the set of $\mathbf{w}_s$ normalized outcomes in the representation triangle yielding this conclusion are

$$\mathcal{C}_{c_1 \succ c_3} \cap \mathcal{C}_{c_2 \succ c_3} \cap \mathcal{CH}(\mathbf{w}_s) = \mathcal{R}(1) \cup \mathcal{R}(6) \cup \mathcal{R}(12).$$

Again, this set is the intersection of convex sets, so it is convex. (This convex set is given by the three ranking regions abutting the bottom edge of the representation triangle.) Using the convexity arguments of Sect. 1.4, the corresponding profile set is convex, so the procedure is weakly consistent.

Instead of choosing a top-ranked candidate, consider selecting the second-ranked candidate. Why? Well, in the newspapers, in congressional debates, and during campaign speeches we hear about the plight of the "average voter," or the "average consumer." A group wanting to identify this "average" individual needs a procedure to find the voters' middle-ranked candidate. As a more practical example, every spring attention is focused on two different collegiate basketball tournaments in the USA. The better teams go to the NCAA, the teams with the next level of ability go to the NIT, and, presumably, the rest of the teams return to the classroom. Instead of waiting to learn which teams are selected for the NCAA tournament, suppose we want to identify who goes to the NIT. This requires a procedure to identify the middle-ranked candidates.

The natural way to select an average candidate is to choose the $\mathbf{w}_s$ middle-ranked candidate. This procedure, however, is *not* weakly consistent. To see why, notice that the region where c_1 is middle-ranked is $\mathcal{R}(3) \cup \mathcal{R}(6) \cup \mathcal{R}(13)$; it is the union of two triangular regions that meet at the point $\mathcal{I}$. (In Fig. 4.1.1b, this is the union of the two shaded regions containing a dot.) As this set clearly fails a convexity test, this middle-seeking procedure is not weakly consistent.

Because the "middle-choosing" procedure fails weak consistency, it is worth using it to learn how to create profile examples to illustrate this deficiency. This is easy; as the nonconvexity (illustrated in Fig. 4.1.1b) causes the problem, it must be used to generate examples. As illustrated in the figure, choose $\mathbf{q}_1 \in \mathcal{R}(3)$ and $\mathbf{q}_2 \in \mathcal{R}(6)$ around the indentation so that the connecting line passes outside of the region. Any point on the portion of the line outside of $\mathcal{R}(3) \cup \mathcal{R}(6) \cup \mathcal{R}(13)$ defines a λ value where $\mathbf{q}_\lambda \notin \mathcal{R}(3) \cup \mathcal{R}(6)$. Obviously, there are numerous choices of $\mathbf{q}_1$, $\mathbf{q}_2$. Then, use the coordinate representations and the $\mathbf{q}_j$ points to compute supporting profiles.

An alternative way to select the "average candidate" is to choose the "winner" of the scoring election $\mathbf{sc} = (\frac{1}{6}, \frac{5}{6}, 0)$. It is left for the reader to determine whether this process is weakly consistent. (It is.)

The example about choosing the middle-ranked candidate along with the profiles used for the Dean's Council election provides insight (but not a proof) why a simple runoff is not weakly consistent. In the $\mathbf{w}_s$-runoff, the two $\mathbf{w}_s$ top-ranked candidates are advanced to the runoff. If c_1 is the winner, then, clearly, she is one of the advanced candidates. The problem is caused by the two choices for the other candidate; the set of normalized $\mathbf{w}_s$ election outcomes must allow the candidates advanced to the runoff to be $\{c_1, c_2\}$ or $\{c_1, c_3\}$. This set is illustrated by the shaded region of Fig. 4.1.1b. As this forked region fails to be convex, it is easy to create examples whereby c_1 is one of the two top-ranked candidates for each subcommittee, but she is bottom-ranked in the committee of the whole. (This is precisely what happens in the Dean's Council example.) This geometry, however, does not explain the runoff problems because it does not indicate what happens in the pairwise elections. $\square$

As illustrated by the above examples, the analysis of weak consistency is reasonably simple for choice procedures based on positional and scoring methods. Call such a procedure a *scoring based choice procedure*. What simplifies the analysis is that, in order to determine whether a scoring based choice procedure is weakly consistent, we only need to check the convexity properties of the sets of normalized election outcomes. Clearly, the geometry of the representation cube and triangle are much easier to understand than the esoteric geometry of the profile space $Si(6)$.

Theorem 4.1.2. *For a specified scoring based choice procedure, f, let $\mathcal{A}(\alpha)$ be the set of scoring election outcomes where the set of candidates $\alpha \in \mathcal{P}$ is selected. The procedure f is weakly consistent iff $\mathcal{A}(\alpha)$ is a convex set for all $\alpha \in \mathcal{P}$.*

The proof of this theorem, as well as illustrations, are given in Example 4.1.1.

4.1.1 Other Uses of Convexity

It is worth pointing out that these convexity arguments apply to the wide spectrum of issues that arise whenever two or more groups of voters combine forces. Such situations occur, for instance, when different political parties form a coalition, when new voters arrive at a meeting, when the Chair is permitted to vote in a group decision, etc.

To illustrate, suppose one group has c_1 $\mathbf{w}_s$ top-ranked while a second group has c_2 $\mathbf{w}_s$ top-ranked. When the two groups join, which candidate will be $\mathbf{w}_s$ top-ranked? With these geometric arguments, it is easy to show that it could be neither; c_3 could be the candidate of choice for the full group! This is because the region where either c_1 or c_2 is top-ranked fails a convexity test. In the representation triangle, this region is everything in the hull $CH(\mathbf{w}_s)$ except $\mathcal{R}(3) \cup \mathcal{R}(9) \cup \mathcal{R}(4)$. (It is everything except those regions with c_3 as a vertex.) Excising this section from the convex hull $CH(\mathbf{w}_s)$ creates an indentation which ensures the nonconvexity. It now is easy to generate examples where c_3 is top-ranked.

So, whatever the issue, whenever the problem is to compare how the outcomes of the parts (the choices of the different groups) relates to the whole (the outcome when the diverse groups come together), convexity prevails as a powerful, yet elementary tool of analysis. In this manner, other interesting examples follow by considering what happens when more than two groups unite, when different groups use different procedures to reach their outcome, etc. For instance, suppose each of two groups select c_1, but one group uses the agenda $< c_1, c_2, c_3 >$ and the other uses a plurality runoff procedure. Need they select c_1 as a full group with a plurality runoff? (No.) If the Chair, whose top-choice is c_1, is permitted to vote to break a tie between c_1 and c_2, are there procedures where the Chair's sincere participation causes c_3 to be selected? (Yes.) What happens when there are three or more groups?

4.1.2 An L of an Agenda

On the theoretical level it is easy to understand the source of weak consistency; the set of profiles supporting each outcome must be convex. What remains is the practical problem to determine whether a specified procedure satisfies this convexity condition. For instance, is an agenda weakly consistent?

To analyze an agenda, it suffices to consider the specific choice $< c_1, c_2, c_3 >$. The analysis, of course, involves the geometric structure of the representation cube reproduced in Fig. 4.1.2. In order for c_1 to win, she needs to beat c_2 in the first election and c_3 in the second. Consequently, c_1 is the $< c_1, c_2, c_3 >$ agenda winner iff she is the Condorcet winner. Thus, $\mathcal{A}(\{c_1\})$ is the convex set defined by the cube region where $x > 0$, $z < 0$.

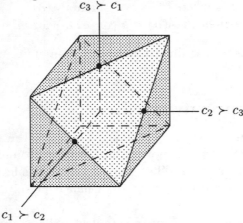

$$c_3 \succ c_1$$

$$c_2 \succ c_3$$

$$c_1 \succ c_2$$

Fig. 4.1.2. The representation cube

To understand whether $\mathcal{A}(\{c_1\})$ is convex, treat each orthant of the representation cube as a child's building block. (As true with most children's toys, each block is mutilated. In our case the mutilation is caused by the faces T_1, T_2.) The set of normalized outcomes leading to the selection of c_1, $\mathcal{A}(\{c_1\})$, consists of placing two blocks together along a common face. Clearly, this (somewhat) rectangular region is convex. Alternatively, because

$$\mathcal{A}(\{c_1\}) = \{\mathbf{q} \,|\, x > 0\} \cap \{\mathbf{q} \,|\, z < 0\}$$

is the intersection of two convex portions of the representation cube (where each portion is half of the cube), it is a convex set.

The convexity of $\mathcal{A}(\{c_1\})$ ensures that if $\mathbf{p}_1$ and $\mathbf{p}_2$ are profiles where c_1 wins (i.e., $f(\mathbf{p}_j) = \{c_1\}$), then $f(\lambda \mathbf{p}_1 + (1 - \lambda)\mathbf{p}_2) = \{c_1\}$ for any $\lambda \in [0, 1]$. Consequently, if c_1 wins with each subcommittee, she wins with the combined group. A similar assertion holds for c_2 because $\mathcal{A}(\{c_2\})$ is the convex set $\{\mathbf{q} \,|\, y > 0,\ x < 0\}$.

Now consider the set $\mathcal{A}(\{c_3\})$. Of the eight orthants in the representation cube, four have been assigned to the other two candidates. Thus, the remaining four orthants must be in $\mathcal{A}(\{c_3\})$. Two of these regions (where $y < 0$, $z > 0$) define c_3 as the Condorcet winner; the other two are the cyclic regions where, as we have seen, the last listed candidate in an agenda always wins. Thus, we have that

$$\mathcal{A}(\{c_3\}) = \{\mathbf{q}\,|\,y < 0, z > 0\} \cup \{\mathbf{q}\,|\,x > 0, y > 0, z > 0\} \cup \{\mathbf{q}\,|\,x < 0, y < 0, z < 0\}.$$

To visualize this region, notice that $\mathcal{A}(\{c_3\})$ includes three of the four orthants above the x-y plane (where $z > 0$). (This is given by $\{\mathbf{q}\,|\,y < 0, z > 0\} \cup \{\mathbf{q}\,|\,x > 0, y > 0, z > 0\}$.) Using the building block construction, start by first placing together all four blocks (orthants) where $z > 0$ to form a convex region. Next, remove one of the blocks (the one where $x < 0$, $y > 0$, $z > 0$; it is part of the c_2-Condorcet region) to destroy convexity. Consequently, because the two cyclic regions are added to the c_3 victory region, both the convexity of $\mathcal{A}(\{c_3\})$ and any chance for the agenda $< c_1, c_2, c_3 >$ to be weakly consistent are lost.

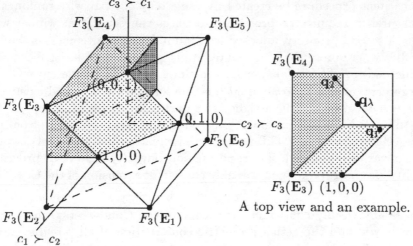

Fig. 4.1.3. The L non-convexity of $\mathcal{A}(c_3)$ for $< c_1, c_2, c_3 >$

This L of a construction proving that an agenda is not weakly consistent is illustrated in Fig. 4.1.3. (To keep the figure from becoming overly complicated, only the c_3-Condorcet and positive cyclic regions are shaded. Missing is the negative cyclic region.) It is easy to use the geometry to create examples showing that an agenda is not weakly consistent; just exploit the "L" indentation of $\mathcal{A}(\{c_3\})$. Because the indentations are caused by adding the cyclic regions to the c_3-Condorcet regions, *all illustrating examples must involve at least one cyclic region.*

To create an example, choose $\mathbf{q}_1$ in the positive cyclic region and $\mathbf{q}_2$ in the other L leg – the orthant where $x < 0, y < 0, z > 0$. If, as illustrated in Fig. 4.1.3, both points are chosen far enough out in the legs of the L (or close enough to the boundary), the connecting line must pass through the removed orthant where $x < 0, y > 0, z > 0$. An appropriate choice of λ generates an example where c_3 wins with both subcommittees, but c_2 wins with the full committee. Notice, if $\mathbf{q}_1$, $\mathbf{q}_2$ are sufficiently close to the boundary, then almost any λ value suffices.

As an aside, the above geometry describing the $\mathcal{A}(\{c_j\})$ regions reinforces my earlier comment that there is a large set of pairwise election outcomes that favor the selection of the last listed candidate in an agenda. The first two candidates can win only by being the Condorcet winner; the last listed candidate can win by being a Condorcet winner or if there is a cycle. Consequently, *with any reasonable definition of a probability distribution of profiles, the last listed candidate in an agenda always has the probabilistic advantage of being selected.* For instance, for any distribution of the profiles where it is equally likely for any candidate to be a Condorcet winner, if the probability of a cycle is nonzero, then the last listed candidate in an agenda has a distinct probabilistic advantage of being selected.

4.1.3 Condorcet Extensions

If an agenda is not weakly consistent, then what pairwise procedure is? Can a weakly consistent procedure be created by using only the pairwise rankings? If so, it is natural to require the procedure to select the Condorcet winner when one exists. A second property, imposed to avoid indecisive outcomes, is that the set of profiles where more than one candidate is selected is of lower dimension. Do such methods exist? The answer is immediate from the geometry: NO!

The argument goes as follows. If such a Condorcet extension did exist, then each open cyclic region must be assigned to a particular choice of $\mathcal{A}(\{c_j\})$. (This is due to the decisiveness requirement outlawing open sets of profiles from supporting indecisive outcomes.) This assignment recreates the L problem discussed above, so convexity is violated. The resulting nonconvexity of $\mathcal{A}(\{c_j\})$ proves the impossibility of constructing such a weakly consistent extension of the Condorcet winner.

Are there *any* weakly consistent extensions of the Condorcet winner? Here the answer is yes, and the actual geometric construction of all possible choices is left to the reader. As a hint, notice that there are seven subsets of candidates in $\mathcal{P}$; so the 27 ranking regions (eight are the open orthants, 12 are portions of coordinate planes, six are portions of coordinate lines, and the last is $\mathcal{I}$) of Fig. 4.1.2 must be combined into seven convex regions. Once the representation cube is divided into these seven convex regions, each region is assigned a subset from $\mathcal{P}$.[2] The only constraint on the assignment is that the singletons, $\{c_j\}$, must be assigned to a region containing c_j as a Condorcet winner (this is the Condorcet requirement). Other restrictions emerge from the geometry. For instance, as $\{c_1, c_2, c_3\}$ can be assigned to at most one cyclic region, at least one cyclic region must be assigned a two-candidate outcome. This choice, however, means that the procedure cannot satisfy neutrality. (Why?) It is left to the reader to discover other properties of the assignment process.

---

[2] This construction holds only for $n = 3$. For $n \geq 4$, there are 2^n orthants in R^n. The geometric assignment of the $n!$ orthants defining Condorcet winners leaves behind a region so divided that it is impossible to combine the orthants into the required $2^n - 1$ convex sets. (The problem is made worse when the regions of coordinate planes and axes are introduced [S12].) Thus, the construction of a weakly consistent extension of the Condorcet winner based on rankings, is doomed for failure for $n \geq 4$.

Corollary 4.1.3. *There does not exist a weakly consistent procedure based on the pairwise rankings of candidates that selects the Condorcet winner, when one exists, and that satisfies either of the following conditions.*

a. *The procedure is neutral.*

b. *The set of profiles assigned to a subset of more than one candidate is lower dimensional.*

The above corollary demonstrates the limited ability to extend the Condorcet winner. After all, to be useful, the Condorcet winner must shed its "sometimes it can be used, sometimes it can't" limitation. This requires extending the concept to all pairwise outcomes. As the above corollary proves, trying to extend the Condorcet winner carries the heavy price of losing weak consistency and, say, neutrality. Instead of using the pairwise rankings, maybe we should modify the Condorcet concept by using the actual pairwise election outcomes. To preserve weak consistency, we end up, as described in Chap. 2, with the Condorcet Improvement procedure which is equivalent to the BC.

4.1.4 Other Pairwise Procedures

One might wonder what happens if, instead of the aggregated pairwise vote (which is equivalent to the BC), a generalized pairwise method is used. (See Sect. 3.5.) In other words, instead of using just the rankings of the pairs, use the election tallies and a G-binary method. In what follows, while I restrict attention to smooth functions $G : [0, 1] \to [0, 1]$,[3] the result is more general and it holds for $n \geq 3$. The next theorem asserts that the only choices of G admitting weak consistency are equivalent to $G(x) = x$; this is the BC.

Theorem 4.1.4. *If $G : [0, 1] \to [0, 1]$ is a smooth function defining an generalized pairwise aggregation method that is weakly consistent, then G is equivalent to $G(x) = x$ and the aggregation process is equivalent to the BC.*

There are several ways to prove this theorem. One is to apply (and slightly extend) the L theorem found at the end of this section. A direct approach is given next. Because the following proof involves calculus, intuition is provided for the reader unfamiliar with this important technical tool.

As we have seen, if the space of profiles $Si(6)$ is to be divided into 13 convex regions (one convex region for each ranking of the three candidates), the boundaries of each region must consist of linear objects defined by planes or the intersections of planes. (If not, then some region has a bulge. But, one region's bulge is another region's indentation. Consequently, nonconvexity must arise.) The next step is to show that the linear boundaries force the defining function G to be linear. As shown in the last section, a linear G is equivalent to $G(x) = x$. Only the assertion that G is linear requires calculus. Therefore, only skeptics are encouraged (no, required!) to read the proof.

---

[3] For the reader familiar with calculus, this means that at least the first and second derivatives of G are defined and continuous. For the reader still waiting to be initiated into the Calculus Club, treat G as a function where the graph can be smoothly drawn.

Proof. We need to show that G' is a constant. As advertised, this requires calculus. The boundary defined by $c_1 \sim c_2$ is given by

$$F = G(q_{1,2}) + G(q_{1,3}) - [G(q_{2,1}) + G(q_{2,3})] = 0.$$

The properties of the level set $F^{-1}(0)$ are determined by the properties of ∇F evaluated along the boundary. A direct computation, using the definition of $q_{i,j}$, yields

$$\nabla F = G'(q_{1,2})(1,1,1,0,0,0) + G'(q_{1,3})(1,1,0,0,0,1) -$$
$$[G'(q_{2,3})(1,0,0,0,1,1) + G'(q_{2,1})(0,0,0,1,1,1)],$$

which, after collecting terms and using $G'(x) = G'(1-x)$ (which results from differentiating $G(x) = 1 - G(1-x)$), becomes

$$\nabla F = (G'(q_{1,2}) + G'(q_{1,3}) - G'(q_{2,3}), G'(q_{1,2}) + G'(q_{1,3}), G'(q_{1,2}),$$
$$-G'(q_{1,2}), -G'(q_{1,2}) - G'(q_{2,3}), G'(q_{1,3}) - G'(q_{1,2}) - G'(q_{2,3})).$$
$$(4.1.2)$$

The boundary is a linear set, so, on each component, $\nabla F / \|\nabla F\|$ is an orthogonal constant unit vector. This condition forces each component of ∇F to be a multiple of the other components. So, by comparing the second and third components, we have that along the boundary $G'(q_{1,2})$ is a multiple of $G'(q_{2,3})$; $G'(q_{1,2}) = mG'(q_{1,3})$ for some scalar m. Similarly, $G'(q_{1,2})$, $G'(q_{1,3})$, and $G'(q_{2,3})$ are all fixed scalar multiples of the others.

The key is that the $q_{i,j}$ variables are independent variables. So, by keeping $q_{1,3}$ fixed and varying $q_{1,2}$, it follows from $G'(q_{1,2}) = mG'(q_{1,3})$ that G' must be a constant over certain domain values. Using the same approach with the other relationships, if follows that G' is a constant over all domain values represented by this $c_1 \sim c_2$ boundary.

To show that G' is a constant over $[0,1]$, it suffices to show that the domain for G leading to $F = 0$ is the full interval $[0,1]$. To do so, consider profiles $x[\mathbf{E}_1 + \mathbf{E}_6] + y[\mathbf{E}_2 + \mathbf{E}_5] + z[\mathbf{E}_3 + \mathbf{E}_4]$ where $x + y + z = \frac{1}{2}$, $x, y, z \geq 0$. (By neutrality, they are in the profile set supporting $F = 0$.) Such a profile defines $q_{1,2} = q_{2,1} = \frac{1}{2}$ and $q_{2,3} = q_{1,3} = 2x + y$. Therefore, the profiles supporting the equation $F = 0$ correspond to the possible $2x + y$ values allowed by the constraint $x + y + z = \frac{1}{2}$. As this includes all values in $[0,1]$, the proof is completed. $\square$

4.1.5 Maybe "if's " and "and's", but no "or's" or "but's"

Figure 4.1.4 displays the geometric fact that the intersection of convex regions is a convex set, but the union of convex sets need not be convex. (The heavily shaded region is the convex intersection. The totally shaded area, including the inward dents near the top and bottom where the circles join, is the union.) A point surviving an intersection satisfies the membership requirements of both groups, where the connecting word *"and"* signals this geometric process. Similarly, because a union allows a qualified point to be in one set *or* in the other, "or" is a reasonable indicator that a geometric union is involved. So, while not infallible, we should question the weak consistency of a procedure requiring an "or" to describe how a subset of candidates is selected.

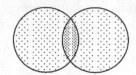

Fig. 4.1.4. Convex sets

Example 4.1.2. For the agenda $< c_1, c_2, c_3 >$, c_1 wins {if she beats c_2 } *and* { if she beats c_3 }. This region, $\mathcal{A}(\{c_1\})$, is convex. On the other hand, c_3 wins { if c_1 beats c_2 *and* c_3 beats c_2 } *or* { if c_2 beats c_1 *and* c_3 beats c_2 }. The "and" in the two bracketed conditions makes each a convex set; it is the lone "or" connecting these sets that destroys the convexity along with any hope of weak consistency.

Consider the extensions of a Condorcet winner which involve a union. When a cyclic region is assigned to a particular candidate, say c_1, the connecting word "or" is needed to describe how c_1 can be selected. Namely, c_1 wins { if $c_1 \succ c_2$ *and* $c_1 \succ c_3$ } *or* { if $c_1 \succ c_2$, $c_2 \succ c_3$, and $c_3 \succ c_1$. } The extension is not weakly consistent as suggested by the "or."

To choose c_1 as the second-ranked candidate from an election, the description is { the $\mathbf{w}_s$ ranking is $c_2 \succ c_1 \succ c_3$ } *or* { the $\mathbf{w}_s$ ranking is $c_3 \succ c_1 \succ c_2$ }. These procedures are not weakly consistent. On the other hand, we can describe how the top (or bottom) ranked candidates are selected by using only the word "and". Hence, one can correctly guess that these are weakly consistent methods. Alternately, by listing the names of all of the admissible ranking regions, the description of this weakly consistent procedure now uses the connecting "or" word. Thus, an "or" only suggests that weak consistency is absent; it is not a proof. □

Runoffs and But's. The description how c_1 is the $\mathbf{w}_s$ runoff winner is { if c_3 is $\mathbf{w}_s$ bottom-ranked *and* $c_1 \succ c_2$ in the pairwise election } *or* { if c_2 is $\mathbf{w}_s$ bottom-ranked *and* $c_1 \succ c_3$ in the pairwise election }. Thus, it is reasonable to expect a proof illustrating the weak consistency problems of a $\mathbf{w}_s$-runoff to involve showing that the two bracketed (convex) sets have a non-convex union. This is correct, and I will leave it to the reader to construct this argument. Instead, I will use a closely related demonstration to illustrate the importance of the *"but"* word – a term used to signal that a portion of a set has been removed. (Clearly, removing a portion from a convex set can destroy convexity.)

Start with the convex hull of profiles causing a c_1 and c_2 pairwise tie. Using cyclic coordinates, it follows that this hull is defined by the nine boundary profiles $\{\mathbf{v}_{i,j} = \frac{1}{2}\mathbf{E}_i + \frac{1}{2}\mathbf{E}_j\}_{i,=1,2,3,j=4,5,6}$. The corresponding positional election outcomes, the convex hull defined by the vertices $\{f(\mathbf{v}_{i,j}, \mathbf{w}_s)\}$, is illustrated by the darkly shaded region in Fig. 4.1.5 for the plurality and BC methods.

The dark region of Fig. 4.1.5 indicates those positional election outcomes that can accompany a pairwise $c_1 \sim c_2$ outcome. By use of the cyclic-positional coordinates, it follows that for *any point* inside the dark shaded region, there is a profile leading to the pairwise outcome $c_1 \succ c_2$ and a profile leading to $c_2 \succ c_1$. To "see" this important fact, notice for any $\mathbf{q}$ in the shaded area, there are many choices of supporting profiles where α_s and β_s permit $d > \frac{1}{2}$; in other words, many profiles support both the positional outcome $\mathbf{q}$ and the $c_1 \succ c_2$ pairwise vote. Likewise, other supporting outcomes have $d < \frac{1}{2}$.

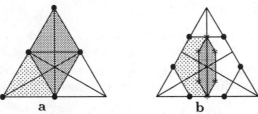

Fig. 4.1.5. The outcomes associated with pairwise $c_1 \succ c_2$.
a. Plurality outcomes. **b.** BC outcomes

The lightly shaded regions are where an election outcome must be accompanied by the pairwise ranking $c_1 \succ c_2$. Consequently, with the possible exception of the line segment separating the shaded from the clear region, any point in the shaded region can be supported by a profile whereby the pairwise ranking is $c_1 \succ c_2$.

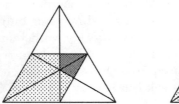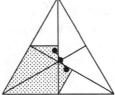

Fig. 4.1.6. The Dean's Council

Using the same argument (or a "name change" with $\sigma = (2,3)$), there is a symmetric region where the election outcome can be supported by a profile with the pairwise outcome $c_1 \succ c_3$. The intersection of the two regions defines a convex region of points that are supported by a profile with the pairwise outcome $c_1 \succ c_2$ and/or $c_1 \succ c_3$. For the plurality vote, this is the shaded region in Fig. 4.1.6a.

It is time to consider the $\mathbf{w}_s$-runoff. For c_1 to win, she must avoid being $\mathbf{w}_s$ bottom-ranked. This means the $\mathbf{w}_s$ outcome cannot be in the heavily shaded part of Fig. 4.1.6a. But, once the heavily shaded region is removed, the remaining region, indicated in Fig. 4.1.6b, looses all claims to convexity!

The lack of convexity of Fig. 4.6.1b not only makes it clear that the runoff is not weakly consistent, but also how to construct illustrating examples. Geometrically, such an example is given by the dots and the connecting line near the inward dent of the shaded region in Fig. 4.1.4b. The upper dot is assigned a profile with the pairwise ranking $c_1 \succ c_3$ while the lower dot is assigned a profile where $c_1 \succ c_2$. Indeed, the profiles for the subcommittees of the Dean's Council example were derived in this manner; coordinate representations were used to find profiles supporting the end points of the line segment.

To ensure that this proof holds for all choices of $\mathbf{w}_s$, modify the argument by including the $\mathcal{CH}(\mathbf{w}_s)$ set, and the regions where the pairwise outcome can be $c_1 \sim c_2$. We already know that this set is the smallest for the BC. Hence, the same proof applies. $\square$

Theorem 4.1.5. *Let $\mathbf{w}_s$ and a scoring vector $\mathbf{sc}$ be given. The $\mathbf{w}_s$ simple runoff and the $\mathbf{w}_s - \mathbf{sc}$ runoff procedures are not weakly consistent.*

4.1.6 A General Theorem

From the abundance of examples, it is reasonable to suspect there is a general theorem. The idea is based on the above "or", "but" comments by being precise in the following definition about what it means for there to exist several options to reach the same outcome. Examples illustrating the definition follow.

Definition 4.1.2. A non-constant scoring based choice procedure is *varied* if it uses the ordinal rankings of two or more subsets of candidates so that the following is true. For some $\alpha \in \mathcal{P}$, and for some choice of subsets of candidates S', S'', there are ways where α is selected independent of the rankings of the candidates in S', and there are other ways where specific rankings of the S' candidates must occur. Namely, there are choices of the rankings for subsets of candidates defining α where no restrictions are placed on the ranking of S', but there are restrictions on the ranking of S''. Then, there are choices of rankings where the ranking of subset S' must be restricted in order to obtain the outcome α. $\square$

Example 4.1.3. Consider the various ways c_3 can be selected with the agenda $< c_1, c_2, c_3 >$. The first is if $c_1 \succ c_2$ and $c_3 \succ c_1$. In this scenario, the ranking of the set $\{c_2, c_3\}$ is immaterial, so let $S' = \{c_2, c_3\}$. Now, we need to show there is another way to elect c_3 that restricts the ranking for $\{c_2, c_3\}$. This is, of course, if $c_2 \succ c_1$. In this setting, for c_3 to be selected, we need $c_3 \succ c_2$. Thus, an agenda is a varied procedure.

A runoff is a varied procedure because one way to elect c_1 is with the rankings $c_1 \succ c_2 \succ c_3$ and $c_1 \succ c_2$. This choice imposes no restriction on the ranking of, say, $\{c_1, c_3\}$. Now, we need to find a second way for c_1's selection that imposes restrictions on the $\{c_1, c_3\}$ ranking. This is if $c_3 \succ c_1 \succ c_2$ with the restriction $c_1 \succ c_3$. $\square$

The examples prove that it is easy to determine whether a choice procedure is, or is not varied. The definition is in terms of rankings; it does not require us to determine whether the particular listing of rankings can occur.

Theorem 4.1.6. *A varied positional choice procedure is not weakly consistent.*

This theorem fails to characterize all procedures that violate weak consistency. For instance, the procedure that selects the second-ranked candidate of a $\mathbf{w}_s$ election only involves the election rankings of the set $\{c_1, c_2, c_3\}$, so it is *not* varied. Yet, as shown above, this procedure is not weakly consistent. (A complete characterization of weakly consistent methods can be fashioned out of the theorem describing positively involved procedures that is found at the end of Sect. 4.2.)

The reason Theorem 4.1.6 holds is that, by being varied, a procedure must create an L in some $\mathcal{A}(c_j)$ set. This L destroys both the convexity of $\mathcal{A}(c_j)$ and the weak consistency of the procedure. This L can be illustrated with *Black's procedure*. D. Black argues [Bl] that whenever a Condorcet winner exists, she should be selected. If there is no Condorcet winner, then the BC winner should be selected.[4] Because of the relationship between pairwise and BC rankings, Black's procedure comes close to being weakly consistent.

Corollary 4.1.7. *Black's procedure is varied. Therefore, Black's procedure is not weakly consistent.*

Proof. To show that Black's procedure is varied, let $S' = \{c_1, c_2, c_3\}$ for two scenarios that select c_1. If the pairwise rankings crown c_1 as the Condorcet winner, then we don't care about the associated BC rankings of S'. But, when no Condorcet winner exists, then c_1 must be BC top-ranked; this restricts the S' rankings to $\mathcal{R}(1) \cup \mathcal{R}(7) \cup \mathcal{R}(2)$. The conclusion follows from Theorem 4.1.6. □

To motivate the proof of the theorem, I describe two ways to see the non-convexity of Black's method. The first approach is based on the relationship where the BC tally is uniquely determined by the pairwise tallies. The difference between regions in the representational cube where c_1 is BC top-ranked and where c_1 is the Condorcet winner is depicted in Fig. 4.1.7. Here, the shaded region represents the BC ranking $c_1 \succ c_2 \succ c_3$ while the dashed lines outline the boundary of the c_1-Condorcet region. The obvious non-convexity is created because part of the c_1-Condorcet region is removed from the BC region and because regions of the cyclic pairwise rankings are assigned to this BC ranking.

With this geometry, the design of supporting examples becomes standard. Let $\mathbf{q}_1$ be in the c_1-Condorcet region near the point $(0, 1, 0)$ and let $\mathbf{q}_2$ be near $\mathcal{I}$ and the $c_1 \sim c_2$ BC boundary in the $c_1 \succ c_2 \succ c_3$ BC region. For $\mathbf{q}_1, \mathbf{q}_2$, the Black method outcome is c_1. However, there are large sets of λ values where the $\mathbf{q}_\lambda$ outcome is c_2.

---

[4] It is clear from the earlier analysis of the BC that strong arguments can be advanced showing that just the BC should be used. The "contributions" offered by the myopic Condorcet approach can be misleading, so they should be ignored.

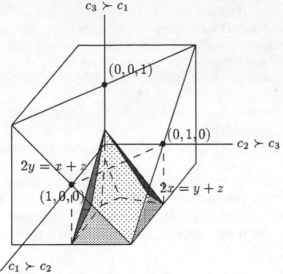

Fig. 4.1.7. The shaded region is the BC ranking $c_1 \succ c_2 \succ c_3$.
The dashed lines have this ranking for pairwise votes.

An alternative approach to visualize the non-convexity uses the fat triangle (the product of the representation triangle with [-1,1]). If c_1 is the Condorcet winner, she must beat c_2, so the point must be at the back half of the fat triangle. In the BC election, she receive at least one-third of all votes. This means that the BC tally must be on the c_1 side of a line passing through $\mathcal{I}$. Thus, points allowing c_1 to be selected in this manner are represented in Fig. 4.1.8a by the triangular region in the back of the fat triangle.

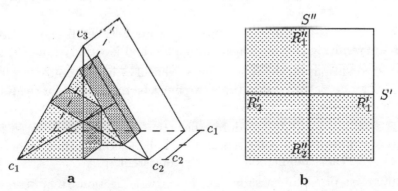

Fig. 4.1.8. Varied procedures. **a.** Black nonconvexity. **b.** A varied L

If there is a negative cycle, then c_1 must be the BC top-ranked candidate. This region is represented by region in the front half of the triangle. Here we can only use points in the representation triangle where c_1 is BC top-ranked. The L non-convexity is evident. Creating examples becomes simple with the geometry and the coordinate representations for profiles.

Proof of the Theorem. A varied procedure offers at least two scenarios for the selection of a particular outcome $\alpha \in P$. One scenario has α selected based on the rankings of sets other than S'; say, it depends upon specified rankings of $\{S'', \ldots, S^*\}$. Once these rankings are specified, α occurs independent of how the candidates in S' are ranked. The second scenario restricts the rankings of S'; but for this scenario to occur, the rankings of $\{S'', \ldots, S^*\}$ must be other than the specified ones.

What this means is that there is some subset (or subsets) S'' so that if S'' is not involved, then the ranking of S'' cannot be R'', but it could be R_2''. On the other hand, if the ranking of R_1'' occurs, then the ranking of S' must be R_1', but not R_2'.

The "L" non-convexity is created in the following manner. The Cartesian product $S' \times S$ contains the four paired ranking regions (R_i', R_j''), for $i, j = 1, 2$. For α to be the outcome, the paired region (R_2', R_1'') cannot occur. But, by excising this region, the L non-convexity is created. See Fig. 4.1.8b. $\square$

The abstract construction of Fig. 4.1.8b is illustrated with specific examples in Figs. 4.1.3, 4.1.7, 4.1.8. In all cases, because a restriction was imposed upon the rankings of one of the sets, a portion of the product of ranking regions must be removed; this creates the non-convexity forcing weak consistency not to hold.

4.1.7 Exercises

4.1.1. Show that the threshold methods are weakly consistent.

4.1.2. By dividing the representation triangle (or the representation cube) into any seven convex sets, define a weakly consistent procedure.

4.1.3. Find a profile demonstrating that the Coombs method is not weakly consistent.

4.1.4. Take G to be 0 at 0, and 1/2 for all points between 0 and 1. Determine whether the resulting G-binary aggregation method is weakly consistent.

4.1.5. Find conditions on the $\mathbf{w}_s$ election so that if c_1 is the top-ranked for group 1 and c_2 for group 2, then one of these two must be top-ranked for the full group. Do the same for the agenda $< c_1, c_2, c_3 >$.

4.1.6. For middle-ranked procedure, show that there exists a sc so that the winner really indicates, in some sense, who is the average person. Then find all choices of sc so that the method is weakly consistent.

4.1.7. Suppose a procedure asserts that, in pairwise elections, if c_1 beats c_2, then c_3 wins; otherwise, c_3 must beat c_2. If not, then c_2 wins. Show by the geometry that this is not weakly consistent. Also show it is varied.

4.1.8. Prove via the union method that a simple runoff or a runoff with scoring elimination is not weakly consistent.

4.1.9. Construct a profile where the procedure line is a point in the region $c_1 \succ c_2 \succ c_3$ and c_2 is the runoff winner. Next, construct a degenerate procedure line with the ranking $c_3 \succ c_2 \succ c_1$ with c_2 as the runoff winner. Construct the first point near the $c_1 \sim c_2$ boundary and the second one near the $c_2 \sim c_3$ boundary.

Thus, for an interval of choices of λ, c_2 is bottom-ranked in a combined election. This one example, then, proves Theorem 4.1.5 for all choices of positional voting methods.

4.1.10. Show when a $\mathbf{p}$-favored candidate exists, it defines a weakly consistent method.

4.1.11. Show that the $\mathbf{w}_{s_1}$, $\mathbf{w}_{s_2}$ comparison method is not weakly consistent.

4.1.12. Show how to extend Theorem 4.1.6 to more general procedures where the outcome depends upon the tallies.

4.1.13. By using the procedure line, show that it is possible for one subcommittee to have c_1 plurality top-ranked, another to have c_1 Borda top-ranked, but when they gather as a full committee, c_2 is the plurality top-ranked candidate.

4.1.14. Use orthogonality arguments of the form used to prove Theorem 4.1.6 to find a shorter proof that a $\mathbf{w}_s$-runoff and a $\mathbf{sc}$-runoff are not weakly consistent.

4.1.15. Suppose when two subcommittees each use a plurality runoff, both select c_1. Find a sufficient condition on the plurality rankings to ensure that c_1 is in the runoff for the full group. Need she win the runoff? Use the geometry of the representation cube to show the new non-convexity. (Examine Fig. 3.3.3.)

4.2 From Involvement and Monotonicity to Manipulation

Among the fascinating multiple profile consequences that can be understood with geometry, I now turn to the counter-intuitive, yet important and widely discussed "responsiveness" issues; this includes *monotonicity* and *manipulability*. Responsive issues explore the common sense notion that a candidate is helped when she receives added support. Shockingly, as we'll discover, this need not be true. Instead, we'll encounter several uneasy situations where voters can wreak planned and/or unintentional damage upon the group outcome.

The terminology and issues of this section differ from our previous discussion, but the analysis does not. The principal geometric tools are those developed in Sect. 4.1; the main difference is that extra restrictions are imposed upon the profiles. For instance, to explore the wishful myth that a candidate's chances always improve with more supporters, I start with a profile $\mathbf{p}_2$ supporting c_1's selection. Then, I restrict the profile $\mathbf{p}_1$ so that it consists only of voters with c_1 top-ranked. The goal is to determine whether $\mathbf{p}_1$ can be chosen so that c_1 is elected with $\mathbf{p}_2$, but *not* with $\mathbf{p}_2 + \mathbf{p}_1$.

To continue to let the geometry do the talking, geometric intuition is exploited as much as possible. As the geometry of the representation triangle and cube is easier than that of $Si(6)$, much of the discussion emphasizes election outcomes rather than profiles. This simplification, however, carries us only so far. To obtain a satisfying characterization of those procedures that do, and do not, respect different responsive issues, we must appeal to the geometry of the profile space $Si(6)$. After all, as we've learned, it is the geometric obstacles created by the higher dimensional properties of profiles that force a procedure to fail specified properties.

4.2.1 A Profile Angle

Important to our analysis is the angle formed by two profiles, $\mathbf{p}_1$, $\mathbf{p}_2$. This angle is conveniently described with the *scalar* or *dot* product. Recall that the scalar product between the two n-dimensional vectors $\mathbf{a} = (a_1, a_2, \ldots, a_n)$ and $\mathbf{b} = (b_1, b_2, \ldots, b_n)$ is

$$(\mathbf{a}, \mathbf{b}) = \sum_{j=1}^{n} a_j b_j = \|\mathbf{a}\| \|\mathbf{b}\| cos(\theta), \tag{4.2.1}$$

The summation, which defines the scalar product, is easy to compute; just add the indicated products. What makes the scalar product particularly powerful is the standard, yet amazing fact captured by the second equality; *this sum always agrees with the product of the lengths of the two vectors times the cosine of the angle, θ, between them.* Of particular concern to us is the *sign* of the scalar product; if it is zero, then the vectors are orthogonal ($\theta = 90^o$), if it is positive, then the vectors point in the same general direction ($|\theta| < 90^o$; they form an acute angle); and if it is negative, then the vectors point in widely different directions ($|\theta| > 90^o$; they form an obtuse angle).

As immediate examples, the orthogonality of the two vectors $\mathbf{e}_1$, $\mathbf{e}_2$ is reflected by the zero value of the scalar product $((1,0,0),(0,1,0)) = 1 \cdot 0 + 0 \cdot 1 + 0 \cdot 0 = 0$. Likewise, the fact the vectors $\mathbf{a} = (1,0)$ and $\mathbf{b} = (-1,0)$ point in opposite directions is in accord with the negative value of $(\mathbf{a}, \mathbf{b}) = (1)(-1) + (0)(0) = -1$. The power of the inner product is reflected by choosing $\mathbf{a} = (3,6,7)$ and $\mathbf{b} = (2,-1,0)$. It is not obvious that $\mathbf{a}$ and $\mathbf{b}$ are orthogonal; yet, the simple computation $(\mathbf{a}, \mathbf{b}) = (3)(2) + (6)(-1) + (7)(0) = 0$ proves that they are.

4.2.2 Positively Involved

A candidate works the precincts to get out the vote because, "clearly," her chances improve with added supporters. Stated in another way, a voter joins a group with the expectation that his sincere vote will advance, not hinder his beliefs. If by voting, a voter's ballot changes the group decision from an acceptable outcome (had he abstained) to one that is personally worse, then we must severely question the legitimacy of the procedure! Yet, such procedures are commonly used. When such a method is used, one can imagine situations where a voter is overjoyed with his good fortune – his car got a flat tire on a busy street during a heavy rainstorm; consequently, he couldn't vote!

Definition 4.2.1. A procedure is called *positively involved* if when c_j is the selected outcome for a profile and when a group of new voters, all with the same voter type with c_j top-ranked, join the group, then c_j remains the selected candidate. □

Upon reflection, we must anticipate that there are procedures where a person's vote can be counter-productive. After all, a similar troubling election phenomenon occurs when a procedure is not weakly consistent. Here, each of two groups reach the same conclusion, but their joint outcome is something different. Now, if one of these groups consists of voters of the same type, then positive involvement is violated. Consequently, all procedures failing weak consistency must be placed on the suspect list as potential positive involvement violators.

Example 4.2.1. An agenda fails to be weakly consistent, and, as shown next, *an agenda is not positively involved.* In fact, the same L geometry causing the weak consistency problems forces an agenda to fail positive involvement. Thus, the proof requires explaining how the L nonconvexity allows q_1 to be an unanimity outcome.

Assume, as in Sect. 4.1, that the agenda is $< c_1, c_2, c_3 >$. As shown in Fig. 4.2.1, one of the L legs forcing the nonconvexity of $\mathcal{A}(c_3)$ contains $F_3(\mathbf{E}_4)$, the unanimity outcome for the ranking $c_3 \succ c_2 \succ c_1$. Let $q_1 = F_3(\mathbf{E}_4)$ and choose q_2 in the other L leg so that the line connecting q_1 and q_2 passes through the c_2-Condorcet region. (For instance, choose q_2 close to the $x = 0$ coordinate plane separating the positive cyclic region and the c_2-Condorcet region.) The portion of the line in the c_2-Condorcet region defines a rich selection of λ values (indicating how many type-four voter have been persuaded to vote) requiring q_λ to be in the c_2-Condorcet region. So, by staying home to watch TV instead of voting, these type-four voters would have been rewarded with the election of their top-choice c_3; by being good citizens and voting, their punishment is the selection of a lesser good: c_2.

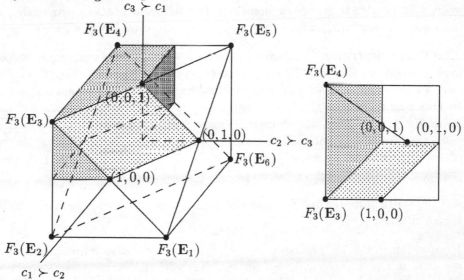

Fig. 4.2.1. Lack of positive involvement for $< c_1, c_2, c_3 >$

How bad can it be? How many, or how few type-four voters are needed to create examples? The answer, again, comes from the L geometry.

First, I show that only one type-four voter is needed. According to the geometry, a lower bound for λ requires q_2 to be as close to the c_2-Condorcet region as possible (so that small λ values force $q_\lambda \in \mathcal{A}(c_2)$). To locate q_2, start with $\mathbf{q}$ on the $x = 0$ coordinate plane where the positive cyclic region is separated from the c_2-Condorcet region. The rankings associated with $\mathbf{q}$ are $c_1 \sim c_2, c_2 \succ c_3, c_3 \succ c_1$.

A profile supporting $\mathbf{q}$ creates headaches for the agenda with its tie vote on the very first pairwise election. This conflict could be resolved with a tie-breaker. If the tie-breaker chooses c_1 for $\mathbf{q}$ (or for a profile supporting $\mathbf{q}^5$), then c_1 is advanced to the next election. But, in this second election, c_1 loses to c_3. Consequently, with the tie breaker, either $\mathbf{q} \in \mathcal{A}(c_3)$ or a profile defining $\mathbf{q}$ leads to the selection of c_3. By choosing $\mathbf{q}_2 = \mathbf{q}$, any $\lambda > 0$ - even a λ value corresponding a single voter - suffices to establish the conclusion.

If the tie-breaker for $\mathbf{q}$ favors c_2, then, in the second election, c_2 beats c_3; thus $\mathbf{q} \in \mathcal{A}(c_2)$. To allow a single type-four voter to change the election outcome, just go one voter "deeper" into $\mathcal{A}(c_3)$. Namely, choose an integer profile $\mathbf{p}$ with at least one type-four voter that supports $\mathbf{q}$. (Recall from the profile coordinate representations that large sets of such profiles exist.) Let $\mathbf{p}'$ be the integer profile obtained by taking away one of the type-four voters from $\mathbf{p}$, and let $\mathbf{q}_2 = F_3(\mathbf{p}')$. (So, if $\mathbf{p}$ requires n voters, then $\mathbf{q}_2$ is defined by the equation $\mathbf{q} = \frac{n-1}{n}\mathbf{q}_2 + \frac{1}{n}\mathbf{q}_1$.) By construction, $F_3(\mathbf{p}') = \mathbf{q}_2$ is an outcome where, by adding the single type-four voter back to the profile (which returns us to $\mathbf{p}$), the outcome shifts from c_1 to c_2. This is the single type-four voter that breaks c_1's back.

So, with an agenda that incorporates tie breakers, it is easy to create examples where a *single voter can, unintentionally, act against his own best interests by voting*. If we wish to ignore tie breakers, then the same analysis proves that there are many choices of $\mathbf{q}_2$ where only two type-four voters suffice for an example.

The Other Extreme. The other λ extreme concerns the maximum number of type-four voters that can be added to the system without forcing the outcome back to c_1. Again, the answer comes from the geometry; this bound is determined by choosing $\mathbf{q}_2$ so that the longest possible portion of the $\mathbf{q}_1$ - $\mathbf{q}_2$ connecting line is in $\mathcal{A}(c_2)$. The geometric construction is obvious; start with $\mathbf{q} = (0, 1, 0)$ and use an argument similar to the above to find $\mathbf{q}_2$. Then, by examining the values of λ that keep the y component of $\mathbf{q}_\lambda = \lambda(-1, -1, 1) + (1 - \lambda)(0, 1, 0)$ positive (so $\mathbf{q}_\lambda \in \mathcal{A}(c_2)$), the upper bound of $\lambda = \frac{1}{2}$ is found. $\square$

An Agenda Theorem. Some of the points from the example are collected in the next statement.

Proposition 4.2.1. *The agenda $< c_1, c_2, c_3 >$ is positively involved for c_1 and c_2; it is not positively involved for c_3. Namely, there exist profiles where the group outcome is c_3, and, if joined by a new group of voters who are all of the same voter type with c_3 top-ranked, then the outcome no longer is c_3. If tie breakers for pairwise elections are involved, the number of voters in this new group can be anywhere from one, to one fewer than the number of the original*

---

[5] Recall, the tie breaking scheme may depend on the vote totals rather than the ranking. If so, we must examine the set of supporting profiles.

group. If there are more voters in the new group than in the original group, then the outcome must be c_3.

Much of what we have learned from the agenda discussion extends to other procedures. In particular, *should a procedure with tie breakers fail to be positively involved, then there exist examples where only a single voter of a particular voter type exhibits the lack of positive involvement.* On the other hand, finding upper bounds on the number of voters is a more subtle computation because it depends upon the geometry of the regions $\mathcal{A}(c_j)$ defined by the procedure.

Sly Manipulators. Just think of the opportunities – and dangers – offered by a procedure that fails to be positively involved. It allows a person to pretend to be "one of the boys" while working against their interests. To see this, call a procedure *slyly manipulable* if a voter can manipulate the system to his true choice of c_2 by *voting as though* he is supporting the group's choice of c_1. Here, the manipulating voter can summon all possible self-righteousness, even announcing and openly marking his ballot for the group's choice of c_1, safe in the knowledge that his actions have sabotaged c_1's chances to the advantage of c_2. The above results prove that *a procedure that is not positively involved can be slyly manipulated!*

Weak Consistency Versus Positive Involvement. It is tempting to conjecture that all procedures failing to be weakly consistent also fail to be positively involved. This is false; this assertion follows by constructing a procedure where a unanimity outcome can not be used to exploit the nonconvexities. For instance, suppose a procedure selects a Condorcet winner when one exists, otherwise the outcome is $\{c_1, c_2, c_3\}$. Because the union of the two cyclic regions is not a convex set, this procedure fails to be weakly consistent. However, the regions defining the nonconvexity have no unanimity outcomes. Consequently, positive involvement is satisfied by default.

As this example demonstrates, because positive involvement is more selective about what new outcomes q_1 are admitted, there are positively involved procedures that are not weakly consistent. Upon reflection, this makes sense. Positive involvement requires the outcome to remain the same when selective types of new voters are added. On the other hand, with its more liberal admissions policy, weak consistency must accommodate not only these selective types of new voters, but also new voters of more general types. Thus, it is more difficult for a procedure to satisfy weak consistency. Consequently, we reach the conclusion of Proposition 4.2.2. First, we use a useful definition introduced by P. Young [Y2].

Definition 4.2.2. A procedure is *faithful* if for an unanimity profile, the top-ranked candidate is chosen. $\square$

The role played by faithfulness is that it requires the unanimity profiles with c_j top-ranked to be in $\mathcal{A}(c_j)$. Once we know where the unanimity profiles are, the following statement follows immediately.

Proposition 4.2.2. *A faithful, weakly consistent scoring based procedure is positively involved, but a faithful, positively involved scoring based procedure need not be weakly consistent.*

Instead of proving the proposition, I offer the following more general comments which underscore the essential geometric differences between weak consistency and positive involvement. Recall, the convexity of weak consistency requires all points on the profile line connecting *any* two supporting profiles to support the same outcome. Positive involvement has the same line segment condition, but one of the endpoints is a unanimity profile. Thus, the stricter convexity requirements of weak consistency are replaced with a "starlike" convexity which requires only that lines starting from a unanimity profile can't leave a region and then re-enter. The significant difference between the two requirements has a "L" demonstration; even though the "L" destroys convexity, it is a starlike region with respect to the vertex joining the two "L" legs.

Guided by the light of "starlike convexity," it becomes easy to decide whether a procedure is positively involved. For instance, if an outside surface of the $\mathcal{A}(c_j)$ region "faces" an unanimity outcome with c_j top-ranked, then a connecting line from this boundary to the unanimity outcome lies, in part, outside of $\mathcal{A}(c_j)$. This is illustrated with the following example.

Example 4.2.2. Black's method is not weakly consistent, but it is positively involved. The explanation follows from the positioning of the L in Fig. 4.1.7-8. In a representation cube, the two unanimity outcomes with c_1 top-ranked are $(1, \pm 1, -1)$. Neither of these points is in a position to exploit the L nonconvexity of the region.

Choosing "the average person" by selecting the $\mathbf{w}_s$ second-ranked candidate is not weakly consistent. The non-convexity is created because this region is the union of two ranking regions that are opposite each other in the representation triangle. For instance, if c_1 is middle-ranked, then this is the union of the type-three and six regions. A "unanimity outcome" having c_1 middle-ranked would be either $[\mathbf{w}_s]_3$ or $[\mathbf{w}_s]_j$. This region is not starlike with respect to these two unanimity outcomes; there are plenty of lines starting from each point that leave the region only to re-enter again. Thus, this method is *not* positively involved.
□

4.2.3 Monotonicity

Positive involvement allows only voters of one type to be added. To be more flexible, how about adding voters subject only to the restriction that each of them provides added support for the winning candidate? (To keep the same candidate elected, the region must be "starlike" with respect to any profile in the hull defined by the appropriate unanimity profiles.) As a different scenario, let the group of voters remain the same, but suppose that during the campaign some voters gain respect for the winning candidate. Can added support be too much of a good thing because it causes her to lose? If so, imagine the anomalistic situation of a candidate campaigning for her opponent because the extra support will hurt her!

These two situations – one involves new voters joining the group and the second involves voters changing their minds – are different, yet a slight modification of the geometry allows them to be analyzed together. This is because both cases involve a comparison of election outcomes for two different profiles. As the election outcomes depend on what fraction of all voters are of each type, rather than the exact integer profiles, the only difference in analyzing the two responsiveness issues is the type of restrictions imposed upon q_1 relative to the positioning of q_2.

While all responsiveness questions can be analyzed with an appropriate "starlike" geometry, I will introduce a new approach. Following the starlike analysis, choose q_2 and *the possible directions of the connecting line*. The goal is to determine whether the admissible directions admit any adverse positionings of the endpoint q_1

Definition 4.2.3. A choice procedure is *monotonic* if when c_j is chosen with profile $\mathbf{p}$, and when the only voters to change their preferences change them to give c_j a higher ranking (hence, preserving the original relative ranking of the other candidates), then c_j is elected with the new profile $\mathbf{p}'$. $\square$

Just imagine what can happen with a non-monotonic procedure. After the polls trumpet the inevitable election of c_1, a bandwagon effect sets in where previously reluctant voters, in an attempt to finally be on the winning side, now rank c_1 higher. With her added support, she loses!

Monotonicity restricts how voters can change their minds to rank c_1 higher; they are listed in the following table. In this table, each row indicates the current voter type, the column indicates a changed voter type. An "o" is where there is no change; an "x" is an admissible change according to the restrictions of monotonicity. For example, the "x" in the third row indicates that a type-three voter can change into a type-two voter to give c_1 a higher ranking. There is no entry under this row in the 1 column because changing a type-three voter to type-one alters the relative ranking of c_2 and c_3.

	1	2	3	4	5	6
1	o					
2		o				
3		x	o			
4		x	x	o		
5	x				o	x
6	x					o

$$(4.2.2)$$

When a $\mathbf{w}_s$ positional method is used, a geometric representation of the changes of Eq. 4.2.2 is as indicated by the arrows in Fig. 4.2.2a. For example, the two arrows from $[\mathbf{w}_s]_4$ indicate that a type-four voter could change to become type-two or three. (Compare this with Table 4.2.2.) By changing voter type, he would cast either the ballot $[\mathbf{w}_s]_2$ or $[\mathbf{w}_s]_3$.

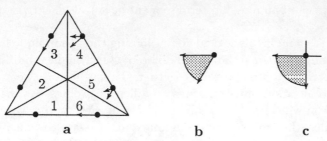

$$\underset{a}{} \qquad \underset{b}{} \qquad \underset{c}{}$$

Fig. 4.2.2. Profile changes admitted with monotonicity

To further refine the geometry of Fig. 4.2.2a, consider how a $\mathbf{w}_s$ outcome can change after monotonic changes in preferences that favor c_1. From any base outcome $\mathbf{q}_2$, the direction lines of monotonic changes from $\mathbf{q}_2$ is given by the "b-cone;" this cone (Fig. 4.2.2b) contains all admissible changes in $[\mathbf{w}_s]$ votes allowed by Fig. 4.2.2a. The boundaries of the b-cone are independent of the choice of $\mathbf{w}_s$. Indeed, one cone edge is horizontal (corresponding to the voter type changes $4 \rightarrow 3$, $6 \rightarrow 1$) and pointing to the left while the other edge points downwards and to the left at $60°$ (caused by changes of voter types $5 \rightarrow 6$, $3 \rightarrow 2$). By taking various combinations, any directional change in the cone is possible.

For the pairwise rankings, the possible directions of change in the representation cube are indicated the "c-cone" represented in Fig. 4.2.2c. There is no possible change in the y direction (because the relative rankings of c_2 and c_3 are held fixed). The changes along the x axis correspond to where *only* c_1 and c_2 are interchanged (changes in types $4 \rightarrow 3$, $6 \rightarrow 1$) while changes downward along the vertical axis require only c_1 and c_3 to be interchanged ($3 \rightarrow 2$, $5 \rightarrow 6$).

What Is Monotonic? From the figure and the cones of admissible directions[6] for the connecting line, it is easy to use the geometry of the $\mathcal{A}(c_j)$ regions to determine which procedures are, and are not, monotonic. For those procedures failing monotonicity, the geometry can be used to characterize the profiles that force this unfortunate change in the outcome. In this manner, it is easy to generate examples.

Example 4.2.3. To illustrate the geometry, start with the procedure that selects the $\mathbf{w}_s$ top-ranked candidate where, by neutrality, I assume she is c_1. The region

$$\mathcal{A}(c_1) = [\mathcal{R}(1) \cup \mathcal{R}(7) \cup \mathcal{R}(2)] \cap \mathcal{CH}(\mathbf{w}_s)$$

are the three regions sharing the c_1 vertex. This is the shaded region of Fig. 4.2.3a to the left of the vertical boundary line ($\mathcal{R}(12)$) and below the upward slanting boundary line ($\mathcal{R}(8)$). It is obvious that if $\mathbf{q}_2 \in \mathcal{A}(c_1)$, then the b-cone of admissible monotonicity changes also is in this region. (The dark region is one such cone.) This procedure is monotonic.

---

[6] For the reader who knows the terms, observe that this process of specifying a line emanating from a point and then analyzing the changes in the procedure, corresponds to the "directional derivatives" of the procedure.

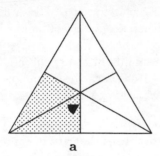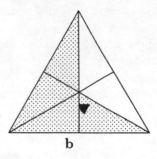

a   b

Fig. 4.2.3. Responsiveness of the cone

Now consider the procedure that selects the two top-ranked candidates from a $\mathbf{w}_s$ election. Again, this procedure is monotonic. For example, if c_1 is one of the two top-ranked candidates and the target for an analysis of monotonicity, then we are interested in the geometry of the region encompassed by $\mathcal{R}(1) \cup \mathcal{R}(2) \cup \mathcal{R}(3) \cup \mathcal{R}(6)$ (and the obvious indifference regions) which is the shaded region of Fig. 4.2.3b. The boundary of this region is a vertical line ($\mathcal{R}(9)$) and a line sloping downward and to the right ($\mathcal{R}(11)$), so it follows that starting from a base point in this region, the b-cone also remains in this region.

Next, consider the agenda $< c_1, c_2, c_3 >$; a procedure that has failed all of the other responsiveness criteria. To see that monotonicity is preserved, at least for c_1 and c_2, recall that $\mathcal{A}(c_1)$ is the c_1-Condorcet region consisting of the region $z < 0$, $x > 0$. Starting from any point in this region, it is clear that a "c - cone" (a sector of the type given by Fig. 4.2.2c) must also be in this region. A similar argument holds for c_2.

If monotonicity difficulties are to plague $< c_1, c_2, c_3 >$, they must be caused by the cyclic regions (in $\mathcal{A}(c_3)$). (The reader is encouraged to examine Fig. 4.1.3.) The monotonicity cone of directions admissible for c_3 requires the x value to remain fixed (reflecting the requirement that the relative rankings of c_1 and c_2 are held fixed) while $z \geq 0$, $y \leq 0$. Starting from any point in the c_3-Condorcet region ($z > 0$, $y < 0$), the c-cone only enhances c_3's victory. In the positive cyclic region ($x > 0, y > 0, z > 0$), changes admitted by the cone have no effect on the x value; they improve upon (or leave untouched) the z values, but they can decrease the y values. However, smaller y values push the outcome into a c_3-Condorcet region. A similar argument holds for the negative cyclic region. Consequently, *an agenda is monotonic.* $\square$

As shown, the geometric argument supporting the monotonicity of a procedure is easy to use. To further illustrate this approach, I use it to show that Black's method, and all of the obvious $\mathbf{w}_s$ modifications, are monotonic.

Definition 4.2.4. The $\mathbf{w}_s$-*Black's method* is where c_j is declared the winner if she is a Condorcet winner. Otherwise, the top-ranked candidate from a $\mathbf{w}_s$ election is selected. $\square$

This "either/or" aspect is what preserves monotonicity. To start, suppose $\mathbf{p}$

requires the selection of c_1. If she wins because she is a Condorcet winner, then any c-cone change provides a more imposing victory. If $\mathbf{p}$ is in a cyclic region, then, as shown above, a c-cone change either keeps the outcome in the same cyclic region, or it forces the outcome toward the c_1-Condorcet region where c_1 has a guaranteed victory. If the outcome remains in the cyclic region, then we need to consider the impact of the b-cone. However, these changes just add to c_1's $\mathbf{w}_s$ victory margin. Consequently, *all $\mathbf{w}_s$- Black's methods are monotonic.*

What Isn't Monotonic? It is easy to verify that a monotonic procedure is monotonic, and it is equally easy to find procedures that are not monotonic. All we need is to find a procedure where combined movements of the types indicated in Fig. 4.2.2b and c lead to c_1's defeat. An obvious choice is a $\mathbf{w}_s$ simple runoff.

For several profiles, a runoff is monotonic. For instance, if c_1 is the winner of a $\mathbf{w}_s$-runoff and if the profile defines a point in the c_1-Condorcet region, then any admissible monotonic change still selects c_1. This is because the b-cone keeps c_1 as one of the two top-ranked candidate and the c-cone forces the pairwise outcome deeper into the c_1-Condorcet region. Similarly, if $\mathbf{q}_2$ is positioned so that the cone of admissible changes allows the same two candidates to be top-ranked, then c_1 will remain the winner. (The $\mathbf{w}_s$ change of a b-cone advances the same two candidates to the runoff; the c-cone pairwise change improves c_1's standing.)

What remains is if the original outcome $\mathbf{q}_2$ is such that:

a. $\mathbf{q}_1$ and $\mathbf{q}_2$ have different candidates top-ranked.

b. The pairwise outcome is cyclic for both profiles.

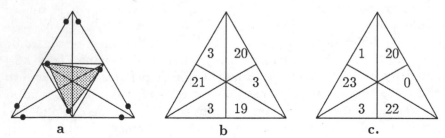

Fig. 4.2.4. Monotonicity and runoffs. **a.** Negative cycles.
b. An example. **c.** A position line example

These two conditions can be satisfied simultaneously. For instance, in Fig. 4.2.4a, the shaded region are those $\mathbf{w}_s$ outcomes which can be accompanied with a negative cycle. (The profile vertices for the negative cycles are $\frac{1}{2}(\mathbf{E}_i + \mathbf{E}_j)$ where i and j are even. Each vertex of the shaded region, the midpoint between $[\mathbf{w}_s]_i$, $[\mathbf{w}_s]_j$ where i and j are even integers, is the $\mathbf{w}_s$ image of one of these profile vertices.) So, choosing a profile for such a $\mathbf{q}_2$ outcome in $\mathcal{R}(2)$ means that c_1 and c_3 are advanced to the runoff. In the runoff, the negative cycle anoints c_1 as the winner.

The key to the geometry is that the $c_2 \sim c_3$ indifference line $\mathcal{R}(7)$ forms a $30°$ angle while the bottom edge of the b-cone forms a $60°$ angle – it is this difference in angles that begs to be exploited. Namely, to show that monotonicity is violated, exploit the geometry promising that if $q_2 \in \mathcal{R}(2)$ is sufficiently close to $\mathcal{I}$ and the $c_2 \sim c_3$ indifference line, then the b-cone enters $\mathcal{R}(1)$. With $q_1 \in \mathcal{R}(1)$, the runoff is between c_1 and c_2 where the negative cycle favors c_2. In other words, the additional support c_1 receives will sabotage her winning position!

Example 4.2.4. Armed with the geometric description, it now is an exercise to construct illustrating examples; I will describe the creation of the one illustrated in Fig. 4.2.4b. We need a negative cycle for the pairs, so start with a profile that creates the most extreme negative cycle. This requires an equal division of the even voters, such as $(0, 19, 0, 19, 0, 19)$. The profile needs to be modified so that:

  a. A negative cycle is preserved.

  b. The plurality outcome is in $\mathcal{R}(2)$.

To change the plurality outcome, add voters with the appropriate voter types obtaining, say, $(0, 21, 0, 20, 0, 19)$.

To defy monotonicity, we need to exploit the $60°$ slope of the b-cone. According to Table 4.2.2 or Fig. 4.2.2a, this slope is defined by changes in voter types from $3 \to 2$ and/or $5 \to 6$. However, before these voters can change their types, we need some of them. So, add a small number of odd voters equally distributed among the three types obtaining, for instance, the profile of Fig. 4.2.4b; $\mathbf{p} = (3, 21, 3, 20, 3, 19)$, with the plurality outcome $c_1 \succ c_3 \succ c_2$.

If only two type-three votes from $\mathbf{p}$ convert to type-two's, then the "c_1 improved profile" is $\mathbf{p}_1 = (3, 23, 1, 20, 3, 19)$. Clearly $\mathbf{p}_1$ preserves the negative cycle and defines the plurality outcome $c_1 \succ c_2 \succ c_3$. As c_2 wins the runoff, monotonicity is violated. $\square$

In Example 4.2.4, I used a voter change of the $3 \to 2$ kind because a change in $\mathbf{p}$ involving only voter types moving from $5 \to 6$ has no impact upon the outcome. This is because $[\mathbf{w}_0]_5 = [\mathbf{w}_0]_6$. Similarly, a voter type change $3 \to 2$ doesn't affect a $\mathbf{w}_{\frac{1}{2}}$ antiplurality outcome, whereas a voter change from $5 \to 6$ does attain influence with $\mathbf{w}_{\frac{1}{2}}$. The effect of a voter change, then, depends on who changes types and which $\mathbf{w}_s$ is being used. Thus, if $\delta_{i,j}$ represents the amount of votes changing from type-j to type-i, the impact upon the $\mathbf{w}_s$ election outcome is

$$\delta_{i,j}[[\mathbf{w}_s]_j - [\mathbf{w}_s]_i]. \tag{4.2.3}$$

The above comments show that to change a plurality outcome of $\mathbf{p}$, it is advantageous to use a type change $3 \to 2$; to change the antiplurality outcome, $5 \to 6$ type changes are needed. *By using both changes and the procedure line, we can create examples where monotonicity fails for all $\mathbf{w}_s$-runoffs.* To do so, observe that the above profile $\mathbf{p}$ defines the plurality outcome $c_1 \succ c_3 \succ c_2$ while the antiplurality outcome is $c_3 \succ c_1 \succ c_2$. Thus, the $\mathbf{p}$ procedure line has c_1 and c_3 as the two top-ranked candidates. Now, let two type-3 voters become type-2 and three type-5 voters become type-6; this defines the profile $\mathbf{p}_2$ represented in Fig. 4.2.4c. A simple computation proves that the negative cycle is preserved with $\mathbf{p}_2$ and that the $\mathbf{p}_2$ procedure line is in the $c_1 \succ c_2 \succ c_3$ ranking region.

Thus *changing from* $\mathbf{p}$ *to* $\mathbf{p}_2$ *displays the simultaneous lack of monotonicity for all possible* $\mathbf{w}_s$-*runoffs.*

4.2.4 A General Theorem Using Profiles

The responsiveness discussion of positive effectiveness and monotonicity emphasizes the geometry of the representation triangle and cube. The real issue, however, concerns changes in profiles. Here, the natural setting is the space of normalized profiles $Si(6)$. There is a cost; when these issues are considered in the five-dimensional space of profiles, $Si(6)$, we lose natural geometric insight. What we gain are techniques that extend to any number of candidates. Moreover, even for three candidates, the technical proofs are simpler.

The idea is to start with a base profile, $\mathbf{p}_2 \in f^{-1}(\mathcal{A}(c_j))$, in the profile set supporting the selection of c_j. A specified responsiveness property is violated if an admissible profile, $\mathbf{p}_1$, is such that $\mathbf{p}_2 + \mathbf{p}_1 \notin f^{-1}(\mathcal{A}(c_j))$. For this to occur, the direction of change must pass through the boundary of $f^{-1}(\mathcal{A}(c_j))$. Therefore, by understanding what admissible directions pass through the boundary, we can determine whether a specified responsiveness property is preserved.

What simplifies the analysis is that the boundaries of $f^{-1}(\mathcal{A}(c_j))$ typically are expressed as linear equations set equal to zero. So, the coefficients of the boundary equation define a normal vector (that is, an orthogonal, or perpendicular vector) to the boundary surface. To see why this is so, observe from the definition of the scalar product that the equation $\sum a_j p_j = 0$ can be reexpressed as $(\mathbf{a}, \mathbf{p}) = 0$ where $\mathbf{a} = (a_1, \ldots, a_6)$. As the scalar product is zero, it follows from Eq. 4.2.1 that the vectors $\mathbf{a}$ and $\mathbf{p}$ are orthogonal.

If $\mathbf{a}$ is perpendicular to the boundary, then so is $-\mathbf{a}$. One of these vectors points to the inside of the $\mathcal{A}(c_j)$ region; this vector is called an *inner normal vector*. By virtue of pointing toward the interior of $\mathcal{A}(c_j)$, the inner normal indicates the direction of profile changes that assist, rather than hurt, the selection of c_j. Consequently, if all admissible directions for changes in profiles are in the same general direction as the inner normal, we cannot expect a profile change starting near this boundary to be detrimental to c_j's chances of being selected.

On the other hand, an admissible direction forming an angle of more than 90° with the inner normal crosses the boundary should the base point be sufficiently near the boundary. What we have, then, is that

> *the dot product between the inner normal and the admissible directions of changes in profiles forms a powerful tool for the analysis of responsiveness concerns; a tool that is technically easy to use.*

Namely, if the dot product between the inner normal and some admissible direction is negative (indicating a movement in the choice of profiles away from the interior of $\mathcal{A}(c_j)$), then examples can be constructed to violate the responsiveness concept.

Example 4.2.5. To illustrate the dot product technique, first consider positive responsiveness. If c_1 is the winner for a procedure, then there are only two admissible directional changes for a profile; $(1,0,0,0,0,0)$[7] or $(0,1,0,0,0,0)$. These vectors are not profiles; they indicate directional changes in profiles. As such, $(1,0,0,0,0,0) \neq \mathbf{E}_1$. Nevertheless, with an abuse of notation, identify $(1,0,0,0,0,0)$ with $\mathbf{E}_1$ and $(0,1,0,0,0,0)$ with $\mathbf{E}_2$. Similarly, the profile directions for c_2 and c_3 are indicated, respectively, as $\mathbf{E}_5$ or $\mathbf{E}_6$ and as $\mathbf{E}_3$ or $\mathbf{E}_4$.

For the agenda $< c_1, c_2, c_3 >$, one of the boundaries for $\mathcal{A}(c_1)$ is the $x = 0$ coordinate plane (or $c_1 \sim c_2$ region). Any profile defining this boundary outcome satisfies the equation

$$p_1 + p_2 + p_3 - p_4 - p_5 - p_6 = 0,$$

and its coefficients define the inner normal vector $\mathbf{N}_{1,2} = (1,1,1,-1,-1,-1)$. (To see that this is an "inner" normal vector, notice that the positive components identify the voter types where more of them will help c_1 defeat c_2.) Because $(\mathbf{N}_{1,2}, \mathbf{E}_1) = (\mathbf{N}_{1,2}, \mathbf{E}_2) = 1 > 0$, all admissible unanimity changes in profiles move in the general direction of the inner normal – toward the interior of the region electing c_1. This supports the notion of positive involvement. Similar simple computations hold for the other boundary.

Next consider the fate of c_3. Any profile leading to a cyclic outcome crowns c_3 as the winner. Boundaries for both cyclic regions include profiles where $c_1 \sim c_2$. Thus, $\mathbf{N}_{1,2}$ must be a normal vector for this portion of the boundary. In fact, using the same argument as above, $\mathbf{N}_{1,2}$ is an inner normal for the positive cyclic region because this region has the ranking $c_1 \succ c_2$. (Again, the positive components determine the voter types where more of them help improve the outcome.)

The two unanimity profiles for c_3 are $\mathbf{E}_3$ and $\mathbf{E}_4$. Even though $(\mathbf{N}_{1,2}, \mathbf{E}_3) = 1 > 0$, we have that $(\mathbf{N}_{1,2}, \mathbf{E}_4) = -1 < 0$. This means that by choosing the original profile close to this boundary and then adding type-four voters to the original profile, the outcome will cross the boundary and c_3 will be defeated. Indeed, this is the earlier constructed example.

For the negative cyclic region, the inward normal vector for the boundary is $-\mathbf{N}_{1,2}$. This change in direction of $\mathbf{N}$ reflects the requirement that the cycle must feature $c_2 \succ c_1$, so the inward direction needs to favor c_2. With this change in sign, $(-\mathbf{N}_{1,2}, \mathbf{E}_3) = -1 < 0$. It now follows that positive involvement can be violated by starting with a profile sufficiently near this boundary and adding type-three voters. What we have, then, is that *analyzing positive involvement for a procedure reduces to checking the signs of certain components of the inner normal vectors!* $\square$

Theorem 4.2.3. *A sufficient condition for a procedure to be positively involved is if the scalar product of all the inner normals for the boundaries of $f^{-1}(\mathcal{A}(c_j))$*

---

[7]More accurately, the sum of the components of a directional change in $Si(6)$ must add to zero because the sum of the components of the defining difference $\mathbf{p}_1 - \mathbf{p}_2$ do. Therefore, a more accurate choice is $(\frac{5}{6}, -\frac{1}{6}, -\frac{1}{6}, \dots, -\frac{1}{6})$. As it is easy to prove, however, nothing is changed in the results by using the simpler choice given above. See the exercises.

form a positive scalar product with the two unanimity profiles having c_j top-ranked. A sufficient condition for a procedure to violate positive involvement is if one of these scalar products is negative.

Example 4.2.6. With this theorem, it now becomes much easier to show that a $\mathbf{w}_s$-runoff is not positively involved. To do so with c_1, all we need show is that the inner normal vector for some boundary has a negative value for either the first or second component. The boundary dividing whether c_2 or c_3 is advanced to the runoff is a portion of the plane of profiles where the c_2, c_3 relative ranking is $c_2 \sim c_3$. This set of profiles is given by the equation $[p_1 s + p_4 s + p_5(1 - s) + p_6(1 - s)] - [p_2 s + p_3(1 - s) + p_4(1 - s) + p_5 s] = 0$. After collecting terms, the normal vector is

$$\mathbf{S}_{2,3} = (s, -s, s - 1, 2s - 1, 1 - 2s, 1 - s). \qquad (4.2.4)$$

Whether $\mathbf{S}_{2,3}$ or $-\mathbf{S}_{2,3}$ is the inner normal vector depends upon whether the pairs are in the positive or negative cyclic region. If the pairs define a positive cycle (so $c_1 \succ c_2$, $c_3 \succ c_1$), then it is to c_1's advantage to be in the runoff with c_2. Thus, $\mathbf{S}_{2,3}$ is the inward normal. As the second component is negative for $s \neq 0$, positive involvement can be violated by starting with a profile near this boundary and adding type-two voters. With a negative cycle, the inward normal becomes $-\mathbf{S}_{2,3}$ with its negative first component. Consequently, *with the sole exception of the plurality system, the violation of positive involvement of a runoff can be illustrated by using type-one voters.*

To handle the plurality system, we need to use the boundaries given by the $\mathbf{w}_s$ relative rankings $c_1 \sim c_2$ and $c_1 \sim c_3$ where c_1 is struggling to be one of the two top-ranked candidates. For example, $\mathbf{S}_{1,3} = (1 - 2s, 1 - s, s, -s, s - 1, 2s - 1)$, in the inward normal for the region with boundary $c_2 \succ c_1 \sim c_3$. As the first two components are positive, positive involvement cannot be violated. Indeed, by checking the remaining boundaries, it follows that *although the $\mathbf{w}_0$ simple runoff is not weakly consistent, it is positively involved. In fact, it is the only $\mathbf{w}_s$ simple runoff that is positively involved.* $\square$

To develop a similar analysis for monotonicity, we just need to list the admissible directions of profile changes. The directions associated with an "improvement" for c_1 can be read off from Table 4.2.1 or Fig. 4.2.2; they are linear combinations (with non-negative scalar multiples indicating how many voters change) of the vectors

$$\mathbf{d}_{3\to 2} = \mathbf{E}_2 - \mathbf{E}_3, \; \mathbf{d}_{4\to 2} = \mathbf{E}_2 - \mathbf{E}_4, \; \mathbf{d}_{4\to 3} = \mathbf{E}_3 - \mathbf{E}_4$$
$$\mathbf{d}_{6\to 1} = \mathbf{E}_1 - \mathbf{E}_6, \; \mathbf{d}_{5\to 1} = \mathbf{E}_1 - \mathbf{E}_5, \; \mathbf{d}_{5\to 6} = \mathbf{E}_6 - \mathbf{E}_5,$$

where $k\mathbf{d}_{i\to j}$ means that k voters of type-i, adhering to their firm evanescent standards, now count themselves as belonging among the type-j voters.

As an illustration, with the agenda $< c_2, c_3, c_1 >$, one of the inner normal vectors for profiles leading to the $y = 0$ (or $c_2 \sim c_3$) coordinate plane which is a boundary for the positive cyclic region is

$$\mathbf{N}_{2,3} = (1, -1, -1, -1, 1, 1, 1). \qquad (4.2.5)$$

However, the scalar product of $(\mathbf{N}_{2,3}, \mathbf{d}_{i \to j}) = 0$. Geometrically, this zero scalar product occurs because all changes of voter types keep the relative ranking of c_2, c_3 invariant. These are the only interesting boundaries, so we have reestablished the monotonicity of the agenda.

The scalar products changes with a runoff. Here, for example, a simple computation proves that $(\mathbf{S}_{2,3}, \mathbf{d}_{6 \to 1}) = 2s - 1 < 0$ if $s \neq \frac{1}{2}$). The vector $\mathbf{S}_{2,3}$ is an inner normal for regions with a positive cycle (because it points to the direction where c_2 is selected over c_3, and we need $c_1 \succ c_2$ in the runoff). It follows, therefore, that with the exception of the antiplurality runoff, examples are easy to design to show the lack of monotonicity for $\mathbf{w}_s$-runoffs just by using voter type changes $6 \to 1$. For an antiplurality example, the dot product shows a $4 \to 2$ change is needed. On the other hand, because $(\mathbf{S}_{2,3}, \mathbf{d}_{5 \to 1}) = 3s - 1 < 0$ if $s < \frac{1}{3}$, the voter type changes $5 \to 1$ can only be used to demonstrate this conclusion only with a limited number of $\mathbf{w}_s$-runoffs. The same kind of analysis extends to the $\mathbf{sc} - \mathbf{w}_s$ runoffs.

4.2.5 Other Admissible Directions

Responsiveness issues start with an election outcome, specify the admissible kinds of changes for the supporting profiles, and then examine whether desired goals for the new profiles are met. When stated in this more general manner, it becomes clear that the above topics just sample the kinds of questions and issues that can be raised. For example, we have not investigated what happens with ties; that is, when two candidates, $\{c_i, c_j\}$, are selected. One should expect that added support in favor of c_i would lead to her selection; but does it? This statement defines the starting configurations (profiles leading to tie votes), the directions of change (adding more support for c_i), and the goal (the selection of c_i). Using the above scalar product analysis, it is not overly difficult to characterize all procedures that do, and do not, satisfy these objectives.

Indeed, I suspect that with sufficient imagination, it is possible to start with almost any set of admissible directions that could be used to change a base profile, and then invent an interesting story to justify its importance for voting theory. For instance, we could modify positive involvement by using other choices of unanimity profiles. Instead of admitting unanimity profiles where c_1 is top-ranked, what about considering what happens if unanimity profiles are added where she is bottom ranked? Where she is middle-ranked? The immediate response should be "why! WGAD!" Actually, with only slight experimentation, a story can be fashioned to justify such an investigation.

To illustrate with a middle-ranked change, suppose c_1 would be elected with profile $\mathbf{p}$. Now, a type-three voter trying to decide whether to vote, is not overly pleased by this situation because c_1 is only his second-place candidate; yet, this outcome is preferable to c_2's selection. So, to show support for c_3, this voter votes; c_2 is selected!

This disturbing situation can occur with the $\mathbf{w}_s$-runoff. All we need is a setting where the pairwise votes are $c_1 \succ c_2$, $c_2 \succ c_3$. So, if the runoff is between c_1 and c_2, c_1 wins. But should the runoff be between c_2 and c_3, the feared c_2 is victorious. This means we need to investigate the boundary between selecting c_1 and c_3 for the runoff; the inner normal (favoring c_1) is

$$\mathbf{S}_{1,3} = (1 - s, 1 - 2s, 2s - 1, s - 1, -s, s).$$

As $(\mathbf{S}_{1,3}, \mathbf{E}_3) = 2s - 1 < 0$ for $s < \frac{1}{2}$, it is clear the above scenario can occur. All we need do is choose $\mathbf{p}$ sufficiently near this boundary with a positive cycle, and the behavior is ensured.[8] Even though the plurality runoff is positively involved, it can still cause middle-ranked involvement problems. But such problems must be expected from the runoff, the agenda, and other varied procedures; their many available boundaries in the profile space provides all sorts of opportunities for changes in profiles to have an unexpected effect!

As another example, consider what happens when only bottom-ranked unanimity profiles are added. Common sense dictates that adding these voters must hurt c_1's chances. To see that this need not be so, consider $\mathbf{S}_{2,3}$, one of the inner normals for the boundary of a $\mathbf{w}_s$-runoff when there is a positive cycle. The interesting fact is that $(\mathbf{S}_{2,3}, \mathbf{E}_5) = 1 - 2s > 0$ if the antiplurality procedure is not used. This positive value for the inner product means that by including a type-five voter, this act of voting can *assist* the election of his bottom-ranked candidate c_1! To create an example, instead of starting with a profile near this boundary leading to the election of c_1, choose a profile on the other side of the boundary where c_2 is elected. With such a base profile, if this type-five voter $(c_2 \succ c_3 \succ c_1)$ stays home on election day, the runoff will be between c_1 and c_3, and his second-ranked candidate, c_3 wins. Perhaps motivated to vote to avoid c_1 getting elected, or just being a good citizen, by casting his ballot our type-five voter's day is ruined with the selection of the candidate he despises, c_1.

Using the same type of analysis as above, examples are easy to create for a procedure where one of its inner normals for a region supporting the selection of c_j has a positive value for a component corresponding to a voter type with c_j bottom ranked. In this manner, the *negative involvement* of procedures can be characterized.

In fact, one of the underlying themes of this section is that with three (or more) candidates, there is a wide variance in the orientations of the boundary regions of profiles for reasonable procedures. This is particularly true for procedures that involve rankings of candidates from different subsets of candidates. The extra boundaries facing different directions makes a difference in the number and kind of inner normal vectors that are admitted. In turn, this makes it difficult for the procedure to satisfy responsiveness properties. The above discussion concerns positional voting and the linear boundaries between profile sets. If non-linear procedures are used with curved surfaces separating profile sets, then a richer set of inner normals arise. The cost which accompanies this rich supply of directions is that it becomes even more difficult to satisfy responsiveness!

---

[8] This "middle-ranked involvement" seems to include the "abstention" paradox which seems to have been discovered by Smith [Sm], significantly advanced for the plurality runoff by Brams and Fishburn [BF3], and then described in more general settings by Saari [S9].

A Simple Analysis. From the above inner normal vector argument, it is obvious that the more admissible directions of change that are admitted, the more difficult it is to find procedure to satisfy a specified goal. For instance, for a procedure to be positively involved for c_1, no inward normal for $f^{-1}(\mathcal{A}(c_1))$ can have a negative first or second component. For monotonicity, these two conditions are supplemented with a larger list of other restrictions. For instance, to ensure that the direction $\mathbf{E}_2 - \mathbf{E}_3$ does not suffice, the second component of an inward normal must be at least as large as the third component; the admissible directions of change, $\mathbf{E}_1 - \mathbf{E}_5$, $\mathbf{E}_1 - \mathbf{E}_6$ require the first component of all inward normals to be at least as large as the fifth and the sixth; etc.

This geometry reduces the responsiveness analysis to a simple game. To illustrate, suppose an hypothetical procedure has $(1, 2, 3, -1.4, -3.2, -1.4)$ as an inward normal for $f^{-1}(\mathcal{A}(c_1))$.

- The first two components are positive, so, at least with respect to this inner normal, the hypothetical procedure is positively involved for c_1.

- If the profile is on the boundary between c_1 and c_3, then the procedure is not positively involved for c_3. (The third component is positive, so a type-three voter improves c_1's chances.)

- Because the third coefficient is larger than the second, this procedure is not monotonic.

- The third coefficient is larger than the first, so this procedure would not survive a responsiveness issue allowing a $3 \to 1$ voter type change. As this is a change from $c_3 \succ c_1 \succ c_2$ to $c_1 \succ c_2 \succ c_3$, it does not fall under the category of monotonicity (because the c_2, c_3 ranking is changed). However, $3 \to 1$ change does provide c_1 with added support, so all we need do is to invent a responsiveness issue that admits a $3 \to 1$ type change. For instance, if we allow type changes from where c_1 is middle-ranked to where c_1 is top-ranked, we are in business.

- Because the first three components are larger than the last three in sign, but not in magnitude, we don't want to encourage any voter type change from the first three voter types to the last three. However if this boundary is between c_1 and c_3, then a type-3 voter would be inspired to pretend to be a type-4 because the change $\mathbf{E}_4 - \mathbf{E}_3$ would ensure a c_3 victory. On the other hand, if the boundary is between c_1 and c_2, then, if a type-six voter acts like type-five, c_2 becomes the victor.

The point is made; with a given inner normal, all sorts of scenarios considering responsiveness issues can be invented. There is a second point; this discussion illustrates why so many responsiveness problem occur for procedures that use the rankings from different subsets of candidates. Each set of candidates defines its own set of boundaries, so with several subsets, there are more boundaries. More boundaries yield more choices of inner normals. More kinds of inner normals provide more opportunities for something to go wrong with respect to certain responsiveness issues.

4.2.6 Gibbard-Satterthwaite and Manipulable Procedures

If we can examine a given inner normal for $f^{-1}(\mathcal{A}(c_j))$ to decide what responsiveness issues will and will not be satisfied, then maybe we can go the other direction. Maybe we can start with a specified responsiveness issue and then design a procedure that satisfies it. This requires the chosen responsiveness issue to restrict the choices of the inner normals. I will do this for the responsiveness issue of sincere voting.

Definition 4.2.5. A choice procedure is called *strategy proof* if there do not exist situations where a voter cannot obtain a more preferred outcome by voting as though his voter type is different than his actual voter type. □

The problem is to determine whether there exists a strategy proof procedure. This issue has been resolved in a general setting by Gibbard [Gi] and Satterthwaite [Sa], where, essentially, they proved the stunning conclusion that if at least three choices can be chosen, then either the procedure is dictatorial, or it is not strategy proof – it can be manipulated. Consider the same question here, but in terms of the responsiveness issue and "linear" and "smooth" procedures. First, assume that the choice procedure selects only a single candidate.

The idea of the proof is simple; by emphasizing how to design a strategy-proof mechanism the basic problems are isolated. For instance, if a voter pretends to be of a different type, he changes the sincere profile to a manipulated one. So, to ensure that the change is not to the voter's advantage, we admit only those inner normals where the manipulative change is not beneficial; this seriously restricts the admissible inner normals. Central to the analysis is the observation that with three or more candidates the space of profiles must be divided into at least three regions, $\{f^{-1}(\mathcal{A}(\{c_j\}))\}_{j=1,2,3}$. The geometry of profile space imposes a second constraint; partitioning a space into three or more regions requires using a certain number of inner normals. The two sets of restrictions about the inner normals conflict with each other, so the conclusion follows.

The responsiveness issue has been defined; we need to determine the properties a procedure needs to satisfy to be strategy proof. To start, notice that each voter can assume a voter type only if it improves his outcome. So, if we consider inner normal vector $\mathbf{n} = (n_1, n_2, \ldots, n_6)$ for $f^{-1}(\mathcal{A}(c_1))$ on the boundary separating $f^{-1}(\mathcal{A}(c_1))$ and $f^{-1}(\mathcal{A}(c_2))$, then only those voters preferring $c_2 \succ c_1$ would be inspired to examine their strategies. These are the voters of types 4, 5, 6. If any of the last three components of $\mathbf{n}$ is positive (indicating a vote from a voter of this type helps c_1 over c_2), then these voters can pretend to be of a type with a negative n_j to help c_2. Thus, to be strategy-proof, the last three values of n_j are negative.

Similarly, to insure that these voters cannot gain advantage just by changing their ranking of c_2 and c_3, it must be that

$$n_4 = n_5 = n_6 < 0.$$

(For instance, if $n_4 > n_6$, then a type change $4 \to 6$ would define the direction $\mathbf{E}_6 - \mathbf{E}_4$ and the scalar product $(\mathbf{n}, \mathbf{E}_6 - \mathbf{E}_4) = n_6 - n_4 < 0$, so an example can be created where this strategic vote leads to c_2's victory instead of c_1's – exactly what a type-four strategic voter prefers.)

With the above interpretation for $\mathbf{n}$, it follows that $-\mathbf{n}$ is the inner normal for $f^{-1}(\mathcal{A}(c_2))$. The same argument, applied to the ways in which supporters with $c_1 \succ c_2$ would vote, indicates that $n_1 = n_2 = n_3 > 0$. But, a direction change for profiles in $Si(6)$ must have the components add to zero, so we can choose

$$\mathbf{n} = \mathbf{N}_{1,2} = (1, 1, 1, -1, -1, -1). \tag{4.2.6}$$

If the choice really is between c_1 and c_2, then in our design of a procedure, it must be that the above inner normal applies everywhere on the boundary separating c_1 and c_2. This means that the outcome of the procedure must be determined by the sign of

$$p_1 + p_2 + p_3 - (p_4 + p_5 + p_6) + a$$

where a is some constant. If $a = 0$, then we have the usual pairwise majority vote scheme between c_1 and c_2 where a positive value shows that c_1 wins and a negative value supports c_2. If $a \neq 0$, we still have a pairwise vote, except now the sign of a provides a bias for a particular candidate.

If it is possible for c_3 to win, then we need to consider the inner boundary between c_1 and c_3 and between c_2 and c_3. The same arguments show that, to be strategy proof, there is no flexibility in their choices – the normal vectors must be $\mathbf{N}_{1,3}$ and $\mathbf{N}_{2,3}$. Therefore, for some choice of scalars $a_{i,j}$, a strategy proof procedure must be based on the signs of the outcomes of

$$((\mathbf{N}_{1,2}, \mathbf{p}) - a_{1,2}, (\mathbf{N}_{2,3}, \mathbf{p}) - a_{2,3}, (\mathbf{N}_{3,1}, \mathbf{p}) - a_{3,1}) = F_3(\mathbf{p}) - (a_{1,2}, a_{2,3}, a_{3,1}). \tag{4.2.7}$$

For example, if the first component is positive and the third is negative, then c_1 must be selected. If the first component is negative and the second is positive, then c_2 must be selected.

So, if a strategy proof procedure exists, it must be a translated version of the Condorcet winner! That is, the outcome must be in terms of the pairwise votes, where bias may be introduced. Namely, the image of the sought after procedure must be in the representation cube with the only difference being that the division between the different sets $\mathcal{A}(c_j)$ need not be at the origin; instead it is at $\mathbf{a} = (a_{1,2}, a_{2,3}, a_{3,1})$. Call this procedure an $\mathbf{a}$-biased Condorcet winner. It remains to see how to choose $\mathbf{a}$.

If $\mathbf{a}$ is in the interior of the representation cube, then the division creates eight open regions; two of them correspond to translated versions of the cyclic regions. This geometry returns to the essence of the agenda problem; each cyclic region needs to be assigned to a candidate c_j. Suppose one of these cyclic regions is assigned to c_1. The cyclic region has three sides, so it has three different inward normals. In $Si(6)$ this means that either $\mathbf{N}_{2,3}$ or $-\mathbf{N}_{2,3}$ is an inward normal for $f^{-1}(\mathcal{A}(c_1))$. But this leads to a contradiction because, to be strategy proof, the only admissible inner normals are $\mathbf{N}_{1,2}$ or $-\mathbf{N}_{3,1}$.

The only way out of this problem is to choose **a** on a boundary surface of the representation cube, and this must be done so that both the positive and negative cyclic regions are eliminated. This is geometrically impossible. As such, no strategy proof mechanism exists.

The above argument used the assumption that the procedure selects only a single candidate. This is not necessary; we can assume it selects any number of them. All we need is an agreement that a voter with $c_j \succ c_i$ prefers $\{c_j\}$ over $\{c_i, c_j\}$, and $\{c_i, c_j\}$ over $\{c_i\}$. What emerges are the same kinds of boundary conditions.

Theorem 4.2.4. *Consider the procedure $f : Si(6) \to \mathcal{P}$ where the boundaries between profile sets supporting different outcomes are are smooth. If for each c_j there is one outcome of f that does not contain c_j and at least one other outcome that does, then f is not strategy proof.*

For example, if the admissible outcomes of a procedure include the sets

$$\{c_1, c_2\}, \{c_2, c_3\}, \{c_3\},$$

then it is not strategy proof.

Proof. If the boundaries are smooth, then they can be represented as $F(\mathbf{p}) = 0$. The inner normal vectors are given by $\nabla F(\mathbf{p})$. The above argument shows that $\nabla F(\mathbf{p})/\|\nabla F\| = \mathbf{N}_{i,j}$. Thus, the boundaries are linear. The proof follows from the above argument. $\square$

It is easy to extend this proof to where the separating boundaries are not smooth. After all, the lack of smoothness just introduces more "directions," and hence, more opportunities to manipulate the system.

In light of the expanding literature about manipulation, incentive schemes, and strategy-free mechanisms, it is worth pausing to emphasize what the geometry tells us. Observe that the choice of admissible inner normal vectors forces a *strategy-free procedure to resemble the one-dimensional setting of a two-alternative choice.* Indeed, it isn't difficult to show that a strategy-free mechanism requires, in some crude manner, the voters to use only one-dimensional kinds of profile changes.[9] How these one-dimensional changes are obtained is flexible; e.g., we could impose severe behavioral assumptions about how the voters would try to manipulate the system. As an example, we might believe that a specified goal drives the actions of manipulating voters (e.g., it might be the outcome of a pre-election survey), or we may assert that voters cheat in only one behavioral way, etc. For instance, if voters can only manipulate the system by trying to assume the reversed voter type (so, a type-four voter must pretend to be a type-one voter), then much more flexibility is gained in the choice of the inner normals $\mathbf{N}$. Instead of $\mathbf{N}_{1,2} = (1, 1, 1, -1, -1, -1)$, we have that $\mathbf{N}_{1,2} = (x, y, z, -x, -y, -z)$ for any positive choices of x, y, z. Namely, if the assumptions allow a voter a multi-dimensional set of options, then the admissible $\mathbf{N}$

---

[9] This can be made precise by using concepts from algebraic or differential geometry.

must reduce this choice set to something that is, essentially, single-dimensional. On the other hand, should a voter starts with a single-dimensional choice set, then there is a wider selection of choices for admissible inner normals **N**.

In essence, this means that the heavy cost of having a strategy-proof procedure is to impose appropriate behavior assumptions about how voters will strategically vote (which strains credibility because we are asked to accept that a strategic voter will be so only in nice, acceptable ways), profile restrictions (which eliminates the robustness of procedures), or sequential procedures where one-dimensionality is enforced. But all of these procedures impose a heavy cost on the kind of outcomes that attained when all voters are sincere. There must be a compromise; this is addressed in the next section.

4.2.7 Measuring Suspectibility to Manipulation

The departmental election for a Chair from the fable, where all but one voter adopted a strategic approach, demonstrates how to manipulate the BC. That the BC can be manipulated has been recognized since the gloreous days of Condorcet and Borda in the 1780s; periodically, this BC defect is resurrected to argue against the adoption of the BC. But, as the Gibbard-Satterthwaite Theorem and Theorem 4.2.4 prove, *all* methods have this defect. The next natural question, then, is to determine whether any one procedure is less susceptible to being manipulated than another.

One way to understand which positional methods are less susceptible to being manipulated is to examine what happens when a small percentage of all voters try to change the outcome. This *micromanipulation* is in the spirit of a Nash equilibrium which examines what happens when a single voter changes strategy. In some sense, using a "small percentage" approach allows more general conclusions; by concentrating on a small percentage rather than a single voter, the coordinated actions of larger groups of voters can be included with the class of manipulators. On the other hand, one out of three voters is not a small percentage.

The basic idea is natural; count those profiles where a small percentage of the voters could successfully manipulate the outcome. Obviously, the more profiles that permit the outcome to be successfully manipulated, the more susceptible the system. The difficulty is to develop a mathematically tractable technique to measure this level of *susceptibility to manipulation*.

To be successfully manipulated, a sincere profile, $\mathbf{p}_s$, must be in the set of profiles supporting the sincere outcome, while the manipulated profile, $\mathbf{p}_m$, is the profile set supporting a different (the manipulated) outcome. The profile difference,

$$\mathbf{v} = \mathbf{p}_m - \mathbf{p}_s, \tag{4.2.8}$$

determines what voter types are involved in the manipulative attempt. Since only a small number of strategic voters are allowed, the magnitude $\|\mathbf{v}\|$ must be a small. This requires both $\mathbf{p}_s, \mathbf{p}_m$ to be on opposite sides but near the profile boundary separating these two outcomes. Thus, the above count only involves profiles near the boundary.

The Choice of w_s. In analyzing a successful manipulation, there are two main factors. The first is the choice of a voting system, w_s, and the second concerns the abundance of opportunities for a successful manipulation.

Both issues can be illustrated with the departmental election of the fable (which involves a massive, highly coordinated strategic action) by comparing $f(\mathbf{p}_s, \mathbf{w}_s)$ and $f(\mathbf{p}_m, \mathbf{w}_s)$ where $\mathbf{p}_s = (\frac{7}{15}, 0, \frac{1}{15}, 0, 0, \frac{7}{15})$ and the manipulated profile $\mathbf{p}_m = (0, \frac{7}{15}, \frac{1}{15}, 0, \frac{7}{15}, 0)$. The plurality vote acknowledges only a voter's top-ranked candidate, so both profiles define the same outcome $A \sim B \succ C$ with the same normalized vote $(\frac{7}{15}, \frac{7}{15}, \frac{1}{15})$. On the other hand, as described in the fable, the BC outcomes for these profiles radically differ; while the BC sincere outcome is $A \succ B \succ C$ with the normalized tally $(\frac{22}{45}, \frac{21}{45}, \frac{2}{45})$, the BC manipulated outcome is $C \succ A \succ B$ with the normalized tally $(\frac{15}{45}, \frac{14}{45}, \frac{16}{45})$.

To see what can happen with other choices of $\mathbf{w}_s$, recall that two $\mathbf{w}_s$ election tallies for a profile determine the unique procedure line. So, as demonstrated in Fig. 4.2.5, if any $\mathbf{w}_s$, $s \geq \frac{1}{3}$, is used, the difference between the sincere and the coordinated manipulation becomes exaggerated reaching an extreme at the antiplurality outcome. Different choices of $\mathbf{w}_s$ can make dramatic differences in the outcomes. (In the figure, the sincere procedure line is the small dash protruding into $\mathcal{R}(1)$, while the manipulated one is the longer line ending in $\mathcal{R}(3)$.)

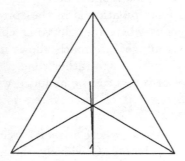

Fig. 4.2.5. Manipulated and sincere procedure lines

The choice of $\mathbf{w}_s$ also affects what constitutes a *successful strategic action*. This can be seen most clearly if the assigned procedure is the plurality vote. If a single candidate is to be selected, a voter might recognize that his top-ranked candidate is going to loose independent of how he votes. Therefore, rather than "wasting a vote," he might vote for his second- ranked candidate. In the fable, for instance, had the plurality vote been used and had our Chair been more worldly, he would have voted for his second-ranked Abbott to ensure an outcome more to his liking. This is strategic action, but rather than being nocuous, I find it to be intelligent. On the other hand, when the identity of the second-ranked candidate is important (such as when the two top-ranked candidates are selected), then similar "idealist justifications" reek of rationalization

Any $\mathbf{w}_s$, $s > 0$, offers ample opportunities to vote strategically by maximizing the point differential between the top two contenders. Obviously, the power of such strategic action increases with the value of $s \in [0, \frac{1}{2}]$, with the antiplurality vote offering the maximal power to block a second-ranked candidate.

Why wouldn't strategic action always be used? The answer is obvious; it depends on what you know. If you know that your first and second-ranked candidates are the only real contenders, then such strategic action may be difficult to resist. If you do not know (or suspect) who are the true contenders, then it is irrational to vote in a manner than could empower your bottom-ranked candidate! *A prerequisite for strategic action, then, is prior knowledge or expectation about the sincere election outcome!*

Macromanipulation. Similar, but more extreme conditions hold for massive coordinated strategic action. It is worth exploring these problems because they serve as part of my motivation for investigating micro- rather than macromanipulation.

A micro analysis requires only a few voters to know, or suspect the sincere election outcome. With only a few voters, it is reasonable to expect them to design and discharge a coordinated strategic action. A macro-strategic analysis, on the other hand, requires:

1. Wide-spread prior knowledge of "who are the real competitors."
2. A coordinator to ensure that the correct number of voters vote strategically (After all, by not voting sincerely, too many votes can lead to an undesired outcome – as in the fable).
3. A way to impose discipline so that the designated voters obediently carry out the planned action.

Situations, such as legislative bodies, almost beg for macromanipulation. With the public, rather than secret ballot, the vote of a person is known. Discipline is imposed by withholding favors. (For instance, a US Senator from Alabama embarrassed Vice President Gore on TV over the Clinton's proposed 1993 budget. Among the ways he was instantly "disciplined" was in terms of his invitations to the Presidential reception for the 1992 National Collegiate Football Champions, the University of Alabama. Anyone fortunate enough to be in Alabama on a "football Saturday" recognizes that this is "political hardball.") However, other than in such open forums, I find it difficult to believe that such carefully disciplined, coordinated action can be sustained. Accompanying this comment is the caveat that strategic voting requires a voter to vote for someone other than his or her top choices. Consequently, macromanipulation does not apply to "bloc voting" by environmental groups, labor organizations, and other special interest groups (unless a multiple system such as Approval Voting is used.) Rather than voting strategically, it is arguable that these groups try to increase the number of sympathetic voters.

Perhaps the most serious difficulty in accepting macromanipulation is the required obedience where large numbers of voters vote *strategically* as instructed. Instead, with the secret ballot and as events reported by the news media suggest (but don't prove), the solidarity of bloc voting tends to be inversely proportional to the level of political awareness and independence of the voters. Indeed, the coordination problem is so severe that it is difficult to accept such carefully arranged block strategic action as a common event.[10]

Opportunities for Micromanipulation. Finally, we arrive at the issue about the availability of opportunities. As noted, the choice of strategic action changes with the choice of $\mathbf{w}_s$. However, a more subtle and significantly more important aspect concerns the geometry of the profile boundaries separating different outcomes. Neutrality ensures that with each $\mathbf{w}_s$ i the same proportion, $\frac{1}{6}$, of the profiles in $Si(6)$ support a specified ranking $c_i \succ c_j \succ c_k$. But, as emphasized in Chap. 3, this profile set changes with different choices of $\mathbf{w}_s$. Consequently, the geometry of the boundary separating different profile sets varies with $\mathbf{w}_s$.

The importance of this geometry is clear; the micromanipulability of a system depends upon how many profiles are near the boundary. Obviously, a smaller boundary admits fewer near-by profiles. Therefore, we can expect the geometry and size of the boundary to limit the number of situations where a small percentage of voters can successfully manipulate the outcome.

This difference is geometry is demonstrated in Fig. 4.2.6 where a unit square is divided into four equal parts in two different ways. In each setting, a sector has area $\frac{1}{4}$, but the perimeter dividing the sectors is smaller (by a factor of $\sqrt{2}$) in the division on the right. (To see this, superimpose the second square upon the first to define several right triangles. The hypotenuse of these triangles define the two segments of a boundary for the division on the left, while two legs are used for the division on the right.) Thus, if these divisions corresponded to profile regions, the procedure on the right, with its shorter boundary, offers fewer opportunities for a micromanipulation.

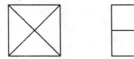

Fig. 4.2.6. Equal areas; different perimeters

These boundary regions can be thought of in terms of the above description of the Gibbard-Satterthwaite Theorem. The proof showed that the only way to avoid manipulation is to create a procedure that essentially restricts voters to one-dimensional options. Positional methods offer more. However, by reducing

---

[10] For any statement that can be made about decision analysis and politics, a reasonable argument can be made to support either side. In a personal communication (4/92), K. Saari argues that such macromanipulation is related to party formation; the different effects of $\mathbf{w}_s$ influence the outcome of how many parties can be formed. This, she argues, is an approach to analyze Duverger's law and what Riker [R2] calls Duverger's hypothesis.

the boundary size, we "reduce" the higher-dimensional options which allow the system to be manipulated. This is what the proof of the following theorem shows.

Which $\mathbf{w}_s$ has the smallest boundary? Intuition comes from mathematics where a standard problem to find the region with the smallest perimeter with a specified area. The answer is clear for rectangles. If the area is 9, then a 1×9 box satisfies the area constraint, but its perimeter is 20. On the other hand, a 3×3 square has perimeter 12. Common sense suggests (and mathematical techniques confirm) that the more symmetric the figure – allowing for a more compact arrangement of the region – the smaller the perimeter. Hence, solutions to this mathematical problem are squares, cubes, circles, spheres, etc.

In voting, then, we should expect the minimal boundary area – the minimal exposure of opportunities to be successfully manipulated – to be associated with the $\mathbf{w}_s$ that allows the greater symmetry. This happens; the most symmetric procedure is, of course, the BC.

Assumptions for the Theorems. Central to an analysis of manipulation are the questions "Who knows what?" (prior information) and "Who is saying what to whom?" (coordination). To see how different answers affect the outcome, suppose an architect of a "one time only" system is confronted with an electorate similar to that found in the departmental election. She knows that c_1 and c_2 will closely contest the election, and that either only very few voters have c_3 top-ranked, or everyone with c_3 top-ranked will vote sincerely. As already demonstrated, the plurality vote, $\mathbf{w}_0$, is the method that optimally encourages a sincere vote, while the worse system in the antiplurality vote $\mathbf{w}_{\frac{1}{2}}$. Conversely, if nobody ranks c_3 in last place, then a plurality system encourages voters with c_3 top-ranked to vote strategically, while the antiplurality system can encourage a stronger sincere vote. In fact, this theme generalizes; it turns out (Theorem 4.2.7) that for any $\mathbf{w}_s$, distributions of profiles can be found where $\mathbf{w}_s$ minimizes the susceptibility to manipulation. Namely, with appropriate assumptions, with a correctly constructed scenario, any system can be justified as being strategically the best. This means we must treat with suspicion any assertion about the manipulability of a system that relies on a finite number of examples or on restrictive assumptions.

The above comments concern a "one-shot voting system;" we want to design a system for long term usage. Here, we do not know the distribution of the profiles, how it will evolve, how many voters are involved, or what pair of candidates are the target of a manipulation. This leads to the first assumptions.

1. *All profiles from $Si(6)$ are equally likely.*
2. *Each pair of alternatives is equally likely to be the target of an attempted manipulation.*

Using neutrality and these assumptions, assume that *the strategic voters are attempting to change the sincere relative ranking of $c_2 \succ c_2$ to $c_1 \succ c_2$.* Thus, the only voters wanting to change this relative ranking must have the relative ranking $c_1 \succ c_2$, so they are of types one, two, or three. Now, a type-one voter, with his ranking $c_1 \succ c_2 \succ c_3$ can maximize the differential of his vote for these two candidates by pretending to be of type-two with $c_1 \succ c_3 \succ c_2$. The same argument hold for a type-three voter. As the type-two voter already has maximized the point differential, his only option is to vote sincerely. So, which kind of voter is manipulative? Keeping to the theme of neutrality, we obtain the third assumption.

3. *It is equally likely for a manipulating voter to be of any strategic type. Such a voter assumes a strategy to maximize the effect of the manipulation.*

Averaging over the actions of the two types, leads to the *Expected Manipulation Vector (EMV)*

$$\lambda \mathbf{v} = \lambda(-\frac{1}{2}, 1, -\frac{1}{2}, 0, 0, 0). \tag{4.1.9}$$

where λ indicates the proportion of all voters acting strategically, and the components of the vector indicate that half of the strategic voters are of type-one, half of type-three, and both of their actions is to pretend to be of type-two. (For the reader concerned about situations, such as the departmental election with a plurality vote, where a type-one voter has no realistic strategic options, don't worry. This fact comes out in the analysis. At this point, $\mathbf{v}$ only indicates who would want to manipulate the outcome.)

Definition 4.2.5. For m voters and a specified $\lambda \mathbf{v}$, let $\mu(\mathbf{w}_s, \lambda \mathbf{v}, m)$, *the m voter measure of binary susceptibility of* $\mathbf{w}_s$, *be the number of m voter profiles,* $\mathbf{p} \in Si(6)$, *where the relative ranking of* $f(\mathbf{p}, \mathbf{w}_s)$ *is* $c_2 \succ c_1$ *but the relative ranking of* $f(\mathbf{p} + \lambda \mathbf{v})$ *is* $c_1 \succ c_2$.

A positional voting method $\mathbf{w}^*$ is *susceptibility efficient* if

$$\mu(\mathbf{w}^*, \lambda \mathbf{v}, m) \leq \mu(\mathbf{w}_s, \lambda \mathbf{v}, m), \forall s \in [0, \frac{1}{2}]. \quad \square$$

While this definition appears to model our objective, it has flaws. For instance, it allows an infinite number of different answers where the answer can change with the number of voters. To illustrate, with 100 voters, there is no difference in the election rankings of $(1, 0, 0)$ and $(0.9999, 0.0001, 0)$, but there can be a significant change with 10,000 voters. To discover a single answer, we use the following definition which, essentially, requires a susceptibility efficient procedure to hold for all values of m. (This is different from and more inclusive than considering the limit as $m \to \infty$ as the limit only emphasizes large numbers of voters.)

Definition 4.2.6. For sufficiently small values of $\mathbf{v}$, let $\mu(\mathbf{w}_s)$ be the volume of $\{\mathbf{p} \in Si(6) | f(\mathbf{p}, \mathbf{w}_s)$ has the relative ranking $c_2 \succ c_1$ while $f(\mathbf{p} + \mathbf{v}, \mathbf{w}_s)$ has the relative ranking $c_1 \succ c_2\}$. $\square$

Susceptibility Theorems. We now come to one of the main conclusions.

Theorem 4.2.5. *For* $s \in [0, \frac{1}{2}]$, $\mu(\mathbf{w}_s) = \mu(\mathbf{w}_s^r)$, *and for* $0 \leq s_1 < s_2 < \frac{1}{3}$,

$$\mu(\mathbf{w}_{\frac{1}{3}}) < \mu(\mathbf{w}_{s_2}) = \mu(\mathbf{w}_{s_2}^r) < \mu(\mathbf{w}_{s_1}) = \mu(\mathbf{w}_{s_1}^r). \tag{4.2.10}$$

In words, *the BC is the unique method which is the least susceptible for micromanipulations.* Moreover, the more a procedure differs from the *BC*, the more its susceptibility measure increases. (As the proof shows, this is because the boundary area where profiles are vulnerable to manipulation increases in size.) The two procedures most susceptible to manipulation are the plurality and antiplurality votes.

The plurality vote does not fare very well by this theorem. But, as noted above, it is easy to invent arguments illustrating where strategic voting is of the benign type that I called "intelligent voting." This is true, but it does not support the choice of the plurality outcome. By examining the profiles which can be plurality manipulated, it becomes clear that many of them provide a strong incentive to vote strategically – this is because the sincere outcome severely violates the true beliefs of the voters! Thus, a voter needs to worry about "wasting" his or her vote only because of the stupidity of the sincere election outcome. We've already seen this with the beverage paradox from the fable. Practical examples can be found by examining the New Hampshire Presidential primarily election outcomes from almost any election year. Here, it is not unusual for a candidate second-ranked by most voters to do poorly.

One might (accurately) complain that Theorem 4.2.5 allows the close election to be between second and third place. Second place is interesting in horse races, but not in an election where the "winner takes all." The next statement asserts that nothing changes when only the top-ranked candidates are considered.

Theorem 4.2.6. *When attempted manipulations involve only the two top-ranked candidates, then a comparison of the levels of susceptibility of different* $\mathbf{w}_s$ *choices remains as asserted in Theorem 4.2.5.*

One way to indicate how changes in the profile or assumptions about what voters are "strategic," is to redefine the *EMV* $\mathbf{v}$ so that the fraction c of the strategic voters, instead of $\frac{1}{2}$ of them, are of type-one. This defines the *EMV* $\lambda\mathbf{v}_c = \lambda(-c, 1, 1-c, 0, 0, 0)$. The value of c is called *the electorate's manipulation characteristic.* Using $\lambda\mathbf{v}_c$, and its defining assumptions, suggests that the susceptibility efficient method might change. The choice is based on finding the $\mathbf{w}_s$ which, for a sufficiently small $\lambda\mathbf{v}_c$, minimizes the volume of

$\{\mathbf{p} \in Si(6) | f(\mathbf{p}, \mathbf{w}_s)$ has the relative ranking $c_2 \succ c_1$ while $f(\mathbf{p} + \mathbf{v}_c)$ has the relative ranking $c_1 \succ c_2\}$.

The next assertion shows that c can be chosen to "prove the superiority" of any $\mathbf{w}_s$.

Theorem 4.2.7. *For each* $\mathbf{w}_s$ *there exists a value of* c, *the electorate's manipulation characteristic, so that* $\mathbf{w}_s$ *is the least susceptible for manipulation.*

In words, this statement proves that with isolated examples and carefully constructed assumptions, any $\mathbf{w}_s$ can be justified as "being the best." When exposed to such arguments, watch your wallet.

As a related issue, how about *sensitivity?* This can be defined as where a small group of voters can alter the election outcome. Sensitivity differs from manipulation in that the outcome need not benefit these voters. Thus, this term captures the danger of the lunatic fringe, where small numbers of voters can alter the outcome; it captures the effects of an outcome changing when small numbers of voters just plain screw up their ballots and vote for the wrong person. Consequently, a highly sensitive system can generate serious unintended problems. A fairly accurate measure of sensitivity is the number of profiles subject to such a change. This is, of course, measured by the size of the profile boundary separating different ranking regions.

Theorem 4.2.8. *The methods* $\mathbf{w}_s$ *and* $\mathbf{w}_s^r$ *are equally sensitive. The least sensitive procedure is the BC. Indeed, as the value of s increases its distance from $\frac{1}{3}$, the degree of sensitivity increases.*

Taking all of these factors into account, the conclusion is, again, that the BC is the optimal system.

Proof of the Susceptibility Theorem. Instead of using the earlier notation of $\mathbf{w}_s = (1 - s, s, 0)$, a more convenient representation for the study of profiles is $(1, u, -1)$. Here, the BC, the plurality vote, and the antiplurality vote are given, respectively, by $u = 0, -1, 1$. In general, $\mathbf{w}_s$ has the representation

$$\mathbf{w}_s \approx (1, \frac{3s - 1}{1 - s}, -1),$$

and, if $\mathbf{w}_s \approx (1, u_1, -1)$, then $\mathbf{w}_s^r \approx (1, -u_1, -1)$.

An inner normal vector for c_1 on the boundary defining a $c_1 \sim c_2$ outcome is

$$\mathbf{N}_u = (1 - u, 2, u + 1, -(1 + u), -2, -(1 - u)).$$

The goal is to find the volume of $\mathbf{p}$'s close enough to this profile boundary so that $\mathbf{p} + \lambda\mathbf{v}$ crosses it. Only the ratio of measures for different $\mathbf{w}_s$ needs to be computed, so common multiples, including the value of λ, are ignored. This reduces the effective computation to the product of the surface area of the boundary plane, $S(H_u)$, with the length of the component of $\mathbf{v}$ orthogonal to it. (This orthogonality aspect identifies which voter types have a true ability to influence the outcome.) As such,

$$\mu((1, u, -1)) \propto < \frac{\mathbf{N}_u}{|\mathbf{N}_u|}, \mathbf{v} > S(H_u). \tag{4.2.11}$$

An elementary computation proves that

$$< \frac{\mathbf{N}_u}{|\mathbf{N}_u|}, \mathbf{v} > = \frac{3}{2\sqrt{3 + u^2}}. \tag{4.2.12}$$

It remains to compute the four-dimensional surface area $S(H_u)$. This is done with two changes of variables to reduce the problem to one of integration over a region in R^4. The first change uses the defining equation for $Si(6)$, $\sum_{j=1}^{6} p_j = 1$, to define

$$y_1 = p_1, y_2 = p_2, y_3 = p_3, y_4 = p_4, y_5 = p_6, p_5 = \left(1 - \sum_{k=1}^{5} y_k\right).$$

The reason p_5 is chosen to be eliminated is that the corresponding component in $\mathbf{N}_u$ is a scalar. The integrating factor for this change of variables is a constant $(\sqrt{6})$, so it is suppressed. The domain for the new variables is

$$y_k \geq 0, \quad \sum_{k=1}^{5} y_k \leq 1$$

and the boundary equation $< \mathbf{N}_u, \mathbf{p} >= 0$ becomes

$$< \mathbf{N}_u^*, \mathbf{y} >= 2; \quad \mathbf{N}_u^* = (3 - u, 4, u + 3, 1 - u, 1 + u).$$

The only scalar component of $\mathbf{N}_u^*$ is the second one, so use a change of variables to eliminate y_2. The new variables are

$$x_1 = y_1, x_2 = y_3, x_3 = y_4, x_4 = y_5,$$

and y_2 is found by solving $< \mathbf{N}_u^*, \mathbf{y} >= 2$ for y_2. The integrating factor is a scalar multiple of $\sqrt{9 + u^2}$, so the functional part is retained. The geometry of the domain for the $\mathbf{x} = (x_1, x_2, x_3, x_4)$ variables is given by

$$x_i \geq 0, \quad < \mathbf{N}_u^j, \mathbf{x} >\leq 2, \quad (4.2.13)$$

where $\mathbf{N}_u^1 = (1 + u, 1 - u, 3 + u, 3 - u)$ and $\mathbf{N}_u^2 = (3 - u, 3 + u, 1 - u, 1 + u)$.

The volume of the region defined by Eq. 4.2.13 can be determined by elementary techniques. If $\mathbf{e}_j$ is the unit vector with unity in the jth component, then the convex region defined by $< \mathbf{N}_u^1, \mathbf{x} >\leq 2$ has the profile vertices

$$\mathbf{0}, \frac{2\mathbf{e}_1}{1 + u}, \frac{2\mathbf{e}_2}{1 - u}, \frac{2\mathbf{e}_3}{3 + u}, \frac{2\mathbf{e}_4}{3 - u}$$

while the convex region $< \mathbf{N}_u^2, \mathbf{x} >\leq 2$ is defined by the profile vertices

$$\mathbf{0}, \frac{2\mathbf{e}_4}{1 + u}, \frac{2\mathbf{e}_3}{1 - u}, \frac{2\mathbf{e}_2}{3 + u}, \frac{2\mathbf{e}_1}{3 - u}.$$

As the domain defined by Eq. 4.2.13 is the intersection of these two regions, it is the union of two congruent regions where one is the convex hull of the vertices

$$\mathbf{0}, \frac{2\mathbf{e}_1}{3 - u}, \frac{2\mathbf{e}_2}{3 + u}, \frac{1}{2}(\mathbf{e}_1 + \mathbf{e}_4), \frac{1}{2}(\mathbf{e}_2 + \mathbf{e}_3).$$

The four-dimensional volume is a scalar multiple of $(9 - u^2)^{-1}$, so, when the integrating factors are included, we have that

$$\mu((1, u, -1)) \propto \left\{ \frac{3 + u^2}{(9 - u^2)(81 - u^4)} \right\}^{\frac{1}{2}}.$$

The conclusion now follows. □

Proof of Theorem 4.2.7. Replace $\mathbf{v}$ with $\mathbf{v}_c$. The main difference is that $< \mathbf{N}_u, \mathbf{v}_c >= 3 + u(1 - 2c)$. In turn,

$$\mu_c((1, u, -1)) \propto \frac{(3 + u(1 - 2c))\sqrt{3 + u^2}}{\sqrt{(9 - u^2)(81 - u^4)}}.$$

For $c = 1, \frac{1}{2}, 0$, the minimum value is, respectively, $u = 1$ (the antiplurality method), $u = 0$ (the BC), and $u = -1$ (the plurality method). The minimum point is a continuous function of c, so it follows from the intermediate value theorem that any choice of u is the optimal choice for some value of $c \in [0, 1]$. □

4.2.8 Exercises

4.2.1. For the agenda $< c_1, c_2, c_3 >$, what must be the choices of the unanimity profiles to force the positive involvement to fail? Find a general statement identifying the kinds of unanimity profiles that can, and cannot cause a profile to show positive involvement.

4.2.2. For Example 2.2.4, start with the $(0, 21, 0, 20, 0, 19)$ profile and obtain type-three voters by subdividing the voters with c_3 top-ranked into two groups to get $(0, 21, 2, 18, 0, 19)$. Show that a $3 \to 2$ change will create an example where monotonicity is violated. Are there changes of this kind that can be made so that an antiplurality method also leads to an example? Find the minimum number of voters needed to create an example illustrating that a $\mathbf{w}_0$-runoff is not monotonic. Find the minimum number of voters needed so that the same example proves that all $\mathbf{w}_s$-runoffs are not monotonic.

4.2.3. For Example 4.2.1, only one boundary surface for the cyclic regions was considered. Determine what happens with the other surfaces.

4.2.4. Once $n \geq 4$, the cyclic regions of pairs are replaced by even more adventurous possibilities for pairs, for rankings of the different triplets, etc. While geometry is higher dimensional, ideas and lessons from $n = 3$ apply. In particular, don't expect weak consistency, positive involvement, monotonicity, etc. for procedures that higher dimensionality of profiles comes into being; when procedures involve rankings of subsets of different numbers of candidates, boundaries can force unusual orientations. It is these different orientations that lead to conclusions. For $n = 4$, analyze the runoff $< c_1, c_2, c_3, c_4 >$.

4.2.5. Re-do Theorem 4.2.4 with smooth surfaces. Here, note that ∇F must assume a required form. Examine the proof for the procedure where, if all voters are of type-one, then c_1 is selected, if all are type-six, c_2 is elected, otherwise c_3 is selected.

4.2.6. By use of the ideas of Theorem 4.2.4, for each of the following procedures construct an example where c_1 wins thanks to a strategy adopted by one voter: the top-choice from a $\mathbf{w}_s$ election, an agenda, Black's procedure, a $\mathbf{w}_{\frac{1}{3}} - (0, 0, 1)$ runoff.

4.2.7. Characterize the scoring rule runoffs with respect to the responsiveness issues.

4.2.8. Suppose G is a smooth function that is not linear. What responsiveness properties does the corresponding G binary procedure satisfy?

4.2.9. For a $\mathbf{w}_s$ election, find example showing how a voter can manipulate the outcome. By use of the inner product, investigate whether it is possible for a voter to manipulate the outcome from his bottom ranked candidate to his top-ranked candidate.

4.2.10. For each $\mathbf{w}_s$, design a profile distribution demonstrating that $\mathbf{w}_s$ is the least susceptible to manipulation.

4.2.11. Find an agenda and a profile where the sincere outcome is c_1, the outcome is c_2 is certain voters abstain, and c_3 if certain voters try to manipulate the outcome.

4.3 Proportional Representation

Proportional representation (PR) is the "fair division problem" that arises when more than one person, party, or alternative is to be selected from a given list. The noble intention that guides PR is to ensure that the division is in accord with what the voters want. The idea is that only when the division of power within a country matches its diversity of beliefs are the legislative outcomes representative. But, as often true, while the driving motivation may be to establish "fairness," the resulting procedure could introduce an intriguing selection of paradoxes and new types of inequities. Indeed, proportional representation has a delightfully emotional history full of charges and countercharges arguing the pros and cons. Supporting examples are easy to find in the many books written on this topic between 1860 and 1945.

The intent of PR is to select candidates in proportion to the number of voters supporting them. While there are many ways to do this, one fact is clear. Should candidates be chosen in this manner from a general group (as opposed to selecting the winners from "winner takes all" district races), then candidates from minority groups have a better chance to be selected. Historically, persuasive arguments of this type have been advanced to promote various PR procedures.

A humbling yet appealing aspect about politics is that its rich history provides numerous examples to serve as counterarguments for almost any claim. This is because procedures are without idology; they are agnostic to the changing nature of practical politics. With identical force, a PR procedure correctly protects the minority rights of ethnic, racial, and special interest groups, as well as empowering those fringe groups, such as the one formed by A. Hitler, that intend to abridge these same rights. The fact is, with repeated failure at the election booth, minorities tend to be absorbed by major groups. "There is every reason to believe that in the absence of PR [this absorption effect] would have been the same outcome so far as Hilter's party was concerned. All that kept it alive was its chance to obtain some measure of success in every election in which it participated. Otherwise it would probably have disbanded, and Hitler might have resumed the peaceful profession of painting houses."[11]

There are many examples where PR appears to work as intended, and others where it does not. Indeed, in early 1993 the PR effect of encouraging small parties was blamed for the scandals of the Italian Government. In reaction, there was an overwhelming 82.7% referendum vote on April 20, 1993, to change procedures. The thought was that "[t]he new method would end the strict proportional representation that gave Italy 51 post-war governments and as many political parties as there are varieties of pasta. ... This would revolutionize politics by eliminating small parties that have always fluttered around democracy's flame: no more Party of Love led by porno stars, no more electoral victories for Mussolini's granddaughter." (New York Times, April 21, 1993, p.3) Clearly, the philosophical debate as to whether the objective of an election is to achieve consensus or (PR) divide according to census continues.

Critical comments in the spirit of what motivates our analysis are the fears that "The vague phrases which [PR advocates] think convey fundamental truths are not analyzed. 'The rights of minorities,' 'the tyranny of majorities,' 'the necessity for men of ability in Parliament,' and many other such phrases, are used as bases not to be questioned." [Ho] Echoing my earlier "No good deed goes unpunished" warning about the design of election procedures is the worry that "[PR supporters] advocate changes without calculating the effect on the abstract ideas for which they profess love unless and until a crisis arises."

These concerns are not restricted to PR; before springing any procedure upon a trusting, unsuspecting public, it should be carefully analyzed to determine what can go right, and what can go wrong. Toward this end, in this section I'll introduce some of the interesting geometry needed to describe certain PR methods. (Even the dynamical instabilities of "Chaos" play a role.) As we should expect, the geometry exposes and explains hidden but fascinating faults about widely used procedures. Some of these faults have led to Presidential vetoes (e.g., by George Washington), court cases, and even helped determine the current size of the US House of Representatives. To indicate that passions remain high even today, I'll briefly describe a US Supreme Court case involving apportionment procedures.

4.3.1 Hare and Single Transferable Vote

A sizable portion of the emotional PR history centers around the various mod-

---

[11] [He] It is clear from the publication date of this book (1940) that this warning was written before the true consequences of these comments were known.

ifications of the Hare procedure also called the "single transferable vote." By modifying the geometric constructions already developed in this book, it is not overly difficult to create a geometric theory for this procedure, so I'll just introduce the method, suggest issues to investigate, and then move on.

PR is needed when more than one candidate is to be selected. Examples of the type given earlier, where 80% of the voters have the ranking $c_1 \succ c_2 \succ c_3$ while the rest have the ranking $c_3 \succ c_2 \succ c_1$, cast serious doubt whether a plurality second-ranked c_3 deserves to be one of the two selected candidates. On the other hand, the weakness of the procedure (generating the foolish outcome) can be corrected with carefully coordinated strategic voting. After all, to be elected, each of the two candidates needs just over one-third of the vote; all additional votes are superfluous. The extreme popularity of c_1 in this profile forces many of her supporters to "waste their vote;" extra votes for c_1 are lost. The price is that these voters' second-ranked candidate loses. If it were possible to coordinate the voters' actions so that half sincerely vote for c_1 while the other half strategically vote for c_2, they could achieve the reasonable choice of $\{c_1, c_2\}$ that more accurately mirrors these voters' wishes.

To recognize what is involved, consider a hypothetical small New England town where voting for the three candidates is done in the following quaint manner. Each candidate stands in an assigned corner of the high school gymnasium. Instead of casting ballots, her supporters stand by her when the count starts at 7 PM. If two candidates are to be selected by the 100 voters, a candidate is assured of selection once she has at least 34 votes. Now, if at 6:50 PM, Helvi has 52 voters standing around her, instead of "wasting their vote," 18 of them would be well advised to move and stand by their second-ranked candidate.

This illustrates where strategic action is to be applauded; it is needed to overcome a distinct defect of the procedure. But, don't allow the noise of the applause to drown out realism; this action probably wouldn't occur in practice. Unless the voters are stuck in a snowbound Vermont gym, the severe informational and group discipline prerequisites for the success of a massive coordinated action makes it highly unlikely that it will occur outside of theory. On the other hand, if we like the process, then we could design a procedure to institutionalize the behavior. This is the Hare method.

The procedure goes as follows. After all voters rank the candidates, the candidates are plurality ranked. To be selected, a candidate needs one more than one-third of the vote. All candidates satisfying this criteria on the first ballot are selected. If only one candidate, say c_1, is selected, then all of her extra votes are proportionally distributed among the remaining two candidates where the proportion is based on voters' preferences. (This corresponds to voters migrating within the gym.) With the adjusted profile (unless a tie), two candidates are selected. When k out of n candidates are chosen, a candidate needs one more than $\frac{1}{k+1}$ of the vote, and several adjusted profiles may be required.

To illustrate with 100 ballots, suppose Helvi, c_1, receives 52 votes where 30 of the voters have the ranking $c_1 \succ c_2 \succ c_3$ and 22 have the ranking $c_1 \succ c_3 \succ c_2$. As Helvi only needs 34 votes to be selected, the extra $52 - 34 = 18$ votes are redistributed among the remaining two candidates on a proportional basis. That is, c_2 receives $\frac{30}{52} \times 18 = 10.38$ extra votes while c_3 receives $\frac{22}{52} \times 18 = 7.62$ extra votes. After the reallocation, Helvi and another candidate should receive the required quota. The reallocation can be viewed as converting 10.38 type-one voters into type-six voters, while 7.62 of the type-two voters now are of type-three.

The procedure captures the spirit of the above common sense approach by automatically moving ballots (rather than voters) from one candidate to another. So, this "institutionalized strategic voting" procedure eliminates the practical difficulties that makes coordinated strategic voting unrealistic; i.e., the gathering and coordinating of information about "who might vote for whom," enforcing coalitional agreements, as well as those complicating personality factors where a voter is too shy to move from one corner of the gym to another, etc. Of course, it is easy to invent all sorts of embellishments and modifications of this procedure, and probably all of them are already described in the literature if not actually used in practice. (For instance, another approach is to transfer *all* votes of a successful candidate to each voter's second preference. This is a form of a runoff, so it can be analyzed with the techniques of Sect. 4.2. Other procedures differ on how the transferred votes are selected, etc.) In fact, variations of this procedure have been used all over Europe, in various cities of the USA (e.g., Cincinnati), Japan, etc. as well as the American Mathematical Society among other organizations.

The properties of the Hare method derive from its multiprofile definition. The original profile, $\mathbf{p}_1$, is used to define the reallocation profile $\mathbf{p}_2$. More precisely, should c_1 win the first election with $\mathbf{p}_1 = (p_1, \ldots, p_6)$, the vote is reallocated in the following manner where, for simplicity, $\frac{1}{3}$ is used instead of "one vote above one-third." Of the votes for c_1, $\frac{p_1}{p_1+p_2}$ are from type-one voters and $\frac{p_2}{p_1+p_2}$ from type-two voters. Therefore, $\frac{p_1}{p_1+p_2}(p_1 + p_2 - \frac{1}{3})$ votes are transferred from type-one to type-six, with a similar expression for the transfer from type-two to type-three. Thus,

$$\mathbf{p}_2 = (\frac{1}{3}\frac{p_1}{p_1 + p_2}, \frac{1}{3}\frac{p_2}{p_1 + p_2}, p_3 + p_2 - \frac{1}{3}\frac{p_2}{p_1 + p_2}, p_4, p_5, p_6 + p_1 - \frac{1}{3}\frac{p_1}{p_1 + p_2}).$$

Aha! Already the source of problems is apparent. The nonlinear nature of $\mathbf{p}_2$ promises that the inner normal on the profile boundary separating different conclusions varies through a spectrum of values. This, in turn, ensures that the theory of Sect. 4.2 can be used to extract the various responsiveness and strategic difficulties that exist. Related problems derive from the multiprofile nature of the method; similar to truncation methods, approval voting, etc., the increase in the number of variables can alter the outcomes (but, not as dramatically).

Other types of issues are immediate. Does the Hare method agree with a plurality runoff? (No.) With any positional method? (No.) How does the Hare method agree with pairwise rankings. (Better than the plurality vote, but it still has problems.) What happens if $\mathbf{w}_0$ is replaced with $\mathbf{w}_s$ in the two elections?

(Some problems, such as allowing the Condorcet loser to be the first selected candidate, are mitigated the closer $\mathbf{w}_s$ is to the BC; they are eliminated once the BC is used.) Issues and comparisons of these kinds can be handled by modifying the geometry of earlier sections. Therefore, after a parting comment, I turn to methods where new geometry is involved.

Related to the Hare procedure is where the BC, rather than the plurality vote, is used for the elections. To avoid the responsiveness problems caused by nonlinearities, the BC should be used directly. Thus, a quite reasonable PR procedure is the BC without any reallocation of ballots. Indeed, as developed in Chap. 3, the BC already achieves the desired proportional representation of the candidates without all of the difficulties.

4.3.2 The Apportionment Problem

The US Constitution requires "Representatives shall be apportioned among the several states according to their respective numbers, counting the whole number of persons in each State ... ." This means, for instance, if the US House of Representatives consisted of $h = 15$ members and a state has one third of the total US population, then that state is entitled to $\frac{1}{3} \times 15 = 5$ representatives. Similarly, with $h = 16$ seats, that same state is entitled to $\frac{1}{3} \times 16 = 5\frac{1}{3}$ representatives.

The fractional part introduces a problem; how should the seats be allocated when the exact apportionment is a mixed number? Some readers may argue for fractional power; some might even argue that occasionally only a third of a representative actually goes to Congress – maybe the wrong third. Fractional representation is not the answer because current interpretations of the Constitution require an integer number of representatives from each state. The resolution is obvious; just "round off" $5\frac{1}{3}$. But, how?

The political need to "round off" an exact apportionment extends beyond the American boundaries to create problems in Europe and all other locales where the PR assignment of seats to different political parties is based on how many voters voted for each party. In what is called the "list system," voters vote for the list of candidates provided by each party. Then, the number of candidates selected from each list is determined by the share of vote a party receives.[12] Fractions are to be expected, so how are they handled? Indeed, this need for rounding off is a standard complexity accompanying any integer allocation problem. As such, similar serious difficulties arise in military manpower decisions where the number of people to be conscripted from different regions must be determined, from economics where the goal is to determine the optimal number of automobiles of different styles to be ordered by a dealer, etc. But, as shown here, "rounding off" looses its simplicity once there are more than two parties. Moreover, "rounding

---

[12] Often the political party determines how the candidates are ordered on a list. Alternatively, such as in Brazil, the voters can influence this ordering by voting for particular candidates.

off" can be an explosive political issue if it introduces an unexpected shift in power or resources. I'll give a recent example later in this section.

To illustrate the problems, suppose 25 seats are to be allocated among three states in accordance with the population figures specified in the next table. The numbers total 10,000, so, a decimal point in front of each population figure specifies the fractional size of that state. The exact apportionment for a state is the product of the decimal value with house size 25. The resulting exact apportionment, however, requires the barbaric act of cutting a representative to size. To find a resolution, start by listing the minimal integer number of representatives each state should have; this *minimal allocation* is in the next to last column.

State	Population	Exact Rep.	Min	Hamilton	
A	4520	11.30	11	11	
B	4136	10.34	10	10	(4.3.1)
C	1344	3.36	3	4	
Total	$\overline{10,000}$	$\overline{25}$	$\overline{24}$	$\overline{25}$	

The minimal allocation settles 24 of the 25 available seats; which state deserves the last one? The standard "rounding off" fails because the fractional part of the exact apportionment for each state is less than the magical $\frac{1}{2}$ division point; each state would be rounded down leaving the assignment problem unresolved.

The usual $\frac{1}{2}$ value is ineffective because there are three, not two states. So, to resolve the problem, we might exchange the cutoff value of $\frac{1}{2}$ with $\frac{1}{3}$; all states with a fractional part greater than $\frac{1}{3}$ would be rounded up. A minor flaw of this approach is that it is useless. In the above table, the fractional portion for two states exceeds $\frac{1}{3}$, yet only one can be rounded up.

The next obvious approach is to rank the states according to the fractional parts, and assign remaining seats to states with the largest fractions. The fractional parts for the example are $C(0.36) \succ B(0.34) \succ A(0.30)$, so this *Hamilton apportionment scheme* (due to the controversial American statesman Alexander Hamilton) awards C the remaining seat. The final Hamilton apportionment is listed in the last column.

Hamilton's Method seems to be reasonable, and it was used for a considerable period of time in the USA. But, when first proposed, Thomas Jefferson helped persuade George Washington to veto the bill.[13] Jefferson's method, described later, was adopted.

Hamilton's Method. Actually, Hamilton's method is closely related to our standard procedure that rounds off, say, the value 34.62 upwards to 35. The two candidates to replace 34.62 are 34 and 35; 35 is chosen because it is closest to

---

[13] In part, this is because with the population of the day Hamilton's method would award Connecticut more representatives than permitted by the Constitutional bound of no more than one representative per 30,000 persons. See [Mon, Mas, BY1].

34.62. Similarly, Hamilton's method is equivalent to first selecting the candidates for the rounding off, and then choosing the one closest to the exact value. To illustrate with the above example where one extra seat is to be awarded, the three ways $(11.30, 10.34, 3.40)$ can be rounded off while satisfying $h = 25$ are

$$(11, 10, 4), \ (11, 11, 3), \ \text{and} \ (12, 10, 3).$$

A computation shows that $(11, 10, 4)$ is the closest to $(11.30, 10.34, 3.36)$ (with distance 0.7843). (The distances of $(11.30, 10.34, 3.40)$ from the other two points $(11, 11, 3)$ and $(12, 10, 3)$ are, respectively, 0.8094 and 0.8574.)

Thus, Hamilton's method is the natural extension of the familiar rounding off process already learned as a young child. The general situation for m states (or parties, or ...) is described in the following definition where the jth component of $\mathbf{p}$ represents the fraction of all people that reside in the jth state and where h is the house size. (In the above example, $m = 3$, $\mathbf{p} = (0.4520, 0.4136, 0.1344)$, and $h = 25$.)

Definition 4.3.1. Let

$$\mathbf{p} = (p_1, p_2, \ldots, p_m) \subset Si(m) = \{\mathbf{p} \mid \sum_{j=1}^{m} p_j = 1, \ p_j \geq 0.\}$$

For an integer h, the Hamilton apportionment of $h\mathbf{p} = (hp_1, hp_2, \ldots, hp_m)$ is the vector of integers $\mathbf{a} = (a_1, a_2, \ldots, a_m)$, $\sum_{j=1}^{m} a_j = h$, that is closest to $h\mathbf{p}$. $\square$

Apportionment Cubes. To understand what kinds of problems we can have with Hamilton's method, I describe the procedure in terms of the geometry of the *apportionment cube* in R^3. This cube is defined by the eight vertices generated by how each component of $h\mathbf{p}$ (i.e., each state's exact apportionment) can be rounded up and down; the sum of the components of these vertices need not equal h. (So, for $m \geq 2$ parties, the apportionment cube has 2^m vertices.) In the example problem with $25(0.4520, 0.4136, 0.1344) = (11.30, 10.34, 3.36)$, the eight vertices of the apportionment cube are

$$
\begin{array}{llll}
(11, 10, 3) & & & h = 24 \\
(11, 10, 4) \quad (11, 11, 3) \quad (12, 10, 3) & & & h = 25 \\
(12, 11, 3) \quad (12, 10, 4) \quad (11, 11, 4) & & & h = 26 \\
(12, 11, 4) & & & h = 27
\end{array}
\qquad (4.3.2)
$$

The vertex in the first row, the *minimal apportionment*, is where every state is rounded down, while the entry in the last row, the *maximal apportionment* is where every state is rounded up. Each entry in the second row rounds up a single component of $h\mathbf{p}$; so these are the ways a single additional seat can be assigned to some state. The third row has two values of $h\mathbf{p}$ rounded up, so it represents the situation where two additional seats are to be assigned.

The *base cube* is the apportionment cube where the eight vertices have entries of 0 or 1. Equivalently, the base cube is the apportionment cube defined by $\mathbf{p}$

and $h = 1$. Observe that each apportionment cube is obtained by adding (or translating) the base cube to the minimal apportionment. For instance, the apportionment cube of Eq. 4.3.2 is given by adding the minimal apportionment values, $(11, 10, 3)$, to each vertex of the base cube. In general,

Apportionment cube = Minimal apportionment + Base cube.

$$(4.3.3)$$

The vertices of the base cube designate which states receive extra seats.

Those vertices of an apportionment cube that correspond to where k extra seats are being allocated define the "k – *assignment triangle*." For the example, the $k = 1$ assignment triangle is defined by the vertices in the second row of 4.3.2, while the $k = 2$ assignment triangle is defined by the vertices of the third row. By virtue of Relationship 4.3.3, the geometry of a k - assignment triangle of an apportionment cube is the same as the respective assignment triangle in the base cube. In the base cube, the $k = 1$ triangle is the intersection of the base cube with the plane $x + y + z = 1$ (So its vertices are $(1,0,0), (0,1,0), (0,0,1)$), while the $k = 2$ triangle is given by the intersection of the base cube with the plane $x + y + z = 2$. (The region between these two planes resembles the representation cube.)

As seats are awarded to the states according to the "closer is better" principle, each assignment triangle is divided into three geometrically similar regions. Therefore, these *apportionment regions* are created by the lines of midpoints determined by different pairs of vertices. In this manner, the seat assignment for the different states is specified by the vertex of the region containing $h\mathbf{p}$. These triangles, along with the base cube, are displayed in Fig. 4.3.1.

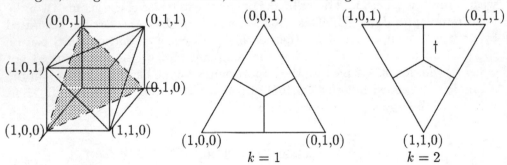

Fig. 4.3.1. The assignment triangle geometry of the base cube

Because Hamilton's method is based on a distance, the apportionment regions of the assignment triangle are similar to the regions of the representation triangle of Chaps. 2 and 3 used to determine where c_j, $j = 1, 2, 3$, is top-ranked. Observe how the geometry of the apportionment cube forces the assignment triangles for $k = 1$ and $k = 2$ to flip in a manner analogous to the "flipping" of T_1 and T_2 from the representation cube. Also observe that the barycentric points of the two assignment triangles have the fractional parts

$$k(\frac{1}{3}, \frac{1}{3}, \frac{1}{3}), \quad k = 1, 2. \tag{4.3.4}$$

Again, this comes from the geometry of a cube; a similar relationship emerged with the indifference points of T_1 and T_2 of the representation cube.

4.3.3 Something Must Go Wrong – Alabama Paradox

Once there are three or more states (or parties), we must anticipate that the process is vulnerable to the counterintuitive peculiarities of higher dimensional geometries; peculiarities that can force unwanted consequences upon voting procedures. In more common language, "Now what can go wrong!"

In Sect. 4.2, we explored how "generosity" toward a candidate, manifested by her receiving added support, can hurt her. A similar "more can cause less" problem arises with Hamilton's apportionment procedure; when an increase in house size provides extra seats, a previously held seat can be *taken* away from a state. Congressional seats represent important political power, so this subtraction phenomenon can trigger political "chaos!"

To see the difficulties, suppose an act of Congress changes the house size of the example to $h = 26$. The following computation shows that states A and B each receive one of the two extra seats.

State	Population	Exact Rep.	Min	Hamilton	
A	4520	11.7520	11	12	
B	4136	10.7536	10	11	(4.3.5)
C	1344	3.4944	3	3	
Total	10,000	26	24	26	

According to the last columns of 4.3.1 and 4.3.5, the generosity of increasing the house size *cost* state C 25% of its original representation! This is not just an amusing academic exercise; such problems have occurred in practice. For instance, before fixing the size of the US House of Representatives at 435, the house size could and did change. And, when the house size grew, states did lose representation!

The first US state to be victimized by the geometry of higher dimensions was Alabama; subsequently, other states such as Maine and Colorado suffered from this "Alabama Paradox." Although a different apportionment method was use, the current size of the US House of Representatives, 435, derived in part from trying to avoid the Alabama Paradox with the 1910 census figures. (For all sorts of climatic, census, and political reasons, the house size remained at 435 from then until it was fixed by law in November, 1941.)

It is clear why this paradox occurs; state C has such a small population fraction that when it is added to the previous figure (from table 4.3.1), the larger fractions that are added for the other states quickly jumps their fractional part to the top of the list. To extract more subtle properties, we need a geometric explanation.

The Alabama Paradox can be understood with the algebraic expression

$$(h+1)\mathbf{p} = h\mathbf{p} + \mathbf{p}. \qquad (4.3.6)$$

The exact apportionment $25\mathbf{p}$ is in the $k = 1$ assignment triangle region defined by the vertex $(11, 10, 4) = (11, 10, 3) + (0, 0, 1)$. For the paradox to occur, the point $(25 + 1)\mathbf{p}$ must be in the $k = 2$ assignment triangle region with vertex $(12, 11, 3) = (11, 10, 3) + (1, 1, 0)$. By examining the alignment of two assignment triangles, it is clear how this can happen. (See Fig. 4.3.1.) First, the base point $25\mathbf{p}$ must be near the barycentric point of the $k = 1$ assignment triangle. (So, the fractional values of $25\mathbf{p}$ are close to $(\frac{1}{3}, \frac{1}{3}, \frac{1}{3})$.) Then the strong "tilt" $\mathbf{p}$ acquires from the smaller population of state C forces the point $25\mathbf{p} + \mathbf{p}$ to slide into the $(11, 10, 3) + (1, 1, 0)$ region of the $k = 2$ assignment triangle.

Swatting Flies. As an intuitive way to understand the Alabama Paradox, consider the problem of swatting a fly on the screen of a door during a hot, humid summer day. For sanitary reasons, a jar lid should be used instead of the left hand. To avoid cutting the screen, keep the jar lid parallel to the screen while moving it toward the screen. Fly-killing expertise can be demonstrated by squashing a single fly on an edge of the lid. This may require an appropriate selection of the size of the jar lid.

In the apportionment problem, the screen represents S_h – the space of all apportionments with house size h (i.e., all vectors where the sum of the components equals h) and the "flies" are the integer apportionments. The center of the jar lid is moved along the *exact apportionment* line $t\mathbf{p}$ where $t \in (0, \infty)$ designates how far the lid is from the origin; when t has an integer value, it represents the house size. Aligning the orientation of the jar lid with the screen ensures that the moved disk is on S_h, while the radius of the lid measures how far points are from the exact apportionment $h\mathbf{p}$. The squashed fly is the Hamilton apportionment. Finding the Hamilton apportionment (the integer apportionment minimizing the distance from the exact apportionment) corresponds to choosing an appropriately sized lid to hit a single fly with the lid edge.

Now suppose there are screens on the main door and storm door, both closed. (So, the screens are parallel but separated by a distance.) Furthermore, suppose the flies have become so irritating that we will ignore the cost of repairing the destruction caused by trying to hit a particular fly on the first screen (representing the $k = 1$ assignment triangle) and, continuing the motion, to hit a specified fly on the second screen (representing the $k = 2$ assignment triangle). By carefully choosing how to move the lid, this clearly can be done. Similarly, by choosing an appropriate "tilt" for $\mathbf{p}$, an Alabama Paradox is created.

The Mathematics of Fly Swatting. To analyze the "fly swatting – Alabama Paradox phenomenon" mathematically, we need to determine how to tilt $\mathbf{p}$ so that the jar lid starts from the $(0, 0, 1)$ region of the $k = 1$ assignment triangle and ends up in the $(1, 1, 0)$ region of the $k = 2$ assignment triangle. Start with the special case where $h\mathbf{p}$ is at the barycentric point on the $k = 1$ assignment triangle and $\mathbf{p} = (\frac{1}{3}, \frac{1}{3}, \frac{1}{3})$. The direction from one barycentric point to the other is $(\frac{1}{3}, \frac{1}{3}, \frac{1}{3})$, so, by Eqs. 4.3.4, 4.3.6, $(h + 1)\mathbf{p}$ is at the barycentric point of the $k = 2$ assignment triangle.

A "tilt" in $\mathbf{p}$ (i.e., $\mathbf{p} \neq (\frac{1}{3}, \frac{1}{3}, \frac{1}{3})$) forces $(h + 1)\mathbf{p}$ off of the barycentric point of the $k = 2$ triangle into a region that disfavors the state with the smallest population. Indeed, exploiting the tilt, the base point, $h\mathbf{p}$, can be moved in the $k = 1$ triangle while keeping the tip, $(h + 1)\mathbf{p}$, in the designated region of the $k = 2$ triangle. Of course, a stronger tilt of $\mathbf{p}$ (i.e., a greater divergence in the populations of the states), defines a larger region for the base point $h\mathbf{p}$.

When moving the base point $h\mathbf{p}$ (in the $k = 1$ triangle) we want to keep it in the region where $h\mathbf{p}$ awards the state with the smallest population the sole extra seat; denote this region by $AP(\mathbf{p})$. (This is the shaded region in Fig. 4.3.2.) By construction, $h\mathbf{p} \in AP(\mathbf{p})$ forces an Alabama Paradox because at house size $h + 1$, the state with the smallest population is denied a previously held seat!

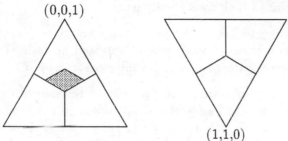

Fig. 4.3.2. The $AP(\mathbf{p})$ region

The above description (aided by the geometry of Fig. 4.3.2) shows that $AP(\mathbf{p})$ includes an open set of possibilities. Remember, the geometry of $AP(\mathbf{p})$ does not depend on h; it only depends upon the chosen $\mathbf{p}$. As noted, the more extreme the tilt of $\mathbf{p}$ (i.e., the larger the disparity between the populations of the states), the bigger the region $AP(\mathbf{p})$. And, as long as $\mathbf{p} \neq (\frac{1}{3}, \frac{1}{3}, \frac{1}{3})$, the region $AP(\mathbf{p})$ must contain an open set.

Cut and Slide Processes. To repeat, once $h\mathbf{p} \in AP(\mathbf{p})$ in an apportionment cube, an Alabama Paradox follows. A potential escape clause from this negative conclusion is the hope that only rare choices of $\mathbf{p}$ allow $h\mathbf{p} \in AP(\mathbf{p})$ for some value of h. As the next theorem asserts, this wishful conjecture is false; for almost all choices of $\mathbf{p} \in Si(m)$, the Alabama Paradox is lurking in the background just waiting to pounce upon some unsuspecting state once an appropriate value of h is reached.

Theorem 4.3.1 [S2]). *For $m \geq 3$, almost all $\mathbf{p} \in Si(m)$ have an Alabama Paradox for some house size h.*

The technical term "almost all"[14] means that those population sizes that manage to escape the Alabama Paradox are rare; consequently, this paradoxical phenomenon is to be expected. Verifying this statement requires proving that most choices of $\mathbf{p}$ admit an integer h so that $h\mathbf{p} \in AP(\mathbf{p})$ in the $h\mathbf{p}$ apportionment cube. This is demonstrated in the following plausibility argument where the missing formal details are easy to fill in. First, I show why the geometry of a

---

[14] For the mathematicians, this could be taken in the sense of Lebesgue measure, or as being an open-dense set. Actually, by examining the proof, more exacting algebraic requirements of excluding a finite number of points can be imposed.

donut plays a critical role for *all* integer apportionment problems. (This includes integer programming problems from economics, and so forth.)

An easy way to relate successive $h\mathbf{p}$ points is to connect them with the *exact apportionment line*

$$t\mathbf{p}, \quad t \in [0, \infty). \tag{4.3.7}$$

Of course, the integer points, $t = h$; $h = 1, 2, \ldots$, on the apportionment line recapture Eq. 4.3.6. The rounding off process involves only the fractional parts of the exact apportionment; for instance, the fractional parts of $(23\frac{1}{3}, 45\frac{2}{3})$ and $(62\frac{1}{3}, 2\frac{2}{3})$ agree, so both terms are rounded off in the same manner. This suggests identifying points in terms of their fractional parts.

Definition 4.3.2. Two vectors $\mathbf{x} = (x_1, x_2, \ldots, x_m)$ and $\mathbf{y} = (y_1, y_2, \ldots, y_m)$ are *fractionally equivalent*, $\mathbf{x} \approx_{frac} \mathbf{y}$, if, when expressed in decimal form, the decimal portion of x_j agrees with that of y_j for all $j = 1, \ldots, m$. $\square$

The theorem is proved by exploiting the equivalence relationship $\mathbf{x} \approx_{frac} \mathbf{y}$. To do so, replace a vector $\mathbf{x}$ with its fractional equivalent in the base cube. For instance, $(36\frac{2}{3}, 78\frac{3}{4}) \approx_{frac} (57\frac{2}{3}, 34\frac{3}{4}) \approx_{frac} (\frac{2}{3}, \frac{3}{4})$, so, for each of these two vectors, only the same fractional point in the base cube is plotted. A geometric way to do this is illustrated in Fig. 4.3.3.

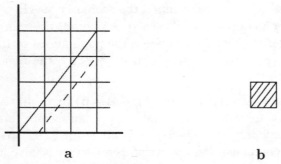

a   b

Fig. 4.3.3. Cutting and sliding the $t\mathbf{p}$ apportionment line.
a. A line in space. **b.** The transposed line

Figure 4.3.3 indicates the lattice of apportionment cubes for $m = 2$. The line $t\mathbf{p}$ leaves the base cube by passing through the horizontal line $y = 1$ at $t\mathbf{p} = (x, 1) \approx_{frac} (x, 0)$. This point of departure is plotted as $(x, 0)$. Retaining only the fractional part of $t\mathbf{p}$ is equivalent to cutting the exact apportionment line where it leaves the base cube at $(x, 1)$ and then shifting the infinite portion of the cut line downwards until it hits the x axis ($y = 0$) at the point $(x, 0)$. The shifted line, the dashed line in Fig. 4.3.3a, is parallel to the original one; it differs only by a change in the integer assignment values.

Now, trace the future of the translated dashed line. It departs the base cube at $(1, y)$ when it passes through the vertical line $x = 1$. As $(1, y) \approx_{frac} (0, y)$, the same "cut and slide" process is used. Namely, cut the translated line where it leaves the base cube at $(1, y)$ and slide the infinite portion to the left so that its base is at the point $(0, y)$.

By continuing this process of taking a translated version of $t\mathbf{p}$, finding where it leaves the base cube, using the appropriate "cut and slide" process, and then continuing with the newly translated version of $t\mathbf{p}$, we end up with a figure similar to that given in Fig. 4.3.3b. In this figure, for instance, the small line segment in the lower right hand corner corresponds to the first cut and slide. The segment just above the diagonal represents the second cut, etc. (Another way to obtain Fig. 4.3.3b is to cut out all squares from Fig. 4.3.3a that are crossed by the apportionment line $t\mathbf{p}$ and then stack them in a pile.) Figure 4.3.3b is a geometric representation of all possible fractional parts arising from $t\mathbf{p}$. A similar geometric process applies for all values of $m \geq 3$, the only difference is that the square is replaced by a m-dimensional base cube.

The Surface of a Donut. If the parallel translates of this "cut and slide" process are sufficiently close to one another, then, clearly, some of them cut across a specified open region in the base cube; say, $AP(\mathbf{p})$. In other words, if $\mathbf{p}$ forces the parallel translates to fill in the base cube, then an Alabama Paradox probably occurs for some h. What remains is to determine how and when this happens.

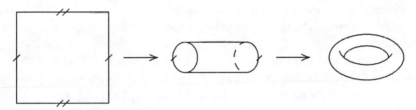

Fig. 4.3.4. Converting a square into a donut

One way to envision these disjoint parallel lines is to reconnect them. To see how to do this, observe from the construction that the two horizontal edges of the base cube are identified with each other; they pinpoint where a translate of the exact apportionment line $t\mathbf{p}$ is cut and slid downwards. So, by gluing these two edges together to create a cylinder, as indicated in the middle portion of Fig. 4.3.4, the horizontal cut segments of the line $t\mathbf{p}$ are reconnected.

Similarly, the side edges of the base cube establish where the exact apportionment line is cut and slid to the left. Gluing these two edges together reconnects the remaining position where translates of $t\mathbf{p}$ are cut. (This second gluing corresponds to connecting the two ends of the cylinder.) What results from this second gluing is the figure on the right of Fig. 4.3.4 – the surface of a donut, or a torus. Now that the edges of the base are connected to form a torus, T^2, the cut parallel lines are reconnected into one long line wrapping around T^2.

A similar cut and regluing operation holds for all values of $m \geq 2$. Here, when the exact apportionment line $t\mathbf{p}$ hits a surface of the base cube, it is cut and moved directly to the opposite surface so that the fractional part of all components remain the same. As above, the parallel translates of the line $t\mathbf{p}$ drawn in the base cube register the fractional portions for each state's exact apportionment. The lines are reconnected when opposite surfaces of the base cube are glued together to create T^m; this is an *m-dimensional torus.*

A problem with trying to construct the torus T^m is that, physically, it can't be done once $m \geq 3$; the folding requires us to reside in a $m + 1$-dimensional space. The reason, suggested by the folding of the square, is that at least one of the gluing steps requires moving "outwards" in a new dimension. It is this extra-dimensional movement that forces T^2 to inhabit a three-dimensional space. Similarly, for $m = 3$ the gluing requires residence in a four-dimensional space. Such physical limitations, constitute a problem only when the physical act is attempted. We do not need the actual physical torus, the mathematical construction more than suffices. Notice, however, the amusing conclusion that

> *the political apportionment problems caused by the US Constitution are subject to the geometric intricacies of a fifty-dimensional donut, T^{50}, residing in a 51- dimensional space.*

No wonder there are so many difficulties! But try (as I once attempted) to explain this to your congressman!

Properties of a Torus. What remains is to show how the reconnected line wraps around the torus. These well understood properties are described in most books on modern dynamics. The explanation is critical for understanding various subtleties of the Alabama Paradox and other apportionment methods, so a brief description is offered.

For $m = 2$ assume the populations of the two states are 1000 and 2000; this defines $\mathbf{p} = (\frac{1}{3}, \frac{2}{3})$. The exact apportionment line $t\mathbf{p}$ crosses an edge of the base cube whenever tp_1 or tp_2 is an integer j; for instance, whenever $t\frac{2}{3} = j$, or $t = \frac{3j}{2}$. Consequently, by inserting $t = \frac{3j}{2}$ into $t\mathbf{p}$ and using $j = 0, 1, 2, \ldots$, we have the points $(0,0)$, $(\frac{1}{2}, 1)$, $(1, 2)$, $(\frac{3}{2}, 3), \ldots$. Using the fractional equivalent, it follows that the line segments in the base cube connect the points $(0,0) \rightarrow (\frac{1}{2}, 1) \approx_{frac} (\frac{1}{2}, 0)$ and $(\frac{1}{2}, 0) \rightarrow (1, 1) \approx_{frac} (0, 0)$. Once the line returns to the starting point $(0, 0)$, everything is repeated. Therefore, the base cube has only two line segments (so the reconnected line circles the torus twice) that, measured in a horizontal direction, are distance $\frac{1}{2}$ apart. This wide separation makes it is easy for the line on the torus (or the two line segments in the base cube) to miss a fairly large open set. This typifies settings where we might expect paradoxes to be avoided.

From the above, we now know that to compute the "cut and slide" points for $t\mathbf{p}$ we first solve $t(p_1, p_2) = (tp_1, tp_2)$ for t values where one component is an integer. The fractional value of the other component locates the "cut and slide" point on the base cube. For example, if $t\mathbf{p}$ has an integer value j for the second state, the value of t is $tp_2 = j$, or $t = \frac{j}{p_2}$. For this value of t, the cutting point is at

$$t\mathbf{p} = \frac{j}{p_2}(p_1, p_2) = j(\frac{p_1}{p_2}, 1). \tag{4.3.8}$$

Equation 4.3.8 offers a simple equation to determine the x values which are cut and slide points; they are at the fractional part of $j\frac{p_1}{p_2}$, $j = 0, 1, \ldots$.

To illustrate Eq. 4.3.8 with numbers from the two state example, suppose a child is born in the first state to change the population figures to 1001 and 2000. This trivial change in population unleashes a major change in the geometry and positioning of the line segments! Equation 4.3.8 now requires the $t\mathbf{p}$ line to cross the x axis in the base cube at the fractional part of the points $j\frac{1001}{2000}$; these points are

$$0, \frac{1001}{2000}, \frac{2}{2000}, \frac{1003}{2000}, \frac{4}{2000}, \frac{1005}{2000}, \ldots$$

So, instead of only two lines in the base cube, *the new population figure forces 2000 line segments to cross the x axis of the base cube, and they are only the distance* $\frac{1}{2000}$ *apart!* Here, the line segments are so close together that it would be difficult for all of them to miss a reasonably sized open set in the base cube. Thus, if entering a particular open set ensures the existence of a paradox (as true for the Alabama Paradox), we must expect the paradox to occur for some value of h. What a difference a birth can make; many new little paradoxes!

The same construction holds for all $m \geq 3$. For example, if $\mathbf{p} = (0.1, 0.3, 0.6)$, then we are interested in learning how the translates of the exact apportionment line pass through, say, the bottom surface (the $z = 0$ surface) of the base cube. Following the derivation of Eq. 4.3.8, these points are the fractional equivalents of $j(\frac{1}{6}, \frac{1}{2}, 0)$. A simple computation confirms that there are only the six points,

$$(0,0,0), (\frac{1}{6}, \frac{1}{2}, 0), (\frac{2}{6}, 0, 0), (\frac{3}{6}, \frac{1}{2}, 0), (\frac{4}{6}, 0, 0), (\frac{5}{6}, \frac{1}{2}, 0)$$

which are reasonably far apart. (The minimum distance is $\frac{1}{3}$.)

Compare the above computation for $\mathbf{p}$ with the almost identical choice of $\mathbf{p}' = (0.1001, 0.2999, 0.6000)$ caused by a single person moving from the second state to the first. Now the points on the bottom surface of the base cube are determined by the fractional parts of $j(\frac{1001}{6000}, \frac{2999}{6000}, 0)$. Instead of only six points, we end up with $(6000)^2 = 36,000,000$ different crossing points on the bottom of the base cube that are closer than $\frac{1}{18,000,000}$ units apart! Using $\mathbf{p}$, it is reasonable to expect that a large open set can be chosen in the base cube which is missed by all of the line segments. Clearly, this same assertion does not hold for $\mathbf{p}'$.

With a little thought, these statements make sense. Compare it with the "savings program" where each evening all pocket change is saved. Each day, there is only a trivial change in total savings. But, the accumulated value over a period of time can be substantial. This *"A little each day makes a lot in a week"* philosophy extends to apportionment problems. A small change in the population figures is trivial in the short run (i.e., for small h values), but the accumulated effect can be substantial in the long run (for larger h values).

Back to the Alabama Paradox. Armed with the wealth of line segments, return to the Alabama Paradox. By construction, minor changes in the value of $\mathbf{p} = (0.1, 0.3, 0.6)$ introduce only trivial changes in the size and shape of the region $AP(\mathbf{p})$; consequently, $AP(\mathbf{p})$ and $AP(\mathbf{p}')$ are almost identical. Now, $\mathbf{p}$ may avoid the Alabama Paradox because $t\mathbf{p} \notin AP(\mathbf{p})$ for any $t \geq 0$. This is true if the line segments are sufficiently far enough apart so that all of them miss the open region $AP(\mathbf{p})$. On the other hand, the line segments for $\mathbf{p}'$ are so close to each other, that many of them must enter the nearly identical region $AP(\mathbf{p}')$. A population change of a single person can trigger the paradox!

In general, most $\mathbf{p}$ values pack the line segments in the torus (or base cube) close enough so that some of them must enter the open, Alabama Paradox generating region $AP(\mathbf{p})$. In fact, as indicated by the above examples, we have an amusing conclusion. The natural approach to try to avoid apportionment difficulties by using more accurate census figures can be penalized; *the added accuracy can force the exact apportionment line* $t\mathbf{p}$ *to unleash an Alabama Paradox.*

Theorem 4.3.2. *For $m \geq 3$, arbitrarily close to any $\mathbf{p} \in Si(m)$, there is a $\mathbf{p}'$ leading to an Alabama Paradox.*[15]

4.3.4 A Better Improved Method?

Can we find a better, improved apportionment method by inventing new procedures? Instead of choosing the integer apportionment $\mathbf{a} = (a_1, a_2, \ldots, a_m)$ which minimizes the distance $\|\mathbf{a} - h\mathbf{p}\|$, maybe the Alabama Paradox can be avoided by using another function $g(\mathbf{x})$. With such a g, the goal is to find the integer apportionment $\mathbf{a}$ which satisfies the house size and minimizes the value of

$$g(\mathbf{a} - h\mathbf{p}). \tag{4.3.9}$$

Approaches of this type have been proposed. Of course, fairness and common sense impose certain requirements upon g. The first is that, because the goal is to "round off," we only need to consider the base cube. Computationally, this means that g only needs to be defined for values in this cube.

Second, it is reasonable to assume that g is continuous. After all, a g with discontinuities allows a slight change in the value of $\mathbf{a} - h\mathbf{p}$ to force a jump, or huge change in the rounding off at a particular house size. Enough problems already occur with continuity, so there is no reason to beg for more difficulties by dropping smoothness.

Next, we require:

1. $g(\mathbf{0})$ is the unique minimum value for g and that $g(\lambda \mathbf{x})$ increases with larger values of λ.

This condition just means that when the exact apportionment for each state is an integer, that should be the apportionment. The monotonicity assumption excludes stupid choices of g where the round off favors a state when it is far from the exact apportionment but not when it is close.

A last condition, *neutrality*, ensures that each state is treated the same. Namely, if the population figures for the different states are interchanged, then so are the allocations. (Neutrality is not necessary, but it is so natural that I included it.)

---

[15] Indeed, the set of $\mathbf{p} \in Si(m)$ that generates an Alabama Paradox includes an open dense set.

Theorem 4.3.3. *Suppose the rounding off process is determined by minimizing the value of Eq. 4.3.9 in the base cube where the choice of a continuous, neutral g satisfies 1. Almost all choices of* $\mathbf{p} \in Si(m)$ *have an Alabama Paradox for some house size h.*

One way to think of this theorem is that the g function only changes the shape of the jar lid used to squash flies. Instead of a circle (where $g(\mathbf{x}) = \|\mathbf{x}\|$), it could be a triangle ($g(\mathbf{x}) = \sum_j |x_j|$), a square ($g(\mathbf{x}) = max(|x_j|)$), or even an object crudely resembling a snowflake ($g(\mathbf{x}) = \sum_j |x_j|^{\frac{1}{4}}$). In fact, one of the proposed procedures was $g(\mathbf{x}) = max(\sqrt{x_j(x_j + 1)})$. The motivation for this and other g choices is given in the description near Eq. 4.3.23.

Whatever the choice of g, it is possible to move (i.e. by appropriately choosing $\mathbf{p}$) the newly shaped jar lid so that, in the two screen problem, designated flies on each screen can be killed even if they are in widely separated regions. In other words, don't blame the choice of a round off procedure g for the difficulties, the Alabama Paradox is caused by the enormous geometric flexibility in movement (determined by population figures) in going from one house size to another.

Outline of Proof. By neutrality, the point $k(\frac{1}{3}, \frac{1}{3}, \frac{1}{3})$ (or, more generally, for $m \geq 3$, $(\frac{l}{m}, \frac{l}{m}, \ldots, \frac{l}{m})$) corresponds to complete ties on a k assignment triangle. By continuity and monotonicity, there is an open set on the $k + 1$ triangle where c_j receives an extra seat and where indifference point is a boundary point. In the same manner as above, an open $AP(\mathbf{p})$ region is defined for $\mathbf{p} \neq (\frac{1}{3}, \frac{1}{3}, \frac{1}{3})$. Thus, the conclusion follows from the properties of the exact apportionment line $\mathbf{p}$. $\square$

A Chaotic Aside. As a digression intended for readers familiar with nonlinear dynamics, let me indicate how the apportionment problem can be identified with "chaos." The reader who has yet to become conversant with these important concepts should skip ahead to the next subsection.

Of the many definitions for "chaos," most include irrational flows on a torus. So, by choosing $\mathbf{p}$ to be irrational and by considering the dynamic of Eq. 4.3.2 on a tori, it is clear that chaos occurs. However, I use a slightly different explanation based on the definition of chaos found in the seminal Li - Yorke paper [LY]. They require the system to have:

1. Sensitive dependence on initial conditions.
2. A dense set of periodic orbits.
3. A topologically transitive orbit.

Instead of a traditional dynamical system, consider the system

$$\frac{d\mathbf{x}}{dt} = \mathbf{P}, \qquad (4.3.10)$$

where $\mathbf{p} \in Si(m)$ serves both as an initial condition and the defining right-hand side. If $\mathbf{p} \neq \mathbf{p}'$, then, clearly, $t|\mathbf{p} - \mathbf{p}'|$ grows to become arbitrarily large. Consequently, arbitrarily small differences in initial conditions must lead to arbitrarily large differences in outcome. This satisfies the sensitivity property.

The second property follows from choosing **p** to have rational entries; it defines a periodic orbit on T^m. Moreover, it is known that these periodic orbits are dense.

The last condition is satisfied by any choice of **p** with completely irrational entries.

4.3.5 More Surprises, but not Problems

Even in the relatively simplistic setting of $m = 3$ states, the assignment triangles so closely resemble the representation triangle that we must anticipate Hamilton's method to suffer many of the same problems endured by voting methods. Actually, because the assignment regions are duplicated in *each* apportionment cube, much more can happen. As the approach used to discover these issues mimics that developed in previous sections, I'll just explore one unusual concern based on responsiveness.[16]

If you think the Alabama Paradox is troublesome, just wait until you learn about its other problems. To start, suppose as part of a population change, people from state 1 move to state 2. "Clearly" this migration enhances the second state's position to receive more representation. But, this need not happen with Hamilton's method; instead, state 1 could win one of state 2's representatives! This is outrageous; such intolerable behavior should disqualify Hamilton's method! Perhaps, but perhaps (as I argue next) Hamilton's outcome is reasonable and the misguided rage is due to how we analyze the problem.

To demonstrate this behavior with numbers, the original population in the following example awards state 1 a single representative while state 2 has 27. Now suppose after the census is corrected it is discovered that 20 of the people credited to state 1 really live in state 2. Rather than improving state 2's position, the new figures reassign one of state 2's seats to state 1!

State	Pop.	200**p**	Apport	New Pop	200**p**$'$	Apport
1	1570	1.57	1	1550	1.52	2
2	26630	26.630	27	26650	26.11	26
3	171800	171.80	172	175900	172.37	172

This is mysterious; how can a state lose a representative after its population grows? To understand the reasons, represent the population change from **p** to **p**$'$ by $\mathbf{v} = (v_1, v_2, v_3) = \mathbf{p}' - \mathbf{p}$. (So, $\sum_{j=1}^{3} v_j = 0$.) Following the lead of Sect. 4.2, **v** alters the apportionment iff it crosses a boundary line in the assignment triangle. (That is, iff **p**$'$ is in a different apportionment region.) If the outer normal of the original region is **n**, then the population change **v** moves toward a new region should $(\mathbf{n}, \mathbf{v}) > 0$. As we have learned from voting methods, this inequality offers ample opportunities to choose **v**'s to generate paradoxes.

---

[16]Other issues, such as when subcommittees unite, are left to the reader. Such questions have relevance for those countries using the "list" PR method. For instance, if the outcome in two regions places party 1 in the top-ranks, must the combined outcome also favor this party?

To illustrate, suppose $h\mathbf{p}$ is such that states 2 and 3 are rounded up while state 1 is rounded down. Geometrically, in Fig. 4.3.1, $h\mathbf{p}$ is in the region of the $k = 2$ assignment triangle with the dagger. The outer normal vectors for the two boundaries of this region are $\mathbf{n}_1 = (1,0,1) - (0,1,1) = (1,-1,0)$ (for the vertical boundary) and $\mathbf{n}_2 = (1,0,-1)$. Thus, should either $(\mathbf{n}_1, \mathbf{v}) = v_1 - v_2 > 0$ or $(\mathbf{n}_2, \mathbf{v}) = v_1 - v_3 > 0$ be satisfied, then when $h\mathbf{p}$ is sufficiently close to the appropriate boundary, the outcome will change to benefit state 1.

To show how to use these responsiveness to design scenarios, I'll use the vertical boundary; here the conditions are $v_1 > v_2$, $v_1 + v_2 + v_3 = 0$, and a change in outcome helps state 1 at the expense of state 2. Can state 2 lose a seat after a population increase? Yes, because $v_2 > 0$ does not preclude the possibility that $v_1 > v_2$ (which forces $v_3 = -(v_1 + v_2) < 0$.) So, even with a population increase, state 2 can lose representation! On reflection, this makes sense; state 2 lost out because its increase is relatively smaller population than other states.

A more creative situation requires $v_1 < 0$; here state 1 gains power after losing population. The responsiveness conditions requires $0 > v_1 > v_2$, so $v_3 > 0$. It now is easy to design settings where after state 1 *suffers a loss in population, it is awarded an extra representative!* This is illustrated with the following example which makes sense; although state 1 suffered a loss in population, it is relatively less than that of other states $(0 > v_1 > v_2)$.

State	Pop.	100p	App	New Pop.	% Change	v_j	100p'	App
1	20650	20.65	20	20610	−0.19	−.00042	20.61	21
2	59670	59.67	60	59600	−0.117	−.00076	59.59	59
3	19680	19.68	20	19800	1.12	.00118	19.80	20

Notice the peculiarity where even though state 1 had a higher percentage loss than state 2 (a multiple of about 1.6), it ended up with more representatives! Actually, such a comparison is misleading; it is caused by a misuse of percentages. It is similar to a rural Northern Michigan community demanding more money for traffic control than Detroit because last year they suffered a 300% increase in traffic accidents and Detroit did not. (The year before they had one accident.) Namely, when decisions are being considered among many alternatives, the non-linear form of percentages, with a different denominator for each state, leads to an "apple – orange" comparison. This occurs in the example where, because of its smaller size, state 1 suffers a larger percentage drop in population even though it lost fewer people. The resolution, of course, is to use a common base – this is Hamilton's method.

We now are prepared to understand why a state with an increase in population can lose a seat to a state with a declining population. The answer is that the true comparison is not between two states, but among all of them. As already shown with voting methods, binary comparisons tend to discard vital information. This is what happens with the original example; state 1's loss of population is reflected by its negative v_1 value (in the following table). With only two states, state 2's position would improve with its larger population. However, state 3 enjoyed such a large increase that state 2's relative position declined (as shown by the negative v_2 value). In other words, the example combines two natural forces – a change in the relative standing of the two states, and a change in their position relative to all other states. When all states are compared with the same base, state 1's small population makes v_1 larger than $p_2 - p'_2 = v_2 < 0$. So, although state 2 grew, relative to other states it declined. When viewed in terms of pairwise comparisons, something seems to be seriously wrong! But when viewed in terms of the whole, the outcome becomes reasonable.

State	Pop.	200**p**	New Pop.	% Change	v_j	200**p**′
1	1570	1.57	1550	–	−.00026	1.52
2	26630	26.63	26650	.07	−.0025	26.11
3	171800	171.80	175900	2.39	.00283	172.37

(Incidentally, the above discussion underscores the dangers of the axiomatic approach that is so commonly used in choice theory. An "axiom" is a specific property, so by concentrating on specified axioms, we impose blinders to evaluate procedures strictly in terms of these properties. For instance, it is easy to package the above population responsiveness property as an appealing axiom and then use it to disqualify Hamilton's method. However, Hamilton's method is not at fault; the property is. This concern extends; for instance, as I show in the problems at the end of Sect. 4.5, it is easy to construct two sets of axioms where one set indicates that a particular procedure is "the best," while the other set "proves" that the same procedure is so bad that it must be disqualified. The message is clear; rather than concentrating on specific properties – axioms – we should attempt to discover all properties.)

With so much offered by the limited $m = 3$ assignment regions, just imagine the more imaginative examples permitted by geometry for $m > 3$ states. Using the same approach, interesting examples can be constructed, but I'll leave the fun to the interested reader. The reason more can happen is that there are even more boundaries, the representation regions no longer are triangular, and, with more states, there are more ways to vary the v_j values to satisfy the responsiveness conditions $(\mathbf{n}, \mathbf{v}) > 0$. A shameless way to generate attention about the designed paradoxes is to describe the population changes with other measures (such as percentage change within specific states, etc.) rather than in terms of v_j values.

These examples require $h\mathbf{p}$ to be sufficiently close to an appropriate boundary of assignment regions so that $h\mathbf{p}' = h(\mathbf{p} + \mathbf{v})$ crosses into another region. This suggests that such problems are rare and occur only in concocted examples. If the analysis required using only one apportionment cube, this assertion would be true. However, changes in h and $\mathbf{p}$ change which cube is of interest. When the outcomes from all possible cubes are combined, it turns out that these conclusions are quite likely. The mathematical tool permitting this analysis is my earlier discussion about the "flow on the torus." In other words, whenever a property can be described geometrically as $h\mathbf{p}$ entering an open region which is similar for all apportionment cubes, then the torus argument ensures that the property eventually (i.e., for some h) is satisfied for almost all $\mathbf{p}$.

This torus argument applies to the properties described by population changes $\mathbf{v}$, after all, $\mathbf{v}$ defines an open region near appropriate boundaries of each assignment region. (In fact, the region grows in size with the value of h.) Thus, *the above conclusions must be expected to occur for some value of h for almost all choices of $\mathbf{p}$.* There are certain restrictions; for instance, the phenomenon where a state loses population yet can win a seat requires a "large state – small state" comparison that is combined with a much larger total population growth; therefore they hold for almost all choices of $\mathbf{p}$ satisfying the appropriate inequalities. Notice, however, that since the early 1800s, these "large state – small state" conditions have been typical with the population growth in the United States; therefore it should be easy to find numerous examples from almost any stage of history. Here, $\mathbf{v}$ could reflect estimates on population growth from one year to another or errors in census (or vote) counts. (Such examples are easy to construct with the 1990 US census.)

Observation. *Let $m \geq 3$ and $\mathbf{v} = (v_1, \dots, v_m)$, $\sum_{j=1}^{m} v_j = 0$ be such that $v_1 > v_2$. For almost all choices of $\mathbf{p} \in Si(m)$, there exists a house size h so that a change from $\mathbf{p}$ to $\mathbf{p} + \mathbf{v}$ takes a seat from state 2 and awards it to state 1.*

As a final comment, the phrase "takes a seat from state 2 and awards it to state 1" is a technically inaccurate comment of the type often used to attract attention. It is true only if there are only two states; with $m \geq 3$, there is a reallocation among all states where state 2 loses a seat and state 1 is awarded an extra one. With $m \geq 3$, everything is "relative."

4.3.6 House Monotone Methods

If geometry prohibits Hamilton's Method and its natural extensions from avoiding the Alabama Paradox, then we should look elsewhere. An obvious solution is to *impose* the desired monotonicity. Instead of recalculating the apportionment when a new seat is available, just assign it to the most deserving state. This requires inventing a "fairness measure" $F(a_j, p_j)$, which, presumably, indicates the level of representation enjoyed by the jth state. The idea is that the state with the minimum $F(a_j, p_j)$ value is underrepresented, so it deserves the extra seat.

To convert this common sense into a *house monotone* technique, start with an initial assignment of seats to the states. This could be zero or some other value; for instance, to satisfy the US Constitution, each state could be initially assigned a single seat. The starting apportionment of $h \geq 0$ seats provides the jth state with $a_j(h)$ representatives, $j = 1, \dots, m$. Now, when a seat is added to enlarge the house size to $h + 1$, it goes to the most underrepresented state as identified by the smallest $F(a_j(h), p_j)$ value. Once assigned, add another seat and give it to the state with the smallest $F(a_j(h + 1), p_j)$ value. Continue by induction until all seats are assigned. (In the USA, this is 435.) Because seats are *added* at each house size – nothing else is changed so nothing is subtracted – such methods avoid the Alabama Paradox. This appears to be a perfect scheme; but, as we now should expect, the solution of one problem can give birth to new ones.

Stability and Fairness Measures. The critical defining factor of a house monotone method is the "fairness measure" $F(a_j, p_j)$; different choices (there are an infinite number of them) distinguish among the procedures. It is natural, for instance, to equalize the number of representatives per population. Clearly, the state with the smallest $\frac{a_j(h)}{p_j}$ value is underrepresented at house size h, so it is entitled to the next available seat. Therefore, in going from house size h to $h + 1$, the *Smallest Divisors* method awards the new seat to the state j with the minimum value of

$$F_{SD}(a_j(h), p_j) = \frac{a_j(h)}{p_j}. \tag{4.3.11}$$

One might argue that "fairness" should emphasize the division of the new house size $h + 1$ rather than worrying about past inequities at old values of h. As this forward looking philosophy requires examining what happens to each state *if* it receives the extra seat, the relevant fraction is

$$F_J(a_j, p_j) = \frac{a_j + 1}{p_j}. \tag{4.3.12}$$

$F_J(a_j, p_j)$ measures state j's level of representation at the new house size, so, in moving from house size h to $h + 1$, the *Jefferson* method (named after Thomas Jefferson) awards the extra seat to the state that minimizes $F_J(a_j(h), p_j)$.

As a compromise to try to heal the wounds of the past while seeking fairness in the future, we could use a weighted average between F_{SD} and F_J; this defines

$$F_{W,\gamma}(a_j, p_j) = \frac{a_j + \gamma}{p_j}, \quad \gamma \in [0, 1]. \tag{4.3.13}$$

Again, the state with the minimum $F_{W,\gamma}(a_j(h), p_j)$ value at house size h is entitled to the extra seat for house size $h + 1$. Different γ values define different techniques; $F_{W,0} = F_{SD}$, $F_{W,1} = F_J$, and $F_{W,\frac{1}{2}} = F_W$ is the *Webster method*.

The method currently used in the USA, *Equal Proportions*, is based upon a more sophisticated premise. E. V. Huntington [Hu1-2] reasoned that a distribution of seats is "fair" if there does not exist a reallocation that achieves a "fairer" division. Mathematically, state j has an advantage (more seats per voter) over state i should $\frac{a_j}{p_j} > \frac{a_i}{p_i}$, or, by dividing, should

$$1 > \frac{\frac{a_i}{p_i}}{\frac{a_j}{p_j}} = \frac{a_i p_j}{a_j p_i}. \tag{4.3.14}$$

This last ratio, then, measures the disadvantage experienced by state i with respect to j; the smaller the value, the more state i is underrepresented.

If state j has a relative overrepresentation, shouldn't one its seats be given to state i? Perhaps; but this might tip the scales so that state i now has an undue advantage over j! Using the same measure, the relative disadvantage state j suffers after a reallocation is $\frac{(a_j-1)p_i}{(a_i+1)p_j}$; the smaller the value, the more state j is underrepresented. Therefore, the new distribution creates an even greater disparity should

$$1 > \frac{a_i p_j}{a_j p_i} \geq \frac{(a_j - 1)p_i}{(a_i + 1)p_j}. \tag{4.3.15}$$

Stated in another way, if Inequality 4.3.15, or its equivalent versions $\frac{a_i(a_i+1)}{p_i^2} \geq \frac{a_j(a_j-1)}{p_j^2}$, or

$$\frac{\sqrt{a_i(a_i + 1)}}{p_i} \geq \frac{\sqrt{a_j(a_j - 1)}}{p_j}, \tag{4.3.16}$$

are satisfied, then there is no reason to give state i one of j's seats; the relative relationship between these two states is stable. In turn, to achieve this stability, the goal is to make the values

$$F_{EP}(a_i, p_i) = \frac{\sqrt{a_i(a_i + 1)}}{p_i} \tag{4.3.17}$$

as equal as possible over the states. The *Equal Proportions* method used by the USA, then, awards the new seat obtained by going from house size h to $h+1$ to the state with the minimum $F_{EP}(a_j(h), p_j)$ value.

The remaining procedure that Huntington calls "workable" is the *Harmonic Mean* defined by

$$F_{HM}(a_j, p_j) = \frac{2a_j(a_j + 1)}{p_j(2a_j + 1)}. \tag{4.3.18}$$

This strange looking choice of F results from trying to equalize the number of citizens per representative by emphasizing the ratio $\frac{p_i}{a_j}$. State j is at a disadvantage with respect to i if $\frac{p_j}{a_j} - \frac{p_i}{a_i} > 0$, where the level of disadvantage is determined by the value of this difference. So, using the stability analysis to decide which of two states is more deserving of a newly available seat in terms of the absolute differences between the fractions, state j is more deserving than i should

$$\frac{p_j}{a_j + 1} - \frac{p_i}{a_i} \geq \frac{p_i}{a_i + 1} - \frac{p_j}{a_j} > 0. \tag{4.3.19}$$

Collecting terms (and taking the reciprocal so "smaller" means "more underrepresented") leads to Eq. 4.3.18.

The description for each method sounds reasonable; so, which one should be used? As described below, each has serious problems. In other words, when grappling with problems based on higher dimensional geometry, be careful – standard "common sense" honed from experiences in our limited three-dimensional world can mislead severely. This continues to underscore the fact that while the defining properties or axioms of a procedure may appear to be acceptable, the consequences may not be!

The Differences Make a Difference. Although it usually is asserted that five of the above methods are the only "workable" allocation procedures (e.g., see [Hu1, Mas]), it takes only minimal imagination to invent an infinite number of other reasonable methods. We could, for instance, modify the derivation for F_{EP} by emphasizing the *new* allocation rather than the current one. Or, to combine the advantages of using relative differences (F_{EP}) and absolute differences (F_{HM}) of different a_i, p_i ratios, we might use the weighted average $F_{L,\gamma}(a_j, p_j) = (1 - \gamma)F_{EP}(a_j, p_j) + \gamma F_{HM}, \gamma \in [0,1]$. Indeed, by modifying the following geometric description, the reader can invent any number of distinctly new approaches.

The main point, which we should anticipate from our discussion of positional methods, is that *different choices for F can result in significantly different apportionments*. Just as a single profile can support many different election rankings, the same population figures can define different allocations of seats as the choice of F varies. Huntington demonstrated this rich divergence with delightful examples typified by the following one where three methods define three different apportionments for three states.

State	Pop.	HM	EP	W
A	729	7	7	8
B	534	5	6	5
C	337	4	3	3
	1600	16	16	16

(4.3.20)

The concerns generated by Huntington's examples underscores the need to understand apportionment methods. What theory has emerged is, for the most part, based on the construction of clever examples or computer simulations. (See [Hu1, Mas, BY1].) As such, this leaves unanswered important concerns. For instance, how prevalent are these paradoxes? When should we worry about them? How can we compare methods? What else can go wrong? Why do the paradoxes occur? In order to correct *what can happen* we need to know *why it can happen*. More generally, I appeal to the lesson already learned – when a procedure is described in terms of the motivation behind its development or certain axioms it possesses, it may sound great. A more practical measure is to understand all of its hidden but serious consequences. This requires a more careful geometric analysis of the procedure.

The similarity of the examples of apportionment paradoxes with those from voting suggests that a geometric theory for apportionments can be designed – a theory closely related to that developed in Chaps. 2 and 3 for voting methods. (For instance, the class of $F_{W,\gamma}$ methods define a version of the procedure line.) This can be done, and (because of the nonlinearities of methods such as EP) the resulting geometry is richer than that for voting. Moreover, all of the concerns from voting, such as responsiveness, comparing what happens when a new candidate or state is admitted, etc., have direct counterparts. While space limitations permit me to present only a hint of what is possible, enough geometry is offered so that the reader can develop intuition about what happens and why. In this way, we overcome Huntington confession that "crucial examples of this sort are not easy to construct, ..." Once we understand *why* something happens, constructing examples becomes an exercise. Dependence on computer simulations no longer is necessary.

4.3.7 Unworkable Methods

In his remarkable paper [Hu1], Huntington describes and then dismisses certain methods as being "unworkable." Although he justifies his comments with examples, he does not explain this curiosity. An explanation, however, shows how to create illustrating examples while underscoring the close connection between apportionment problems and voting. Therefore, I digress to explain his preference for "relative differences" of fractions over "absolute;" a preference that has been widely quoted and adopted, but, seemingly, only superficially explored.

Two fractions, $\frac{x_1}{y_1}, \frac{x_2}{y_2}$, can be compared with the absolute difference, $\frac{x_1}{y_1} - \frac{x_2}{y_2}$, or the relative difference $\frac{x_1}{y_1} / \frac{x_2}{y_2}$. The advantage of using the relative difference is that a number, $F(a_j, p_j)$, is defined to rank the states. What is wrong with relative differences?

To illustrate the problems, suppose absolute difference are used with, say, an approach that compares $\frac{a_i}{a_j}$ with $\frac{p_i}{p_j}$. Ideally, $\frac{a_i}{a_j} = \frac{p_i}{p_j}$, so, a positive value for $\frac{a_i}{a_j} - \frac{p_i}{p_j}$ indicates that state i is overrepresented. This indicator of overrepresentation combined with the stability analysis determines which of two states are more deserving of an extra representative. Clearly, the inequality

$$\frac{a_j + 1}{a_i} \quad \frac{p_j}{p_i} \geq \frac{a_i + 1}{a_j} - \frac{p_i}{p_j}, \tag{4.3.21}$$

favors state i over j.

Herein lies the problem. Using only the ordinal information from absolute differences harbors the possibility of cycles; cycles generate the inability to decide. As shown next, this happens! Recall, however, that the above derivation of the Harmonic Mean is based on absolute differences. What saves HM is that, instead of using the ordinal rankings for each pair, the *value* of the difference is used to generate a number for each state. Ranking states according to these numbers avoids cycles, so the most "underrepresented" can be determined. Therefore, by incorporating the *level of intensity of representation*, rather than just ordinal pairwise comparisons, the cycle problem is evaded. Observe how this resolution is related to my earlier discussion about avoiding voting cycles.

Theorem 4.3.4. *Consider the method where if the value of the difference*

$$\frac{overrepresented\ state}{underrepresented\ state} - \frac{Population\ of\ overrepresented\ state}{Population\ of\ underrepresented\ state} \tag{4.3.22}$$

can be reduced by a transfer of representatives from one state to the other, then this transfer should be made. For $m \geq 3$, this method admits cycles. Indeed, for $n = 3$ and for any set of positive integers (a_1, a_2, a_3) so that

$$a_1 a_3 (a_3^3 - a_1^3) + a_2 a_3 (a_2^3 - a_3^3) + a_1 a_2 (a_1^3 - a_2^3) \neq 0, \tag{4.3.23}$$

there exists an open set of choices of **p** *so that a cycle occurs when an extra seat is added to create house size* $h = a_1 + a_2 + a_3 + 1$.

As already argued, cycles make it impossible to decide which state deserves the next seat. The above asserts that cycles exist, and it suggests that they are abundant. Indeed, with a little extra effort (combining notions described in the proof with the earlier "flow on a torus" description), an assertion of the type in Theorem 4.3.1 holds. In fact, I view the proof of Theorem 4.3.4 to be more important than the statement because it indicates how to extend the conclusion to other settings that rely upon ordinal rankings. The proof and a method to find examples are motivated by the following.

Example 4.3.1. Suppose the population figures and apportionment for three states and house size nine are

State	Population	Apportionment
1	4593	4
2	3327	3
3	2080	2
Total	10,000	9

Who should get the extra seat at house size 10? The stability comparison between states one and two leads to the inequality $\frac{4+1}{3} - \frac{p_1}{p_2} = 0.286 > \frac{4}{3+1} - \frac{p_2}{p_1} = 0.276$. Thus, state 2 deserves the seat more than state 1; $2 \succ 1$. Similarly, comparing states two and three, $\frac{3+1}{2} - \frac{p_2}{p_3} = 0.400 > \frac{3}{2+1} - \frac{p_3}{p_2} = 0.375$, shows that $3 \succ 2$. The last comparison between states three and one, $\frac{2+1}{4} - \frac{p_3}{p_1} = 0.297 > \frac{4+1}{2} - \frac{p_1}{p_3} = 0.2918$, completes the cycle with $1 \succ 3$. Observe that the apportionment figures for $h = 9$ satisfy Eq. 4.3.23.

To see how to construct this and other examples, reexpress Eq. 4.3.21, which designates $i \succ j$ (i deserves the seat more than j), as

$$\frac{a_j + 1}{a_i} - \frac{a_i + 1}{a_j} \geq \frac{p_j}{p_i} - \frac{p_i}{p_j}, \qquad (4.3.24)$$

For temporary notation, call the left side the (j, i) *adjustment ratio* and the right side the *population ratio*. A $2 \succ 1, 3 \succ 2, 1 \succ 3$ cycle, then, is created if Eq. 4.3.24 is satisfied for the (j, i) choices $(1, 2), (2, 3), (3, 1)$. (The reverse cycle is created if the inequalities or the (j, i) pairs are reversed.)

Using these inequalities and the figures from the example, cycles can be created from solutions of

$$x - \frac{1}{x} < \frac{8}{12}, \ y - \frac{1}{y} < 1, \ z - \frac{1}{z} < -\frac{7}{4},$$

where $x = \frac{p_1}{p_2}, y = \frac{p_2}{p_3}, z = \frac{p_3}{p_1}$. Each inequality reduces to a quadratic inequality; e.g., the first one is $x^2 - \frac{8}{12}x - 1 < 0$. Thanks to the quadratic formula, we have

$$x < 1.3874, \ y < 1.618, \ z < 0.4537.$$

Because $xy = \frac{p_1}{p_2}\frac{p_2}{p_3} = \frac{p_1}{p_3} = \frac{1}{z}$, x and y need to satisfy not only the above inequalities, but (and this is where the difficulty arises) also $xy = \frac{1}{z} > \frac{1}{0.4537} = 2.2037$. Thus, while values such as $x = \frac{4}{3}, y = \frac{3}{2}$ satisfy the first two inequalities, the product fails to satisfy the third. Larger values, such as $x = 1.38, y = 1.60$ satisfy all requirements, so set $\frac{p_1}{p_2} = 1.38, \frac{p_2}{p_3} = 1.60$, and adjust the value of p_3 so that numbers come out in a nice fashion. This is how the example was generated.

If we knew that the algebraic approach always worked, the proof would be completed. It does not. With the above figures, for instance, it is impossible to construct a $1 \succ 2, 2 \succ 3, 3 \succ 1$ cycle. This is because any supporting population figures must reverse all of the inequalities to satisfy $x > 1.387, y > 1.618, xy < 2.2037$. But, even the minimal $y = 1.618$ value imposes the contradictory $x < 1.362$.

As another illustration, the apportionment $a_1 = a_2 = 2$, $a_3 = 1$ leads to the quadratic equations $x^2 < 1$, $y^2 - 2y - 1 < 0$, $z^2 + 2z - 1 < 0$, or the inequalities $0 < x < 1$, $0 < y < 1 + \sqrt{2}$, $xy > \frac{1}{-1+\sqrt{2}} = 1 + \sqrt{2}$. These inequalities impose the impossible situation where $y < xy$ and $x < 1$. Similarly, reversing the inequalities leads to the impossible setting of $y > xy, x > 1$. Notice that because $a_1 = a_2$, Eq. 4.3.23 is not satisfied. $\square$

The theorem is proved, then, if Eq. 4.3.23 ensures that the inequalities comparing the adjustment and population ratios can be solved to define cycles. I prove this, of course, via geometric arguments. As a bonus, the geometry shows how the sign of the expression of Eq. 4.3.23 indicates which cycle can be created.

Outline of Proof. I will indicate how to prove the theorem for $m = 3$; a similar proof holds for $m \geq 3$. Equation 4.3.24 forces a cycle if the $(1,2),(2,3),(3,1)$ adjustment values are either all above, or all below the corresponding population values. So, if a coordinate system is placed at the vector of population ratios, then the vector of adjustment values is in the positive or negative orthant. This approach (resembling the representation cube analysis) is how the theorem is proved.

The geometry is based on the population ratios; in particular, on the graph of the mapping $G(x,y,z) = (x - \frac{1}{x}, y - \frac{1}{y}, z - \frac{1}{z})$. Because $z = \frac{p_3}{p_1} = [\frac{p_1}{p_2}\frac{p_2}{p_3}]^{-1} = (xy)^{-1}$, the image set is a two dimensional surface; it is crudely represented in Fig. 4.3.5.

Following standard mathematical procedures, replace the more complicated image set of G with an object easier to comprehend – its approximating tangent plane at each point. (This plane is the shaded region in the figure.) A tangent plane is uniquely determined by a normal vector, so, with the help of calculus, for specified values of $x = \frac{p_1}{p_2}, y = \frac{p_2}{p_3}, z = \frac{p_3}{p-1}$ a normal vector is

$$\mathbf{N(p)} = (\frac{(p_1^2 + p_3^2)(p_2^2 + p_3^2)}{p_3}, \frac{(p_1^2 + p_3^2)(p_1^2 + p_2^2)}{p_1}, \frac{(p_1^2 + p_2^2)(p_2 + p_3^2)}{p_2}). \quad (4.3.25)$$

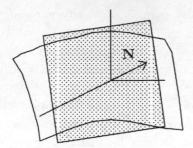

Fig. 4.3.5. The G-surface with a coordinate system

As the components of $\mathbf{N}(\mathbf{p})$ are positive, if the origin of a coordinate system is located at $G(\frac{p_1}{p_2}, \frac{p_2}{p_3}, \frac{p_3}{p_1})$, then *the graph does not enter either the positive or the negative orthants.* This makes sense; if it did, there would be pairs of population figures where one is a cycle relative to the other.

Decomposing the adjustment values into the two terms

$$\frac{a_j + 1}{a_i} - \frac{a_i + 1}{a_j} = [\frac{a_j}{a_i} - \frac{a_i}{a_j}] + \frac{a_j - a_i}{a_i a_j}, \qquad (4.3.26)$$

the term in the brackets (from the $h = \sum a_j$ apportionment) defines a point on the G surface and the second defines a vector of potential changes, $\mathbf{v} = (\frac{a_1 - a_2}{a_1 a_2}, \frac{a_2 - a_3}{a_2 a_3}, \frac{a_3 - a_1}{a_3 a_1})$. In this manner, the dot product

$$(\mathbf{N}((a_1, a_2, a_3)), \mathbf{v}) = \frac{a_1 a_3(a_3^3 - a_1^3) + a_2 a_3(a_2^3 - a_3^3) + a_1 a_2(a_1^3 - a_2^3)}{a_1 a_2 a_3}$$

locates where the adjustment values are relative to the approximating tangent plane (defined at $G(\frac{a_1}{a_2}, \frac{a_2}{a_3}, \frac{a_3}{a_1})$). Namely, if the numerator (which is Eq. 4.3.23) is positive (i.e., the angle is less than 90°), then the vector of adjustment values is above the plane (on the same side as $\mathbf{N}((a_1, a_2, a_3))$); if it is negative (the angle is more than 90°), the adjustment vector is below the plane.

To find a $\mathbf{p}$, project the vector of adjustment values to the plane. If the origin of a coordinate system (x', y', z') were placed at this point, then the vector of adjustment values would be located at $x' = y' = 0$, $z' \neq 0$. So, adjust the location of the origin so that all components of the adjustment values have the same sign. Trivially, this can be done. The location of the new coordinate system defines population figures leading to an example.

To complete the proof, the last geometric step needs to be done with the G surface rather than the approximating tangent plane. However, the details are essentially the same and not particularly illuminating for voting theory, so they are skipped.[17] This completes the proof. $\square$

---

[17] For the mathematically curious, recognize that because $G(x, y, z) : R_+^3 \rightarrow R^3$ has a diagonal Jacobean with entries $(1 + x^{-2}, 1 + y^{-2}, 1 + z^{-2})$, it is locally invertible. Showing it is globally invertible is standard. A foliation on R_+^3 defined by the positive values of c in $xyz = c$ defines a foliation for R^3 where the above image set is on the leaf corresponding to the $xyz = 1$ leaf in the domain. Cycles are created iff the vector of adjustment values is on a different leaf. The condition avoiding cycles corresponds to a lower dimensional algebraic set.

As a parting comment, observe that when three reasonable (i.e., not "too wild") lines are drawn on a two-dimensional surface, seven open regions are usually defined. The special case, where all three lines intersect at a common point, creates only six regions. So, an alternative but closely related proof can be based on the geometry of the apportionment triangles. The three lines in the triangle are "indifference lines" of $\mathbf{p}$ values defined by pairs of vertices where $\frac{a_i+1}{a_j-1} - \frac{a_j+1}{a_i-1} = \frac{p_i}{p_j} - \frac{p_j}{p_i}$. Each side of the line represents where stability favors one state over the other for a representative. The expressions are nonlinear, so, in general, the three lines do not pass through a common point; i.e., in general seven regions emerge. The seventh region, of course, defines the population figures forcing cycles. Using arguments (but more delicate) of the type developed for the discussion of the Alabama Paradox, extra conclusions can be extracted.

4.3.8 Who Cares About Quota?

The telling clue that house monotone methods experience problems comes from Huntington's comment,

> "Now it is a common misconception that in a good apportionment the actual assignment should not differ from the exact quota by more than one whole unit; for example, if the exact quota is 5.21 or 5.76, then it is often assumed that the actual assignment should not be less than 5 nor more than 6."

Sure seems like a reasonable assumption to me! If my state is entitled to 62.76 seats, why should we remain politically content when assigned only 58 seats! Yet, Huntington's comment must have its supporters; such exaggerated round-offs seem to be sanguinely accepted in Europe where allocations of seats to parties can be rounded up or down by more than unity. I am unaware of any sustained outcry of, "Foul! Foul!" Maybe they are intimidated by the mathematics.

Huntington demonstrates one such ("good"?) apportionment with the following example where state A, with its exact apportionment of 92.15, is awarded only 90 seats. This is a "large - small" state comparison, so, with the current USA population figures, citizens from California and New York should pay particular attention.

State	Pop.	EP	State	Pop.	EP	
A	9215	90	D	157	2	
B	159	2	E	156	2	(4.3.27)
C	158	2	F	155	2	
				10,000	100	

Concerned citizens from states with smaller populations, such as Vermont or Alaska, should not allow this example to lull them into smug complacency; the next Huntington example allows the EP to award a large state 90 seats although only entitled to 87.85 representatives! One must wonder which small states sacrificed seats so that A can indulge in its added political power.

State	Pop.	EP	State	Pop.	EP
A	8785	90	F	122	1
B	126	1	G	121	1
C	125	1	H	120	1
D	124	1	I	119	1
E	123	1	J	118	1
			K	117	1
				$\overline{10,000}$	$\overline{100}$

$$(4.3.28)$$

As I indicate next, much more can happen!

The Humane Way to Catch Flies. What is going on? To understand the apportionment paradoxes, return to the fly killing exercise. Squashing flies on a screen leaves a mess, so, instead of killing flies, catch them by replacing the lid with a jar. (Surprisingly, the "shape" of the jar is the same for all F functions! Thus, just by introducing new shapes, unexplored classes of methods are invented.) Holding the jar with an orientation to be specified later, move it as close as possible to the screen to catch a single fly on a side of the jar. (As before, the movement is determined by the exact apportionment line $t\mathbf{p}$.) For comfort, each jar could be held in a different manner. (How the "jar" is held distinguishes the different choices of F.) Obviously, by holding the jar in different ways, different flies can be caught. (This explains the differences in the apportionments for the same $\mathbf{p}$.)

To equate fly hunting with house monotone methods, let $F_g(a_j, p_j) = \frac{g(a_j)}{p_j}$ for function g. Of course, to be realistic, $g(0) \geq 0$ and g needs to be monotonically increasing where $\lim_{x \to \infty} g(x) = \infty$. If $F_g(a_j, p_j) \geq \lambda$, then

$$g(a_j) \geq \lambda p_j, \quad \forall j. \qquad (4.3.29)$$

Equation 4.3.29 makes sense. The term $\lambda\mathbf{p} = (\lambda p_1, \ldots, \lambda p_m)$ is a point on the exact apportionment line, while $g(x)$ measures the number of representatives assigned to a state. This equation, then, asserts that the g measure should approximate the exact apportionment λp_j. (Well, if $\lambda = h$.) Indeed, for years, a closely related approach, based on Jefferson's choice of $g(a) = a + 1$, was used in the USA. After a value of λ was chosen, state j was assigned k_j seats where k_j is the first integer so that $g_J(k_j) = k_j + 1$ is greater than or equal to λp_j. By allowing the value of h to depend upon the choice of λ and $\mathbf{p}$, the house size could and did vary.

The "fly catching jar" is defined by $J_g(\mathbf{a}, \mathbf{p}, \lambda) = (g(a_1) - \lambda p_1, \ldots, g(a_m) - \lambda p_m)$ where an apportionment, $\mathbf{a}$, is "inside" the jar iff each component of J_g is nonnegative. Thus the jth side of the jar is determined by the unique x_j value

$$g(x_j) = \lambda p_j; \quad x_j = g^{-1}(\lambda p_j).$$

(All positive numbers are in the image of g, so x_j is defined; g is strictly increasing, so x_j is unique.) For example, to find the x value for EP, solve

$\sqrt{x(x+1)} = \lambda p$, or $x^2 + x - (\lambda p)^2 = 0$, to obtain (via the quadratic formula), $x = \frac{-1 + \sqrt{1 + 4(\lambda p)^2}}{2}$, a value that is less than λp. For the methods described above, the solutions are

Method	$g(x)$	$x = g^{-1}(\lambda p)$	
SD	x	$x = \lambda p$	
J	$x + 1$	$x = \lambda p - 1$	
W, γ	$x + \gamma$	$x = \lambda p - \gamma$	(4.3.30)
EP	$\sqrt{x(x+1)}$	$x = \frac{-1 + \sqrt{1 + 4(\lambda p)^2}}{2}$	
HM	$\frac{2x(x+1)}{2x+1}$	$x = \frac{\lambda p - 1 + \sqrt{1 + (\lambda p)^2}}{2}$	

Example 4.3.2. For two states,[18] suppose $\mathbf{p} = (\frac{1}{5}, \frac{4}{5})$ and $\lambda = 10$. According to the table 4.3.29, the sides of the SD jar are $x = \lambda p_1 = 2$, $y = \lambda p_2 = 8$. So, the SD jar is defined by

$$J_{SD} = \{(x, y) \mid x \geq 2, y \geq 8\}.$$

In other words, the J_{SD} jar is just a translated positive quadrant where the origin now is at the point $\lambda \mathbf{p} = (2, 8)$. This is the shaded region depicted in Fig. 4.3.6.

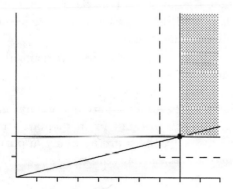

Fig. 4.3.6. Comparison between SD and Jefferson jars

For the same $\lambda \mathbf{p}$ values, the sides of the Jefferson jar are $x = \lambda p_1 - 1 = 1$, $y = \lambda p_2 - 1 = 7$. Consequently, the J_J jar for $\lambda \mathbf{p}$ is

$$J_J = \{(x, y) \mid x \geq 1, y \geq 7\}.$$

Again, J_J is a translated positive quadrant; the difference between J_{SD} and J_J is how they are held. The translated origin for J_J is at the point $\lambda \mathbf{p} - (1, 1)$, rather than on the exact apportionment line! The boundaries for this J_J region

---

[18] No serious problems occur for $m = 2$, but pictures are easy to draw.

are the dashed lines depicted in Fig. 4.3.6. This means that *the J_J jar is held in a lagging, asymmetric manner as it is moved along the exact apportionment line.*

As a third example using these $\lambda \mathbf{p}$ values, J_{EP} is defined by

$$\{(x,y) \mid x \geq \frac{-1+\sqrt{17}}{2} \approx 2 - 0.4384, \, y \geq \frac{-1+\sqrt{257}}{2} \approx 8 - 0.4844\}.$$

Again, J_{EP} is obtained by sliding the positive quadrant in a lagging, asymmetric manner to a point near, but *never on* the exact apportionment line $\lambda \mathbf{p}$. In fact, with the EP, the direction and amount of translation from $\lambda \mathbf{p}$ changes with the value of $\lambda \mathbf{p}$. $\square$

For any number of states, *the jar $J_g(\mathbf{x}, \mathbf{p}, \lambda)$ always is a translated positive orthant.* The differences between F_g methods, therefore, are uniquely determined by the location of the translated origin. Expressing this point as

$$\lambda \mathbf{p} + T_g(\lambda \mathbf{p}) = \lambda \mathbf{p} + [(g^{-1}(\lambda p_1), \ldots, g^{-1}(\lambda p_m)) - \lambda \mathbf{p}],$$

the term in the brackets, $T_g(\lambda \mathbf{p})$, indicates the position of the translated origin relative to the reference point $\lambda \mathbf{p}$ on the exact apportionment line. In words, this translation term determines how the jar J_g is held as it moves. With the exception of the SD, the jar always is held in a lagging, asymmetric manner as it moves according to the exact apportionment line.

For the methods described above, all components of the translation term $T_g(\lambda \mathbf{p})$ are between -1 and 0. Therefore, if the *translation cube* is defined as $TC = [-1, 0]^m$, then *the translation term, $T_g(\lambda \mathbf{p}) \in TC$, uniquely determines the properties of F_g.* (In Fig. 4.3.6, TC is the small square defined by the dashed and solid lines; the location of the translation point in this square determines which procedure is being used.) Conversely, there are as many apportionment methods as there are ways to define the translation vector.

4.3.9 Big States, Small States

Once we recognize that the properties of a method are determined by the translation term $\mathbf{T}_g(\lambda \mathbf{p}) \in TC$, it is easy to see why different methods lead to different apportionments. Figure 4.3.7 depicts the impact of different choices of $\mathbf{T}_g(\lambda \mathbf{p})$ with the same $\lambda \mathbf{p}$ value. Obviously, certain approaches (e.g., J_a in the figure) favors states with large populations, while others (e.g., J_b in the figure) favor small population states. By positioning the orthant so that it is further along the axis representing the state with the larger population, as true with J_a, a distinct bias is interjected; for the same population figures, the large state gets more seats.

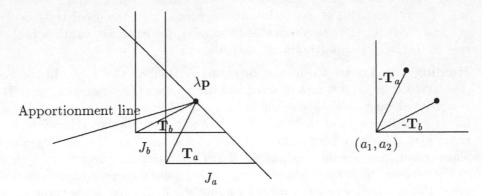

Fig. 4.3.7. A comparison of different jars

It is possible to coax an useful inequality out of the geometry that determines which methods favor large or small population states. The approach is based on comparing the (ratio of) population figures that different methods require to assign the same relative allocation (a_1, a_2), $a_1 > a_2$. To see what we are looking for, suppose method g_a assigns (a_1, a_2) with population figures $(500, 100)$ while method g_b requires $(1,000, 100)$. By awarding the large state the allocation a_1 with the smaller population figure of 500, or with the ratio $\frac{p_2}{p_1} = \frac{1}{5}$, method g_a displays its distinct bias in favor of larger states. Method g_b, on the other hand, forces a large population state to have a much larger population before justifying this allocation; here the ratio is $\frac{p_2}{p_1} = \frac{1}{10}$. So, for a given allocation, the larger the value of $\frac{p_2}{p_1}$ (where $p_1 > p_2$) required for a specific allocation (i.e., the sooner a large population state gets a particular apportionment), the more bias a method discloses toward larger states.

To describe this measure in geometric terms, place the vertex of two jars at the same (a_1, a_2) point. The exact apportionment line supporting this outcome is found by adding $-T_g$ to the origin. (See Fig. 4.3.7.) In the example, $-T_a$ locates a point above $-T_b$. This means that the exact apportionment line for g_a allows a larger slope than that g_b, $\frac{p_2^a}{p_1^a} > \frac{p_2^b}{p_1^b}$; this reinforces the earlier observation that g_a favors larger states.

Translating this description into the geometry of TC, two methods, g_a, g_b are compared in the following manner. Draw a line from $(0,0)$ through T_{g_b}. If T_{g_a} is to the south of this line, or on the line but farther along, then g_a favors large states more than g_b; otherwise g_a favors the small state. With this elementary comparison technique, it follows that *the SD favors small states more than any other procedure; the Jefferson method favors large states more than any other procedure.* Also, if $\gamma_1 > \gamma_2$, then W, γ_1 favors large states over W, γ_2. Reexpressing the geometry in terms of the g functions, g_a favors large states if for all $s > t$,

$$\frac{g_a(t)}{g_a(s)} > \frac{g_b(t)}{g_b(s)}. \qquad (4.3.31)$$

The above comments suggest that SD and J play a role analogous to $\mathbf{w}_0$ and $\mathbf{w}_{\frac{1}{2}}$ from voting. This suspicion becomes accurate when the other vertices of TC are included. Thus, it is reasonable to wonder, for instance, which g plays the role of the BC for apportionment methods, etc.[19]

Holding the Jar to Collect a Specimen. Holding the J_g jar in the above prescribed manner, it is moved according to the exact apportionment line. There is a critical value $\lambda = \lambda_h$ so that for $\lambda > \lambda_h$ all apportionments inside the jar have house sizes greater than h – we've moved the jar too far. Therefore, at the value $\lambda_h \mathbf{p}$, those apportionments in J_g with house size h are the ones we examine. These candidates are on a side of J_g (if any apportionment of house size h were in the interior, then λ_h is not at its maximum value), and usually, there is only one – this is the F_g apportionment for house size h. If there are several qualified apportionments, then there is a tie in the choice, so use a tie-breaker.

Example 4.3.3. The geometric description is invaluable for understanding the properties of an apportionment procedure, but, in practice, a computational scheme is used. As described above, the value of λ_h is such that $g(a_j(h)) = \lambda_h p_j$ for some state. For all other states, say the kth, find the smallest value of a_k satisfying $\frac{g(a_k)}{p_k} = \lambda^{(k)} \geq \lambda_h$. Then, the seats are assigned to states according to the $\lambda^{(k)}$ values where smaller values are served first.

Actual computations are fairly simple. With a spreadsheet, compute for each state the values of $\frac{g(a_i)}{p_i}$ for various consecutive choices of a_i. At house size h, λ_h must be one of the computed values. The jth state receives the smallest value of a_j so that $\frac{g(a_j)}{p_j} \geq \lambda_h$. To illustrate with the EP, $h = 100$, and the population figures of Eq. 4.3.27, suppose we thought that the accurate apportionment would assign state B a single seat. If so, then it must be that $\frac{g(1)}{0.0159} = \lambda^{(B)} = 88.944 \geq \lambda_{100}$. In turn, the ratios $\frac{g(a_j(100))}{p_j}$, $j = A, \ldots, F$, must be as close to this value as possible. With the smaller populations of states $C - F$, the inequalities $\frac{g(1)}{p_j} > \frac{g(1)}{0.0159}$ for $j = C, D, E, F$, ensures that B is entitled to a second seat before any of these four states.

For state A, $\frac{g(81)}{0.9215} = 88.4411$ while $\frac{g(82)}{0.9215} = 89.5263$. Thus, as long as B has only a single representative, state A is entitled to at most 82 seats. All together, this adds up to 87 seats; 13 more to go. The only way extra seats can be added legitimately is to relax the assumption restricting state B to only one seat. Therefore, $\lambda_{100} > \frac{g(1)}{0.0159}$, so B must be assigned another seat.

---

[19] Regional voting in Congress is becoming increasingly important for many policy factors. Indeed, for many issues, the concerns of a region overtake those of the individual states. Wendy Ramsbottom explored this question (in her 1993 Northwestern University Senior Thesis) by comparing the number of representatives from all states in a region with the number of representatives the region would receive if it were a state. In this way, she demonstrated that certain regions are short-changed in political power; a factor that can be critical on a close vote. (She identified issues where this could have been a deciding factor in several Congressional votes.) The natural question raised by her work is whether there is a method of the above kind which keeps both kinds of apportionments – state and region – as consistent as possible. This is the Borda issue.

The much larger $\lambda^{(B)} = \frac{g(2)}{0.0159} = 154.0560$ value, obtained when B has two seats, eliminates the restricting logjam; now seats can be assigned to other states. Nevertheless, until F secures its second seat, state A's apportionment is restricted to the smallest value of a so that $\frac{g(a)}{0.9215} \geq \frac{g(1)}{0.0155} = 91.2396$, or $a_A = 84$. This leaves us still far below the designated value of $h = 100$, so F also gets a second seat.

Now that the small population states have two seats, the apportionment for state A defines the value λ_h. In fact, each new seat must be assigned to A until the first integer value of a where $\frac{g(a)}{0.9215} \geq \lambda^{(B)} = \frac{g(2)}{0.0159} = 154.0560$. With a simple computation, this means that for all house sizes from 94 to 151, states $B - F$ remain fixed at two representatives and A gets the rest. The figures for the final apportionment of 100 seats follow.

State	EP	$\frac{g_{EP}(a_j)}{p_j}$	State	EP	$\frac{g_{EP}(a_j)}{p_j}$	
A	90	98.2079	D	2	156.0185	
B	2	154.0559	E	2	157.01857	(4.3.32)
C	2	155.0400	F	2	158.0360	

From this computation, we have that

$$\lambda_{100} = \lambda^{(A)} = 98.2079,$$
$$\mathbf{T}_{EP}(\lambda_{100}\mathbf{p}) = -(0.4986, 0.4219, 0.4214, 0.4210, 0.4205, 0.4200).$$
$$(4.3.33)$$

In this example where the large population state is rounded down by more than unity, $\lambda_h < h$. For the population figures of Eq. 4.3.32, where the large population state is rounded upwards, $\lambda_{100} = \lambda^{(A)} = 103.0149$ while $\lambda^{(j)}, j = B, \ldots, K$, range in value from 112.2392 to 120.8730. $\square$

4.3.10 The Translation Bias

The lesson learned from the example is that the F_y methods do not base the apportionment on the values of $h\mathbf{p}$, but rather on some other value $\lambda_h\mathbf{p}$ where λ_h can be larger or smaller than h. That is not all; fresh bias is manufactured by the lagging, asymmetric motion of the jar held away from the apportionment line (as established by T_g)! With all of this hidden, very real bias, something serious must go wrong. But what and why?

The answer, as always, comes from the geometry. There are only two elements; the slope of the apportionment line $\lambda\mathbf{p}$ and the translation of the jar, $T_g(\lambda\mathbf{p})$. Perhaps the easiest way to see how they interact is to run the "fly catching" film backwards. Choose the unique $\lambda = \lambda^*$ value which positions the origin of the jar right at $\mathbf{x}^*$ on the simplex $S_h = \{\mathbf{x} \in R_+^m \mid \sum_{j=1}^m x_j = h\}$. Even a slight increase in $\lambda > \lambda^*$ forces the jar to totally miss S_h. On the other hand, a $\lambda < \lambda^*$ value requires the jar to meet a portion of the simplex including $\mathbf{x}^*$. Should all components of $\mathbf{x}^*$ be integers, $\mathbf{x}^*$ is the apportionment at house size h. If not, then "back up" by choosing smaller values of λ until an integer apportionment on S_h is obtained. This backwards approach is, of course, equivalent to the earlier description.

The bias introduced by the translation term $T_g(\lambda \mathbf{p})$ permits – at times demands – the point $\mathbf{x}^*$ to be quite distant from the apportionment cube defined by $h\mathbf{p}$. With $\mathbf{x}^*$ in a different cube, this makes it easy for the backing up process to catch an apportionment that doesn't satisfy quota. Examples now become trivial to construct. For instance, for $m = 3$, choose $\mathbf{x}^* = (95, 1, 1)$; the entries are integers, so $\mathbf{x}^*$ is the apportionment for $h = 97$. All we need is to find the corresponding $\mathbf{p}$ for a specified method. To illustrate with the Jefferson method, the translation term $T_J = (-1, -1, -1)$ shows that the point on the exact apportionment line is $\mathbf{x}^* - T_J = \lambda_{97}\mathbf{p} = (95 + 1, 1 + 1, 1 + 1)$; so $\mathbf{p} = (0.96, 0.02, 0.02)$ defines fractional population figures. With this $\mathbf{p}$, the exact apportionment at $h = 97$ is $(93.12, 1.94, 1.94)$; as we might conjecture from Fig. 4.3.7, the large state is rounded up by more than one seat.

Maybe creating examples is not completely trivial; there are no population figures which allows the above $\mathbf{x}^*$ to be the basis of a paradox for the Webster or EP methods. Again, the explanation comes from the geometry. For the Webster method, the distance between $\|\lambda_{97}\mathbf{p} - \mathbf{x}^*\| = \| - T_W\| = \|(\frac{1}{2}, \frac{1}{2}, \frac{1}{2})\| = \frac{\sqrt{3}}{2}$ is insufficient to push $h\mathbf{p}$ and $\mathbf{x}^*$ into different apportionment triangles that don't share common vertices; i.e., apportionments. For $m \geq 4$ states, however, the increased value of $\|T_W\| = \frac{\sqrt{m}}{2}$ puts added distance between a chosen point $\mathbf{x}^*$ and $h\mathbf{p}$ which allows examples to be created. So, if $\mathbf{x}^* = (95, 1, 1, 1)$, then $\mathbf{x}^* - T_W = 100\mathbf{p} = 100(0.955, 0.015, 0.015, 0.015)$. The exact $h = 98$ allocation for the large state with $\mathbf{p}$ is 93.59, thus this illustrates that the Webster method can round this state up by more than one.

Of course, larger values of m increases the value of $\|T_g\|$, which allows even more extreme examples to be created. For instance, let $\mathbf{x}^* = (51, 1, \ldots, 1)$ be the $h = 100$ apportionment for $m = 50$ states. With Jefferson's method, the associated $\lambda \mathbf{p} = \mathbf{x} * -T_J = (52, 2, \ldots, 2)$, so $\mathbf{p} = (0.265, 0.015, \ldots, 0.015)$ and the exact apportionment is $(34.67, 1.33, \ldots, 1.33)$. Here, Jefferson's method rounds the large state upwards not by one, but by 17. EP does not do much better; here the exact apportionment is 42.63, so the large state is rounded upwards by 9 rather than unity.

Indeed, *the bias of $T_g \in TC$ tends to try to violate the upper quota*. As T_J is an extreme vertex of TC, it designates the upper bound on how badly upper quota can be violated. More generally, for method g, if there exists a value $\gamma > 0$ so that each component of T_g is bounded above by $-\gamma$, then examples (by choosing appropriate values of m and $\mathbf{p}$) can be created showing that instead of rounding up to the nearest integer, g can round up by a value as large as desired! Enough geometry has been described to make the proofs of these assertions an exercise.

Conversely, $T_{SD} = \mathbf{0}$, so we must expect that *the SD never violates upper quota*. The proof of this assertion also follows from the geometry. With SD, $\mathbf{x}^*$

is the exact apportionment $h\mathbf{p}$; that is, for each state $\frac{x_i^*}{p_i} = h < \frac{x_i^*+1}{p_i}$. If $\mathbf{x}^*$ is an integer vector, then it is the apportionment. If not, then the backward motion requires $\lambda_h < h$. So, for state i, the apportionment is the smallest integer a_i satisfying $\frac{x_i^*+1}{p_i} > \frac{g_{SD}(a_i)}{p_i} = \frac{a_i}{p_i} \geq \lambda_h$, or $x_i^*+1 > a_i$. This means that a_i can be no larger than rounding x_i^* upwards.

4.3.11 Sliding Bias

By forcing the jar off the apportionment line, the translation term creates an obvious bias that attempts to violate upper quota. More subtly, but with equal force in the "other direction," the sliding action of the jar determined by the slope of the apportionment line plays a critical role.

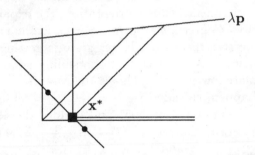

Fig. 4.3.8. The sliding bias of the apportionment line

Figure 4.3.8 demonstrates the influence (i.e., bias) the slope of $\lambda\mathbf{p}$ has on the "backing up" process for $m = 2$; even a large difference in λ values admits only a trivial change in the height of the horizontal edge (i.e., where the jar edge for the large state passes through S_h). The starting position of $\mathbf{x}^*$ is closest to an apportionment favoring the large state; the "backing-up" process forces the jar edge to hit an apportionment less favorable to the large state. This makes sense; the flatter the apportionment line is in a direction, the less change there will be in the edge of the jar in this direction. Therefore, the real change in the jar, which ends up determining the apportionment, is in the other directions. Observe who is being "helped;" by keeping the value for the larger state essentially fixed but varying the edge for the small state, the smaller population state gains an advantage!

The limited interval geometry associated with $m = 2$ forces the sliding action of the jar to hit an endpoint of the interval containing $\mathbf{x}^*$. More adventure is created once $m \geq 3$. This is illustrated in Fig. 4.3.9 with $m = 3$. Each triangle in the grid corresponds to either a $k = 1$ or $k = 2$ assignment triangle. The jar, with its edges parallel to the coordinate axis of R^3, always create a triangle with the same orientation as the $k = 1$ assignment triangle; the size of the triangle depends upon the value of λ.

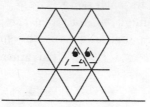

Fig. 4.3.9. Bias due to geometry and sliding

The two dots in the figure represent different values of $\mathbf{x}^*$; because they are nearby, they correspond to similar population values. The two dashed triangles describe how the jar intersects with S_h; the asymmetric positioning about the respective $\mathbf{x}^*$ position is attributed to the sliding bias introduced by the apportionment line $\lambda \mathbf{p}$ as described above. In this depiction, the geometry of the expanding triangle on the right must hit a vertices of the assignment triangle containing $\mathbf{x}_2^*$. This need not be the situation with the expanding triangle on the left. Because of the assignment triangle orientation, the expanding triangle can miss all of these vertices to first hit a bottom vertex in the assignment triangle below! But, a lower vertex means the larger state is getting a smaller apportionment. Therefore, we must suspect that the sliding action might cause the apportionment to violate lower quota. This is the case!

To see what can happen, consider the $h = 150$, $m = 50$, SD apportionment where the large state has population 5051 and each of the 49 small states has the population of 101. For a small state, $\frac{g_{SD}(1)}{p_1} = \frac{1}{0.0101} = 99.010$ while $\frac{2}{0.0101} = 198.020$. For the large state, $\frac{g_{SD}(51)}{0.5051} = 100.970$, $\frac{100}{0.5051} = 197.981$. Thus, when $h = 100$, we have that $\lambda_{100} = \frac{1}{0.0101} = 99.010$ leading to the quite reasonable apportionment where each small state has a single representative and the large state has 51. But, for house sizes from $h = 101, \ldots, 198$, we have that $\lambda_h = \frac{g_{SD}(51)}{0.5051} = 100.970$. In particular, the $h = 198$ apportionment has two seats for each small state and the same 51 for the large state. As the exact apportionment for the large state is 100.010, the state is rounded down not by unity, but by 49 seats! In contrast, EP would assign the large state 71 seats (some small states receive two and rest, three seats.) Here, rounding down violates lower quota by "only" 29 seats. The reasonable apportionment, where quota is met, comes from the Jefferson approach which assigns the large state 100 seats, and 2 seats for each small state.

What is going on is that the bias of the sliding action tries to violate lower quota. Countering this effect is the upward bias of the translation term T_g; if it is sufficiently large, then lower quota need not be violated. In particular, *the Jefferson apportionment never violates lower quota.* The proof of this assertion is elementary. If $\mathbf{y}^* = h\mathbf{p}$ is the exact quota, then for each i,

$$h = \frac{y_i^*}{p_i} = \frac{(y_i^* - 1) + 1}{p_i} = \frac{g_J(y_i^* - 1)}{p_i}.$$

The sum of the values $\sum_{i=1}^m (y_i - 1) = \sum_{i=1}^m y_i - m = h - m$, so the above values cannot be apportionments for house size h; that is, $\lambda_h > h$. Consequently, the Jefferson apportionment for state i is the smallest integer a_i satisfying

$$\frac{g_J(a_i)}{p_i} = \frac{a_i + 1}{p_i} \geq \lambda_h > h = \frac{g_J(hp_i - 1)}{p_i},$$

or $a_i \geq hp_i$. This completes the proof.

Other assertions now can be proved. For instance, it turns out that if a procedure is bounded away from the Jefferson method, then values of m, h, and **p** can be chosen so that the method rounds down by any desired amount. It can be shown that if a procedure is bounded away from the boundary of TC (so, it can't be J or SD), then almost all population figures satisfying a specified ratio between the populations of densely and sparsely populated states will eventually round apportionments up and down by more than unity. With so many problems, one must wonder why these procedures are used!

Compensating Actions and Constructing Examples. What a mess! The translation term tries to violate upper quota while the sliding effect attempts to violate lower quota. This means the Jefferson - Small Divisor methods play extreme roles most similar to that played by the plurality - anti-plurality methods for positional voting. The SD favors small states by trying to abuse lower quota – Jefferson favors large states by trying to break upper quota. All other methods attempt a balance between these two evils; they combine the negatives of both approaches. So, using these methods becomes a gamble where the hope is that "compensating errors" will enable reasonable outcomes!

The following is a small sample of what else can be extracted from the geometry. Here, as above, $\mathbf{x}^*$ is the last point on S_h hit by the apportionment jar.

- Slightly changing the population can vary the location of $\mathbf{x}^*$. But, different choices can induce radically different "sliding actions." Thus, for any g, there are situations where a slight change in population can make a drastic change in apportionments.
- The admissible changes are determined by the geometry of the assignment triangles. All of the admissible, different directions defined by the boundaries between regions promise that apportionment methods are subject to all sorts of responsiveness difficulties. For instance, for any g, there are situations where, after a state has an increase in its relative population, it loses seats.
- For any g, with enough states, the rounding off process can be as bad as desired.

These two compensating elements – the translation term and the sliding effect – provides enough tools to put a grin even on Steven, the jolly anarchist, as he strokes his long, greying beard while contemplating how to construct examples to demonstrate the inadequacies of structured government. The building blocks are boundary conditions (e.g., tied outcomes) separating different outcomes. To illustrate, I show how to construct examples for a specified g where a small change in population – say, no more than two voters – can alter the allocations.

Corresponding to states A, B, C, let a, b, c be positive integers – potential numbers of seats – where $a + b + c + 1 = h$ and choose population figures so that

$$\lambda^A = \frac{g(a)}{p_a} > \lambda^B = \frac{g(b)}{p_b} = \frac{g(c)}{p_c} = \lambda^C > \frac{g(a-1)}{p_a}. \tag{4.3.34}$$

The key is the tied outcome between B and C. There is an extra seat to be assigned, and who gets it depends upon the $g(b+1), g(c+1)$ values. On the other hand, suppose the tie vote is broken because C's population is ever so slightly increased so that $p_c^+ > p_c$; the operative inequalities now are $\frac{g(a)}{p_a} > \frac{g(b)}{p_b} = \lambda^B > \frac{g(c)}{p_c^+} = \lambda^C$. It cannot be that $\lambda_h = \lambda^C$ because this would lead to the A, B, C allocation of (a, b, c); one seat remains to be assigned. Therefore, $\lambda_h = \lambda^B > \lambda^C$, so B gets b seats, A gets a seats, and, as $\frac{g(c+1)}{p_c^+} > \lambda^B > \frac{g(c)}{p_c^+}$, C gets $c + 1$ seats. To create other scenarios, just play with the p_j values. For example, if p_c decreases, p_b increases, or p_b increases more than p_c, then B gets the extra seat. With all of this flexibility created by the radical changes in values of fractions with small changes in denominators with small values, all sorts of examples are forthcoming.

The starting point to create examples, then, is where there is equality of the $\frac{g}{p_j}$ values. Then, slight changes in the population figures can make a radical difference in the allocation. This is how I constructed the above examples demonstrating the differing bias of T_g and the sliding action. (The reader familiar with "singularity" or "catastrophe" theory will recognize similarities where qualitatively different outcomes occur with certain small perturbations from a specified singular, boundary condition. Mathematically, there is a close relationship.)

Example 4.3.4. Let $(a, b, c) = (6, 8, 5)$ and $h = 20$. For the EP, Eq. 4.3.34 becomes

$$\frac{\sqrt{42}}{p_a} > \frac{\sqrt{72}}{p_b} = \frac{\sqrt{30}}{p_c},$$

so population figures for examples can be constructed from 64750 ($< 10^4\sqrt{42}$), 84852 ($\approx 10^4\sqrt{72}$), 54772 ($\approx 10^4\sqrt{30}$). The following illustrates that when only two people move from C to A, B's apportionment can change.

State	Population	EP	Population	EP
A	64750	6	64752	6
B	84852	8	84852	9
C	54772	6	54770	5

Similarly, C would benefit if only a couple of people moved from B to A.

The same figures can be used to construct examples where even after an *increase in a state's population, the apportionment goes down.* With the first figures, suppose a mini-migration from state A has two people moving to C and five people moving to B. Before the migration, C had six seats; after the migration, even with its increased population, C is assigned only five seats. (The population figures $(64743, 84857, 54774)$ have the EP apportionment $(6, 9, 5)$.) The disturbing, but not uncommon theme from voting – more can mean less – applies again.

The remaining changes in these figures, where people move from A to just one of the states, or where people move from, say, B to C, provide no surprises. This can be corrected by admitting more states. With more states, there are more ways to move the population from one group of states to another; hence, there are more surprises. These are left for the entertainment of the reader. $\square$

Of course, EP is used above because it is the technique of choice for the USA; similar assertions hold for all choices of g. In fact, by attaching what we learned about the motion on a torus onto the above comments, it can be shown that while the construction of these assertions involves boundary values, almost all population figures eventually will satisfy these conditions. So, for instance, if only a specified ϵ percentage of the voters can change states, for almost all choices of $\mathbf{p}$, there are house sizes where certain changes within these bounds will alter the apportionments in the above indicated manner.

As for a choice of ϵ, recognize that the 1990 census of the USA was about 2.1% short. (For instance, see the discussion in the Congressional Record, July 30, 1991, S11316-S11327.) Although statistical procedures were offered (and declined) to correct the situation, an error of 2.1% was considered quite accurate. Thus, a reasonable value to use with the above comments is half of that – $\epsilon = 0.01$.

4.3.12 If the State of Washington Had only 836 More People

If changes in apportionments are likely, then why do we not observe it in practice? Actually, we do; based on the 1990 census a small change in the population of New Jersey, New York, and Massachusetts would have caused changes in the apportionment of other states. As true in giving course grades, some student is right on the dividing line between and A and B; a very slight change in the grade of even a quiz would change the grades. Similarly, for 1990 and EP, the dividing value of $\lambda_{435} = 432.5043$ is defined by Massachusetts; it has 10 seats. Other nearby values are for New Jersey, with its population of 7,730,188 and 13 seats is $\lambda_{NJ} = 432.99037$ while New York, with its population of 17,990,455 has $\lambda_{NY} = 434.35646$. Currently, Oklahoma has six seats; its EP values are $\frac{g_{EP}(6)}{p_{OK}} = 511.15877$; $\frac{g_{EP}(5)}{p_{OK}} = 432.008$. So, a slight increase in the populations of New Jersey, New York, or Massachusetts that force their λ value below 432.008 would result in Oklahoma losing a seat to that state. To assist the reader in designing examples to show how increase in populations would lead to decrease in seats, etc., a listing of the states with λ values near the division line are given below.

In this table, a_i is the current apportionment; p_j is defined by dividing the population of each state by 248, 103, 333; the total population of the 50 states.

(This excludes the population of Washington DC. Using the full population of 248,709,873 changes the λ_j values, but not their ordering, so it does not affect the apportionment.)

State	Pop	a_j	$\frac{g_{EP}(a_j)}{p_j}$	$\frac{g_{EP}(a_j-1)}{p_j}$
Florida	12,937,926	23	450.54427	431.3633
Massachusetts	6,016,425	10	432.5043	391.2149
Montana	799,065	1	440.1755	∞
Mississippi	2,573,216	5	528.10099	431.19265
New Jersey	7,730,188	13	432.99037	400.87119
New York	17,990,455	31	434.35646	420.56384
Tennessee	4,877,185	9	482.59701	431.64789
Washington	4,866,692	9	483.63753	432.57855

These figures display the peculiar fact that *the 1990 apportionment of Congressional seats appears to be wrong!* According to the census figures (as recorded in the Congressional Record, specified by the census bureau, and listed in any number of almanacs) the state of Washington should receive 8, rather than the assigned 9 seats. In fact, $\frac{g_{EP}(9)}{p_{WA}} = 483.6375$ while $\frac{g_{EP}(8)}{p_{WA}} = 432.57855 > \lambda_{435}$. These figures require Washington to have 8, rather than 9 representatives, and that $\lambda_{435} = \frac{g_{EP}(8)}{p_{WA}} = 432.57855$. Namely, Washington is the true state on the dividing line! In turn, Massachusetts is entitled to Washington's extra seat!

From several perspectives, assigning Massachusetts 11 seats and Washington eight makes sense. Currently, Massachusetts has 11% more representatives than Washington (10 to 9). With the swap leading to 11 and eight seats, Massachusetts would have 25% more representatives matching its 23% larger population (6,016,425 to 4,866,692). Moreover, such representation would provide parity between Massachusetts and Virginia (pop 6,187,358). It is a close call, with only about 840 more people in Washington – no more than a reasonable turnout for a small town high school football game – the apportionment is correct! This constitutes less than $\frac{2}{100}$ of a percent change!

So, what happened? The answer is that for only the second time since 1900, the Census Bureau allocated Department of Defense's overseas employees for purposes of reapportionment. (The other time was in 1970 during the Vietnam War.) As shown above, a small change will benefit Washington at Massachusetts' expense, and it happened. Consequently, as one might expect, Massachusetts went to court. The District Court ruled that the "decision to allocate the employees and to use home of record data was arbitrary and capricious." [Mas] But, on June 26, 1992, the US Supreme Court ruled against Massachusetts on technical grounds involving "the separation of powers and the unique constitutional position of the President." (This is because the President is charged with calculating and transmitting the apportionment to Congress. See [Mas, Mon]; the decision includes a nice description of the history.)

Around the same time, Montana also issued a legal challenge prompted by the fact that the 1990 census caused it to lose one of its two representatives. As they argued, the average population of a district in the US is 572,466 as compared to the much larger 803,655 for Montana. (The inflated number is due to the overseas employee count.) Essentially, they attacked the EP method; "Montana alleged that the 'method of the harmonic mean' or the 'method of smallest divisors' would yield a fairer result." [Mon, p4] It is no surprise to see Montana championing SD because, as shown above, it favors small states. But as demonstrated by the above discussion, for selecting a procedure, the 1990 figures are immaterial; it is easy to demonstrate other figures where the outcome is distinctly biased! Indeed, all of these procedures are subject to creating serious difficulties! Montana lost in the Supreme Court. [Mon]

4.3.13 A Solution

With so many problems generated by these procedures, what should we do? Personally, I find that the house monotone methods violate the initial intent in the design of PR methods far more than Hamilton's Method. Think about it; the serious bias pulling in both directions leaves us hostage to "compensating errors." That doesn't seem to be a reasonable way to conduct serious business. Anyway, the main reason we dropped Hamilton's method is to avoid the Alabama Paradox. This paradox requires changes in house size, so in the many situations where the house size is fixed, the political ramifications of the Alabama Paradox no longer remain relevant. Consequently, whenever the house size is fixed, as for the US Congress, Hamilton's method is most reasonable! In fact, Montana's argument about district size is an argument for a return to Hamilton.

Of course, for the intellectual challenge and for those countries using the "list system," we can develop procedures that avoid the Alabama Paradox while preserving quota but, yes, with the price of introducing still new problems. The approach I suggest is based on standard techniques from optimization theory. Before selecting an "optimal" choice, first we find all viable candidates. Similarly, before designing selection methods, we must first identify *all house monotone paths that satisfy quota*. Call this set $\mathcal{E}(\mathbf{p})$.

An entry of $\mathcal{E}(\mathbf{p})$ is a listing of apportionments starting at house size $h = 0$ and going as far as needed; even to $h = \infty$. Each apportionment in the listing differs from the previous apportionment in that one state has an extra seat (house monotone). Secondly, for each h, the apportionment for h is a vertex on the apportionment cube containing $h\mathbf{p}$ (respects quota). Once $\mathcal{E}(\mathbf{p})$ is given, then the reader's favorite method can be used to select the actual apportionment – Hamilton's method, toss of the dice, whatever. For instance, suppose $\mathbf{a}(h)$ is the apportionment at house size h. In moving to house size $h + 1$, consider all paths in $\mathcal{E}(\mathbf{p})$ that pass through $\mathbf{a}(h)$. The $h + 1$ *eligible set* are all apportionment at house size $h + 1$ that are on one of these paths. So, choose one of the eligible apportionments. This procedure eliminates all worries about the Alabama Paradox as well as the more serious concerns introduced by the normal house monotone methods.

On the other hand, once some vertices (apportionments) are eliminated (because they are not in $\mathcal{E}(\mathbf{p})$), we have changed the geometry; e.g., the boundary of $\mathbf{p}$ values dividing one type of outcome from another is significantly altered. As we have learned, changes in the boundary structure can be accompanied a host of new kinds of paradoxes. This happens; for instance, more serious "population paradoxes" than that described earlier for Hamilton's method occur; some of these problems cannot be dismissed. (To find them, apply the earlier discussion involving the inner normals to the new inner normals that are defined by the new boundaries.)

Finding the Entries of $\mathcal{E}(\mathbf{p}) \neq \emptyset$. It is easy to show for $m = 3$ that $\mathcal{E}(\mathbf{p})$ is not empty. More challenging is to prove this for $m \geq 4$. To conclude this section, I indicate why this is so.

The exact apportionment line for a given $\mathbf{p}$ passes through the interiors of various apportionment cubes. Label them in ascending order; so, cube 1 is the base cube, 2 is the second cube along the line, and so forth. For the kth cube, let $t_e(k)$ and $t_x(k)$ be, respectively, the minimum and maximum value of t with $t\mathbf{p}$ in the cube – this just identifies where the exact apportionment line enters and exits the cube. When $t_e(k)\mathbf{p}$ enters this cube, it passes through a face, an edge, or a vertex; choose the geometric construct with minimal dimension. (So, if it passes through an edge, ignore that the edge is on several faces.) Call this object the kth *entering face*. Similarly, $t_x(k)\mathbf{p}$ identifies where the exact apportionment line leaves the cube, so the geometric object containing this point is called the kth *exiting face*. What helps in this description is that the kth exiting face is the $k + 1$th entering face.

Let $[x]$ be the greatest integer function; this is the function that replaces x with the largest integer smaller than or equal to x. For instance, $[4.89] = 4$, $[7] = 7$. The *candidate entering apportionments* are all apportionments on the kth entering face that satisfy house size $[t_e(k)]$; similarly, the *candidate leaving apportionments* are all apportionments on the k exiting face that satisfy house size $[t_x(k)]$.

To illustrate with numbers, let $\mathbf{p} = (\frac{3}{12}, \frac{5}{12}, \frac{1}{12}, \frac{3}{12})$. The exact apportionment line leaves the base cube and enters cube # 2 when $t = \frac{12}{5}$ at $t\mathbf{p} = (\frac{3}{5}, 1, \frac{1}{5}, \frac{3}{5})$. Thus, the vertices of the first exiting and second entering faces are all vertices where the second component is unity, and all others are either zero or unity. As $[t_e(2)] = [\frac{12}{5}] = 2$, the entering apportionments for the second cube (and exiting apportionments for the first one) are $(1, 1, 0, 0), (0, 1, 1, 0), (0, 1, 0, 1)$.

The next time there is an integer value for $t\mathbf{p}$ is when $t = \frac{12}{3} = 4$ and the point is $4\mathbf{p} = (1, \frac{5}{3}, \frac{1}{3}, 1)$. Here, the $k = 2$ exiting face (and $k = 3$ entering face) is the set of points $(1, x, y, 1)$ where $1 = [\frac{5}{3}] \leq x \leq [\frac{5}{3}] + 1 = 2$, $0 = [\frac{1}{3}] \leq y \leq [\frac{1}{3}] + 1$. As $[4] = 4$, the exiting apportionments are $(1, 1, 1, 1)$ and $(1, 2, 0, 1)$.

The purpose of the candidate entering and exiting apportionments is to ensure that an apportionment is on the correct apportionment cube for each value of h. Clearly, an entry of $\mathcal{E}(\mathbf{p})$ crosses the kth cube from a candidate entering apportionment to a candidate exiting one. What we want to do is to construct all possible ways there are to go between them in a house monotone fashion. Any such listing is a *path* for the k cube. To illustrate with numbers, there are two paths going from $(1,1,0,0)$ to $(1,2,0,1)$; one has the intermediate point $(1,2,0,0)$ and the other has the intermediate point $(1,1,0,1)$. On the other hand, there are *no* paths going from $(0,1,1,0)$ to $(1,2,0,1)$.

In the natural way, the paths in $\mathcal{E}(\mathbf{p})$ are constructed by tying together all of the paths from the cubes. Some of these paths can end in a cube, so they cannot be continued. For instance, as shown above, there is no way to get from $(0,1,1,0)$ to $(1,2,0,1)$. It turns out that by working forwards, we can encounter many of these "dead-ends." So, the better approach mimics how some students try to do homework – start at the answer and work backwards to the problem. The trouble here is to avoid starting at the impossible $h = \infty$. Thus, we need ways to identify intermediate starting points; these are juncture points through which all paths pass.

To define an intermediate starting point, call the candidate entering apportionments *strong entering apportionments* if there is a house monotone path from *each* entering apportionment of the cube to *each* exiting apportionment of the cube! The advantage of these points is that they impose no complications in the construction of forward paths. Choose such an apportionment in a cube larger than needed for the problem (say, for the US Congress, in a cube where $t_e(k) > 435$), these points serve as the starting "answers" for the backwards iteration.

A sufficient condition for there to be strong entering apportionments in the kth cube is if the candidate entering apportionment is the minimal apportionment for the cube. This is satisfied whenever $\sum_{i=1}^{m}(t_e(m)p_i - [t_e(m)p_i]) < 1$. The inequality means that the exact apportionment is very close to the minimal apportionment. For theoretic purposes, observe that this inequality defines an open set about the minimal apportionment. This open set permits the earlier arguments about the line on a torus to be used to show that *for all* $\mathbf{p}$, *there are an infinite number of cubes with a strong entering apportionment.* In the example problem, for instance, whenever $t = 12j$, the exact apportionment passes through the minimal apportionment point, so a strong entering apportionment is defined.

Each strong entering apportionment for cube k also is an exiting apportionment for the $k-1$ cube. In this $k-1$ cube, find all paths connecting entering and exiting apportionments. All entering apportionments, then, serve as the exiting apportionments on the $k-2$ cube. Continue this process.

To demonstrate that $\mathcal{E}(\mathbf{p})$ is nonempty, we only need to construct one such path. To do this, apportionments are chosen to mimic the "cut and side" points. At house size h, initially assign each state its minimal apportionment as determined by $h\mathbf{p}$. This leave $\beta(h)$ extra seats to be assigned. We want to assign extra seats according to "need;" the states where tp_j first turns into an integer needs an extra representative to protect quota. Therefore, order the states according to the value of $t > h$ that make tp_j an integer; a state with a smaller t value needs an extra representative sooner than others. Of course, there can be ties. If so, then break them according to the "next" values of t. Use this ranking to assign $\beta(h)$ states an extra seat. To illustrate with the above example for $t = 10$, $10\mathbf{p} = (2\frac{1}{2}, 4\frac{2}{12}, \frac{10}{12}, 2\frac{3}{4})$. Thus, the initial allocation is $(2, 4, 0, 2)$ and $\beta(10) = 2$. The next value of $t > 10$ when tp_j is an integer for any state is $t = 12$; unfortunately, this is true for *all* four states. To invoke the tie breaker, find the smallest $t > 12$ values where tp_j is an integer. As they are $12 + 4, 12 + 2.4, 12 + 12, 12 + 4$, the second state gets one seat. The last tie cannot be broken (the states have the same population), so flip a coin to assign the next seat to get $(3, 5, 0, 2)$. At $h = 11$, the apportionment is $(3, 5, 0, 3)$, and at $h = 12$, it is $(3, 5, 1, 3)$.

The hard part is done; showing that this assignment process is in $\mathcal{E}(\mathbf{p})$ is left as an exercise.

4.3.14 Exercises

4.3.1. Explain why $AP((0.35, 0.34, 0.31))$ is smaller than $AP((0.6, 0.3, 0.1))$. Find a geometric description for each. (Hint: To find the $AP((0.35, 0.34, 0.31))$ boundary, consider the line $\mathbf{p} + \mathbf{d} = (0.35, 0.34, 0.31) + (d_1, d_2, d_3)$ where $\mathbf{d} \in Si(3)$. Now, set $\mathbf{p} + \mathbf{d}$ equal to a boundary point where the first and second state are awarded an extra seat, but not the first. The values of $\mathbf{d}$ describe the boundaries of $AP((0.35, 0.34, 0.31))$.)

4.3.2. Can an Alabama Paradox occur for $m = 2$? Use the fact there is only one assignment triangle in each apportionment cube to explain your answer.

4.3.3. The description of the Alabama Paradox describes when $h\mathbf{p}$ is in the $k = 1$ assignment triangle, and $(h + 1)\mathbf{p}$ is in the $k = 2$ assignment triangle. To develop other ways this can happen, create an example where $(h + 1)\mathbf{p}$ is an integer vector, $h\mathbf{p}$ is not an integer vector, and in the process of going from h to $h + 1$, an Alabama Paradox occur. This illustrates the folklore story where p_i represents the share of inheritance to be received by the ith brother, $i = 1, 2, 3$. The inheritance requires dividing up h cows. Because $h\mathbf{p}$ does not provide an integer division, two of the brothers "graciously" buy another cow to be added, free of charge, to the division so that an integer number will occur. Of course, their graciousness gives the remaining brother the "Alabama." Find a geometric representation for this description.

4.3.4. The set $A(\mathbf{p})$ is designed so that the state with the lowest population loses a representative at the next step. Can this be done so the state with the second highest population that loses a seat? What is the situation with $m \geq 4$ states?

4.3.5. For the populations of the three states specified in the introductory example, find $AP(\mathbf{p})$. Next, find the smallest integer h so that $h\mathbf{p} \in AP(\mathbf{p})$. As a more challenging problem, for a given $\mathbf{p} \neq (\frac{1}{3}, \frac{1}{3}, \frac{1}{3})$ find a way to determine a lower bound on the value of h that could cause an Alabama Paradox. As another challenging problem, which leads to an analysis of responsiveness questions, for each AP region given by the introductory example, plot the corresponding set of points on the simplex with the initial population figures.

4.3.6. Show that $\mathbf{x} \approx_{frac} \mathbf{y}$ is an equivalence relationship. Show that for any $\mathbf{x}$ and for any apportionment cube, there exists a unique $\mathbf{y}$ in the specified apportionment cube so that $\mathbf{x} \approx_{frac} \mathbf{y}$.

4.3.7. Show that Hamilton's method gives the same answer independent of the choice of the distance. Namely, we could use $d(\mathbf{a}, \mathbf{b}) = \sum |a_j - b_j|$ or, say, $(\sum [a_j - b_j]^2)^{\frac{1}{2}}$.

4.3.8. Compare the lines in the base cube for $\mathbf{p} = (0.50, 0.50)$ and for $\mathbf{p}' = (0.49, 0.51)$. Next try $\mathbf{p}'' = (0.499, 0.501)$. Notice how a slight change in the population, or in the degree of accuracy can radically change how the base cube is filled. From this observation, create a three state example where no Alabama Paradox occurs for $\mathbf{p}$. but, when just a couple people move from one state to another, a paradox does occur for some h.

4.3.9. Rederive Eq. 4.3.17 by assuming the a_j values are the allocation at a given house size and another seat is added. That is, derive the formula showing which state most deserves the extra seat.

4.3.10. If one uses the value of the absolute difference in Eq. 4.3.20, can a transitive method be defined?

4.3.11. The Harmonic mean is based upon a number obtained by taking absolute differences. If only the ordinal relationship is retained, is it possible to have cycles?

4.3.12. There is a significant difference between $m > 3$ and $m = 3$. For $m = 3$, the k-assignment triangles are defined by three vertices in the base cube. Show that for $m \geq 4$, what replaces the k-assignment triangle is defined by $\binom{m}{k}$ vertices, $k = 1, \ldots, m - 1$. Find the distance from the center of this object (given by $k(\frac{1}{m}, \ldots, \frac{1}{m})$) to one of these vertices, and compare this distance to the distance between points $k(\frac{1}{m}, \ldots, \frac{1}{m})$ and $(k + 1)(\frac{1}{m}, \ldots, \frac{1}{m})$. Finally, to appreciate the bias introduced by the translation $T_g(\lambda \mathbf{p})$, compute the length of T_g for EP, for J, and for W with m states.

4.3.13. Use Eq. 4.3.30 to show that the Jefferson method favors large states more than EP. Compare g_J with HM and SD. How does HM compare with EP?

4.3.14. To show that $\mathcal{E}(\mathbf{p}) \neq \emptyset$, we need to show that the path constructed in the concluding subsection has all of the correct properties. First, use the fact that the apportionment is defined in terms of the apportionment cube to show that it is quota preserving. Next, show that all apportionments within a particular cube are house monotone. What remains is to show that the apportionment cannot jump by more than one seat. (This takes care of the transition between cubes.)

4.4 Arrow's Theorem

My discussion of multiprofile conclusions has emphasized issues such as "responsiveness" or "apportionments." The last two sections provide a significant change of pace. Now, differences between profiles are used to prove and extend certain important theorems. The one examined here is Arrow's Impossibility Theorem; in Sect. 4.5 I examine Young's characterization of scoring rules. In both sections, my emphasis is on the informational content about the profiles allowed by the imposed axioms.

With all of the paradoxical difficulties that arise with positional voting methods, it is natural to try to design better selection approaches. Surely, with imagination and creativity, we could invent a procedure where the ranking of three candidates always is compatible with how the different pairs are ranked. However, Kenneth Arrow [Ar] proved that no such procedure exists.

4.4.1 A Sen Type Theorem

Even though there are many proofs of Arrow's Theorem, his mysterious conclusion continues to serve as an intellectual magnet. The attracting force is that it seems to be impossible for his assertion to be true; but it is. What I offer is an extension of his conclusion where my emphasis is to remove the mystery by identifying the informational obstacles preventing the design of such a procedure. (These results hold for $n \geq 3$ candidates.) Once we understand why Arrow's Theorem holds, it is easy to circumvent the difficulties.

Example 4.4.1. To motivate the geometry of this section, I will describe a situation related to Sen's Theorem [Se1,2]. Here, we consider those situations where a particular person has the right to decide the relative ranking of certain alternatives. For instance, I, rather than society, should determine whether I wear a sport coat or my favorite torn and worn sweater when lecturing. Clearly, there are many situations where the relative ranking of certain sets of alternatives are strictly in the purview of a particular agent.

Such a common sense requirement should be easy to accommodate. For instance, suppose I retain the right to decide the relative ranking of $\{c_1, c_2\}$ while Lillian has full power over the relative ranking of $\{c_2, c_3\}$. It is not clear how the relative ranking of $\{c_1, c_3\}$ should be handled, but, at a minimum, it is reasonable to accept that when we agree in our ranking of this pair, that is the chosen ranking.

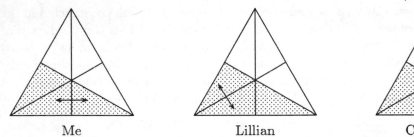

| Me | Lillian | Combined |

Fig. 4.4.1. A special case of Sen's Theorem

While these seemingly innocuous requirements sound reasonable, they are incompatible; there exist situations where they are in conflict with one another. To see why, suppose we both have the ranking $c_1 \succ c_3$; this is, by agreement, our joint ranking of the pair. In the representation triangles of Fig. 4.4.1, this ranking is indicated by the shaded region.

The arrow in the first representation triangle shows how I can satisfy the

$c_1 \succ c_3$ condition while changing my $\{c_1, c_2\}$ ranking, while those in the second representation triangle indicate how Lillian observes the $c_1 \succ c_3$ ranking while altering her ranking of $\{c_2, c_3\}$. The third representation triangle demonstrates the conflict. Our unanimous agreement on $c_1 \succ c_3$ dictates that the outcome must be in the shaded region. However, if my ranking is $c_2 \succ c_1$, as indicated by the bullet on the bottom edge, and Lillian's ranking is $c_3 \succ c_2$, as indicated by the dagger on the side edge, it follows (by intersecting the two binary triangles) that the joint ranking is $c_3 \succ c_2 \succ c_1$, the region with a black square. This outcome is not in the shaded region, so there is a conflict among the imposed conditions. $\square$

These seemingly reasonable assumptions are incompatible because of an interesting mixture of flexibility, yet restrictiveness admitted by the geometry of the representation triangle. The flexibility is manifested by the freedom a voter has to vary the relative rankings of a particular pair while keeping the relative rankings of the other two pairs fixed. Observe that while this motion preserves the relative ranking of the two pairs, the intensity of these binary relationships changes.

The restriction nature of the geometry is indicated with the third representation triangle. Here, two carefully chosen pairwise rankings can dictate the ranking of the last pair. In the example, the choice forces the ranking of $c_3 \succ c_1$. To see what else can happen, let $\mathbf{p}_1$ be the profile for our preferences as specified in the figure. Now let $\mathbf{p}_2$ be where only Lillian changes her ranking to $c_1 \succ c_2 \succ c_3$. Our two binary preferences defining $\mathbf{p}_2$ and the selection rules limit the outcome to either $c_2 \succ c_1 \succ c_3$ or $c_2 \succ c_3 \succ c_1$, where the first is selected according to our unanimity requirement. If I, too, change my ranking (as allowed by the arrow) to define $\mathbf{p}_3$, then our two binary decisions force the outcome to be $c_1 \succ c_2 \succ c_3$. Thus the $\mathbf{p}_1 \rightarrow \mathbf{p}_2 \rightarrow \mathbf{p}_3$ profile change converts one restrictive setting to the other.

It is this geometric conflict of a representation triangle permitting flexibility in inputs while requiring restrictiveness of conclusions – this algebraic sense of having too many unknowns (voters' preferences) with too many equations (the three pairs)– that explains Arrow's Theorem and most other "impossibility" conclusions from social choice. But first, the basic axioms need to be introduced.

4.4.2 Universal Domain and IIA

The most obvious property a procedure should preserve is the democratic principle that *each voter is free to strictly rank the candidates in any desired manner*. No "Big Brother" is permitted in the voting booth to ensure that the voter votes in a particular manner. This is the *universal domain* condition.

The second requirement is a restatement of our goal to invent approaches that eliminate the election paradoxes. Namely, we are seeking a procedure where its ranking of the three candidates always agrees with the rankings of the pairs. The goal, then, is to characterize all ways there are to rank the pairs of candidates and to rank triplets so that the rankings of all four sets always agree.

As Example 4.4.1 shows, this compatibility condition fails even when we allow the ranking of each of two pairs to be determined by different individuals while unanimity decides the ranking of the last pair. On the other hand, it is easy to find procedures where compatibility is achieved. The natural approach, which mimics the way election rankings often are used, is to select a procedure to rank all three candidates and then *state* that the ranking of a pair is determined by its relative rankings in the election ordering. Unfortunately, decision by assertion does not resolve the paradoxes, it attempts to hide them. The problem is that the imposed pairwise rankings may suffer any credibility. This is demonstrated by the plurality ranking of $c_1 \succ c_3 \succ c_2$ for the profile where 9,999,999 people have the preference $c_1 \succ c_2 \succ c_3$ where only c_3 has the preference $c_3 \succ c_2 \succ c_1$. The imposed pairwise ranking is $c_3 \succ c_1$ even though the voters obviously prefer $c_1 \succ c_3$.

On the other hand, there are credible pairwise ranking procedures where the goal can be obtained. For instance, the pairwise rankings of the intensity of comparison approach developed in Sect. 3.1 always agree with the BC ranking (as shown in Sect. 3.2). The reason for the compatibility, of course, is that the intensity of comparison approach is specifically designed to integrate the higher dimensional information about the profile that is available when comparing three (or more) alternatives.

It is reasonable to wonder whether the "intensity of comparison – BC" success can be duplicated by using only the weaker information about the relative rankings of pairs. The information theoretical question, then, is to determine whether the information about each voter's relative ranking of each pair suffices to design a procedure to rank all three candidates. This goal is made precise with the condition of *Independence of Irrelevant Alternatives* (IIA). *IIA requires the relative ranking of a pair of candidates to be determined strictly by the voters' relative rankings of the same pair.* Information about how the remaining candidate is ranked is irrelevant.

With a little thought, it is clear that IIA captures what we want. This can be seen by the considering the problems experienced by a committee ranking three candidates for a prize after they announce that Poinchoff is the winner by virtue of their ranking of Poinchoff $\succ$ Poincare $\succ$ Birkhoff. After reporting their decision to an assembly, suppose the committee tries to explain to the very vocal Birkhoff supporters that, "Well, yes, we do believe that Birkhoff is a better choice than Poinchoff. But, well, because Poincare also was a candidate, we came to the conclusion that Poinchoff is top-ranked. But, should Poincare withdraw, then there is no question – we definitely would choose Birkhoff over Poinchoff!" I wouldn't want to speculate about the committee's popularity quotient after such a report. This is precisely the type of problem IIA is designed to avoid. The relative ranking of two candidates should be determined by their relative merits. Conversely, if a procedure fails to satisfy IIA, then, unless a committee recognizes the critical importance of the intensity of binary ranking, (along with its signal that the voters are rational, rather than confused), we must expect the possibility of embarrassing reports that are difficult to defend.[20]

4.4.3 Involvement and Voter Responsiveness

As three candidates are to be compared, we must eliminate all procedures that do not really consider all three candidates. For instance, the constant procedure that reports the same ranking of $c_1 \succ c_2 \succ c_3$, independent of what the voters believe, is useless. Similarly, a procedure that just changes the rankings of the top or the bottom two candidates is not really a three-candidate procedure. If, for example, the only two outcomes of a procedure are $c_1 \succ c_2 \succ c_3$ and $c_2 \succ c_1 \succ c_3$, then c_3 is not really a choice; the real decision is between c_1 and c_2 with c_3 always relegated to last place.

What we want, then, is a weak condition to ensure that all candidates are, in some manner, involved. Observe that with any two pairs of candidates, say $\{c_2, c_3\}$ and $\{c_1, c_3\}$, all three candidates appear. So, the weakest condition to impose, "Involvement," is that *for at least each of two pairs of candidates $\{c_i, c_j\}$ the outcome changes; there is an outcome with the relative ranking $c_i \succ c_j$ and another outcome with the relative ranking $c_j \succ c_i$.*

If a procedure truly involves all three candidates, even in a minimal fashion, then it satisfies involvement. Involvement, for instance, includes *Arrow's unanimity condition* where, if all voters have the same ranking, then that is the group outcome. Unanimity, of course, forces all strict rankings to be admissible group outcomes, so, for each pair $\{c_i, c_j\}$, there are rankings where $c_i \succ c_j$ and others where $c_j \succ c_i$.

"Involvement" is so inclusive that we do not even need all six rankings to satisfy the definition. To illustrate, suppose for reasons of cost, or whatever, it is impossible to accept a group ranking where c_2 is top-ranked. Here, we might modify the traditional assumption of unanimity to require unanimity to be honored *except* in the two proscribed situations. It is easy to check that the remaining four admissible group outcomes easily suffice to satisfy the involvement condition.

Involvement only depends upon the admissible outcomes – it is not concerned with how the outcomes are related to voters' preferences. Consequently, this condition is satisfied for perverse approaches where, if the voters are unanimous, then the outcome chosen by an "Ivan the Terrible" is the reverse of what they want. In fact, involvement is as weak of a condition as can be imposed; even if a procedure admits just the two outcomes $c_1 \succ c_2 \succ c_3$ and $c_3 \succ c_2 \succ c_1$, it satisfies "involvement" for all three pairs. This is because for each pair $\{c_i, c_j\}$, the relative ranking admitted by one outcome is $c_i \succ c_j$ and $c_j \succ c_i$ for the other one. Consequently, replacing "unanimity" with "involvement" we are permitted to consider a much richer set of procedures.

Finally, we do not want the outcome of a procedure to depend only upon the rankings of a particular voter; dictators need not apply! Thus the last condition,

---

[20] Examples abound in professional and academic circles and anywhere else where committee members seem afflicted with a driving need to pontificate upon their decisions.

"Voter Responsiveness," requires that the outcomes of the procedure cannot always agree with those of another procedure where its outcomes are determined by the rankings of a single voter.

Examples where voter responsiveness[21] is not satisfied can be found in the corporate world where the number of votes a voter has equals her stock holdings. If a voter has a sufficient number of stocks, she is a de facto dictator; the beliefs of the other voters are amusing footnotes with no bearing on the outcome. Thus, voter responsiveness eliminates the explicit or implicitly defined dictatorship where the wishes of one voter, the dictator, always are granted. As another example, voter responsiveness rules out an anti-dictator where the group ranking always reverses the voter's ranking. As such, it rules out those situations of a sufficiently annoying voter where, just to spite him, the procedure always selects the opposite of what he wants.

4.4.4 Arrow's Theorem

The goal is to find all procedures satisfying the above four conditions. While the requirements are basic, and seemingly innocuous, they are not compatible; no such procedure exists. The reason for the conflict is closely related to that described in Example 4.1.1.

Theorem 4.4.1. *No procedure exists that satisfies universality of domain, IIA, involvement, and voter responsiveness.*

If a procedure yielding strict rankings of the three candidates satisfies universality of domain, IIA, and involvement, then it must be a dictatorship or an anti-dictatorship.

An immediate consequence of Theorem 4.4.1 is Arrow's famous conclusion.

Arrow's Theorem. *If a procedure yielding the strict rankings of the three candidates satisfies universality of domain, IIA, and unanimity, then it must be a dictatorship.*

For simplicity, I have restricted attention to strict rankings. Also, some formulations of Arrow's Theorem are stated in terms of choice procedures where the goal is to select a candidate rather than a ranking of the candidates. Outlines how to extend Arrow's Theorem and Theorem 4.4.1 to choice procedures, for group rankings with a tie (or indifference) between certain candidates are in the exercises. In either formulation, the key is IIA.

The next formal statement, which is a corollary of the proof of Theorem 4.4.1, asserts that it is impossible to design pairwise procedures that are compatible with a way to transitively rank all three candidates. This statement, therefore, subsumes Example 4.4.1.

---

[21] If each of 60 voters has t votes and I have 120, then as long as $t \in [0, 2)$, I am the de facto dictator. As $t \to 0$, this becomes the usual dictator. Thus, these procedures can be expressed as belonging to the same homotopy class. See [Ch].

Corollary 4.4.2. *Suppose for each pair of candidates a procedure F_{c_i,c_j} is used to find a strict ranking for $\{c_i, c_j\}$ where only the voters' rankings of these two candidates is used. Suppose at least two of these pairwise procedures are non-constant. Furthermore, assume that at least one of these procedures satisfies the voter responsiveness requirement. If there are no restrictions on profiles, then there exist profiles so that the pairwise rankings define a cycle.*

4.4.5 A Dictatorship or an Informational Problem?

Rather than endorsing dictatorships, these assertions just prove that we can not always get what we want. The theorems assert that for any procedure, there exist profiles where the ranking of some pair is not compatible with how the procedure ranks all three candidates. Actually, this is a familiar theme from our earlier analysis of positional and pairwise procedures.

Instead of describing the draconian conclusions suggested by Arrow's Theorem, I will offer a benign interpretation. Recall, the motivation for IIA (given above) is to decide whether we can construct a procedure using only a certain type of restricted information about profiles – the relative ranking of each pair. Arrow's Theorem asserts that the answer is no. From an informational perspective, then, *Arrow's Theorem proves that the informational requirements of a choice or ranking procedure involving three or more candidates must extend beyond the relative rankings of pairs.* With three or more candidates we have access to the refined information about the intensity of pairwise rankings; Arrow's Theorem requires information of this type to be included.[22] Stated in another way, when the pairwise rankings are determined, we must retain, in some manner, the assumption that voters have transitive preferences! IIA dismisses this transitivity information, so Arrow's Theorem can be treated as wondering whether there exists a procedure serving both transitive and confused cyclic voters where the outcome is transitive. When posed in this fashion, the answer is clear; of course not!

These important theorems can be understood by appealing to elementary algebra. One of the first lessons of algebra is to expect solutions for a system of m equations in n unknowns, $n \geq m$. Technically, a "rank" requirement, which means that there truly are m independent equations, needs to be verified. What I show is that the above choice theorems can be understood in these terms.

To see the connection between the above assumptions and the algebra model, start with the IIA assumption; it is used below to define $m = 3$ equations. "Involvement" guarantees that at least two of these equations are non-constant; this ensures that there are at least $m \geq 2$ equations to be "solved."

The "unknowns" correspond to a voter's preferences. The roles of "universal domain" and "voter responsiveness" (which requires at least two voters to be involved) ensures that the number of variables satisfies the relationship $n \geq m$.

---

[22] I do not assert that the pairwise rankings *and* the intensity of these rankings constitutes the minimal informational requirement, because it is easy to prove that such a statement is false. However, to avoid stilted methods, this is close to being the minimal requirement.

The rank condition, to ensure that at least two equations are independent, remains to be verified. The rank conditions turn out to be related to the geometric arguments used in Fig. 4.4.1.

IIA and Three Pairwise Procedures. To make the precise central ideas, Theorem 4.4.1 is proved first for the special case of $n = 2$ voters. Here, each voter's ranking of the three candidates is represented by a strict ranking from $Si(3)$, so, according to the universality of domain condition, we search for a mapping

$$F : Si(3) \times Si(3) \to Si(3). \tag{4.4.1}$$

The jth term of the product $Si(3) \times Si(3)$ represents the jth voter's ranking of the three candidates, $j = 1, 2$.

Assume the theorem is false because there exists such a mapping F. Function F combined with IIA implicitly defines the three functions $(F_{c_1,c_2}, F_{c_2,c_3}, F_{c_3,c_1})$ where $F_{c_i,c_j}(\mathbf{p})$ is the $\{c_i, c_j\}$ relative ranking obtained from $F(\mathbf{p})$. For instance, if $F(\mathbf{p}) = c_2 \succ c_1 \succ c_3$, then $F_{c_1,c_2}(\mathbf{p}) = c_2 \succ c_1$, $F_{c_2,c_3}(\mathbf{p}) = c_2 \succ c_3$, and $F_{c_3,c_1}(\mathbf{p}) = c_1 \succ c_3$. In other words, *the F_{c_i,c_j} functions are the imposed rankings of the pairs as determined by the F outcome;* if F exists, these functions are always defined. Moreover, because F defines transitive rankings, the pairwise rankings obtained by the F_{c_i,c_j} functions never define cycles.

Instead of using rankings, let $F_{c_i,c_j} = 1$ if $c_i \succ c_j$, and $F_{c_i,c_j} = -1$ if $c_j \succ c_i$. With this convention, the outcome for the above profile is

$$F^*(\mathbf{p}) = (F_{c_1,c_2}(\mathbf{p}), F_{c_2,c_3}(\mathbf{p}), F_{c_3,c_1}(\mathbf{p})) = (-1, 1, -1);$$

thus, the image of $F^*(\mathbf{p})$ is a vertex of the cube $[-1, 1]^3$. The theorem follows if we can show that one of the cyclic vertices, $(1, 1, 1)$ or $-(1, 1, 1)$, is in the F^* image set. In other words, the theorem is proved once we "solve" either the three equations $F^*(\mathbf{p}) = (1, 1, 1)$, or the system $F^*(\mathbf{p}) = (-1, -1, -1)$.

Now that the three F_{c_i,c_j} functions are defined, we need to describe the relevant variables. An important aspect of IIA is that the outcome of $F_{c_i,c_j}(\mathbf{p})$ is determined simply by knowing each voter's relative ranking of the pair. Thus, $F_{c_1,c_2}(\mathbf{p})$ uses only the restricted information about whether the relative ranking of each voter is $c_1 \succ c_2$ or $c_2 \succ c_1$. As a consequence, $F_{c_1,c_2}(\mathbf{E}_1, \mathbf{E}_6) = F_{c_1,c_2}(\mathbf{E}_2, \mathbf{E}_4)$ because there is no change in each voters $\{c_1, c_2\}$ ranking. (The first profile is indicated by the bullets in Fig. 4.4.2, while the second profile is represented by the daggers.)

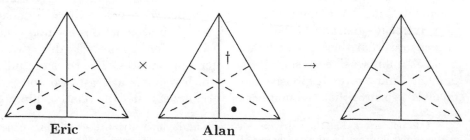

Fig. 4.4.2. Geometry of IIA for $\{c_1, c_2\}$

From IIA, the mapping F_{c_1,c_2} admits a geometrical representation similar to the pairwise vote for $\{c_1, c_2\}$; we only care about which side of the $c_1 \sim c_2$ line contains each voter's preference, the mapping can be expressed as in Fig. 4.4.2. A similar geometric representation holds for each F_{c_i,c_j} mapping as determined by the $c_i \sim c_j$ line.

4.4.6 Elementary Algebra

Comparing Fig. 4.4.2 with the description of the pairwise vote makes it clear that both the $\{c_i, c_j\}$ majority vote and the F_{c_i,c_j} procedure are based upon the myopic, one-dimensional information concerning which voters have preferences on each side of the $c_i \sim c_j$ indifference line. Another interpretation of Arrow's Theorem, then, is that it seeks to determine whether there are ways to define pairwise voting procedures F_{c_i,c_j} using the same restrictive information available to the pairwise majority vote, but where the outcomes now are transitive. The answer is no.

The relationship between the pairwise majority vote and the design of the F_{c_i,c_j} functions suggests that intuition for the proof of Theorem 4.4.2 can be derived by better understanding the relationship between the two approaches. Recall that the pairwise vote defines the three equations in six unknowns

$$x_1 + x_2 + x_3 - x_4 - x_5 - x_6 = q_{1,2}$$
$$x_1 - x_2 - x_3 - x_4 + x_5 + x_6 = q_{2,3}$$
$$-x_1 - x_2 + x_3 + x_4 + x_5 - x_6 = q_{3,1}. \qquad (4.4.2)$$

To show that cycles exist, we just need to show that there are solutions satisfying $\sum_{j=1}^{6} x_j = 1$ where all $q_{i,j}$ values have the same sign. This is true if the system of four equations in six unknowns has rank of four. It does, so solutions exist for any $q_{i,j}$ values; in particular, by choosing the $q_{i,j}$ values to have the same sign, cycles occur.

Compare the pairwise voting problem with our goal of solving the three equations $F^*(\mathbf{p}) = \pm(1, 1, 1)$. Again, we need to establish that the system of equations has an appropriate "rank." However, we don't know the definition of F, so a standard computational approach does not apply to F^*. We don't, for instance, have any idea whether the components of F^* are algebraic or even differentiable. Thus, we need to invent an alternative, geometric way to analyze the rank of a system based on its properties.

To demonstrate the ideas with a simple system, the level sets of the equations

$$x + y = q_1, \; x - y = q_2, \qquad (4.4.3)$$

are given in Fig. 4.4.3. (The downward sloping lines are the level sets for $x+y$; the upward sloping dashed lines are level sets for $x-y$.) These two equations are clearly independent, so they satisfy the rank condition. In turn, Eq. 4.4.3 can be solved for any choice of (q_1, q_2). In fact, because each downward sloping line defines the (x, y) values leading to a particular q_1, we can think of the q_1 value as the identifying name of the line. Similarly, the name of each upward sloping line identifies a q_2 value.

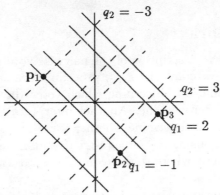

Fig. 4.4.3. Level set solution for an algebraic system

To complicate the trivial problem of finding a solution for $(q_1, q_2) = (2, 3)$, suppose only the geometry of the level sets can be used. The appropriate geometric approach is intuitively clear. Choose an arbitrary point, say $\mathbf{p}_1 = (-2, 1)$. This point defines the values $(q_1, q_2) = (-1, -3)$, so it needs to be modified to solve the posed problem. To do so, solve the problem an equation at a time. Namely, modify $\mathbf{p}_1$ so that the $q_1 = -1$ name remains fixed (i.e., change $\mathbf{p}_1$ by staying on the same downward slanting level set $x + y = -1$). Keeping changing the profile until reaching the dashed line level set with the name $x - y = 3$ (at $\mathbf{p}_2 = (1, -2)$). (This is equivalent to solving a series of problems of the form $x + y = -1$, $x - y = q$.)

The point $\mathbf{p}_2$ solves the $x - y = 3$ equation. To solve the second equation, start from $\mathbf{p}_2$, modify the $\mathbf{p}$ value by moving on the dashed line level set $x - y = 3$. By staying on this dashed line, the solution for the first equation remains intact. Keep moving $\mathbf{p}$ until reaching the downward sloping level set of $x + y = 2$. This point, $\mathbf{p}_3 = (2.5, -.5)$, is a solution. The rank condition for the linear equations guarantees that this $\mathbf{p}_1 \to \mathbf{p}_2 \to \mathbf{p}_3$ adjustment process works.

Cycle Construction. To use this $\mathbf{p}_1 \to \mathbf{p}_2 \to \mathbf{p}_3$ to construct a pairwise cycle (for Eqs. 4.4.2), start with an arbitrary profile $\mathbf{p}_1$ where we assume it defines the value $q_{1,2} > 0$. To create the cycle, change the profile keeping the value of $q_{1,2}$ fixed but allowing the values of $q_{2,3}, q_{3,1}$ to vary. The objective is to make them positive. That is, modify $\mathbf{p}_1$, on the level set of the first equation, so that the value of the second equation changes; keep changing until arriving at $\mathbf{p}_2$ where $q_{2,3} > 0$. The final stage is change $\mathbf{p}_2$ by staying on the level sets of the first two equations while changing the value of the third equation until it becomes positive at profile $\mathbf{p}_3$. The success of this $\mathbf{p}_1 \to \mathbf{p}_2 \to \mathbf{p}_3$ construction, which creates a positive cycle, is guaranteed by the rank conditions.

Not only does the rank condition allow this $\mathbf{p}_1 \to \mathbf{p}_2 \to \mathbf{p}_3$ approach to work, but, with some added conditions, this $\mathbf{p}_1 \to \mathbf{p}_2 \to \mathbf{p}_3$ process is a geometric way to determine the "rank." This technique, used in Example 4.4.1, is how I prove Theorem 4.4.1. Namely, the goal of the approach developed here is to convert the proof of Arrow's Theorem into a discrete version of the standard algebra conclusion about "m equations and n unknowns."

First, Who Can Do What? In any system of equations, the first step is to determine what variables change the values of which equations. To see the importance with the system $x + y = 6$, $y - z = 7$, the only interesting variables for the first equation are x and y. Similarly, we need to understand which variables can change the F_{c_i,c_j} values.

As involvement requires F to have at least two different outcomes, there exist profiles $\mathbf{p}, \mathbf{p}'$ where $F(\mathbf{p}) \neq F(\mathbf{p}')$. The two F rankings are different iff the relative ranking of some pair changes iff for some pair $\{c_i, c_j\}$ we have that $F_{c_i,c_j}(\mathbf{p}) \neq F_{c_i,c_j}(\mathbf{p}')$. If $\mathbf{p}_{c_i,c_j}$ denotes the relative c_i, c_j rankings of the profile, then IIA requires that

$$F_{c_i,c_j}(\mathbf{p}_{c_i,c_j}) \neq F_{c_i,c_j}(\mathbf{p}'_{c_i,c_j}). \tag{4.4.4}$$

According to Eq. 4.4.4, $\mathbf{p}_{c_i,c_j} \neq \mathbf{p}'_{c_i,c_j}$, so, at least one of the voters, Eric or Alan, had to change his relative ranking of $\{c_i, c_j\}$. If only one of them switched $\{c_i, c_j\}$ rankings, then this identifies a situation where a single voter changing his $\{c_i, c_j\}$ ranking forces the F_{c_i,c_j} ranking to vary.

A second possibility is that both Eric's and Alan's relative $\{c_i, c_j\}$ rankings differ in the profiles $\mathbf{p}_{c_i,c_j}$ and $\mathbf{p}'_{c_i,c_j}$. So, let $\mathbf{p}''_{c_i,c_j}$ represent the change of $\mathbf{p}_{c_i,c_j}$ defined when only Eric changes his $\{c_i, c_j\}$ ranking. Thus, the change in profiles

$$\mathbf{p}_{c_i,c_j} \to \mathbf{p}''_{c_i,c_j} \to \mathbf{p}'_{c_i,c_j} \tag{4.4.5}$$

is a stepwise process where first Eric changes his pairwise preference, and then Alan does. Clearly, at least two of the outcomes of $F_{c_i,c_j}(\mathbf{p}), F_{c_i,c_j}(\mathbf{p}), F_{c_i,c_j}(\mathbf{p})$ differ, so *there always exists a situation where when a single voter changes his* $\{c_i, c_j\}$ *ranking, the* F_{c_i,c_j} *ranking changes.*

According to involvement, there are at least two pairs $\{c_i, c_j\}$ where F_{c_i,c_j} changes rankings with changes in profiles. Using the above argument, a change in the F_{c_i,c_j} ranking, always can be identified with at least one situation where a single voter varies his relative ranking. The worst possible setting is if, for all possible situations and for all pairs, it is the same voter – say, Eric – who must reverse his ranking. If so, the only way F can change is according to Eric's preferences. This, of course, violates the voter responsiveness condition. (A word of warning: This statement does not mean that every voter can influence the relative ranking of every pair. Instead, it could be that Eric *always* determines the $\{c_1, c_2\}$ and $\{c_1, c_3\}$ relative rankings, and sometimes he determines the $\{c_2, c_3\}$ relative rankings. Nevertheless, to satisfy voter responsiveness, there always exists at least one situation where, if Eric has a particular $\{c_2, c_3\}$ relative ranking, then Alan's preferences determine the F_{c_2,c_3} outcome.)

What we gain from the voter responsiveness condition is that each voter influences the outcome of a different pair of candidates, say, Eric could be assigned $\{c_1, c_2\}$ while Alan is assigned $\{c_2, c_3\}$. Of course, it may be that only when Alan has a particular $\{c_1, c_2\}$ ranking, can Eric's preferences over this pair vary the F_{c_1,c_2} ranking. (In the example, Lillian and I altered rankings of our specified pairs independent of what the other person believed about that pair. So, to avoid the same impossibility difficulty, a procedure may impose a constraint upon Eric's influence in terms of Alan's choices.) Similarly, in order for Alan's preferences over $\{c_2, c_3\}$ to influence the F_{c_2,c_3} ranking, Eric might need to have a particular $\{c_2, c_3\}$ ranking. These requirements define portions of the F_{c_i,c_j} level sets.

4.4.7 The F_{c_i,c_j} Level Sets

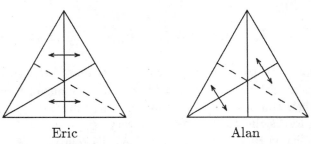

Eric   Alan

Fig. 4.4.4. Changing level sets keeping $\{c_1, c_3\}$ fixed

The rank conditions are proved with a $\mathbf{p}_1 \to \mathbf{p}_2 \to \mathbf{p}_3$ adjustment argument. First assign Eric the $\{c_2, c_3\}$ ranking that permits Alan to effect the F_{c_2,c_3} outcome. If it is $c_2 \succ c_3$, then by varying between type-one and six, Eric keeps the same $\{c_1, c_3\}$ and $\{c_2, c_3\}$ relative ranking, while changing the $\{c_1, c_2\}$ relative ranking. Alternatively, if Eric must have a $c_3 \succ c_2$ ranking, then he varies between type-three and four. Eric's choices are indicated by arrows in Fig. 4.4.4. Observe the similarity between this figure and Fig. 4.4.1.

Assignment for Eric	Voter type	Assignment for Alan	Voter type
$c_2 \succ c_3$	1 and 6	$c_1 \succ c_2$	1 and 2
$c_3 \succ c_2$	3 and 4	$c_2 \succ c_1$	4 and 5

(4.4.6)

Similarly, it may be that only when Alan has a particular $\{c_1, c_2\}$ ranking can Eric's preferences change the F_{c_1,c_2} ranking. Whatever the assignment, Alan's possible voter types can be chosen so that his $\{c_1, c_3\}$ relative ranking remains fixed, his $\{c_1, c_2\}$ relative ranking is the assigned one, and his $\{c_2, c_3\}$ relative ranking varies. Thus, the assignment for the voters is as given in Fig. 4.4.4 and

Eq. 4.4.6. Observe that while the permitted moves for Eric and for Alan keep invariant the binary rankings of two pairs, the *intensity level* changes. Namely, this is precisely where IIA ignores the intensity information.

To prove the theorem, choose a profile where Eric has the $\{c_2, c_3\}$ ranking to enfranchise Alan over this pair, and Alan has the $\{c_1, c_2\}$ ranking that unleashes Eric's influence over the F_{c_1,c_2} outcome. By choosing the profile satisfying this condition, and along the appropriate arrows, we have the profile $\mathbf{p}_1$ and the value for $F_{c_3,c_1}(\mathbf{p})$. Now, as Eric varies his ranking between the two admissible voter types, both Alan's and Eric's $\{c_2, c_3\}$ and the c_3, c_1 rankings remain fixed, (so there is no change in F_{c_2,c_3} and F_{c_3,c_1}), but the F_{c_1,c_2} value changes. Choose Eric's ranking to define a profile $\mathbf{p}_2$ where

$$F_{c_3,c_1}(\mathbf{p}_1) = F_{c_1,c_2}(\mathbf{p}_2).$$

As Eric did not change $\{c_2, c_3\}$ or $\{c_3, c_1\}$ rankings, the profile change $\mathbf{p}_1 \to \mathbf{p}_2$ is on the level sets of F_{c_2,c_3} and F_{c_3,c_1}.

Next, change the profile $\mathbf{p}_2$ by allowing Alan to change his $\{c_2, c_3\}$ rankings between the two indicated voter types. This, of course, changes the F_{c_2,c_3} value without affecting the value of the other two functions. (The change is on level sets of the other two functions because the relative ranking of $\{c_1, c_2\}$ and $\{c_1, c_3\}$ remain the same.) Thus, $\mathbf{p}_2$ can be changed to $\mathbf{p}_3$ where

$$F_{c_1,c_2}(\mathbf{p}_3) = F_{c_2,c_3}(\mathbf{p}_3) = F_{c_3,c_1}(\mathbf{p}_3).$$

As the profile $\mathbf{p}_3$ defines a cycle for F^*; and as a cycle cannot be defined from a transitive ranking, the assumed F does not exist.

To extend the proof to $n \geq 2$ voters, just mimic the argument used in Eq. 4.4.5. From involvement, there are profiles whereby $F_{c_i,c_j}(\mathbf{p}) \neq F_{c_i,c_j}(\mathbf{p}')$. Converting profile $\mathbf{p}_{c_i,c_j}$ into $\mathbf{p}'_{c_i,c_j}$ is broken down into steps where one voter at a time changes these pairwise rankings. In this manner, a change in F_{c_i,c_j} can be identified with a situation where one voter changed his rankings and all other voters have specified rankings of this pair. Thus, we can identify situations where when David changes, say, $\{c_1, c_2\}$ relative rankings, then F_{c_1,c_2} changes value, and there exist situations where when Adrian changes, say, $\{c_2, c_3\}$ rankings, the F_{c_2,c_3} value changes. Using the profile $\mathbf{p}_1 \to \mathbf{p}_2 \to \mathbf{p}_3$ argument, only David and Adrian change rankings; all other voters remain fixed at the specific required rankings.

Dictator or Anti-Dictator. We have established that if a procedure satisfies involvement, universality of domain, and IIA, it must depend upon the ranking of a particular voter. But, this conclusion should be expected. After all, if the procedure is defined in terms of a one-dimensional type of information, then the resulting procedure should be single-dimensional in nature – it should depend upon the preferences of a single voter. Stated in another way, the IIA assumption makes it impossible for the procedure to determine whether it is dealing with a rational or a confused voter, so it must serve the needs of either kind obediently.

(See Sect. 2.5.) But, if the voter is rational, this critical assumption should manifest itself in the relationship between the outcome of the procedure and the voter's ranking. As asserted, this must define a dictatorship or an anti-dictatorship.

The "level set" proof of Theorem 4.4.1 exploited the flexibility of movement in a profile while keeping two relative rankings fixed. To prove this assertion, the restrictiveness feature, where the relative ranking of one pair is uniquely determined by the relative rankings of the other two pairs, is used. (See Example 4.4.1.)

Involvement requires the rankings of at least two F_{c_i,c_j} functions to vary. Assume they are F_{c_1,c_2} and F_{c_2,c_3}, and assume the F_{c_i,c_j} ranking of each pair agrees with the voter's relative ranking. Thus, if $\mathbf{p} = c_1 \succ c_2 \succ c_3$, then $F_{c_1,c_2}(\mathbf{p}) = c_1 \succ c_2$, $F_{c_2,c_3}(\mathbf{p}) = c_2 \succ c_3$. In turn, because F provides a transitive ranking, we have that $F_{c_3,c_1}(\mathbf{p}) = c_1 \succ c_3$. Similarly, if the voter has the reversed ranking of $c_3 \succ c_2 \succ c_1$, the transitivity of F forces $F_{c_3,c_1}(c_3 \succ c_1) = c_3 \succ c_1$. In other words, if two of the three F_{c_i,c_j} functions agree with the voter's relative ranking of the pair, then so must the third. This is a dictatorship. A similar argument shows that if two of the F_{c_i,c_j} functions reverse the voter's relative ranking, then so must the third. This defines an anti-dictatorship.

The remaining possibility is if one function, say F_{c_1,c_2}, agrees with the voter's relative ranking, and another function, say F_{c_2,c_3}, reverses this ranking. Now consider F_{c_3,c_1}. If it reverses or retains the voter's ranking of the pair, then at least two of the F_{c_i,c_j} functions have the same effect on the ranking. This causes a contradiction because it requires the third to be of the same type. Therefore, F_{c_3,c_1} must be a constant mapping. Without loss of generality, assume $F_{c_3,c_1}(\mathbf{p}) = c_1 \succ c_3$.

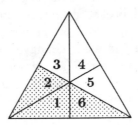

Fig. 4.4.5. Impossibility of F_{c_3,c_1} being constant

These assumptions require the ranking type of an F outcome to be one of $\{1,2,6\}$. (See the shaded region of Fig. 4.4.5.) The contradiction, which is determined by following the lead of Example 4.4.1, is obtained by showing there is a $\mathbf{p}$ where $F(\mathbf{p})$ must be a prohibited type-four ranking. For this to occur, we need $F_{c_1,c_2} = c_2 \succ c_1$, so the voter's relative ranking of this pair is $c_2 \succ c_1$. To have $F_{c_2,c_3} = c_3 \succ c_2$, the reversal nature of this mapping requires the voter to have the ranking $c_2 \succ c_3$. Combining this information, if the voter is either of type-three or four, we obtain the outlawed $F_{c_3,c_1} = c_3 \succ c_1$. Thus, F_{c_3,c_1} cannot be constant, and the conclusion follows. $\square$

4.4.8 Some Existence Theorems

The proof of Theorem 4.4.1 (or of Arrow's Theorem) is similar to the problem of solving m equations in n unknowns, $n \geq m$. This suggests that to avoid the negative statement of Arrow's Theorem, the number of independent equations and/or the number of unknowns must be reduced. Actually, *if any condition of Theorem 4.4.1 is weakened, a possibility theorem emerges*. As this means that Theorem 4.4.1 describes the boundary between possibility and impossibility theorems, I will show why this statement is true. (A weakening of IIA is described later in this section.)

The only way "involvement" can be relaxed is to admit procedures that change the rankings of a single pair of candidates (rather than at least two). This reduces the design problem to a single-dimension, so it is trivial to find such procedures. For instance, if this pair is $\{c_1, c_2\}$, then all outcomes could vary between type-one and six; i.e., between the rankings $c_1 \succ c_2 \succ c_3$ and $c_2 \succ c_1 \succ c_3$. One such procedure satisfying the remaining requirements is the majority vote.

The next goal is to relax the universal domain condition to define profile restrictions. Here, rather than providing a complete discussion,[23] examples are offered to suggest the rich selection of issues.

Example 4.4.2. "Universal domain" does not hold iff some candidate is prohibited from achieving a particular ranking. So, assume Alfred has no restriction on his preferences, but Gene is prohibited from choosing just one ranking; say, $c_1 \succ c_3 \succ c_2$. As a single ranking is forbidden for one agent, this profile restriction is as close as possible to satisfying the universal domain condition without doing so. Nevertheless, this minimal restriction permits a procedure to exist that satisfies the remaining assumptions.

To design this procedure, observe from Fig. 4.4.6 that by keeping Gene away from $c_1 \succ c_3 \succ c_2$, he has only weak $c_1 \succ c_2$ rankings. In particular, it is impossible for Gene to keep fixed the ranking $c_1 \succ c_2$ and that of another pair while varying the ranking of the third pair. Consequently, the above impossibility proof fails if Gene needs to have the ranking $c_1 \succ c_2$ when Alfred decides the $\{c_1, c_2\}$ ranking. The procedure follows from this observation. (Notice, by excluding this ranking, it doesn't matter whether Gene is transitive–at least with this pair.)

Let Gene be the dictator with respect to the $\{c_1, c_3\}$ and the $\{c_2, c_3\}$ relative rankings. Indeed, go a step further; if Gene prefers $c_2 \succ c_1$, then that is the procedure's pairwise ranking. On the other hand, when Gene has the ranking $c_1 \succ c_2$, Alfred's relative ranking of this pair determines its relative ranking.

---

[23] The interested reader should consult [S14].

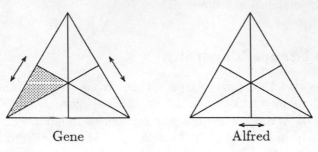

Fig. 4.4.6. A possibility example

To see that this procedure is well defined, observe that if Gene has the relative rankings $c_3 \succ c_1$ and $c_3 \succ c_2$, or if he has $c_1 \succ c_3$ and $c_2 \succ c_3$, then the two possible group outcomes are distinguished by the $\{c_1, c_2\}$ relative ranking – at times, this is Al's choice. The remaining case is where Gene has the rankings $c_3 \succ c_1$ and $c_2 \succ c_3$; here the outcome must be $c_2 \succ c_3 \succ c_1$ and the $\{c_1, c_2\}$ ranking corresponds to Gene's preference of $c_2 \succ c_1$. (It is impossible for Gene to have the rankings $c_1 \succ c_3$ and $c_3 \succ c_1$ because it would force him to have the proscribed ranking $c_1 \succ c_3 \succ c_2$.) Therefore, except where Gene has the relative ranking $c_2 \succ c_1$, the $\{c_1, c_2\}$ ranking is free to be decided. Consequently, the above procedure is well-defined.

While the procedure is defined, its quasi-dictatorial nature disqualifies it from service as a paradigm for emerging democracies. Instead, this procedure can be viewed as combining two one-dimensional methods; it specifies when each procedure is operative. The stilted nature is to be expected; as long as a choice method relies upon lower dimensional information (as required by IIA), only lower dimensional procedures can emerge.

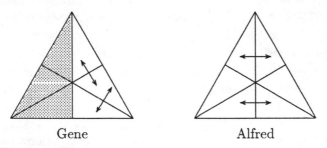

Fig. 4.4.7. Too much of a restriction reverts to impossibility

Because the above procedure can be defined with Gene's profile restriction, imagine the multitude of possible procedures if we impose an even more severe restriction on him. For instance, suppose Gene is not permitted to have any ranking where $c_1 \succ c_2$; thus any ranking in the shaded region of Fig. 4.4.7 is off-limits for him. The surprising fact is that, with this more severe restriction, no procedure exists!

Gene does not change $\{c_1, c_2\}$ rankings, so the earlier procedure becomes a vacuous campaign promise; there never is a situation where Alfred can decide. To define a different procedure, there must exist situations where Gene can influence the outcome of a pair; that pair must be $\{c_1, c_3\}$ and/or $\{c_2, c_3\}$. Al has to decide at least the $\{c_1, c_2\}$ outcome. Now, a further restriction can't be imposed upon Gene in order for Alfred to decide this outcome; Gene already has the ultimate restriction of always staying with the ranking $c_2 \succ c_1$. As shown in the figure, Gene can vary his ranking of any pair to satisfy this condition and to keep the relative ranking of the remaining pair fixed. The rest of the proof follows from the $\mathbf{p}_1 \rightarrow \mathbf{p}_2 \rightarrow \mathbf{p}_3$ rank argument.[24]

4.4.9 Intensity IIA

Theorem 4.4.1 asserts the impossibility of defining a reasonable procedure by using only the one-dimensional information about the relative ranking of pairs. In fact, the $\mathbf{p}_1 \rightarrow \mathbf{p}_2 \rightarrow \mathbf{p}_3$ profile change argument depended on IIA admitting so little information about the profile that we cannot be sure even whether the voters have transitive preferences! Such a proof, however, fails when information about the "intensity of pairwise rankings" is admitted; the intensity identifies that transitive preferences are used.

To see the limiting effect of the intensity information, recall that both Eric and Alan varied between a weak and a strong intensity of the two fixed binary rankings. Recall in Example 4.4.2 that just by keeping Gene away from a strong binary ranking of one pair, a procedure could be constructed. Therefore, it appears that by including the information about the intensity of pairwise rankings, a wider variety of procedures could be defined. This is the case.

To add intuition, return to Eq. 4.4.6 and the accompanying Fig. 4.4.4. Suppose for Alan to change the F_{c_2, c_3} value, Eric must have the *strong* binary ranking $c_2 \succ c_3$. As this restricts Eric to the ranking $c_2 \succ c_1 \succ c_3$, he has no way to vary his ranking. Similarly, if Eric is required to have a weak ranking of $c_2 \succ c_3$, then, to retain the same $\{c_1, c_3\}$ ranking (critical for the proof), Eric must have the preference $c_1 \succ c_2 \succ c_3$. This lack of movement kills the proof and the geometric rank condition. Consequently, we must expect possibility assertions when intensity information is allowed.

Definition 4.4.1. The *intensity IIA* condition is where the relative ranking of any two candidates, c_i, c_j, depends only on each voter's relative ranking of these candidates and the intensity of this ranking. $\square$

The main conclusion, which shows that procedures exist which are acceptable in polite groups, follows.

Theorem 4.4.3. *There exist procedures satisfying universal domain, unanimity, intensity IIA, and voter responsiveness. One such procedure is the BC. Indeed, the BC is the only positional method to satisfy these conditions.*

Example 4.4.2 can be modified to create an procedure satisfying universal domain, involvement, voter responsiveness, and where IIA is satisfied for all

---

[24]See [S14] for more general conditions that ensure a possibility or impossibility theorem.

agents but one; for this agent (Gene) the intensity IIA condition applies to
one pair and IIA to all others. In other words, even the slightest change of
the assumptions in Theorem 4.4.1 changes the conclusions. The main point,
however, is that a simple change in the informational requirements transforms
an impossible mission into a reasonably comfortable setting. Again, the BC
moves to center stage!

4.4.10 Exercises

4.4.1. Theorem 4.4.1 holds even if indifference among rankings is admitted.
Change the involvement condition to read that for at least two pairs, the relative
ranking can be two of the three possible choice. (For instance, this would be
satisfied if F had the rankings $c_1 \sim c_2 \succ c_3$ and $c_1 \succ c_2 \sim c_3$ because the $\{c_1, c_2\}$
and the $\{c_2, c_3\}$ rankings change while the $\{c_1, c_3\}$ ranking remains the same.)
Show that with this weaker condition, the theorem still holds. (Now, however,
the dictator may get only indifference with certain strict pairwise rankings.)

4.4.2. For the plurality method, find an example where IIA is not satisfied.

4.4.3. a. In the proof showing that when F must depend upon the ranking of
a single voter, one step assumed that F_{c_1,c_2} corresponded to the voter's ranking
of the pair, F_{c_2,c_3} reversed it, and the last mapping was the constant $F_{c_3,c_1} =
c_3 \succ c_1$. Carry out the same argument with the assumption that the constant
mapping is $F_{c_3,c_1} = c_1 \succ c_3$.
b. Exercise 4.4.1 extends the theorem to where the outcome can be indifference.
Suppose the only two outcomes admitted by F_{c_1,c_2} are $c_1 \succ c_2$ and $c_1 \sim c_2$.
What replaces the dictator and anti-dictator?
c. One way to view Theorem 4.4.1 is that we are trying to create a procedure
so that when all voters have transitive preferences, the outcome is transitive.
However, IIA allows the same procedure also to serve confused voters (voters
without transitive preferences.) The result is that, by trying to accommodate two
radically different groups, only the wishes of a single voter can be considered. If
this voter is transitive, then the procedure is either a dictator or an anti-dictator.
What happens if the single empowered voter is cyclic?

4.4.4. The proof of most theorems in this section depended upon the fact that
there are rankings of two pairs which uniquely determine the ranking of the
third, and there are other rankings of these two pairs where the ranking of the
third pair is free to be determined. Describe these two situations in terms of the
rankings of the first two pairs.

4.4.5. Show that IIA, involvement, and the fact that F depends upon a single
voter's preferences requires $F_{c_i,c_j}(\mathbf{p}^r) = F^r_{c_i,c_j}(\mathbf{p})$.

4.4.6. For choice functions, the IIA condition is that if $F(\mathbf{p}) = c_i$, and if $\mathbf{p}'$ is a
profile where each voter's relative ranking of $\{c_i, c_j\}$ remains the same in both
profiles, then $F(\mathbf{p}') \neq c_j$. This means, for example, that by knowing what voters
are on which side of the $c_1 \sim c_2$ line, we can determine whether the outcome
is in $\{c_1, c_3\}$ or $\{c_2, c_3\}$ However, which choice is made cannot be determined

just from the $\{c_1, c_2\}$ information. Thus, when choice procedures are used, IIA implicitly defines three mappings $F_{c_1,c_2}, F_{c_2,c_3}, F_{c_3,c_1}$. (Geometrically, the image of F_{c_1,c_2} is in either the union

$$\mathcal{R}(1) \cup \mathcal{R}(2) \cup \mathcal{R}(3) \cup \mathcal{R}(4),$$

or in

$$\mathcal{R}(6) \cup \mathcal{R}(5) \cup \mathcal{R}(4) \cup \mathcal{R}(3).)$$

So, if there are only two voters with fixed $\{c_1, c_3\}$ rankings, the outcome set is either from $\{c_1, c_2\}$ or $\{c_3, c_2\}$. (These sets replace the rankings $c_1 \succ c_3, c_3 \succ c_1$ from the above proof of Theorem 4.4.1.) Suppose it is the first. To prove the choice function version of Theorem 4.4.1, it suffices to show that it is possible to change the $\{c_1, c_2\}$ rankings (altering the choice between $\{c_1, c_3\}$ and $\{c_2, c_3\}$) and $\{c_2, c_3\}$ rankings (altering the outcome between $\{c_2, c_1\}$ and $\{c_3, c_1\}$) so that c_3 is the outcome. (This is when one outcome requires $\{c_3, c_1\}$ and the other has $\{c_3, c_2\}$.) This is a contradiction.

The other possibility is if the fixed $\{c_1, c_3\}$ outcome must be in $\{c_3, c_2\}$. Here, the goal is to show that c_1 can be the forced outcome from two voters. The problem, should you choose to accept it, is to carry out the details.

4.4.7. In Example 4.4.2, suppose the profile restriction is that Gene cannot have any of the three even rankings. Does a procedure exist? If so, characterize all of them. If not, explain why.

4.5 Characterizations of Scoring, Positional and Borda

Our discussion of Arrow's Theorem identifies why procedures do not do what we want them to do. More precisely, the kind of data admitted by IIA is too narrow for the design of three (or more) candidate voting procedures. On the other hand, as we now know, once the IIA condition is relaxed, procedures including the BC are admitted. In this section I examine other conditions that allow reasonable choice procedures. Of the many choices of axioms that could be used, I will follow the lead of P. Young [Y1-2] by characterizing all choice procedures (so, a subset of candidates, rather than a ranking, is selected) that satisfy certain desirable properties.

The procedures that emerge are *scoring rules*. With additional conditions, the set of procedures is reduced to the positional voting methods. A different refinement isolates the BC. Then, *generalized positional voting procedures* are introduced. As these conditions provide an axiomatic characterization of the procedures examined throughout this book, it is a natural way to conclude.

In this analysis, the powerful consequences of certain natural assumptions, such as *neutrality* become clear. When described in words, these requirements sound like innocuous "Motherhood and Apple Pie" constraints. Who could be against them? What difference do they make? Thus, a secondary theme is to use their mathematical consequences to demonstrate the highly selective nature of these assumptions.

Anonymity and Neutrality. By serving as social decision processes, elections can unleash changes in political power and social policies. This creates incredibly strong incentives to try to influence how the voters vote. Consequently, safeguards have been developed to protect that delicate dividing line between "influencing voters" through campaign rhetoric, and "coercing voters" to vote in ways they do not want to vote. This is why there are rules forbidding anyone to join a voter in the voter booth. Another major advance is the secret ballot; the way a voter votes is disguised by the cloak of anonymity. The importance of this condition is captured by the comments of a UN official describing the insistence of a Mogadishu leader that he would win the most votes in a free election. "I told him, 'If you're holding a gun to a person's head, of course he's going to vote for you.' "[25] *Anonymity*, therefore, is a natural condition to impose upon a choice procedure.

To be more specific, *anonymity requires the outcome to depend upon the portion of voters that are of each type.* This means that the outcome does not depend upon *who* votes for what candidate, but rather upon *how many* voters vote for her. Namely, the intent of anonymity is to protect against "Big Brother" as well as the dictators and anti-dictators of the last section. In terms of our notation, *anonymity requires the outcome to depend upon the choice of the normalized profile* $\mathbf{p} \in Si(6)$ where there is no restriction on the choice of $\mathbf{p}$.

A second "fairness" condition, *neutrality*, requires all candidates to be treated equally. We should, for example, seriously question the equity of a procedure where Andrew needs 60% of the vote to win, while Carl needs only 50%. Fairness dictates that the criteria for winning must not depend on the candidates' names, but rather on the support they receive from the voters. With a fair procedure, if Carl wins, then Andrew would have won if their names were interchanged.

Using the notation of Sect. 3.1, where the concept of neutrality is extensively explored, if σ represents a change of the candidates' names and if f is the procedure, then neutrality requires

$$f(\sigma_T(\mathbf{p})) = \sigma(f(\mathbf{p})). \tag{4.5.1}$$

As a specific example, if $f(\mathbf{p}) = \{c_1, c_2\}$ and $\sigma = (2,3)$, (so, this name change examines whether the treatment accorded to c_2 agrees with that required of c_3), then $\sigma_T(\mathbf{p})$ is the profile where the voters interchange their ranking of c_2 and c_3. According to neutrality, it must be that $f(\sigma_T(\mathbf{p})) = \sigma(\{c_1, c_2\}) = \{c_1, c_3\}$.

4.5.1 Strong and Weak Consistency

The third condition, *strong consistency*, involves changes in a profile – the theme of this chapter. Recall from Sect. 4.1 that a procedure is *weakly consistent* if when two groups are in complete agreement, this common choice is the conclusion for the united group. "Strong consistency," as introduced by Young [Y2], goes a step further to specify the outcome when there is only partial agreement

---

[25] New York Times, February 21, 1993, p. 3.

between the groups. To motivate the definition with the Dean's Council selection problem (Sect. 1.1), suppose the first subcommittee can't decide between Ann and Barb, and the second subcommittee can't decide between Ann and Carol. It is reasonable to expect the common choice for both subcommittees, Ann, to be selected by the full committee.

In terms of integer profiles, strong consistency requires if $f(\mathbf{p}_1) \cap f(\mathbf{p}_2) \neq \emptyset$, then $f(\mathbf{p}_1 + \mathbf{p}_2) = f(\mathbf{p}_1) \cap f(\mathbf{p}_2)$. With normalized profiles, the relative size of each subgroup is measured by the value of $\lambda \in (0, 1)$, so our definition is as follows.

Definition 4.5.1. A choice procedure f is *strongly consistent* if $f(\mathbf{p}_1) \cap f(\mathbf{p}_2) \neq \emptyset$ for $\mathbf{p}_1, \mathbf{p}_2 \in Si(6)$ implies that

$$f(\lambda \mathbf{p}_1 + (1 - \lambda)\mathbf{p}_2) = f(\mathbf{p}_1) \cap f(\mathbf{p}_2), \quad \lambda \in (0, 1). \quad \square \qquad (4.5.2)$$

Weak and strong consistency are natural conditions, so it is worth exploring how they agree and differ.

Proposition 4.5.1. a. *A strongly consistent procedure is weakly consistent, but there are weakly consistent procedures that are not strongly consistent.*

b. *For a given scoring rule* **sc**, *the procedure that selects the* **sc** *top-ranked candidate(s) is both weakly and strongly consistent.*

c. *Suppose a strongly consistent choice procedure admits all singleton outcomes. (That is, there are profiles where each candidate is the sole choice.) The set of profiles defining a non-singleton outcome is a convex subset contained in a lower dimensional subset of the profile space $Si(6)$. Indeed, for two subsets of candidates, $\beta \subset \alpha$, the profile set $f^{-1}(\alpha)$ is in the boundary of the profile set $f^{-1}(\beta)$.*

Proof. The first assertion of part a is obvious; if g is a strongly consistent procedure and if $\mathbf{p}_1, \mathbf{p}_2$ satisfy $g(\mathbf{p}_1) = g(\mathbf{p}_2)$, then weak consistency is assured by Eq. 4.5.2. The second part follows from the observation that the threshold methods are weakly consistent but not strongly consistent procedures. (See Exercise 2.1.5.) To illustrate with a particular threshold procedure, suppose a candidate wins if she receives at least 50% of the plurality vote. If no candidate wins, then the two top-ranked candidates are chosen should the total of their plurality tallies exceed 60% of the vote. The integer profile $\mathbf{p}_1$ where 45 voters are of type 1, 45 are of type 6, and 10 are of type 3 has a plurality outcome of $(45, 45, 10)$, so $g(\mathbf{p}_1) = \{c_1, c_2\}$. If $\mathbf{p}_2 = \mathbf{E}_1$ is a single person profile, then $g(\mathbf{p}_2) = \{c_1\}$. The plurality outcome for $\mathbf{p}_2 + \mathbf{p}_1$ is $(46, 45, 10)$, so the $g(\mathbf{p}_1 + \mathbf{p}_2)$ outcome remains $\{c_1, c_2\}$; this is *not* the required $g(\mathbf{p}_1) \cap g(\mathbf{p}_2) = \{c_1\}$ needed to qualify g as a strongly consistent procedure. In other words, with a "strongly consistent" procedure, a tie *always* can be broken just by introducing a single voter of the correct type. This need not happen with weakly consistent methods.

Part b of the proposition follows immediately from the straight line relationship dictated by the election mapping

$$f(\lambda \mathbf{p}_1 + (1 - \lambda)\mathbf{p}_2, \mathbf{sc}) = \lambda f(\mathbf{p}_1, \mathbf{sc}) + (1 - \lambda)f(\mathbf{p}_2, \mathbf{sc}), \qquad (4.5.3)$$

and the convex geometry of the ranking regions of the representation triangle. It is clear from the representation triangle geometry that the union of all ranking regions with the same candidate(s) top-ranked is a convex set. Thus, if $f(\mathbf{p}_1, \mathbf{sc})$, $f(\mathbf{p}_2, \mathbf{sc})$ have the same top-ranked candidates, then these are the top-ranked candidates for all outcomes on the line connecting $f(\mathbf{p}_1, \mathbf{sc})$, $f(\mathbf{p}_2, \mathbf{sc})$.

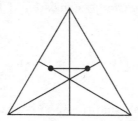

Fig. 4.5.1. The consistency of scoring methods

Finally, suppose $f(\mathbf{p}_1, \mathbf{sc}) \neq f(\mathbf{p}_2, \mathbf{sc})$, but $f(\mathbf{p}_1, \mathbf{sc}) \cap f(\mathbf{p}_2, \mathbf{sc}) \neq \emptyset$. This scenario requires $f(\mathbf{p}_1, \mathbf{sc})$ and/or $f(\mathbf{p}_2, \mathbf{sc})$ to have a top-place tie vote between two candidates or among all three. The election points are in different ranking regions, and the tie vote regions are either line segments or the point $\mathcal{I}$. Therefore, any election point on the line (Eq. 4.5.3) corresponding to a value of $\lambda \in (0, 1)$ must be off of this tied vote ranking region. Moreover, the top-ranked candidate(s) of $\lambda f(\mathbf{p}_1, \mathbf{sc}) + (1 - \lambda)f(\mathbf{p}_2, \mathbf{sc})$ are determined by which candidates are top-ranked for both endpoints of the line; they are $f(\mathbf{p}_1, \mathbf{sc}) \cap f(\mathbf{p}_2, \mathbf{sc})$. This completes the proof. Figure 4.5.1 depicts the setting where $f(\mathbf{p}_1, \mathbf{w}_s) \in \mathcal{R}(c_1 \sim c_3 \succ c_2)$ while $f(\mathbf{p}_2, \mathbf{w}_s) \in \mathcal{R}(c_2 \sim c_3 \succ c_1)$, so the connecting line is in the region where c_3 is top-ranked.

The proof of part c is a technical version of the observation that, with a strongly consistent procedure, a tie vote can be broken by adding a single voter. This sensitivity requires the profile sets for tie votes to reside in a lower dimensional space. More formally, the convexity of the profile set $f^{-1}(\alpha)$ follows from weak consistency. Using the earlier convexity arguments, this requires the boundary between two profile sets $\{f^{-1}(\alpha_j)\}_{j=1}^{2}$ to be in a plane.

Suppose $c_1 \in \alpha$ where $|\alpha| \geq 2$ and $\mathbf{p}_1$ is such that $f(\mathbf{p}_1) = \{c_1\}$. If, contrary to the assertion, $\mathbf{p}_2$ is an interior point of $f^{-1}(\alpha)$, then $\lambda \mathbf{p}_1 + (1 - \lambda)\mathbf{p}_2 \in f^{-1}(\alpha)$ for sufficiently small values of $\lambda > 0$. If f were strongly consistent, c_1, not α, would be the outcome for this profile.

This argument proves that $f^{-1}(\alpha)$ is in the boundary of $f^{-1}(\{c_1\})$; this boundary is a portion of a plane. The more general assertion that $f^{-1}(\alpha)$ is in the boundary of $f^{-1}(\beta)$ involves a similar argument. $\square$

An important difference between weak and strong consistency is that weak consistency permits a tie outcome to be supported by an open set of profiles while strong consistency does not. Thus the threshold methods, which prohibit a candidate with a single vote margin from being declared victorious, are weakly consistent but not strongly consistent. Part c, asserting that strong consistency requires the profile sets for tie votes to be in lower dimensional planes, is important for our analysis.

Equivalence. Before stating the theorems, the "equivalence" of choice procedures is defined.

Definition 4.5.2. Two choice procedures, f, g, are equivalent (denoted as $f \sim g$) iff $f(\mathbf{p}) = g(\mathbf{p})$ for all $\mathbf{p} \in Si(6)$. $\square$

Example 4.5.1. Even though the definitions of procedures differ, they are equivalent if they always choose the same set of candidates.

a. Let f be the top-ranked candidate from the intensity of comparison approach and g be the BC top-ranked candidate. Even though f and g have different definitions, they are equivalent. (See Sect. 3.2.)

b. Let g be the procedure that chooses the plurality top-ranked candidate if she has less than 80% of the vote; otherwise g chooses the $(.9, .1, 0)$ top-ranked candidate. Let f choose the top-ranked plurality candidate. The candidate rankings for f and g can differ, but both procedures always have the same top-ranked candidates. After all, if $(.9, .1, 0)$ to be used, a candidate is top-ranked by at least 80% of the voters, so she is top- ranked with both procedures.[26] $\square$

4.5.2 Characterization of Scoring Rules

Strong consistency, anonymity, and neutrality are satisfied by the commonly used procedure where the top-ranked candidate from a scoring election is chosen. The following theorem asserts that is all there is; a procedure satisfying these conditions is equivalent to choosing a scoring-rule top-ranked candidate. There is an embellishment; ties can be broken with a second or third election. Thus, up to the equivalence of procedures and the runoffs, the above natural conditions characterize scoring rules. While the following statement slightly extends P. Young's theorem [Y2] and the proof is different, the basic ideas were pioneered by Young. (These results hold for all $n \geq 3$. See [Y2, S12].)

Theorem 4.5.2. *A non-constant choice procedure that satisfies anonymity, neutrality, and strong consistency is equivalent to one of the following three kinds of procedures.*

a.   For a scoring vector $\mathbf{sc}_1$, the $\mathbf{sc}_1$ top-ranked candidate is chosen.

b.   If more than one candidate is top-ranked in part a, then the tie can be broken with a $\mathbf{sc}_2$ runoff election. This $\mathbf{sc}_2$ runoff involves all three candidates; the $\mathbf{sc}_2$ relative ranking of the top-ranked candidates at the end of the first stage determines who is selected.[27]

---

[26] Observe, equivalence can be described in a topological manner.
[27] For $n \geq 4$ candidates, there can be more runoffs.

  c.   If $\mathbf{sc}_1$, $\mathbf{sc}_2$ are *not both positional methods*, then a third $\mathbf{sc}_3$ can be selected for a third runoff involving all three candidates.

Part a describes the commonly used method where the top-ranked candidate from an election is selected. To break ties, part b allows a runoff. But, what a weird runoff! For reasons of efficiency, or a minimal sense of decency, a runoff should involve only the candidates eligible to be selected. That is not the case here; a Young runoff involves *all candidates*–even those already eliminated from further consideration! Then, although the dropped candidate is in the runoff, we ignore how she does! She serves as a benchmark because only the relative ranking of the eligible candidates is used.

Example 4.5.2. Suppose a plurality election ($\mathbf{sc}_1 = (1,0,0)$) is used to rank the candidates and the BC ($\mathbf{sc}_2 = (\frac{2}{3}, \frac{1}{3}, 0)$) is used for a runoff. If the $\mathbf{sc}_1$ ranking is $c_1 \sim c_3 \succ c_2$, then c_2 is dropped from further consideration while $\{c_1, c_3\}$ await the verdict of the Young runoff. With the BC outcome $c_2 \succ c_3 \succ c_1$, c_3 is the chosen candidate. (By using the procedure line, it is easy to find profiles with these outcomes.)

Even though c_2 is victorious in the second election, it doesn't matter. The only relevant information is the relative ranking $c_3 \succ c_1$. It doesn't take undue imagination to invent scenarios of public outrage and clamor (particularly from c_2 supporters) about the "unfairness" and "stupidity" of this method. The theorem, however, asserts that this is a cost of being decisive (by insisting on a runoff), or, perhaps, of being unimaginative in describing the procedure. (Remember, the procedure is *equivalent* to this runoff; it need not be defined this way.) □

To understand why strong consistency requires a Young runoff, observe that if it involves only the tied candidates, it is one of traditional approaches analyzed in Sect. 4.1. As these runoffs fail to be weakly consistent, they cannot be strongly consistent. Consequently, to preserve consistency while breaking ties via a runoff, the information about *all* candidates is needed. (By doing so, information about the "intensity" of the relative rankings of the remaining candidates is included.) Weird? Yes, but that is the hidden informational price accompanying these reasonable assumptions.

An Outline of the Proof. A detailed proof is given at the end of this section, but it is worth outlining why it is true. First, just by assuming there are at least two admissible subsets of candidates (the choice procedure is nonconstant), *all* subsets of candidates are admissible. For instance, if a pair, say $\{c_1, c_2\}$, is admissible, then neutrality (i.e., by applying various "name changes") ensures that, all pairs are admissible. Once two pairs are admissible, say $\{c_1, c_2\}$ and $\{c_1, c_3\}$, then strong consistency forces their intersection, $\{c_1\}$, to be admissible. If $\{c_1\}$ is admissible, then, by neutrality, all singleton subsets are admissible outcomes.

What brings scoring methods to the forefront is convexity. The source of this geometry is that the profiles sets supporting $\{c_1\}$ and $\{c_2\}$ are convex (by weak consistency) and their separating boundary is a lower dimensional set (by strong consistency and convexity) in a hyperplane. (Remember, one set's bulge is another set's indentation, so if the boundaries of $f^{-1}(\{c_1\})$ are not portions of planes, then some profile set $f^{-1}(\alpha)$ fails to be convex.) This boundary plane can be defined by

$$(\mathbf{a}, \mathbf{p}) = \sum_{j=1}^{6} a_j p_j = 0. \qquad (4.5.4)$$

If the theorem is true, then the hyperplane of Eq. 4.5.4 agrees with the hyperplane defined by a scoring rule tie vote. With $\mathbf{sc} = (s_1, s_2, s_3)$, c_1 receives

$$s_1 p_1 + s_1 p_2 + s_2 p_3 + s_3 p_4 + s_3 p_5 + s_2 p_6$$

points while c_2 receives

$$s_2 p_1 + s_3 p_2 + s_3 p_3 + s_2 p_4 + s_1 p_5 + s_1 p_6$$

points. Therefore, a tie vote between these candidates is the profile set where both sums agree; this is the profile set

$$\{\mathbf{p} \,|\, (s_1 - s_2)p_1 + (s_1 - s_3)p_2 + (s_2 - s_3)p_3$$
$$+ (s_3 - s_2)p_4 + (s_3 - s_1)p_5 + (s_2 - s_1)p_6 = 0.\}$$
$$(4.5.5)$$

The theorem claims there exist s_1, s_2, s_3 so that each p_j coefficient in Eq. 4.5.4 equals the corresponding p_j coefficient from Eq. 4.5.5.

The trick to prove that the a_j coefficients have the desired expression is to derive appropriate linear equations in the a_j variables. To find these "appropriate" equations, just "work backwards from the answer." Namely, properties of the coefficients of Eq. 4.5.5 define algebraic relationships among the s_j terms. Then, the tools of neutrality and strong consistency are used to show that the same algebraic relationships hold for the a_j coefficients. For instance, the sums of the odd and of the even coefficients of Eq. 4.5.5 are zero, so we want to establish that

$$a_1 + a_3 + a_5 = a_2 + a_4 + a_6 = 0. \qquad (4.5.6)$$

The fact the sum of the odd coefficients of Eq. 4.5.5 equals zero is equivalent to the assertion that $\mathbf{p} = \frac{1}{3}(\mathbf{E}_1 + \mathbf{E}_3 + \mathbf{E}_5)$ defines a $\mathbf{sc}$ tie vote between c_1 and c_2. (Observe that this is a $\sigma = (1, 2, 3)$ orbit from Sect. 3.1.) Similarly, the odd coefficient expression in Eq. 4.5.6 is true iff this profile $\mathbf{p}$ can be used with Eq. 4.5.4. It can be used iff $\mathbf{p}$ is a boundary profile of $f^{-1}(\{c_1\})$ and $f^{-1}(\{c_2\})$.

To verify that $\mathbf{p}$ is a boundary profile, observe that $\mathbf{p}$ is invariant with respect to repeated applications of the name change $\sigma = (1, 2, 3)$, so, by neutrality, $\mathbf{p} \in f^{-1}(\{c_1, c_2, c_3\})$. Strong consistency (Proposition 4.5.1c) now requires $\mathbf{p}$ to be a boundary point of $f^{-1}(\{c_1, c_2\})$. Consequently, $\mathbf{p}$ satisfies Eq. 4.5.4, and the odd equation for Eq. 4.5.6 is true. The other algebraic equations needed to show that f is equivalent to using a scoring method are discovered in a similar manner.

In this outline, the hyperplanes are determined by strong consistency, and the form of the equations for tie votes is determined by neutrality. Where do we need anonymity? Can this condition be dropped? I leave this as an exercise for the reader. (Hint: Think about weighted voting.)

The Young Runoff. It remains to explain where the Young runoff enters. Equation 4.5.4 defines a four-dimensional space of profiles. It is worth wondering whether this huge space of indecisive profiles can be reduced in size by using tie-breaking methods. This is equivalent to partitioning this four-dimensional space so that some of its profiles are assigned to $\{c_1\}$ and some to $\{c_2\}$. The division process has to be done in a symmetric fashion (to satisfy neutrality) while ensuring that the defined sets are convex (as dictated by consistency). Thus, this division is defined by another equation $(\mathbf{a}_1, \mathbf{p}) = 0$. Again, similar to above, neutrality is used to establish that $\mathbf{a}_1$ comes from a scoring rule $\mathbf{sc}_2$. This scoring rule defines the first Young runoff.

With the runoff, the set of tie votes now defines a three-dimensional space. (There are six variables and three equations. Two equations are defined by the tie votes, one comes from the definition of the simplex.) So, why not try a second run-off? We can, but it is useless if the first two elections used positional voting methods. This is because, if both positional rankings keep the same two (or more) candidates tied, then, as established in Sect. 2.4 in the discussion of the scoring hull, the outcome for *all scoring methods* would keep the same two candidates tied. On the other hand, if the two scoring methods are not on the same leg of the scoring hull, another runoff election is possible. More runoffs, of course, add no additional information. Thus, only two runoffs are needed.

4.5.3 Positional Voting Methods

A scoring method $\mathbf{sc} = (s_1, s_2, s_3)$ is a positional method iff $s_1 \geq s_2 \geq s_3$ and $s_1 > s_3$. So, to characterize positional methods, the weights $\{s_j\}$ need to respect these monotonicity conditions; correspondingly, the choice functions must satisfy appropriate monotonicity assumptions. A condition from the last section is *faithfulness*; here, for a single voter profile $\mathbf{p}$, $f(\mathbf{p})$ is the voter's top-ranked candidate. But faithfulness requires $s_1 > max(s_2, s_3)$, so it excludes the antiplurality method. We need a weaker, more inclusive requirement.

Definition 4.5.3. A choice procedure is *somewhat faithful* if there is a single-voter profile $\mathbf{p}$ where the voter's *bottom ranked candidate* is not in $f(\mathbf{p})$. $\square$

Again, the power of neutrality is exhibited; if a procedure is somewhat faithful for a single-voter profile, it is somewhat faithful for all single-voter profiles. The difference between faithfulness and somewhat faithful is characterized by the restriction

$$max(s_1, s_2) > s_3. \tag{4.5.7}$$

From this equation, it follows that being "somewhat faithful" protects us from adopting rules such as $\mathbf{sc} = (2, 0, 3)$, but it doesn't save us from $\mathbf{sc}_1 = (2, 3, 0)$, or even $(3, 0, 2)$. These somewhat faithful vectors satisfy anonymity, neutrality, and strong consistency, but, they fail to be positional methods, so we need additional monotonicity assumptions. Clearly, these new requirements must distinguish between a first and second ranked candidate. (Mathematically, these conditions just eliminate vectors from an unwanted leg, or portion of a leg, of the scoring hull.) One such condition follows.

Definition 4.5.4. A choice procedure, g, is *eventually responsive* if, for any $\mathbf{p}$ and c_j, there is a unanimity ranking, $\mathbf{E}_k$, with c_j in top-place and a value λ^* so that for all $\lambda \geq \lambda^*$, $g(\lambda \mathbf{E}_k + (1-\lambda)\mathbf{p}) = \{c_j\}$. $\square$

Eventually responsiveness means that when enough voters with c_j top- ranked join a group, c_j will be chosen. A related monotonicity condition concerns the outcome of a two-voter profile where both voters have the same two candidates top-ranked. Surely, at least one of these candidates should be selected.

Definition 4.5.5. Suppose $\mathbf{p}_1 \neq \mathbf{p}_2$ are single voter profiles where c_i, c_j are the two top-ranked candidates for each voter. A choice procedure is *balancing* if c_i or c_j are in $f(\frac{1}{2}(\mathbf{p}_1 + \mathbf{p}_2))$. $\square$

Theorem 4.5.3. *Suppose a choice procedure is balancing, anonymous, neutral, strongly consistent, and eventually responsive. This procedure is either equivalent to choosing the top-ranked candidates from a positional election, or to choosing the top-ranked candidates from a positional election supplemented with a Young runoff. Conversely, all positional methods satisfy these conditions.*

4.5.4 Axiomatic Characterizations of the BC

An axiomatic representation for the BC is accomplished by imposing appropriate conditions to separate the BC from the other scoring procedures. Somewhat surprisingly, this is easy. According to Chap. 3, any condition relating the rankings of pairs to the chosen alternative either is satisfied by the top-ranked BC candidate, or it is not satisfied by any scoring method. Consequently, any BC-pairwise ranking property can be used to separate the BC from all other positional methods. The following is a sample.

Theorem 4.5.4. *Suppose a choice procedure g is anonymous, neutral, and strongly consistent.*

a. *If $g(\mathbf{p}) = \{c_1, c_2, c_3\}$ for all choices of $\mathbf{p}$ leading to tie votes for all three pairs, and if g is somewhat faithful, then g is equivalent to choosing the BC top-ranked candidate.*

b. *If g never selects the Condorcet loser, then g is equivalent either to choosing the BC top-ranked candidate, or to breaking a BC tie with a Young runoff.*

c. *No procedure g can guarantee the selection of a Condorcet winner.*

A surprise from this theorem is that so few assumptions dictate that the procedure is the BC! Moreover, these assumptions are so natural and acceptable that it is difficult to argue against them. Incidentally, observe that this theorem dispenses with the earlier monotonicity assumptions required to separate positional methods from scoring procedures. This is because the BC provides its own monotonicity (coming from the structure of the pairs, see Sect. 3.2.)

Proof. As already shown, the BC and the reversed BC, $\mathbf{sc} \approx (0, 1, 2) \approx \mathbf{w}_{\frac{1}{3}}$, are the only scoring rules where a tied pairwise vote ensures that the scoring outcome is also a tied vote. The somewhat faithful assumption eliminates the possibility that the scoring vector is $(0, 1, 2)$. As a runoff could break the tie vote, there can be no runoffs.

For part b, observe that only the BC ensures that a Condorcet loser cannot be top-ranked, nor tied for top-rank. Thus, we do not need the assistance of somewhat faithfulness. There is no reason to exclude runoffs.

For part c, all scoring rules, including the BC, can rank the Condorcet winner in second place. $\square$

4.5.5 Generalized Positional Voting

In positional voting, the points assigned to a candidate c_j are determined by how she is ranked on each ballot, but there remains more information that can be extracted from a profile. For instance, we could consider all ways c_1 is compared with another candidate, say c_2, relative to the last candidate c_3. One way to capture this information is to assign points to c_1 for each of the six possible ways she can be compared to c_2 in a ranking of three candidates. The choice of these points reflects a belief, or bias, about the importance of certain kinds of rankings.

I call the general class of procedures defined by this extra information *generalized positional voting methods.* What makes these methods interesting is that *generalized positional voting methods are the procedures that arise when weak consistency replaces strong consistency in Theorem 4.5.3.* As such, the generalized positional methods include positional voting, the threshold methods introduced in the exercises of Sect. 2.1, as well as other approaches.

These procedures utilize more fully the geometry of the space of profiles. The motivation comes from scoring rules where candidate c_1 is **sc** ranked above c_2 if she is assigned more points. This higher ranking holds if the value of the linear expression in Eq. 4.5.5 is positive; namely, Eq. 4.5.5 transfers the emphasis of a scoring election from the points received by each candidate to the geometry of the profile space $Si(6)$. Scoring rules partition $Si(6)$ in a restricted manner; generalized positional methods relax certain restrictions.

Thus, a generalized positional method is defined by a partitioning of the profile space into seven convex regions. (The number seven corresponds to the number of nonempty subsets of candidates while the convexity is required to satisfy weak consistency.) These sets must satisfy certain symmetry properties in order to obey the dictates of neutrality. For instance, whatever the final definition, the profile sets assigned to $\{c_i\}$ and to $\{c_j\}$ must be geometrically similar because neutrality requires σ_T (defined by $\sigma = (i, j)$) to convert the first set into the second.

Actually, thanks to convexity, the partitioning is reasonably straightforward because the boundaries of the regions must be portions of planes. Consequently, to define the partitioning, it suffices to describe the boundaries between

  a. the sets of profiles where a single candidate is chosen and where a pair is selected,

  b. the profile sets where a single candidate is chosen and where all three candidates are selected, and

c.   the profile sets where a pair is selected and where all three candidates are selected.

The boundaries between these convex regions are portions of hyperplanes, so the boundaries, and hence the procedure, can be described by scalar products not unlike those used in Eq. 4.5.5. For instance, the boundary between where $\{c_1\}$ and where $\{c_1, c_2\}$ are selected is given by an equation

$$\tau(\mathbf{p}; \mathbf{a}, c_1, \{c_1, c_2\}) = \sum_{j=1}^{6} a_j p_j \qquad (4.5.8)$$

where a zero value is the boundary, and the sign of $\tau(\mathbf{p}; \mathbf{a}, c_1, \{c_1, c_2\})$ indicates the side of the boundary where $\mathbf{p}$ resides. The convention I adopt is that a positive value favors the smaller subset of candidates. So, a positive value requires a profile to be on the $\{c_1\}$ side of the hyperplane. (Conditions on the coefficients defining $\mathbf{a}$ are specified below.) A decision must be made whether a zero value of τ is pro $\{c_1\}$ or $\{c_1, c_2\}$.

A interesting feature emerges. Even if $\mathbf{p}$ is on the $\{c_1\}$ side of the boundary hyperplane, it doesn't follow that $\{c_1\}$ is the $\mathbf{p}$ outcome; all we know is that $\{c_1, c_2\}$ is *not* the outcome. After all, the profile set supporting $\{c_1\}$ has other boundaries, such as that between $\{c_1\}$ and $\{c_3\}$, that need to be investigated. Consequently, we have an *elimination procedure* where, a negative τ value only determines that $\mathbf{p}$ cannot be in the $\{c_1\}$ region while a positive τ value excludes $\{c_1, c_2\}$ from further consideration.

The definition of $\tau(\mathbf{p}; \mathbf{a}, c_i, \{c_i, c_j\})$, to determine between sets $\{c_i\}, \{c_i, c_j\}$, follows immediately from neutrality. If σ is the name change where $i \to 1, j \to 2$, then the profile $\sigma_T(\mathbf{p})$ requires c_1 to have the same relationship with c_2 that c_i has with c_j. This leads to the definition

$$\tau(\mathbf{p}; \mathbf{a}, c_i, \{c_i, c_j\}) = \tau(\sigma_T(\mathbf{p}); \mathbf{a}, c_1, \{c_1, c_2\}). \qquad (4.5.9)$$

Similarly, vectors $\mathbf{b} = (b_1, b_1, b_2, b_3, b_3, b_2)$ and $\mathbf{d} = (d_1, d_2, d_3, d_3, d_2, d_1)$ are chosen to determine, respectively, the boundary between $\{c_1\}$ and $\{c_1, c_2, c_3\}$ and between $\{c_1, c_2\}$ and $\{c_1, c_2, c_3\}$. (To suggest why these vectors have the particular form where certain coefficients are repeated, note that because the type-one and two voters have c_1 top-ranked, they prefer her to $\{c_1, c_2, c_3\}$. To combine their votes, b_1 is the common multiple for p_1, p_2.) Thus, for instance, if $\tau(\mathbf{p}; \mathbf{d}, \{c_1, c_2\}, \{c_1, c_2, c_3\}) > 0$, the profile favors the smaller set, so $\{c_1, c_2, c_3\}$ is eliminated from further consideration. The definition for $\tau(\mathbf{p}; \mathbf{b}, \{c_i\}, \{c_1, c_2, c_3\})$ and $\tau(\mathbf{p}; \mathbf{d}, \{c_i, c_j\}, \{c_1, c_2, c_3\})$ are determined by name changing permutations as in Eq. 4.5.9.

All subsets of candidates are compared; at each stage one of the two compared subsets is dropped from further consideration. At the end, a single subset remains; this is the chosen subset. Of course, conditions need to be imposed upon the a_j, b_i, d_k values to ensure that a unique set of candidates is determined for each profile. These are

$$a_1, a_2 \geq 0; a_3 + a_4 \leq 0, a_1 + a_6 \leq 0, a_2 + a_5 \leq 0, a_1 a_2 \leq a_5 a_6.$$

If $a_1 + a_2 > 0$; $a_2 a_6 \leq a_1 a_3, a_1 a_5 \leq a_2 a_4, a_1 a_6 \leq a_2 a_3, a_2 a_5 \leq a_1 a_4$,

$$a_1(\sum a_j) \geq a_2(\sum a_j), a_2 \geq a_1. \tag{4.5.10}$$

$$b_1 \geq 0, \sum b_j \leq 0, b_1(\sum a_j) \geq (a_1 + a_2)(\sum b_j)$$
$$\sum d_i \leq 0. \tag{4.5.11}$$

The first row of conditions ensure that the profile regions supporting a single candidate do not overlap. The rest of the conditions on a_j's ensure convexity of profile sets by preventing the linear boundaries from creating a "V" indentation. Just as the definition of the threshold methods from Sect. 2.1 required a compatibility condition between the different values, a compatibility condition needs to be imposed on the **a** and **b** vectors; these are the conditions relating b_j and a_i terms.

If vectors **a**, **b**, **d** satisfy these conditions, they define a generalized positional voting method; that is, an appropriate geometric partitioning of $Si(6)$. Such awkward descriptions are not needed, as illustrated by the following.

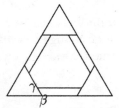

Fig. 4.5.2. A threshold method

- The positional method $(w_1, w_2, 0)$ is where $\mathbf{a} = (w_1 - w_2, w_1 - w_3, w_2 - w_3, w_3 - w_2, w_3 - w_1, w_2 - w_1)$ and **d** has the property $d_1, d_2 > 0, d_1 + d_2 + d_3 = 0$.
- The threshold method indicated in Fig. 4.5.2 has $\mathbf{a} = (1, 1, 0, 0, -1, -1)$, $b_1 = 1 - \beta, b_2 = b_2 = -\beta$, and $d_1 = d_2 = 1 - \gamma, d_3 = \gamma$. A more civilized description is the one given in Chap. 2. □

For details concerning the reason for the restrictions on the coefficients of **a**, **b**, **d**, and a proof of the following theorem, see [S12]. (The interesting part of the proof mimics that given below. What remains are the straightforward, tedious computations to verify that the above equations perform as advertised.)

Theorem 4.5.5. *A generalized positional voting method is anonymous, neutral, weakly consistent, balancing, and eventually responsive. Conversely, a neutral, anonymous, weakly consistent choice procedure that is balancing and eventually responsive is equivalent to choosing the top-ranked candidate from a generalized* *positional voting method, or choosing the top-ranked candidate from a generalized positional method where ties are broken by Young runoffs based on other generalized positional methods.*

The theorems of this section establish, then, that remarkably few natural and most acceptable assumptions force attention upon the positional or generalized positional methods. The message is that not only are these procedures natural to use, but, when basic axioms are specified, they are the only procedures that are allowed. So, if positional methods are not used, what is the cost?

The Proof of Theorem 4.5.2. The power of neutrality is captured by the following lemma.

Lemma 4.5.6. *Let g be a neutral choice procedure. If a profile $\mathbf{p}$ is invariant with respect to a subset of candidates B (that is, for all σ such that $\sigma(B) = B$, $\sigma_T(\mathbf{p}) = \mathbf{p}$), then either $g(\mathbf{p}) \supset B$ or $g(\mathbf{p}) \cap B = \emptyset$.*

Proof. If false, there are two candidates, say $c_1, c_2 \in B$, where $c_1 \in g(\mathbf{p})$, $c_2 \notin g(\mathbf{p})$. Using the permutation $\sigma = (1, 2)$, it follows that $c_2 = \sigma(c_1) \in \sigma(g(\mathbf{p})) = g(\sigma_T(\mathbf{p})) = g(\mathbf{p})$. The contradiction proves the assertion. $\square$

Corollary 4.5.7. *If a non-constant choice procedure g is neutral and strongly consistent, then:*

a.   *$\{c_1, c_2, c_3\}$ is an admissible set where its supporting profile set includes the line*

$$\mathcal{I} = \{\mathbf{p} \mid \mathbf{p} = (\lambda \mathbf{p}_1 + (1 - \lambda)\mathbf{p}_2), \lambda \in [0, 1]\} \qquad (4.5.12)$$

   where $\mathbf{p}_1 = \frac{1}{3}(\mathbf{E}_1 + \mathbf{E}_3 + \mathbf{E}_5)$ and $\mathbf{p}_2 = \frac{1}{3}(\mathbf{E}_2 + \mathbf{E}_4 + \mathbf{E}_6)$.

b.   *All nonempty subsets of candidates are admissible outcomes for g.*

Proof. Part a follows from the fact that both $B = \{c_1, c_2, c_3\}$ and the profiles of Eq. 4.5.12 are invariant with respect to all name changes. As the complement of B is the empty set, the conclusion follows from the lemma.

As $\{c_1, c_2, c_3\}$ is an admissible g outcome (part a), g has at least one other admissible subset. If it is a pair, then, by neutrality, all pairs are admitted. Thus $\{c_1, c_2\}$ and $\{c_2, c_3\}$ are admissible outcomes, and, from strong consistency, so is the intersection $\{c_2\}$. The conclusion follows from neutrality. If a pair is not admitted, then the extra set is a singleton and, by neutrality, all singletons are admitted.

It remains to prove that a pair always is admissible. As the profiles

$$\frac{1}{2}[\mathbf{E}_1 + \mathbf{E}_6], \frac{1}{2}[\mathbf{E}_2 + \mathbf{E}_5], \frac{1}{2}[\mathbf{E}_3 + \mathbf{E}_4] \qquad (4.5.13)$$

are invariant with respect to $\sigma = (1, 2)$ name changes, the outcomes for these profiles, and for any profile in its convex hull, is restricted (according to the lemma) to $\{c_1, c_2\}$, $\{c_1, c_2, c_3\}$, or $\{c_3\}$. The profile $(\frac{1}{6}, \ldots, \frac{1}{6}) \in \mathcal{I}$, the barycentric point of the equilateral triangle convex hull, is a profile supporting $\{c_1, c_2, c_3\}$. I show that not all profiles in this hull support $\{c_1, c_2, c_3\}$.

If all the profiles of Eq. 4.1.13 support $\{c_1, c_2, c_3\}$, then, by neutrality, so would $\frac{1}{2}[\mathbf{E}_1 + \mathbf{E}_4]$, $\frac{1}{2}[\mathbf{E}_5 + \mathbf{E}_6]$. (This assertion follows from applying the name change $(2, 3)$ to the vectors of Eq. 4.5.13. Alternatively, one can find the corresponding profiles from the representation triangle.) As this would identify five *linearly independent profiles* from a five-dimensional space ($Si(6)$) that support $\{c_1, c_2, c_3\}$, it would mean there is an open set of profiles that supports $\{c_1, c_2, c_3\}$. This contradicts Proposition 4.5.1c.

The worse case (for $\{c_1, c_2\}$ being an admissible outcome) is if all profiles in this hull support only $\{c_3\}$ and $\{c_1, c_2, c_3\}$. To show that this can't be so, observe by combining convexity (weak consistency) and the fact that the barycentric profile $(\frac{1}{6}, \ldots, \frac{1}{6}) \in \mathcal{I}$ supports $\{c_1, c_2, c_3\}$ that there must be a line dividing the convex hull where the line passes through the barycentric point. This line either separates the profiles supporting $\{c_3\}$ and $\{c_1, c_2, c_3\}$, or it is in the set supporting $\{c_1, c_2, c_3\}$. If no profile supports $\{c_1, c_2\}$, an open region of this convex hull, which includes at least one vertex and portions of two edges connecting this vertex with the two remaining vertices, must be in the support of $\{c_1, c_2, c_3\}$. By neutrality, it now is easy to find a linearly independent set of five profiles in the support of $\{c_1, c_2, c_3\}$. This creates the contradiction that an open set of profiles supports $\{c_1, c_2, c_3\}$. Consequently, there is a profile set that supports $\{c_1, c_2\}$. By strong convexity, this profile set includes an open set (of the hull) along with one of the vertices. $\square$

Weak consistency ensures that each profile set $f^{-1}(\alpha)$ is a convex subset of $Si(6)$. As $Si(6)$ is partitioned into seven convex sets, one of them contains an open set of $Si(6)$. If α consists of more than one candidate, then Proposition 4.5.1c requires the profile set $f^{-1}(\alpha)$ to be in a lower dimensional plane. Therefore, only the profile sets supporting a singleton contain open subsets of $Si(6)$.

By the power of neutrality, if $f^{-1}(\{c_i\})$ contains an open set, then so does $f^{-1}(\{c_j\})$ for each j. Assisted by the various name changes, σ, the associated permutations of voter types, σ_T, ensure that each of these regions are geometric copies of the others. Therefore, all three $f^{-1}(\{c_j\})$ sets contain open sets; moreover, whatever is said about the geometry of one set is true for the other two.

The convex geometry forces the boundaries for $f^{-1}(\{c_1\})$ to be portions of planes. An analytic expression for the boundary between c_1 and c_2, then, is a subset of the set

$$(\mathbf{a}, \mathbf{p}) = \sum_{j=1}^{6} a_j p_j = e, \qquad (4.5.14)$$

where $\mathbf{a} = (a_1, a_2, \ldots a_6)$ is a vector to be determined and e is a scalar. Decompose $\mathbf{a}$ into a component in the direction $(\frac{1}{6}, \ldots, \frac{1}{6})$ and a component orthogonal to this vector, $\mathbf{a} = \mathbf{a}_1 + b(\frac{1}{6}, \frac{1}{6}, \ldots, \frac{1}{6})$. Using this decomposition with a profile proves that $b = e$. Namely, the e value describes the behavior of the boundary plane off of the simplex $Si(6)$. This is irrelevant, so we can and do assume that $e = 0$. Thus $(\mathbf{a}, (1, \ldots, 1)) = \sum_{j=1}^{6} a_j = 0$.

The boundary equation is of the form $(\mathbf{a}, \mathbf{p}) = 0$, so $\mathbf{a}$ is a normal vector for the profile boundary. To eliminate the ambiguity whether $\mathbf{a}$ is an inner or an outer normal vector, let $\mathbf{a}$ be the inner normal for the profile set supporting $\{c_1\}$.

An important part of the proof is to show that all profiles satisfying $\sigma_T(\mathbf{p}) = \mathbf{p}$ for $\sigma = (1, 2)$ satisfy Eq. 4.5.14. As Eq. 4.5.14 defines a linear subspace, the linear span of a profile set satisfying Eq. 4.5.14 also satisfies the equation. So, because the proof of Corollary 4.5.7 shows that an open set of profiles from the hull defined by Eq. 4.5.13 satisfies Eq. 4.5.14, the span of this open set, which includes the hull, satisfies Eq. 4.5.14.

To show that $\mathbf{a}$ can be expressed in terms of a scoring rule (as indicated by Eq. 4.5.5), substituting the profiles of Eq. 4.5.13 into Eq. 4.5.14 defines the relationships

$$a_1 = -a_6, \ a_2 = -a_5, \ a_3 = -a_4; \tag{4.5.15}$$

equalities that mimic the corresponding $s_i - s_j = -(s_i - s_j)$ relationship from Eq. 4.5.5. Choose scalars s_1, s_2, s_3 satisfying $a_1 = s_1 - s_2$, $a_2 = s_1 - s_3$. (Observe that the derivation of Eq. 4.5.5 has the vector defined by the coefficients as an inner normal for the set $\{c_1\}$.) According to Eq. 4.5.6, it follows that $a_3 = s_2 - s_3$. Thus, $\mathbf{a}$ can be expressed in a form so that Eq. 4.5.5 is recaptured.

To complete the proof, use the muscle power of neutrality to determine the equations for the plane dividing c_1-c_3 and c_2-c_3. With the name changes $\sigma_1 = (2, 3)$, $\sigma_2 = (1, 3)$ and the associated profile permutations $\sigma_{1,T} = (1, 2)(3, 6)(4, 5)$, $\sigma_{2,T} = (1, 4)(2, 3)(5, 6)$, these equations are

$$(\mathbf{a}, \sigma_{1,T}(\mathbf{p})) = a_2 p_1 + a_1 p_2 + a_6 p_3 + a_5 p_4 + a_4 p_5 + a_3 p_6 = 0$$
$$(\mathbf{a}, \sigma_{2,T}(\mathbf{p})) = a_4 p_1 + a_3 p_2 + a_2 p_3 + a_1 p_4 + a_6 p_5 + a_5 p_6 = 0$$
$$\tag{4.5.16}$$

Courtesy of the standard associative and commutative rules of addition and multiplication is the relationship

$$(\mathbf{a}, \sigma_{j,T}(\mathbf{p})) = (\sigma_{j,T}(\mathbf{a}), \mathbf{p}) = 0; \ j = 1, 2. \tag{4.5.17}$$

The conclusion now follows. $\square$

As a comment about the runoffs, notice that Eq. 4.5.5 defines a four dimensional space of profiles. On the other hand, neutrality only requires that the profiles in this set are those in the convex hull with vertices in Eq. 4.5.13. The runoffs define ways of passing planes through this two dimensional space so that the convexity conditions are satisfied. While a simple description of these cutting planes is the Young runoffs, it is not overly difficult to invent other formulations.

4.5.6 Exercises

4.5.1. Show for $\sigma = (1, 2)$ that the line with endpoints $\frac{1}{3}(\mathbf{E}_1 + \mathbf{E}_3 + \mathbf{E}_5)$ and $\frac{1}{3}(\mathbf{E}_2 + \mathbf{E}_4 + \mathbf{E}_6)$ is invariant with respect to σ_T.

4.5.2. A choice procedure g is called "majority preserving" if, when a profile $\mathbf{p}$ has more than half of the voters with c_j top-ranked, then $g(\mathbf{p}) = \{c_j\}$. Show that if majority preserving is added to the conditions of Theorem 4.5.3, then the system must be equivalent to choosing the top-ranked candidate from the plurality vote (with the possibility of Young runoffs).

4.5.3. Suppose a profile $\mathbf{p}$ is such that at least one voter less than two-thirds of all voters has c_j bottom ranked. A choice function g is "minimally respectable" if for all such profiles, $g(\mathbf{p}) \neq \{c_j\}$. Show that if in addition to the conditions of Theorem 4.5.3 a procedure is *not minimally respectable*, then these axioms define the plurality vote.

The conditions of Example 4.5.2 are attractive while those of Example 4.5.3 are not. Yet, both conditions characterize the plurality voting system. The purpose of these exercises is to demonstrate the danger of relying upon an isolated set of axioms as the decisive factor in selecting a voting system. By accepting a particular set of axioms without knowing what else can happen is akin to buying a Rolex watch in a dark alley from a vendor who keeps his merchandise carefully arranged and attached to the inside of his coat.

4.5.4. Show how each of the monotonicity conditions of Theorem 4.5.3 (balancing, etc.) exclude portions of the scoring hull. Assuming Theorem 4.5.2, prove Theorem 4.5.3.

4.5.5. By use of the BC properties, derive axiomatic representations for the BC that differ from Theorem 4.5.4. (For instance, what about the reversal symmetry?)

4.5.6. For the profile $\frac{2}{9}\mathbf{E}_1 + \frac{1}{3}\mathbf{E}_3 + \frac{4}{9}\mathbf{E}_6$, show that the generalized election outcome for $\mathbf{a} = (3, 2, 1, -2, -2, -3)$, $\mathbf{b} = (1, 0, -2)$, is $\{c_1, c_3\}$.

4.5.7. Show that the threshold methods are generalized positional voting methods. Find the corresponding values of $\mathbf{a}$, $\mathbf{b}$, $\mathbf{d}$ for each method.

4.5.8. Find all generalized positional voting procedures where $a_1 = a_2 = 0$. (One procedure is where a candidate is selected if and only if she is top-ranked by all voters.)

4.5.9. Notice for $\sigma_T = (1, 6)(2, 5)(3, 4)$ (corresponding to $\sigma = (1, 2)$ that

$$< \mathbf{a}, \sigma_T(\mathbf{p}) > = a_1 p_6 + a_2 p_5 + a_3 p_4 + a_4 p_3 + a_5 p_2 + a_6 p_1$$
$$= < \sigma_T(\mathbf{a}), \mathbf{p} > .$$

Generalize this relationship to all choices of σ used in neutrality. Then, use your result to find a simpler expression for Eq. 4.5.9.

4.5.10. Show that any convex partitioning of the profile space $Si(6)$ into seven sets defines a weakly consistent, anonymous procedure.

4.5.11. Create an example to show that if anonymity is not used, then Theorem 4.5.2 does not hold. Where is anonymity used in the proof? (Hint: weighted voting.)

NOTES

What follows are informal notes, suggestions how results can be extended, and references for readers wanting to learn more about particular topics. By no means are the references complete; they are places to start. In addition to these suggestions and their references, I recommend Kelly's *Social Choice Bibliography* [K3]. At the end of these notes is an outline how the basic mathematical results for this book (and my more general research program of $n \geq 3$ candidates) were discovered. Hopefully, the person comfortable with advanced mathematics can use this description to unify and extend the results described and developed here.

Chapter 2

Section 2.1-3. The geometry of the representation triangle, ranking regions, the space of voting profiles, the normalized form for voting vectors, and the convex hull $\mathcal{CH}(\mathbf{w}_s)$ are natural, but it appears to have been first developed in [S1, 3-6]. (I have not found it elsewhere. Instead, for example, most results are described with specific methods in analytic formulations rather than considering all possibilities.) This geometric approach has become my standard tool.

Section 2.4. Already during the exciting years of debate between Borda and Condorcet, it was understood that the same profile can define different outcomes as $\mathbf{w}_s$ varies. In more recent time, others, including Steven Brams, Peter Fishburn, Herve Moulin, and Phil Straffin have created provocative and amusing examples (e.g., see [F1-3, Str]). However, this earlier discussion tends to be limited to special examples for specific procedures. The first approach to understand everything that can happen for all $n \geq 3$ for all positional methods is [S1, 3-4].

The geometric theory and results in this section are new and specifically designed for this book. Originally all results for the book were for $n \geq 3$ candidates, but realism required limiting discussion to $n = 3$ candidates. After the decision was made, Benoit wrote his delightful paper [Be] applying these paradoxes to the selection of the MVP in baseball. Partially as a rejoinder in an enjoyable, joking debate between us whether there existed a method that would choose the MVP from one of my favorite teams, portions of the original material for $n \geq 3$ were resurrected and modified to write [S15]. Consequently, [S15] indicates how to extend the procedure line to the "procedure hull." Combining techniques from [S15] and this section, the reader can extend the results from Sec. 2.4 (e.g., the scoring hulls and shells, the precise conditions on the permissible locations for the procedure hull, etc.) from $n = 3$ to all $n \geq 3$ candidates.

Section 2.5. A complete history about the rankings of pairs probably would include everybody who has written or experimented with voting! For previous work, I suggest starting with the books and survey articles by Black [Bl], Fishburn [F1], Niemi and Riker [NR], Nurmi [Nu], and Sen [Se2]. While the explanation of the Condorcet cycle in terms of the irrational voter is new; hints are in [S1, 19]. (The reader knowledgable about algebraic group theory will find several extensions both in terms of subgroup constructions and for $n \geq 3$. See the concluding comments.) The material from 2.5.3 to the end of 2.5 is newly developed for this book.

Originally I had planned to include a section on computing the probability of cycles and other types of voting behavior. My goal was to start with the seminal work of Gehrlein [G1,2] and his joint work with Fishburn [GF] and then show how to modify a new approach pioneered by Jill Van Newenhizen [VN] to extend this work to all values of n, a wider class of probability distributions, and all basic questions. However, I now believe that the coordinate representation approach developed in this section and advanced throughout the book is much easier to use, it leads to sharper results, and, because we now can "see" all profiles, it is more informative. Also, as described, it is reasonably easy to use the coordinate representations to completely determine the profile set supporting various conclusions. Thus, we now can answer more ambitious questions from the traditional approach for any number of issues in a fairly elementary manner using more general assumptions. (All of this extends to $n \geq 3$ candidates.)

Cycles arise in almost all areas involving pairwise rankings – economics, statistics, etc. The mathematical reason for these cycles is similar to the confused voter explanation. A reader interested in reading more about this might look at [FS], [Ha], [S5-6]. For different ideas on this and related subjects, I suggest Aizerman's survey paper [A].

Black's conditions are well known and described in most books on this topic; see Black's classic [Bl]. The conditions developed in Sec. 2.5.7 seem to be more general than what is in the literature; it is the only discussion (I know about) based on geometric reasoning. Again, extensions to $n \geq 3$ follow similar geometric arguments.

Spatial voting is an important growth area that provides sensitive insight into varied questions from political science. (The results of this subsection are based on arguments from [S17].) For the reader interested in learning more about this topic, I recommend starting with Steven Brams' book [Br2], progress to the book edited by Enelow and Hinich [EH], and then the references of these books. For a flavor of the serious difficulties, see the many papers and books written by Norman Schofield (e.g., [Sh1, 2]) as well as papers such the one by Le Breton and Salles [LS].

The material in Sec. 2.5.10 about the failings and faults of the Condorcet winners and losers was developed for this book; all of the comments extend with even greater force to the $n \geq 3$ setting. Actually, in higher dimensions, there are even more profiles that demonstrate the serious weakness of conclusions from pairwise ordinal rankings.

Section 2.6.1. Comparing the rankings of pairs and all three candidates is as old as this subject. After all, this was the force of Borda's example in 1770. Extensions to more candidates in terms of specific examples with restrictions on the choice of procedures were made by others – in particular Fishburn. The first theory describing (in certain settings) everything that can happen is in [S1,3,4] and then, in greater generality, in papers starting with [S9]. Everything else in this section is new – in particular, the geometric reasoning.

Chapter 3

Section 3.1. Symmetry and neutrality are well known and carefully described in any number of papers. (This includes the permutation notation used here.) The results about the orbit and exploiting the higher dimensional aspects of profiles is developed for this book. Identifying the Condorcet cycle with an higher dimensional 120° orbit was developed in [S1] and used in several papers; e.g., [S8,19].

At the end of these notes, I'll explain why symmetry plays such a critical role in the geometric development described here. Most of this material (e.g., super-neutrality) is new. (However, portions of this material were needed to prove the major result in [S10]; in particular, I needed a relationship equivalent to Eq. 3.1.6.) In the original manuscript, super-neutrality was developed for all $n \geq 3$; in this version, the basic hints needed for extensions to the general setting are in the footnotes. While the reversal geometry extends to all $n \geq 3$, nice pictures no longer are possible. The easiest analytic way to handle this material is to recognize that the cyclic positional coordinates are based on the two orbits admitted by the permutation $\sigma = (1, 2, 3)$. For $n > 3$ candidates, the orbits of $\sigma = (1, 2, 3, \ldots, n)$ foliate the space in a distinctly higher-dimensional nature. With the coordinate systems, the reversal (as well as higher order symmetry changes) can be computed and the reversal geometry conclusions can be obtained. The Borda Symmetry class is first published with this presentation; using similar geometric techniques, it extends to all $n \geq 3$.

Section 3.2. Some results in the first part of the section probably were known by Borda. (See [D], [B]. I believe this even though others point to the absence of supporting proof (e.g., Borda never made conclusions of the "Condorcet winner not being bottom-ranked" type). However, *nobody* writes down everything they have determined and these conclusions involve only basic algebra, so it is difficult to accept that an applied mathematician of Borda's standing did not recognize these basic relationships.) Included among the 19th and 20th century papers contributing to the BC are Nanson [N], Smith [Sm], Young [Y1], Gehrlein and Fishburn [FG, GF]; an overview is in the expositions [Nu, Str]. For a modern approach that characterizes all of the BC properties for $n \geq 3$ candidates, see [S9, 11, 13] and the extensions to other positional systems in [S16, 17].

The Borda Dictionary and Vector Space come from [S9, 11]. Most of the geometric descriptions, such as the BC cross-sections, Borda cyclic coordinates, are new with this book. Using the above comments about orbits of $\sigma = (1, 2, \ldots, n)$, results depending on the BC cyclic coordinates extend to $n \geq 3$.

Section 3.3. Much of this material is a special case of statements from [S9], but with a new geometric representation; e.g., the cross-section approach has not been previously published.

Section 3.4. To my chagrin, the unimaginative term "multiple voting systems" was coined in [SV1]. Most of the results in this section are extensions (to the restrictive setting of $n = 3$) of comments in [SV1,2]. The heavier emphasis on geometry is new.

Section 3.5. Some of this material is a geometric representation of conclusions from [S9, 11, 12, 13, 15] where the results were established for all $n \geq 3$.

Chapter 4

Section 4.1. Weak consistency was introduced in [S12]. The material in this section relies upon and extends (with a greater emphasis on geometry) the results from this reference. For earlier, related statements, consult Nurmi's and Straffin's expositions [Nu, Str] as well as Moulin's work, e.g., [Mo1].

Section 4.2. The kind of issues described here have consumed much of the social choice literature. Therefore, the interested reader could start with the general books and references mentioned above as well as the work of Plott (a starting point might be the references in his paper [Pl]). It is impossible to do justice to the literature for manipulation and strategic action; after the startling, seminal work of Gibbard [Gi] and Satterthwaite [Sa], there have been many deep contributions to this topic. One starting point might be the work of Barbera [Ba2] and of Schmeidler and Sonnenschein [ScS]. Also, for almost any method, a manipulation analysis can be found; e.g., see Niemi's analysis of Approval Voting [Ni] and Chamberlin's comparison [C]. (Incidentally, many comparisons are based on computer simulations; this no longer is necessary as the method developed in [S10] and reported in this section allows an analytic analysis.) Periodically, when some organization believes they have invented a strategy-proof system, they need to be informed of the errors of their ways by others. This leads to some interesting examples; for instance, S. Brams [Br1] developed one to educate the American Mathematical Society.

Usually, the topics addressed in this section are treated separately. Thus, this geometric treatment seems to be the first to show that all of the questions from monotonicity to manipulation are so intimately connected that they can be addressed in the same general framework while obtaining sharper conclusions. The geometric proof of the Gibbard-Satterthwaite Theorem is new (and I thank Mark Satterthwaite for discussions about it). The susceptibility to manipulation discussion is a more geometric formulation of ideas first developed in [S10].

Section 4.3. While apportionment methods have been widely studied for years, I find the best papers to be Huntington's work from the 1920s – his references [Hu1, 2] are a good place to start. Several papers were published up to the 60s and 70s, but, after the size of Congress was fixed at 435, interest diminished. Then, in 1975, Balinski and Young [BY1] published an entertaining exposition that resurrected interest in the USA and Europe. Also see the book edited by Brams, Lucas and Straffin [BLS].

The presentation about the Alabama Paradox and the method described in the last subsection come from [S2]. In particular, the identification of apportionment and integer programming problems with flows on a torus was first done in [S2]. The material concerning fly-catching leading up to the geometric explanation of the sliding and transition bias is new. (Some of the technical support for [Mas] and [Mon] required computer simulations; this new geometric analysis allows for sharper statements.)

For the readers interested in creating other approaches, let me note that the Hamilton method is based on moving a flat object held parallel to the simplices S_h, while the Huntington methods move an orthant in various lagging and sliding ways. These two methods are special cases of moving a cone according to the exact apportionment line – Hamilton's method is where the vertex angle is $\theta = 180^o$ while Huntington is characterized by $\theta = 90^o$. Let an acute cone be where $|\theta| < 90^o$ while an obtuse cone has $90^o < \theta < 180^o$. It is easy to reject the acute cone (it has all the problems associated with requiring values of $\lambda << h$), but what are the properties of the obtuse cones?

Section 4.4. Arrow's Theorem [Ar] is so shocking that even today, at most conferences involving choice theory, papers are presented trying to unravel the mystery. Explanations use all sorts of techniques: e.g., Barbera [Ba1] emphasizes pivotal voting while Barthelemy [Bar] describes unusual domains. Gibbard, Hylland, and Weymark's paper [GHW] has many surprises. Indeed, to find other earlier approaches, the reader should start with one of the many excellent books on the subject; say, the one by Kelly [K1]. As for earlier work on "possibility theorems" of the "Gene-Alfred" flavor, see the work of Kalai and his coauthors [KM, KR] and their references.

I want to call attention to the insightful work of Chichilinsky [Ch]; she created a subfield by explaining Arrow-type results with algebraic topology. A different abstract approach using algebraic group theory is outlined at the end of [S8]. As the approach from [S8] uses the wreath product of permutation groups – a topic employed in algebraic topology – it probably is related to Chichilinsky's work, but I haven't explored this question.

The approach developed in this section is a benign geometric modification of ideas developed in [S14]. This reference describes results for all values of n as well as showing how the same ideas hold for game theory, probability, economics, etc. The approach was developed to understand the "kind of information" required by certain classes of axioms. To suggest what I mean, Chichilinsky used topology to establish a form of "similarity" among different conclusions. One way to think about "similarity" is that it catalogues procedures into partition sets. The goal of [S14] is to go a step further to characterize these partition sets in terms of the kinds of information involved. Now, a natural partition is defined by level sets of a function, and, more generally, by "foliations." So, [S14] finds discrete versions of "foliations" over the space of all possible procedures. Similarly, other theorems ranging in flavor from that of Blau and Deb [BD] to Brown [Bro] can be extended.

Section 4.5. The first deep work on the topic of this section is by Peyton Young. In two insightful papers [Y1, 2] he found an axiomatic representation of scoring methods and of Borda's method. His proofs are complex; hopefully, the geometric approach developed for this book are simpler.

The geometric proof characterizing scoring methods is new. Finding a further restriction for scoring methods to be positional methods now becomes straightforward once we recognize the role of the geometry of the scoring hull; the set I give is only one of many possible. Be careful, however, because "natural conditions" can be false. (In particular, the exclusion principle in [S12] is wrong; not only does it eliminate the scoring methods, but it also positional methods. So, replace it with the kinds of conditions found in this section. Fortunately, this embarrassing error does not affect the other results in [S12].) The first characterization of the BC is due to Young [Y1]. A method to find all sorts of new, alternative choices of axioms is outlined in [S11, 13, 16]. Actually, now that we know how to extract all possible properties of the Borda Count (as well as all other positional voting methods [S16, 18]), axiomatic representations become almost trivial to construct. This is indicated with the approach used in this section. The generalized positional voting method was introduced in [S12].

A geometric approach

The emphasis in this book has been to find the outcomes of the unanimity profiles and then determine the convex hull described by these vertices. While I hope the reader finds this approach to be natural, it took awhile to discover it. Being a typical mathematician, I enjoy the challenge of envisioning the intricacies of higher dimensional spaces guided by various mathematical tools. Once the basic conclusions are known, the task of translating them from the abstract setting to a more useful language is difficult. This book is a partial translation; what follows is a brief exposition of the conclusions in the original, perhaps unintelligible form.

Symmetry is the key. One role played by symmetry is to partition a space with its orbits. To see what I mean, start with unit vectors in a three-dimensional space; that is, points on a unit sphere S^2. Here, a natural symmetry action is rotation about some axis (a $SO(2)$ action) such as the axis connecting the North and South Poles. The effect of such a symmetry is to identify points on the sphere with other points (as being "similar" with respect to this action); these are the latitude lines in the figure. The circles partition the sphere; by filling in the convex hull formed by each circle the discs partition the solid sphere.

So, the *orbit* of this symmetry action on the unit vector is a circle. The one exception is if the vector being acted upon is on the axis of rotation; then the orbit is a lower-dimensional object – a point. Notice that as the choice of the base point approaches the rotation axis, the size of the orbit shrinks; it gets closer to resembling the lower-dimensional object.

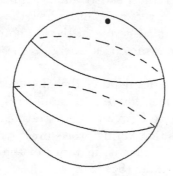

Fig. 5.1. Orbits under symmetry actions

I'm going to use the above to suggest what happens with voting and choice theory. The natural symmetry action in voting is a change in voter type. So, if $A = c_1 \succ c_2 \succ \cdots \succ c_n$, then any other voter type is obtained with an appropriate permutation (i.e., an appropriate name change). Therefore, the permutation group, S_n, replaces the above rotation action. To define a vector, recognize that there are $2^n - (n + 1)$ subsets of two or more candidates. For each subset, assign a normalized voting vector; this assignment defines a *system vector* $\mathbf{W}^n$. In fact, this system vector describes how a ballot for each subset of candidates would be tallied for a type-A voter. Each point on the orbit defined by $\mathbf{W}^n$ under the action of S_n corresponds to a listing of election outcomes for a unanimity profile. The question is to determine whether this action admits a singularity; namely, is there a choice of $\mathbf{W}^n$ that mimics the North Pole because its S_n orbit has the smallest dimension? (Namely, is there a $\mathbf{W}^n$ near the "axis" of this permutation group action.) There is, and it is when the Borda Count is assigned to each subset of candidates. Now, "dimension" corresponds to the number and kinds of paradoxes that can occur, so we must (correctly) expect the BC to minimize the number of things that can go wrong ([S9, 11, 16, 18]). Moreover, just as when points on the sphere approach the North Pole, the orbits decrease in size, as $\mathbf{W}^n$ approaches the Borda Count, the likelihood of these electoral difficulties also decreases.

So, my emphasis on using the geometry created by unanimity outcomes is intended as a translation of this higher dimensional geometry into more useful terms; here I emphasize the setting of $n = 3$ candidates. Each point on the S_n orbit is a unanimity outcome; thus the approach of this book is to find other ways to capture the properties of the orbits of this symmetry action in the higher dimensional geometry. For instance, the geometry dictates that the closer $\mathbf{w}_s$

is to the BC, the smaller the convex hull should be; that is, the less likely it is that problems occur. This is precisely what we have seen with voting vectors when considered with respect to almost any issue. Continuing this analogy, by being a singularity, the North Pole admits other kinds of symmetry relationships that can't be satisfied by other points (except the South Pole). For example, the point remains the same under a flip of a 180° rotation. Similarly, because the BC creates a singularity orbit, it must satisfy added symmetry relationships not available to other system voting vectors. This is how the reversal property described in Sec. 3.1 was found. As suggested in the footnotes in this section, with larger values of n, even more symmetries emerge – these are the "super-neutrality" properties.

Singularity theory from mathematics requires the singularities to form what is called a stratified structure. Thus, for $n > 3$ candidates, we must expect the orbits of system voting vectors to form a similar stratified behavior. When translated into English, this means that voting procedures form a partial order-ing in terms of their consequences – that is, in terms of the kinds of election relationships and paradoxes they admit. (See [S18].)

Abstract social choice. By no means are these symmetry structures restricted to voting vectors; they play a critical role throughout social choice as well as economics, statistics, and anywhere where something resembling the anonymity condition is combined with a universal domain assumption. In more abstract settings, we have to analyze the symmetry action with greater care. To see what is involved, consider the name change $\sigma = (1,3)$ applied to a type-three voter $(c_3 \succ c_1 \succ c_2)$. Over the four subsets of candidates, this changes

$$c_3 \succ c_1 \succ c_2, \, c_1 \succ c_2, \, c_3 \succ c_2, \, c_3 \succ c_1$$

to

$$c_1 \succ c_3 \succ c_2, \, c_1 \succ c_2, \, c_3 \succ c_2, \, c_1 \succ c_3.$$

Thus, the action on each ranking from the four subsets of candidates is repre-sented by (σ, I, I, F) where I is the identity action, and F is the flip. On the other hand, if this same action is applied to a type-one voter, it converts

$$c_1 \succ c_2 \succ c_3, \, c_1 \succ c_2, \, c_2 \succ c_3, \, c_1 \succ c_3$$

to

$$c_3 \succ c_2 \succ c_1, \, c_2 \succ c_1, \, c_3 \succ c_2, \, c_3 \succ c_1$$

which is represented by (σ, F, F, F). This means that the same name change in-duces drastically different outcomes on the symmetry actions of different subsets of candidates; the difference also depends on the voter type the change acts upon. The mathematical development of this topic, where the symmetry action over different sets depends upon the object acted upon, is called the *wreath product of groups*. So, the above symmetry action of voting vectors is the orbit of a wreath product of permutation groups.

We now can extract the mathematical structure of Arrow's IIA. According to IIA, the $\{c_i, c_j\}$ outcome depends only on how the voters rank $\{c_i, c_j\}$; it is immaterial how the remaining candidate is ranked. Using a given pairwise ranking as a reference, the other ranking of this pair can be described in terms of whether the reference ranking is kept (so, we use I) or flipped (i.e., F); this defines the group Z_2. What happens is that IIA requires the group of name changes to be $Z_2 \times Z_2 \times Z_2$ which is of order eight while transitivity can support only the group S_6 of order six. In [S14] (and an earlier version called "Symmetry and Arrow's Theorem") I expressed this symmetry inconsistency in terms of the "kind of information" a subgroup of $Z_2 \times Z_2 \times Z_2$ imposes upon the system. This subgroup is $\{I\} \times Z_2 \times Z_2$ where the action from the first Z_2 subgroup describes $\mathbf{p}_1 \to \mathbf{p}_2$ profile change while the second action defines the $\mathbf{p}_2 \to \mathbf{p}_3$ profile change. In fact, by using various extensions of these techniques, one can obtain extensions of all the results I'm aware of from abstract social choice theory. After all, what is typically involved are larger sets of candidates (rather than pairs), so we just need to bring other product structures to the forefront. For instance, if IIA is applied only to three candidate situations where $n = 4$, then IIA tries to make the outcome $S_3 \times S_3 \times S_3 \times S_3$; a group of order 6^4, instead of the more accurate S_4 which has order 24. (What adds fun comes from the size of $\binom{n}{k}$ when subsets of k candidates are considered.)

From this discussion, the mathematical role of "intensity" becomes clearer. If there is a "weak $\{c_1, c_2\}$" ranking, then a $(1, 2)$ name change effects the set of all 3 candidates and one pair; it leads to a group structure of the (σ, I, I, F) type. But, a strong $\{c_1, c_2\}$ ranking and a $(1, 2)$ name change forces a (σ, F, F, F) kind of outcome. What we have are distinctly different outcomes with name changes and the behavior of the IIA group structure.

REFERENCES

[Ab]   Abbott, E.A., *Flatland; a romance of many dimensions 6th edn.*, Dover Publications, 1952.

[A]   Aizerman, MA, *New problems in the general choice theory: review of a research trend*, Soc Choice Welfare **2** (1985), 235-282.

[Ar]   Arrow KJ, *Social choice and individual values, 2nd edn.*, Wiley, New York, 1963.

[B]   Baker, KM, *Condorcet*, University of Chicago Press, 1975.

[BY1]   Balinski, ML, Young HP, *The quota method of apportionment*, Am Math Mon **82** (1975), 701-730.

[BY2]   Balinski, ML, Young HP, *Fair representation*, Yale University Press, New Haven, 1982.

[Ba1]   Barbera, S, *Pivotal voters: a new proof of Arrow's theorem*, Econ Lett **6** (1980), 13-16.

[Ba2]   Barbera, S, *Strategy-proofness and pivotal voters: a direct proof of the Gibbard-Satterthwaite theorem*, Int Econ Rev **24** (1983), 413-428.

[Bar]   Barthelemy, J-P, *Arrow's theorem: unusual domains and extended co-domains*, Math Soc Sci **3** (1982), 79-89.

[Be]   Benoit, J-P, *Scoring reversals: a major league dilemma*, Soc Choice Welfare **9** (1992), 89-97.

[Bl]   Black, D, *The theory of committees and elections*, Cambridge University Press, London New York, 1958.

[BD]   Blau, JH, and R. Deb., *Social decision functions and veto*, Econometrica **45** (1977), 871-879.

[Bo]   Borda, J-C, *Memoire sur les elections au Scrutin*, Histoire de l'Academie Royale des Sciences (1781).

[Br1]   Brams, SJ, *The AMS nomination procedure is vulnerable to "truncation of preferences"*, Not Am Math Soc **29** (1982), 136-138.

[Br2]   Brams, SJ,, *Spatial Models of Election Competition*, comap, inc., Lexington, MA, 1983.

[BrF1] Brams, SJ, Fishburn, PC, *Approval voting*, Am Polit Sci Rev **72** (1978), 831-847.

[BrF2] Brams, SJ, Fishburn, PC, *Approval voting*, Birkhauser, Boston, 1983.

[BrF3] Brams, SJ, Pishburn, PC, *Manipulability of voting by sincere truncation of preferences*, Public Choice **44** (1984), 397-410.

[BFM]   Brams, SJ, Fishburn, PC, Merril, S III, *The responsiveness of approval voting: comments on Saari and Van Newenhizen*, Public Choice **59** (1988), 121-131.

[BLM]   Brams, S.J. W.F. Lucas, P.D. Straffin, Jr., *Political and Related Models*, Springer-Verlag, Heidelberg, 1983.

[Bro]   Brown, DJ, *Aggregation of preferences*, Quarterly journal of economics **89** (1975), 465-469.

[C]   Chamberlin, JR, *An investigation into the relative manipulability of four voting systems*, Behav Sci **30** (1985), 195-203.

[Ch]   Chichilnisky, G, *The topological equivalence of the Pareto condition and the existence of a dictator*, J Math Econ **9** (1982), 223-234.

[D]   De Grazia, A, *Mathematical derivation of an election system*, Isis **44** (1953), 42-51.

[De]   De Groot, M, *Reaching a consensus*, J Am Stat Assoc **69** (1974), 118-121.

[Do]   Dodgson, CL, *Suggestions as to the best method taking votes when more than two issues are to be voted on*, Oxford, 1874.

[E]   Ellis, GM, *Boso's life of Alexander III*, Rowman and Littlefield, Totawa, New Jersey, 1973.

[EH]   Enelow, JM and Hinich, M (eds.), *Advances in the Spatial Theory of Voting*, Cambridge University Press, 1990.

[F1]   Fishburn, PC, *The theory of social choice*, Princeton University Press, Princeton, 1973.

[F2]   Fishburn, PC, *Paradoxes of voting*, Am Polit Sci Rev **68** (1974), 537-548.

[F3]   Fishburn, PC, *Inverted orders for monotone scoring rules*, Discrete Appl Math **3** (1981), 27-36.

[FG]   Fishburn, PC, Gehrlein, WV, *Borda's rule; positional voting, and Condorcet's simple majority principle*, Public Choice **28** (1976), 79-88.

[Fr]   Francis, MJ, *The Allende victory: an analysis of the 1970 Chilean presidential election*, University of Tuscon Press, Tuscon, 1973.

[FS]   Funkenbusch, WW, Saari, DG,, *Preferences among preferences or nested cyclic stochastic inequalities*, Congressus Numerantium **39** (1983), 419-432.

[G1]   Gehrlein, WV, *Expected probability of Condorcet's paradox*, Econ Lett **7** (1981), 33-37.

[G2]   Gehrlein, WV, *Probability calculations for transitivity of the simple majority rule*, Econ Lett **27** (1988), 311-315.

[GF]   Gehrlein, WV, Fishburn, PC, *Probabilities of election outcomes for large electorates*, J Econ Theory **19** (1978), 38-49.

[Gi]   Gibbard, AF, *Manipulation of voting schemes: a general result*, Econometrica **41** (1973), 587-601.

[GHW]   Gibbard, AF, Hylland, A., Weymark, JA, *Arrow's theorem with a fixed feasible alternative*, Soc Choice Welfare **4** (1987), 105-115.

[H1]   Hansson, B, *The existence of group preferences*, Public Choice **28** (1976), 89-98.

[H2]   Hansson, B, *Voting and group decision functions*, Synthese **20** (1969), 526-537.

[Ha]   Haunsperger, D, *Dictionaries of paradoxes for statistical tests on k samples*, J Am Stat **87** (1992), 149-155.

[He]   Hermens, A., *Democracy and Proportional Representation*, University of Chicago Press, 1940.

[H0]   Horwell, G., *Proportional Representation; its dangers and defects*, George Allen and Unwin LTD, London, 1925.

[Hu1]   Huntington, EV, *The mathematical theory of the apportionment of representatives*, Natl Acad Sci **7** (1921), 123-127.

[Hu2]   Huntington, EV, *The apportionment of representatives in Congress*, Trans Am Math Soc **30** (1928), 85-110.

[KM]   Kalai, E, Muller, E., *Characterization of domains admitting nondictatorical social welfare functions and nonmanipulable voting procedures*, J Econ Theory **16** (1977), 457-469.

[KR]   Kalai, E, Ritz, Z., *Characterization of the private alternatives domains admitting Arrow social welfare functions*, J Econ Theory **22** (1980), 23-36.

[K1]   Kelly, JS, *Arrow impossibility theorems*, Academic Press, New York, 1978.

[K2]   Kelly, JS, *Conjectures and unsolved problems*, Soc Choice Welfare **4** (1987), 235-239.

[K3]   Kelly, JS, *Social choice bibliography*, Soc Choice Welfare **8** (1991), 97-169.

[LS]   Le Breton, M, Salles, M., *On the generic emptiness of the local core of voting games*, Soc Choice Welfare **4** (1987), 287-294.

[LY]   Li T-Y and Yorke, J.A., *Period three implies chaos*, Amer Math Monthly **82** (1975), 985-992.

[M]   Mascart, J, *La vie et les travaux du chevalier Jean-Charles de Borda*, Annales de l'Universite de Lyon **2** (1919).

[Ma]   Maskin, ES, *Implementation and strong Nash-equilibrium*, Aggregation and revelation of preferences (Laffont, J-J, ed.), North-Holland, Amsterdam, 1979, pp. 433-439.

[Mas]   Sec. of Commerce vs. Massachusetts, *US Supreme Court Decision 91-1502* (1992).

[Mo1]   Moulin, H, *Fairness and strategy in voting*, Fair allocation (Young, HP, ed.), AMS, Providence, 1985, pp. 109-142.

[Mo2]   Moulin, H, *Condorcet's principle implies the no show paradox*, J Econ Theory **45** (1988), 53-64.

[Mon]   Montana vs. US Dept of Commerce;, *US Supreme Court Decision 91-860* (1992).

[N]   Nanson, EJ, *Methods of election*, Trans Proc R Soc Victoria **18** (1882), 197-240.

[Ni]   Niemi, RG, *The problem of strategic behavior under approval voting*, American Political Science Review **78** (1984), 952-958.

[NiR]   Niemi, RG, Riker, WH, *The choice of voting systems*, Sci Am **234** (1976), 21-27.

[Nu]   Nurmi, H, *Comparing voting systems*, D. Reidel, Dordrecht, 1987.

[PS]   Packel, EW, Saari, DG, *Strategic equilibria and decisive set structures for social choice mechanisms*, Math Soc Sci **2** (1982), 373-378.

[Pl]   Plott, CR, *Axiomatic social choice theory: an overview and interpretation*, Am J Polit Sci **20** (1976), 511-596.

[P]   Poinchoff, H.,, *The algebraic closing lemma*, Very Unusual Dynamics (Robinson, C., C. Simon, K. Meyer, eds.), Eastern Chicago State Press, 1976, pp. 69f.

[R1]   Riker, WH, *Arrow's theorem and some examples of the paradox of voting*, Mathematical applications in political science (Claunch, JM, ed.), SMU Press, Dallas, 1965, pp. 41-60.

[R2]   Riker, WH, *Liberalism against populism: a confrontation between the theory of democracy and the theory of social choice*, Freeman, San Francisco, 1982.

[R3]   Riker, WH, *The two-party system and Duverger's law: an essay in the history of political science*, Am Polit Sci Rev **76** (1982), 753-766.

[R4]   Riker, WH, *The Art of Political Manipulation*, Yale University Press, 1986.

[S1]   Saari, DG, *The geometry of departmental politics, of the scoring of track meets, and of Arrow's Social Choice Theorem,*, NU mimeo (1978).

[S2]   Saari, DG, *Methods of apportionment and the House of Representatives*, Amer Math Monthly **85** (1978), 792-802.

[S3]   Saari, DG, *Inconsistencies of weighted summation voting systems*, Math Oper Res **7** (1982), 479-490.

[S4]   Saari, DG, *The ultimate of chaos resulting from weighted voting systems*, Adv Appl Math **5** (1984), 286-308.

[S5]   Saari, DG, *Random behavior in numerical analysis, decision theory, and macrosystems: some impossibility theorems*, Dynamics of macrosystems (Aubin, J-P, Saari, DG, Sigmund, K, eds.), Springer, Berlin Heidelberg New York, 1986, pp. 115-126.

[S6]   Saari, DG, *The sources of some paradoxes from social choice and probability*, J Econ Theory **41** (1987), 1-22.

[S7]   Saari, DG, *Chaos and the theory of elections*, Dynamical systems (Kurzhanski, AB, Sigmund, K, eds.), Springer, Berlin Heidelberg New York, 1987, pp. 179-188.

[S8]   Saari, DG, *Symmetry, voting and social choice*, Math Intell **10** (1988), 32-42.

[S9]   Saari, DG, *A dictionary for voting paradoxes*, Jour Econ Theory **48** (1989), 443-475.

[S10]   Saari, DG, *Susceptibility to manipulation*, Public Choice **64** (1990), 21-41.

[S11]   Saari, DG, *The Borda Dictionary*, Soc Choice Welfare **7** (1990), 279-317.

[S12]   Saari, DG, *Consistency of decision processes*, Annals of Operations Research **23** (1990), 103-137.

[S13]   Saari, DG, *Relationship admitting families of candidates*, Soc Choice Welfare **8** (1991), 21-50.

[S14]   Saari, DG, *Calculus and Extensions of Arrow's Theorem*, Jour Math Econ **20** (1991), 271-306.

[S15]   Saari, DG, *Millions of election rankings from a single profile*, Soc Choice Welfare **9** (1992), 277-306.

[S16]   Saari, DG, *Symmetry extensions of "neutrality" I. Advantage to the Condorcet loser*, Soc Choice Welfare **9** (1992), 307-336.

[S17]   Saari, DG, *The aggregate excess demand function and other aggregation procedures*, Economic Theory **2** (1992), 359-388.

[S18]   Saari, DG, *Symmetry extensions of "neutrality" II. Partial Ordering of Dictionaries*, Soc Choice Welfare (1993).

[S19]   Saari, DG, *Inner consistency or not inner consistency; a reformulation is the answer*, Social Choice Welfare (Barnett, W., H. Moulin, H. M. Salles, N. Scholfield, ed.), Springer-Verlag, 1994.

[SvN1]   Saari, DG, van Newenhizen, J, *The problem of indeterminancy in approval, multiple and truncated voting systems*, Public Choice **59** (1988), 101-120.

[SvN2]   Saari, DG, van Newenhizen, J, *Is approval voting an "unmitigated evil"? A response to Brams, Fishburn, and Merrill*, Public Choice **59** (1988), 133-147.

[Sa]   Satterthwaite, MA, *Strategyproofness and Arrow's conditions: existence and correspondence theorems for voting procedures and social welfare functions*, J Econ Theory **10** (1975), 187-217.

[SMR]   Sawyer, J. and MacRae, D., *Game theory and cumulative voting in Illinois:1902-1954*, Amer. Political Science Review **56** (1962), 937f.

[ScS]   Schmeidler, D, Sonnenschein, HF, *Two proofs of the Gibbard-Satterthwaite theorem on the possibility of a strategy-proof social choice function*, Decision theory and social ethics, issues in social welfare (Gottinger, HW, Leinfellner, W, eds.), Reidel, Dordrecht, 1978, pp. 227-234.

[Sh1]   Schofield, N., *Social Equiilibrium and cycles on compact sets*, Jour Economic Theory **33** (1984), 59-71.

[Sh2]   Schofield, N., *Social Choice and Demoncracy*, Springer Verlag, 1985.

[ShT]   Schofield, N. and Tovey, G, *Probability and convergence for supra-majority rule with Euclidean preferences*, Mathl. Comput. Modelling **16** (1992), 41-58.

[Se1]   Sen, AK, *The impossibility of a Paretian liberal*, J Polit Econ **78** (1970), 152-157.

[Se2]   Sen, AK, *Social choice theory*, Handbook of Mathematical Economics, vol III (Arrow, KJ, Intriligator, MD, eds.), North-Holland, Amsterdam, 1986, pp. 1073-1181.

[Sm]   Smith, JH, *Aggregation of preferences with variable electorate*, Econometrica **41** (1973), 1027-1041.

[St]   Stavely, ES, *Greek and Roman voting and elections*, Thames and Hudson, 1972.

[Str]   Straffin, P.D., *Topics in the Theory of Voting*, Birkhauser, Boston, 1980.

[T1]   Taggepera, R, *Seats and votes: a generalization of the cube law of election*, Soc Sci Res **2** (1973), 257-275.

[T2]   Taggepera, R, *Reformulating the cube law for proportional representation elections*, Am Polit Sci Rev **80** (1986), 489-504.

[U]   Ullmann, W, *Principles of government and politics in the middle ages*, London, 1961.

[VN]   Van Newenhizen, J, *The Borda method is most likely to respect the Condorcet principle*, Economic Theory **2** (1992), 69-83.

[W]   Wilson, RB, *Social science without the Pareto principle*, J Econ Theory **5** (1972), 478-486.

[Y1]   Young HP, *An axiomatization of Borda's Theory*, J Econ Theory **9** (1974), 43-52.

[Y2]   Young, HP, *Social choice scoring functions*, SIAM J Appl Math **28** (1975), 824-838.

INDEX

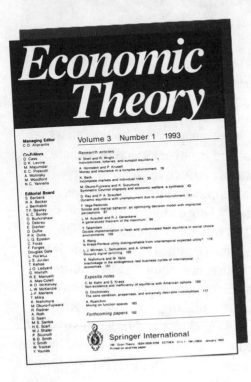

Managing Editor: C. D. Aliprantis, Indianapolis, IN
Co-editors: D. Cass, D. Gale, D. Levine,
M. Majumdar, E.C. Prescott, A. Wolinsky,
M. Woodford, N.C. Yannelis

A selection of recent papers:

D. Cass: Sunspots and incomplete financial markets
S.R. Aiyatari, N. Wallace: Fiat money in the Kiyotaki–Wright model
V. Bala, M. Majumdar: Chaotic Tatonnement
D.G. Saari: The aggregate excess demand function and other aggregation procedures
J. Benhabib, R. Radner: The joint exploitation of a productive asset: a game theoretic approach
C.D. Aliprantis, C.R. Plott: Competitive equilibria in overlapping generations experiments
E. Karni, D. Schmeidler: On the uniqueness of subjective probabilities
L. Koutsougeras, N.C. Yannelis: Incentive compatibility and information superiority of the core of an economy with differential information
T.J. Kehoe, N. Kiyotaki, R. Wright: More on money as a medium of exchange
T.F. Cooley, B.D. Smith: A theory of optimal denominations for government liabilities
P. Aghion, M.P. Espinosa, B. Jullien: Dynamic duopoly with learning through market experimentation
J.M. Lacker, J.A. Weinberg: A coalition proof equilibrium for a private information credit economy

Membership in the **Society for the Advancement of Economic Theory** includes a subscription to this journal. Membership details available from:
Society for the Advancement of Economic Theory, Dept. of Economics, University of Illinois, 330 Commerce Building, 1206 South Sixth Street, Champaign, IL 61820, USA

The purpose of **Economic Theory** is to provide an outlet for research

– in all areas of economics based on rigorous theoretical reasoning, and

– on specific topics in mathematics which are motivated by the analysis of economic problems.

Economic Theory's scope encompasses – but is not limited to – the following fields: classical and modern equilibrium theory; macroeconomics; social choice and welfare; mathematical economics, game theory, uncertainty and information, intertemporal economics; public economics; international economics; financial economics, money and banking; industrial organization.

Springer

Social Choice and Welfare

Social Choice and Welfare publishes original research, survey papers and book reviews on the ethical and positive aspects of welfare economics and collective choice theory. The appropriate topics comprise social choice and voting theory (normative, positive and strategic sides) as well as all aspects of welfare theory (Pareto optimality; welfare criteria; fairness, justice, and equity; externalities; public goods; optimal taxation; incentives in public decision making; cost-benefit analysis; etc.) Articles on choice and order theory may also be published if their results can be applied to these topics. Papers both verbal and formal in style are being solicited.

Membership to the **Society for Social Choice and Welfare** includes subscription to **Social Choice and Welfare.** Please contact M. Salles, Society for Social Choice and Welfare, CREMERC, Université de Caen, 14032 Caen cédex, France

Springer